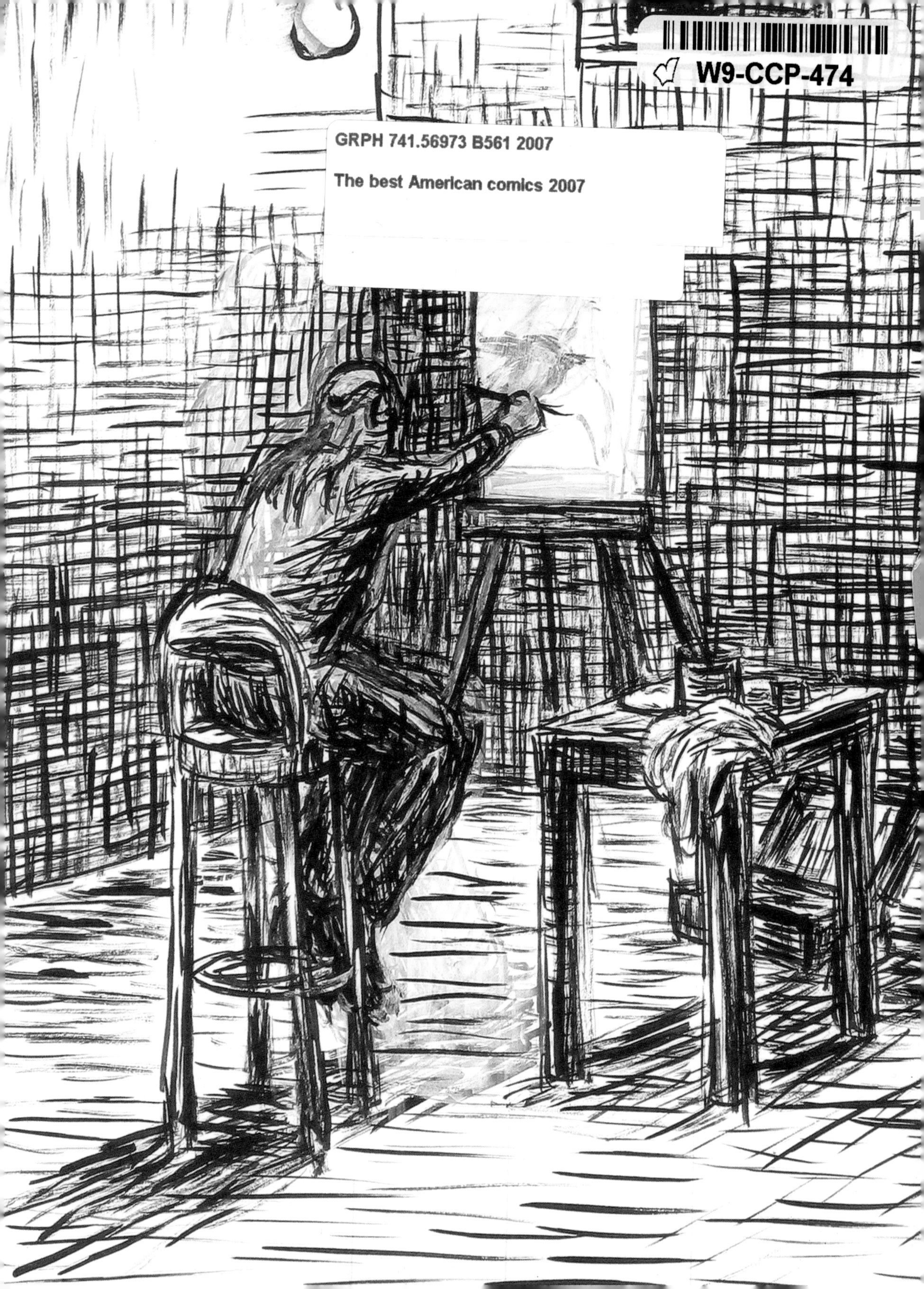

THE BEST AMERICAN

Comics 2007

Guest Editors
of the Best American Comics

2006 HARVEY PEKAR
2007 CHRIS WARE

THE HORROR OF SIMPLY BEING ALIVE

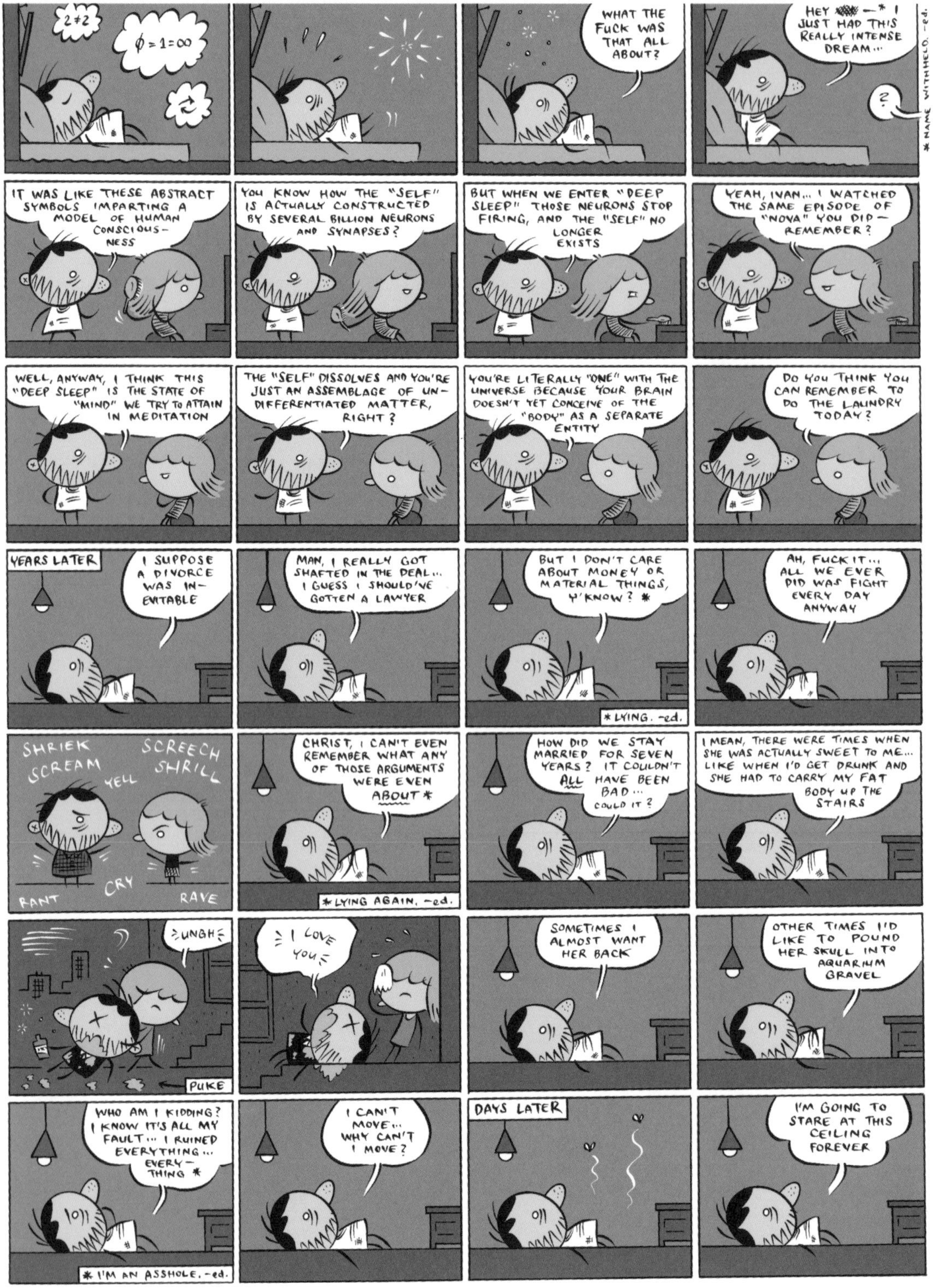

2≠2
φ = 1 = ∞
WHAT THE FUCK WAS THAT ALL ABOUT?
HEY [redacted] —* I JUST HAD THIS REALLY INTENSE DREAM...
?
* NAME WITHHELD. –ed.
IT WAS LIKE THESE ABSTRACT SYMBOLS IMPARTING A MODEL OF HUMAN CONSCIOUS-NESS
YOU KNOW HOW THE "SELF" IS ACTUALLY CONSTRUCTED BY SEVERAL BILLION NEURONS AND SYNAPSES?
BUT WHEN WE ENTER "DEEP SLEEP" THOSE NEURONS STOP FIRING, AND THE "SELF" NO LONGER EXISTS
YEAH, IVAN... I WATCHED THE SAME EPISODE OF "NOVA" YOU DID — REMEMBER?
WELL, ANYWAY, I THINK THIS "DEEP SLEEP" IS THE STATE OF "MIND" WE TRY TO ATTAIN IN MEDITATION
THE "SELF" DISSOLVES AND YOU'RE JUST AN ASSEMBLAGE OF UN-DIFFERENTIATED MATTER, RIGHT?
YOU'RE LITERALLY "ONE" WITH THE UNIVERSE BECAUSE YOUR BRAIN DOESN'T YET CONCEIVE OF THE "BODY" AS A SEPARATE ENTITY
DO YOU THINK YOU CAN REMEMBER TO DO THE LAUNDRY TODAY?
YEARS LATER
I SUPPOSE A DIVORCE WAS IN-EVITABLE
MAN, I REALLY GOT SHAFTED IN THE DEAL... I GUESS I SHOULD'VE GOTTEN A LAWYER
BUT I DON'T CARE ABOUT MONEY OR MATERIAL THINGS, Y'KNOW? *
* LYING. –ed.
AH, FUCK IT... ALL WE EVER DID WAS FIGHT EVERY DAY ANYWAY
SHRIEK
SCREAM
YELL
SCREECH
SHRILL
RANT
CRY
RAVE
CHRIST, I CAN'T EVEN REMEMBER WHAT ANY OF THOSE ARGUMENTS WERE EVEN ABOUT *
* LYING AGAIN. –ed.
HOW DID WE STAY MARRIED FOR SEVEN YEARS? IT COULDN'T ALL HAVE BEEN BAD... COULD IT?
I MEAN, THERE WERE TIMES WHEN SHE WAS ACTUALLY SWEET TO ME... LIKE WHEN I'D GET DRUNK AND SHE HAD TO CARRY MY FAT BODY UP THE STAIRS
UNGH
PUKE
I LOVE YOU
SOMETIMES I ALMOST WANT HER BACK
OTHER TIMES I'D LIKE TO POUND HER SKULL INTO AQUARIUM GRAVEL
WHO AM I KIDDING? I KNOW IT'S ALL MY FAULT... I RUINED EVERYTHING... EVERY-THING *
* I'M AN ASSHOLE. –ed.
I CAN'T MOVE... WHY CAN'T I MOVE?
DAYS LATER
I'M GOING TO STARE AT THIS CEILING FOREVER

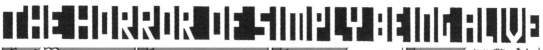

IVAN BRUNETTI

THE BEST AMERICAN

Comics

2007

EDITED *and with an*

INTRODUCTION *by* Chris Ware

ANNE ELIZABETH MOORE,
series editor

HOUGHTON MIFFLIN COMPANY

BOSTON ▪ NEW YORK 2007

PORTRAIT OF THE ARTIST AS A YOUNG %@?☆!

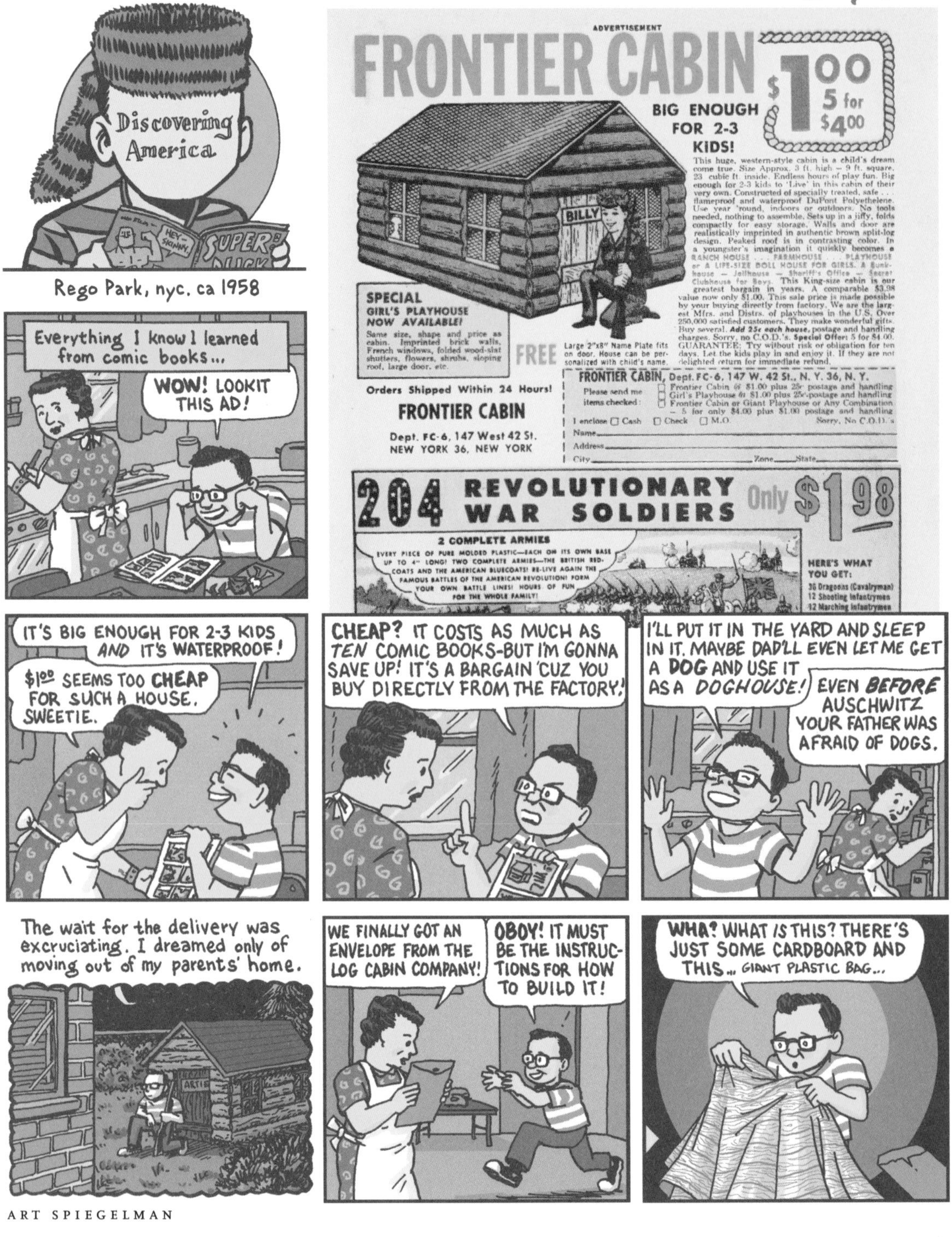
Discovering America
HEY SKINNY
SUPER DUCK
Rego Park, nyc. ca 1958
ADVERTISEMENT
FRONTIER CABIN
$1.00 5 for $4.00
BIG ENOUGH FOR 2-3 KIDS!
This huge, western-style cabin is a child's dream come true. Size Approx. 3 ft. high – 9 ft. square. 23 cubic ft. inside. Endless hours of play fun. Big enough for 2-3 kids to 'Live' in this cabin of their very own. Constructed of specially treated, safe . . . flameproof and waterproof DuPont Polyethelene. Use year 'round, indoors or outdoors. No tools needed, nothing to assemble. Sets up in a jiffy, folds compactly for easy storage. Walls and door are realistically imprinted in authentic brown split-log design. Peaked roof is in contrasting color. In a youngster's imagination it quiskly becomes a RANCH HOUSE . . . FARMHOUSE . . . PLAYHOUSE or A LIFE-SIZE DOLL HOUSE FOR GIRLS. A Bunk-house — Jailhouse — Sheriff's Office — Secret Clubhouse for Boys. This King-size cabin is our greatest bargain in years. A comparable $3.98 value now only $1.00. This sale price is made possible by your buying directly from factory. We are the largest Mfrs. and Distrs. of playhouses in the U.S. Over 250,000 satisfied customers. They make wonderful gifts. Buy several. Add 25¢ each house, postage and handling charges. Sorry, no C.O.D.'s. Special Offer: 5 for $4.00. GUARANTEE: Try without risk or obligation for ten days. Let the kids play in and enjoy it. If they are not delighted return for immediate refund.
BILLY
SPECIAL GIRL'S PLAYHOUSE NOW AVAILABLE!
Same size, shape and price as cabin. Imprinted brick walls, French windows, folded wood-slat shutters, flowers, shrubs, sloping roof, large door, etc.
FREE
Large 2"x8" Name Plate fits on door. House can be personalized with child's name.
Orders Shipped Within 24 Hours!
FRONTIER CABIN
Dept. FC-6, 147 West 42 St. NEW YORK 36, NEW YORK
FRONTIER CABIN, Dept. FC-6, 147 W. 42 St., N. Y. 36, N. Y.
Please send me items checked:
Frontier Cabin @ $1.00 plus 25¢ postage and handling
Girl's Playhouse @ $1.00 plus 25¢ postage and handling
Frontier Cabin or Giant Playhouse or Any Combination – 5 for only $4.00 plus $1.00 postage and handling
I enclose Cash Check M.O. Sorry, No C.O.D.'s
Name
Address
City Zone State
204 REVOLUTIONARY WAR SOLDIERS Only $1.98
2 COMPLETE ARMIES
EVERY PIECE OF PURE MOLDED PLASTIC—EACH ON ITS OWN BASE UP TO 4" LONG! TWO COMPLETE ARMIES—THE BRITISH RED-COATS AND THE AMERICAN BLUECOATS! RE-LIVE AGAIN THE FAMOUS BATTLES OF THE AMERICAN REVOLUTION! FORM YOUR OWN BATTLE LINES! HOURS OF FUN FOR THE WHOLE FAMILY!
HERE'S WHAT YOU GET:
36 Dragoons (Cavalryman)
12 Shooting Infantrymen
12 Marching Infantrymen
Everything I know I learned from comic books...
WOW! LOOKIT THIS AD!
IT'S BIG ENOUGH FOR 2-3 KIDS AND IT'S WATERPROOF!
$1.00 SEEMS TOO CHEAP FOR SUCH A HOUSE, SWEETIE.
CHEAP? IT COSTS AS MUCH AS TEN COMIC BOOKS-BUT I'M GONNA SAVE UP! IT'S A BARGAIN 'CUZ YOU BUY DIRECTLY FROM THE FACTORY!
I'LL PUT IT IN THE YARD AND SLEEP IN IT. MAYBE DAD'LL EVEN LET ME GET A DOG AND USE IT AS A DOGHOUSE!
EVEN BEFORE AUSCHWITZ YOUR FATHER WAS AFRAID OF DOGS.
The wait for the delivery was excruciating. I dreamed only of moving out of my parents' home.
ARTIE
WE FINALLY GOT AN ENVELOPE FROM THE LOG CABIN COMPANY!
OBOY! IT MUST BE THE INSTRUCTIONS FOR HOW TO BUILD IT!
WHA? WHAT IS THIS? THERE'S JUST SOME CARDBOARD AND THIS... GIANT PLASTIC BAG...

ART SPIEGELMAN

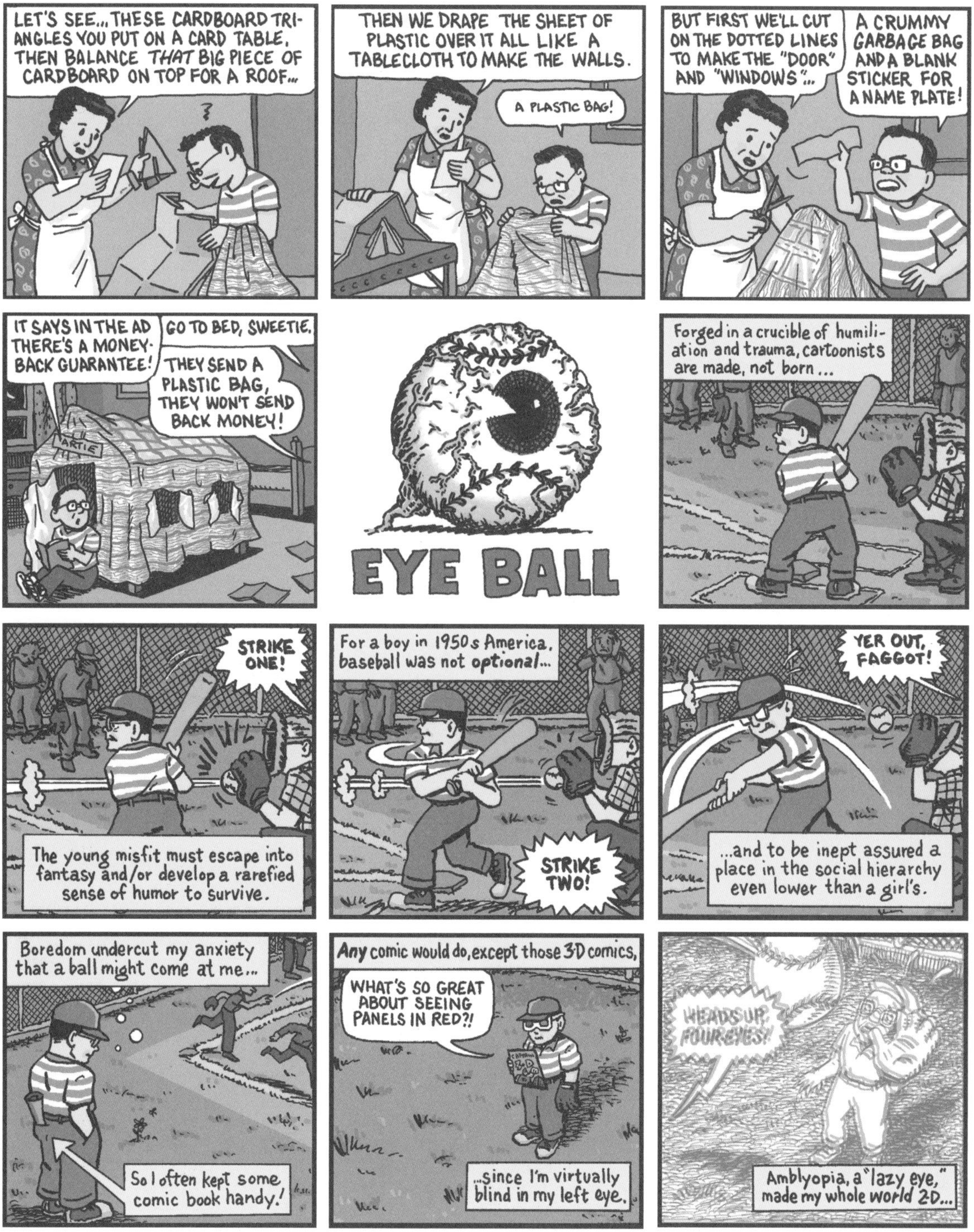
LET'S SEE... THESE CARDBOARD TRIANGLES YOU PUT ON A CARD TABLE, THEN BALANCE *THAT* BIG PIECE OF CARDBOARD ON TOP FOR A ROOF...
?
THEN WE DRAPE THE SHEET OF PLASTIC OVER IT ALL LIKE A TABLECLOTH TO MAKE THE WALLS.
A PLASTIC BAG!
BUT FIRST WE'LL CUT ON THE DOTTED LINES TO MAKE THE "DOOR" AND "WINDOWS"...
A CRUMMY GARBAGE BAG AND A BLANK STICKER FOR A NAME PLATE!
IT SAYS IN THE AD THERE'S A MONEY-BACK GUARANTEE!
GO TO BED, SWEETIE.
THEY SEND A PLASTIC BAG, THEY WON'T SEND BACK MONEY!
ARTIE
EYE BALL
Forged in a crucible of humiliation and trauma, cartoonists are made, not born...
STRIKE ONE!
The young misfit must escape into fantasy and/or develop a rarefied sense of humor to survive.
For a boy in 1950s America, baseball was not *optional*...
STRIKE TWO!
YER OUT, FAGGOT!
...and to be inept assured a place in the social hierarchy even lower than a girl's.
Boredom undercut my anxiety that a ball might come at me...
So I often kept some comic book handy!
Any comic would do, except those 3-D comics,
WHAT'S SO GREAT ABOUT SEEING PANELS IN RED?!
...since I'm virtually blind in my left eye.
HEADS UP, FOUR-EYES!
Amblyopia, a "lazy eye," made my whole *world* 2-D...

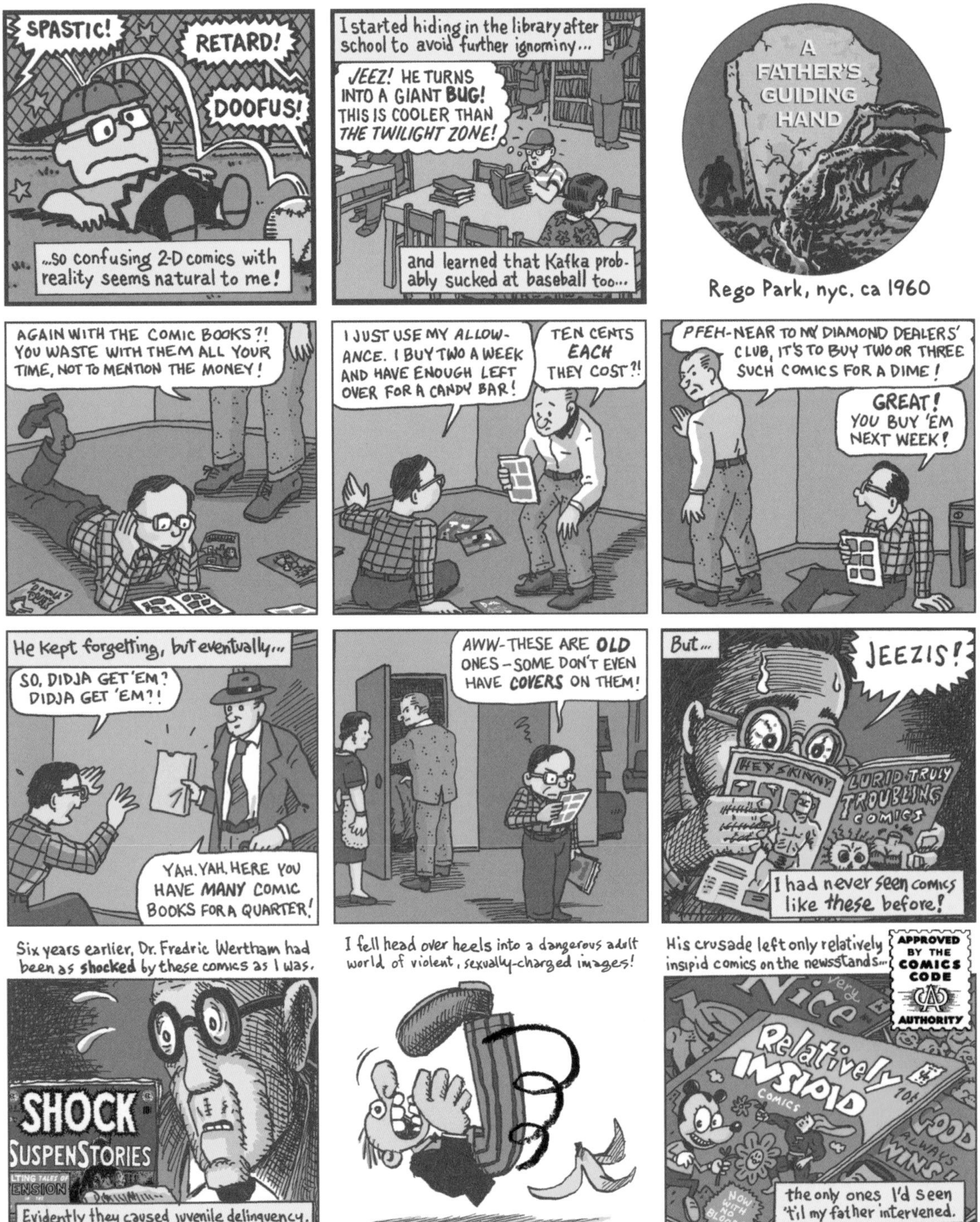
SPASTIC!
RETARD!
DOOFUS!
...so confusing 2-D comics with reality seems natural to me!
I started hiding in the library after school to avoid further ignominy...
JEEZ! HE TURNS INTO A GIANT BUG! THIS IS COOLER THAN THE TWILIGHT ZONE!
and learned that Kafka probably sucked at baseball too...
A FATHER'S GUIDING HAND
Rego Park, nyc. ca 1960
AGAIN WITH THE COMIC BOOKS?! YOU WASTE WITH THEM ALL YOUR TIME, NOT TO MENTION THE MONEY!
I JUST USE MY ALLOWANCE. I BUY TWO A WEEK AND HAVE ENOUGH LEFT OVER FOR A CANDY BAR!
TEN CENTS EACH THEY COST?!
PFEH-NEAR TO MY DIAMOND DEALERS' CLUB, IT'S TO BUY TWO OR THREE SUCH COMICS FOR A DIME!
GREAT! YOU BUY 'EM NEXT WEEK!
He kept forgetting, but eventually...
SO, DIDJA GET 'EM? DIDJA GET 'EM?!
YAH, YAH, HERE YOU HAVE MANY COMIC BOOKS FOR A QUARTER!
AWW-THESE ARE OLD ONES-SOME DON'T EVEN HAVE COVERS ON THEM!
But...
JEEZIS!
HEY SKINNY
LURID-TRULY TROUBLING COMICS
I had never seen comics like these before!
Six years earlier, Dr. Fredric Wertham had been as shocked by these comics as I was.
SHOCK SUSPENSTORIES
Evidently they caused juvenile delinquency.
I fell head over heels into a dangerous adult world of violent, sexually-charged images!
His crusade left only relatively insipid comics on the newsstands...
APPROVED BY THE COMICS CODE AUTHORITY
Very Nice
Relatively INSIPID COMICS
GOOD ALWAYS WINS!
NOW! WITH NO BLOOD!
the only ones I'd seen 'til my father intervened.

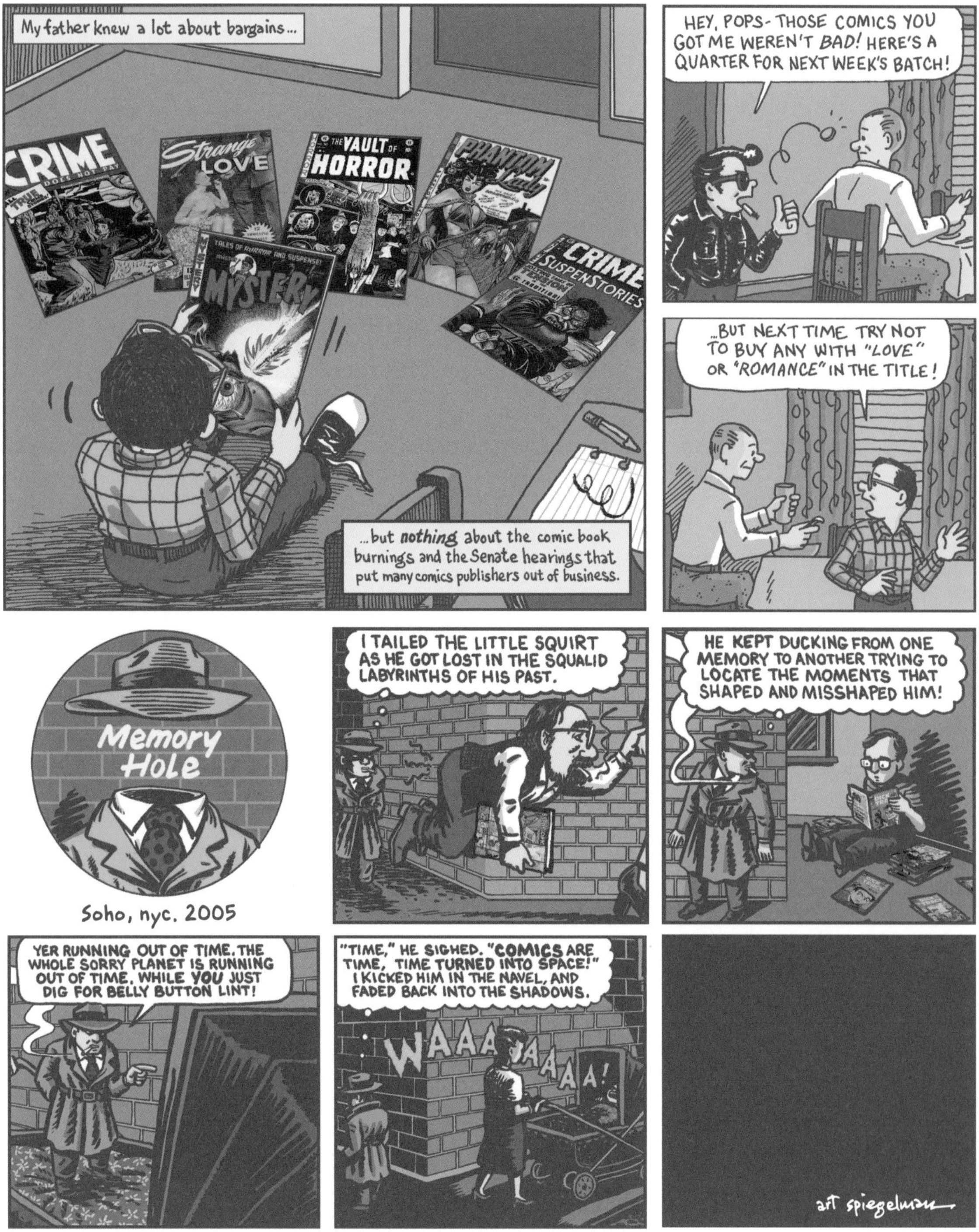
My father knew a lot about bargains...
...but *nothing* about the comic book burnings and the Senate hearings that put many comics publishers out of business.
HEY, POPS- THOSE COMICS YOU GOT ME WEREN'T *BAD!* HERE'S A QUARTER FOR NEXT WEEK'S BATCH!
...BUT NEXT TIME TRY NOT TO BUY ANY WITH "LOVE" OR "ROMANCE" IN THE TITLE!
Memory Hole
Soho, nyc. 2005
I TAILED THE LITTLE SQUIRT AS HE GOT LOST IN THE SQUALID LABYRINTHS OF HIS PAST.
HE KEPT DUCKING FROM ONE MEMORY TO ANOTHER TRYING TO LOCATE THE MOMENTS THAT SHAPED AND MISSHAPED HIM!
YER RUNNING OUT OF TIME. THE WHOLE SORRY PLANET IS RUNNING OUT OF TIME. WHILE **YOU** JUST DIG FOR BELLY BUTTON LINT!
"TIME," HE SIGHED. "**COMICS** ARE TIME, TIME TURNED INTO SPACE!" I KICKED HIM IN THE NAVEL, AND FADED BACK INTO THE SHADOWS.
WAAAAAAA!
art spiegelman

ISBN-13: 978-0-618-71874-0   ISBN-10: 0-618-71874-5

Book design by Robert Overholtzer
Book layout by Chris Ware
Jacket and cover design by David Heatley

PRINTED IN SINGAPORE   TWP 10 9 8 7 6 5 4 3 2 1

Permissions credits are located on page 343.

Contents

Preface

RECENTLY MET A MAN who spent a year living with the Fuerzas Armadas Revolucionarias de Colombia — Ejército del Pueblo, or the FARC-EP, who had taken him by force under the mistaken belief that he was a member of the Central Intelligence Agency. In fact, he was a typical North American college student, suddenly thrust into a world where food was scarce and bad, travel by foot and under duress a constant necessity, and the dangers of new diseases or attacks by strange creatures were common. Also, instead of attending classes, he was a de facto revolutionary. His kidnappers were in their early teens, and occasionally asked his assistance in the difficult tasks involved in maintaining an armed guerilla force — cleaning guns, for example, or battle wounds. At one point, finding a large pile of loaded artillery at his feet and only one lonely guard in sight, he considered escape, which plan was abandoned when he realized he had nowhere to escape to. It was, without a doubt, the strangest story I have ever heard. When his captors eventually released him, having realized some months beforehand that he held little value as a bargaining chip, they first asked if he'd like to join their army. He preferred to return home.

"And *that*," he explained to me in all sincerity, "is when it got really weird."

Perhaps needless to say, I was surprised to hear him calmly relay details from his year in Colombia and follow it up by describing what most of us consider normal life as "really weird." Yet his perspective, despite the extravagant convolutions of his story, should not have surprised me: anyone who spends a year on the lam with a guerilla force must grow, by dint of psychological necessity, to consider it normal eventually. That sense of normality, of reasonability — what we understand to be our background, our setting, our character — dictates what we believe to be logical behavior.

We read constantly in newspapers about bizarre and complex systems of logic unfamiliar and unimaginable to the average reader. The most fascinating, and the most frequently discussed, drive our nation's notorious criminals to acts of villainy. Michael Devlin, for example, who took two boys home to his Saint Louis suburb, told police he'd been "relatively happy" since he had kidnapped them. Former Enron CEO Jeffrey Skilling claimed he knew nothing about the financial distress of the company and moreover had done no wrong. Andrea Yates, who drowned her five children, knew she would be condemned for her actions but wanted to save them from torment by Satan. Less distinctive acts merely give pause, but when the acts committed under such uncomfortable logic hurt others — kidnapping, fraud, conspiracy, murder — we call them deranged.

Yet when a unique pattern of logic is envisioned, drawn out, set to paper, mapped, populated, adhered to over a period of sometimes several years, and released into the world through a series of books, pamphlets, Internet postings, or newspapers, we call them comics.

The best comics create an all-encompassing environment in which characters, actions, and landscape fall into a pattern of decipherable logic. We readers piece this logic together between panels, watching the subtle ways the same object may shift over time, through line variance or plot advancement. We perceive color, or lack thereof, as indications of mood, tone, and lighting. We allow horizon lines to describe gravity, proximity, and believability, but then do not take offense when entire panels are suddenly filled with text. This is not, we know, a strange new weather formation: it is noise. And when suddenly birds talk, or middle schoolers have their own TV shows, we are prepared. Why on earth would they not do these things?

In comics, all things are possible, but only some of them make sense. Some stories do not adhere to earthbound logic. We may read about a world that looks exactly like our own but where a disfiguring condition afflicts teenagers with strange mutations; where giant turnips offer cartooning advice; where aggressors escape retaliation by turning into a wild swirl of colors; or where shoehorns are objects of prophecy. Still, actions proceed naturally from characters' backgrounds, setting, and essential nature. Teenagers remain teenagers: disaffected, moody, interested only in other teenagers. Entire religio-medical practices build up around podiatry. It seems perfectly reasonable.

Some comics trace a logic dictated by common experience, but pressed to extremes by trauma: the Apocalypse; the great Louisville Flood of 1937; the Nazi occupation of Budapest. Others offer prettied up and streamlined versions of the logic that underlies our daily life, and actions are no more than sensible. Cars in such strips are basic and puffy, distinguishable by perfectly round wheels, always viewed only from the side. When people are happy, visible rays of enthusiasm emit from them. Thoughts, even the most mundane, are transcribed into complete sentences for the reader to follow.

My very favorite moments in my most beloved comics, therefore, do not come when the main character is revealed to be some kind of fantastic archetype — or more relevantly to some of the strips that follow, a participant in some excessively unusual circumstance, a Seinfeld cast member, or some general schlub. They do not happen when a moment of off-panel violence has caused a narrative fault line to open, dramatically shifting the way the story can be interpreted. They do not come when a brilliant tree stands for solitude, or loss, or the future. I treasure these moments, do not get me wrong. My favorites, though, come when I look up from reading, glance out the window, and think, "Is that bird trying to tell me something?" or, "I wonder what's on *What's Happening Marlys* tonight."

But I mistype; one does not merely *read* comics, right — one *sees* them. One watches them unfold like a tiny little handheld movie, the language of which you learn to comprehend only as you move through it. And because we can *see it happening with our own two eyes*, because we watch and even force a series of small drawings to fit into a cohesive storyline, as we learn the unique mode of communication offered by each piece, we develop a way to comprehend the events described as logical, sensible, and reasonable. One thing naturally follows from another. The couch, for example, would like for us to skin it; *well lookit that!* It's made out of CDs. And they're great! In almost no time, we've begun to perceive the previously-understood-to-be-normal as, now, really weird.

This edition of the Best American Comics traverses a continuum from autobiography to fiction. It's a continuum that literary comics, and practitioners thereof, are intimate with: as cover artist David Heatley notes at the end of this book, new writers are admonished to "write what you know," and many start with their own lives. Some have yet to cross into pure fiction, but the field continues to expand. Even with 39 stories, and my list of 100 Distinguished Comics, this volume seems insufficient to provide a true slice of the actual best American comics from the past year. Several creators of fiction that didn't find their way into this edition — Jo Dery, Genevieve Elverum, Andrice Arp, and last edition's cover artist Lilli Carré — have produced amazing fictional works in the past twelve months. Megan Kelso's clever biographical work also deserves mention, and Sergio Aragonés's recent autobiographical work for DC's Solo series. Please supplement your reading here with a trip to the local comics shop.

In the last year of comics, exciting new trends have emerged: stories that describe biological events, or suss out prehistorical occurrences; an array of works that describe the contemporary life of queer urban youth, the seemingly regular events that lead up to a high-school massacre, or experiences common to those living with disease or chronic pain. The possibilities for storytelling continue to expand at a dizzying pace. The continual development of innovative narrative structures, plot devices, page layouts, and drawing techniques only multiplies the potential of this developing form.

The tough part of creating an anthology like this is ensuring that the material represented is high quality, yet diverse enough to engage a variety of readers, from all backgrounds and levels of experience. To negotiate this open-mindedly, one strives to read outside one's comfort level. A reader never knows when she or he has fallen into solipsism and mistaken the familiar for the great. Yet I urge you to read through this accusation, should it arise in your mind. Here there may be strips that will challenge new readers, by Tim Hensley, Paper Rad, and C. F., most notably. Follow them closely and allow their unique patterns of logic to melt into your own. Should you find yourself speaking in eloquent but irrelevant phrases, picking up the latest Bill Callahan CD, or singing yourself rhyming little shopping poems — well, all the better for you.

Should you find the challenge agitating, however, console yourself with the works of Lynda Barry, Seth, Alison Bechdel, Gilbert Hernandez, Art Spiegelman, and C. Tyler. The depth and eloquence of their stories set a high standard for comics; I am particularly honored to present their work in this volume.

This year's collection culls from work produced in North America between August 31, 2005, and September 1, 2006, including periodicals, Web comics, traditional pamphlet comic books, graphic novels, anthologies, and mini-comics. Future editions will continue to adhere to this date range, so publishers should send work — no later than September 15, please! — to Best American Comics, Houghton Mifflin Company, 215 Park Avenue South, New York, New York 10003-1603.

Thanks are owed to Jason MacLachlan, Holly Bemiss, Beth Burleigh Fuller, Greg Cook, Ben Russell, Lynda Barry, Christa Donner, Sarah Fan, Andy Yang, Anders Nilsen, the many inhabitants of the Punk Planetarium, and all the great independent bookstores and venues that hosted Harvey Pekar and me on tour with the 2006 edition of Best American Comics. Most, however, I wish to thank you, the early adopter of this series. Comics would not be going through this renaissance without your enthusiastic support, and I sincerely hope to have created a book that incites your passion for more.

ANNE ELIZABETH MOORE

Introduction

FIRST OF ALL, the title: it's misleading. Though I haven't taken a survey, I'd imagine that a good number of the guest editors of all the Best American series have felt compelled to take issue with it, too. To presume that my personal taste defines an objective by which all living cartoonists should be judged is absurd. On top of that, any public competition is antithetical to the spirit of real art, and labeling a widely disseminated collection of artwork as "the best" veers perilously close to suggesting that artists should gauge what they do against some sort of popularity contest for an ancillary reward—notoriety, money, or even inclusion in an anthology—other than the artwork itself. So while I suppose it's probably obvious to the reader that my name as guest editor essentially acts as a sort of aesthetic loophole for the overall series title, it still seems polite and proper to acknowledge it here. In some cases I've chosen stories or excerpts of stories that fulfill what I think I'm regularly looking for from art and literature (which, when boiled down past all the things that don't really matter like a snazzy style and clever writing and accomplished drawing, means "telling the truth"). I've also included work that has stuck in my craw to such a degree that the best I can do is to say that it's interesting, or, in a more conversational way, that it's made me feel really, really old.

As a cartoonist myself, I've been quite heartened at the veritable explosion of intriguing work in a medium that as recently as a decade ago seemed marginal and embarrassing. In fact, it has almost gotten to the point now where a cartoonist doesn't have to explain or qualify what he or she does, let alone not have to launch into a thumbnail history of comics as a commercial-cum-artistic medium to family members at Christmastime. Comics are appearing in bookstores as novels and in museums as art. Even more amazing is that this is all because there really does appear to be a concomitant general increase in interest by the public, one of the most tangible bits of evidence being the very book you now hold.

Even the "Newspaper of Record," long proud of its comic-strip-free pages, has gotten into the game. Aside from introducing a regular weekly feature in its magazine pages wherein a single cartoonist is invited to serialize his or her latest graphic novel for approximately thirty weeks (and, it should be noted, where Jaime Hernandez's full-color "La Maggie La Loca" appeared, inclusion of which in this anthology was precluded by its upcoming collection in a comprehensive art book, despite my editorial wishes), dignified reviews of comics and graphic novels now regularly appear in the *New York Times* book review pages. But for all this general and encouraging bonhomie, the opinions expressed are not always rah-rah; in a June 2006 roundup of various recent comics in the *Times*, the reviewer expressed a certain weariness at the "creeping sameness" to much of what he was leafing through, "semi- or wholly autobiographical sketches of drifting daily life and its quiet epiphanies." Admittedly, as comics have entered their late adolescence as art/literature, a preponderance of autobiographical work has accrued, beginning with the 1960s and 1970s comics of Justin Green, Aline Kominsky (now Kominsky-Crumb), Harvey Pekar, and, of course, Robert Crumb himself. Art Spiegelman has eloquently expressed the difficulty of understanding both the value of and the means to approaching fiction in his recent "Portrait of the Artist as a Young %@#*!" and the three generations of artists C. Tyler, Joe Matt, and Jeffrey Brown have, at least up until now, devoted their oeuvres almost solely to soul-searching self-analyses. I genuinely think that this is a necessity, however, both for the artists and the medium. As cartoonists and comics still attempt to acquaint themselves with not only how to express real human emotion but also try to decide exactly what human emotions are worth expressing, the most facile and immediate way to do it is to write about oneself. Charges of self-indulgence and navel-gazing are inevitable, especially for an artist maturing within an insulated and comparatively worry-free culture such as America's, but isn't art at least partly a means of finding a way out of oneself and then reporting back? The value of trying to see and feel one's own experience is a necessary step toward understanding what communicates and works in a medium, as well as an important bridge to cross toward completely synthetic, or imaginary, storytelling, should any artist want to cross it. (Though things really aren't that different over there, other than the grass is a bit greener—or at least it is if you want it to be.) So in the first part of this anthology there are a number of biographical and autobiographical selections, ranging from C. Tyler's heartbeat-skipping "Once, We Ran" to the ideogrammatically immolating couch-time of Ivan Brunetti—with everything in between. For myself, I genuinely think that one of the real responsibilities of an artist and writer (or, more properly, what I look for in writing and art myself) is a clear, honest communication of what it feels like to be alive to people who haven't been born yet. There's a unique emotional rudder that literature and art can provide to a consciousness drifting through life—not something as banal as a roadmap or a rule book—but a sort of sympathetic rut in the road. And whether that rut is real or imaginary, life is a lot harder to get through without it.

Without tilling too much of the same ground that I always seem to turn over whenever I try to write about comics as a medium, I should reiterate that cartooning takes a really, really long time and is hard, lonely work. Pages upon hundreds of pages are drawn and thrown away before any writer or artist eventually finds him- or herself. The reader may even reliably calculate that the time it takes to read a comic strip story to the time it took to draw it is roughly 1:1,000, and I'm not exaggerating. At the same time, if any art is to endure, the effort expended on its creation is usurped (and one hopes eventually dwarfed) by the work's lasting power. For example, it takes a few days to read *War and Peace,* which took Tolstoy a few years to write, but it has survived and grown exponentially in strength through many generations of readers. Being so faced with eternity, at some point the artist, writer, or cartoonist has to somehow allow his or her work, for lack of any better metaphor, to take on a life of its own — a necessary step that admits instinct, uncertainty, or faith into the act of creation — what is frequently referred to as "taking a risk" in art. Sometimes this yielding can lead to complete failure, other times it can lead to something much larger. I think that in comics it's a necessary step in the regular creative process, and, from the works collected in this volume, it's something that appears to be happening more and more. The traditional, commercially established mode of "scripting" a story and then simply illustrating it does not admit to the endemic potential in comics to literally imagine and see on the page, to say nothing of plumbing areas of imagination and memory that, I think, would otherwise be left inaccessible to words or single pictures alone.

Art in the twentieth century (at least in the West) all but stomped out the idea of storytelling in pictures. Before that, a narrative, whether religious, military, or mythological, practically formed the raison d'être for visual art's existence. Altarpieces, through repeated sequential images, told the story of the Stations of the Cross, and giant tapestries and paintings recounted battles and victories for citizens and subsequent generations to admire and fear. But as the notion of art as essentially conceptual sprouted and eventually grew all over the previous century's museum walls and museumgoers' eyes, paintings or drawings that "showed something" were increasingly dismissed as sentimental, or, even worse, "illustrative." There's a certain logic to this, especially if the urge is toward reducing a medium to its absolute barest skin-and-bones essentials in an attempt to discover its innate truth. Unfortunately, the truth of painting and drawing is that they're actually really great for showing things. (Music, on the other hand, isn't; think of how clunky and disturbing a concrete sound like a car horn is when introduced into a melody line that otherwise seems to be perfectly capturing the ebb and flow of the heart; I don't think it's wrong to think that certain art forms might be better at one thing or another.) Comics, on the third hand (and at about the same time all of this was in full swing in the world of visual art), were showing things, lots of things: rape, murder, and other violence — so much so that in the

1950s comic books were forced to self-censor as activist Fredric Wertham suggested that the corruption of American youth could be directly traced to such pictured acts of horror (the story of which, incidentally, is lyrically illuminated in Art Spiegelman's as-of-yet-unproduced opera *Drawn to Death*). Because of the traditionally narrative basis of the language in which they work, cartoonists are almost always cornered into "showing something." And how lucky we've been! And how lucky painters have been, too, ironically appropriating comic book imagery for decades because it was one of the few permitted territories for visual representation that the art world could stomach, sort of a "cake and eat it too" approach. (I, for one, am actually glad they let me eat cake, even if I had to choke down a little theory with it.)

Ironically, while intellectually dismantling the reasons that people made pictures in the first place, art historians and art theoreticians also fell all over themselves telling us that we lived in an increasingly media-saturated world, an imagecentric, visually overstuffed, nonverbal, and distracted commercial culture barely able to discern what was real from what was advertised, and I guess to a certain degree they were right; I grew up with a mind snot-packed full of camera-cropped visions of superheroes and spaceships, and it's taken me a number of years of school and adulthood to blow my brains free of them all. Additionally, the narrative techniques of filmmaking have infiltrated our consciousness to the degree that we now dream in crosscuts, close-ups, and long shots. We think nothing of zooming in on something in a photograph or a drawing, slicing off arms and legs and even ears as a way of simulating the focus of consciousness and how our minds categorize and order information. But is this really the best, or even the most accurate, way to reflect how we "see" the world? I'm certainly no scientist or perceptual researcher, though I think I can say with a fair degree of certainty that the human invention of language evolved as a means of speedily ordering experience, allowing us to collect and organize the wash of perceptual muck that enters our senses into categorizable and reasonably consistent generalities, all as a means for quick action. Without delving too far into didactic nattering any further than I've already allowed myself, this distinction is more or less what comics are: a language of abbreviated "visual words" having its own grammar, syntax, and punctuation.

I recently came across a very odd but captivating idea in the introduction to a new edition of a collection of Alexander Pushkin's short stories, in which the author, discussing the rise of prose in Russia as contrasted with that of England, suggested that seventeenth-century Elizabethans (who were, I infer, isolated and essentially rural) thought and spoke mainly in poetry. By the eighteenth century, however, poetry had surrendered to the more blunt clarity of prose, finally culminating in an increasingly urban and industrial nineteenth century, where Victorians "talked in fiction."* The

* John Bayley, *Alexander Pushkin: The Collected Stories,* Everyman's Library, p. xxii.

idea that as geography, communication, and society became more tight-knit, individual perceptions and expression began to standardize seems oddly credible to me, despite its broad sweep. And this is more or less exactly the inverse of what's been happening in comics for the last few years. As a medium that was locked into a fairly rigid set of storytelling strictures by a commercial system that encouraged production over insight, the basic "balloon over picture" trope hadn't changed for decades. But even a casual flip-through of the pages of this book will demonstrate a highly individual approach by each and every artist, all with the aim of getting at something new or, more precisely, real. I've said this a few times before, but I wholeheartedly believe that comics are one of the more alive arts currently extant. I eagerly anticipate the newest publications by my favorite cartoonists not only because I love their work, but also so I can see what new approaches to storytelling they've discovered that I can steal. With the recent rise of self-revelatory comics have come a requisite experimentation and pushing forward of the means of expression available to every artist, to say nothing of younger cartoonists no longer having to begin with the stone tools of superhero comics to try and chip out a personal story. (If this isn't the definition of a living language, then I don't know what is.) Sometimes this experimentation can be as straightforward as grafting a naturalistic or literary sensibility to the traditional mode of cartooning and sometimes it can be a complete reassessment of what comics really are, whether illustrated text, a symbolic language, or a series of uncertainly linked and expressively limned drawings. The younger generation, especially, seems to have taken this latter notion and developed it to such a degree that it leaves a creaky, brittle thinker like myself sitting on the edge of the dance floor, earnestly trying to find the beat. In short, I think this is absolutely great. A few years ago I wouldn't have thought that comics could sustain such wrenching around, but I'm delighted to see that as a medium it seems to hold up just fine. The cartoonist Gary Panter has to be given credit more than anyone for this change, in the 1970s and 1980s inventing a new way of visual storytelling that articulated and highlighted the emotional shifts of experience with a pen-on-paper pithing out of synaesthetic sensations of memory into an inseparable alchemy of poetry, calligraphy, and vision that leaves a reader reeling. I think it's fair to opine that he's also singlehandedly paved the way for an entirely new generation of artists. Two of the more individual ones are the art collective "Paper Rad" and C.F., and they appear in this anthology. Whereas for decades it has been the tacit aim of most cartoonists to present a series of pictures that are consistently and clearly linked visually, many of the younger artists make no such concession, allowing for very strange yet oddly real associations and feelings that, to me, are disconcertingly freeing, especially when compared to more conventional and, for lack of a better word, theatrical comics. Reading their work and then returning to a more familiar type of comics is sort of like listening to Louis Armstrong and a Sousa march back-to-back.

Personally, I suffered the very traumatizing experience of reading a large chunk of this material and then returning to my drawing table to suddenly sense a great deficit and lack of internal life to my rigid schemata. Like I mentioned earlier: it makes me feel old.

At the same time, a number of cartoonists whom I admire and deeply respect state with relative certainty that a comic strip without a solid, easily grasped story or explicit moral conflict between characters is not worthy of either reading or writing. I guess I'm not so sure. I think we're at a point now where it's becoming clear that comics can accommodate a variety of sensibilities and wildly divergent dispositions, and I wonder whether the more dramatic mode of presenting scenes and situations is necessarily the only approach. In the interests of full disclosure (and risking the above-mentioned accusations of being self-indulgent and navel-gazing), lately I find myself frequently torn between whether I'm "really" an artist or a writer. I was trained and educated as the former, encouraged into the world of paint-stained pants and a white-walled studio where wild, messy experiments precipitate the incubation of other visual ideas — though I'm just as happy to sit at a desk in clean trousers with a sharp pencil and work on a single story for four or five days in a quiet and deliberate manner. In short, I'm coming to believe that a cartoonist, unlike the general cliché, is almost — bear with me now — a sort of new species of creator, one who can lean just as easily toward a poetic, painterly, or writerly inclination, but one who thinks and expresses him- or herself primarily in pictures. This might sound crazy, but I'm starting to think it's true. I am not, however, advocating some empty approach to a nonobjective sort of cartooning such as what happened to painting in the 1960s and 1970s. But as a possible metaphor for memory and recollection, I definitely think that there are many untapped and untried approaches in comics, and ones that are only now starting to be unearthed. At the very least, cartoonists for decades have been making art — and visual art — about life, and that's something to take note of during a period that art historical naysayers and doomsdayers sometimes label as suffering a "crisis of representation."

Any good annual anthology should have a sort of desert island condensation to it; even if every single comic produced between August 2005 and August 2006 suddenly and mysteriously vaporized, this book should still at least hint at what was happening during those months. As such, I've tried to organize it as cleanly and clearly as possible, but a partly visual, partly literary book like this is not simply a matter of lining all the selections up, drizzling them into a layout program, and then pressing "print." Disturbing conjunctions and abrasions of style, approach, and even something as seemingly inconsequential as conflicting colors can affect the readability and emotional effect of an individual story. Also, cartoonists think in panels, pages, and page spreads, frequently composing their stories so that the simple act of turning the page means that a scene change, an emotional shift, or a visual surprise awaits. Thus, maintaining the integrity of a left/right page orientation sometimes required abutting odd bedfellows, inserting blank or colored page stops, or, at least in one obvious case, restructuring. Miriam Katin's excerpt from her squarely formatted "We Are on Our Own" necessitated the restacking of panels into arrangements that completely destroyed her carefully considered scene changes, here now alluded to by color shifts in the tonalities of the grays. As well, while Adrian Tomine's and Gilbert Hernandez's works were originally printed in stark black and white, in these pages the paper has been tinted (with the artists' permission, of course) as a means of more clearly defining their respective spaces. Finally, though many of these stories appear in their entirety, some are excerpts from much longer works, and so what serves as an ending may actually simply be the extract coming to an abrupt stop; in every case, however, an eye was kept toward readability and the artists consulted as to the beginnings and ends of their respective excerpts (and, of course, the afterword section allows every artist to explain and/or vent an opinion of the stories selected).

A frequent complaint regarding these sorts of collections (and even recent museum shows) is that there aren't enough (or any) women included in them. I should state right here that I am not of the cut of cloth to check an artist's genitalia at the door. Nor in the case of this book did I go out in search of a couple of hermaphrodites to even out the score. What I did include, however, was work that I found to be the most interesting, honest, and revealing to be published in the past year, and that collection, as it turned out, included comics from the pens of both sexes. However, those who still feel compelled to tally points for one or another chromosome may wish to note that Alison Bechdel's *Fun Home* was chosen as the best book of the year by *Time* magazine — the best book, of ALL books, not just the best comic book — and that Marjane Satrapi now ranks as probably one of the best-known and most widely read authors in the United States (though her not living here unfortunately disqualifies her from inclusion in this book). This all brings me to Lynda Barry, who both as a cartoonist and a friend ranks highly in my personal pantheon of greats. I think that her work of all cartoonists was the first to show me how the revelatory experiments of biography can lead into fiction in comics, to say nothing of finding an individual expressive voice in the medium that has had a lasting and powerful influence. The artists Seth and John Porcellino have also both told me on different occasions the profound effect her unpretentious and penetrating work had on them in their formative years. Writing believable fiction in comics (because despite how confessional and autobiographical her work may seem, it is, by and large, fiction) in many ways, I believe, started with her.

I realize as I list off some of the names in this book that I'm not only mentioning artists and writers I admire and who have provided either examples or encouragement to me as a cartoonist, I'm also pretty much making a list of people whom I consider friends. Some are, in fact, very close friends. The careful reader might even notice a name or two cropping up between and within stories; this shouldn't be read as any in joke or intentional insularity on the part of cartoonists but more as an indication of how closely we all pay attention to each other's work, as I mentioned above. As well, because of the great amount of time that cartooning requires, sometimes years pass without a new collected work appearing by any single artist. In light of this, and aside from not being able to include Jaime Hernandez's *Times* strip in this collection, 2006 was a year in which foremost cartoonist and screenwriter Daniel Clowes unfortunately saw nothing published between the August 2005 and August 2006 eligibility dates for this anthology, and the great Joe Sacco, whose emotionally wrenching and life-changing work renders real parts of the world that the nightly news renders emotionless, continues to work on a new book about the Middle East. Finally, I can't claim that I was able to read everything that was published or available in the last year, though I did try, a difficulty which in and of itself is encouraging, because that only confirms the number of cartoonists and graphic novelists working seems now to be greater than ever before. In fact, I sort of hope that somewhere something was published or is about to be published that makes everything in this book seem outmoded and juvenile — though I guess that's for future guest editors to discover and decide upon.

Lastly, since these prefaces always seem to clatter to their end with a tiresomely long list of thanks (which I'm going to avoid here with a blanket, though no less grateful, regards to the patient editors at Houghton Mifflin who have made this new addition to their Best American series tenable), I'd additionally like to single out and acknowledge Dave Eggers for his help and encouragement to cartoonists everywhere over the past few years. From his early, kind (and inaugural) reviews of comics for the *New York Times* to his inviting *McSweeney's* #13 to be an all-comics anthology to his including cartoonists' work as viable contributions to his otherwise all-prose Best American Nonrequired Reading anthologies, it's without a doubt that comics' legitimacy as an increasingly accepted art form owes a lion's share of thanks to him.

CHRIS WARE

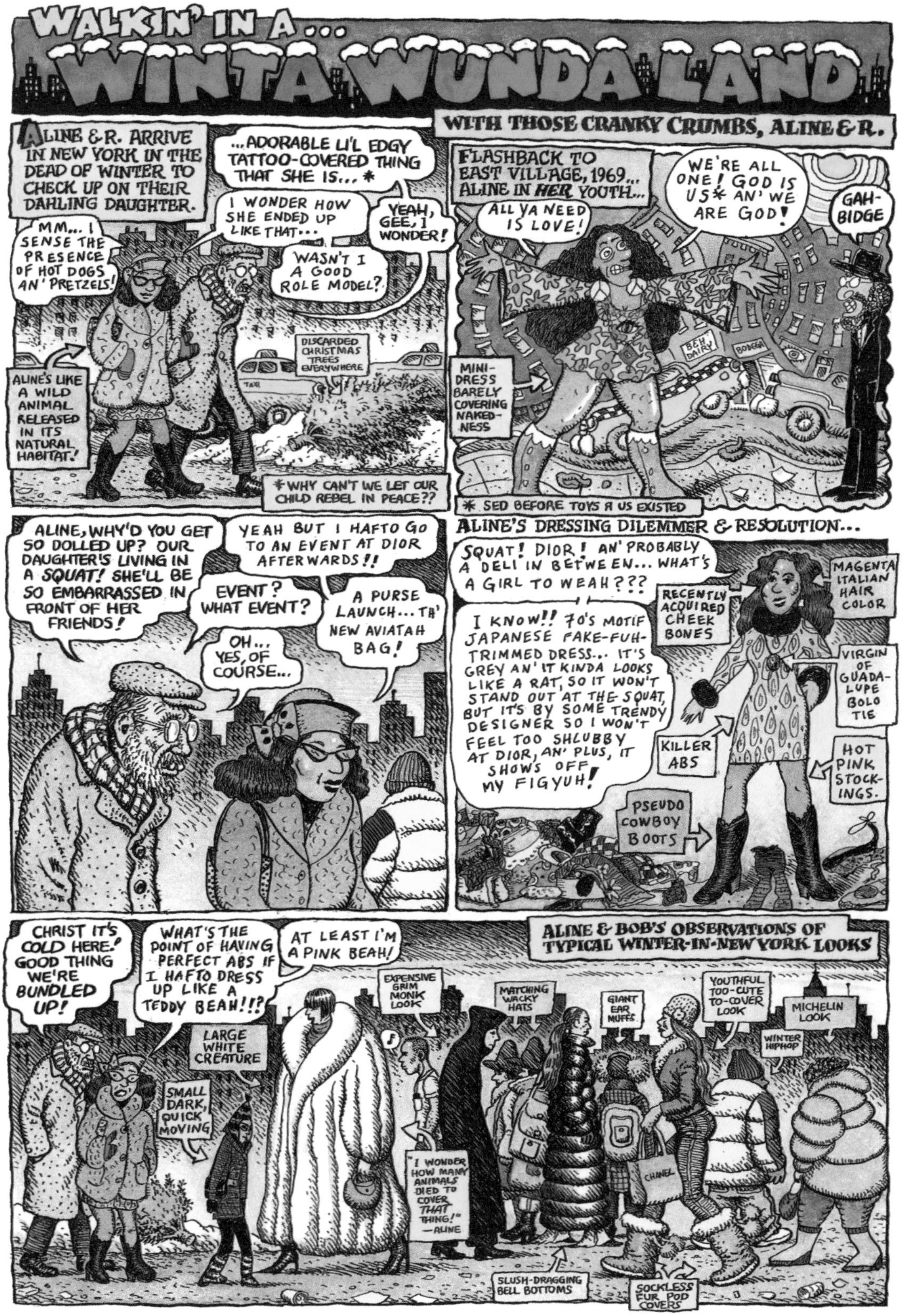
WALKIN' IN A...
WINTA WUNDA LAND
WITH THOSE CRANKY CRUMBS, ALINE & R.
ALINE & R. ARRIVE IN NEW YORK IN THE DEAD OF WINTER TO CHECK UP ON THEIR DAHLING DAUGHTER.
...ADORABLE LI'L EDGY TATTOO-COVERED THING THAT SHE IS... *
MM... I SENSE THE PRESENCE OF HOT DOGS AN' PRETZELS!
I WONDER HOW SHE ENDED UP LIKE THAT...
YEAH, GEE, I WONDER!
WASN'T I A GOOD ROLE MODEL?
DISCARDED CHRISTMAS TREES EVERYWHERE
ALINE'S LIKE A WILD ANIMAL RELEASED IN ITS NATURAL HABITAT!
* WHY CAN'T WE LET OUR CHILD REBEL IN PEACE??
FLASHBACK TO EAST VILLAGE, 1969... ALINE IN HER YOUTH...
ALL YA NEED IS LOVE!
WE'RE ALL ONE! GOD IS US* AN' WE ARE GOD!
GAH-BIDGE
MINI-DRESS BARELY COVERING NAKED-NESS
* SED BEFORE TOYS Я US EXISTED
ALINE, WHY'D YOU GET SO DOLLED UP? OUR DAUGHTER'S LIVING IN A SQUAT! SHE'LL BE SO EMBARRASSED IN FRONT OF HER FRIENDS!
YEAH BUT I HAFTO GO TO AN EVENT AT DIOR AFTERWARDS!!
EVENT? WHAT EVENT?
A PURSE LAUNCH... TH' NEW AVIATAH BAG!
OH... YES, OF COURSE...
ALINE'S DRESSING DILEMMER & RESOLUTION...
SQUAT! DIOR! AN' PROBABLY A DELI IN BETWEEN... WHAT'S A GIRL TO WEAH???
I KNOW!! 70'S MOTIF JAPANESE FAKE-FUH-TRIMMED DRESS... IT'S GREY AN' IT KINDA LOOKS LIKE A RAT, SO IT WON'T STAND OUT AT THE SQUAT, BUT IT'S BY SOME TRENDY DESIGNER SO I WON'T FEEL TOO SHLUBBY AT DIOR, AN' PLUS, IT SHOWS OFF MY FIGYUH!
RECENTLY ACQUIRED CHEEK BONES
MAGENTA ITALIAN HAIR COLOR
VIRGIN OF GUADA-LUPE BOLO TIE
KILLER ABS
HOT PINK STOCK-INGS.
PSEUDO COWBOY BOOTS
CHRIST IT'S COLD HERE! GOOD THING WE'RE BUNDLED UP!
WHAT'S THE POINT OF HAVING PERFECT ABS IF I HAFTO DRESS UP LIKE A TEDDY BEAH!!?
AT LEAST I'M A PINK BEAH!
ALINE & BOB'S OBSERVATIONS OF TYPICAL WINTER-IN-NEW YORK LOOKS
LARGE WHITE CREATURE
SMALL DARK, QUICK MOVING
EXPENSIVE GRIM MONK LOOK
MATCHING WACKY HATS
GIANT EAR MUFFS
YOUTHFUL TOO-CUTE TO-COVER LOOK
MICHELIN LOOK
WINTER HIPHOP
"I WONDER HOW MANY ANIMALS DIED TO COVER THAT THING!" —ALINE
CHANEL
SLUSH-DRAGGING BELL BOTTOMS
SOCKLESS FUR POD COVERS

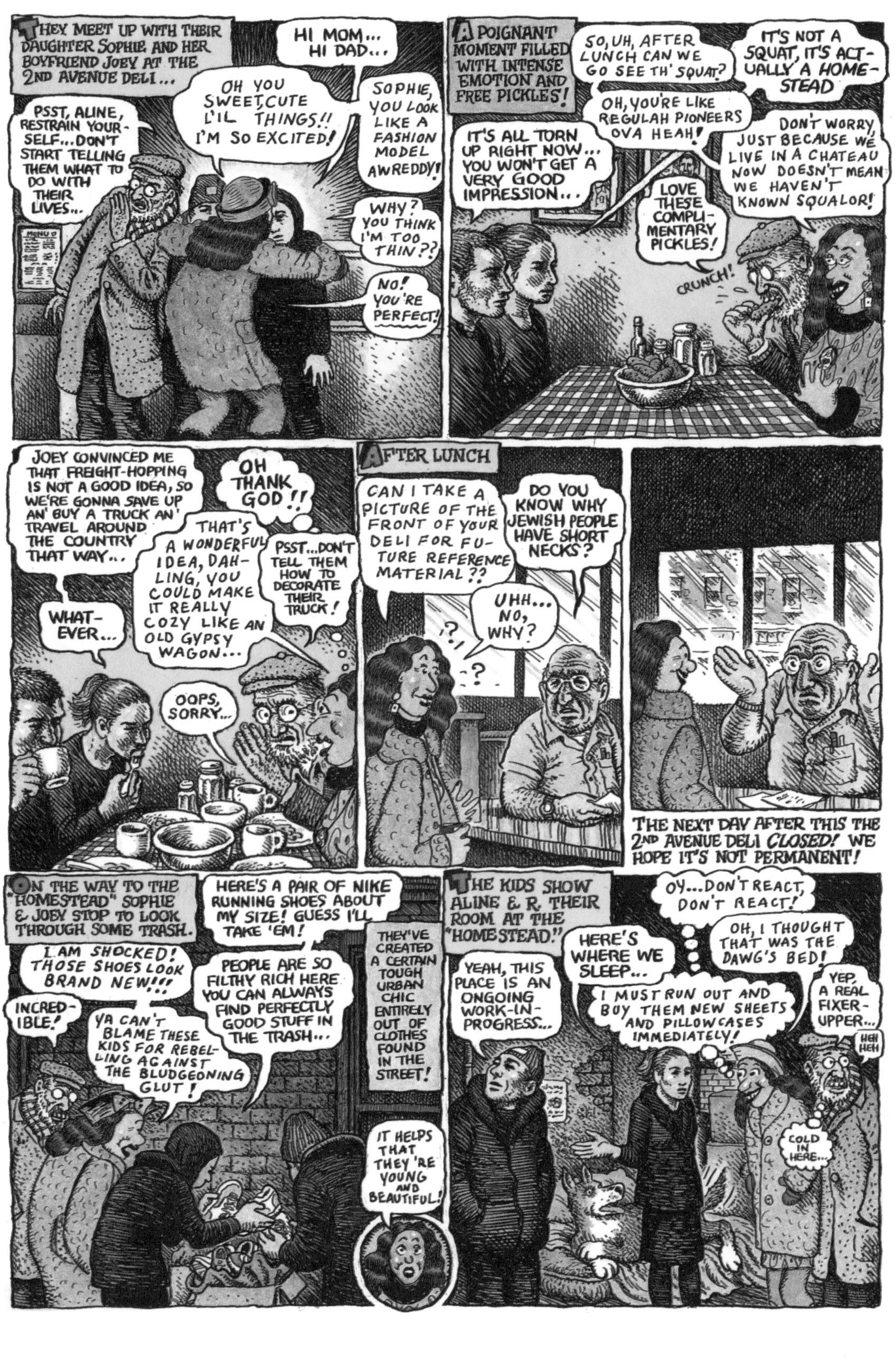
THEY MEET UP WITH THEIR DAUGHTER SOPHIE AND HER BOYFRIEND JOEY AT THE 2ND AVENUE DELI...
HI MOM... HI DAD...
OH YOU SWEET, CUTE L'IL THINGS!! I'M SO EXCITED!
SOPHIE, YOU LOOK LIKE A FASHION MODEL AWREDDY!
PSST, ALINE, RESTRAIN YOURSELF... DON'T START TELLING THEM WHAT TO DO WITH THEIR LIVES...
WHY? YOU THINK I'M TOO THIN??
NO! YOU'RE PERFECT!
A POIGNANT MOMENT FILLED WITH INTENSE EMOTION AND FREE PICKLES!
SO, UH, AFTER LUNCH CAN WE GO SEE TH' SQUAT?
IT'S NOT A SQUAT, IT'S ACTUALLY A HOMESTEAD
OH, YOU'RE LIKE REGULAH PIONEERS OVA HEAH!
IT'S ALL TORN UP RIGHT NOW... YOU WON'T GET A VERY GOOD IMPRESSION...
DON'T WORRY, JUST BECAUSE WE LIVE IN A CHATEAU NOW DOESN'T MEAN WE HAVEN'T KNOWN SQUALOR!
LOVE THESE COMPLIMENTARY PICKLES!
CRUNCH!
JOEY CONVINCED ME THAT FREIGHT-HOPPING IS NOT A GOOD IDEA, SO WE'RE GONNA SAVE UP AN' BUY A TRUCK AN' TRAVEL AROUND THE COUNTRY THAT WAY...
OH THANK GOD!!
THAT'S A WONDERFUL IDEA, DAHLING, YOU COULD MAKE IT REALLY COZY LIKE AN OLD GYPSY WAGON...
PSST...DON'T TELL THEM HOW TO DECORATE THEIR TRUCK!
WHAT-EVER...
OOPS, SORRY...
AFTER LUNCH
CAN I TAKE A PICTURE OF THE FRONT OF YOUR DELI FOR FUTURE REFERENCE MATERIAL??
DO YOU KNOW WHY JEWISH PEOPLE HAVE SHORT NECKS?
UHH... NO, WHY?
THE NEXT DAY AFTER THIS THE 2ND AVENUE DELI CLOSED! WE HOPE IT'S NOT PERMANENT!
ON THE WAY TO THE "HOMESTEAD" SOPHIE & JOEY STOP TO LOOK THROUGH SOME TRASH.
HERE'S A PAIR OF NIKE RUNNING SHOES ABOUT MY SIZE! GUESS I'LL TAKE 'EM!
I AM SHOCKED! THOSE SHOES LOOK BRAND NEW!!!
INCREDIBLE!
PEOPLE ARE SO FILTHY RICH HERE YOU CAN ALWAYS FIND PERFECTLY GOOD STUFF IN THE TRASH...
YA CAN'T BLAME THESE KIDS FOR REBELLING AGAINST THE BLUDGEONING GLUT!
THEY'VE CREATED A CERTAIN TOUGH URBAN CHIC ENTIRELY OUT OF CLOTHES FOUND IN THE STREET!
IT HELPS THAT THEY'RE YOUNG AND BEAUTIFUL!
THE KIDS SHOW ALINE & R. THEIR ROOM AT THE "HOMESTEAD."
OY...DON'T REACT, DON'T REACT!
HERE'S WHERE WE SLEEP...
OH, I THOUGHT THAT WAS THE DAWG'S BED!
YEAH, THIS PLACE IS AN ONGOING WORK-IN-PROGRESS...
I MUST RUN OUT AND BUY THEM NEW SHEETS AND PILLOWCASES IMMEDIATELY!
YEP, A REAL FIXER-UPPER...
HEH HEH
COLD IN HERE...

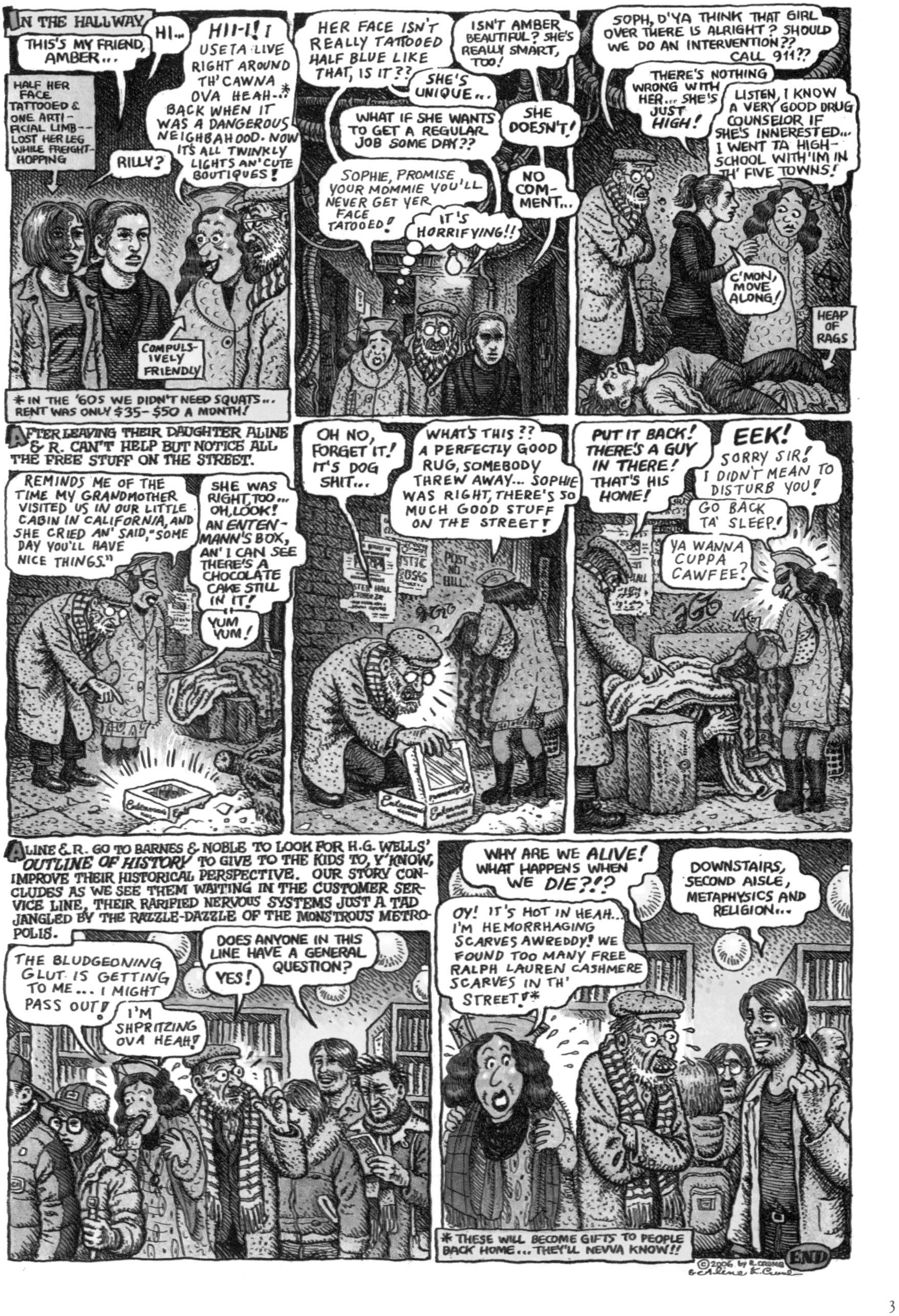
IN THE HALLWAY
THIS'S MY FRIEND, AMBER...
HI...
HII-I!! I USETA LIVE RIGHT AROUND TH' CAWNA OVA HEAH...* BACK WHEN IT WAS A DANGEROUS NEIGHBAHOOD. NOW IT'S ALL TWINKLY LIGHTS AN' CUTE BOUTIQUES!
HALF HER FACE TATTOOED & ONE ARTIFICIAL LIMB-- LOST HER LEG WHILE FREIGHT-HOPPING
RILLY?
COMPULSIVELY FRIENDLY
* IN THE '60S WE DIDN'T NEED SQUATS... RENT WAS ONLY $35-$50 A MONTH!
HER FACE ISN'T REALLY TATTOOED HALF BLUE LIKE THAT, IS IT??
ISN'T AMBER BEAUTIFUL? SHE'S REALLY SMART, TOO!
SHE'S UNIQUE...
WHAT IF SHE WANTS TO GET A REGULAR JOB SOME DAY??
SHE DOESN'T!
SOPHIE, PROMISE YOUR MOMMIE YOU'LL NEVER GET YER FACE TATTOOED!
IT'S HORRIFYING!!
NO COMMENT...
SOPH, D'YA THINK THAT GIRL OVER THERE IS ALRIGHT? SHOULD WE DO AN INTERVENTION?? CALL 911??
THERE'S NOTHING WRONG WITH HER... SHE'S JUST HIGH!
LISTEN, I KNOW A VERY GOOD DRUG COUNSELOR IF SHE'S INNERESTED... I WENT TA HIGH-SCHOOL WITH 'IM IN TH' FIVE TOWNS!
C'MON, MOVE ALONG!
HEAP OF RAGS
AFTER LEAVING THEIR DAUGHTER ALINE & R. CAN'T HELP BUT NOTICE ALL THE FREE STUFF ON THE STREET.
REMINDS ME OF THE TIME MY GRANDMOTHER VISITED US IN OUR LITTLE CABIN IN CALIFORNIA, AND SHE CRIED AN' SAID, "SOME DAY YOU'LL HAVE NICE THINGS."
SHE WAS RIGHT, TOO... OH, LOOK! AN ENTENMANN'S BOX, AN' I CAN SEE THERE'S A CHOCOLATE CAKE STILL IN IT!
YUM YUM!
OH NO, FORGET IT! IT'S DOG SHIT...
WHAT'S THIS?? A PERFECTLY GOOD RUG, SOMEBODY THREW AWAY... SOPHIE WAS RIGHT, THERE'S SO MUCH GOOD STUFF ON THE STREET!
POST NO BILL
PUT IT BACK! THERE'S A GUY IN THERE! THAT'S HIS HOME!
EEK! SORRY SIR! I DIDN'T MEAN TO DISTURB YOU!
GO BACK TA' SLEEP!
YA WANNA CUPPA CAWFEE?
ALINE & R. GO TO BARNES & NOBLE TO LOOK FOR H.G. WELLS' OUTLINE OF HISTORY TO GIVE TO THE KIDS TO, Y'KNOW, IMPROVE THEIR HISTORICAL PERSPECTIVE. OUR STORY CONCLUDES AS WE SEE THEM WAITING IN THE CUSTOMER SERVICE LINE, THEIR RARIFIED NERVOUS SYSTEMS JUST A TAD JANGLED BY THE RAZZLE-DAZZLE OF THE MONSTROUS METROPOLIS.
THE BLUDGEONING GLUT IS GETTING TO ME... I MIGHT PASS OUT!
DOES ANYONE IN THIS LINE HAVE A GENERAL QUESTION?
YES!
I'M SHPRITZING OVA HEAH!
WHY ARE WE ALIVE! WHAT HAPPENS WHEN WE DIE?!?
DOWNSTAIRS, SECOND AISLE, METAPHYSICS AND RELIGION...
OY! IT'S HOT IN HEAH... I'M HEMORRHAGING SCARVES AWREDDY! WE FOUND TOO MANY FREE RALPH LAUREN CASHMERE SCARVES IN TH' STREET!*
* THESE WILL BECOME GIFTS TO PEOPLE BACK HOME... THEY'LL NEVVA KNOW!!
END
©2006 by R. Crumb & Aline K. Crumb

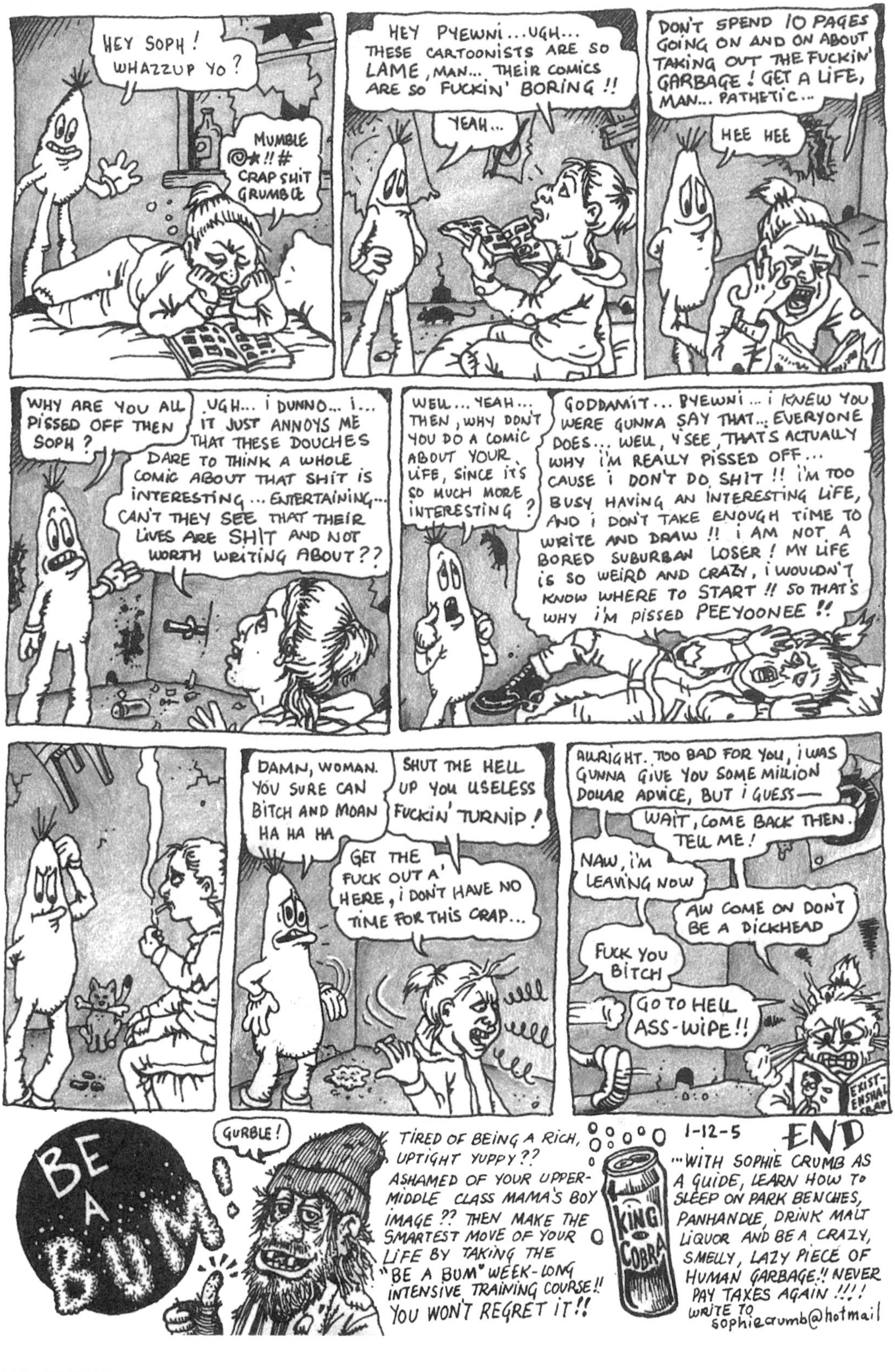
HEY SOPH! WHAZZUP YO?
MUMBLE @*!!# CRAP SHIT GRUMBLE
HEY PYEWNI... UGH... THESE CARTOONISTS ARE SO LAME, MAN... THEIR COMICS ARE SO FUCKIN' BORING!!
YEAH...
DON'T SPEND 10 PAGES GOING ON AND ON ABOUT TAKING OUT THE FUCKIN' GARBAGE! GET A LIFE, MAN... PATHETIC...
HEE HEE
WHY ARE YOU ALL PISSED OFF THEN SOPH?
UGH... I DUNNO... I... IT JUST ANNOYS ME THAT THESE DOUCHES DARE TO THINK A WHOLE COMIC ABOUT THAT SHIT IS INTERESTING... ENTERTAINING... CAN'T THEY SEE THAT THEIR LIVES ARE SHIT AND NOT WORTH WRITING ABOUT??
WELL... YEAH... THEN, WHY DON'T YOU DO A COMIC ABOUT YOUR LIFE, SINCE IT'S SO MUCH MORE INTERESTING?
GODDAMIT... PYEWNI... I KNEW YOU WERE GUNNA SAY THAT... EVERYONE DOES... WELL, Y'SEE, THAT'S ACTUALLY WHY I'M REALLY PISSED OFF... CAUSE I DON'T DO SHIT!! I'M TOO BUSY HAVING AN INTERESTING LIFE, AND I DON'T TAKE ENOUGH TIME TO WRITE AND DRAW!! I AM NOT A BORED SUBURBAN LOSER! MY LIFE IS SO WEIRD AND CRAZY, I WOULDN'T KNOW WHERE TO START!! SO THAT'S WHY I'M PISSED PEEYOONEE!!
DAMN, WOMAN. YOU SURE CAN BITCH AND MOAN HA HA HA
SHUT THE HELL UP YOU USELESS FUCKIN' TURNIP!
GET THE FUCK OUT A' HERE, I DON'T HAVE NO TIME FOR THIS CRAP...
ALRIGHT. TOO BAD FOR YOU, I WAS GUNNA GIVE YOU SOME MILLION DOLLAR ADVICE, BUT I GUESS—
WAIT, COME BACK THEN. TELL ME!
NAW, I'M LEAVING NOW
AW COME ON DON'T BE A DICKHEAD
FUCK YOU BITCH
GO TO HELL ASS-WIPE!!
EXIST-ENSHAL CRAP
BE A BUM
GURBLE!
TIRED OF BEING A RICH, UPTIGHT YUPPY?? ASHAMED OF YOUR UPPER-MIDDLE CLASS MAMA'S BOY IMAGE?? THEN MAKE THE SMARTEST MOVE OF YOUR LIFE BY TAKING THE "BE A BUM" WEEK-LONG INTENSIVE TRAINING COURSE!! YOU WON'T REGRET IT!!
KING COBRA
1-12-5
END
...WITH SOPHIE CRUMB AS A GUIDE, LEARN HOW TO SLEEP ON PARK BENCHES, PANHANDLE, DRINK MALT LIQUOR AND BE A CRAZY, SMELLY, LAZY PIECE OF HUMAN GARBAGE!! NEVER PAY TAXES AGAIN!!!!
WRITE TO sophiecrumb@hotmail

THE CANARY-COLORED CARAVAN OF DEATH

TWO NIGHTS BEFORE MY FATHER DIED, I DREAMED THAT I WAS OUT AT THE BULLPEN WITH HIM. THERE WAS A GLORIOUS SUNSET VISIBLE THROUGH THE TREES.

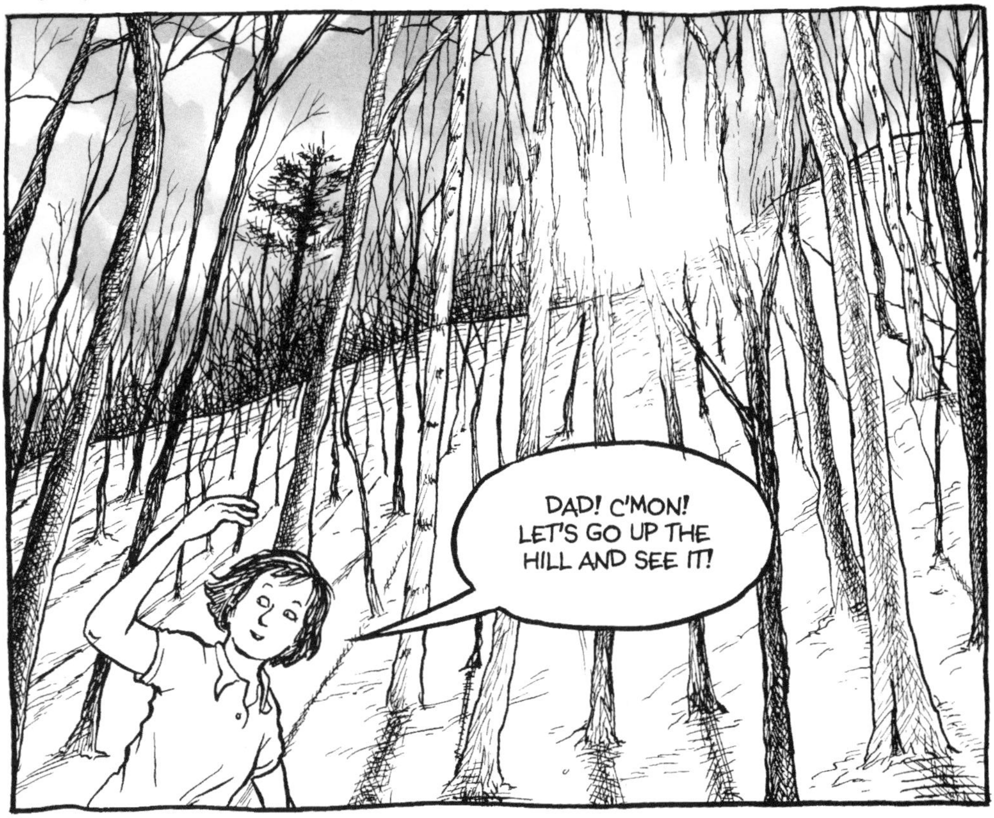
DAD! C'MON! LET'S GO UP THE HILL AND SEE IT!

AT FIRST HE IGNORED ME. I RACED OVER THE VELVETY MOSS IN MY BARE FEET.

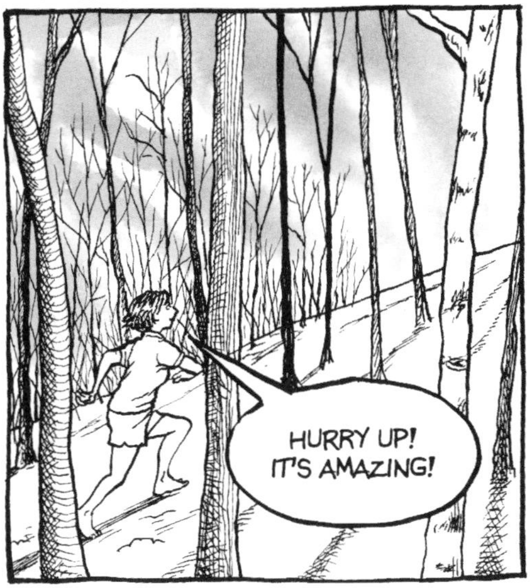
HURRY UP! IT'S AMAZING!

WHEN HE FINALLY GOT THERE, THE SUN HAD SUNK BEHIND THE HORIZON AND THE BRILLIANT COLORS WERE GONE.

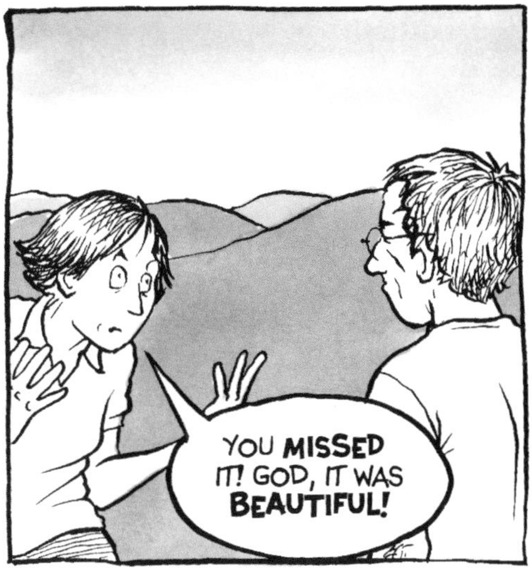
YOU **MISSED** IT! GOD, IT WAS **BEAUTIFUL!**

IF THIS WAS A PREMONITORY DREAM, I CAN ONLY SAY THAT ITS CONDOLENCE-CARD ASSOCIATION OF DEATH WITH A SETTING SUN IS MAUDLIN IN THE EXTREME.

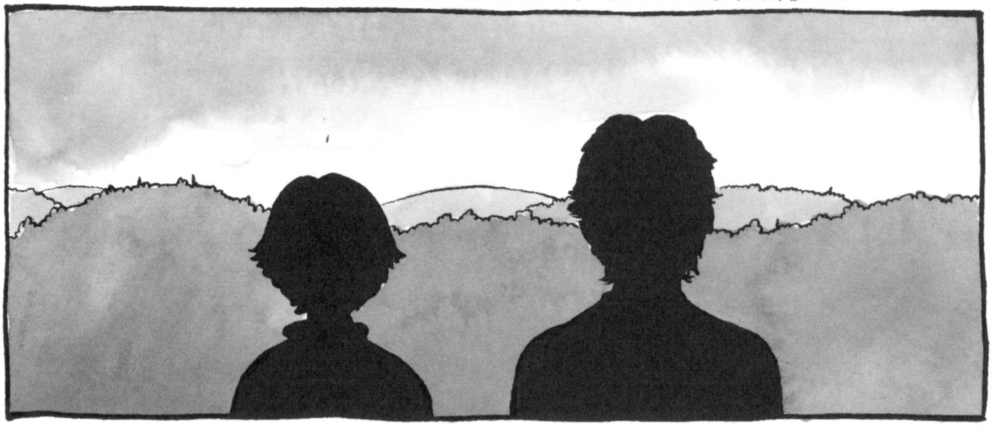

YET MY FATHER DID POSSESS A CERTAIN RADIANCE--

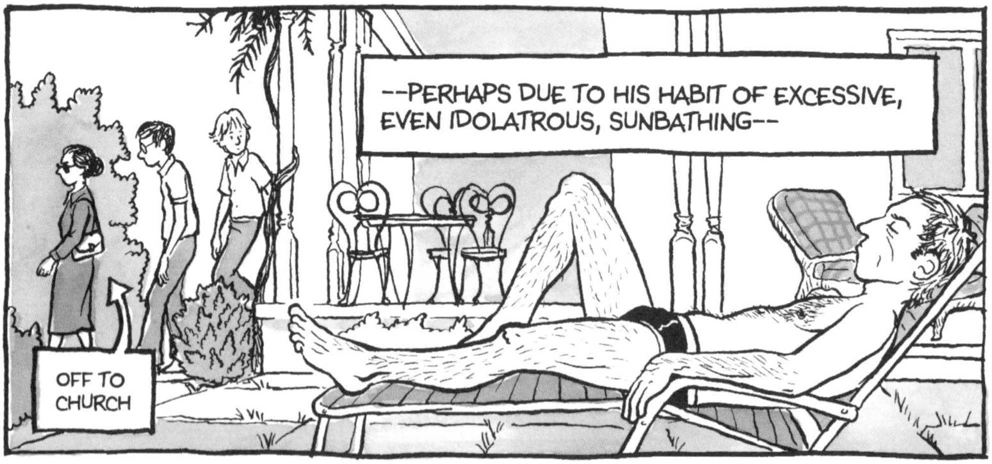
--PERHAPS DUE TO HIS HABIT OF EXCESSIVE, EVEN IDOLATROUS, SUNBATHING--
OFF TO CHURCH

--AND SO HIS DEATH HAD AN INEVITABLY DIMMING, CREPUSCULAR EFFECT. MY COUSIN EVEN POSTPONED HIS ANNUAL FIREWORKS DISPLAY THE NIGHT BEFORE THE FUNERAL.

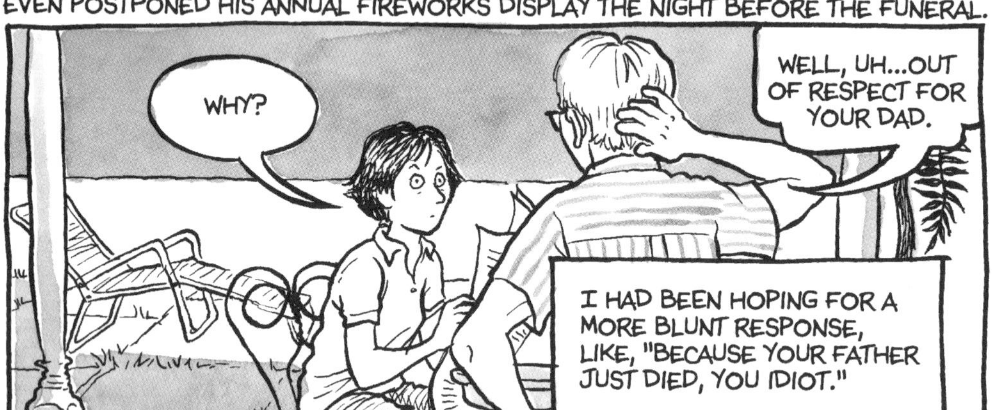
WHY?
WELL, UH...OUT OF RESPECT FOR YOUR DAD.
I HAD BEEN HOPING FOR A MORE BLUNT RESPONSE, LIKE, "BECAUSE YOUR FATHER JUST DIED, YOU IDIOT."

MY NUMBNESS, ALONG WITH ALL THE MEALY-MOUTHED MOURNING, WAS MAKING ME IRRITABLE. WHAT WOULD HAPPEN IF WE SPOKE THE TRUTH?

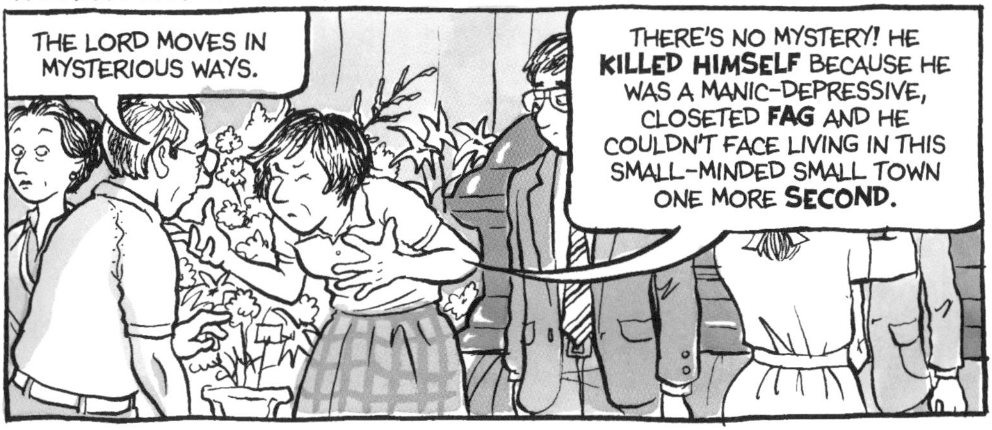
THE LORD MOVES IN MYSTERIOUS WAYS.
THERE'S NO MYSTERY! HE **KILLED HIMSELF** BECAUSE HE WAS A MANIC-DEPRESSIVE, CLOSETED **FAG** AND HE COULDN'T FACE LIVING IN THIS SMALL-MINDED SMALL TOWN ONE MORE **SECOND.**

I DIDN'T FIND OUT.

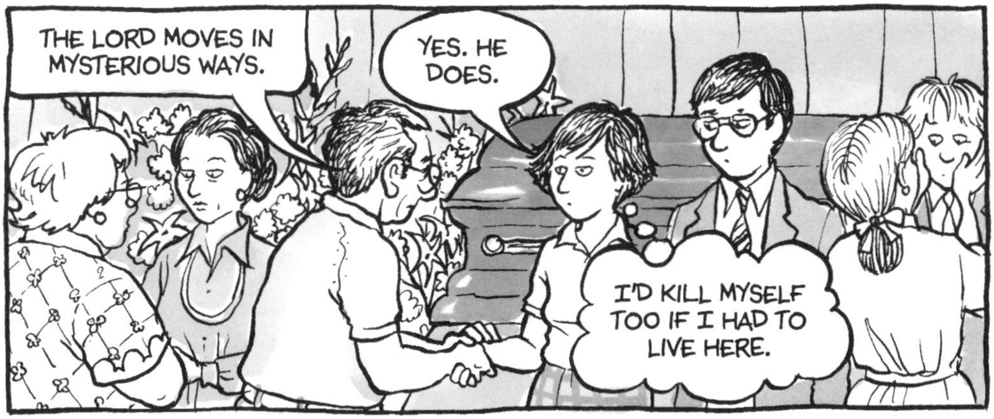
THE LORD MOVES IN MYSTERIOUS WAYS.
YES. HE DOES.
I'D KILL MYSELF TOO IF I HAD TO LIVE HERE.

WHEN I THINK ABOUT HOW MY FATHER'S STORY MIGHT HAVE TURNED OUT DIFFERENTLY, A GEOGRAPHICAL RELOCATION IS USUALLY INVOLVED.

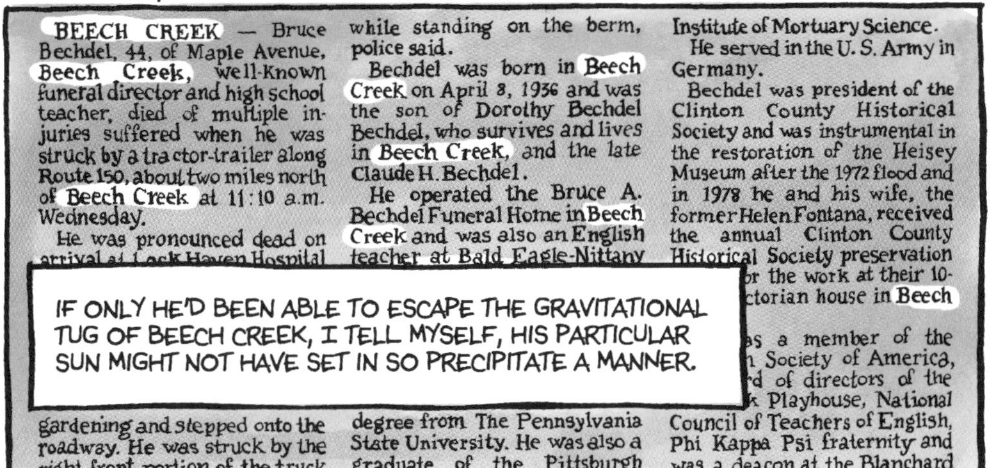
BEECH CREEK — Bruce Bechdel, 44, of Maple Avenue, Beech Creek, well-known funeral director and high school teacher, died of multiple injuries suffered when he was struck by a tractor-trailer along Route 150, about two miles north of Beech Creek at 11:10 a.m. Wednesday.

He was pronounced dead on arrival at Lock Haven Hospital

gardening and stepped onto the roadway. He was struck by the right front portion of the truck while standing on the berm, police said.

Bechdel was born in Beech Creek on April 8, 1936 and was the son of Dorothy Bechdel Bechdel, who survives and lives in Beech Creek, and the late Claude H. Bechdel.

He operated the Bruce A. Bechdel Funeral Home in Beech Creek and was also an English teacher at Bald Eagle-Nittany

degree from The Pennsylvania State University. He was also a graduate of the Pittsburgh Institute of Mortuary Science.

He served in the U. S. Army in Germany.

Bechdel was president of the Clinton County Historical Society and was instrumental in the restoration of the Heisey Museum after the 1972 flood and in 1978 he and his wife, the former Helen Fontana, received the annual Clinton County Historical Society preservation ...r the work at their 10- ...ctorian house in Beech

...s a member of the ...n Society of America, ...rd of directors of the ...k Playhouse, National Council of Teachers of English, Phi Kappa Psi fraternity and was a deacon at the Blanchard

IF ONLY HE'D BEEN ABLE TO ESCAPE THE GRAVITATIONAL TUG OF BEECH CREEK, I TELL MYSELF, HIS PARTICULAR SUN MIGHT NOT HAVE SET IN SO PRECIPITATE A MANNER.

PERHAPS THE PECULIAR TOPOGRAPHY REALLY DID EXERT SOME KIND OF PULL.

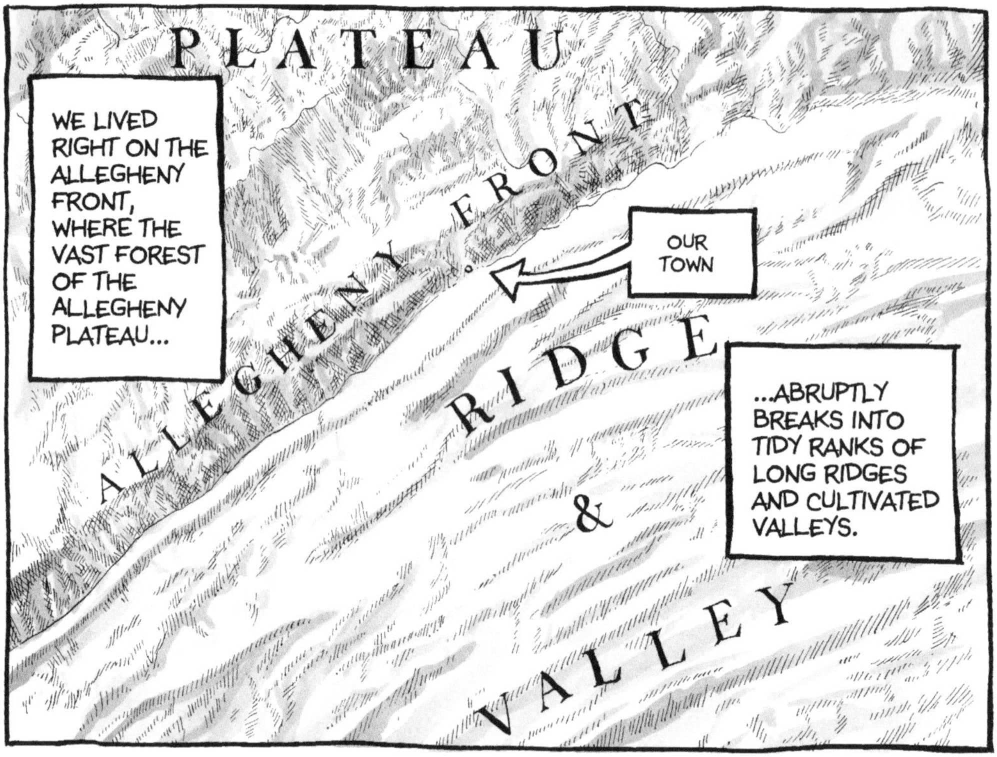
PLATEAU
WE LIVED RIGHT ON THE ALLEGHENY FRONT, WHERE THE VAST FOREST OF THE ALLEGHENY PLATEAU...
ALLEGHENY FRONT
OUR TOWN
RIDGE
&
VALLEY
...ABRUPTLY BREAKS INTO TIDY RANKS OF LONG RIDGES AND CULTIVATED VALLEYS.

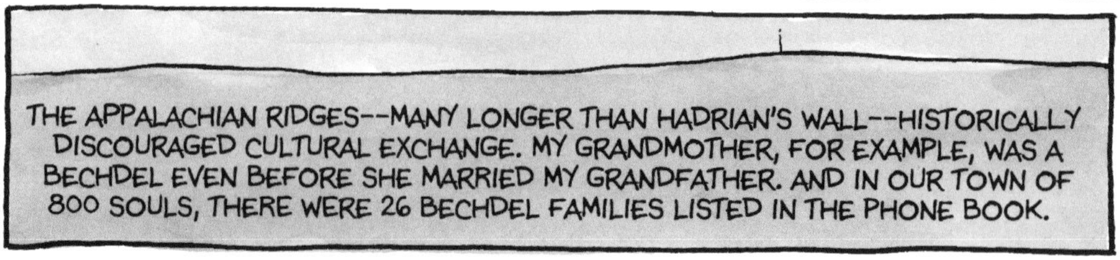
THE APPALACHIAN RIDGES--MANY LONGER THAN HADRIAN'S WALL--HISTORICALLY DISCOURAGED CULTURAL EXCHANGE. MY GRANDMOTHER, FOR EXAMPLE, WAS A BECHDEL EVEN BEFORE SHE MARRIED MY GRANDFATHER. AND IN OUR TOWN OF 800 SOULS, THERE WERE 26 BECHDEL FAMILIES LISTED IN THE PHONE BOOK.

THIS DESPITE THE FACT THAT PEOPLE COULD EASILY DRIVE AROUND THE MOUNTAINS BY THE TIME MY FATHER WAS A CHILD.

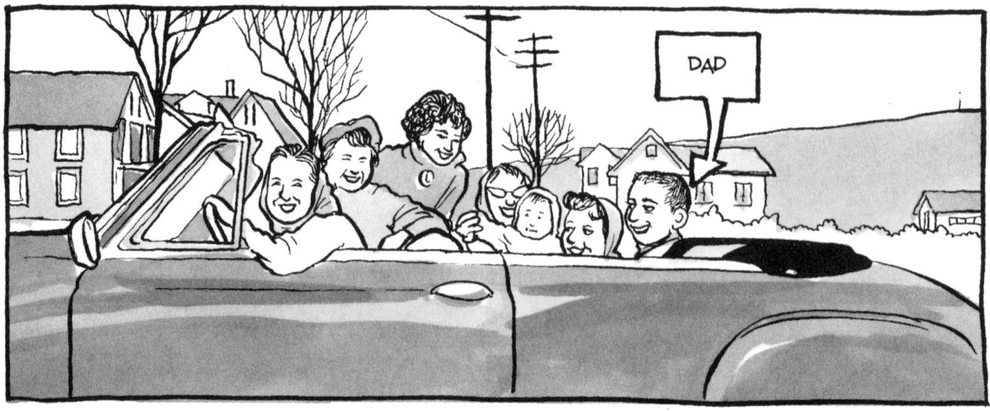
DAD

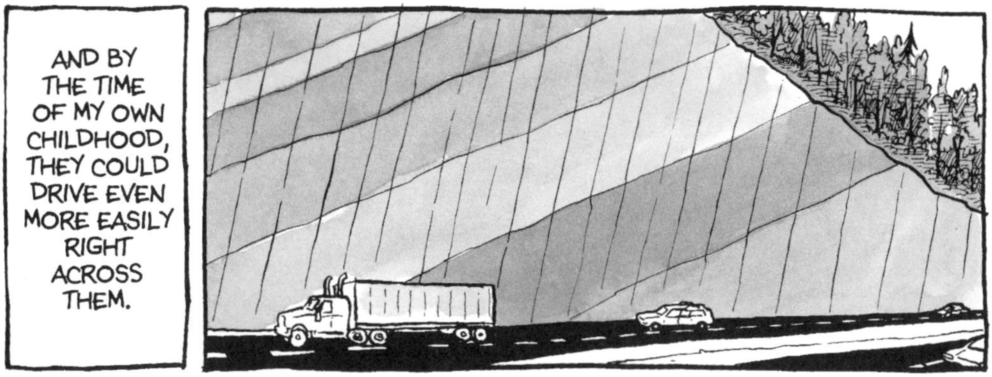
AND BY THE TIME OF MY OWN CHILDHOOD, THEY COULD DRIVE EVEN MORE EASILY RIGHT ACROSS THEM.

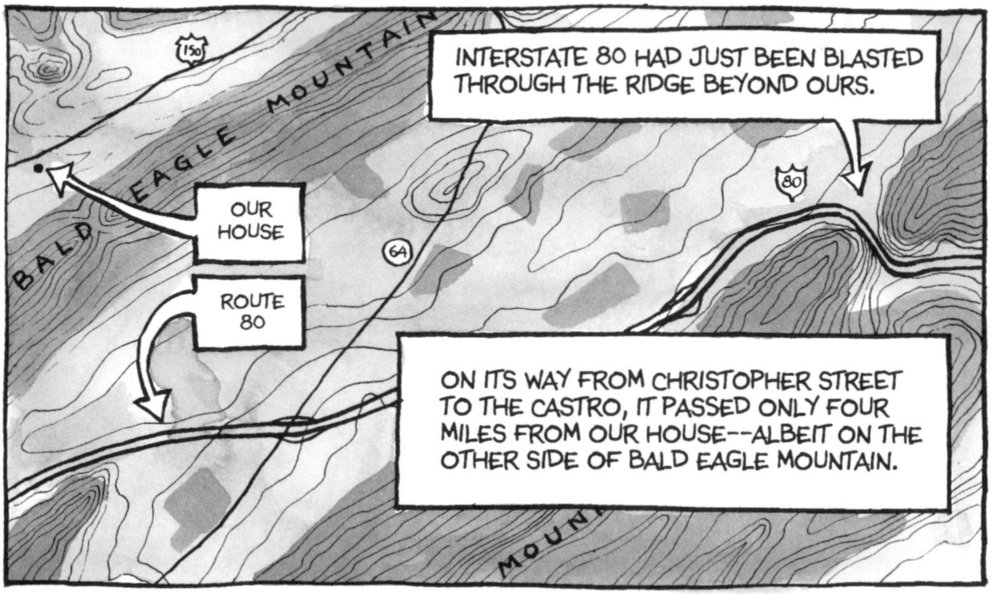
INTERSTATE 80 HAD JUST BEEN BLASTED THROUGH THE RIDGE BEYOND OURS.
BALD EAGLE MOUNTAIN
150
OUR HOUSE
ROUTE 80
64
80
ON ITS WAY FROM CHRISTOPHER STREET TO THE CASTRO, IT PASSED ONLY FOUR MILES FROM OUR HOUSE--ALBEIT ON THE OTHER SIDE OF BALD EAGLE MOUNTAIN.

THIS MASSIVE EARTHEN BERM EFFECTIVELY DEADENED ANY HINT OF NOISE FROM THE GLORIOUS THOROUGHFARE...

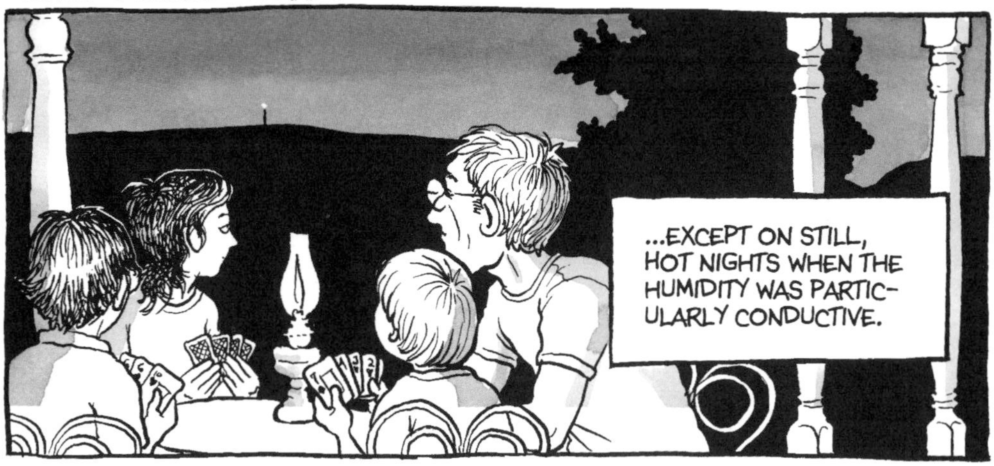
...EXCEPT ON STILL, HOT NIGHTS WHEN THE HUMIDITY WAS PARTICULARLY CONDUCTIVE.

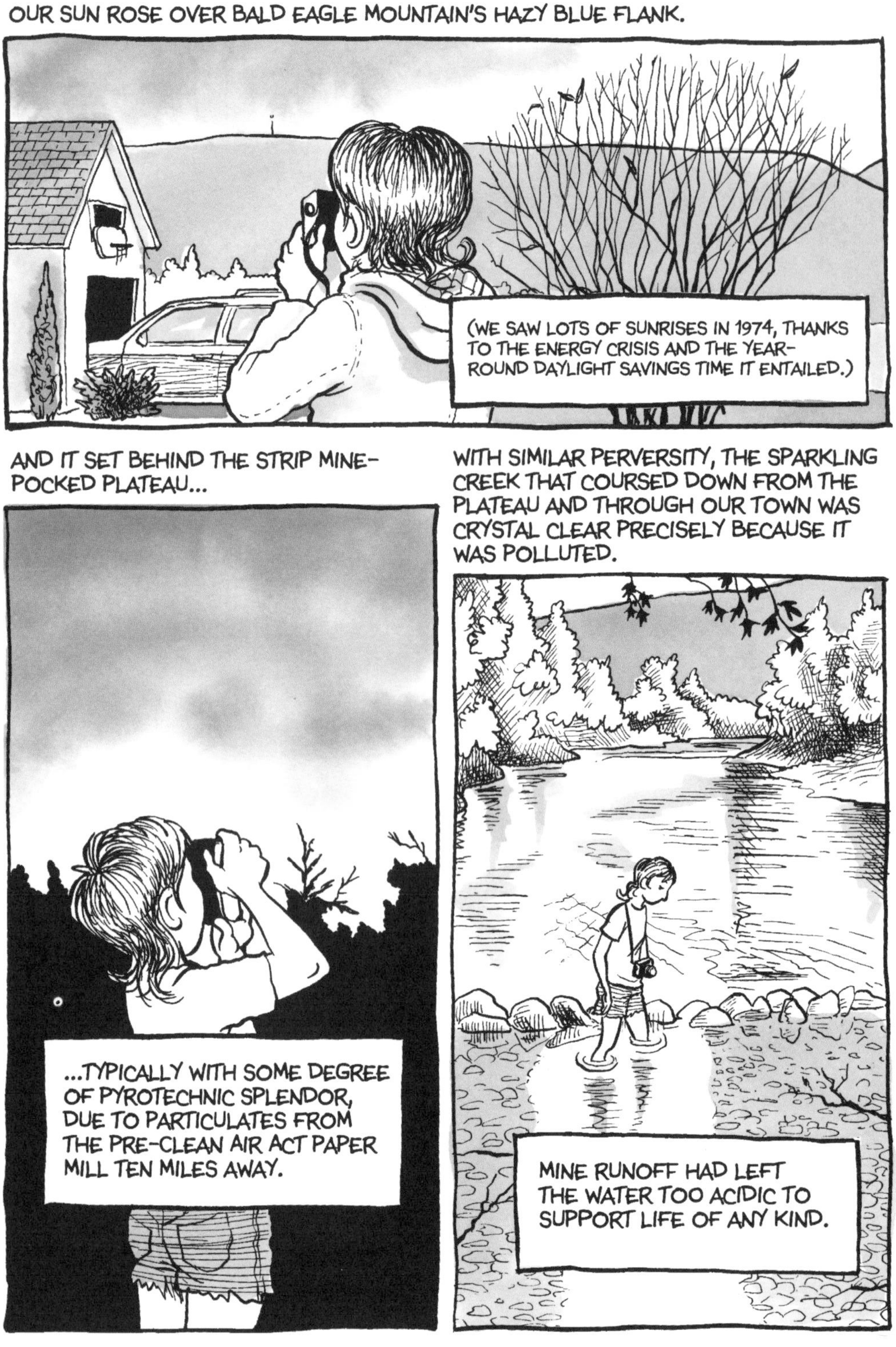
OUR SUN ROSE OVER BALD EAGLE MOUNTAIN'S HAZY BLUE FLANK.
(WE SAW LOTS OF SUNRISES IN 1974, THANKS TO THE ENERGY CRISIS AND THE YEAR-ROUND DAYLIGHT SAVINGS TIME IT ENTAILED.)
AND IT SET BEHIND THE STRIP MINE-POCKED PLATEAU...
...TYPICALLY WITH SOME DEGREE OF PYROTECHNIC SPLENDOR, DUE TO PARTICULATES FROM THE PRE-CLEAN AIR ACT PAPER MILL TEN MILES AWAY.
WITH SIMILAR PERVERSITY, THE SPARKLING CREEK THAT COURSED DOWN FROM THE PLATEAU AND THROUGH OUR TOWN WAS CRYSTAL CLEAR PRECISELY BECAUSE IT WAS POLLUTED.
MINE RUNOFF HAD LEFT THE WATER TOO ACIDIC TO SUPPORT LIFE OF ANY KIND.

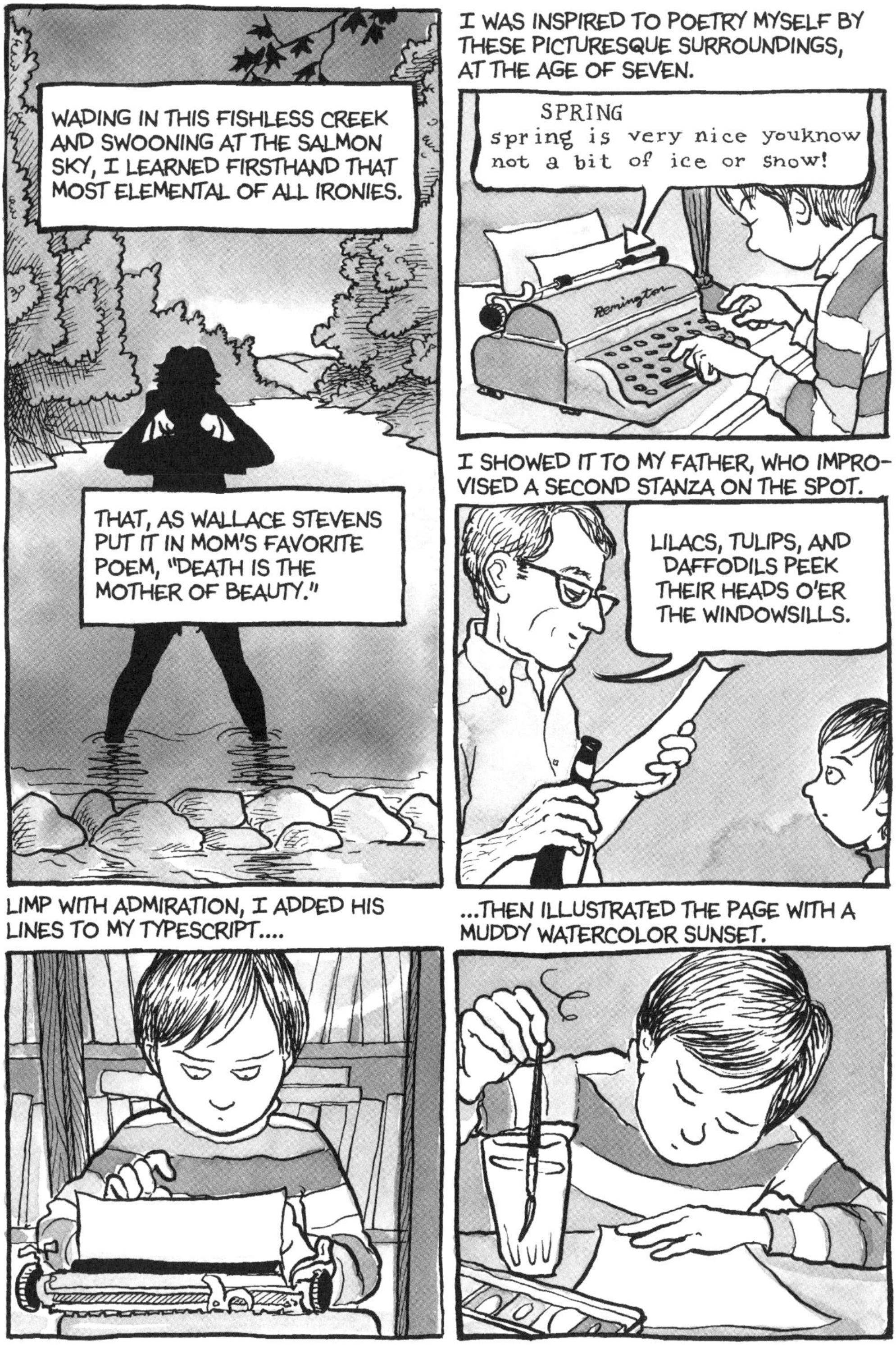
WADING IN THIS FISHLESS CREEK AND SWOONING AT THE SALMON SKY, I LEARNED FIRSTHAND THAT MOST ELEMENTAL OF ALL IRONIES.
THAT, AS WALLACE STEVENS PUT IT IN MOM'S FAVORITE POEM, "DEATH IS THE MOTHER OF BEAUTY."
I WAS INSPIRED TO POETRY MYSELF BY THESE PICTURESQUE SURROUNDINGS, AT THE AGE OF SEVEN.
SPRING
spring is very nice youknow
not a bit of ice or snow!
Remington
I SHOWED IT TO MY FATHER, WHO IMPROVISED A SECOND STANZA ON THE SPOT.
LILACS, TULIPS, AND DAFFODILS PEEK THEIR HEADS O'ER THE WINDOWSILLS.
LIMP WITH ADMIRATION, I ADDED HIS LINES TO MY TYPESCRIPT....
...THEN ILLUSTRATED THE PAGE WITH A MUDDY WATERCOLOR SUNSET.

IN THE FOREGROUND STANDS A MAN, MY SAD PROXY, GAZING ON THE UNTIMELY ECLIPSE OF HIS CREATIVE LIGHT.

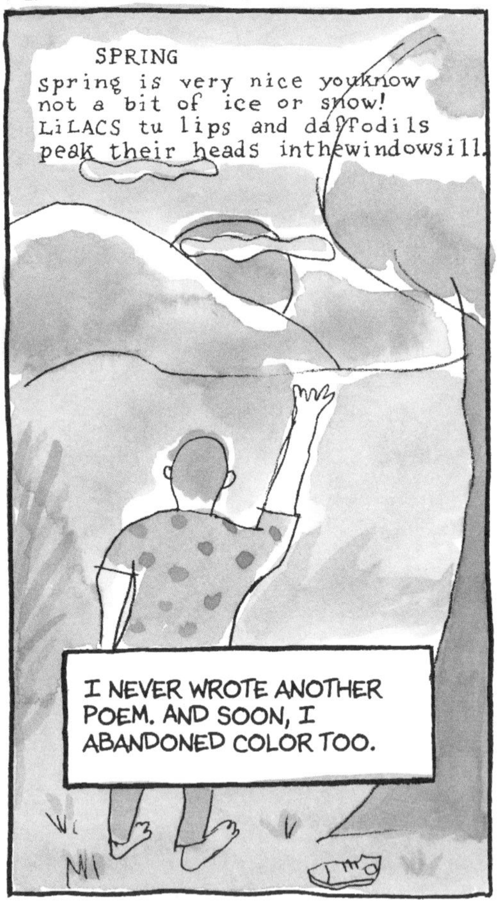
SPRING
spring is very nice youknow
not a bit of ice or snow!
LiLACS tu lips and daffodils
peak their heads inthewindowsill.
I NEVER WROTE ANOTHER POEM. AND SOON, I ABANDONED COLOR TOO.

WE HAD A HUGE, OVERSIZE COLORING BOOK OF E.H. SHEPARD'S ILLUSTRATIONS FOR *THE WIND IN THE WILLOWS*.

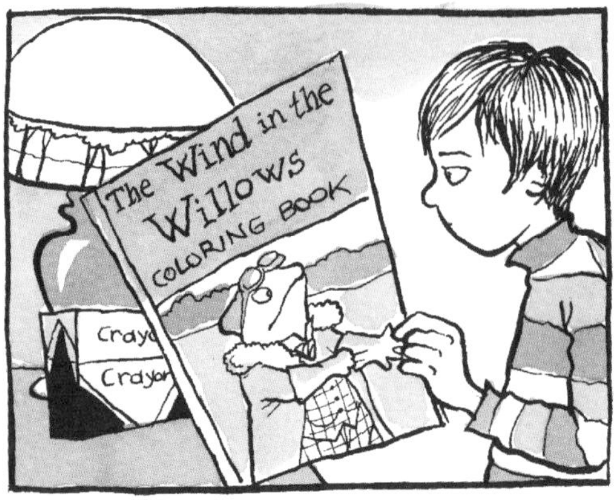
The Wind in the Willows
COLORING BOOK
Crayo
Crayon

DAD HAD READ ME BITS OF THE STORY FROM THE REAL BOOK. IN ONE SCENE, THE CHARMING SOCIOPATH MR. TOAD PURCHASES A GYPSY CARAVAN.

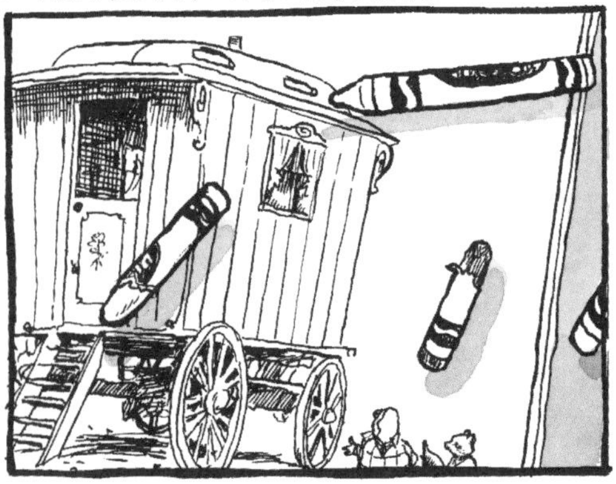

I WAS FILLING THIS IN ONE DAY WITH MY FAVORITE COLOR, MIDNIGHT BLUE.

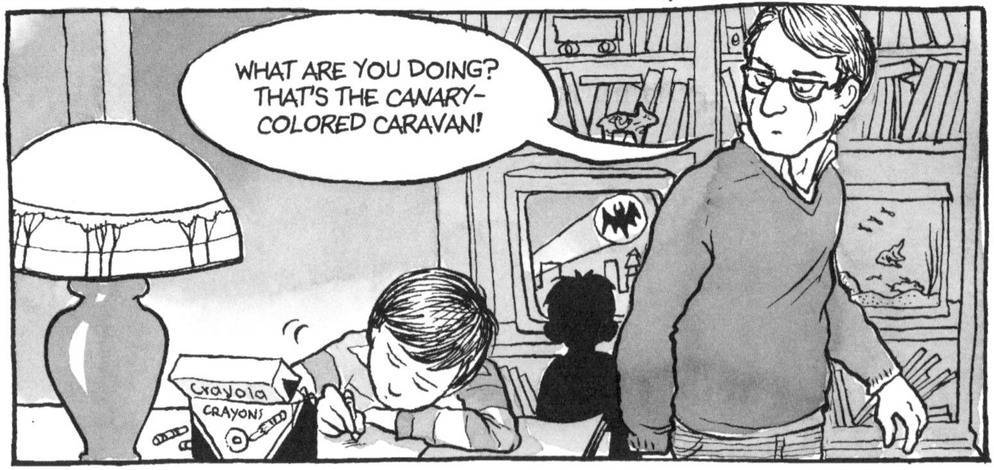
WHAT ARE YOU DOING? THAT'S THE *CANARY-COLORED* CARAVAN!
Crayola
CRAYONS

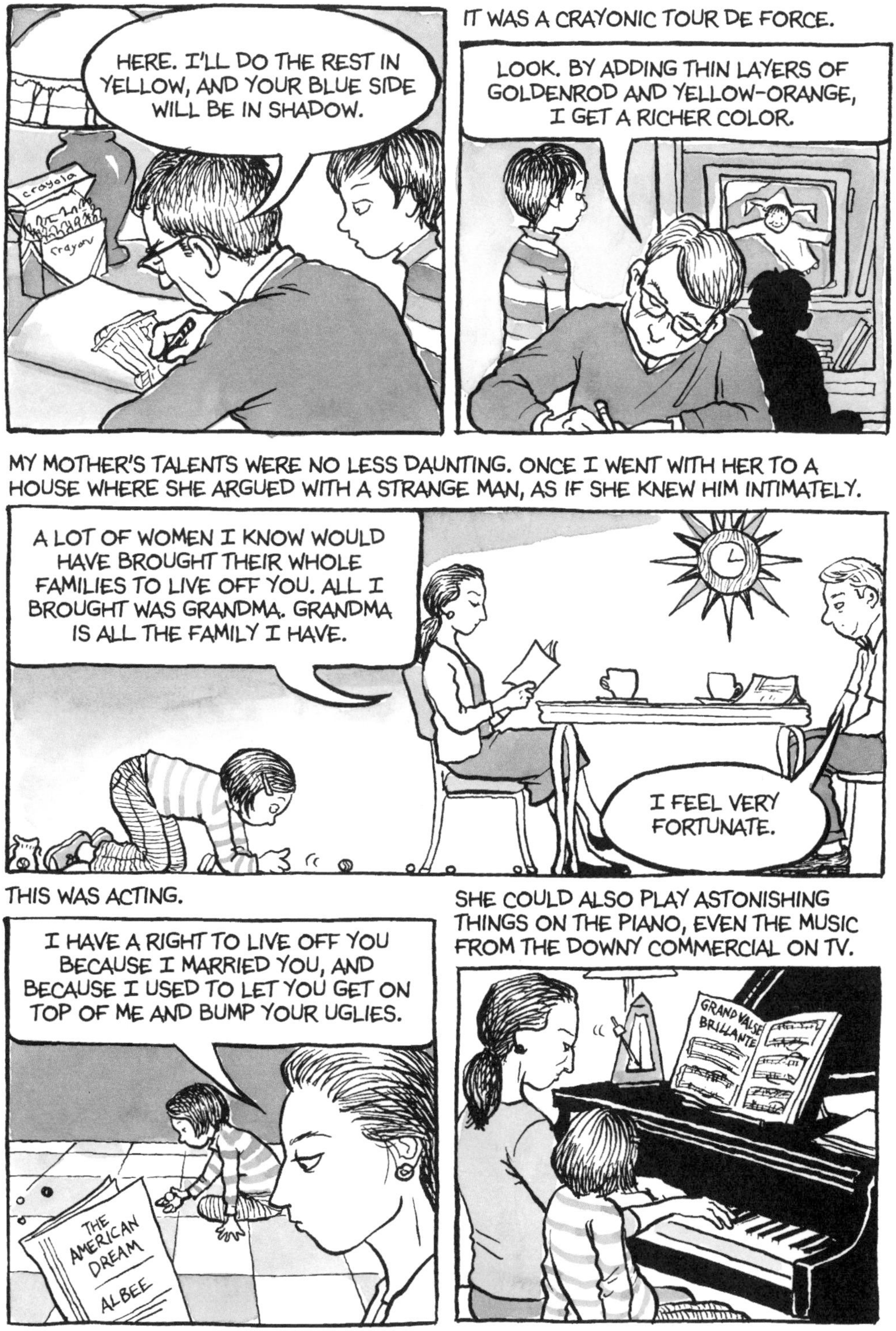
crayola
crayon
HERE. I'LL DO THE REST IN YELLOW, AND YOUR BLUE SIDE WILL BE IN SHADOW.
IT WAS A CRAYONIC TOUR DE FORCE.
LOOK. BY ADDING THIN LAYERS OF GOLDENROD AND YELLOW-ORANGE, I GET A RICHER COLOR.
MY MOTHER'S TALENTS WERE NO LESS DAUNTING. ONCE I WENT WITH HER TO A HOUSE WHERE SHE ARGUED WITH A STRANGE MAN, AS IF SHE KNEW HIM INTIMATELY.
A LOT OF WOMEN I KNOW WOULD HAVE BROUGHT THEIR WHOLE FAMILIES TO LIVE OFF YOU. ALL I BROUGHT WAS GRANDMA. GRANDMA IS ALL THE FAMILY I HAVE.
I FEEL VERY FORTUNATE.
THIS WAS ACTING.
I HAVE A RIGHT TO LIVE OFF YOU BECAUSE I MARRIED YOU, AND BECAUSE I USED TO LET YOU GET ON TOP OF ME AND BUMP YOUR UGLIES.
THE AMERICAN DREAM
ALBEE
SHE COULD ALSO PLAY ASTONISHING THINGS ON THE PIANO, EVEN THE MUSIC FROM THE DOWNY COMMERCIAL ON TV.
GRAND VALSE BRILLANTE

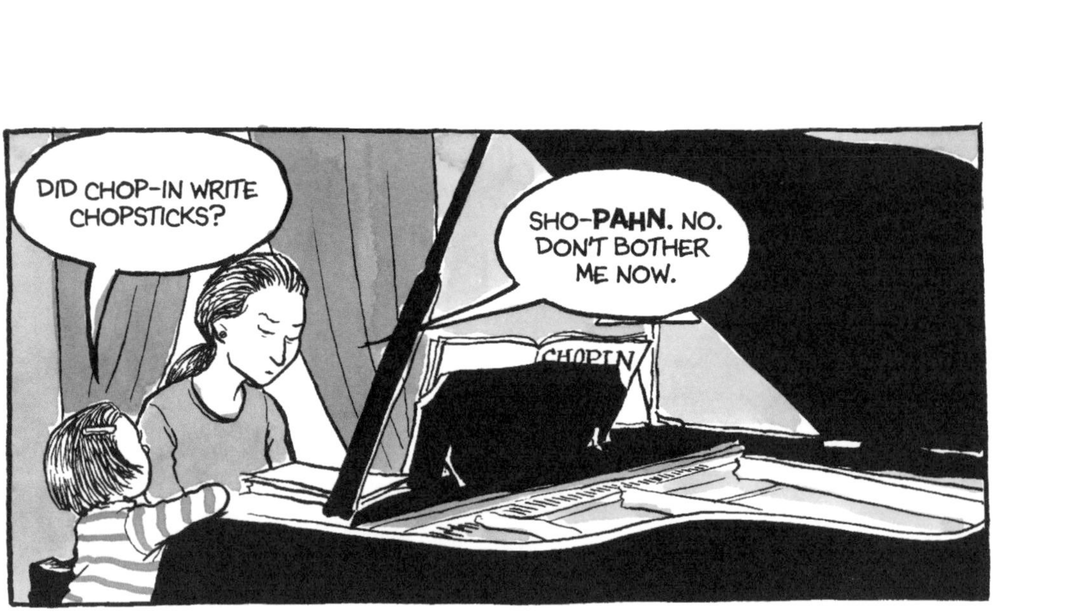
DID CHOP-IN WRITE CHOPSTICKS?
SHO-**PAHN.** NO. DON'T BOTHER ME NOW.
CHOPIN

SEVERAL YEARS AFTER DAD DIED, MOM WAS USING OUR OLD TAPE RECORDER TO REHEARSE FOR A PLAY. SHE READ FROM THE SCRIPT, LEAVING PAUSES WHERE IT WAS HER CHARACTER'S TURN TO SPEAK.

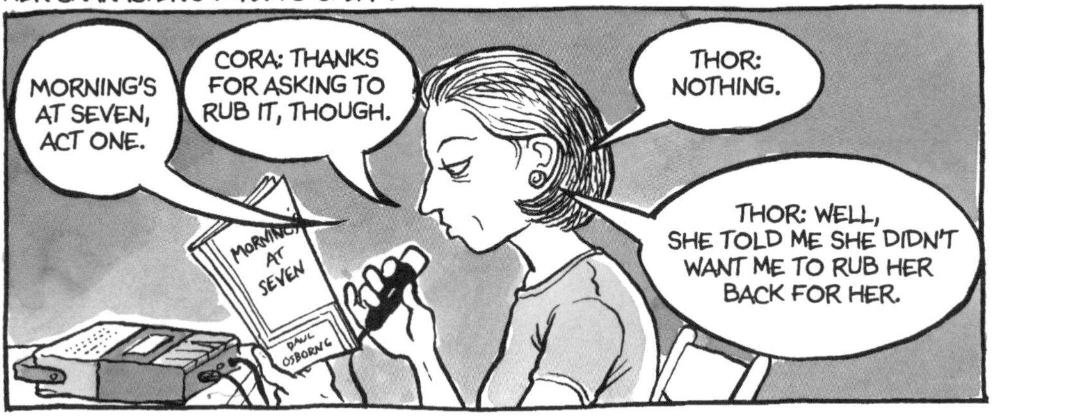
MORNING'S AT SEVEN, ACT ONE.
CORA: THANKS FOR ASKING TO RUB IT, THOUGH.
THOR: NOTHING.
THOR: WELL, SHE TOLD ME SHE DIDN'T WANT ME TO RUB HER BACK FOR HER.
MORNING AT SEVEN
PAUL OSBORNE

WHEN SHE CHECKED TO MAKE SURE THE MACHINE WAS RECORDING PROPERLY...

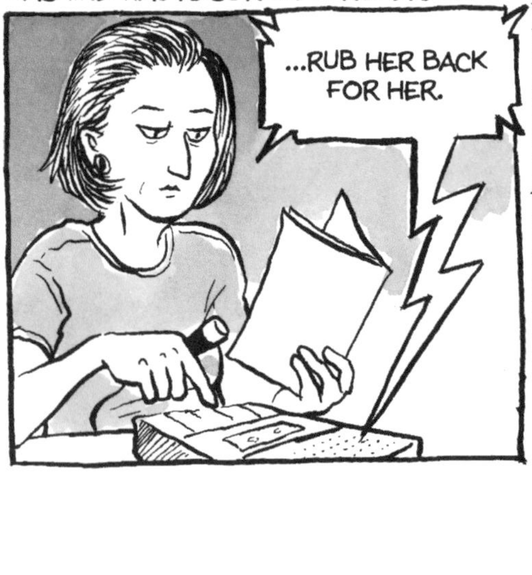
...RUB HER BACK FOR HER.

...SHE REALIZED THAT SHE WAS TAPING OVER MY FATHER'S VOICE.

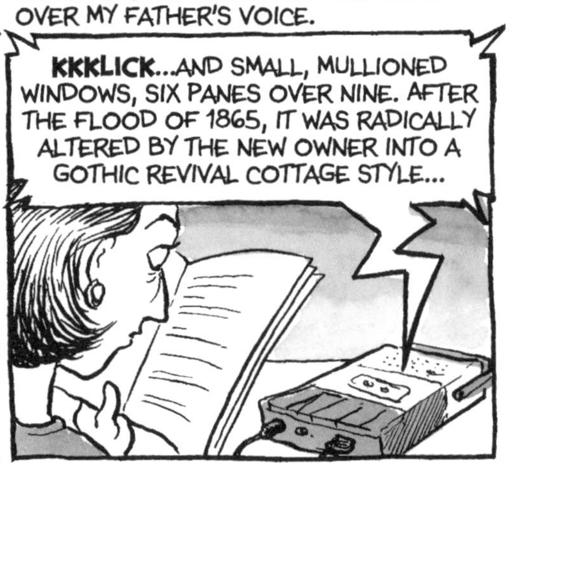
KKKLICK...AND SMALL, MULLIONED WINDOWS, SIX PANES OVER NINE. AFTER THE FLOOD OF 1865, IT WAS RADICALLY ALTERED BY THE NEW OWNER INTO A GOTHIC REVIVAL COTTAGE STYLE...

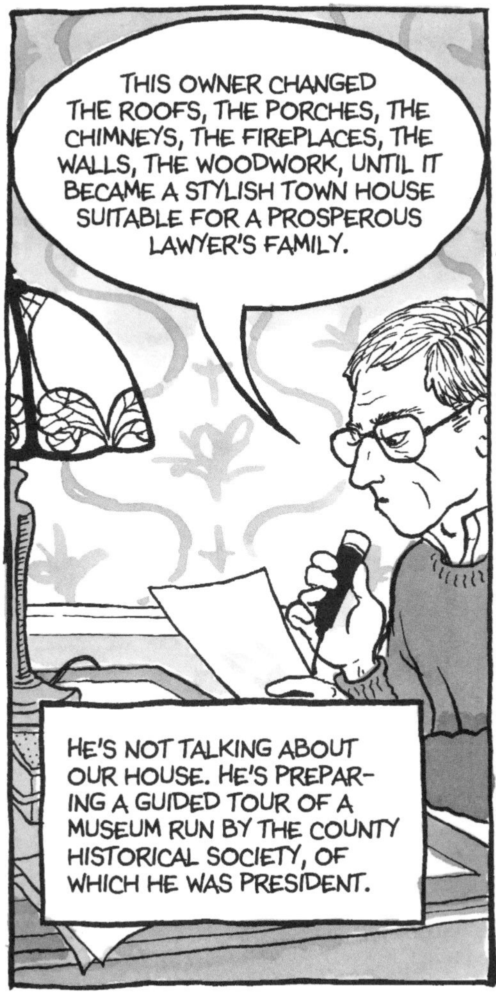
THIS OWNER CHANGED THE ROOFS, THE PORCHES, THE CHIMNEYS, THE FIREPLACES, THE WALLS, THE WOODWORK, UNTIL IT BECAME A STYLISH TOWN HOUSE SUITABLE FOR A PROSPEROUS LAWYER'S FAMILY.
HE'S NOT TALKING ABOUT OUR HOUSE. HE'S PREPARING A GUIDED TOUR OF A MUSEUM RUN BY THE COUNTY HISTORICAL SOCIETY, OF WHICH HE WAS PRESIDENT.

IT'S JARRING TO HEAR MY FATHER SPEAK FROM BEYOND THE GRAVE.

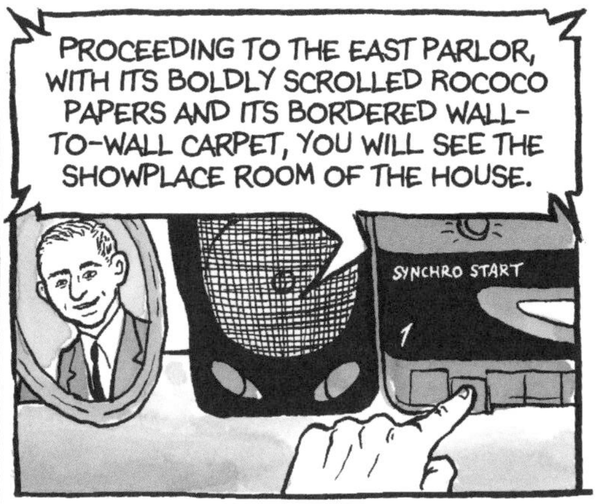
PROCEEDING TO THE EAST PARLOR, WITH ITS BOLDLY SCROLLED ROCOCO PAPERS AND ITS BORDERED WALL-TO-WALL CARPET, YOU WILL SEE THE SHOWPLACE ROOM OF THE HOUSE.
SYNCHRO START
1

BUT THE MOST ARRESTING THING ABOUT THE TAPE IS ITS EVIDENCE OF BOTH MY PARENTS AT WORK, INTENT AND SEPARATE.

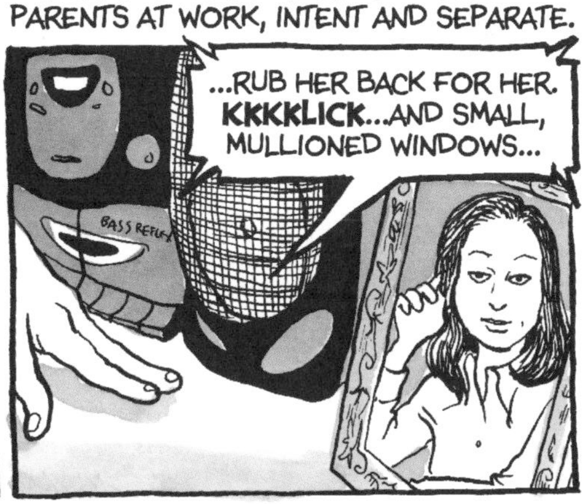
...RUB HER BACK FOR HER. **KKKKLICK**...AND SMALL, MULLIONED WINDOWS...

THEIR RAPT IMMERSION EVOKES A FAMILIAR RESENTMENT IN ME.

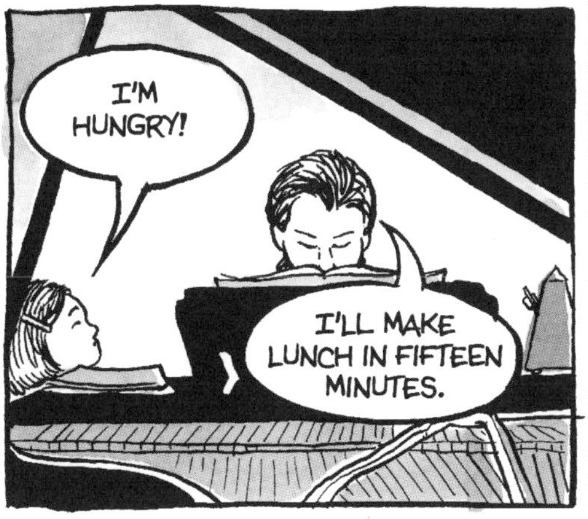
I'M HUNGRY!
I'LL MAKE LUNCH IN FIFTEEN MINUTES.

IT'S CHILDISH, PERHAPS, TO GRUDGE THEM THE SUSTENANCE OF THEIR CREATIVE SOLITUDE.

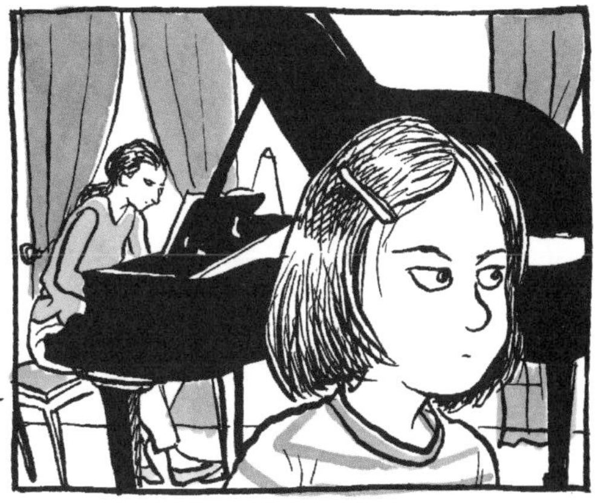

BUT IT WAS *ALL* THAT SUSTAINED THEM, AND WAS THUS ALL-CONSUMING.

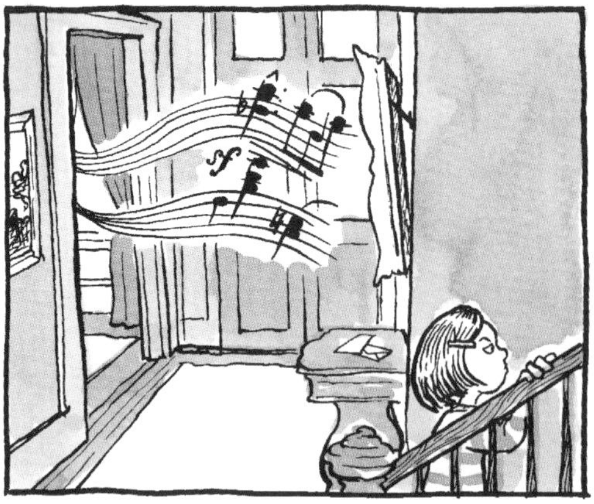

FROM THEIR EXAMPLE, I LEARNED QUICKLY TO FEED MYSELF.

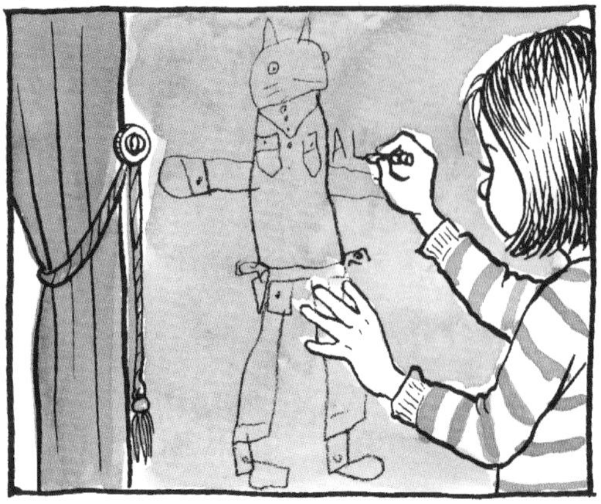

IT WAS A VICIOUS CIRCLE, THOUGH. THE MORE GRATIFICATION WE FOUND IN OUR OWN GENIUSES, THE MORE ISOLATED WE GREW.

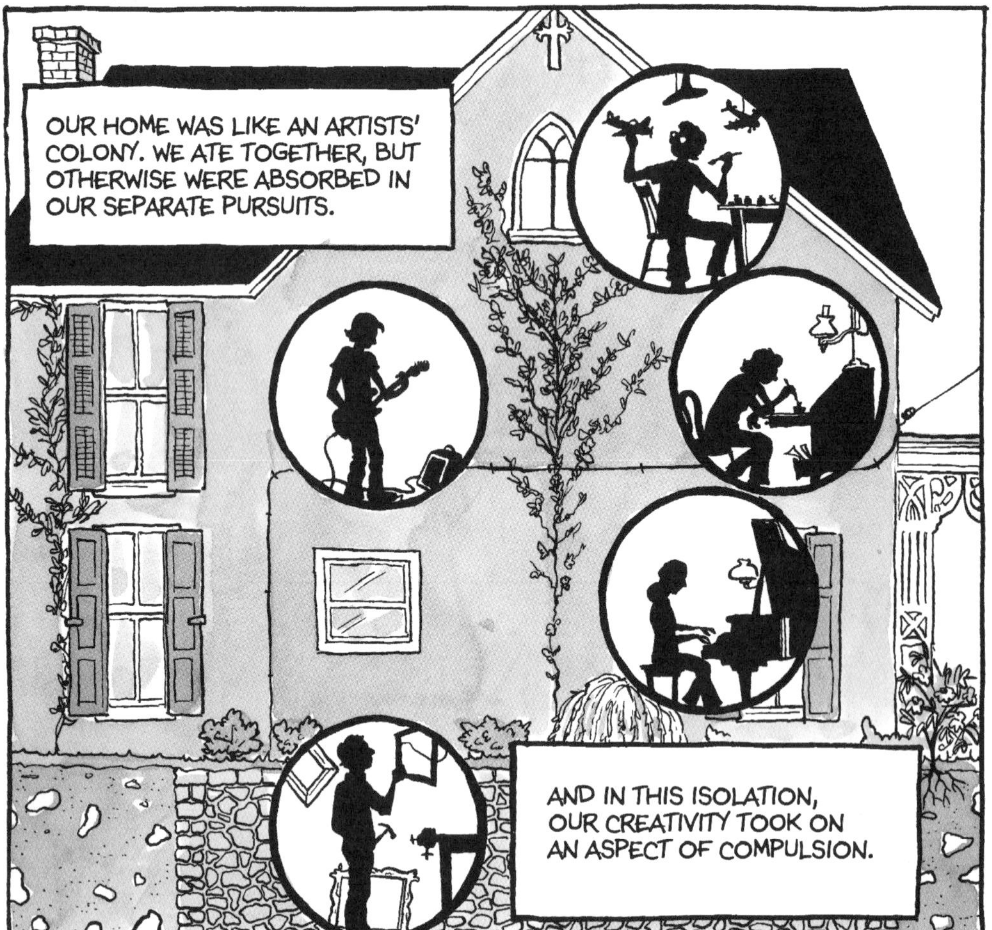
OUR HOME WAS LIKE AN ARTISTS' COLONY. WE ATE TOGETHER, BUT OTHERWISE WERE ABSORBED IN OUR SEPARATE PURSUITS.
AND IN THIS ISOLATION, OUR CREATIVITY TOOK ON AN ASPECT OF COMPULSION.

MY ACTUAL OBSESSIVE-COMPULSIVE DISORDER BEGAN WHEN I WAS TEN.

FIRST IT INVOLVED A LOT OF COUNTING. TRYING TO MANIP-
ULATE THE SLIGHTLY LEAKY BATHTUB FAUCET WITH MY TOE
SO THAT IT WOULD STOP ON AN EVEN NUMBER OF DRIPS.

ODD NUMBERS AND MULTIPLES OF
THIRTEEN WERE TO BE AVOIDED AT
ALL COSTS.

CROSSING THRESHOLDS BECAME A TIME-
CONSUMING PROCEDURE SINCE I HAD TO
TABULATE THE NUMBER OF EDGES OF
FLOORING I SAW THERE.

IF THESE FAILED TO ADD UP TO AN EVEN
NUMBER, I'D INCLUDE ANOTHER
SUBDIVISION, PERHAPS THE SMALL
GROOVES IN THE METAL STRIP.

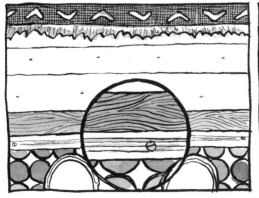

THEN CAME THE INVISIBLE SUBSTANCE
THAT HUNG IN DOORWAYS, AND THAT, I
SOON REALIZED, HUNG LIKE SWAGS OF
DRAPERY BETWEEN ALL SOLID OBJECTS.

THIS HAD TO BE GATHERED AND DISPERSED CONSTANTLY, TO KEEP IT AWAY FROM MY BODY--TO AVOID IN PARTICULAR INHALING OR SWALLOWING IT.

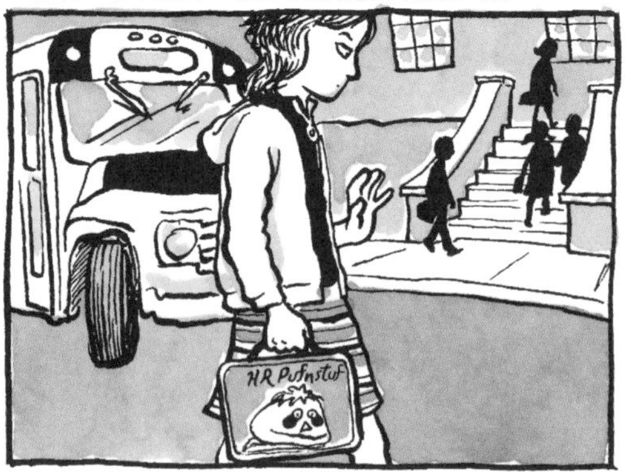
H.R. Pufnstuf

DESPITE MY UNRELENTING VIGILANCE, THESE EFFORTS FELL SHORT. ODD NUMBERS AND MULTIPLES OF THIRTEEN WERE EVERYWHERE.

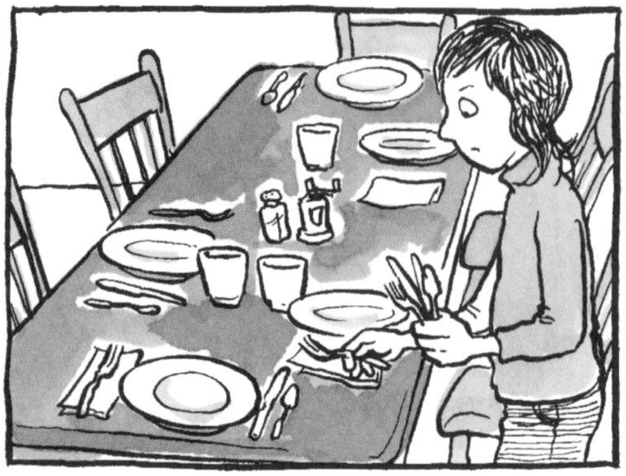

AND FESTOONS OF THE NOXIOUS SUBSTANCE PROLIFERATED BEYOND MY CONTROL. SO MY PREVENTIVE MEASURES SPAWNED MORE STOPGAP MEASURES.

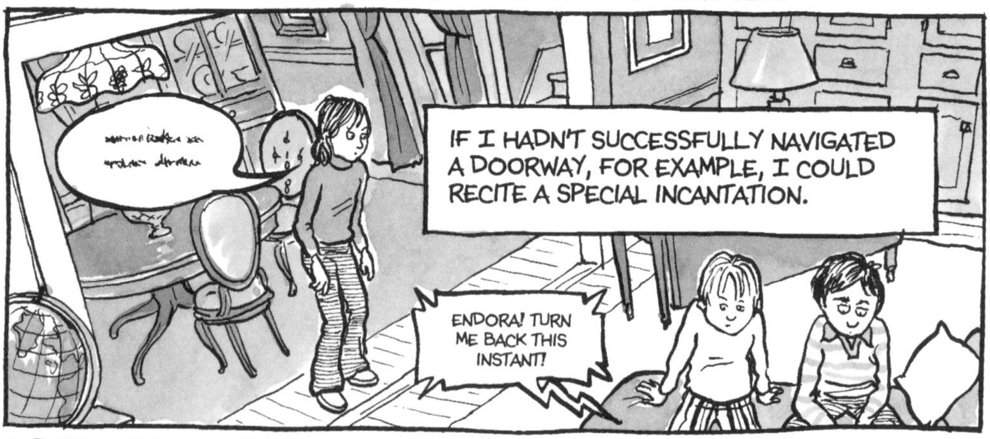
IF I HADN'T SUCCESSFULLY NAVIGATED A DOORWAY, FOR EXAMPLE, I COULD RECITE A SPECIAL INCANTATION.
ENDORA! TURN ME BACK THIS INSTANT!

AND TO ENSURE THAT THE INCANTATION WOULD BE EFFECTIVE, I COULD REPEAT IT, THIS TIME WITH HAND GESTURES.

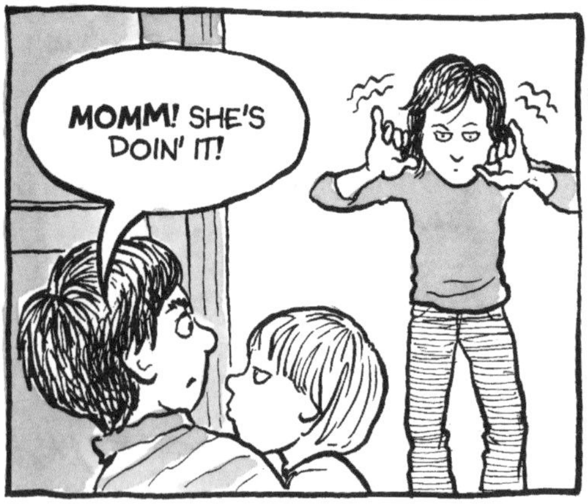
MOMM! SHE'S DOIN' IT!

IF MY DAY WENT WELL, I TRIED TO DUPLICATE AS MANY OF ITS CONDITIONS AS POSSIBLE. AND IF IT DIDN'T, I MADE SMALL ADJUSTMENTS TO MY REGIMEN.

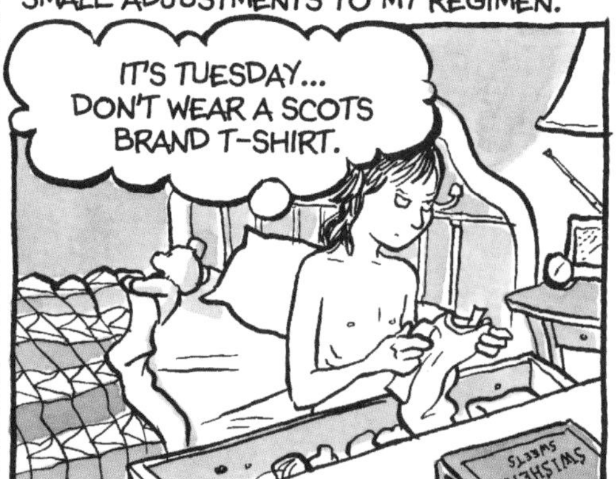
IT'S TUESDAY... DON'T WEAR A SCOTS BRAND T-SHIRT.
SWISHER SWEETS

LIFE HAD BECOME A LABORIOUS ROUND OF CHORES.

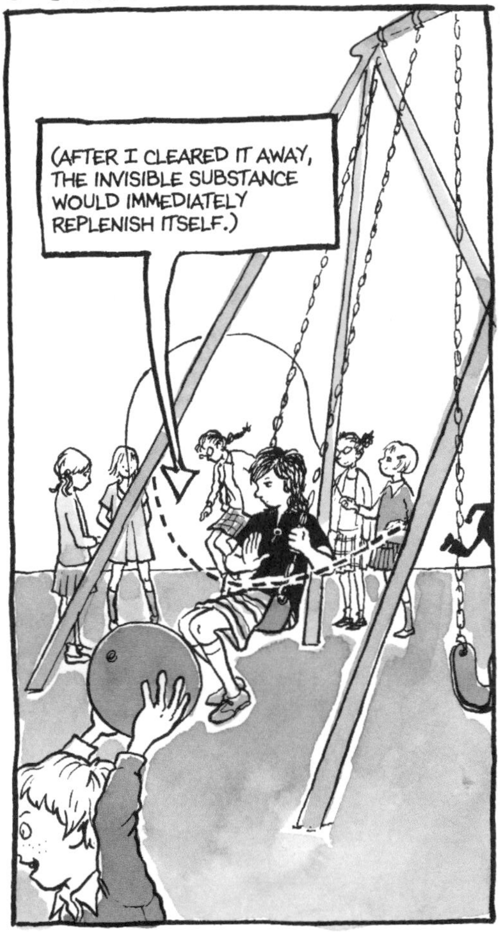
(AFTER I CLEARED IT AWAY, THE INVISIBLE SUBSTANCE WOULD IMMEDIATELY REPLENISH ITSELF.)

AT THE END OF THE DAY, IF I UNDRESSED IN THE WRONG ORDER, I HAD TO PUT MY CLOTHES BACK ON AND START AGAIN.

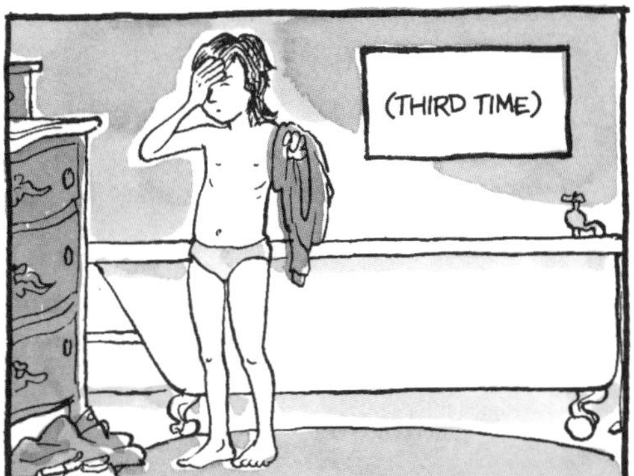
(THIRD TIME)

IT TOOK SEVERAL PAINSTAKING MINUTES TO LINE UP MY SHOES EXACTLY, SO AS TO SHOW NEITHER ONE PREFERENCE.

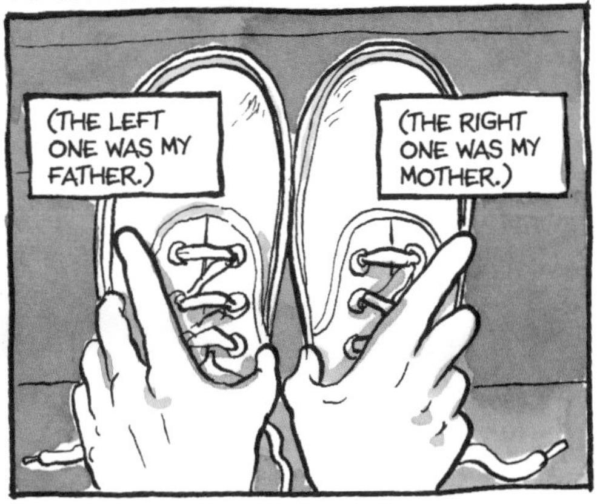
(THE LEFT ONE WAS MY FATHER.)
(THE RIGHT ONE WAS MY MOTHER.)

NO MATTER HOW TIRED I WAS AFTER ALL THIS, I HAD TO KISS EACH OF MY STUFFED ANIMALS--AND NOT JUST IN A PERFUNCTORY WAY. THEN I'D BRING ONE OF THE THREE BEARS TO BED WITH ME, ALTERNATING NIGHTLY BETWEEN MOTHER, FATHER, AND BABY.

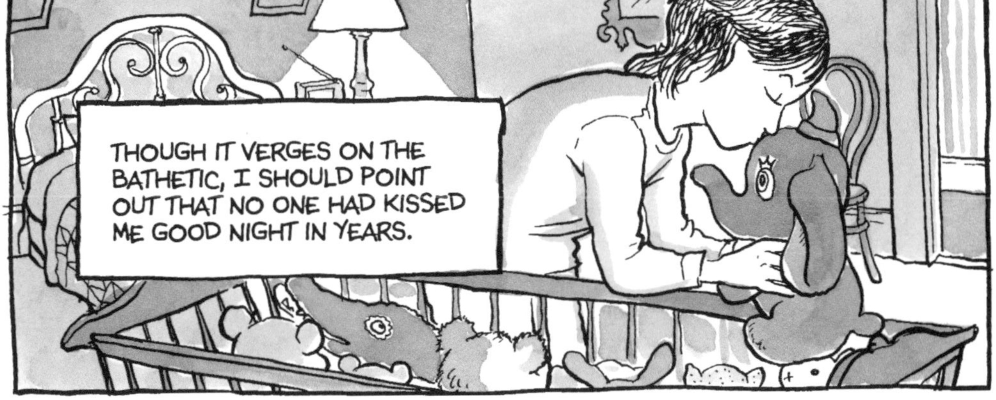
THOUGH IT VERGES ON THE BATHETIC, I SHOULD POINT OUT THAT NO ONE HAD KISSED ME GOOD NIGHT IN YEARS.

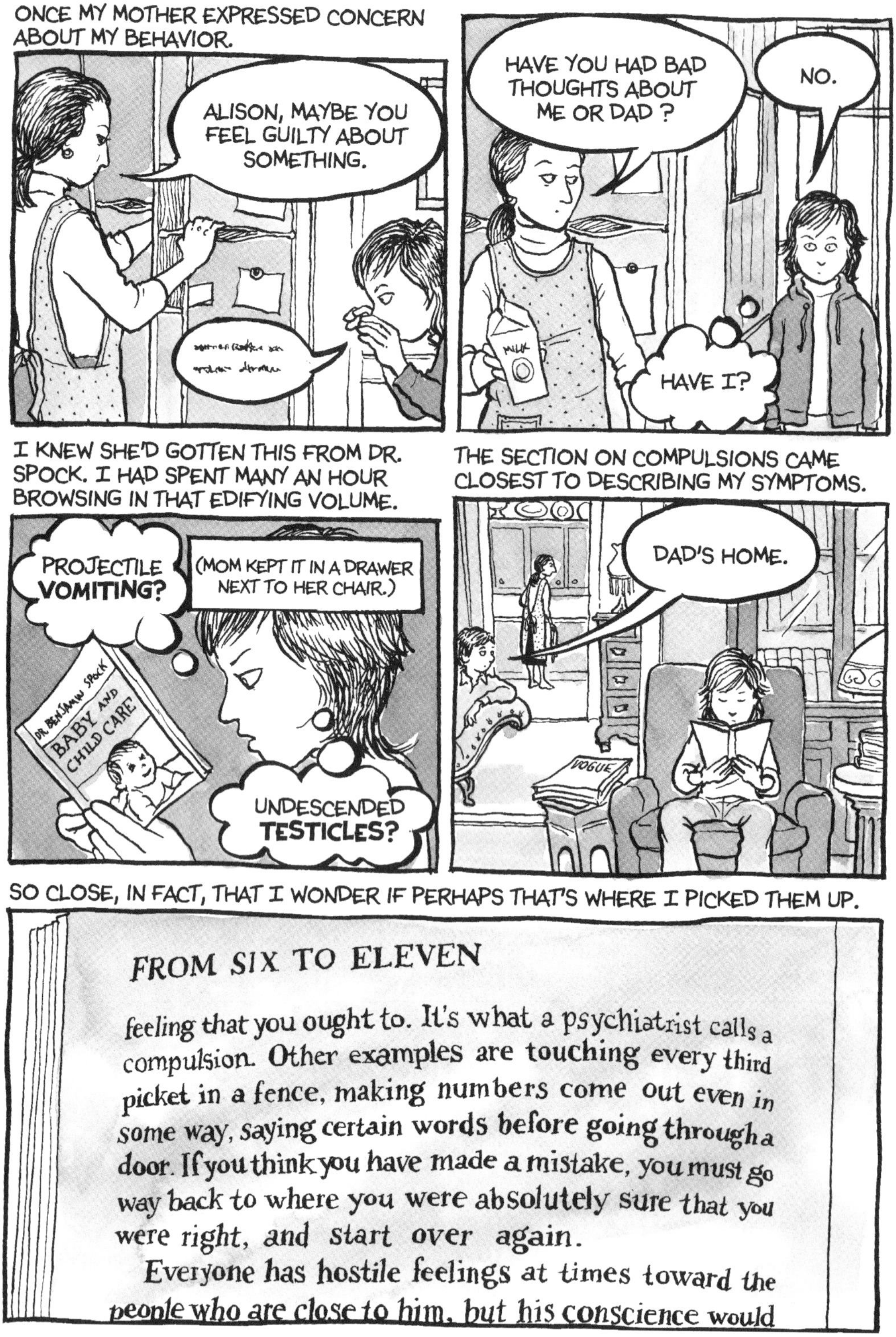
ONCE MY MOTHER EXPRESSED CONCERN ABOUT MY BEHAVIOR.
ALISON, MAYBE YOU FEEL GUILTY ABOUT SOMETHING.
HAVE YOU HAD BAD THOUGHTS ABOUT ME OR DAD ?
NO.
MILK
HAVE I?
I KNEW SHE'D GOTTEN THIS FROM DR. SPOCK. I HAD SPENT MANY AN HOUR BROWSING IN THAT EDIFYING VOLUME.
PROJECTILE VOMITING?
(MOM KEPT IT IN A DRAWER NEXT TO HER CHAIR.)
DR. BENJAMIN SPOCK
BABY AND CHILD CARE
UNDESCENDED TESTICLES?
THE SECTION ON COMPULSIONS CAME CLOSEST TO DESCRIBING MY SYMPTOMS.
DAD'S HOME.
VOGUE
SO CLOSE, IN FACT, THAT I WONDER IF PERHAPS THAT'S WHERE I PICKED THEM UP.
FROM SIX TO ELEVEN
feeling that you ought to. It's what a psychiatrist calls a compulsion. Other examples are touching every third picket in a fence, making numbers come out even in some way, saying certain words before going through a door. If you think you have made a mistake, you must go way back to where you were absolutely sure that you were right, and start over again.
Everyone has hostile feelings at times toward the people who are close to him, but his conscience would

THE EXPLANATION OF REPRESSED HOSTILITY MADE NO SENSE TO ME. I CONTINUED READING, SEARCHING FOR SOMETHING MORE CONCRETE.

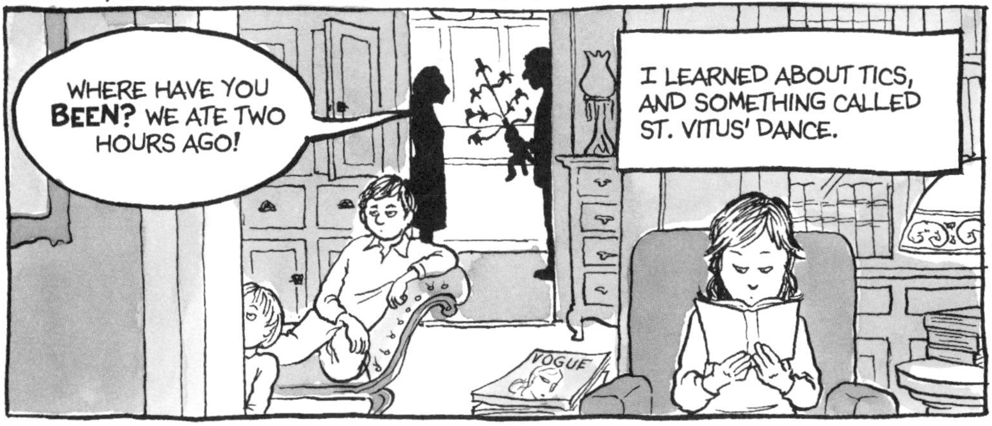
WHERE HAVE YOU **BEEN?** WE ATE TWO HOURS AGO!
I LEARNED ABOUT TICS, AND SOMETHING CALLED ST. VITUS' DANCE.
VOGUE

BUT THESE NERVOUS HABITS AND INVOLUNTARY TWITCHES WERE CHILD'S PLAY TO THE DARK FEAR OF ANNIHILATION THAT MOTIVATED MY OWN RITUALS.

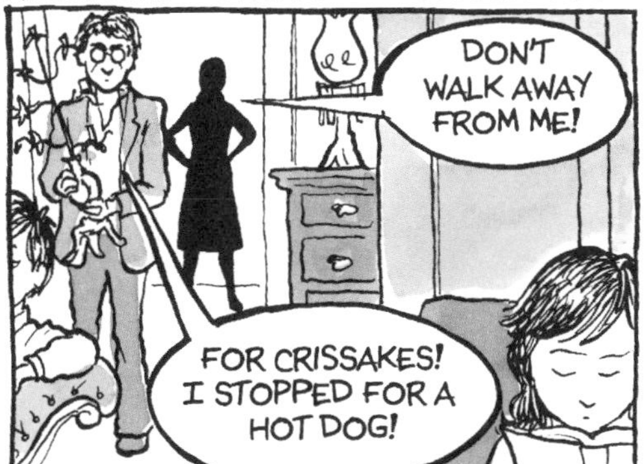
DON'T WALK AWAY FROM ME!
FOR CRISSAKES! I STOPPED FOR A HOT DOG!

STILL, I LIKED DR. SPOCK. READING HIM WAS A CURIOUS EXPERIENCE IN WHICH I WAS BOTH SUBJECT AND OBJECT, MY OWN PARENT AND MY OWN CHILD.

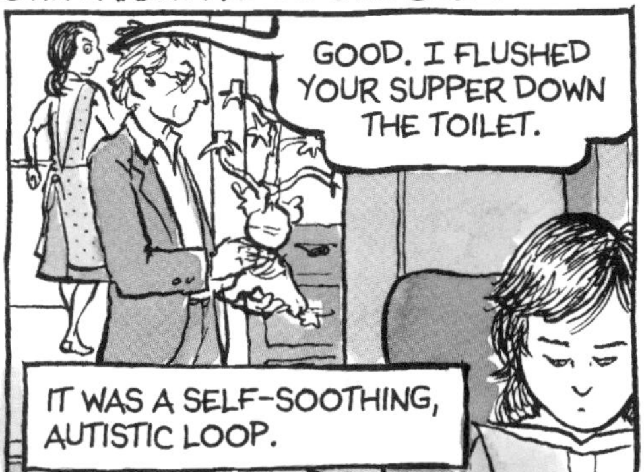
GOOD. I FLUSHED YOUR SUPPER DOWN THE TOILET.
IT WAS A SELF-SOOTHING, AUTISTIC LOOP.

AND INDEED, IF OUR FAMILY WAS A SORT OF ARTISTS' COLONY, COULD IT NOT BE EVEN MORE ACCURATELY DESCRIBED AS A MILDLY AUTISTIC COLONY?

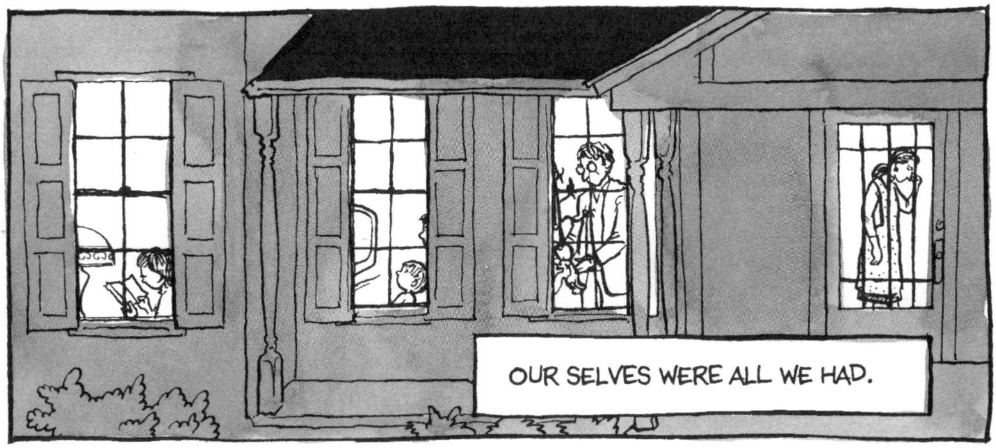
OUR SELVES WERE ALL WE HAD.

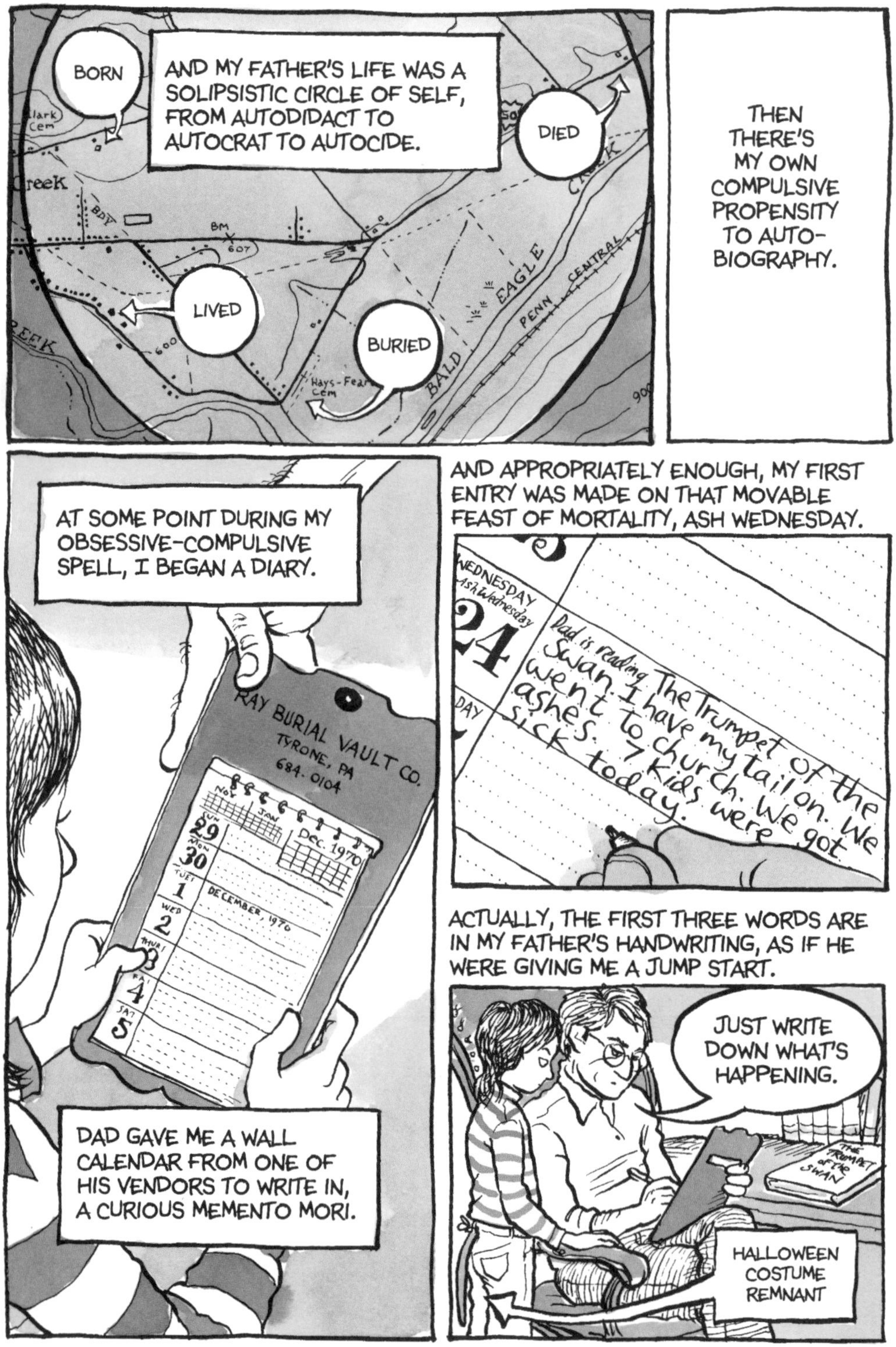
BORN
AND MY FATHER'S LIFE WAS A SOLIPSISTIC CIRCLE OF SELF, FROM AUTODIDACT TO AUTOCRAT TO AUTOCIDE.
DIED
LIVED
BURIED
Hays-Fear Cem
BALD EAGLE
PENN CENTRAL
THEN THERE'S MY OWN COMPULSIVE PROPENSITY TO AUTO-BIOGRAPHY.
AT SOME POINT DURING MY OBSESSIVE-COMPULSIVE SPELL, I BEGAN A DIARY.
RAY BURIAL VAULT CO.
TYRONE, PA
684. 0104
Dec. 1970
DECEMBER, 1970
DAD GAVE ME A WALL CALENDAR FROM ONE OF HIS VENDORS TO WRITE IN, A CURIOUS MEMENTO MORI.
AND APPROPRIATELY ENOUGH, MY FIRST ENTRY WAS MADE ON THAT MOVABLE FEAST OF MORTALITY, ASH WEDNESDAY.
WEDNESDAY
Ash Wednesday
24
Dad is reading The Trumpet of the Swan. I have my tail on. We went to church. We got ashes. 7 kids were sick today.
ACTUALLY, THE FIRST THREE WORDS ARE IN MY FATHER'S HANDWRITING, AS IF HE WERE GIVING ME A JUMP START.
JUST WRITE DOWN WHAT'S HAPPENING.
THE TRUMPET of the SWAN
HALLOWEEN COSTUME REMNANT

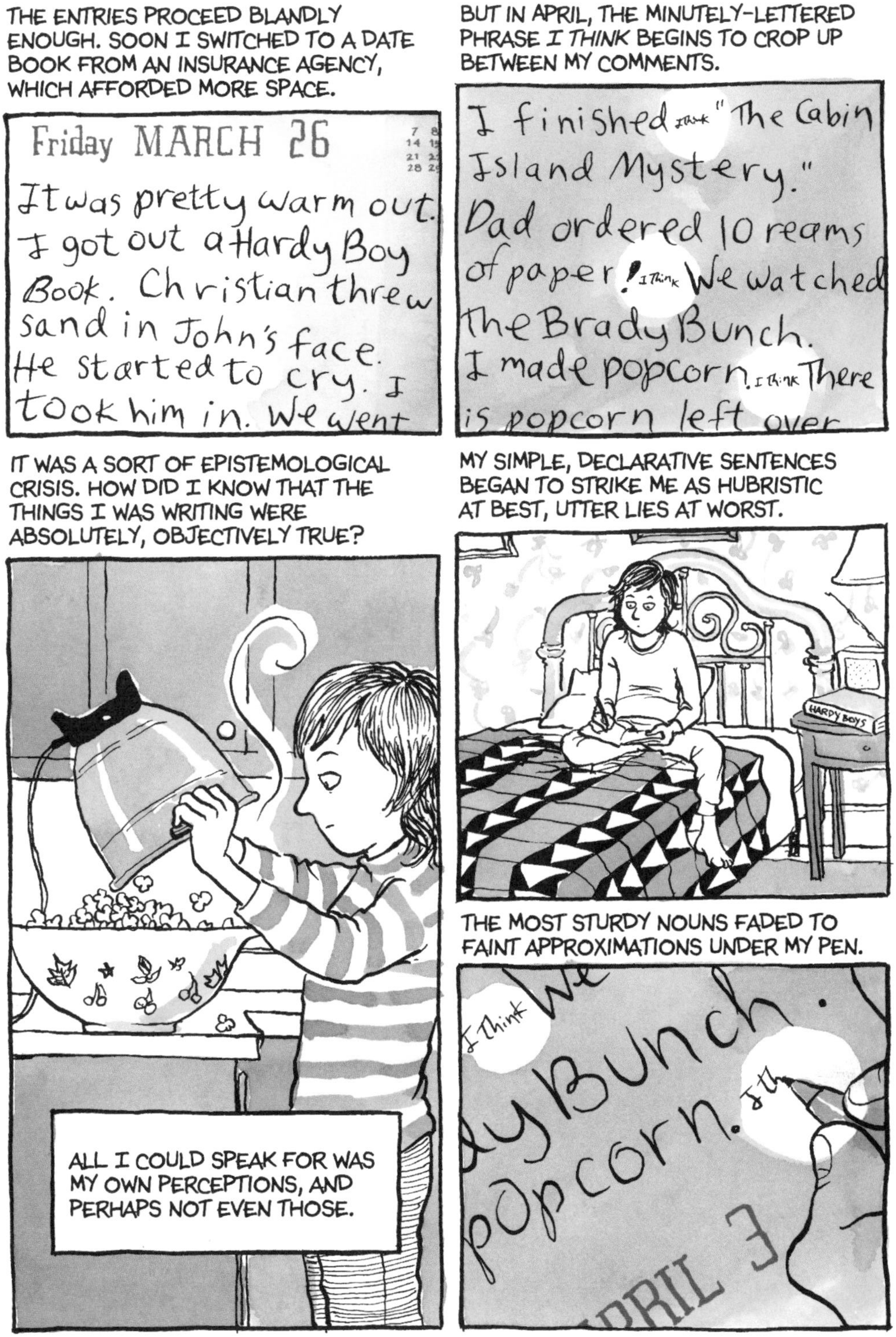
THE ENTRIES PROCEED BLANDLY ENOUGH. SOON I SWITCHED TO A DATE BOOK FROM AN INSURANCE AGENCY, WHICH AFFORDED MORE SPACE.
Friday MARCH 26
It was pretty warm out. I got out a Hardy Boy Book. Christian threw sand in John's face. He started to cry. I took him in. We went
BUT IN APRIL, THE MINUTELY-LETTERED PHRASE *I THINK* BEGINS TO CROP UP BETWEEN MY COMMENTS.
I finished I think "The Cabin Island Mystery." Dad ordered 10 reams of paper! I think We watched the Brady Bunch. I made popcorn. I think There is popcorn left over
IT WAS A SORT OF EPISTEMOLOGICAL CRISIS. HOW DID I KNOW THAT THE THINGS I WAS WRITING WERE ABSOLUTELY, OBJECTIVELY TRUE?
ALL I COULD SPEAK FOR WAS MY OWN PERCEPTIONS, AND PERHAPS NOT EVEN THOSE.
MY SIMPLE, DECLARATIVE SENTENCES BEGAN TO STRIKE ME AS HUBRISTIC AT BEST, UTTER LIES AT WORST.
HARDY BOYS
THE MOST STURDY NOUNS FADED TO FAINT APPROXIMATIONS UNDER MY PEN.
I Think We
dy Bunch.
popcorn.
PRIL 3

MY *I THINKS* WERE GOSSAMER SUTURES IN THAT GAPING RIFT BETWEEN SIGNIFIER AND SIGNIFIED. TO FORTIFY THEM, I PERSEVERATED UNTIL THEY WERE BLOTS.

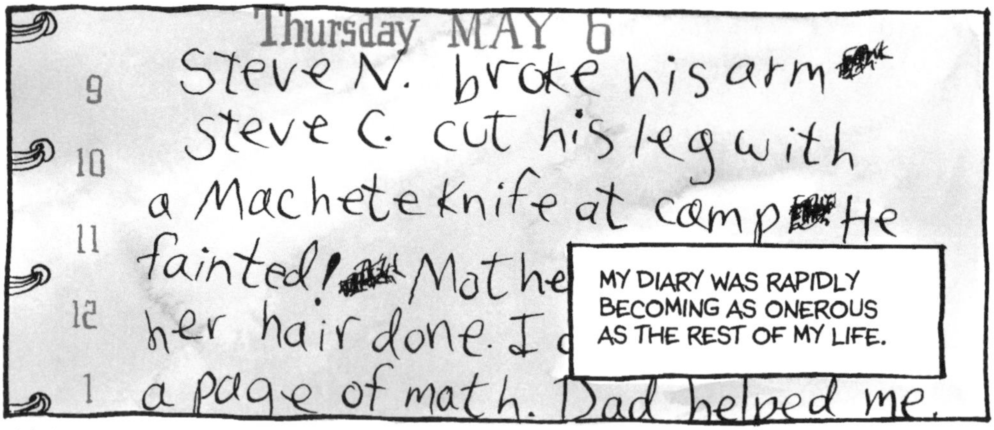
Thursday MAY 6
9 Steve N. broke his arm
10 steve C. cut his leg with
11 a Machete knife at camp He
12 fainted! Mother
her hair done. I
1 a page of math. Dad helped me.
MY DIARY WAS RAPIDLY BECOMING AS ONEROUS AS THE REST OF MY LIFE.

MY MOTHER APPARENTLY DECIDED THAT GIVING ME SOME ATTENTION MIGHT HELP, AND BEGAN READING TO ME WHILE I HAD MY BATH. BUT IT WAS TOO MUCH, TOO LATE.

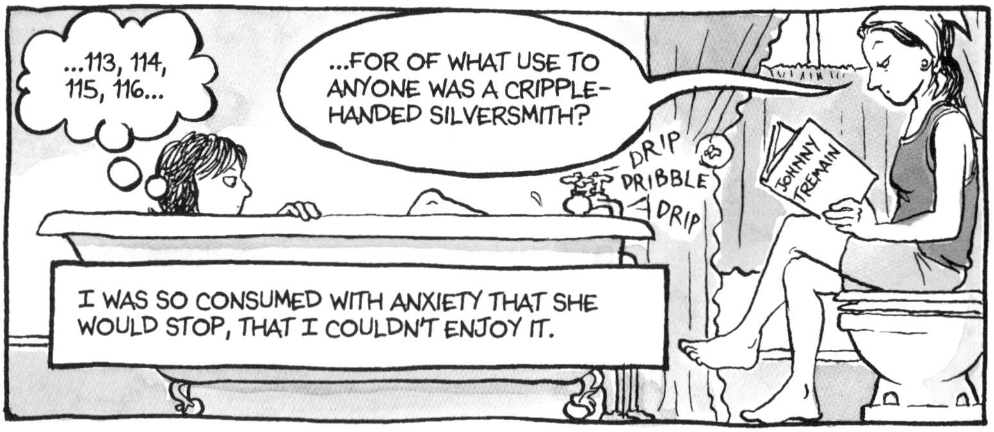
...113, 114, 115, 116...
...FOR OF WHAT USE TO ANYONE WAS A CRIPPLE-HANDED SILVERSMITH?
DRIP
DRIBBLE
DRIP
JOHNNY TREMAIN
I WAS SO CONSUMED WITH ANXIETY THAT SHE WOULD STOP, THAT I COULDN'T ENJOY IT.

MATTERS WORSENED IN MY DIARY. TO SAVE TIME I CREATED A SHORTHAND VERSION OF *I THINK*, A CURVY CIRCUMFLEX.

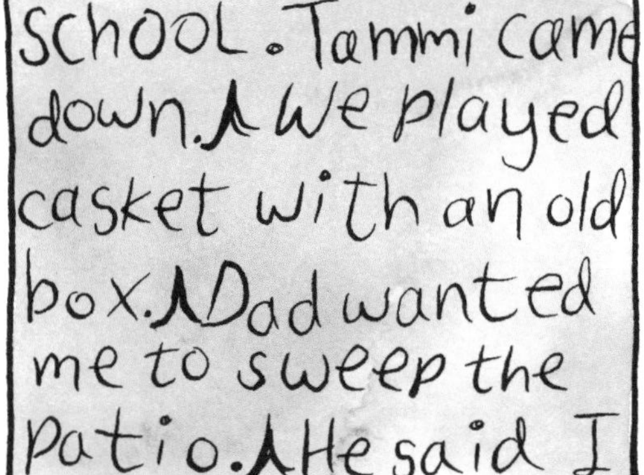
School. Tammi came
down. We played
casket with an old
box. Dad wanted
me to sweep the
patio. He said I

SOON I BEGAN DRAWING IT RIGHT OVER NAMES AND PRONOUNS. IT BECAME A SORT OF AMULET, WARDING OFF EVIL FROM MY SUBJECTS.

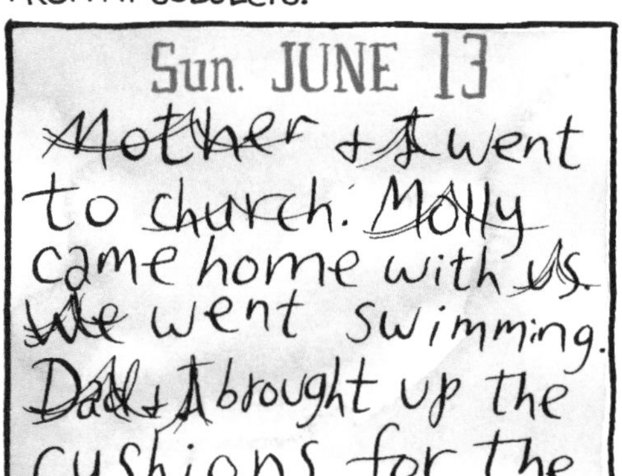
Sun. JUNE 13
Mother & I went
to church. Molly
came home with us.
We went swimming.
Dad & I brought up the
cushions for the

THEN I REALIZED I COULD DRAW THE SYMBOL OVER AN ENTIRE ENTRY.

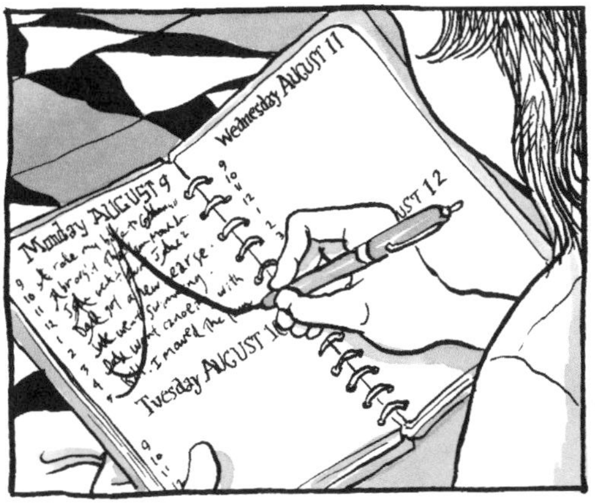
Wednesday AUGUST 11
Monday AUGUST 9
Tuesday AUGUST 10

THINGS WERE GETTING FAIRLY ILLEGIBLE BY AUGUST, WHEN WE HAD OUR CAMPING TRIP/INITIATION RITE AT THE BULLPEN.

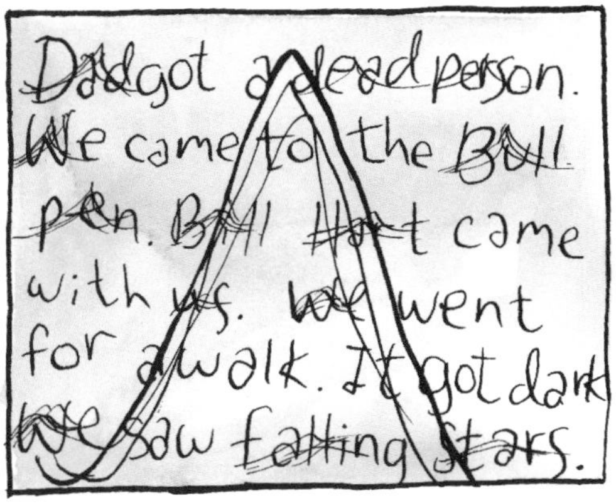
Dad got a dead person.
We came to the Bull
pen. Bill Hat came
with us. We went
for a walk. It got dark
We saw falling stars.

CONSIDERING THE PROFOUND PSYCHIC IMPACT OF THAT ADVENTURE, MY NOTES ON IT ARE SURPRISINGLY CURSORY. NO MENTION OF THE PIN-UP GIRL, THE STRIP MINE, OR BILL'S .22. JUST THE SNAKE--AND EVEN THAT WITH AN EXTREME ECONOMY OF STYLE.

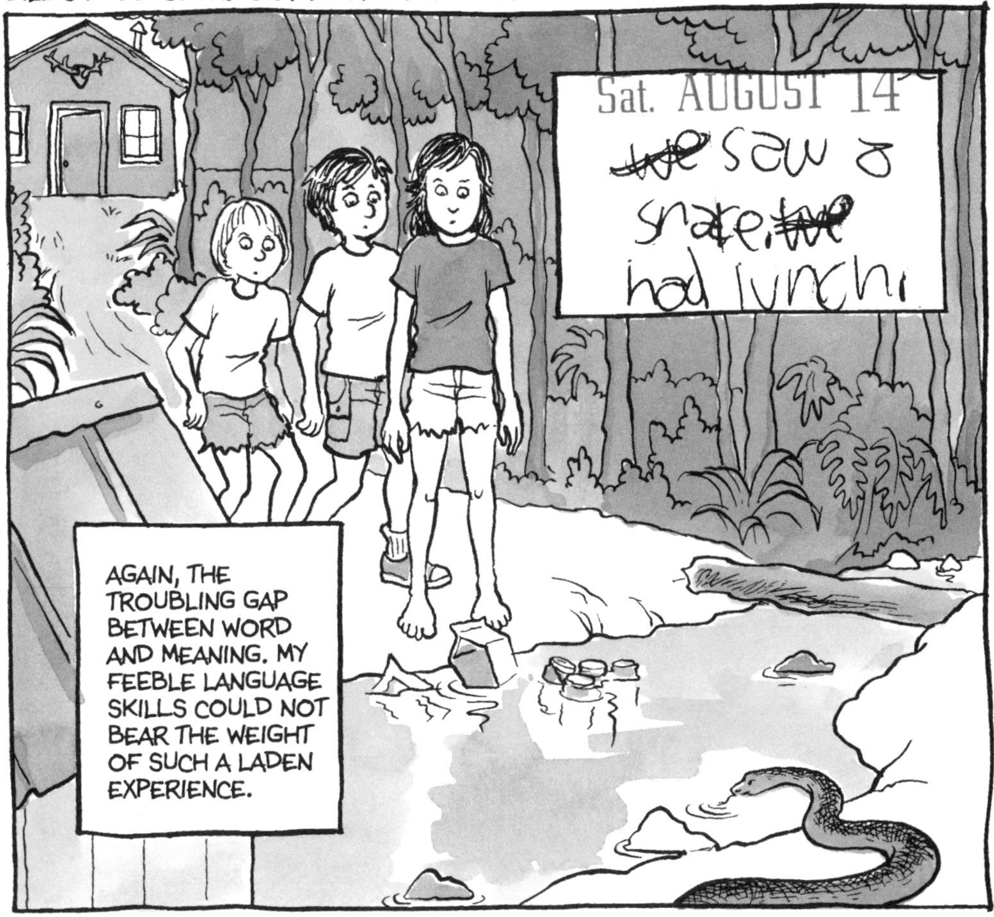
Sat. AUGUST 14
We saw a
snake. We
had lunch.
AGAIN, THE TROUBLING GAP BETWEEN WORD AND MEANING. MY FEEBLE LANGUAGE SKILLS COULD NOT BEAR THE WEIGHT OF SUCH A LADEN EXPERIENCE.

IN A SIMILAR KIND OF LANGUAGE FAILURE, IN THE LOCAL DIALECT THE BULLPEN WAS SAID TO BE SITUATED SIMPLY "OUT ON THE MOUNTAIN," THAT IS, ON THE PLATEAU. IN THE PRIMEVAL WILDERNESS BEYOND THE FRONT, SPECIFICITY IS ABANDONED.

BEECH CREEK
ALLEGHENY FRONT
BALD EAGLE MOUNTAIN
SAND RIDGE
BIG MOUNTAIN
SUGAR VALLEY MOUNTAIN
Sugar Valley
Nippenose Valley
NORTH WHITE DEER RIDGE
SOUTH WHITE DEER RIDGE
NITTANY MTN
Nittany Valley
NITTANY MOUNTAIN
Brush Valley
BRUSH MOUNTAIN
BUFFALO MOUNTAIN
Buffalo Valley
MOUNTAIN

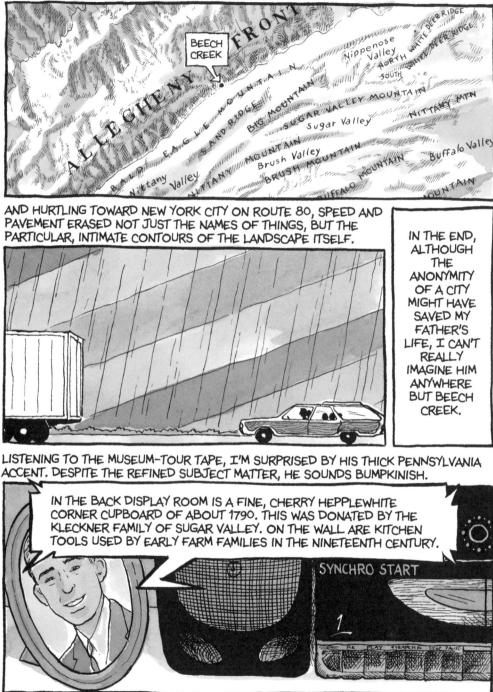

AND HURTLING TOWARD NEW YORK CITY ON ROUTE 80, SPEED AND PAVEMENT ERASED NOT JUST THE NAMES OF THINGS, BUT THE PARTICULAR, INTIMATE CONTOURS OF THE LANDSCAPE ITSELF.

IN THE END, ALTHOUGH THE ANONYMITY OF A CITY MIGHT HAVE SAVED MY FATHER'S LIFE, I CAN'T REALLY IMAGINE HIM ANYWHERE BUT BEECH CREEK.

LISTENING TO THE MUSEUM-TOUR TAPE, I'M SURPRISED BY HIS THICK PENNSYLVANIA ACCENT. DESPITE THE REFINED SUBJECT MATTER, HE SOUNDS BUMPKINISH.

IN THE BACK DISPLAY ROOM IS A FINE, CHERRY HEPPLEWHITE CORNER CUPBOARD OF ABOUT 1790. THIS WAS DONATED BY THE KLECKNER FAMILY OF SUGAR VALLEY. ON THE WALL ARE KITCHEN TOOLS USED BY EARLY FARM FAMILIES IN THE NINETEENTH CENTURY.
SYNCHRO START
1

I HADN'T REMEMBERED THIS ABOUT HIM. BY THE TIME HE DIED, I HAD NEARLY SUCCEEDED IN SCRUBBING THOSE ELONGATED VOWELS FROM MY OWN SPEECH.

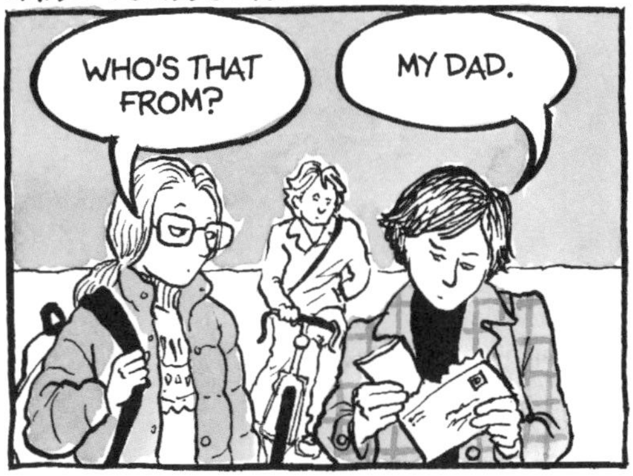
WHO'S THAT FROM?
MY DAD.

MY DERACINATION WAS KINDLY ABETTED BY VARIOUS FRIENDS AT COLLEGE.

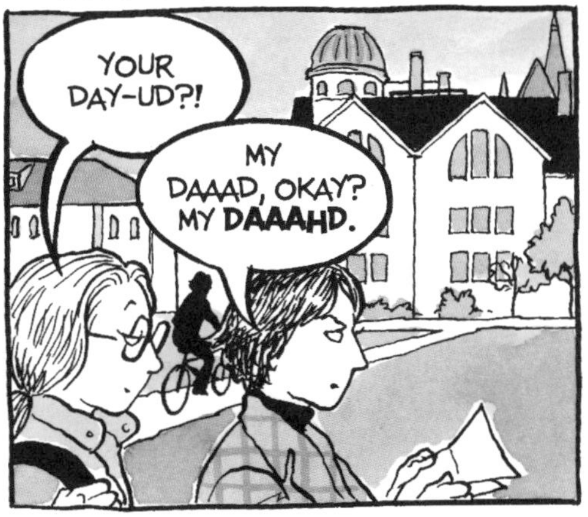
YOUR DAY-UD?!
MY DAAAD, OKAY? MY **DAAAHD.**

BUT MY FATHER WAS PLANTED DEEP.

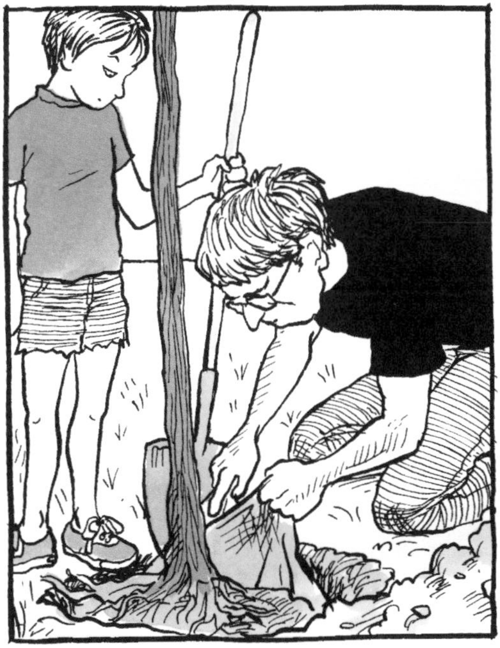

WHEN HE WAS IN THE ARMY AND DATING MY MOTHER, HE MADE PLANS FOR HER TO VISIT HIM AT HIS PARENTS' HOUSE ON AN UPCOMING LEAVE.

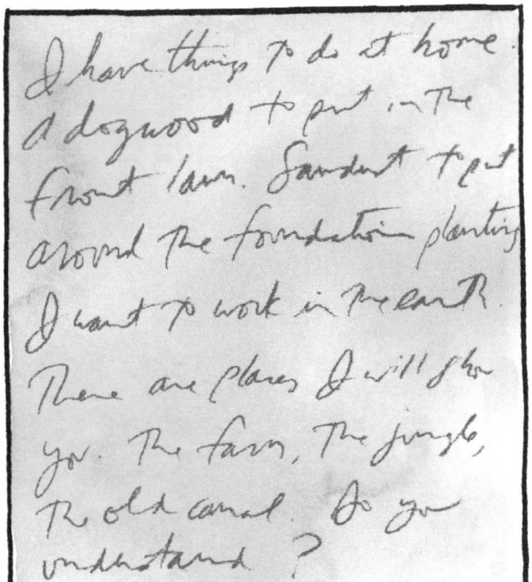
I have things to do at home. A dogwood to put in the front lawn. Sawdust to put around the foundation planting. I want to work in the earth. There are places I will show you. The farm, The jungle, The old canal. Do you understand?

IN AN EARLIER LETTER TO HER, HE DESCRIBES A WINTER SCENE.

Yesterday we skated on Beech Creek for miles through the silvery grey woods. How can I explain the creek? there are holes and crusty spots and solid mirrorlike passageways. It's dark bluish green under the iron bridge. Then on down between the island and the locks of the old canal the ice is like crystal and pale green weeds wave back and forth over blue rocks.

IN OUR *WIND IN THE WILLOWS* COLORING BOOK, MY FAVORITE PAGE WAS THE MAP.

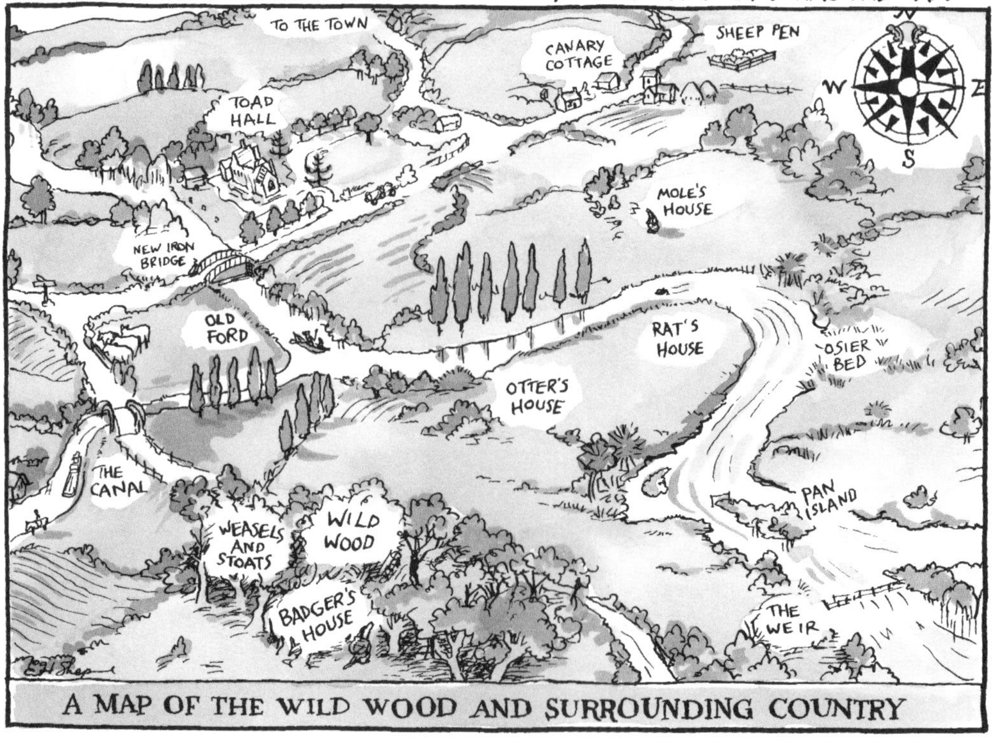
TO THE TOWN
SHEEP PEN
CANARY COTTAGE
TOAD HALL
W
E
S
MOLE'S HOUSE
NEW IRON BRIDGE
OLD FORD
RAT'S HOUSE
OSIER BED
OTTER'S HOUSE
THE CANAL
PAN ISLAND
WEASELS AND STOATS
WILD WOOD
BADGER'S HOUSE
THE WEIR
A MAP OF THE WILD WOOD AND SURROUNDING COUNTRY

I TOOK FOR GRANTED THE PARALLELS BETWEEN THIS LANDSCAPE AND MY OWN. OUR CREEK FLOWED IN THE SAME DIRECTION AS RATTY'S RIVER.

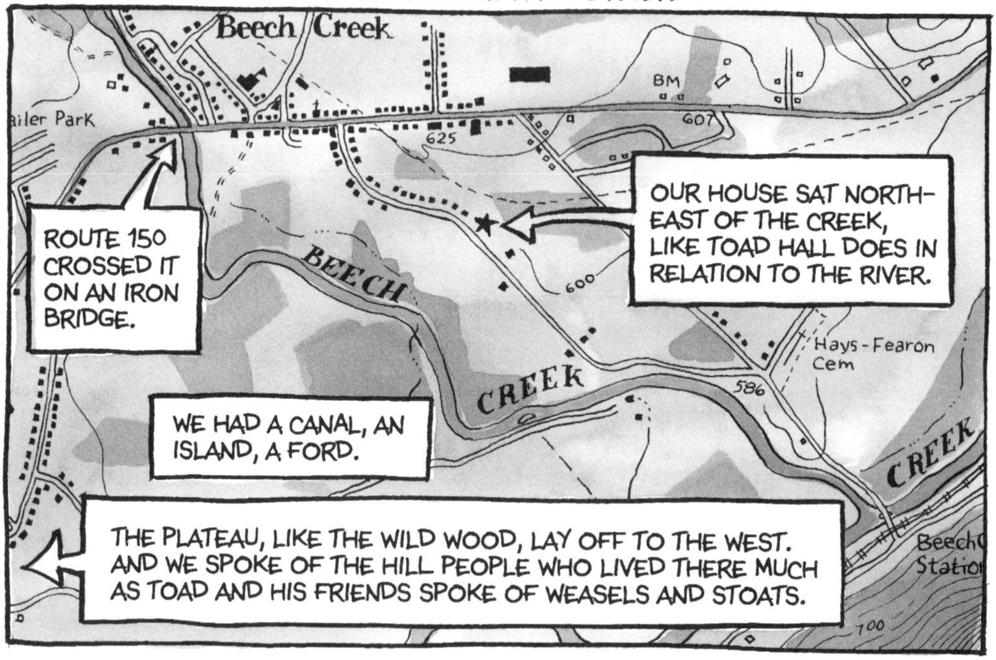
Beech Creek
BM
607
ailer Park
625
OUR HOUSE SAT NORTHEAST OF THE CREEK, LIKE TOAD HALL DOES IN RELATION TO THE RIVER.
ROUTE 150 CROSSED IT ON AN IRON BRIDGE.
BEECH
600
CREEK
Hays-Fearon Cem
586
WE HAD A CANAL, AN ISLAND, A FORD.
CREEK
THE PLATEAU, LIKE THE WILD WOOD, LAY OFF TO THE WEST. AND WE SPOKE OF THE HILL PEOPLE WHO LIVED THERE MUCH AS TOAD AND HIS FRIENDS SPOKE OF WEASELS AND STOATS.
Beech
Statio
700

BUT THE BEST THING ABOUT THE *WIND IN THE WILLOWS* MAP WAS ITS MYSTICAL BRIDGING OF THE SYMBOLIC AND THE REAL, OF THE LABEL AND THE THING ITSELF. IT WAS A CHART, BUT ALSO A VIVID, ALMOST ANIMATED PICTURE. LOOK CLOSELY...

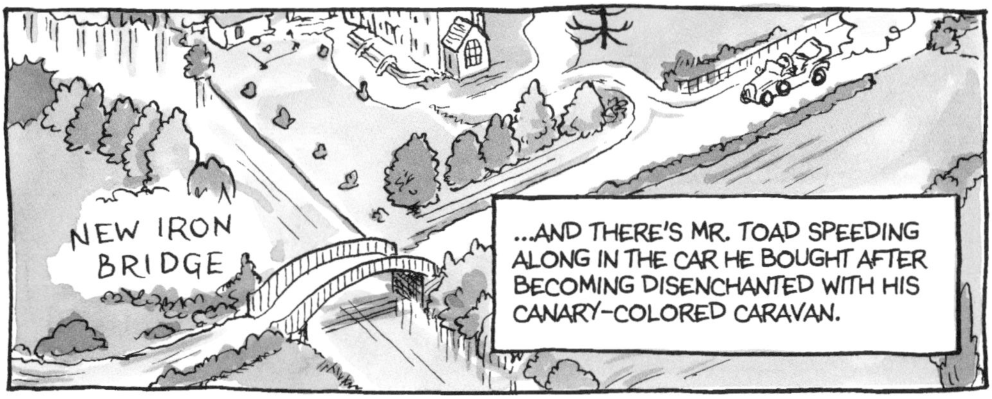
NEW IRON BRIDGE
...AND THERE'S MR. TOAD SPEEDING ALONG IN THE CAR HE BOUGHT AFTER BECOMING DISENCHANTED WITH HIS CANARY-COLORED CARAVAN.

IN SEPTEMBER OF MY OBSESSIVE-COMPULSIVE YEAR, THERE WAS A TERRIBLE ACCIDENT ON ROUTE 150.

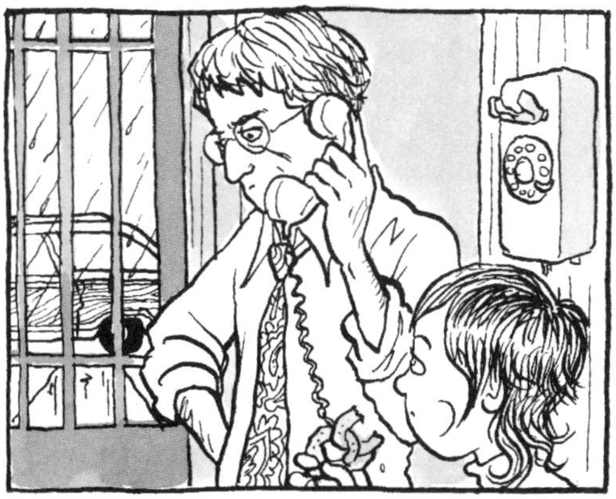

THREE PEOPLE WERE KILLED IN A CRASH ABOUT TWO MILES BEYOND THE SPOT WHERE DAD WOULD DIE NINE YEARS LATER.

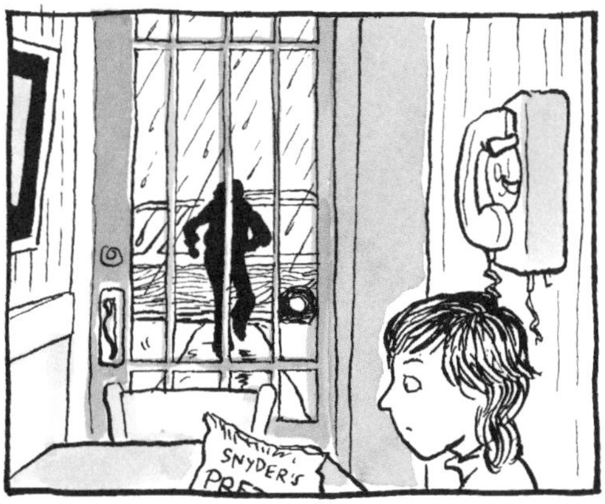
SNYDER'S

WE'D NEVER HAD A TRIPLE HEADER AT THE FUN HOME BEFORE.

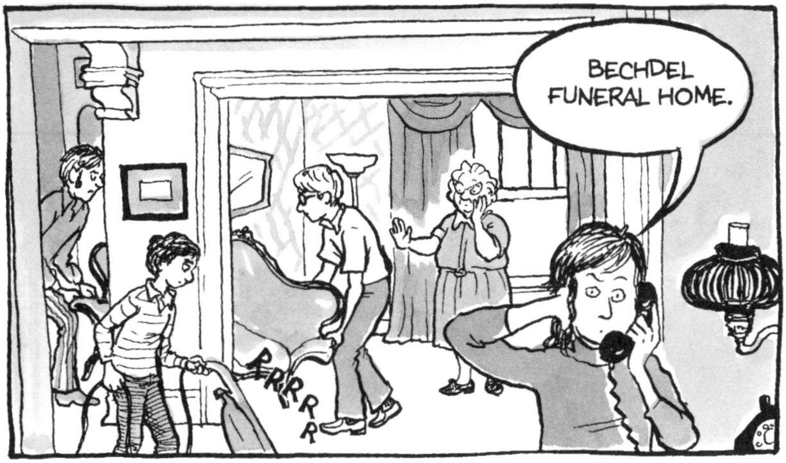
BECHDEL FUNERAL HOME.
RRRRR

ONE OF THE VICTIMS WAS A DISTANT COUSIN OF MINE, A BOY EXACTLY MY AGE.

DAD EXPLAINED THAT HE HAD DIED FROM A BROKEN NECK.

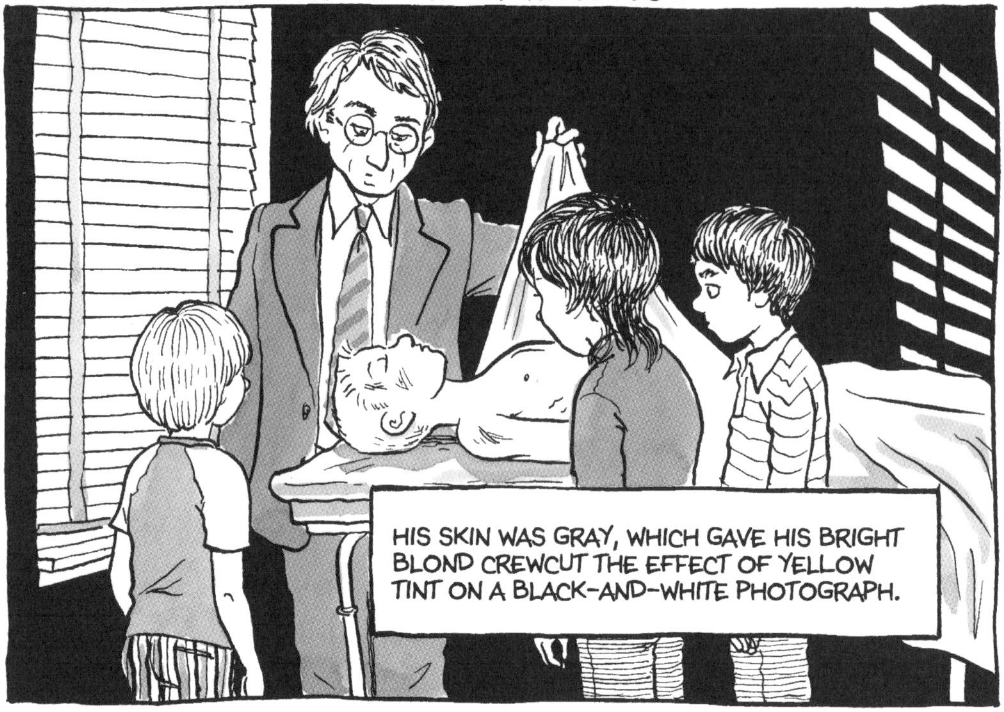
HIS SKIN WAS GRAY, WHICH GAVE HIS BRIGHT BLOND CREWCUT THE EFFECT OF YELLOW TINT ON A BLACK-AND-WHITE PHOTOGRAPH.

MY DIARY ENTRIES FOR THAT WEEKEND ARE ALMOST COMPLETELY OBSCURED.

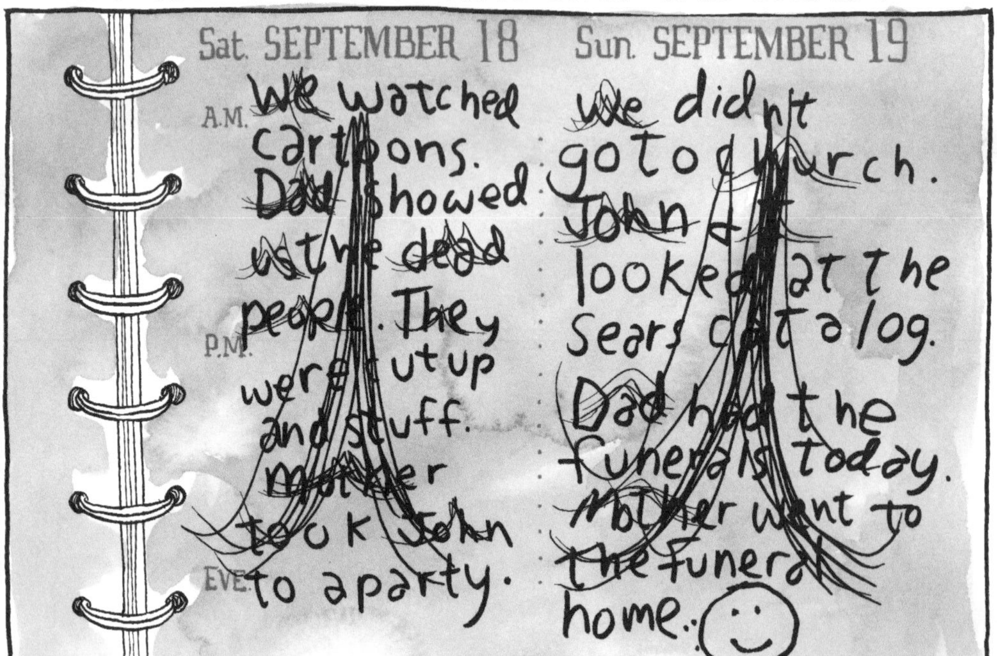
Sat. SEPTEMBER 18
Sun. SEPTEMBER 19
A.M.
P.M.
EVE.
We watched cartoons. Dad showed us the dead people. They were cut up and stuff. Mother took John to a party.
We didnt go to church. John looked at the Sears catalog. Dad had the funerals today. Mother went to the funeral home.

ON MONDAY MY BELABORED HAND IS INTERRUPTED BY MY MOTHER'S TIDY ONE.

FOR THE NEXT TWO MONTHS SHE TOOK DICTATION FROM ME, UNTIL MY "PENMANSHIP" IMPROVED.

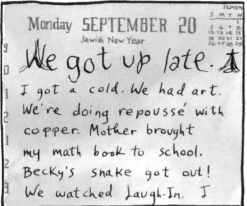

Monday SEPTEMBER 20
Jewish New Year

We got up late.

I got a cold. We had art. We're doing repoussé with copper. Mother brought my math book to school. Becky's snake got out! We watched Laugh-In. I

THERE WAS A FIRE DRILL AND WE GOT FUDGESICLES. UH...I WASHED MY HAIR.

AND SLOWLY, I DID IMPROVE. ON MY WALL CALENDAR, I SET MYSELF DEADLINES BY WHICH TO ABANDON SPECIFIC COMPULSIONS, ONE AT A TIME.

3 Do english workbook out of order	4 Stop folding towels funny.	5 Get out Dad's side of car.	6 Don't worry. You're safe.	7 Toss shoes	8
10	11 Wear "Scots" T-shirt	12	I INTERSPERSED THESE WITH SMALL ENCOURAGEMENTS.		

MY RECOVERY WAS HARDLY A JOYOUS EMBRACE OF LIFE'S ATTENDANT CHAOS——I WAS AS OBSESSIVE IN GIVING UP THE BEHAVIORS AS I HAD BEEN IN PURSUING THEM.

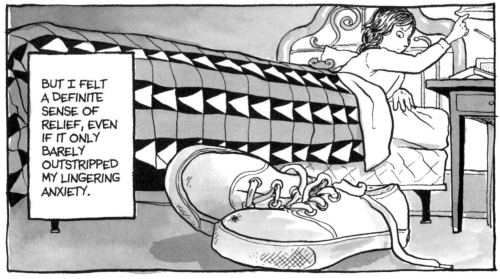

BUT I FELT A DEFINITE SENSE OF RELIEF, EVEN IF IT ONLY BARELY OUTSTRIPPED MY LINGERING ANXIETY.

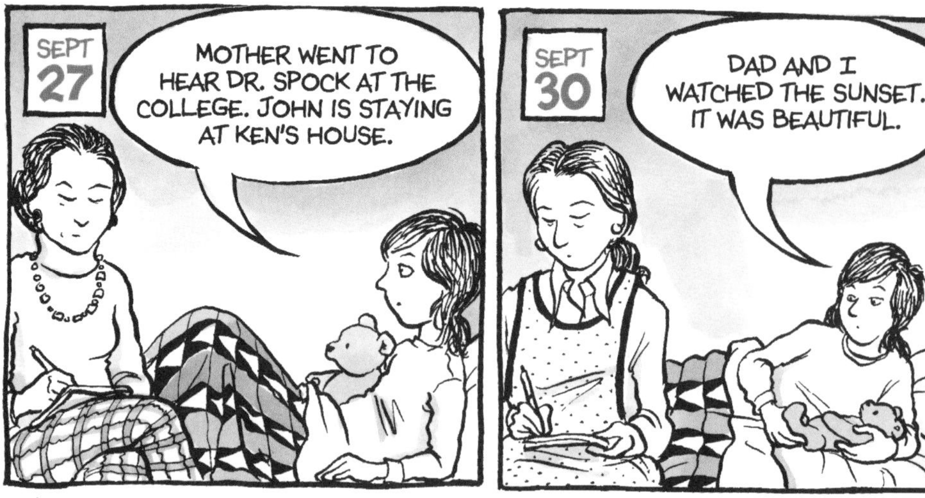
SEPT 27
MOTHER WENT TO HEAR DR. SPOCK AT THE COLLEGE. JOHN IS STAYING AT KEN'S HOUSE.
SEPT 30
DAD AND I WATCHED THE SUNSET. IT WAS BEAUTIFUL.

MY FATHER ONCE NEARLY CAME TO BLOWS WITH A FEMALE DINNER GUEST ABOUT WHETHER A PARTICULAR PATCH OF EMBROIDERY WAS FUCHSIA OR MAGENTA.

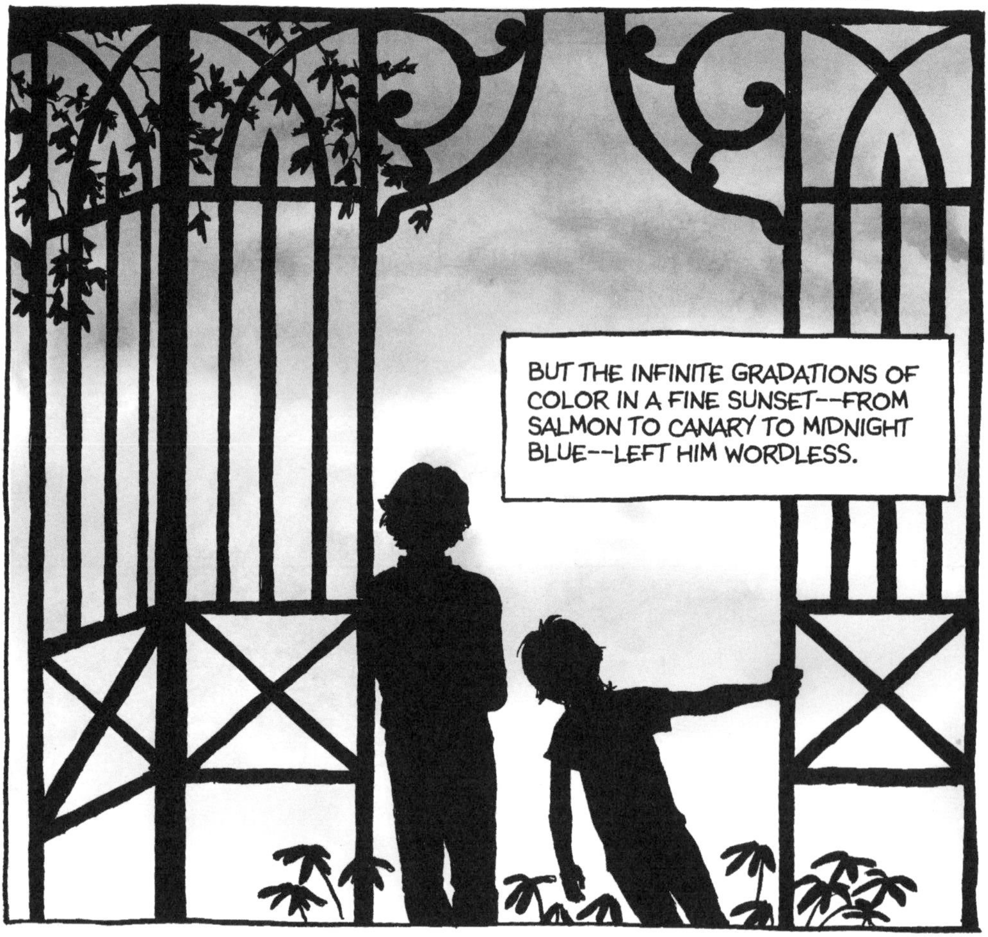
BUT THE INFINITE GRADATIONS OF COLOR IN A FINE SUNSET--FROM SALMON TO CANARY TO MIDNIGHT BLUE--LEFT HIM WORDLESS.

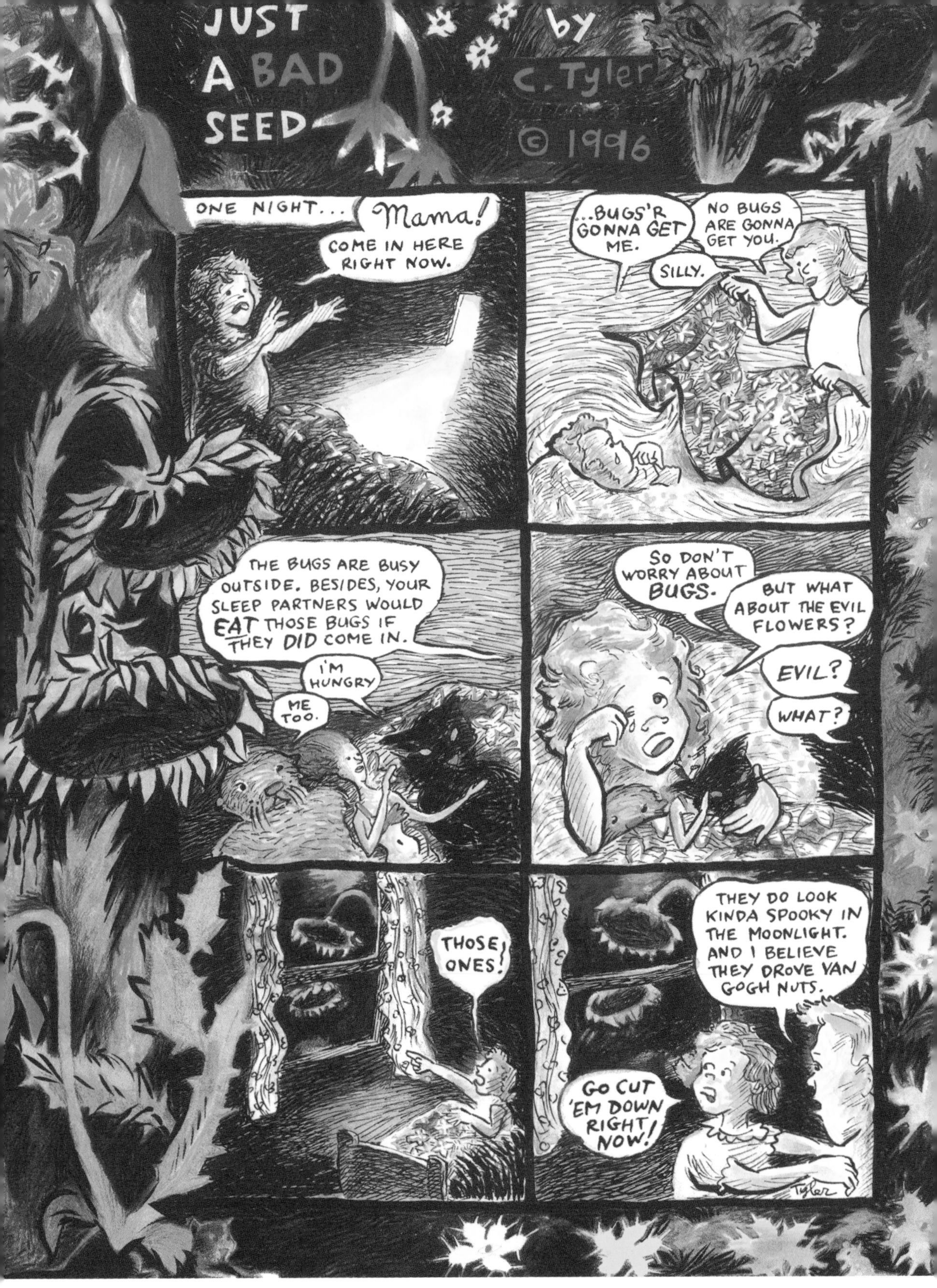
JUST A BAD SEED
by C. Tyler
© 1996
ONE NIGHT...
Mama!
COME IN HERE RIGHT NOW.
...BUGS'R GONNA GET ME.
NO BUGS ARE GONNA GET YOU.
SILLY.
THE BUGS ARE BUSY OUTSIDE. BESIDES, YOUR SLEEP PARTNERS WOULD EAT THOSE BUGS IF THEY DID COME IN.
I'M HUNGRY
ME TOO.
SO DON'T WORRY ABOUT BUGS.
BUT WHAT ABOUT THE EVIL FLOWERS?
EVIL?
WHAT?
THOSE ONES!
THEY DO LOOK KINDA SPOOKY IN THE MOONLIGHT. AND I BELIEVE THEY DROVE VAN GOGH NUTS.
GO CUT 'EM DOWN RIGHT NOW!
Tyler

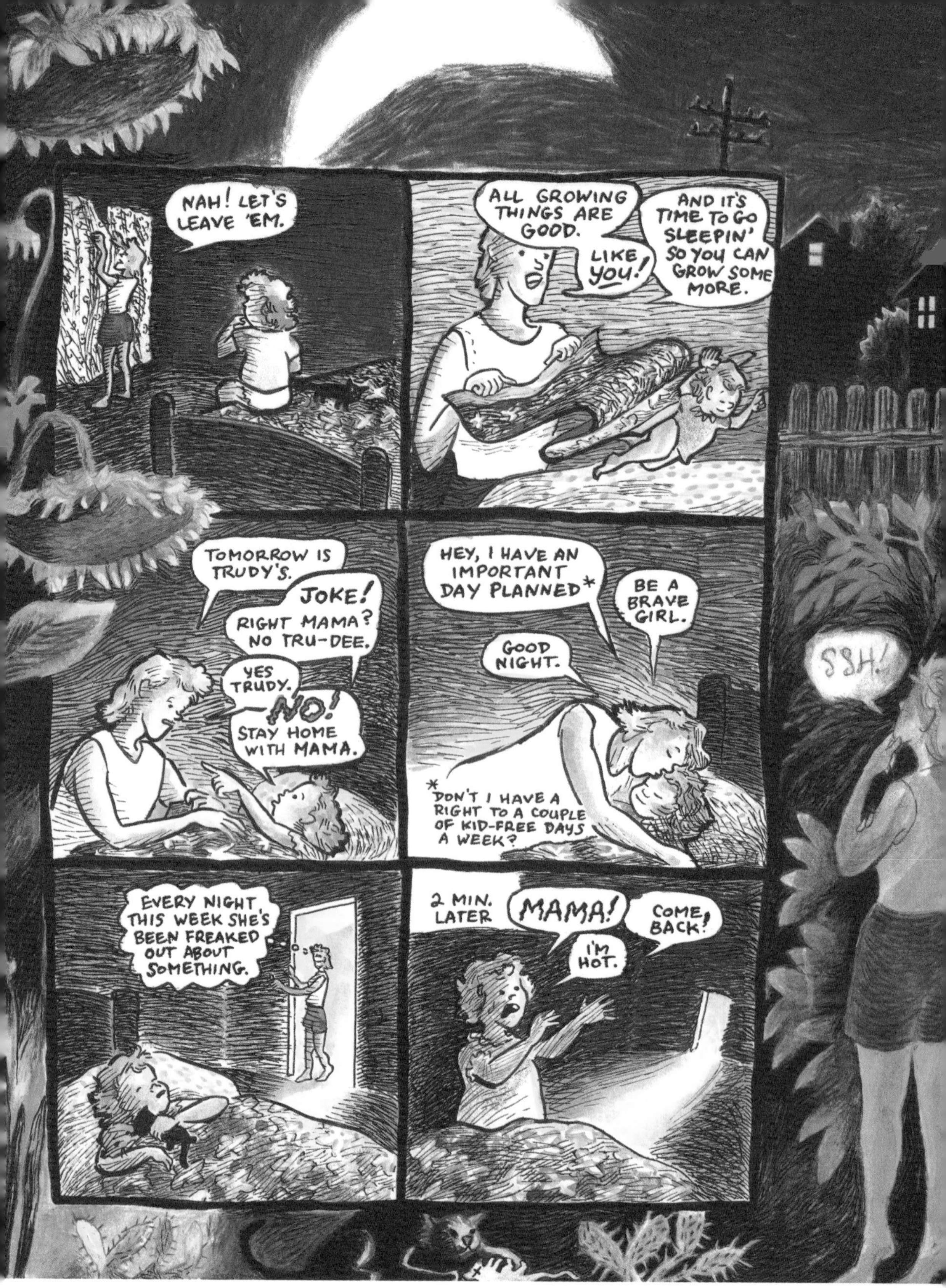
NAH! LET'S LEAVE 'EM.
ALL GROWING THINGS ARE GOOD.
LIKE YOU!
AND IT'S TIME TO GO SLEEPIN' SO YOU CAN GROW SOME MORE.
TOMORROW IS TRUDY'S.
JOKE! RIGHT MAMA? NO TRU-DEE.
YES TRUDY.
NO! STAY HOME WITH MAMA.
HEY, I HAVE AN IMPORTANT DAY PLANNED*
BE A BRAVE GIRL.
GOOD NIGHT.
*DON'T I HAVE A RIGHT TO A COUPLE OF KID-FREE DAYS A WEEK?
EVERY NIGHT THIS WEEK SHE'S BEEN FREAKED OUT ABOUT SOMETHING.
2 MIN. LATER
MAMA!
I'M HOT.
COME BACK!
SSH!

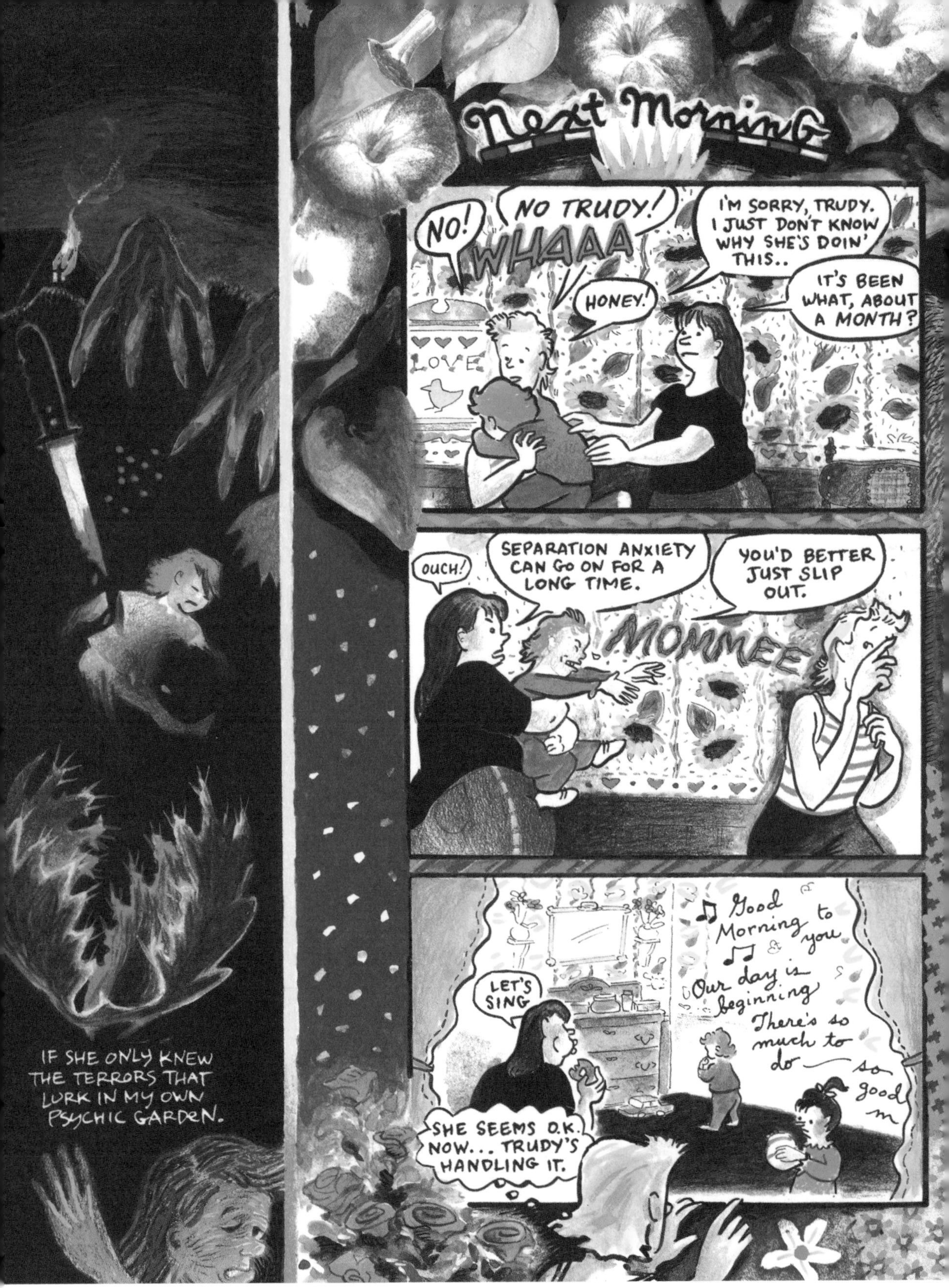
IF SHE ONLY KNEW THE TERRORS THAT LURK IN MY OWN PSYCHIC GARDEN.
Next Morning
NO!
NO TRUDY!
WHAAA
I'M SORRY, TRUDY. I JUST DON'T KNOW WHY SHE'S DOIN' THIS..
HONEY!
IT'S BEEN WHAT, ABOUT A MONTH?
LOVE
OUCH!
SEPARATION ANXIETY CAN GO ON FOR A LONG TIME.
YOU'D BETTER JUST SLIP OUT.
MOMMEE
LET'S SING
Good Morning to you
Our day is beginning
There's so much to do — so good
SHE SEEMS O.K. NOW... TRUDY'S HANDLING IT.

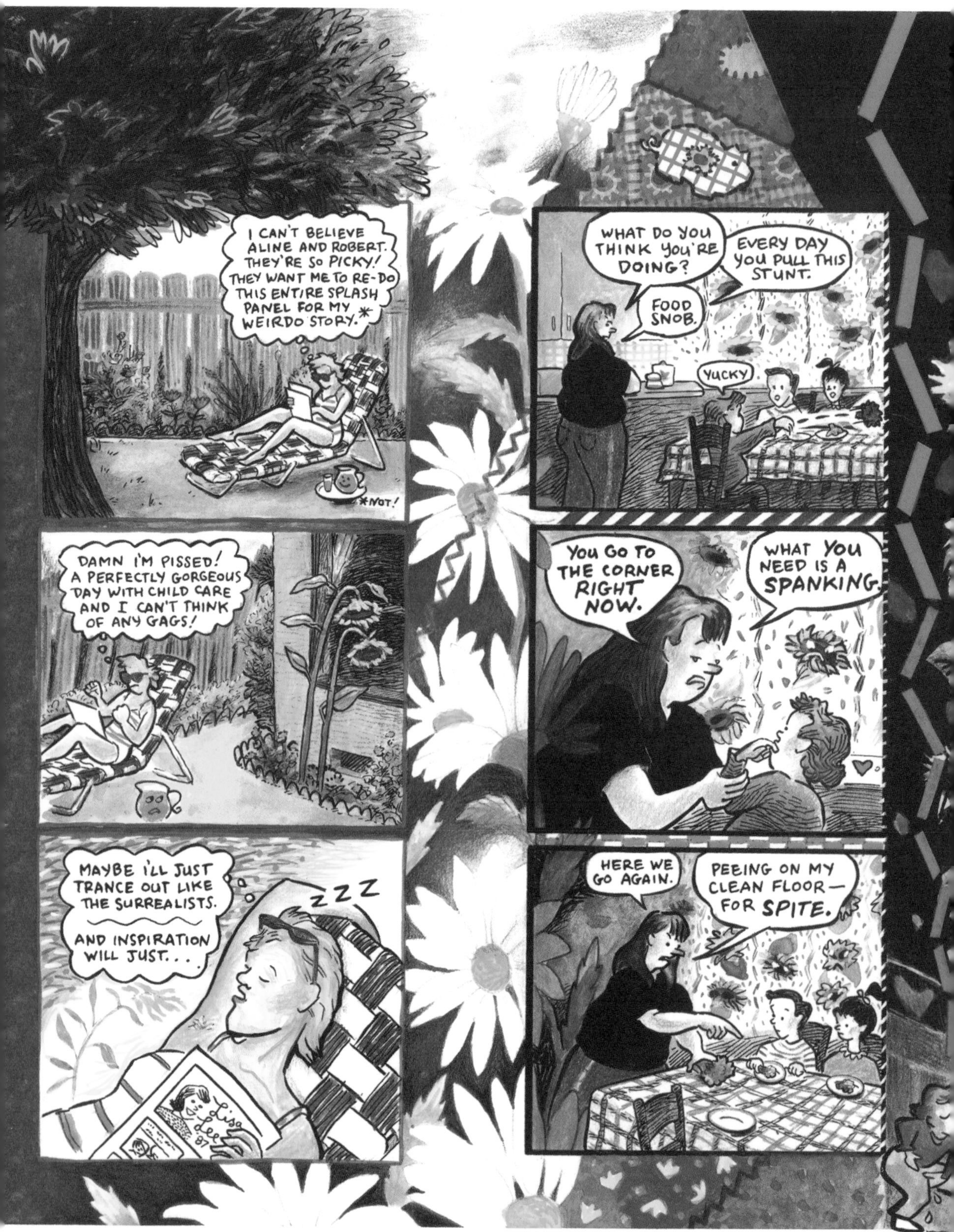
I CAN'T BELIEVE ALINE AND ROBERT. THEY'RE SO PICKY! THEY WANT ME TO RE-DO THIS ENTIRE SPLASH PANEL FOR MY WEIRDO STORY.*
*NOT!
DAMN I'M PISSED! A PERFECTLY GORGEOUS DAY WITH CHILD CARE AND I CAN'T THINK OF ANY GAGS!
MAYBE I'LL JUST TRANCE OUT LIKE THE SURREALISTS.
AND INSPIRATION WILL JUST...
ZZZ
Lisa Lee '87
WHAT DO YOU THINK YOU'RE DOING?
EVERY DAY YOU PULL THIS STUNT.
FOOD SNOB.
YUCKY
YOU GO TO THE CORNER RIGHT NOW.
WHAT YOU NEED IS A SPANKING.
HERE WE GO AGAIN.
PEEING ON MY CLEAN FLOOR— FOR SPITE.

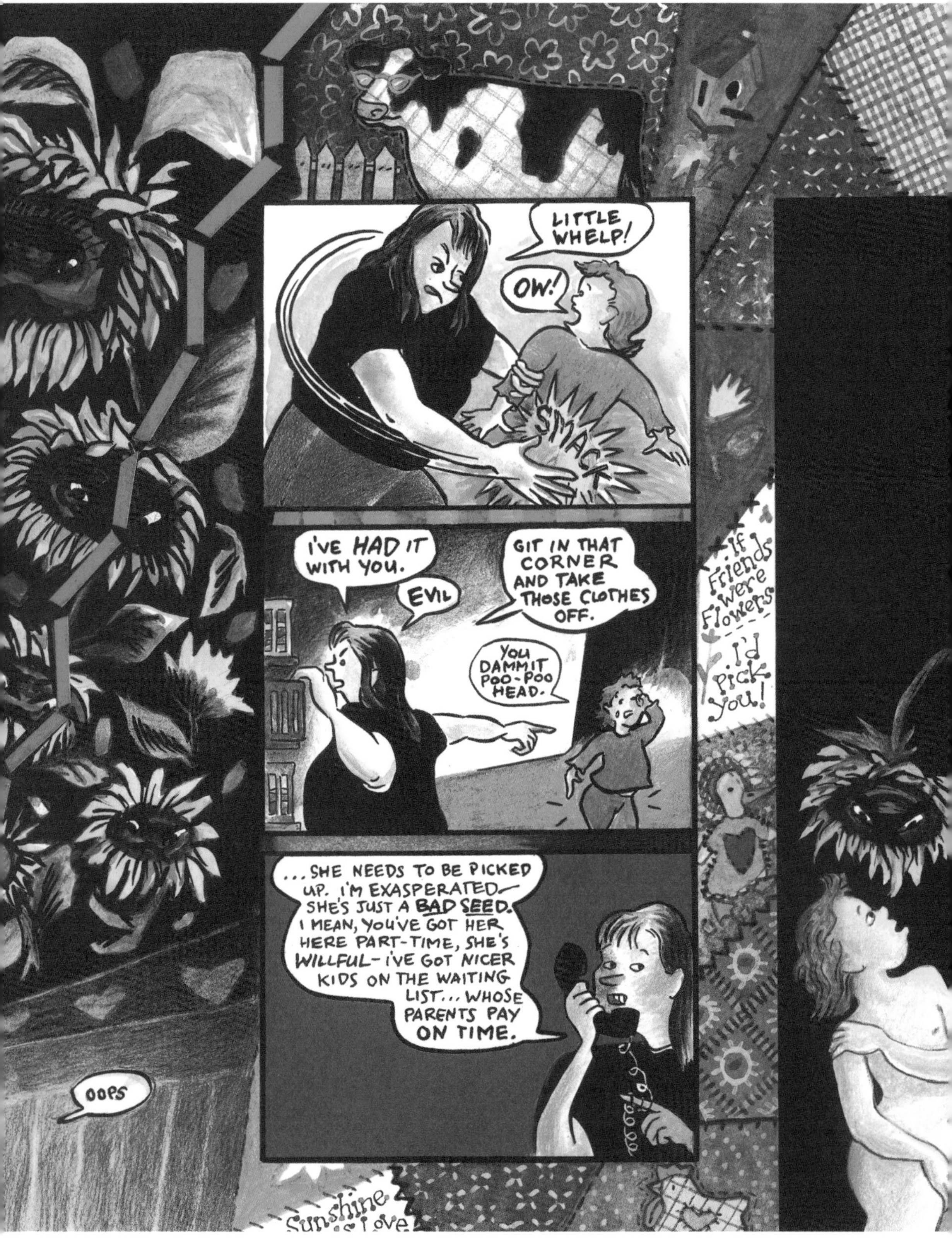
LITTLE WHELP!
OW!
SMACK
I'VE HAD IT WITH YOU.
EVIL
GIT IN THAT CORNER AND TAKE THOSE CLOTHES OFF.
YOU DAMMIT POO-POO HEAD.
...SHE NEEDS TO BE PICKED UP. I'M EXASPERATED— SHE'S JUST A BAD SEED. I MEAN, YOU'VE GOT HER HERE PART-TIME, SHE'S WILLFUL— I'VE GOT NICER KIDS ON THE WAITING LIST... WHOSE PARENTS PAY ON TIME.
OOPS
If Friends were Flowers I'd pick you!
Sunshine is Love

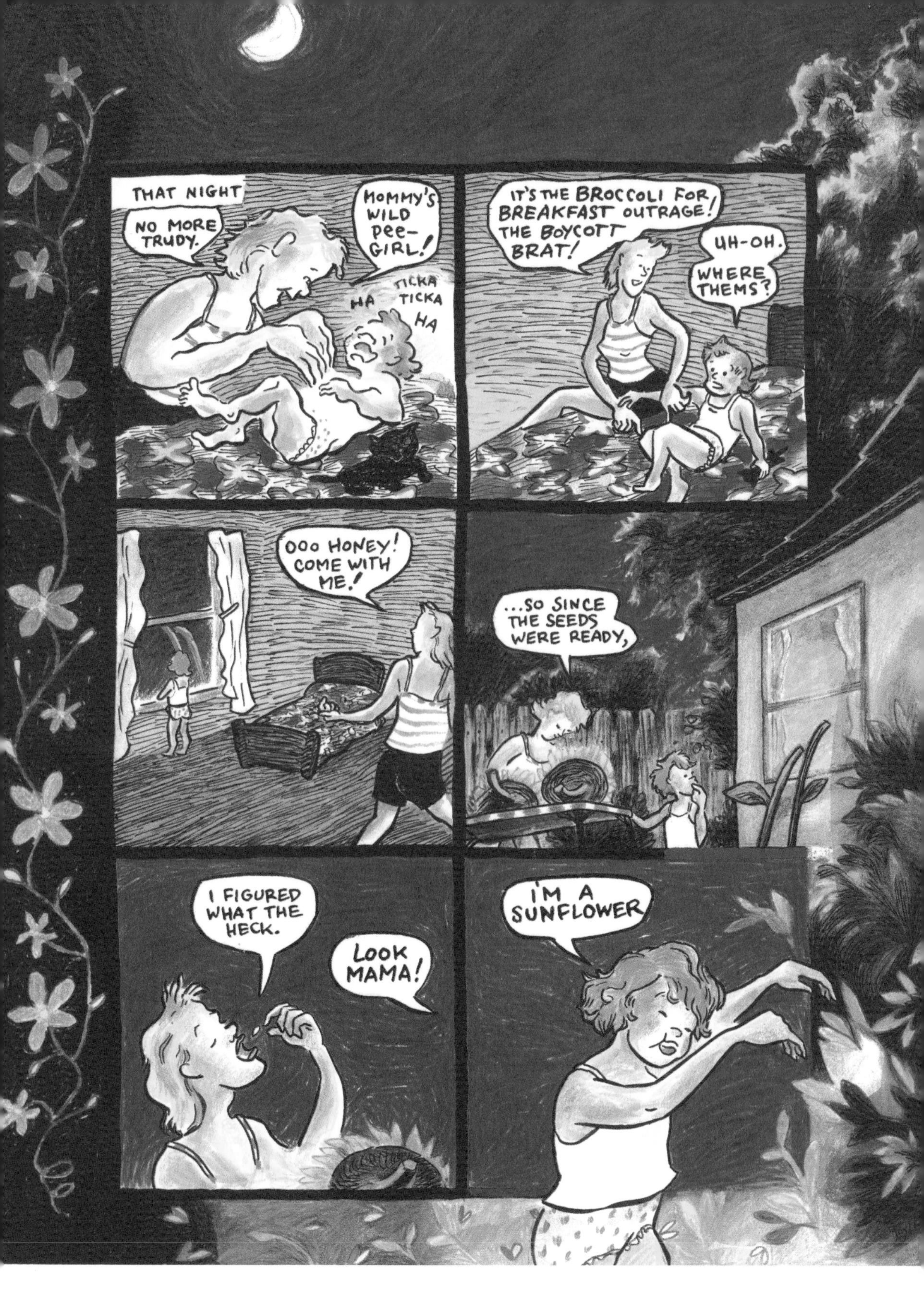
THAT NIGHT
NO MORE TRUDY.
MOMMY'S WILD PEE-GIRL!
HA
TICKA TICKA
HA
IT'S THE BROCCOLI FOR BREAKFAST OUTRAGE! THE BOYCOTT BRAT!
UH-OH.
WHERE THEMS?
OOO HONEY! COME WITH ME!
...SO SINCE THE SEEDS WERE READY,
I FIGURED WHAT THE HECK.
LOOK MAMA!
I'M A SUNFLOWER

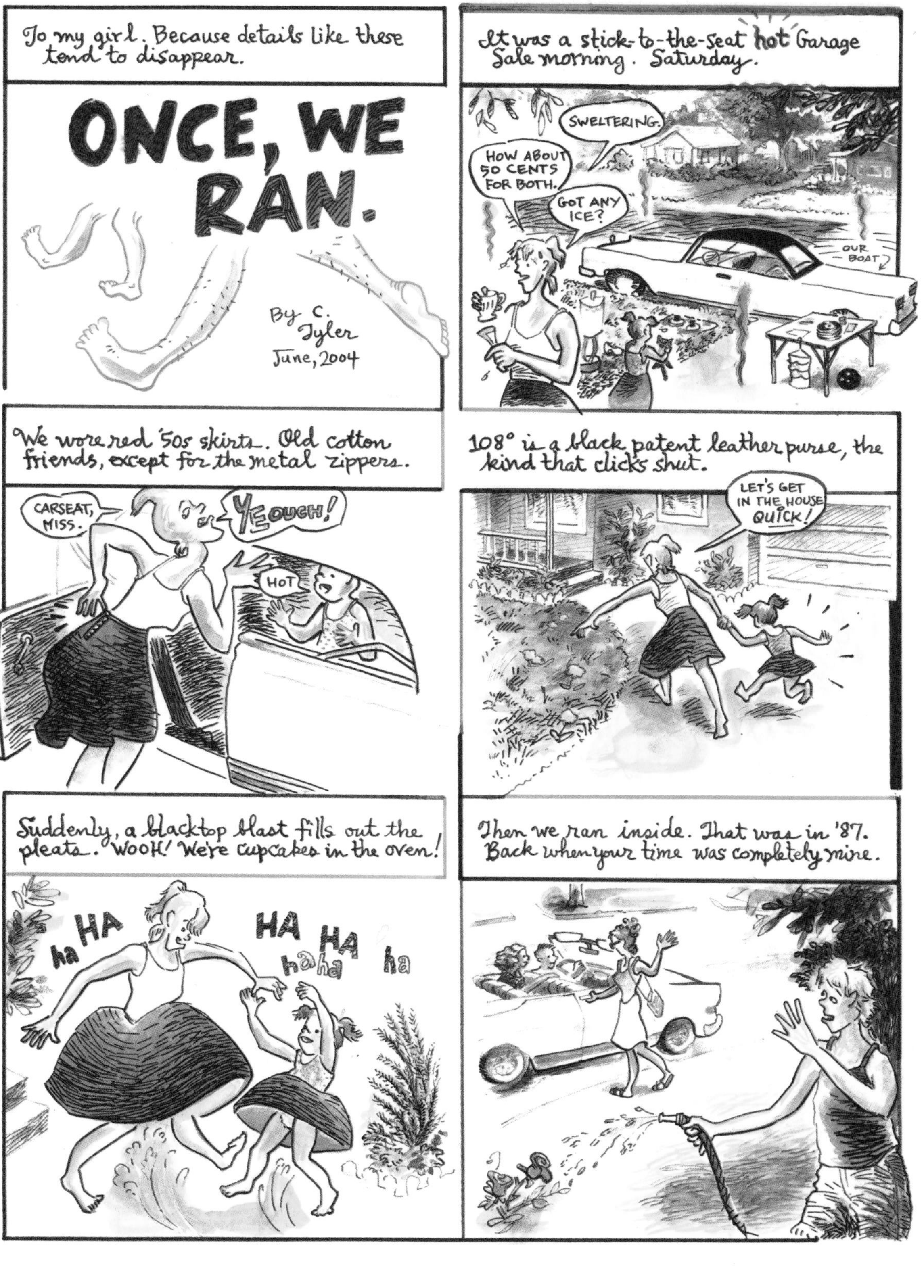

To my girl. Because details like these tend to disappear.
ONCE, WE RAN.
By C. Tyler
June, 2004
It was a stick-to-the-seat hot Garage Sale morning. Saturday.
SWELTERING.
HOW ABOUT 50 CENTS FOR BOTH.
GOT ANY ICE?
OUR BOAT
We wore red '50s skirts. Old cotton friends, except for the metal zippers.
CARSEAT, MISS.
YEOUCH!
HOT
108° is a black patent leather purse, the kind that clicks shut.
LET'S GET IN THE HOUSE QUICK!
Suddenly, a blacktop blast fills out the pleats. WOOH! We're cupcakes in the oven!
ha HA
HA
HA
haha
ha
Then we ran inside. That was in '87. Back when your time was completely mine.

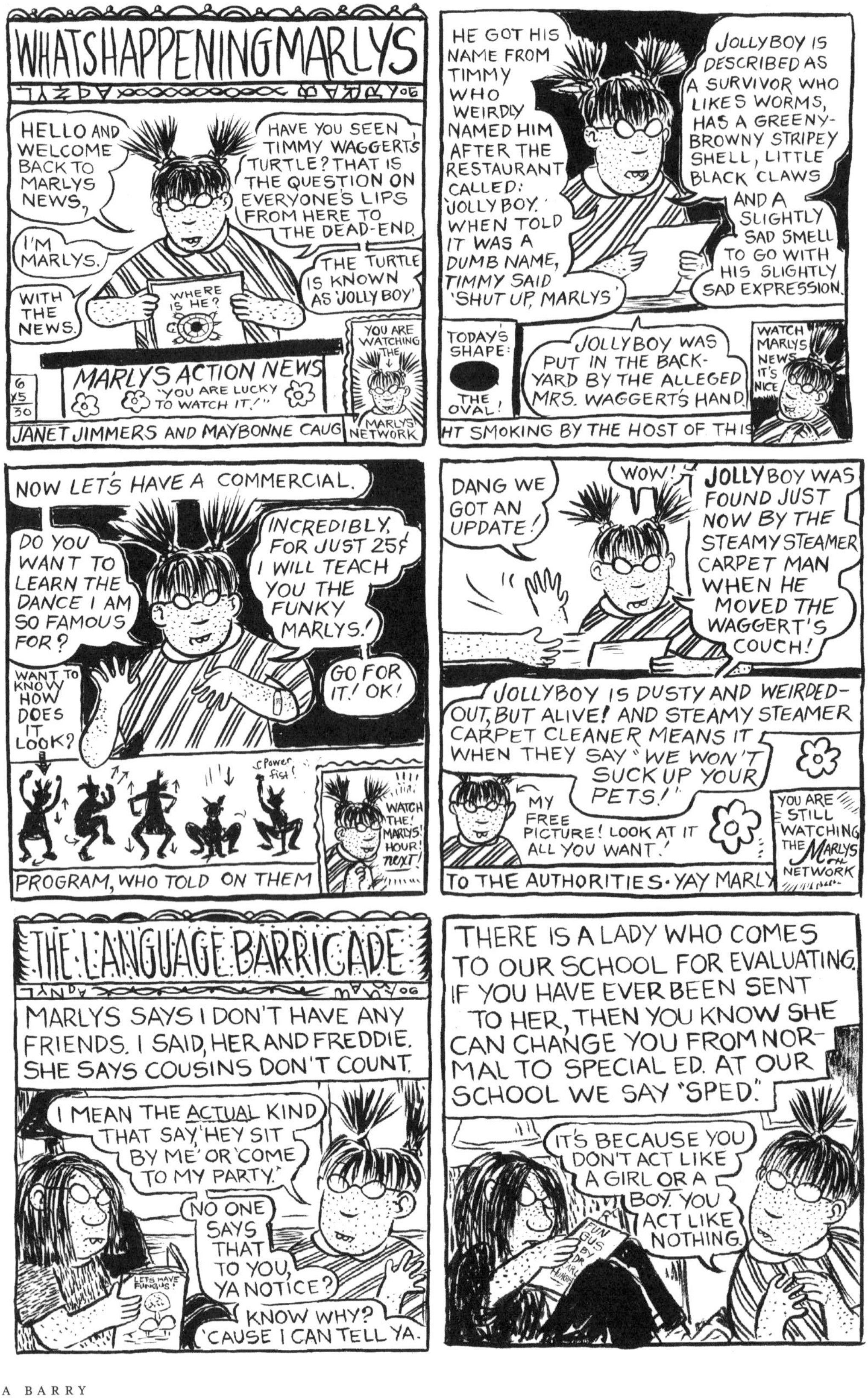
WHATSHAPPENINGMARLYS
LYNDA BARRY ©06
HELLO AND WELCOME BACK TO MARLYS NEWS,
I'M MARLYS.
WITH THE NEWS.
HAVE YOU SEEN TIMMY WAGGERT'S TURTLE? THAT IS THE QUESTION ON EVERYONE'S LIPS FROM HERE TO THE DEAD-END.
THE TURTLE IS KNOWN AS 'JOLLY BOY'
WHERE IS HE?
MARLYS ACTION NEWS
"YOU ARE LUCKY TO WATCH IT!"
6 X5 30
YOU ARE WATCHING THE
MARLYS NETWORK
JANET JIMMERS AND MAYBONNE CAUG
HE GOT HIS NAME FROM TIMMY WHO WEIRDLY NAMED HIM AFTER THE RESTAURANT CALLED: 'JOLLY BOY.' WHEN TOLD IT WAS A DUMB NAME, TIMMY SAID 'SHUT UP, MARLYS'
JOLLYBOY IS DESCRIBED AS A SURVIVOR WHO LIKES WORMS, HAS A GREENY-BROWNY STRIPEY SHELL, LITTLE BLACK CLAWS
AND A SLIGHTLY SAD SMELL TO GO WITH HIS SLIGHTLY SAD EXPRESSION.
TODAY'S SHAPE: THE OVAL!
JOLLYBOY WAS PUT IN THE BACK-YARD BY THE ALLEGED MRS. WAGGERT'S HAND.
WATCH MARLYS NEWS IT'S NICE
HT SMOKING BY THE HOST OF THIS
NOW LET'S HAVE A COMMERCIAL.
DO YOU WANT TO LEARN THE DANCE I AM SO FAMOUS FOR?
INCREDIBLY, FOR JUST 25¢ I WILL TEACH YOU THE FUNKY MARLYS!
GO FOR IT! OK!
WANT TO KNOW HOW DOES IT LOOK?
Power fist!
WATCH THE! MARLYS! HOUR! NEXT!
PROGRAM, WHO TOLD ON THEM
DANG WE GOT AN UPDATE!
WOW!
JOLLY BOY WAS FOUND JUST NOW BY THE STEAMY STEAMER CARPET MAN WHEN HE MOVED THE WAGGERT'S COUCH!
JOLLYBOY IS DUSTY AND WEIRDED-OUT, BUT ALIVE! AND STEAMY STEAMER CARPET CLEANER MEANS IT WHEN THEY SAY "WE WON'T SUCK UP YOUR PETS!"
MY FREE PICTURE! LOOK AT IT ALL YOU WANT.
YOU ARE STILL WATCHING THE MARLYS NETWORK
TO THE AUTHORITIES · YAY MARLY
THE LANGUAGE BARRICADE
LYNDA BARRY ©06
MARLYS SAYS I DON'T HAVE ANY FRIENDS. I SAID, HER AND FREDDIE. SHE SAYS COUSINS DON'T COUNT.
I MEAN THE ACTUAL KIND THAT SAY, 'HEY SIT BY ME' OR 'COME TO MY PARTY.'
NO ONE SAYS THAT TO YOU, YA NOTICE?
KNOW WHY? 'CAUSE I CAN TELL YA.
LET'S HAVE FUNGUS!
THERE IS A LADY WHO COMES TO OUR SCHOOL FOR EVALUATING. IF YOU HAVE EVER BEEN SENT TO HER, THEN YOU KNOW SHE CAN CHANGE YOU FROM NOR-MAL TO SPECIAL ED. AT OUR SCHOOL WE SAY "SPED."
IT'S BECAUSE YOU DON'T ACT LIKE A GIRL OR A BOY. YOU ACT LIKE NOTHING.
FUN GUS BY DR. CARL

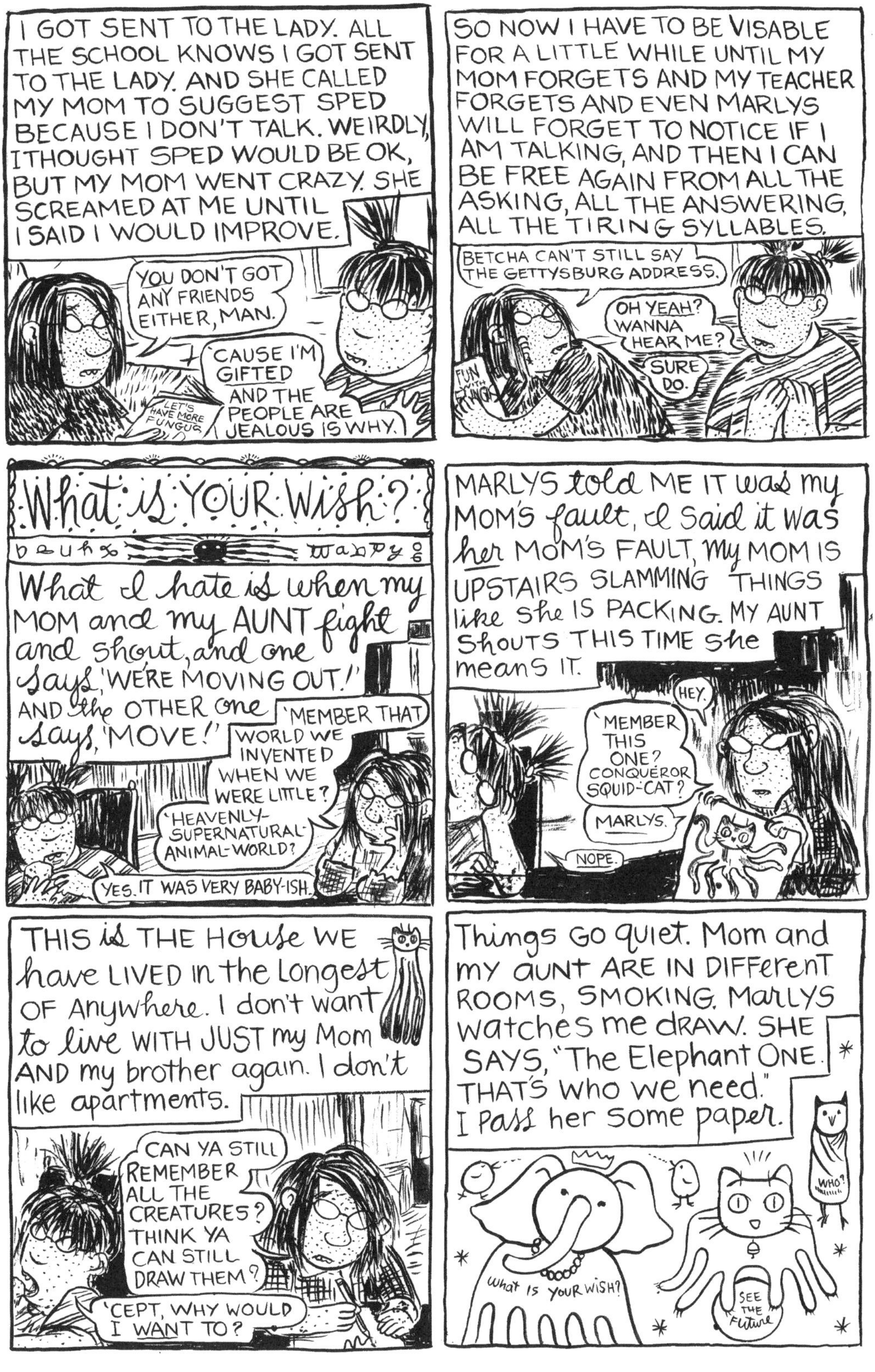
I GOT SENT TO THE LADY. ALL THE SCHOOL KNOWS I GOT SENT TO THE LADY. AND SHE CALLED MY MOM TO SUGGEST SPED BECAUSE I DON'T TALK. WEIRDLY, I THOUGHT SPED WOULD BE OK, BUT MY MOM WENT CRAZY. SHE SCREAMED AT ME UNTIL I SAID I WOULD IMPROVE.
YOU DON'T GOT ANY FRIENDS EITHER, MAN.
'CAUSE I'M GIFTED AND THE PEOPLE ARE JEALOUS IS WHY.
LET'S HAVE MORE FUNGUS
SO NOW I HAVE TO BE VISABLE FOR A LITTLE WHILE UNTIL MY MOM FORGETS AND MY TEACHER FORGETS AND EVEN MARLYS WILL FORGET TO NOTICE IF I AM TALKING, AND THEN I CAN BE FREE AGAIN FROM ALL THE ASKING, ALL THE ANSWERING, ALL THE TIRING SYLLABLES.
BETCHA CAN'T STILL SAY THE GETTYSBURG ADDRESS.
OH YEAH? WANNA HEAR ME?
SURE DO.
What is YOUR Wish?
What I hate is when my MOM and my AUNT fight and shout, and one says, 'WE'RE MOVING OUT!' AND the OTHER one says, 'MOVE!'
'MEMBER THAT WORLD WE INVENTED WHEN WE WERE LITTLE?
'HEAVENLY-SUPERNATURAL-ANIMAL-WORLD?
YES. IT WAS VERY BABY-ISH.
MARLYS told ME IT was my MOM'S fault, I Said it was her MOM'S FAULT, my MOM IS UPSTAIRS SLAMMING THINGS like She IS PACKING. MY AUNT Shouts THIS TIME She means IT.
HEY.
'MEMBER THIS ONE? CONQUEROR SQUID-CAT?
MARLYS.
NOPE.
THIS is THE House WE have LIVED in the Longest of Anywhere. I don't want to live WITH JUST my Mom AND my brother again. I don't like apartments.
CAN YA STILL REMEMBER ALL THE CREATURES? THINK YA CAN STILL DRAW THEM?
'CEPT, WHY WOULD I WANT TO?
Things Go quiet. Mom and my aunt ARE IN DIFFERENT ROOMS, SMOKING. Marlys watches me draw. SHE SAYS, "The Elephant ONE. THAT'S who we need." I Pass her Some paper.
What is YOUR WISH?
WHO?
SEE THE Future

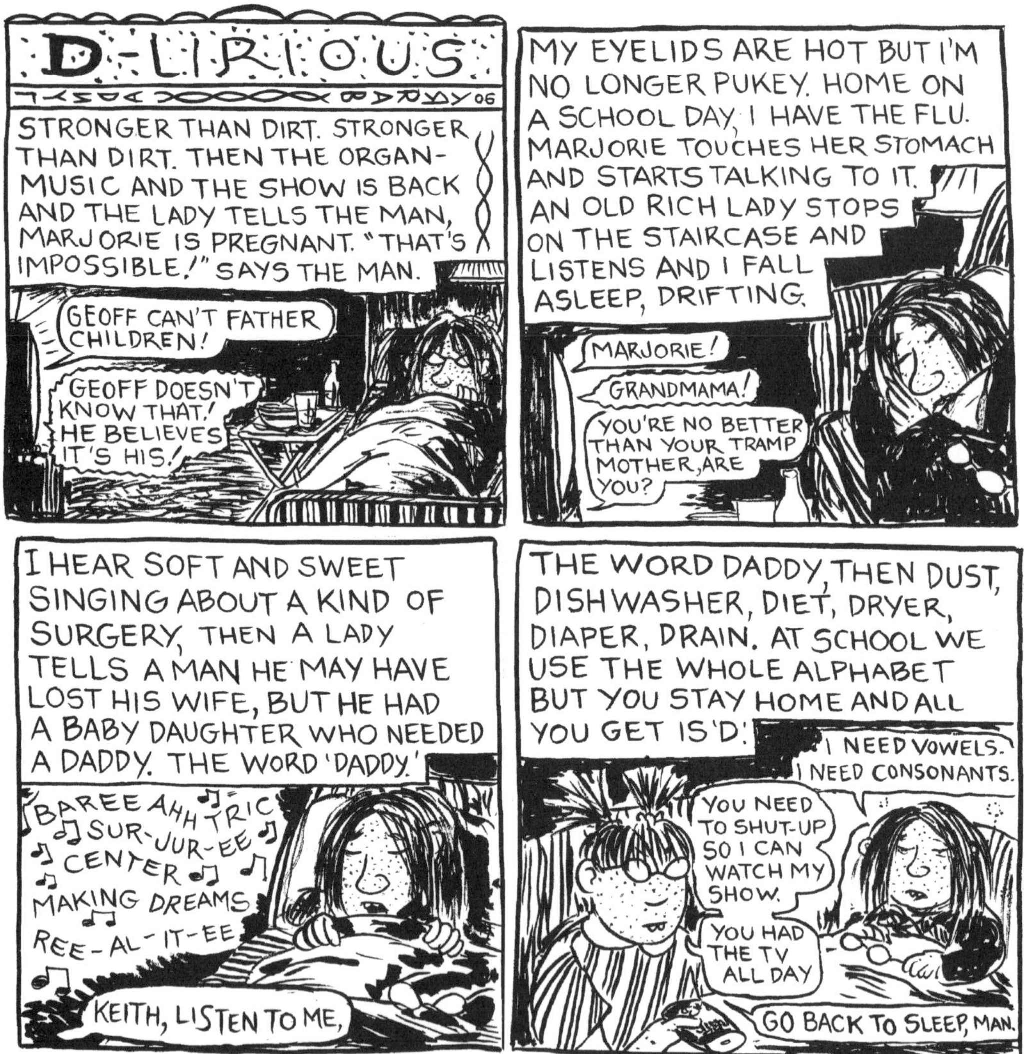
D-LIRIOUS
STRONGER THAN DIRT. STRONGER THAN DIRT. THEN THE ORGAN-MUSIC AND THE SHOW IS BACK AND THE LADY TELLS THE MAN, MARJORIE IS PREGNANT. "THAT'S IMPOSSIBLE!" SAYS THE MAN.
GEOFF CAN'T FATHER CHILDREN!
GEOFF DOESN'T KNOW THAT! HE BELIEVES IT'S HIS!
MY EYELIDS ARE HOT BUT I'M NO LONGER PUKEY. HOME ON A SCHOOL DAY, I HAVE THE FLU. MARJORIE TOUCHES HER STOMACH AND STARTS TALKING TO IT. AN OLD RICH LADY STOPS ON THE STAIRCASE AND LISTENS AND I FALL ASLEEP, DRIFTING.
MARJORIE!
GRANDMAMA!
YOU'RE NO BETTER THAN YOUR TRAMP MOTHER, ARE YOU?
I HEAR SOFT AND SWEET SINGING ABOUT A KIND OF SURGERY, THEN A LADY TELLS A MAN HE MAY HAVE LOST HIS WIFE, BUT HE HAD A BABY DAUGHTER WHO NEEDED A DADDY. THE WORD 'DADDY.'
BAREE AHH TRIC SUR-JUR-EE CENTER MAKING DREAMS REE-AL-IT-EE
KEITH, LISTEN TO ME,
THE WORD DADDY, THEN DUST, DISHWASHER, DIET, DRYER, DIAPER, DRAIN. AT SCHOOL WE USE THE WHOLE ALPHABET BUT YOU STAY HOME AND ALL YOU GET IS 'D.'
I NEED VOWELS. I NEED CONSONANTS.
YOU NEED TO SHUT-UP SO I CAN WATCH MY SHOW.
YOU HAD THE TV ALL DAY
GO BACK TO SLEEP, MAN.

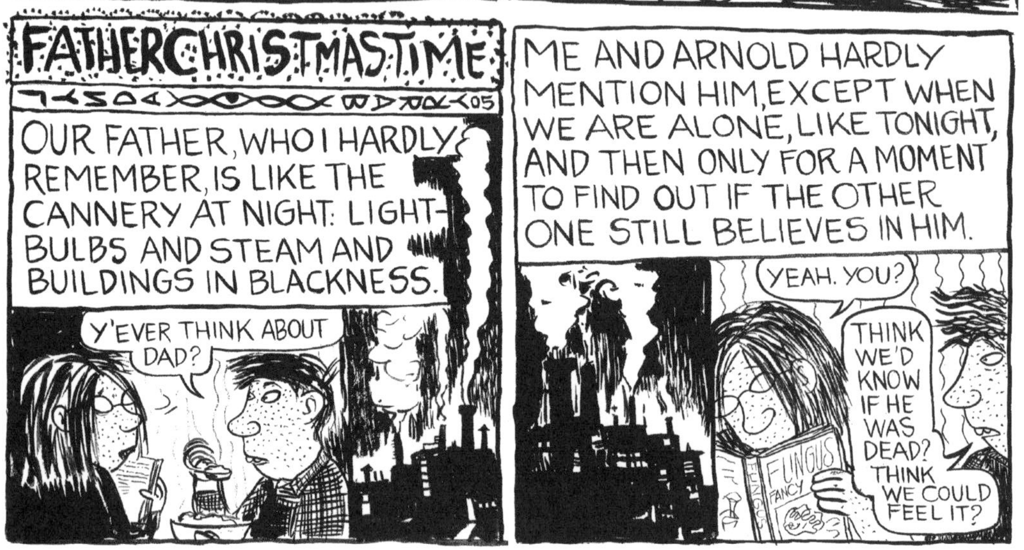
FATHERCHRISTMASTIME
OUR FATHER, WHO I HARDLY REMEMBER, IS LIKE THE CANNERY AT NIGHT: LIGHT-BULBS AND STEAM AND BUILDINGS IN BLACKNESS.
Y'EVER THINK ABOUT DAD?
ME AND ARNOLD HARDLY MENTION HIM, EXCEPT WHEN WE ARE ALONE, LIKE TONIGHT, AND THEN ONLY FOR A MOMENT TO FIND OUT IF THE OTHER ONE STILL BELIEVES IN HIM.
YEAH. YOU?
THINK WE'D KNOW IF HE WAS DEAD? THINK WE COULD FEEL IT?
FUNGUS FANCY

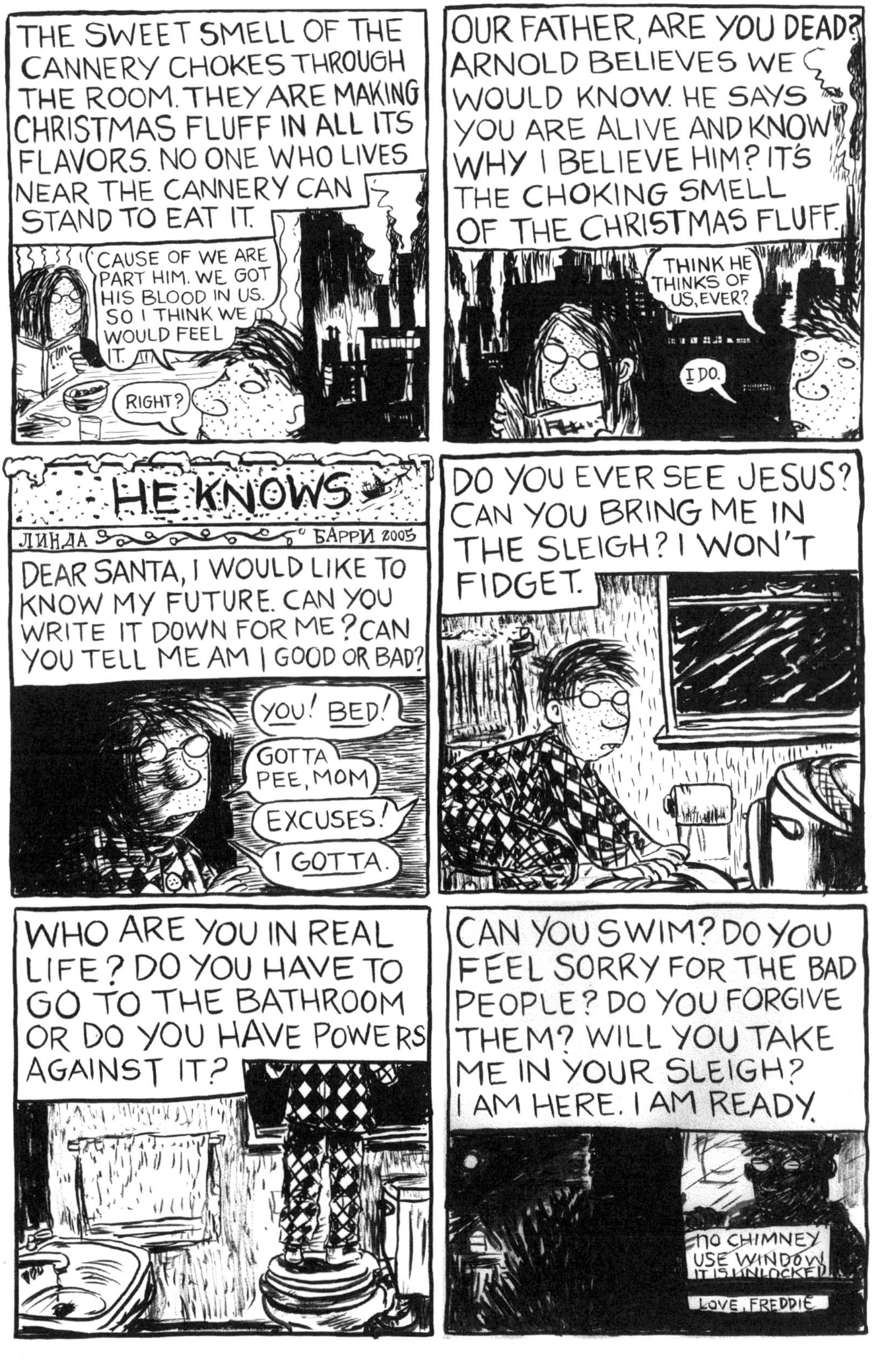
THE SWEET SMELL OF THE CANNERY CHOKES THROUGH THE ROOM. THEY ARE MAKING CHRISTMAS FLUFF IN ALL ITS FLAVORS. NO ONE WHO LIVES NEAR THE CANNERY CAN STAND TO EAT IT.
CAUSE OF WE ARE PART HIM. WE GOT HIS BLOOD IN US. SO I THINK WE WOULD FEEL IT.
RIGHT?
OUR FATHER, ARE YOU DEAD? ARNOLD BELIEVES WE WOULD KNOW. HE SAYS YOU ARE ALIVE AND KNOW WHY I BELIEVE HIM? IT'S THE CHOKING SMELL OF THE CHRISTMAS FLUFF.
THINK HE THINKS OF US, EVER?
I DO.
HE KNOWS
ЛИНДА БАРРИ 2005
DEAR SANTA, I WOULD LIKE TO KNOW MY FUTURE. CAN YOU WRITE IT DOWN FOR ME? CAN YOU TELL ME AM I GOOD OR BAD?
YOU! BED!
GOTTA PEE, MOM
EXCUSES!
I GOTTA.
DO YOU EVER SEE JESUS? CAN YOU BRING ME IN THE SLEIGH? I WON'T FIDGET.
WHO ARE YOU IN REAL LIFE? DO YOU HAVE TO GO TO THE BATHROOM OR DO YOU HAVE POWERS AGAINST IT?
CAN YOU SWIM? DO YOU FEEL SORRY FOR THE BAD PEOPLE? DO YOU FORGIVE THEM? WILL YOU TAKE ME IN YOUR SLEIGH? I AM HERE. I AM READY.
NO CHIMNEY
USE WINDOW
IT IS UNLOCKED
LOVE, FREDDIE

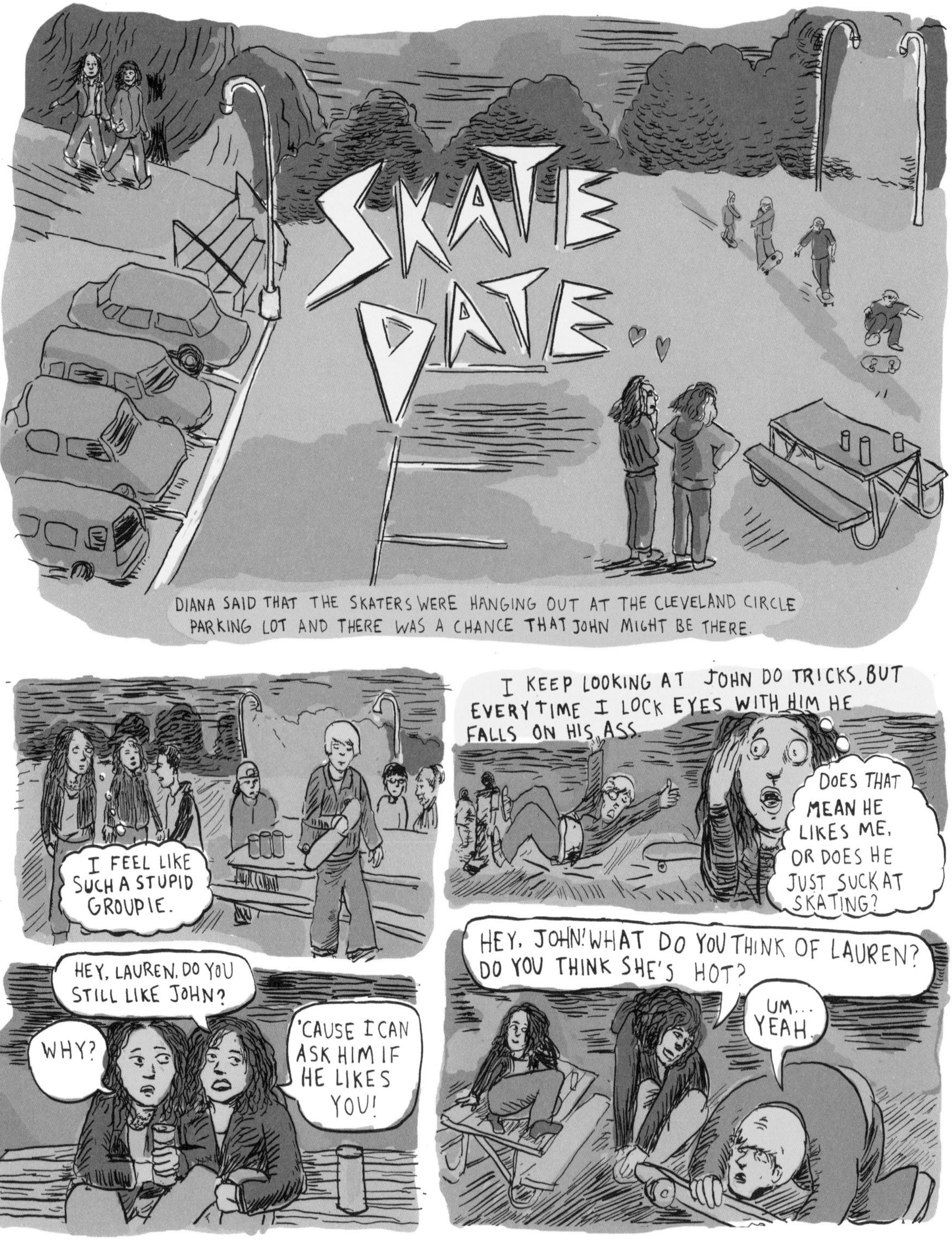
SKATE DATE
DIANA SAID THAT THE SKATERS WERE HANGING OUT AT THE CLEVELAND CIRCLE PARKING LOT AND THERE WAS A CHANCE THAT JOHN MIGHT BE THERE.
I FEEL LIKE SUCH A STUPID GROUPIE.
I KEEP LOOKING AT JOHN DO TRICKS, BUT EVERY TIME I LOCK EYES WITH HIM HE FALLS ON HIS ASS.
DOES THAT MEAN HE LIKES ME, OR DOES HE JUST SUCK AT SKATING?
HEY, LAUREN, DO YOU STILL LIKE JOHN?
WHY?
'CAUSE I CAN ASK HIM IF HE LIKES YOU!
HEY, JOHN! WHAT DO YOU THINK OF LAUREN? DO YOU THINK SHE'S HOT?
UM... YEAH.

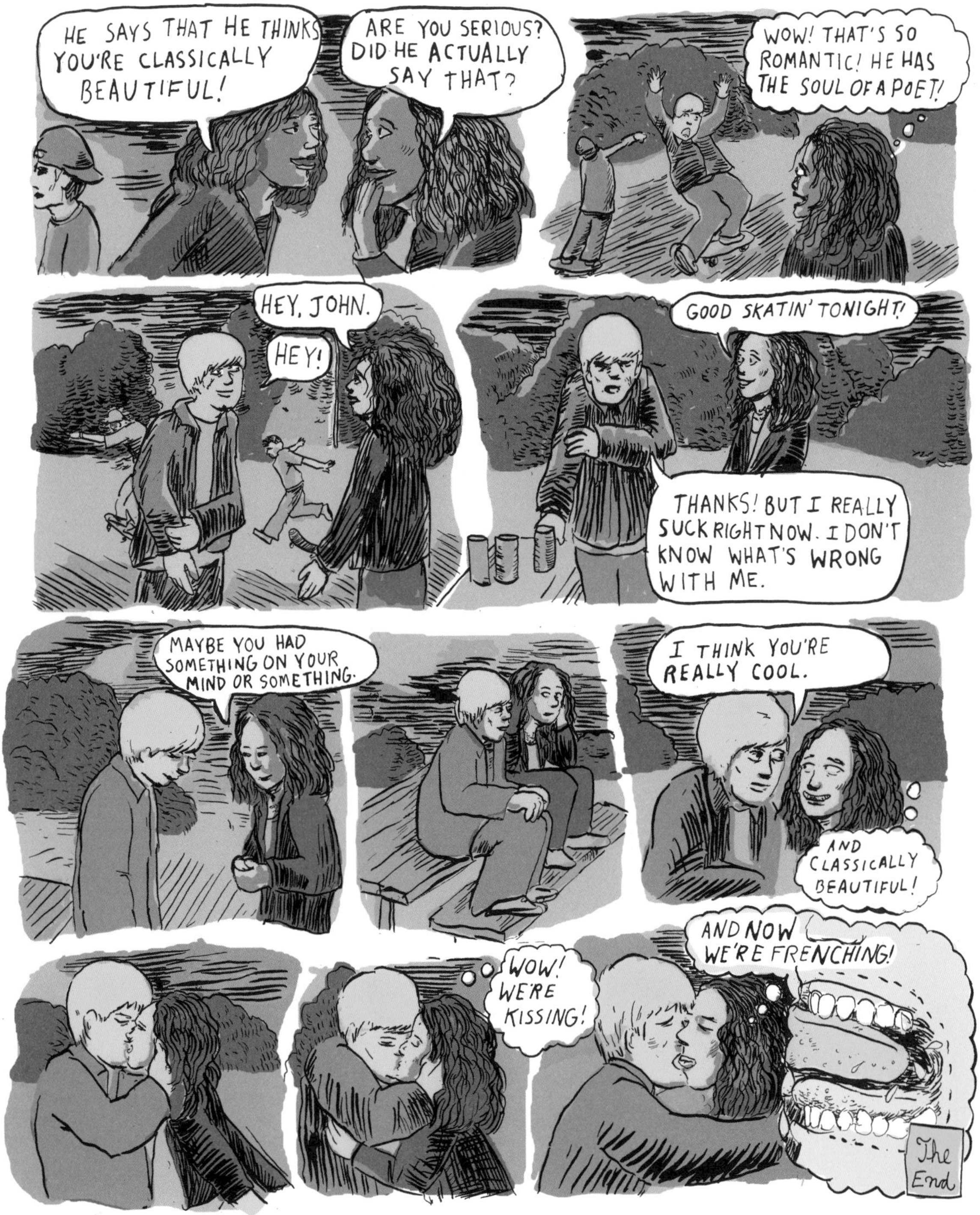
HE SAYS THAT HE THINKS YOU'RE CLASSICALLY BEAUTIFUL!
ARE YOU SERIOUS? DID HE ACTUALLY SAY THAT?
WOW! THAT'S SO ROMANTIC! HE HAS THE SOUL OF A POET!
HEY, JOHN.
HEY!
GOOD SKATIN' TONIGHT!
THANKS! BUT I REALLY SUCK RIGHT NOW. I DON'T KNOW WHAT'S WRONG WITH ME.
MAYBE YOU HAD SOMETHING ON YOUR MIND OR SOMETHING.
I THINK YOU'RE REALLY COOL.
AND CLASSICALLY BEAUTIFUL!
WOW! WE'RE KISSING!
AND NOW WE'RE FRENCHING!
The End

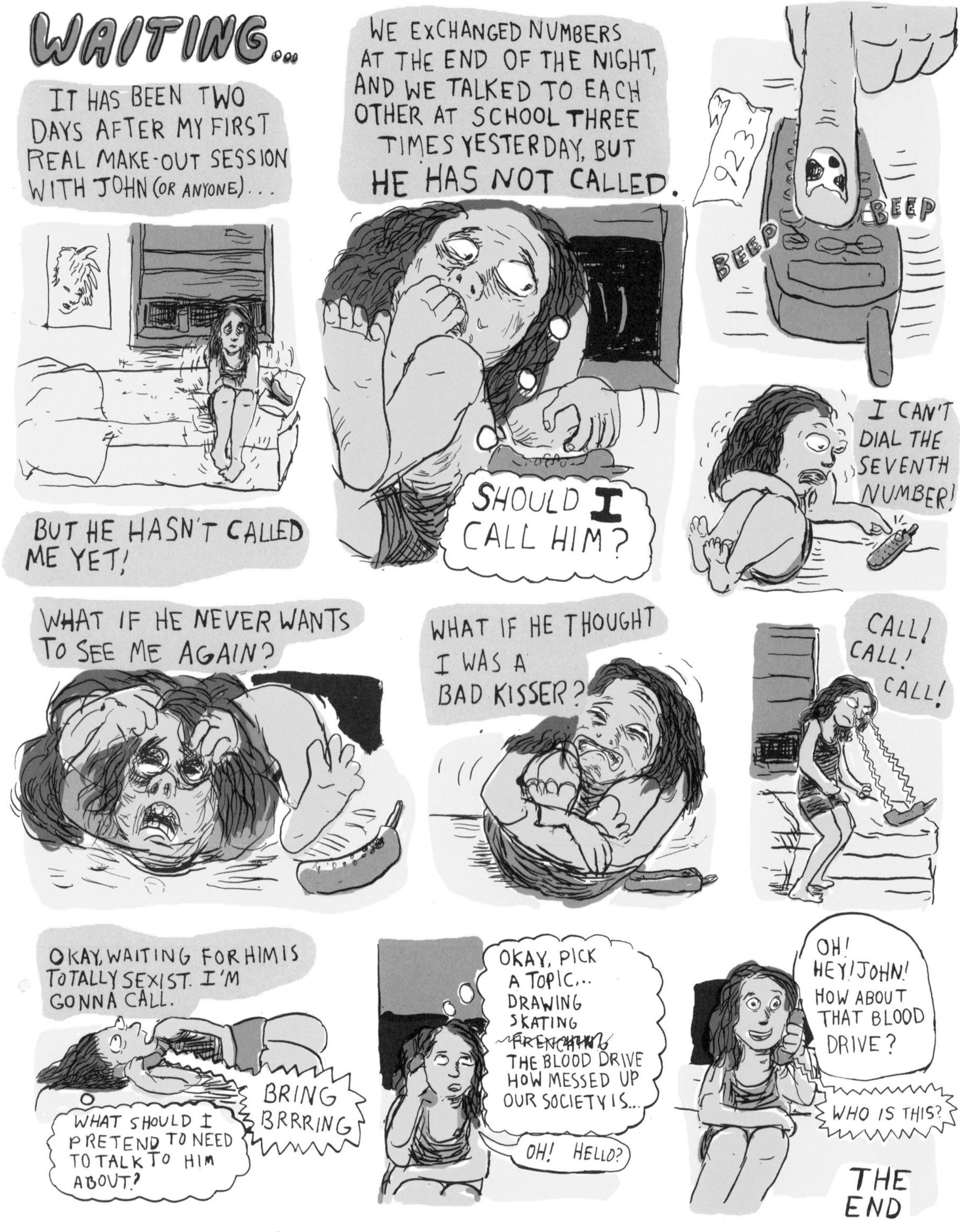
WAITING...
IT HAS BEEN TWO DAYS AFTER MY FIRST REAL MAKE-OUT SESSION WITH JOHN (OR ANYONE)...
BUT HE HASN'T CALLED ME YET!
WE EXCHANGED NUMBERS AT THE END OF THE NIGHT, AND WE TALKED TO EACH OTHER AT SCHOOL THREE TIMES YESTERDAY, BUT HE HAS NOT CALLED.
SHOULD I CALL HIM?
923-
BEEP
BEEP
I CAN'T DIAL THE SEVENTH NUMBER!
WHAT IF HE NEVER WANTS TO SEE ME AGAIN?
WHAT IF HE THOUGHT I WAS A BAD KISSER?
CALL! CALL! CALL!
OKAY, WAITING FOR HIM IS TOTALLY SEXIST. I'M GONNA CALL.
WHAT SHOULD I PRETEND TO NEED TO TALK TO HIM ABOUT?
BRING BRRRING
OKAY, PICK A TOPIC... DRAWING SKATING ~~FRENCHING~~ THE BLOOD DRIVE HOW MESSED UP OUR SOCIETY IS...
OH! HELLO?
OH! HEY! JOHN! HOW ABOUT THAT BLOOD DRIVE?
WHO IS THIS?
THE END

John & I Go to the Movies...

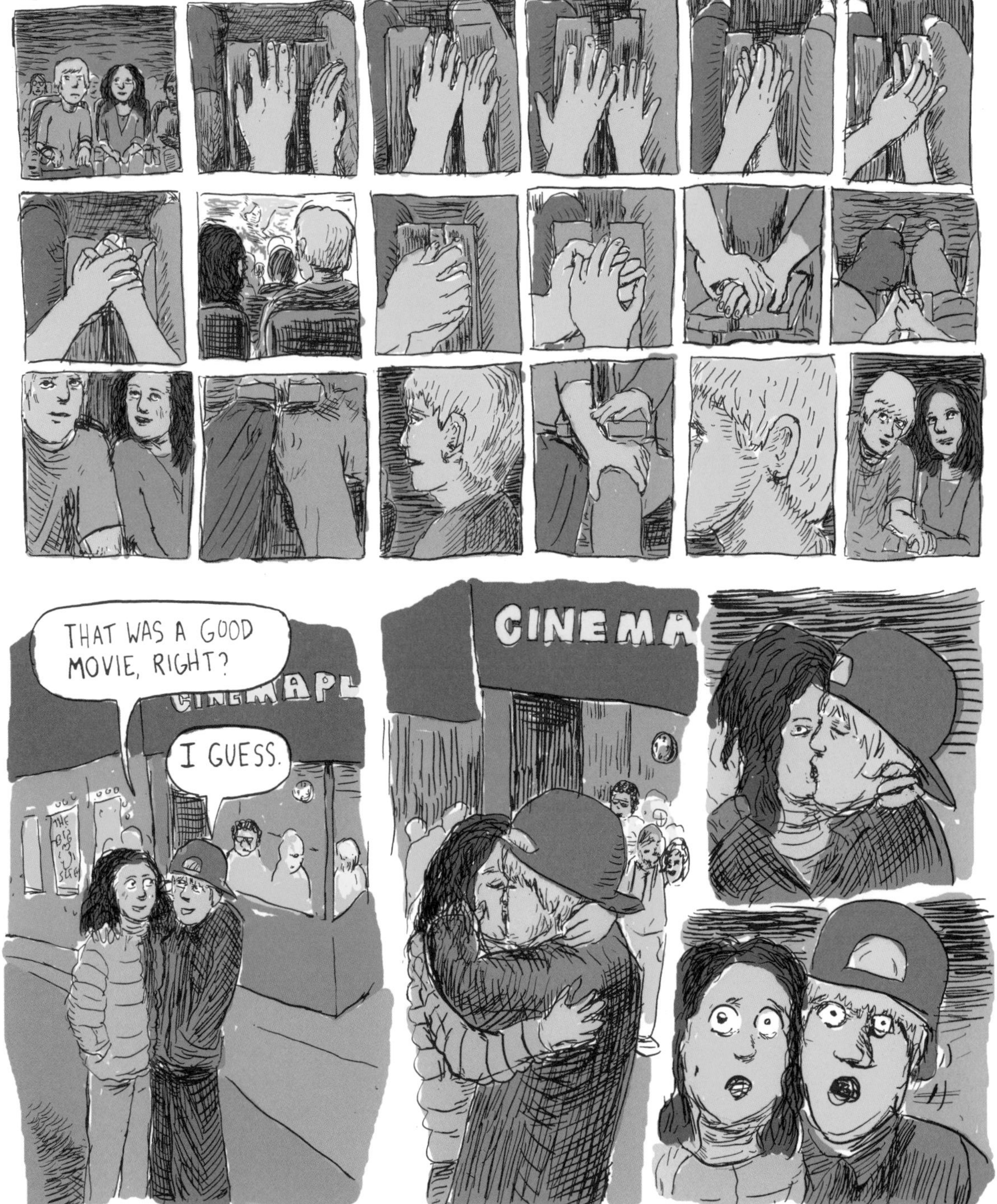
THAT WAS A GOOD MOVIE, RIGHT?
I GUESS.
CINEMA

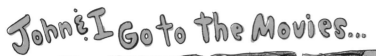

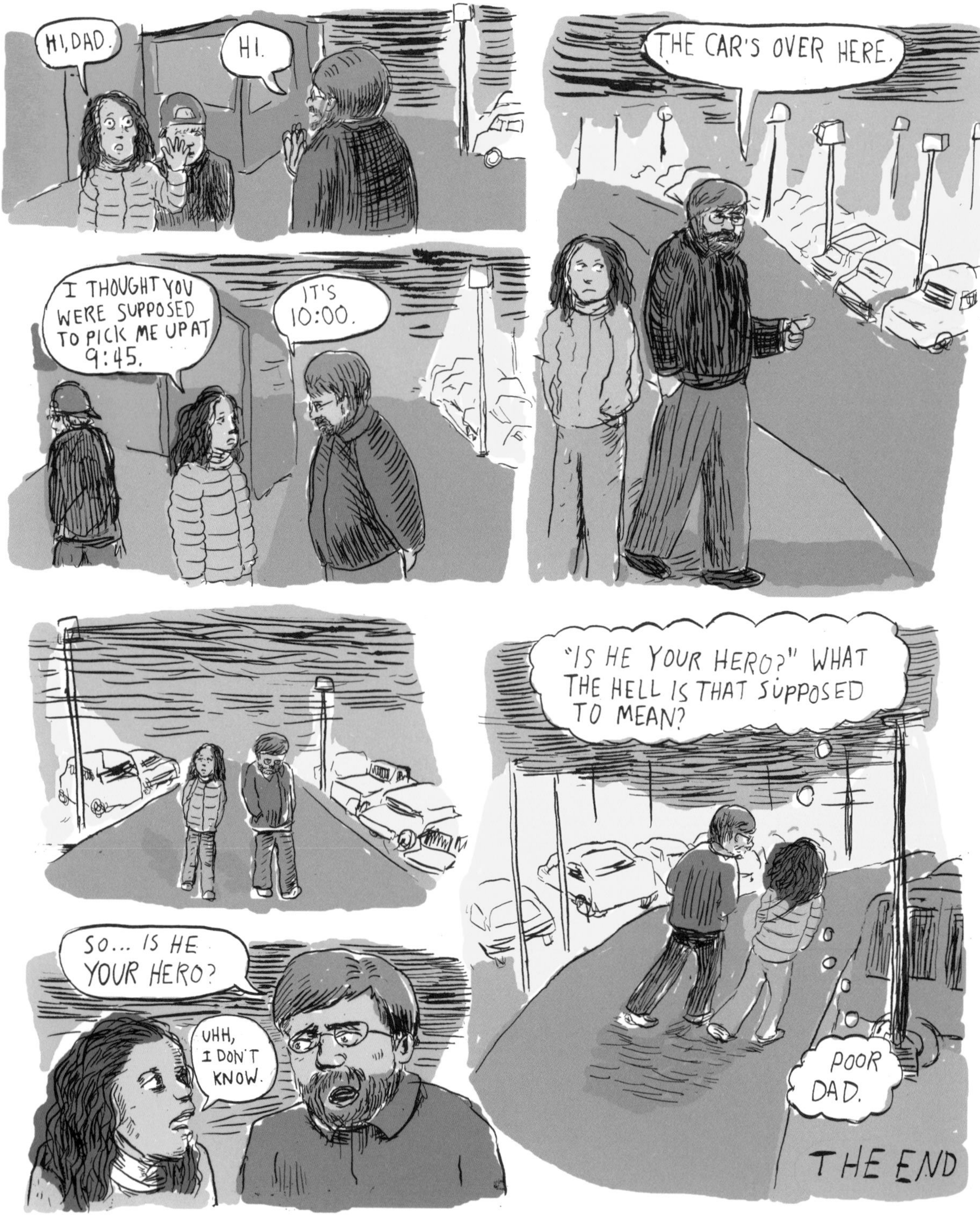
HI, DAD.
HI.
I THOUGHT YOU WERE SUPPOSED TO PICK ME UP AT 9:45.
IT'S 10:00.
THE CAR'S OVER HERE.
SO... IS HE YOUR HERO?
UHH, I DON'T KNOW.
"IS HE YOUR HERO?" WHAT THE HELL IS THAT SUPPOSED TO MEAN?
POOR DAD.
THE END

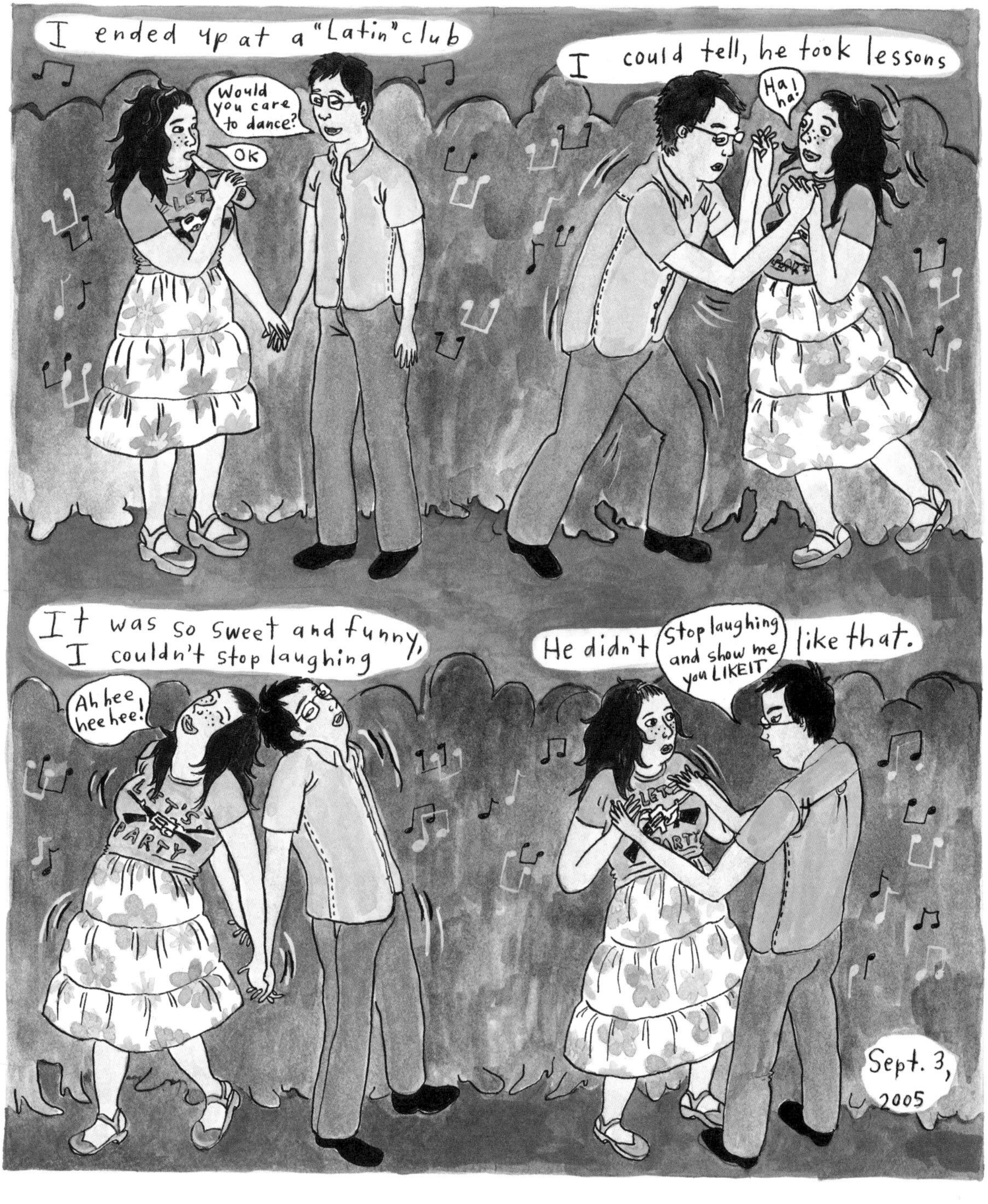
I ended up at a "Latin" club
Would you care to dance?
OK
I could tell, he took lessons
Ha! ha!
It was so sweet and funny, I couldn't stop laughing
Ah hee hee hee!
He didn't
Stop laughing and show me you LIKE IT
like that.
Sept. 3, 2005

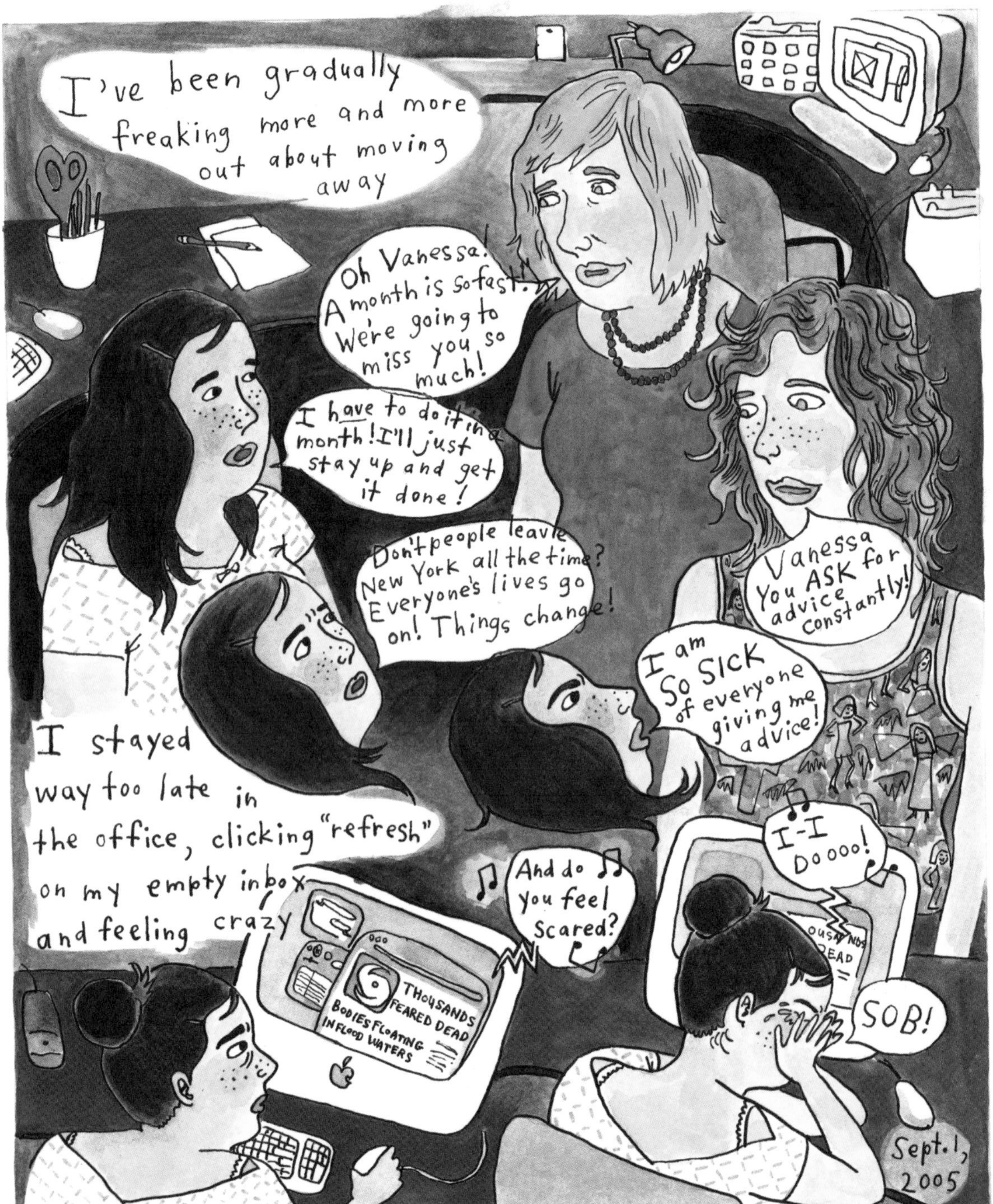
I've been gradually freaking more and more out about moving away
Oh Vanessa! A month is so fast! We're going to miss you so much!
I have to do it in a month! I'll just stay up and get it done!
Don't people leave New York all the time? Everyone's lives go on! Things change!
Vanessa You ASK for advice constantly!
I am So SICK of everyone giving me advice!
I stayed way too late in the office, clicking "refresh" on my empty inbox and feeling crazy
And do you feel Scared?
I-I Doooo!
THOUSANDS FEARED DEAD
BODIES FLOATING IN FLOOD WATERS
SOB!
Sept. 1, 2005

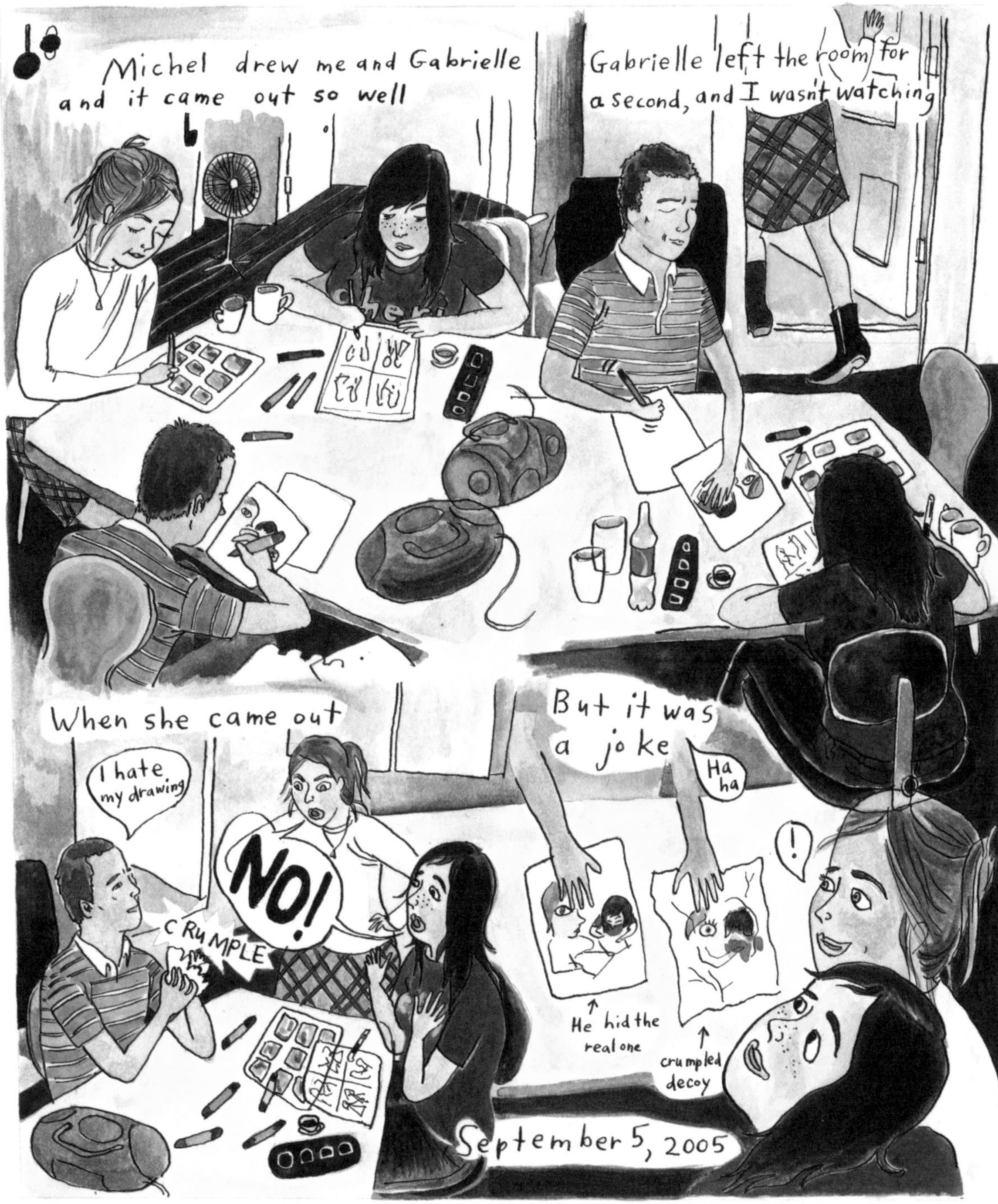
Michel drew me and Gabrielle and it came out so well
cheri
Gabrielle left the room for a second, and I wasn't watching
When she came out
I hate my drawing
CRUMPLE
NO!
But it was a joke
Ha ha
!
He hid the real one
crumpled decoy
September 5, 2005

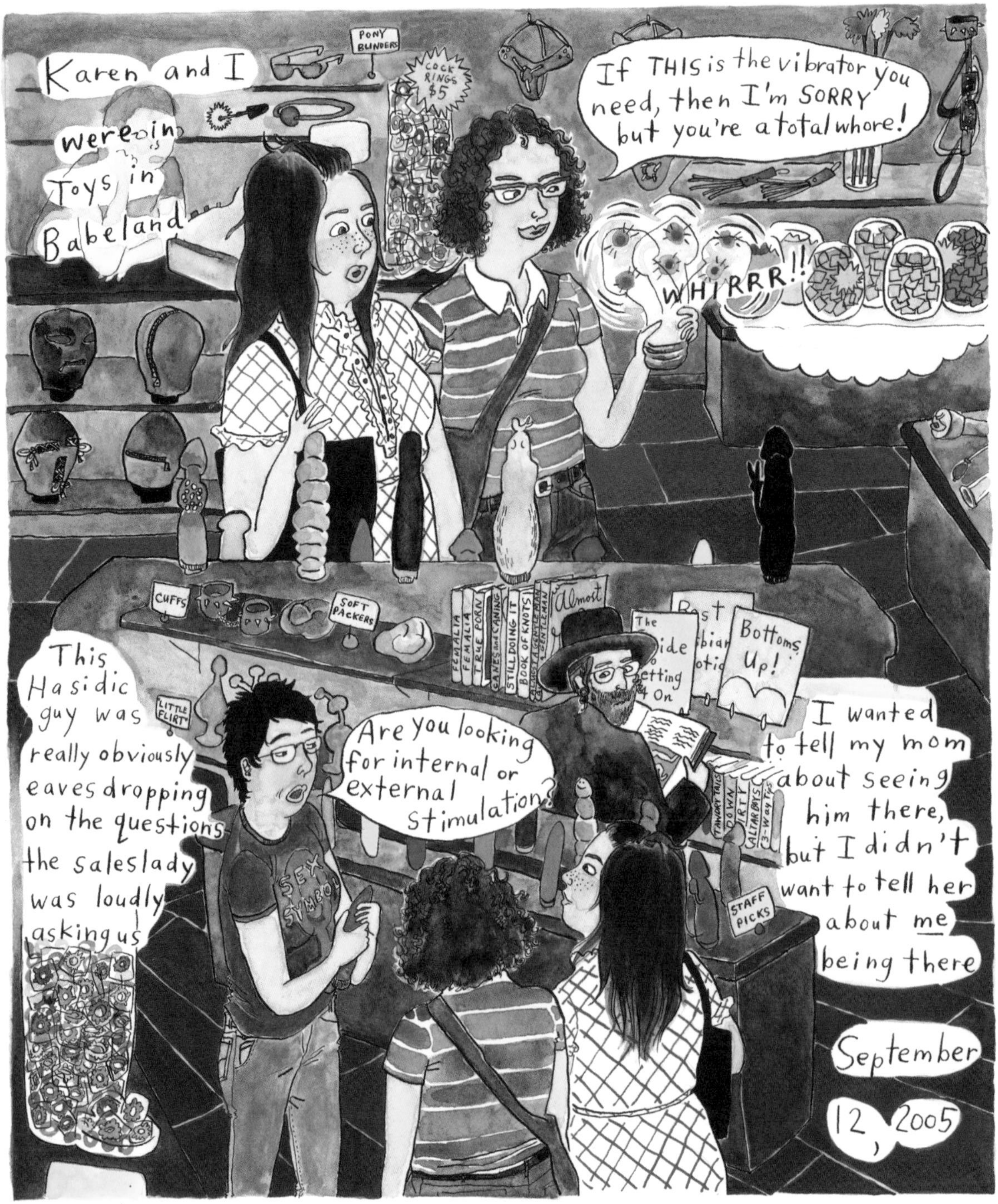
Karen and I were in Toys in Babeland
PONY BLINDERS
COCK RINGS $5
If THIS is the vibrator you need, then I'm SORRY but you're a total whore!
WHIRRR!!
CUFFS
SOFT PACKERS
FEMALIA
FEMALIA
TRUE PORN
STILL DOING IT
BOOK OF KNOTS
Almost
Bottoms Up!
This Hasidic guy was really obviously eavesdropping on the questions the saleslady was loudly asking us
LITTLE FLIRT
Are you looking for internal or external stimulation?
SEX SYMBOL
STAFF PICKS
I wanted to tell my mom about seeing him there, but I didn't want to tell her about me being there
September 12, 2005

March 28th, 2006

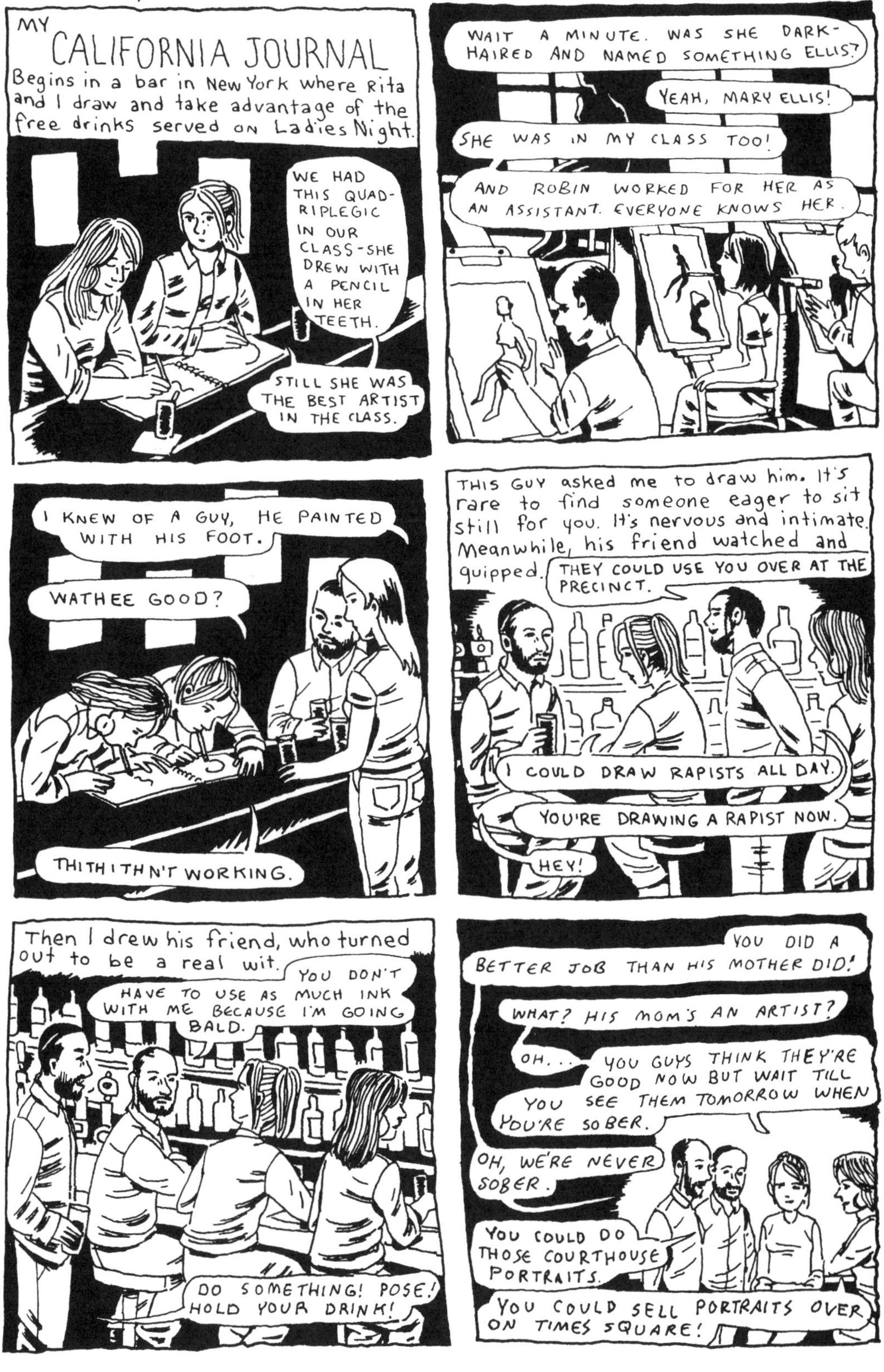

MY CALIFORNIA JOURNAL
Begins in a bar in New York where Rita and I draw and take advantage of the free drinks served on Ladies Night.
WE HAD THIS QUAD-RIPLEGIC IN OUR CLASS-SHE DREW WITH A PENCIL IN HER TEETH.
STILL SHE WAS THE BEST ARTIST IN THE CLASS.
WAIT A MINUTE. WAS SHE DARK-HAIRED AND NAMED SOMETHING ELLIS?
YEAH, MARY ELLIS!
SHE WAS IN MY CLASS TOO!
AND ROBIN WORKED FOR HER AS AN ASSISTANT. EVERYONE KNOWS HER.
I KNEW OF A GUY, HE PAINTED WITH HIS FOOT.
WATHEE GOOD?
THITHITHN'T WORKING.
THIS GUY asked me to draw him. It's rare to find someone eager to sit still for you. It's nervous and intimate. Meanwhile, his friend watched and quipped.
THEY COULD USE YOU OVER AT THE PRECINCT.
I COULD DRAW RAPISTS ALL DAY.
YOU'RE DRAWING A RAPIST NOW.
HEY!
Then I drew his friend, who turned out to be a real wit.
YOU DON'T HAVE TO USE AS MUCH INK WITH ME BECAUSE I'M GOING BALD.
DO SOMETHING! POSE! HOLD YOUR DRINK!
YOU DID A BETTER JOB THAN HIS MOTHER DID!
WHAT? HIS MOM'S AN ARTIST?
OH...
YOU GUYS THINK THEY'RE GOOD NOW BUT WAIT TILL YOU SEE THEM TOMORROW WHEN YOU'RE SOBER.
OH, WE'RE NEVER SOBER.
YOU COULD DO THOSE COURTHOUSE PORTRAITS.
YOU COULD SELL PORTRAITS OVER ON TIMES SQUARE!

March 29th

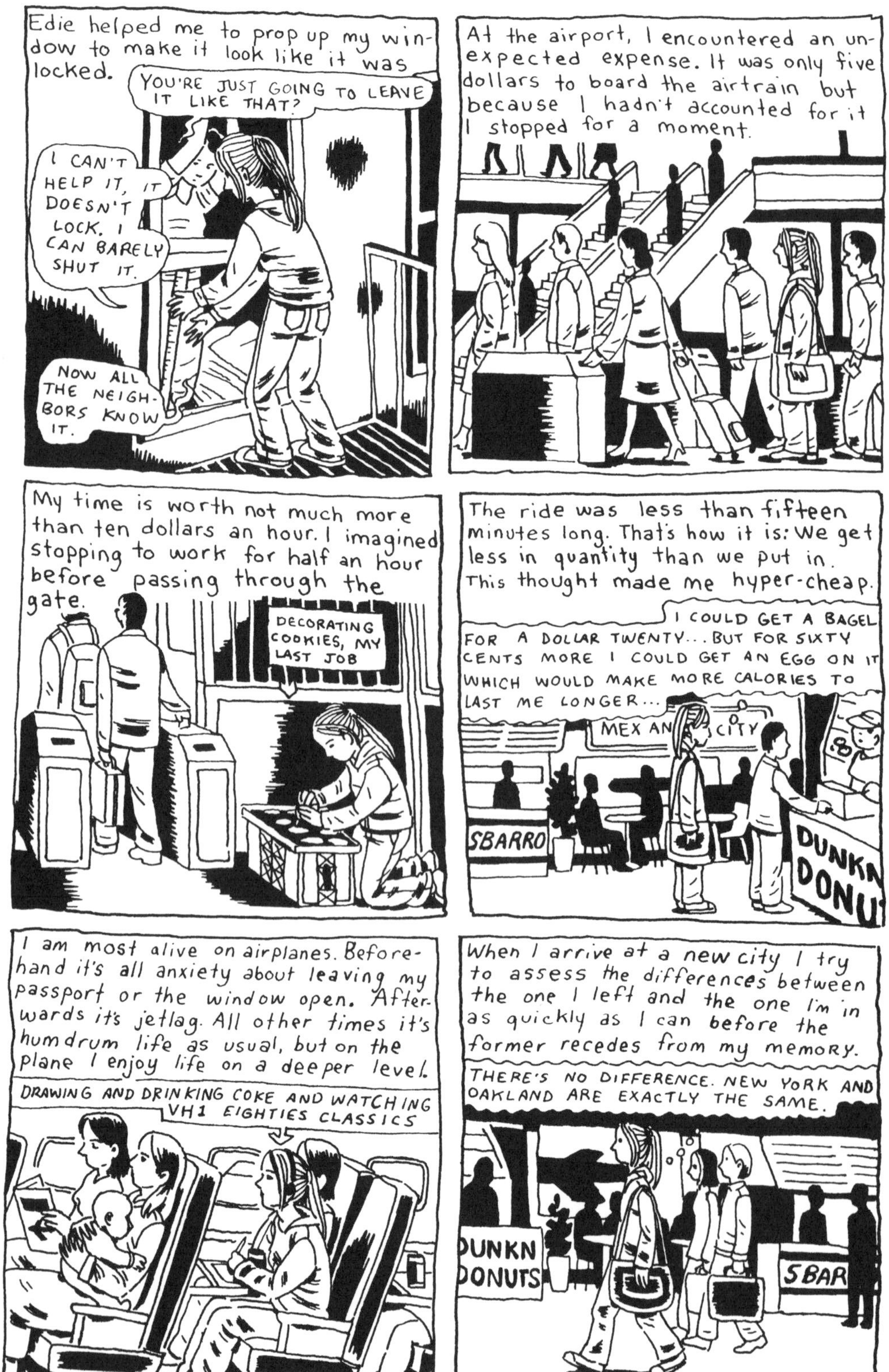

Edie helped me to prop up my window to make it look like it was locked.
YOU'RE JUST GOING TO LEAVE IT LIKE THAT?
I CAN'T HELP IT, IT DOESN'T LOCK. I CAN BARELY SHUT IT.
NOW ALL THE NEIGHBORS KNOW IT.
At the airport, I encountered an unexpected expense. It was only five dollars to board the airtrain but because I hadn't accounted for it I stopped for a moment.
My time is worth not much more than ten dollars an hour. I imagined stopping to work for half an hour before passing through the gate.
DECORATING COOKIES, MY LAST JOB
The ride was less than fifteen minutes long. That's how it is: We get less in quantity than we put in. This thought made me hyper-cheap.
I COULD GET A BAGEL FOR A DOLLAR TWENTY... BUT FOR SIXTY CENTS MORE I COULD GET AN EGG ON IT WHICH WOULD MAKE MORE CALORIES TO LAST ME LONGER...
SBARRO
DUNKN DONU
I am most alive on airplanes. Beforehand it's all anxiety about leaving my passport or the window open. Afterwards it's jetlag. All other times it's humdrum life as usual, but on the plane I enjoy life on a deeper level.
DRAWING AND DRINKING COKE AND WATCHING VH1 EIGHTIES CLASSICS
When I arrive at a new city I try to assess the differences between the one I left and the one I'm in as quickly as I can before the former recedes from my memory.
THERE'S NO DIFFERENCE. NEW YORK AND OAKLAND ARE EXACTLY THE SAME.
DUNKN DONUTS
SBAR

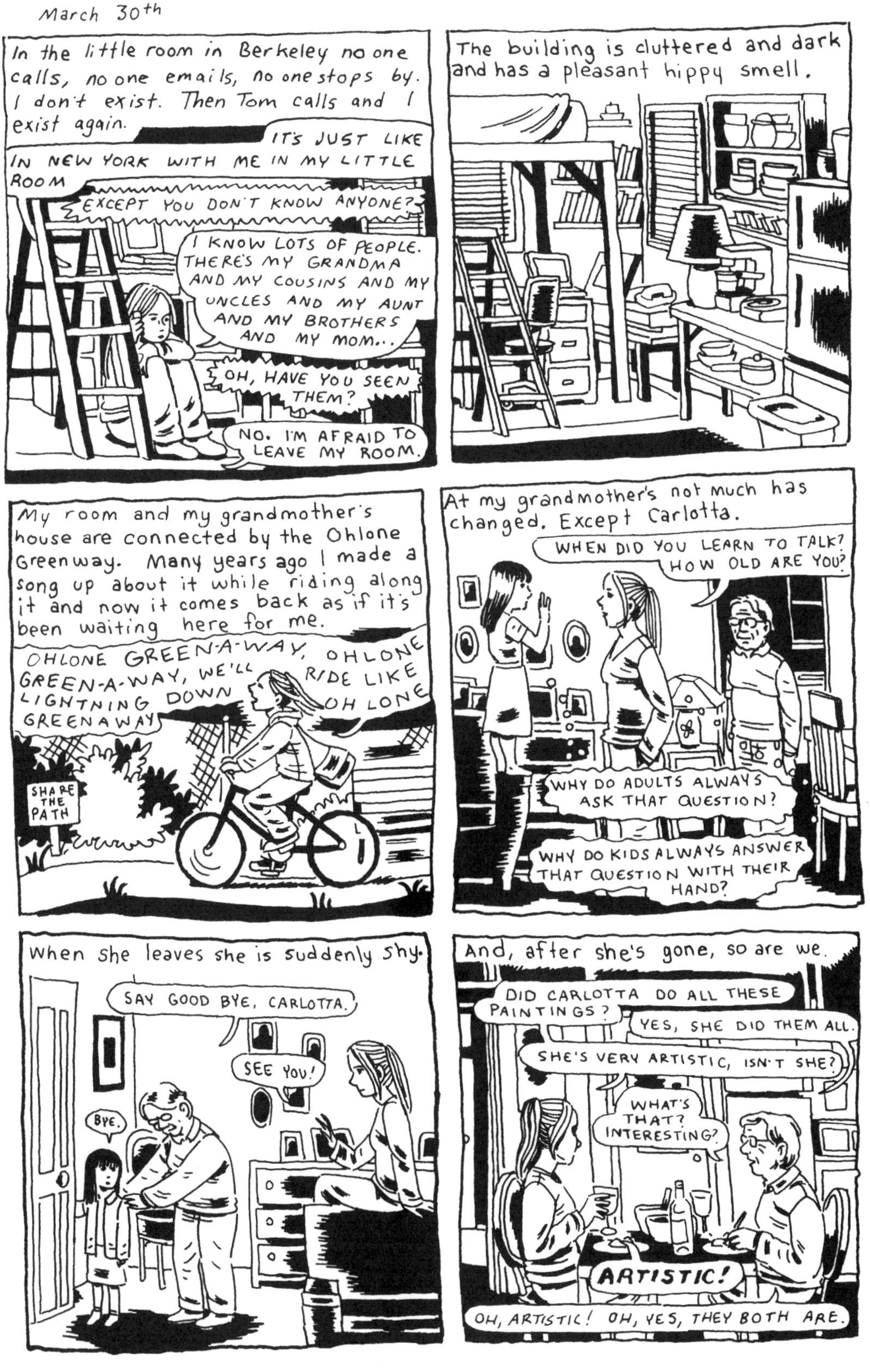
March 30th
In the little room in Berkeley no one calls, no one emails, no one stops by. I don't exist. Then Tom calls and I exist again.
IT'S JUST LIKE IN NEW YORK WITH ME IN MY LITTLE ROOM
EXCEPT YOU DON'T KNOW ANYONE?
I KNOW LOTS OF PEOPLE. THERE'S MY GRANDMA AND MY COUSINS AND MY UNCLES AND MY AUNT AND MY BROTHERS AND MY MOM...
OH, HAVE YOU SEEN THEM?
NO. I'M AFRAID TO LEAVE MY ROOM.
The building is cluttered and dark and has a pleasant hippy smell.
My room and my grandmother's house are connected by the Ohlone Greenway. Many years ago I made a song up about it while riding along it and now it comes back as if it's been waiting here for me.
OHLONE GREEN-A-WAY, OHLONE GREEN-A-WAY, WE'LL RIDE LIKE LIGHTNING DOWN OHLONE GREENAWAY
SHARE THE PATH
At my grandmother's not much has changed. Except Carlotta.
WHEN DID YOU LEARN TO TALK? HOW OLD ARE YOU?
WHY DO ADULTS ALWAYS ASK THAT QUESTION?
WHY DO KIDS ALWAYS ANSWER THAT QUESTION WITH THEIR HAND?
When she leaves she is suddenly shy.
SAY GOOD BYE, CARLOTTA.
SEE YOU!
BYE.
And, after she's gone, so are we.
DID CARLOTTA DO ALL THESE PAINTINGS?
YES, SHE DID THEM ALL.
SHE'S VERY ARTISTIC, ISN'T SHE?
WHAT'S THAT? INTERESTING?
ARTISTIC!
OH, ARTISTIC! OH, YES, THEY BOTH ARE.

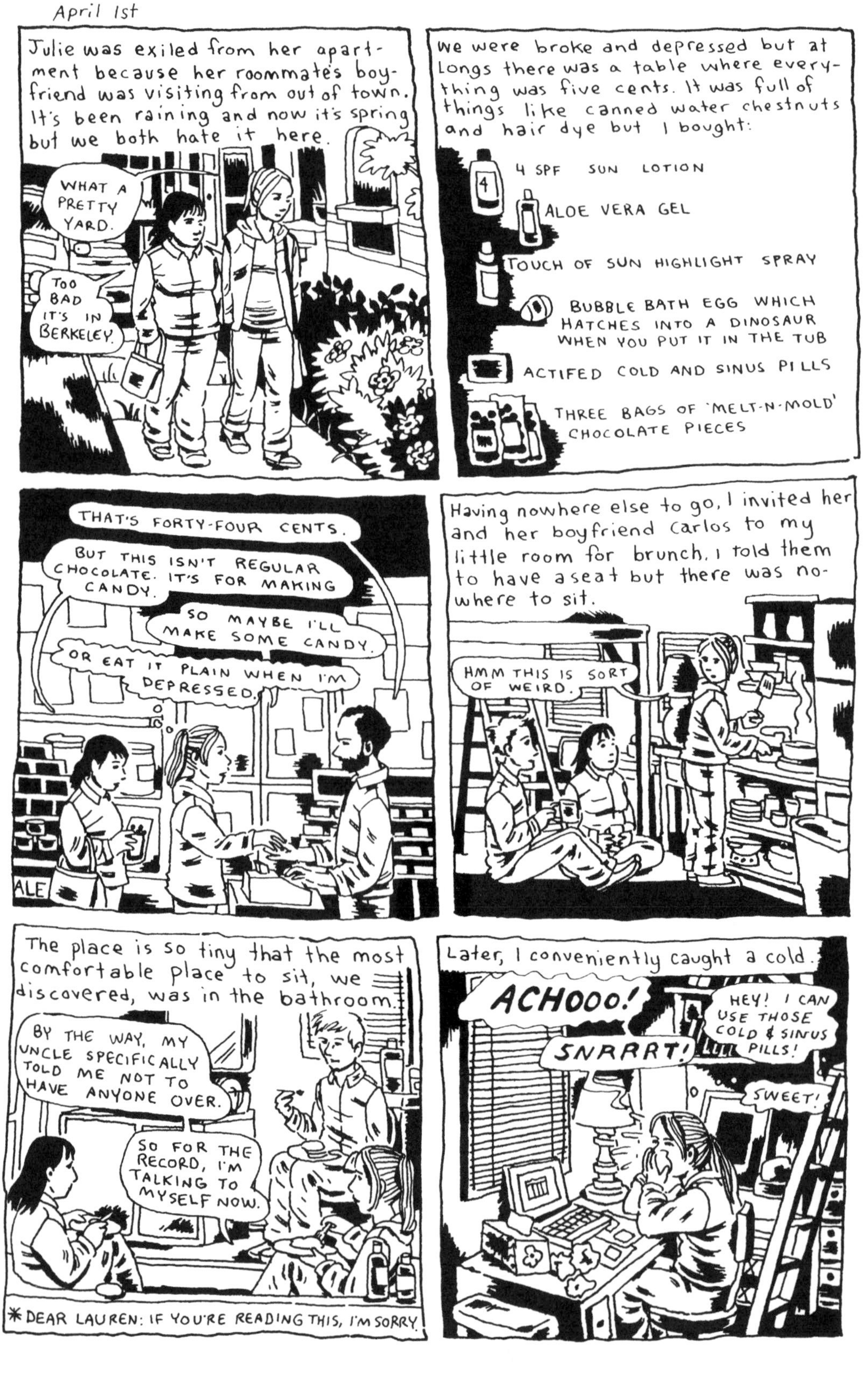
April 1st
Julie was exiled from her apartment because her roommate's boyfriend was visiting from out of town. It's been raining and now it's spring but we both hate it here.
WHAT A PRETTY YARD.
TOO BAD IT'S IN BERKELEY.
We were broke and depressed but at Longs there was a table where everything was five cents. It was full of things like canned water chestnuts and hair dye but I bought:
4 SPF SUN LOTION
4
ALOE VERA GEL
TOUCH OF SUN HIGHLIGHT SPRAY
BUBBLE BATH EGG WHICH HATCHES INTO A DINOSAUR WHEN YOU PUT IT IN THE TUB
ACTIFED COLD AND SINUS PILLS
THREE BAGS OF 'MELT-N-MOLD' CHOCOLATE PIECES
THAT'S FORTY-FOUR CENTS.
BUT THIS ISN'T REGULAR CHOCOLATE. IT'S FOR MAKING CANDY.
SO MAYBE I'LL MAKE SOME CANDY.
OR EAT IT PLAIN WHEN I'M DEPRESSED.
ALE
Having nowhere else to go, I invited her and her boyfriend Carlos to my little room for brunch. I told them to have a seat but there was nowhere to sit.
HMM THIS IS SORT OF WEIRD.
The place is so tiny that the most comfortable place to sit, we discovered, was in the bathroom.
BY THE WAY, MY UNCLE SPECIFICALLY TOLD ME NOT TO HAVE ANYONE OVER.
SO FOR THE RECORD, I'M TALKING TO MYSELF NOW.
*DEAR LAUREN: IF YOU'RE READING THIS, I'M SORRY.
Later, I conveniently caught a cold.
ACHOOO!
SNRRRT!
HEY! I CAN USE THOSE COLD & SINUS PILLS!
SWEET!

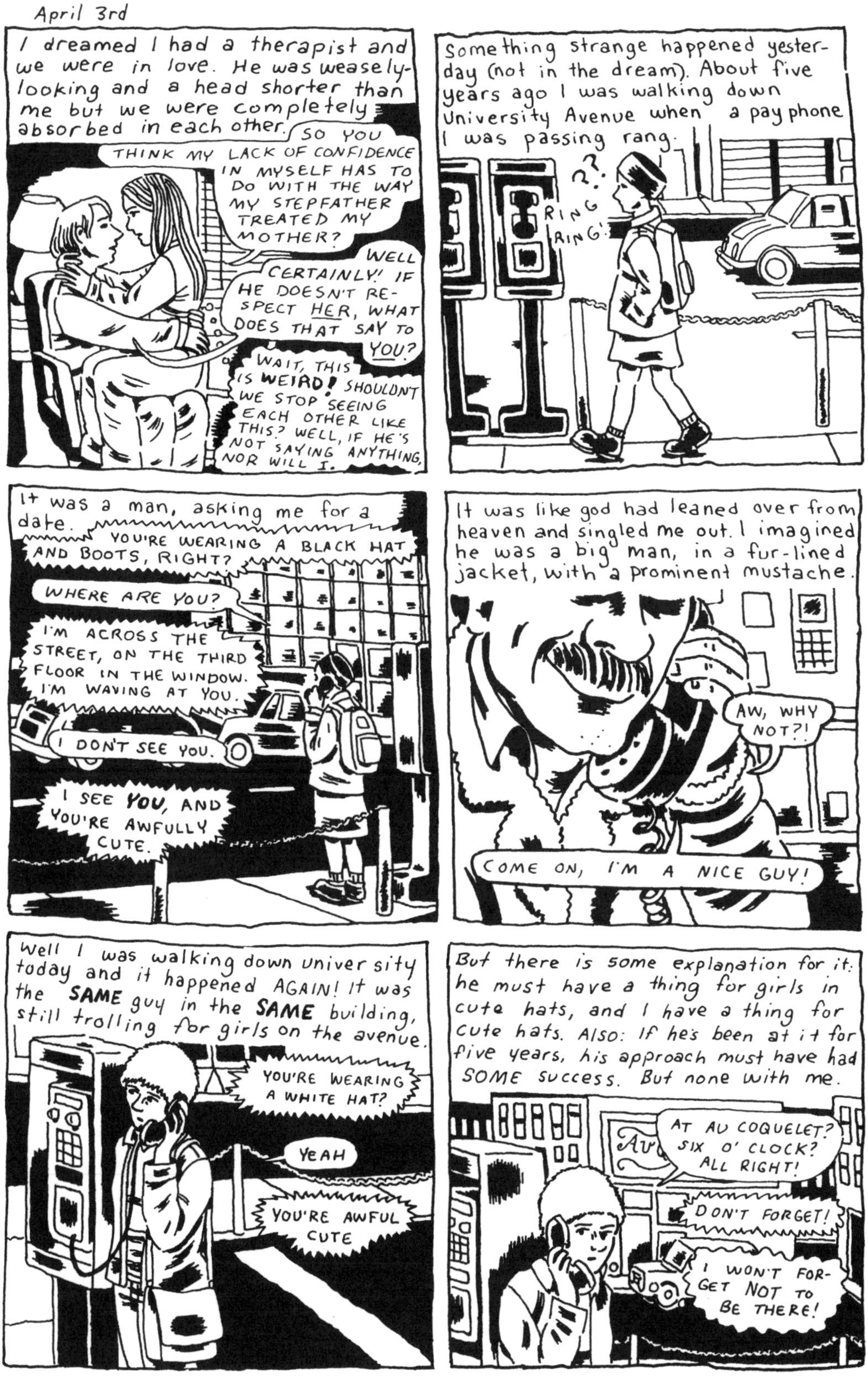
April 3rd
I dreamed I had a therapist and we were in love. He was weasely-looking and a head shorter than me but we were completely absorbed in each other.
SO YOU THINK MY LACK OF CONFIDENCE IN MYSELF HAS TO DO WITH THE WAY MY STEPFATHER TREATED MY MOTHER?
WELL CERTAINLY! IF HE DOESN'T RE-SPECT HER, WHAT DOES THAT SAY TO YOU?
WAIT, THIS IS WEIRD! SHOULDN'T WE STOP SEEING EACH OTHER LIKE THIS? WELL, IF HE'S NOT SAYING ANYTHING, NOR WILL I.
Something strange happened yester-day (not in the dream). About five years ago I was walking down University Avenue when a pay phone I was passing rang.
??
RING RING!
It was a man, asking me for a date.
YOU'RE WEARING A BLACK HAT AND BOOTS, RIGHT?
WHERE ARE YOU?
I'M ACROSS THE STREET, ON THE THIRD FLOOR IN THE WINDOW. I'M WAVING AT YOU.
I DON'T SEE YOU.
I SEE YOU, AND YOU'RE AWFULLY CUTE.
It was like god had leaned over from heaven and singled me out. I imagined he was a big man, in a fur-lined jacket, with a prominent mustache.
AW, WHY NOT?!
COME ON, I'M A NICE GUY!
Well I was walking down University today and it happened AGAIN! It was the SAME guy in the SAME building, still trolling for girls on the avenue.
YOU'RE WEARING A WHITE HAT?
YEAH
YOU'RE AWFUL CUTE
But there is some explanation for it: he must have a thing for girls in cute hats, and I have a thing for cute hats. Also: If he's been at it for five years, his approach must have had SOME success. But none with me.
AT AU COQUELET? SIX O' CLOCK? ALL RIGHT!
DON'T FORGET!
I WON'T FOR-GET NOT TO BE THERE!

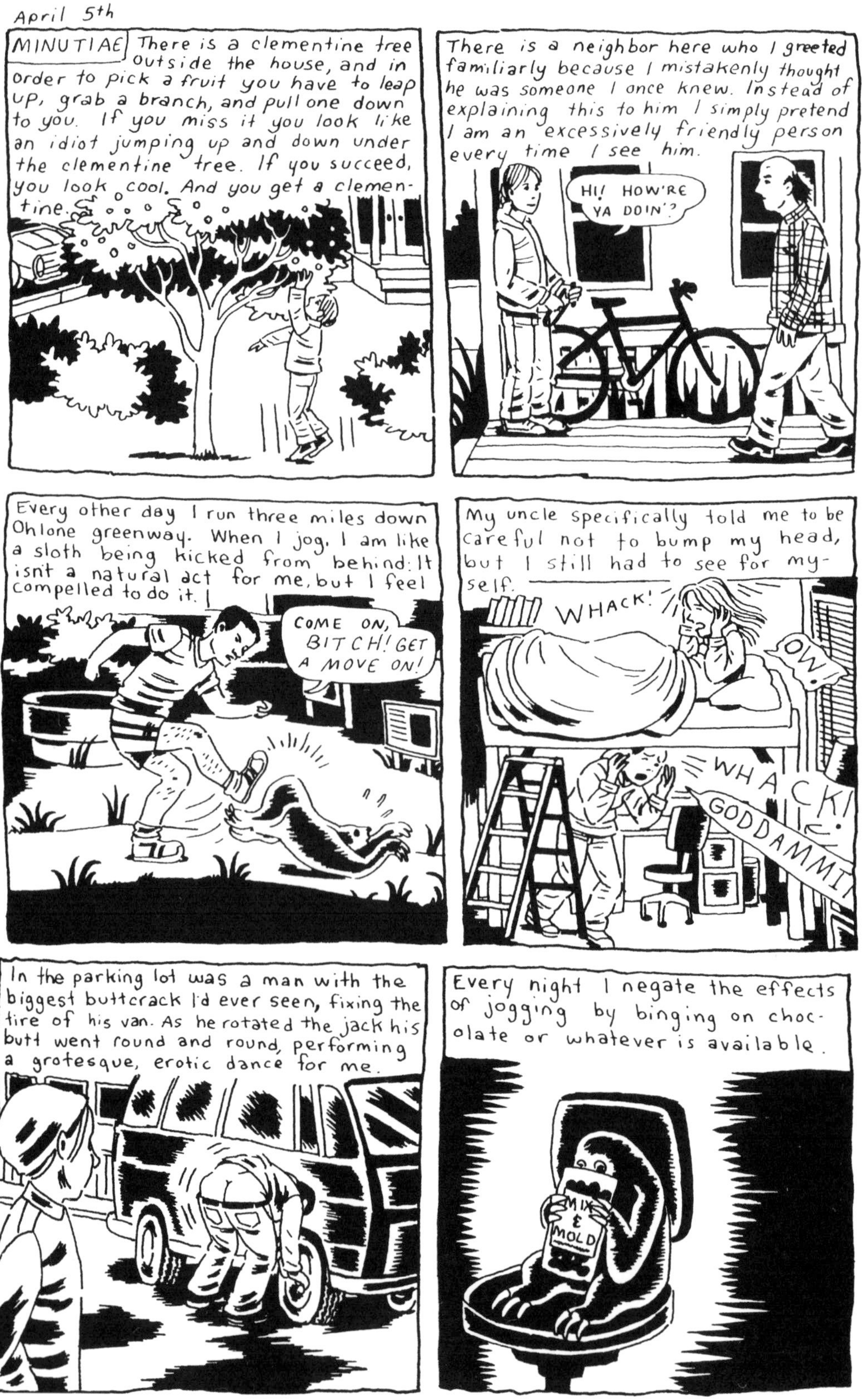
April 5th
MINUTIAE
There is a clementine tree outside the house, and in order to pick a fruit you have to leap up, grab a branch, and pull one down to you. If you miss it you look like an idiot jumping up and down under the clementine tree. If you succeed, you look cool. And you get a clementine.
There is a neighbor here who I greeted familiarly because I mistakenly thought he was someone I once knew. Instead of explaining this to him I simply pretend I am an excessively friendly person every time I see him.
HI! HOW'RE YA DOIN'?
Every other day I run three miles down Ohlone greenway. When I jog, I am like a sloth being kicked from behind: It isn't a natural act for me, but I feel compelled to do it.
COME ON, BITCH! GET A MOVE ON!
My uncle specifically told me to be careful not to bump my head, but I still had to see for myself.
WHACK!
OW
WHACK!
GODDAMMIT
In the parking lot was a man with the biggest buttcrack I'd ever seen, fixing the tire of his van. As he rotated the jack his butt went round and round, performing a grotesque, erotic dance for me.
Every night I negate the effects of jogging by binging on chocolate or whatever is available.
MIX & MOLD

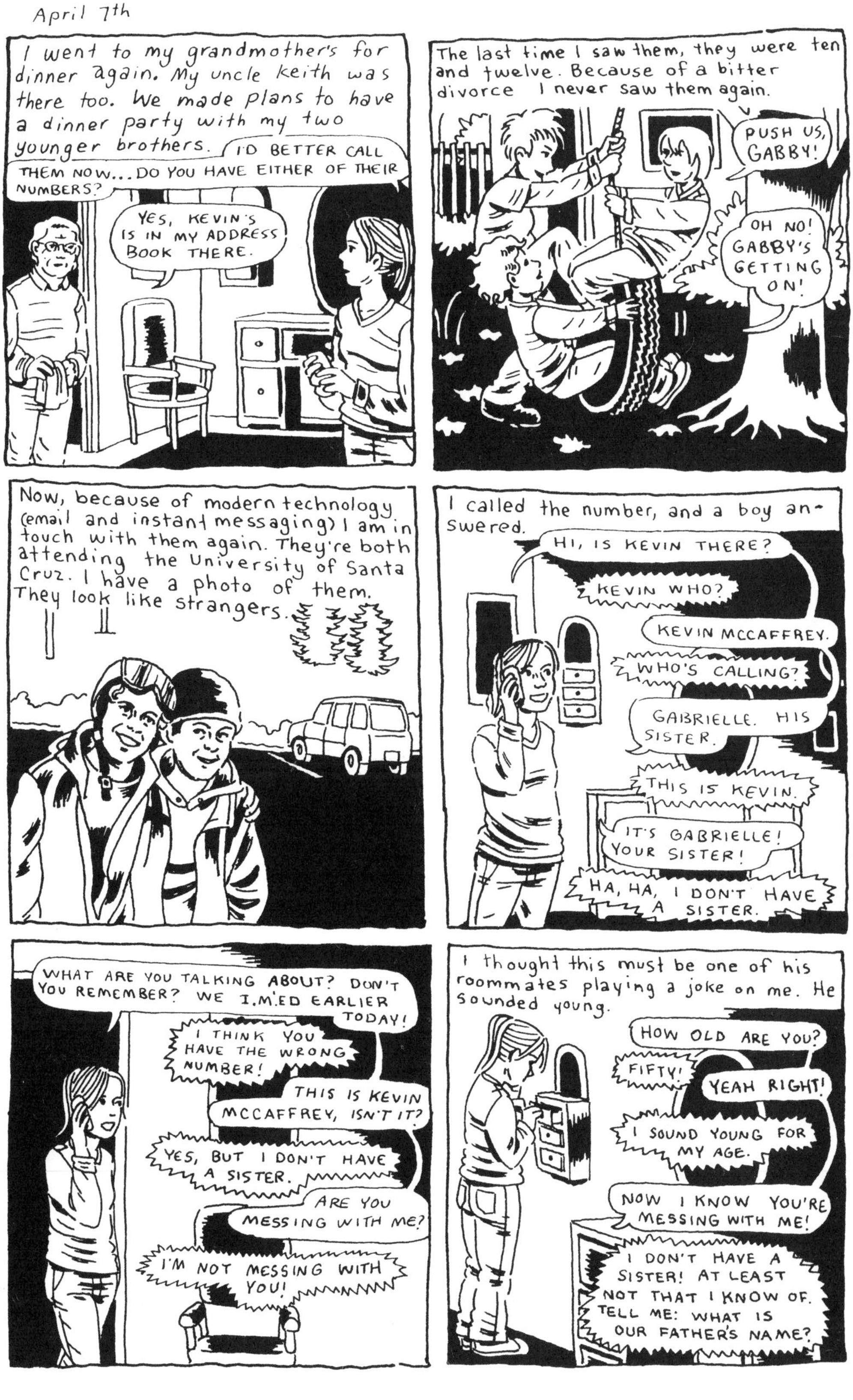
April 7th
I went to my grandmother's for dinner again. My uncle Keith was there too. We made plans to have a dinner party with my two younger brothers.
I'D BETTER CALL THEM NOW... DO YOU HAVE EITHER OF THEIR NUMBERS?
YES, KEVIN'S IS IN MY ADDRESS BOOK THERE.
The last time I saw them, they were ten and twelve. Because of a bitter divorce I never saw them again.
PUSH US, GABBY!
OH NO! GABBY'S GETTING ON!
Now, because of modern technology (email and instant messaging) I am in touch with them again. They're both attending the University of Santa Cruz. I have a photo of them. They look like strangers.
I called the number, and a boy answered.
HI, IS KEVIN THERE?
KEVIN WHO?
KEVIN MCCAFFREY.
WHO'S CALLING?
GABRIELLE. HIS SISTER.
THIS IS KEVIN.
IT'S GABRIELLE! YOUR SISTER!
HA, HA, I DON'T HAVE A SISTER.
WHAT ARE YOU TALKING ABOUT? DON'T YOU REMEMBER? WE I.M.'ED EARLIER TODAY!
I THINK YOU HAVE THE WRONG NUMBER!
THIS IS KEVIN MCCAFFREY, ISN'T IT?
YES, BUT I DON'T HAVE A SISTER.
ARE YOU MESSING WITH ME?
I'M NOT MESSING WITH YOU!
I thought this must be one of his roommates playing a joke on me. He sounded young.
HOW OLD ARE YOU?
FIFTY!
YEAH RIGHT!
I SOUND YOUNG FOR MY AGE.
NOW I KNOW YOU'RE MESSING WITH ME!
I DON'T HAVE A SISTER! AT LEAST NOT THAT I KNOW OF. TELL ME: WHAT IS OUR FATHER'S NAME?

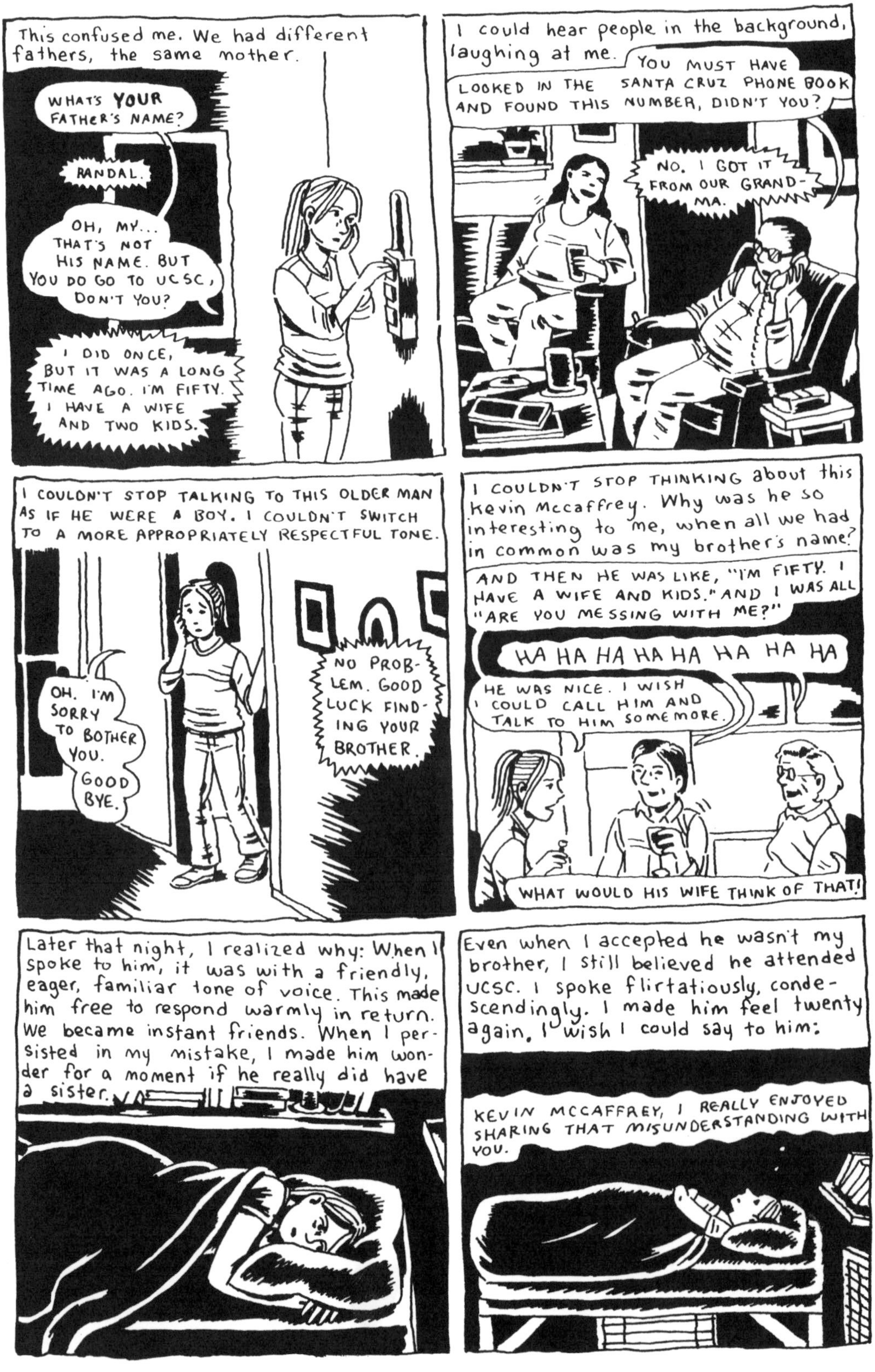
This confused me. We had different fathers, the same mother.
WHAT'S YOUR FATHER'S NAME?
RANDAL.
OH, MY... THAT'S NOT HIS NAME. BUT YOU DO GO TO UCSC, DON'T YOU?
I DID ONCE, BUT IT WAS A LONG TIME AGO. I'M FIFTY. I HAVE A WIFE AND TWO KIDS.
I could hear people in the background, laughing at me.
YOU MUST HAVE LOOKED IN THE SANTA CRUZ PHONE BOOK AND FOUND THIS NUMBER, DIDN'T YOU?
NO. I GOT IT FROM OUR GRANDMA.
I COULDN'T STOP TALKING TO THIS OLDER MAN AS IF HE WERE A BOY. I COULDN'T SWITCH TO A MORE APPROPRIATELY RESPECTFUL TONE.
OH. I'M SORRY TO BOTHER YOU.
GOOD BYE.
NO PROBLEM. GOOD LUCK FINDING YOUR BROTHER.
I COULDN'T STOP THINKING about this Kevin McCaffrey. Why was he so interesting to me, when all we had in common was my brother's name?
AND THEN HE WAS LIKE, "I'M FIFTY. I HAVE A WIFE AND KIDS." AND I WAS ALL "ARE YOU MESSING WITH ME?"
HA HA HA HA HA HA HA HA
HE WAS NICE. I WISH I COULD CALL HIM AND TALK TO HIM SOMEMORE.
WHAT WOULD HIS WIFE THINK OF THAT!
Later that night, I realized why: When I spoke to him, it was with a friendly, eager, familiar tone of voice. This made him free to respond warmly in return. We became instant friends. When I persisted in my mistake, I made him wonder for a moment if he really did have a sister.
Even when I accepted he wasn't my brother, I still believed he attended UCSC. I spoke flirtatiously, condescendingly. I made him feel twenty again. I wish I could say to him:
KEVIN MCCAFFREY, I REALLY ENJOYED SHARING THAT MISUNDERSTANDING WITH YOU.

April 8th

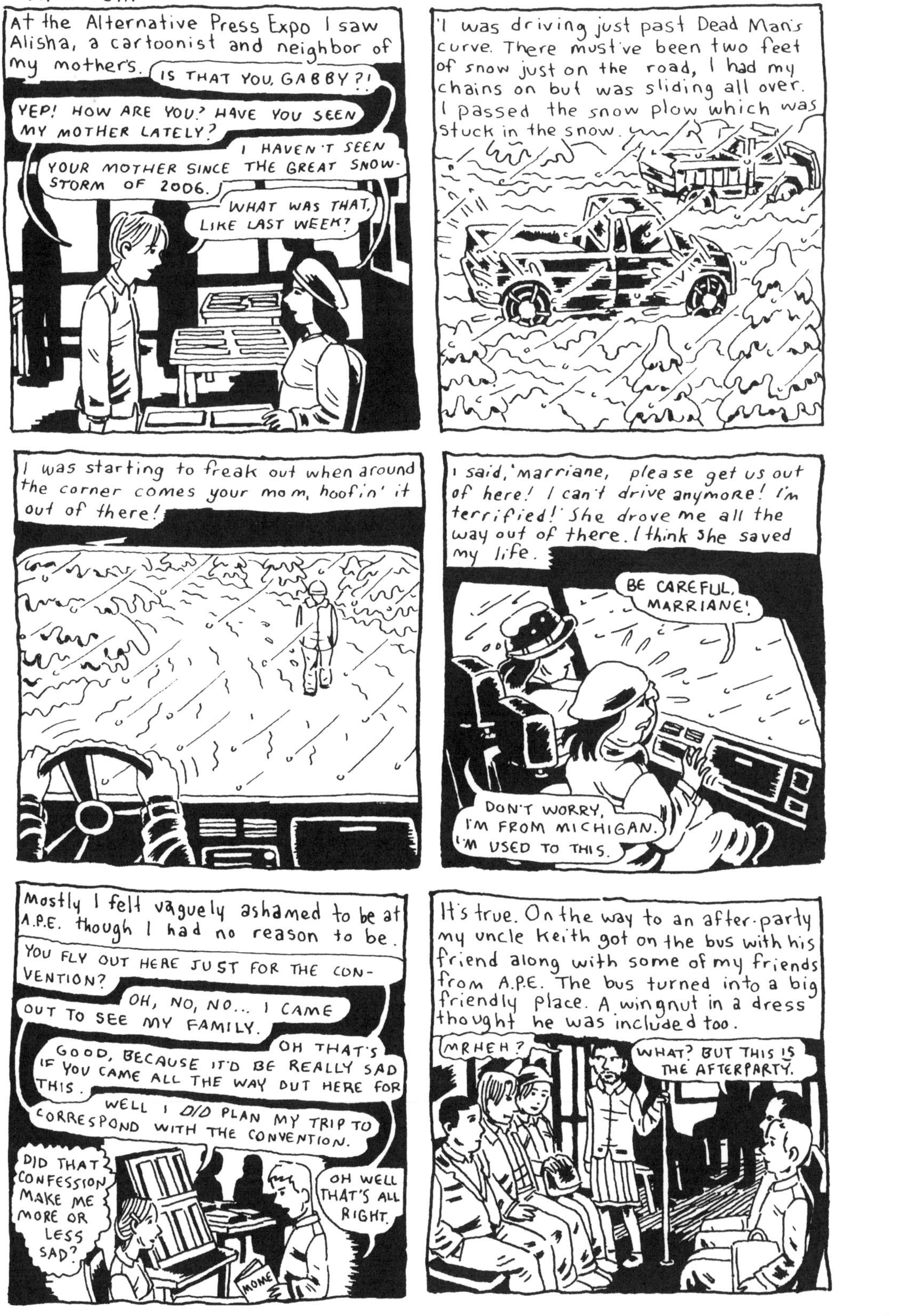
At the Alternative Press Expo I saw Alisha, a cartoonist and neighbor of my mother's.
IS THAT YOU, GABBY?!
YEP! HOW ARE YOU? HAVE YOU SEEN MY MOTHER LATELY?
I HAVEN'T SEEN YOUR MOTHER SINCE THE GREAT SNOW-STORM OF 2006.
WHAT WAS THAT, LIKE LAST WEEK?
'I was driving just past Dead Man's curve. There must've been two feet of snow just on the road, I had my chains on but was sliding all over. I passed the snow plow which was stuck in the snow.
I was starting to freak out when around the corner comes your mom, hoofin' it out of there!
I said, 'Marriane, please get us out of here! I can't drive anymore! I'm terrified!' She drove me all the way out of there. I think she saved my life.
BE CAREFUL, MARRIANE!
DON'T WORRY, I'M FROM MICHIGAN. I'M USED TO THIS.
Mostly I felt vaguely ashamed to be at A.P.E. though I had no reason to be.
YOU FLY OUT HERE JUST FOR THE CONVENTION?
OH, NO, NO... I CAME OUT TO SEE MY FAMILY.
OH THAT'S GOOD, BECAUSE IT'D BE REALLY SAD IF YOU CAME ALL THE WAY OUT HERE FOR THIS.
WELL I *DID* PLAN MY TRIP TO CORRESPOND WITH THE CONVENTION.
DID THAT CONFESSION MAKE ME MORE OR LESS SAD?
OH WELL THAT'S ALL RIGHT.
MOME
It's true. On the way to an after-party my uncle Keith got on the bus with his friend along with some of my friends from A.P.E. The bus turned into a big friendly place. A wingnut in a dress thought he was included too.
MRHEH?
WHAT? BUT THIS IS THE AFTERPARTY.

April 9th

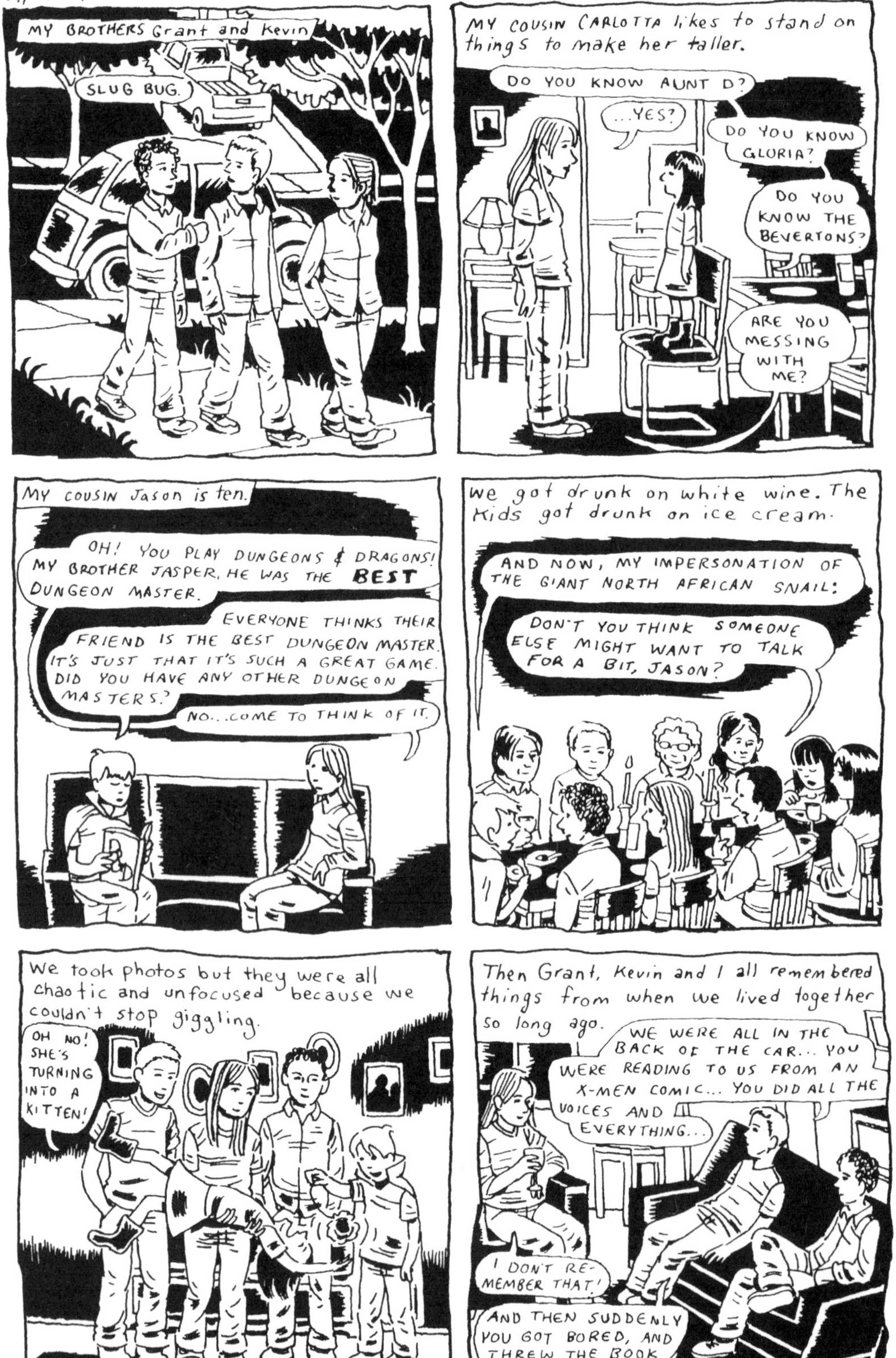
MY BROTHERS Grant and Kevin
SLUG BUG.
MY COUSIN CARLOTTA likes to stand on things to make her taller.
DO YOU KNOW AUNT D?
...YES?
DO YOU KNOW GLORIA?
DO YOU KNOW THE BEVERTONS?
ARE YOU MESSING WITH ME?
My cousin Jason is ten.
OH! YOU PLAY DUNGEONS & DRAGONS! MY BROTHER JASPER, HE WAS THE BEST DUNGEON MASTER.
EVERYONE THINKS THEIR FRIEND IS THE BEST DUNGEON MASTER. IT'S JUST THAT IT'S SUCH A GREAT GAME. DID YOU HAVE ANY OTHER DUNGEON MASTERS?
NO...COME TO THINK OF IT.
We got drunk on white wine. The kids got drunk on ice cream.
AND NOW, MY IMPERSONATION OF THE GIANT NORTH AFRICAN SNAIL:
DON'T YOU THINK SOMEONE ELSE MIGHT WANT TO TALK FOR A BIT, JASON?
We took photos but they were all chaotic and unfocused because we couldn't stop giggling.
OH NO! SHE'S TURNING INTO A KITTEN!
Then Grant, Kevin and I all remembered things from when we lived together so long ago.
WE WERE ALL IN THE BACK OF THE CAR... YOU WERE READING TO US FROM AN X-MEN COMIC... YOU DID ALL THE VOICES AND EVERYTHING...
I DON'T REMEMBER THAT!
AND THEN SUDDENLY YOU GOT BORED, AND THREW THE BOOK DOWN.

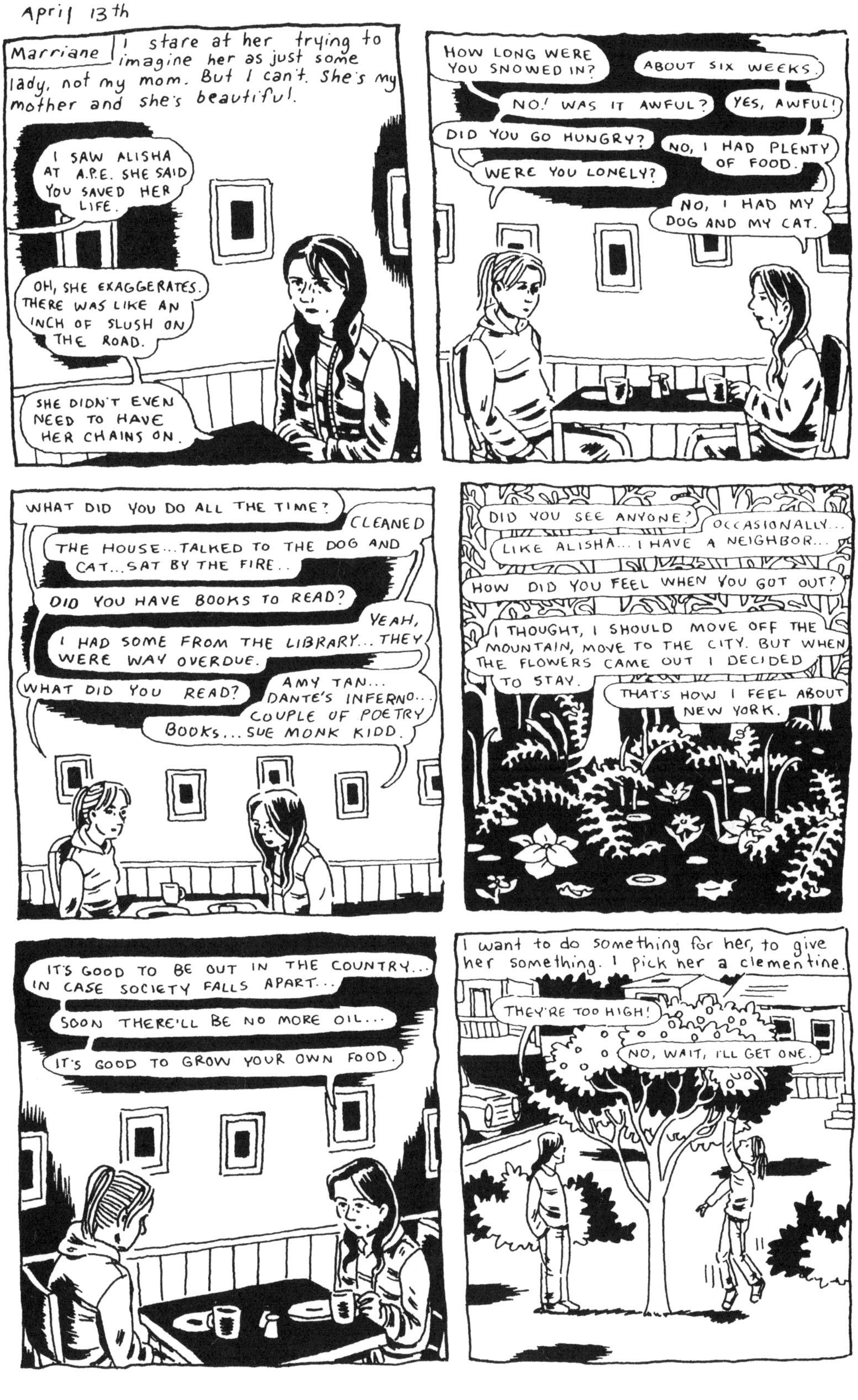
April 13th
Marriane
I stare at her trying to imagine her as just some lady, not my mom. But I can't. She's my mother and she's beautiful.
I SAW ALISHA AT A.P.E. SHE SAID YOU SAVED HER LIFE.
OH, SHE EXAGGERATES. THERE WAS LIKE AN INCH OF SLUSH ON THE ROAD.
SHE DIDN'T EVEN NEED TO HAVE HER CHAINS ON.
HOW LONG WERE YOU SNOWED IN?
ABOUT SIX WEEKS.
NO! WAS IT AWFUL?
YES, AWFUL!
DID YOU GO HUNGRY?
NO, I HAD PLENTY OF FOOD.
WERE YOU LONELY?
NO, I HAD MY DOG AND MY CAT.
WHAT DID YOU DO ALL THE TIME?
CLEANED THE HOUSE...TALKED TO THE DOG AND CAT...SAT BY THE FIRE..
DID YOU HAVE BOOKS TO READ?
YEAH, I HAD SOME FROM THE LIBRARY... THEY WERE WAY OVERDUE.
WHAT DID YOU READ?
AMY TAN... DANTE'S INFERNO... COUPLE OF POETRY BOOKS... SUE MONK KIDD.
DID YOU SEE ANYONE?
OCCASIONALLY... LIKE ALISHA... I HAVE A NEIGHBOR...
HOW DID YOU FEEL WHEN YOU GOT OUT?
I THOUGHT, I SHOULD MOVE OFF THE MOUNTAIN, MOVE TO THE CITY. BUT WHEN THE FLOWERS CAME OUT I DECIDED TO STAY.
THAT'S HOW I FEEL ABOUT NEW YORK.
IT'S GOOD TO BE OUT IN THE COUNTRY... IN CASE SOCIETY FALLS APART...
SOON THERE'LL BE NO MORE OIL...
IT'S GOOD TO GROW YOUR OWN FOOD.
I want to do something for her, to give her something. I pick her a clementine.
THEY'RE TOO HIGH!
NO, WAIT, I'LL GET ONE.

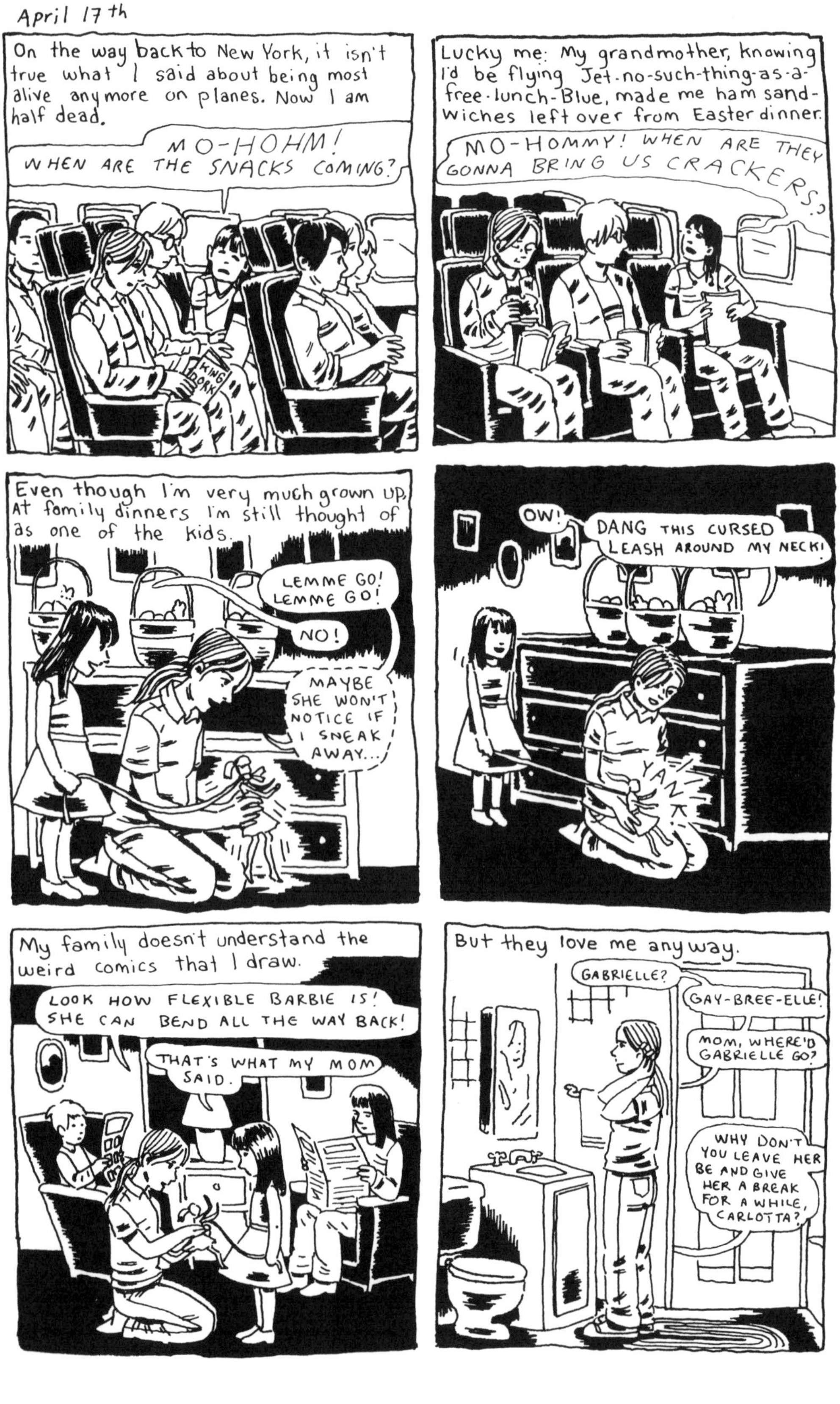
April 17th
On the way back to New York, it isn't true what I said about being most alive anymore on planes. Now I am half dead.
MO-HOHM! WHEN ARE THE SNACKS COMING?
KING DORK
Lucky me: My grandmother, knowing I'd be flying Jet-no-such-thing-as-a-free-lunch-Blue, made me ham sandwiches left over from Easter dinner.
MO-HOMMY! WHEN ARE THEY GONNA BRING US CRACKERS?
Even though I'm very much grown up, at family dinners I'm still thought of as one of the kids.
LEMME GO! LEMME GO!
NO!
MAYBE SHE WON'T NOTICE IF I SNEAK AWAY...
OW!
DANG THIS CURSED LEASH AROUND MY NECK!
YANK
My family doesn't understand the weird comics that I draw.
LOOK HOW FLEXIBLE BARBIE IS! SHE CAN BEND ALL THE WAY BACK!
THAT'S WHAT MY MOM SAID.
But they love me anyway.
GABRIELLE?
GAY-BREE-ELLE!
MOM, WHERE'D GABRIELLE GO?
WHY DON'T YOU LEAVE HER BE AND GIVE HER A BREAK FOR A WHILE, CARLOTTA?

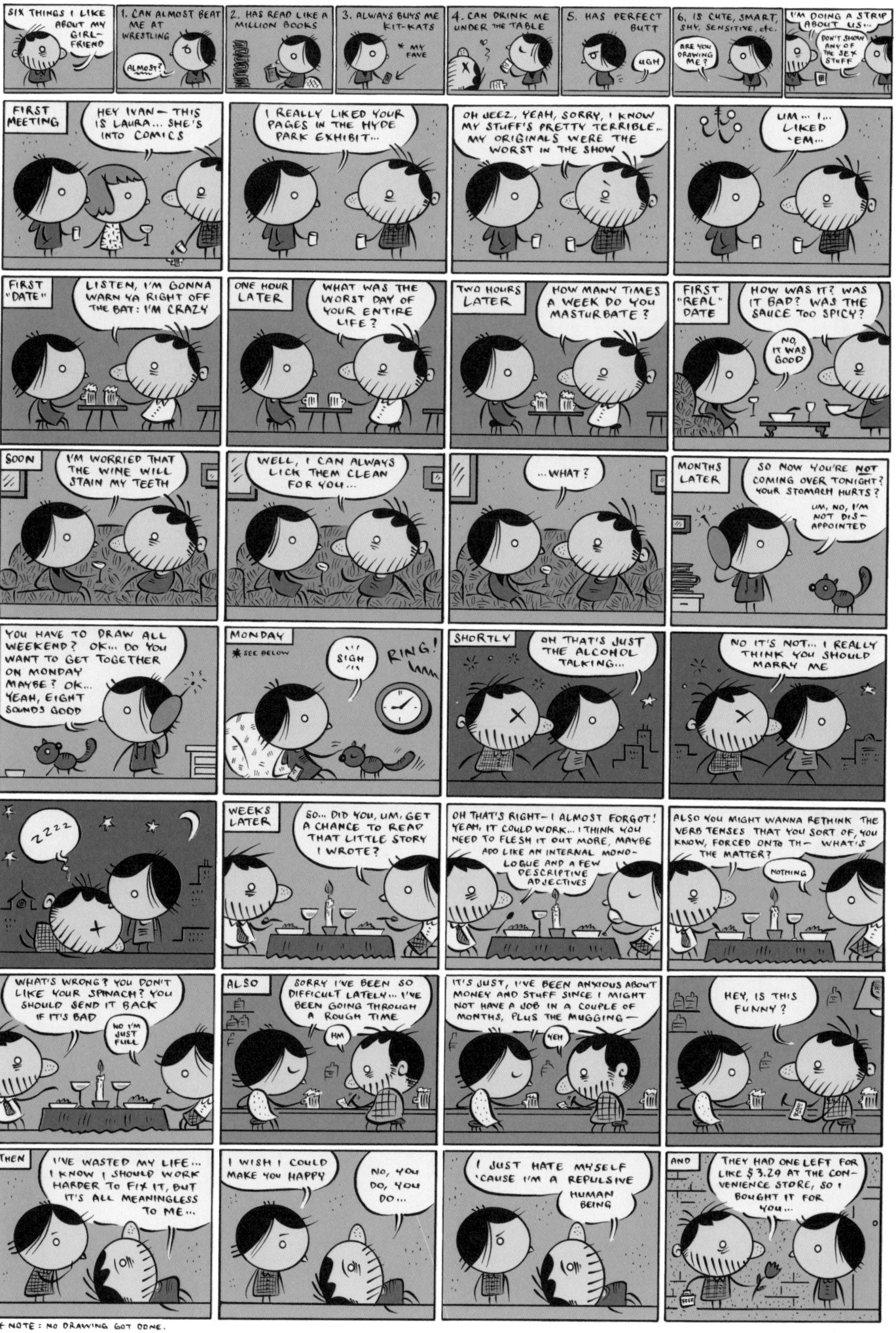
SIX THINGS I LIKE ABOUT MY GIRLFRIEND
1. CAN ALMOST BEAT ME AT WRESTLING
ALMOST?
2. HAS READ LIKE A MILLION BOOKS
3. ALWAYS BUYS ME KIT-KATS
* MY FAVE
4. CAN DRINK ME UNDER THE TABLE
5. HAS PERFECT BUTT
UGH
6. IS CUTE, SMART, SHY, SENSITIVE, etc.
ARE YOU DRAWING ME?
I'M DOING A STRIP ABOUT US...
DON'T SHOW ANY OF THE SEX STUFF
FIRST MEETING
HEY IVAN— THIS IS LAURA... SHE'S INTO COMICS
I REALLY LIKED YOUR PAGES IN THE HYDE PARK EXHIBIT...
OH JEEZ, YEAH, SORRY, I KNOW MY STUFF'S PRETTY TERRIBLE... MY ORIGINALS WERE THE WORST IN THE SHOW
UM... I... LIKED 'EM...
FIRST "DATE"
LISTEN, I'M GONNA WARN YA RIGHT OFF THE BAT: I'M CRAZY
ONE HOUR LATER
WHAT WAS THE WORST DAY OF YOUR ENTIRE LIFE?
TWO HOURS LATER
HOW MANY TIMES A WEEK DO YOU MASTURBATE?
FIRST "REAL" DATE
HOW WAS IT? WAS IT BAD? WAS THE SAUCE TOO SPICY?
NO, IT WAS GOOD
SOON
I'M WORRIED THAT THE WINE WILL STAIN MY TEETH
WELL, I CAN ALWAYS LICK THEM CLEAN FOR YOU...
...WHAT?
MONTHS LATER
SO NOW YOU'RE NOT COMING OVER TONIGHT? YOUR STOMACH HURTS?
UM, NO, I'M NOT DISAPPOINTED
YOU HAVE TO DRAW ALL WEEKEND? OK... DO YOU WANT TO GET TOGETHER ON MONDAY MAYBE? OK... YEAH, EIGHT SOUNDS GOOD
MONDAY
* SEE BELOW
SIGH
RING!
SHORTLY
OH THAT'S JUST THE ALCOHOL TALKING...
NO IT'S NOT... I REALLY THINK YOU SHOULD MARRY ME
ZZZZ
WEEKS LATER
SO... DID YOU, UM, GET A CHANCE TO READ THAT LITTLE STORY I WROTE?
OH THAT'S RIGHT— I ALMOST FORGOT! YEAH, IT COULD WORK... I THINK YOU NEED TO FLESH IT OUT MORE, MAYBE ADD LIKE AN INTERNAL MONOLOGUE AND A FEW DESCRIPTIVE ADJECTIVES
ALSO YOU MIGHT WANNA RETHINK THE VERB TENSES THAT YOU SORT OF, YOU KNOW, FORCED ONTO TH— WHAT'S THE MATTER?
NOTHING
WHAT'S WRONG? YOU DON'T LIKE YOUR SPINACH? YOU SHOULD SEND IT BACK IF IT'S BAD
NO I'M JUST FULL
ALSO
SORRY I'VE BEEN SO DIFFICULT LATELY... I'VE BEEN GOING THROUGH A ROUGH TIME
HM
IT'S JUST, I'VE BEEN ANXIOUS ABOUT MONEY AND STUFF SINCE I MIGHT NOT HAVE A JOB IN A COUPLE OF MONTHS, PLUS THE MUGGING—
YEH
HEY, IS THIS FUNNY?
THEN
I'VE WASTED MY LIFE... I KNOW I SHOULD WORK HARDER TO FIX IT, BUT IT'S ALL MEANINGLESS TO ME...
I WISH I COULD MAKE YOU HAPPY
NO, YOU DO, YOU DO...
I JUST HATE MYSELF 'CAUSE I'M A REPULSIVE HUMAN BEING
AND
THEY HAD ONE LEFT FOR LIKE $3.29 AT THE CONVENIENCE STORE, SO I BOUGHT IT FOR YOU...

* NOTE: NO DRAWING GOT DONE.

IVAN BRUNETTI

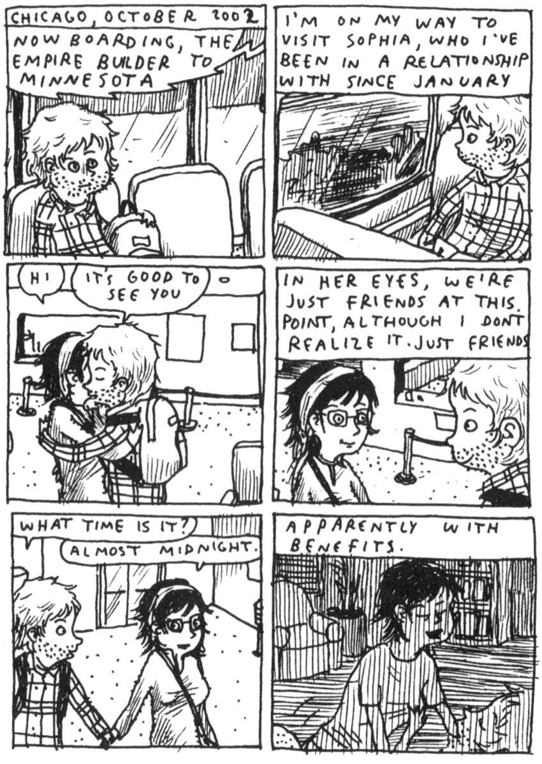
CHICAGO, OCTOBER 2002
NOW BOARDING, THE EMPIRE BUILDER TO MINNESOTA
I'M ON MY WAY TO VISIT SOPHIA, WHO I'VE BEEN IN A RELATIONSHIP WITH SINCE JANUARY
HI
IT'S GOOD TO SEE YOU
IN HER EYES, WE'RE JUST FRIENDS AT THIS POINT, ALTHOUGH I DONT REALIZE IT. JUST FRIENDS
WHAT TIME IS IT?
ALMOST MIDNIGHT.
APPARENTLY WITH BENEFITS.

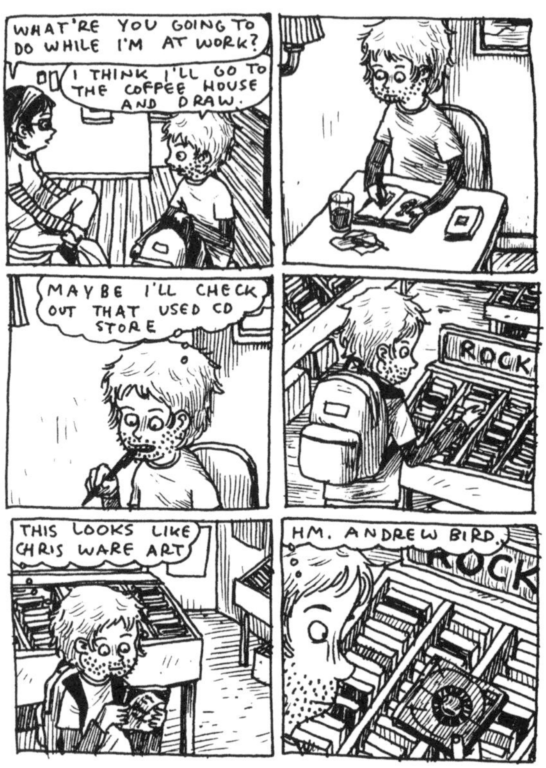
WHAT'RE YOU GOING TO DO WHILE I'M AT WORK?
I THINK I'LL GO TO THE COFFEE HOUSE AND DRAW.
MAYBE I'LL CHECK OUT THAT USED CD STORE
ROCK
THIS LOOKS LIKE CHRIS WARE ART
HM. ANDREW BIRD.
ROCK

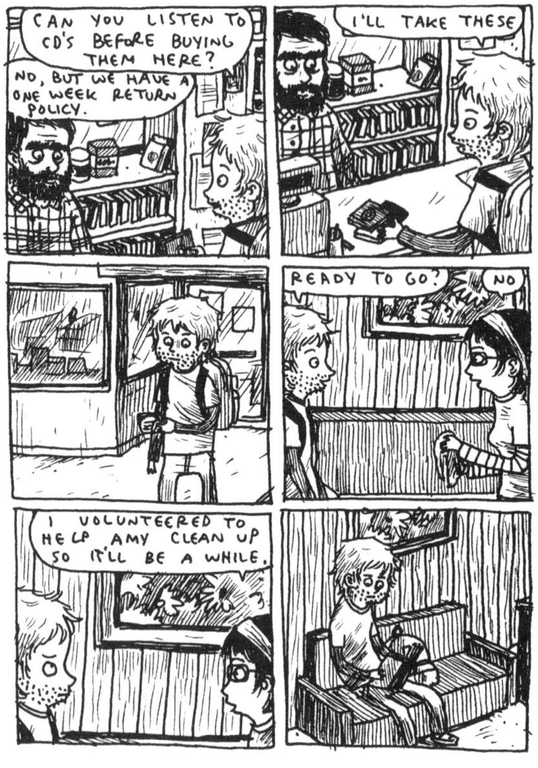
CAN YOU LISTEN TO CD'S BEFORE BUYING THEM HERE?
NO, BUT WE HAVE A ONE WEEK RETURN POLICY.
I'LL TAKE THESE
READY TO GO?
NO
I VOLUNTEERED TO HELP AMY CLEAN UP SO IT'LL BE A WHILE.

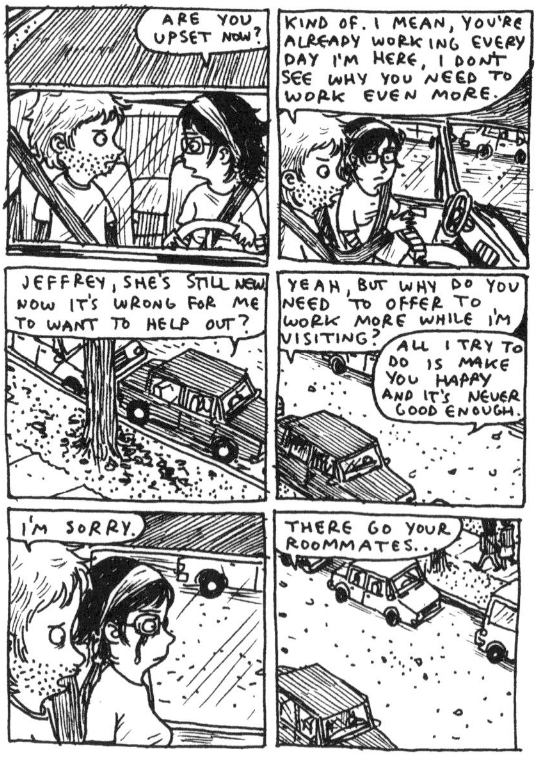
ARE YOU UPSET NOW?
KIND OF. I MEAN, YOU'RE ALREADY WORKING EVERY DAY I'M HERE, I DONT SEE WHY YOU NEED TO WORK EVEN MORE.
JEFFREY, SHE'S STILL NEW NOW IT'S WRONG FOR ME TO WANT TO HELP OUT?
YEAH, BUT WHY DO YOU NEED TO OFFER TO WORK MORE WHILE I'M VISITING?
ALL I TRY TO DO IS MAKE YOU HAPPY AND IT'S NEVER GOOD ENOUGH.
I'M SORRY.
THERE GO YOUR ROOMMATES.

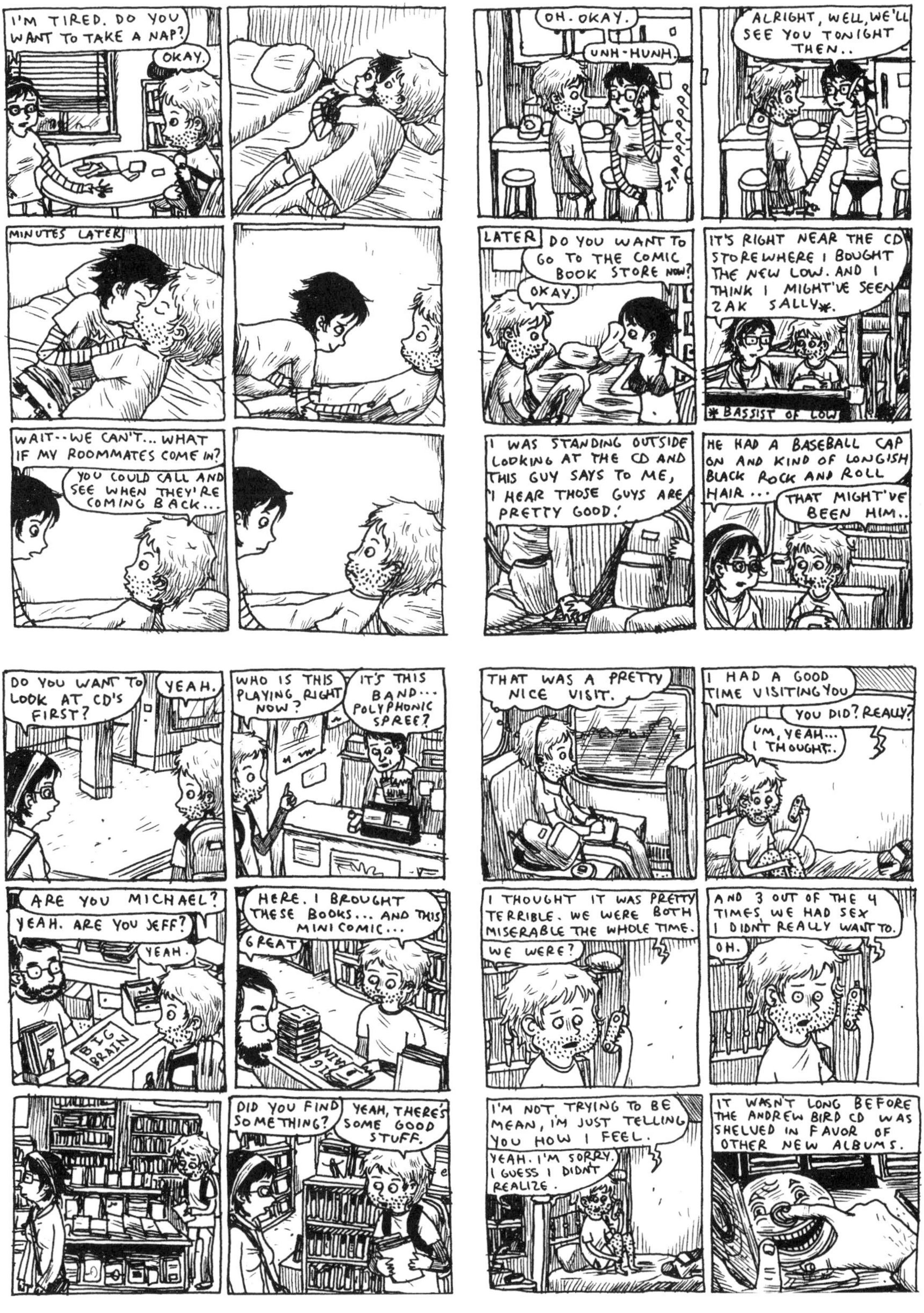
I'M TIRED. DO YOU WANT TO TAKE A NAP?
OKAY.
MINUTES LATER
WAIT.. WE CAN'T... WHAT IF MY ROOMMATES COME IN?
YOU COULD CALL AND SEE WHEN THEY'RE COMING BACK...
OH. OKAY.
UNH-HUNH.
ZIPPPPPP
ALRIGHT, WELL, WE'LL SEE YOU TONIGHT THEN..
LATER
DO YOU WANT TO GO TO THE COMIC BOOK STORE NOW?
OKAY.
IT'S RIGHT NEAR THE CD STORE WHERE I BOUGHT THE NEW LOW. AND I THINK I MIGHT'VE SEEN ZAK SALLY*.
* BASSIST OF LOW
I WAS STANDING OUTSIDE LOOKING AT THE CD AND THIS GUY SAYS TO ME, 'I HEAR THOSE GUYS ARE PRETTY GOOD.'
HE HAD A BASEBALL CAP ON AND KIND OF LONGISH BLACK ROCK AND ROLL HAIR...
THAT MIGHT'VE BEEN HIM..
DO YOU WANT TO LOOK AT CD'S FIRST?
YEAH.
WHO IS THIS PLAYING RIGHT NOW?
IT'S THIS BAND... POLYPHONIC SPREE?
ARE YOU MICHAEL?
YEAH. ARE YOU JEFF?
YEAH.
BIG BRAIN
HERE. I BROUGHT THESE BOOKS... AND THIS MINICOMIC...
GREAT.
DID YOU FIND SOMETHING?
YEAH, THERE'S SOME GOOD STUFF.
THAT WAS A PRETTY NICE VISIT.
I HAD A GOOD TIME VISITING YOU.
YOU DID? REALLY?
UM, YEAH... I THOUGHT..
I THOUGHT IT WAS PRETTY TERRIBLE. WE WERE BOTH MISERABLE THE WHOLE TIME.
WE WERE?
AND 3 OUT OF THE 4 TIMES WE HAD SEX I DIDN'T REALLY WANT TO.
OH.
I'M NOT TRYING TO BE MEAN, I'M JUST TELLING YOU HOW I FEEL.
YEAH. I'M SORRY. I GUESS I DIDN'T REALIZE.
IT WASN'T LONG BEFORE THE ANDREW BIRD CD WAS SHELVED IN FAVOR OF OTHER NEW ALBUMS.

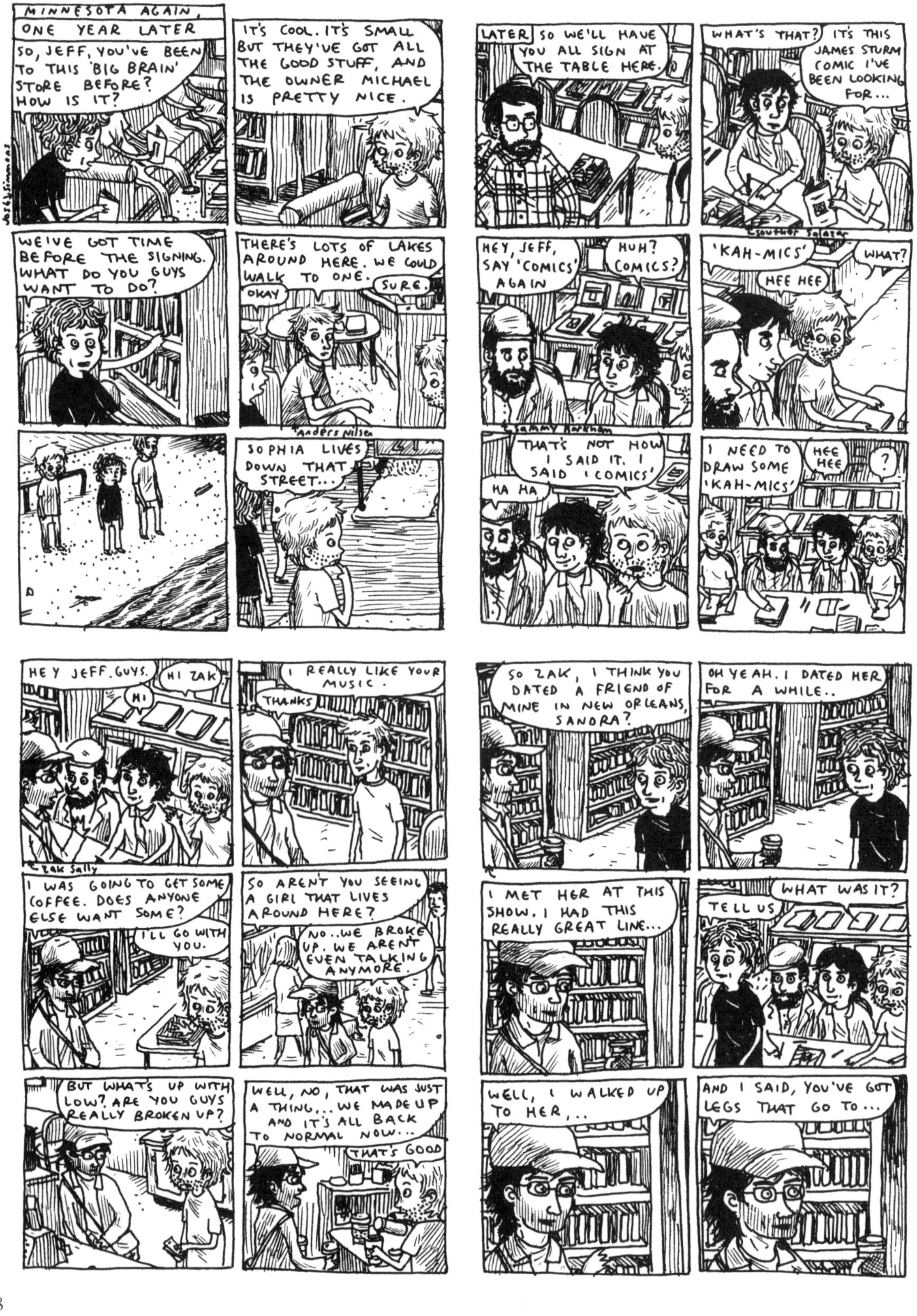
MINNESOTA AGAIN, ONE YEAR LATER
SO, JEFF, YOU'VE BEEN TO THIS 'BIG BRAIN' STORE BEFORE? HOW IS IT?
IT'S COOL. IT'S SMALL BUT THEY'VE GOT ALL THE GOOD STUFF, AND THE OWNER MICHAEL IS PRETTY NICE.
WE'VE GOT TIME BEFORE THE SIGNING. WHAT DO YOU GUYS WANT TO DO?
THERE'S LOTS OF LAKES AROUND HERE. WE COULD WALK TO ONE.
OKAY
SURE.
Anders Nilsen
SOPHIA LIVES DOWN THAT STREET...
LATER
SO WE'LL HAVE YOU ALL SIGN AT THE TABLE HERE.
WHAT'S THAT?
IT'S THIS JAMES STURM COMIC I'VE BEEN LOOKING FOR...
Souther Salazar
HEY, JEFF, SAY 'COMICS' AGAIN
HUH? COMICS?
'KAH-MICS'
WHAT?
HEE HEE
Sammy Harkham
THAT'S NOT HOW I SAID IT. I SAID 'COMICS'
HA HA
I NEED TO DRAW SOME 'KAH-MICS'
HEE HEE
?
HEY JEFF. GUYS.
HI ZAK
HI
Zak Sally
I REALLY LIKE YOUR MUSIC.
THANKS
I WAS GOING TO GET SOME COFFEE. DOES ANYONE ELSE WANT SOME?
I'LL GO WITH YOU.
SO AREN'T YOU SEEING A GIRL THAT LIVES AROUND HERE?
NO.. WE BROKE UP. WE AREN'T EVEN TALKING ANYMORE.
BUT WHAT'S UP WITH LOW? ARE YOU GUYS REALLY BROKEN UP?
WELL, NO, THAT WAS JUST A THING... WE MADE UP AND IT'S ALL BACK TO NORMAL NOW...
THAT'S GOOD
SO ZAK, I THINK YOU DATED A FRIEND OF MINE IN NEW ORLEANS, SANDRA?
OH YEAH. I DATED HER FOR A WHILE..
I MET HER AT THIS SHOW. I HAD THIS REALLY GREAT LINE...
TELL US
WHAT WAS IT?
WELL, I WALKED UP TO HER,..
AND I SAID, YOU'VE GOT LEGS THAT GO TO...

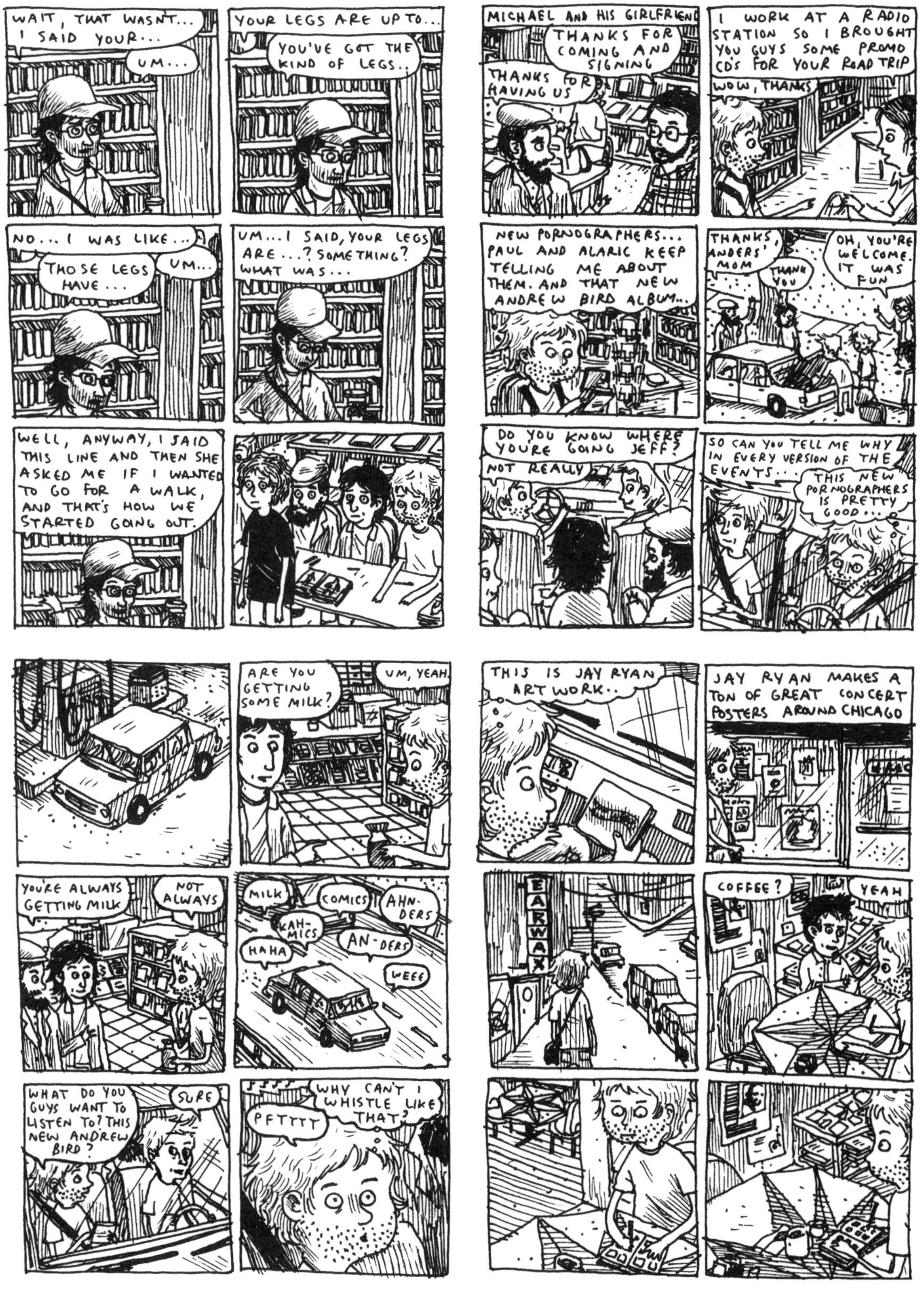
WAIT, THAT WASN'T... I SAID YOUR...
UM...
YOUR LEGS ARE UP TO...
YOU'VE GOT THE KIND OF LEGS..
NO... I WAS LIKE...
THOSE LEGS HAVE...
UM...
UM... I SAID, YOUR LEGS ARE...? SOMETHING? WHAT WAS...
WELL, ANYWAY, I SAID THIS LINE AND THEN SHE ASKED ME IF I WANTED TO GO FOR A WALK, AND THAT'S HOW WE STARTED GOING OUT.
MICHAEL AND HIS GIRLFRIEND
THANKS FOR COMING AND SIGNING
THANKS FOR HAVING US
I WORK AT A RADIO STATION SO I BROUGHT YOU GUYS SOME PROMO CD'S FOR YOUR ROAD TRIP
WOW, THANKS
NEW PORNOGRAPHERS... PAUL AND ALARIC KEEP TELLING ME ABOUT THEM. AND THAT NEW ANDREW BIRD ALBUM...
THANKS, ANDERS' MOM
THANK YOU
OH, YOU'RE WELCOME. IT WAS FUN
DO YOU KNOW WHERE YOU'RE GOING JEFF?
NOT REALLY
SO CAN YOU TELL ME WHY IN EVERY VERSION OF THE EVENTS...
THIS NEW PORNOGRAPHERS IS PRETTY GOOD...
ARE YOU GETTING SOME MILK?
UM, YEAH
YOU'RE ALWAYS GETTING MILK
NOT ALWAYS
MILK
COMICS
AHN-DERS
KAH-MICS
AN-DERS
HAHA
WEEE
WHAT DO YOU GUYS WANT TO LISTEN TO? THIS NEW ANDREW BIRD?
SURE
WHY CAN'T I WHISTLE LIKE THAT?
PFTTTT
THIS IS JAY RYAN ART WORK..
JAY RYAN MAKES A TON OF GREAT CONCERT POSTERS AROUND CHICAGO
EARWAX
COFFEE?
YEAH

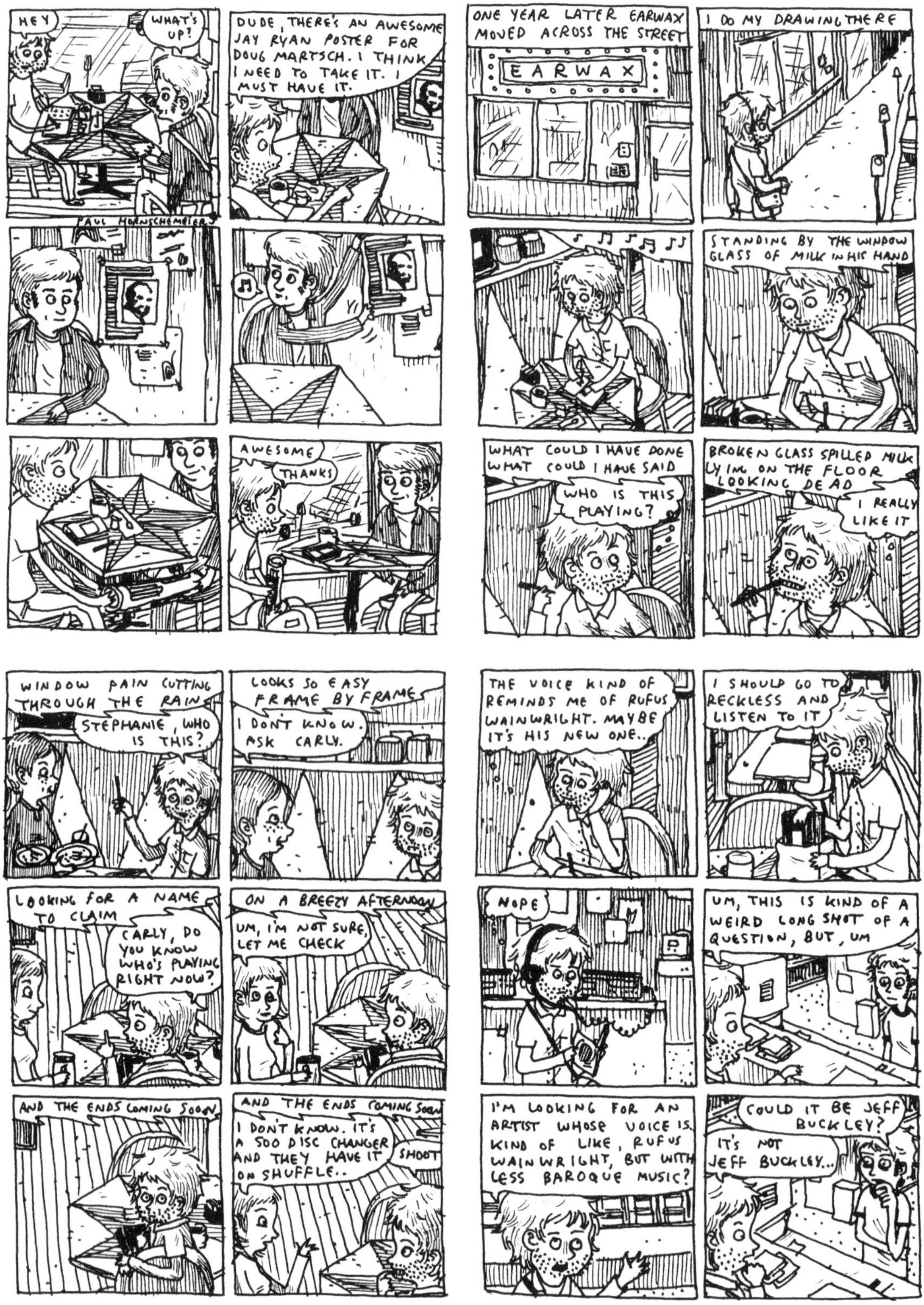

HEY
WHAT'S UP?
DUDE, THERE'S AN AWESOME JAY RYAN POSTER FOR DOUG MARTSCH. I THINK I NEED TO TAKE IT. I MUST HAVE IT.
PAUL HORNSCHEMEIER
AWESOME
THANKS
ONE YEAR LATER EARWAX MOVED ACROSS THE STREET
EARWAX
I DO MY DRAWING THERE
STANDING BY THE WINDOW GLASS OF MILK IN HIS HAND
WHAT COULD I HAVE DONE WHAT COULD I HAVE SAID
WHO IS THIS PLAYING?
BROKEN GLASS SPILLED MILK LYING ON THE FLOOR LOOKING DEAD
I REALLY LIKE IT
WINDOW PAIN CUTTING THROUGH THE RAIN
STEPHANIE, WHO IS THIS?
LOOKS SO EASY FRAME BY FRAME
I DONT KNOW. ASK CARLY.
LOOKING FOR A NAME TO CLAIM
CARLY, DO YOU KNOW WHO'S PLAYING RIGHT NOW?
ON A BREEZY AFTERNOON
UM, I'M NOT SURE, LET ME CHECK
AND THE ENDS COMING SOON
AND THE ENDS COMING SOON
I DON'T KNOW. IT'S A 500 DISC CHANGER AND THEY HAVE IT ON SHUFFLE..
SHOOT
THE VOICE KIND OF REMINDS ME OF RUFUS WAINWRIGHT. MAYBE IT'S HIS NEW ONE..
I SHOULD GO TO RECKLESS AND LISTEN TO IT
NOPE
UM, THIS IS KIND OF A WEIRD LONG SHOT OF A QUESTION, BUT, UM
I'M LOOKING FOR AN ARTIST WHOSE VOICE IS KIND OF LIKE, RUFUS WAINWRIGHT, BUT WITH LESS BAROQUE MUSIC?
COULD IT BE JEFF BUCKLEY?
IT'S NOT JEFF BUCKLEY...

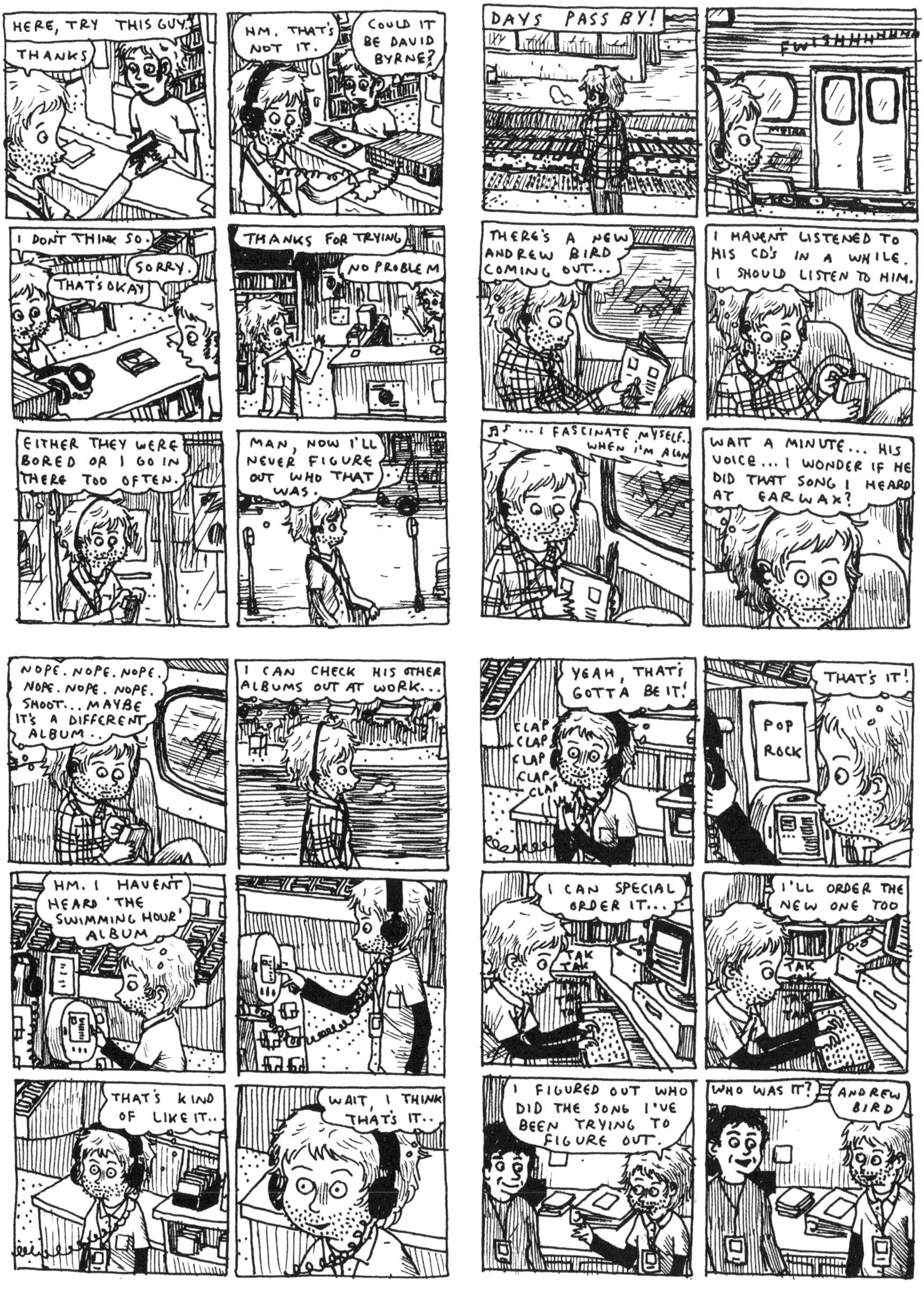
HERE, TRY THIS GUY.
THANKS
HM. THAT'S NOT IT.
COULD IT BE DAVID BYRNE?
I DON'T THINK SO.
SORRY.
THAT'S OKAY
THANKS FOR TRYING
NO PROBLEM
EITHER THEY WERE BORED OR I GO IN THERE TOO OFTEN.
MAN, NOW I'LL NEVER FIGURE OUT WHO THAT WAS.
DAYS PASS BY!
FWISHHHHHHH
THERE'S A NEW ANDREW BIRD COMING OUT...
I HAVEN'T LISTENED TO HIS CD'S IN A WHILE. I SHOULD LISTEN TO HIM.
...I FASCINATE MYSELF. WHEN I'M ALON
WAIT A MINUTE... HIS VOICE... I WONDER IF HE DID THAT SONG I HEARD AT EARWAX?
NOPE. NOPE. NOPE. NOPE. NOPE. NOPE. SHOOT... MAYBE IT'S A DIFFERENT ALBUM..
I CAN CHECK HIS OTHER ALBUMS OUT AT WORK...
HM. I HAVEN'T HEARD 'THE SWIMMING HOUR' ALBUM
THAT'S KIND OF LIKE IT..
WAIT, I THINK THAT'S IT..
YEAH, THAT'S GOTTA BE IT!
CLAP CLAP CLAP CLAP CLAP
THAT'S IT!
POP ROCK
I CAN SPECIAL ORDER IT...
TAK TAK
I'LL ORDER THE NEW ONE TOO
TAK TAK
I FIGURED OUT WHO DID THE SONG I'VE BEEN TRYING TO FIGURE OUT.
WHO WAS IT?
ANDREW BIRD

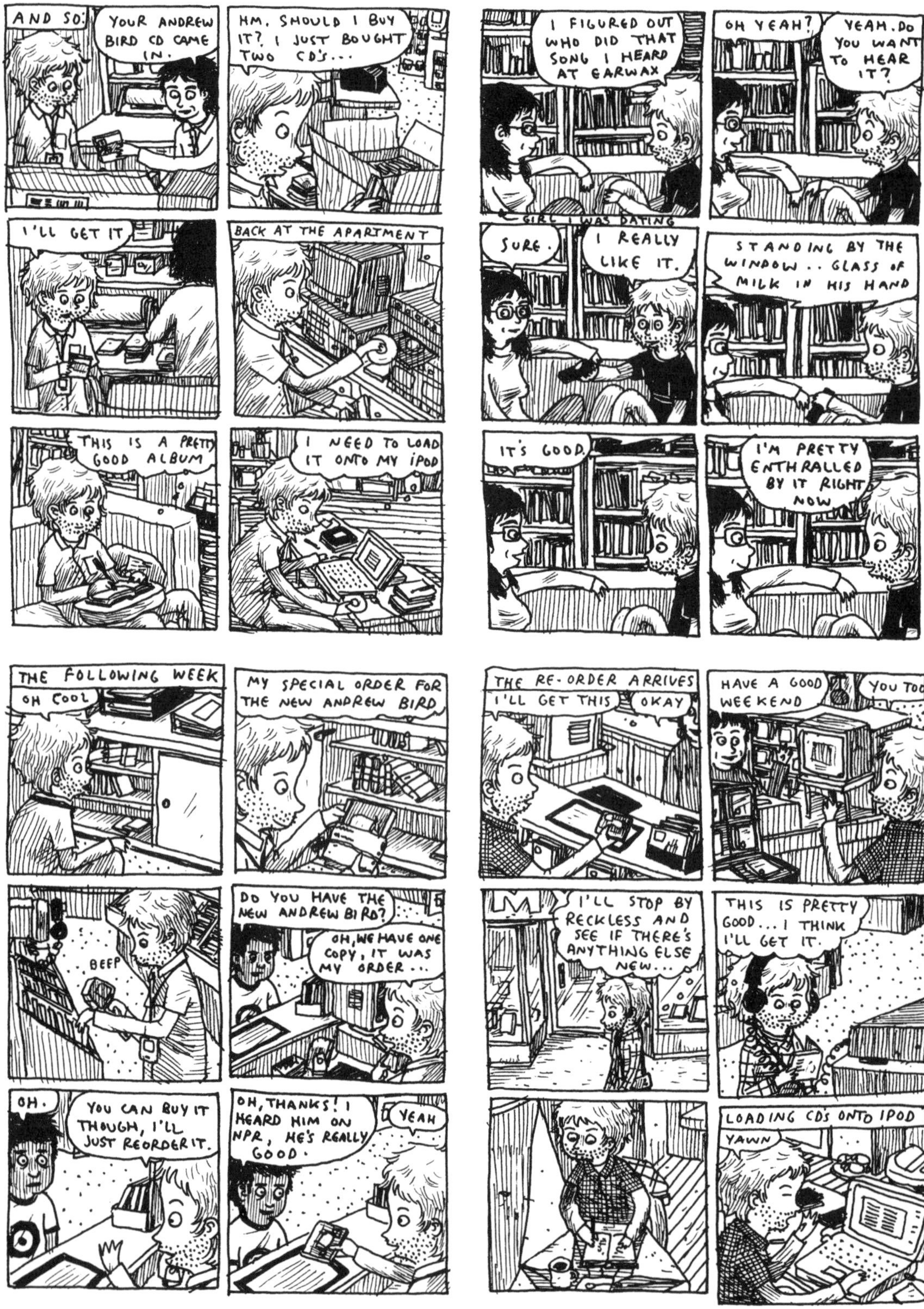
AND SO:
YOUR ANDREW BIRD CD CAME IN.
HM, SHOULD I BUY IT? I JUST BOUGHT TWO CD'S...
I'LL GET IT
BACK AT THE APARTMENT
THIS IS A PRETTY GOOD ALBUM
I NEED TO LOAD IT ONTO MY iPOD
I FIGURED OUT WHO DID THAT SONG I HEARD AT EARWAX
OH YEAH?
YEAH. DO YOU WANT TO HEAR IT?
GIRL I WAS DATING
SURE.
I REALLY LIKE IT.
STANDING BY THE WINDOW.. GLASS OF MILK IN HIS HAND
IT'S GOOD.
I'M PRETTY ENTHRALLED BY IT RIGHT NOW
THE FOLLOWING WEEK
OH COOL
MY SPECIAL ORDER FOR THE NEW ANDREW BIRD
BEEP
DO YOU HAVE THE NEW ANDREW BIRD?
OH, WE HAVE ONE COPY, IT WAS MY ORDER...
OH.
YOU CAN BUY IT THOUGH, I'LL JUST REORDER IT.
OH, THANKS! I HEARD HIM ON NPR, HE'S REALLY GOOD.
YEAH
THE RE-ORDER ARRIVES
I'LL GET THIS
OKAY
HAVE A GOOD WEEKEND
YOU TOO
I'LL STOP BY RECKLESS AND SEE IF THERE'S ANYTHING ELSE NEW...
THIS IS PRETTY GOOD... I THINK I'LL GET IT.
LOADING CDS ONTO IPOD
YAWN

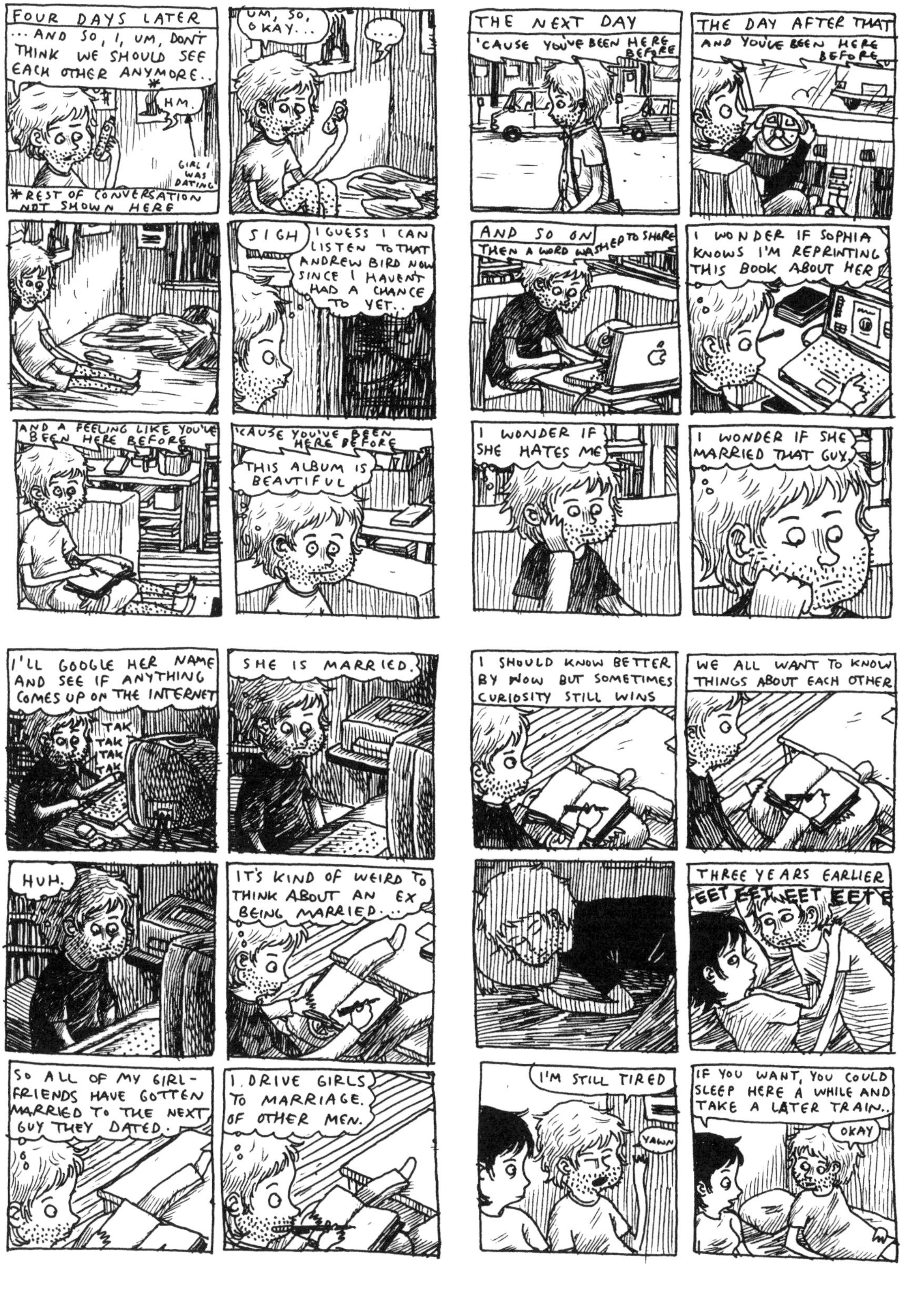
FOUR DAYS LATER
...AND SO, I, UM, DON'T THINK WE SHOULD SEE EACH OTHER ANYMORE..*
HM.
GIRL I WAS DATING
*REST OF CONVERSATION NOT SHOWN HERE
UM, SO, OKAY...
...
THE NEXT DAY
'CAUSE YOU'VE BEEN HERE BEFORE
THE DAY AFTER THAT
AND YOU'VE BEEN HERE BEFORE
SIGH
I GUESS I CAN LISTEN TO THAT ANDREW BIRD NOW SINCE I HAVEN'T HAD A CHANCE TO YET.
AND SO ON
THEN A WORD WASHED TO SHORE
I WONDER IF SOPHIA KNOWS I'M REPRINTING THIS BOOK ABOUT HER
AND A FEELING LIKE YOU'VE BEEN HERE BEFORE
'CAUSE YOU'VE BEEN HERE BEFORE
THIS ALBUM IS BEAUTIFUL
I WONDER IF SHE HATES ME
I WONDER IF SHE MARRIED THAT GUY.
I'LL GOOGLE HER NAME AND SEE IF ANYTHING COMES UP ON THE INTERNET
TAK TAK TAK TAK
SHE IS MARRIED.
I SHOULD KNOW BETTER BY NOW BUT SOMETIMES CURIOSITY STILL WINS
WE ALL WANT TO KNOW THINGS ABOUT EACH OTHER
HUH.
IT'S KIND OF WEIRD TO THINK ABOUT AN EX BEING MARRIED...
THREE YEARS EARLIER
EET EET EET EETE
SO ALL OF MY GIRLFRIENDS HAVE GOTTEN MARRIED TO THE NEXT GUY THEY DATED.
I DRIVE GIRLS TO MARRIAGE. OF OTHER MEN.
I'M STILL TIRED
YAWN
IF YOU WANT, YOU COULD SLEEP HERE A WHILE AND TAKE A LATER TRAIN..
OKAY

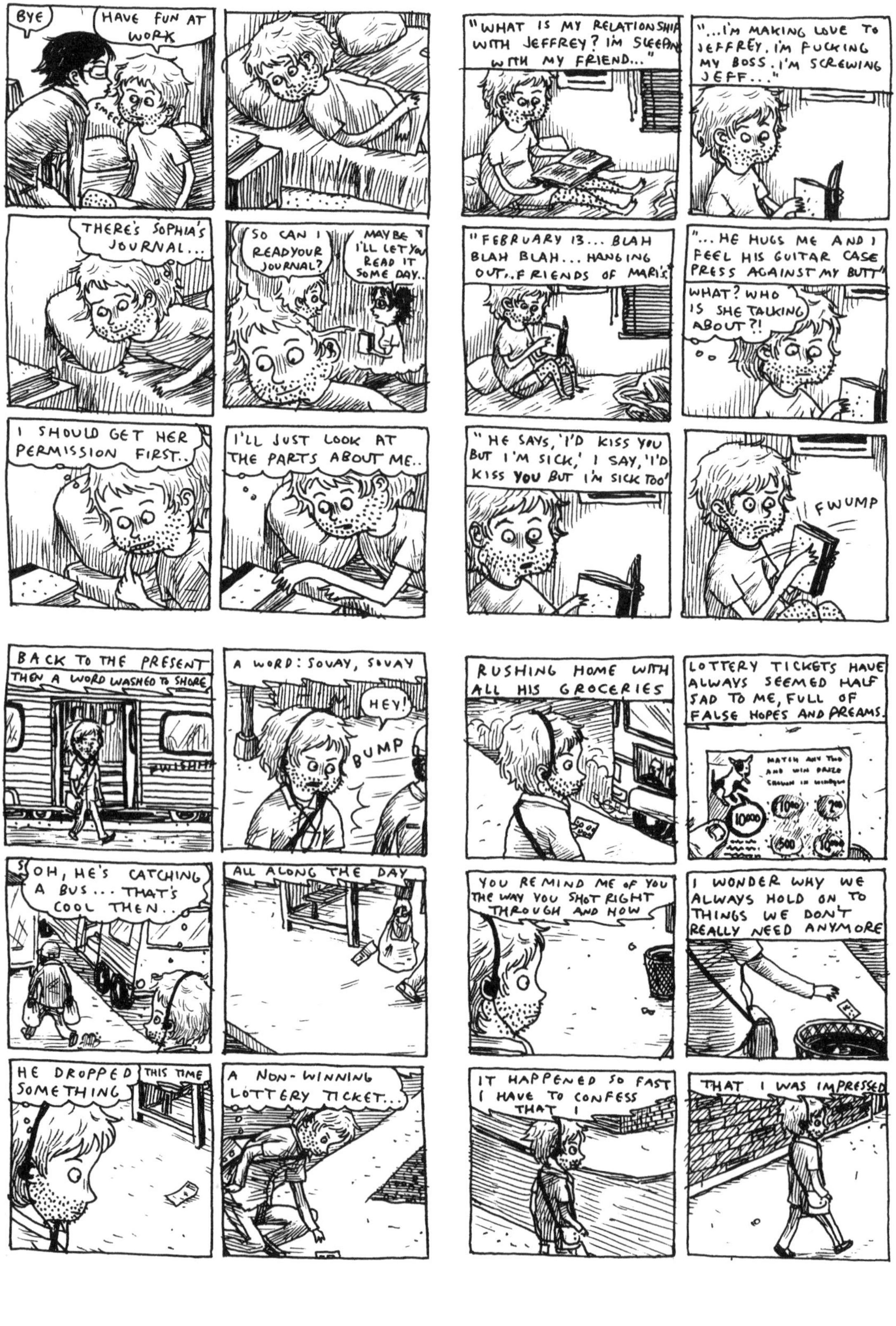
BYE
HAVE FUN AT WORK
SMECK
THERE'S SOPHIA'S JOURNAL...
SO CAN I READ YOUR JOURNAL?
MAYBE I'LL LET YOU READ IT SOME DAY..
I SHOULD GET HER PERMISSION FIRST..
I'LL JUST LOOK AT THE PARTS ABOUT ME..
"WHAT IS MY RELATIONSHIP WITH JEFFREY? I'M SLEEPIN WITH MY FRIEND..."
"...I'M MAKING LOVE TO JEFFREY. I'M FUCKING MY BOSS. I'M SCREWING JEFF..."
"FEBRUARY 13... BLAH BLAH BLAH... HANGING OUT..FRIENDS OF MARI'S"
"...HE HUGS ME AND I FEEL HIS GUITAR CASE PRESS AGAINST MY BUTT"
WHAT? WHO IS SHE TALKING ABOUT?!
"HE SAYS, 'I'D KISS YOU BUT I'M SICK,' I SAY, 'I'D KISS YOU BUT I'M SICK TOO'"
FWUMP
BACK TO THE PRESENT
THEN A WORD WASHED TO SHORE
SWISHH
A WORD: SOVAY, SOVAY
HEY!
BUMP
OH, HE'S CATCHING A BUS... THAT'S COOL THEN..
ALL ALONG THE DAY
HE DROPPED SOMETHING
THIS TIME
A NON-WINNING LOTTERY TICKET...
RUSHING HOME WITH ALL HIS GROCERIES
LOTTERY TICKETS HAVE ALWAYS SEEMED HALF SAD TO ME, FULL OF FALSE HOPES AND DREAMS.
10000
YOU REMIND ME OF YOU THE WAY YOU SHOT RIGHT THROUGH AND HOW
I WONDER WHY WE ALWAYS HOLD ON TO THINGS WE DON'T REALLY NEED ANYMORE
IT HAPPENED SO FAST I HAVE TO CONFESS THAT I
THAT I WAS IMPRESSED

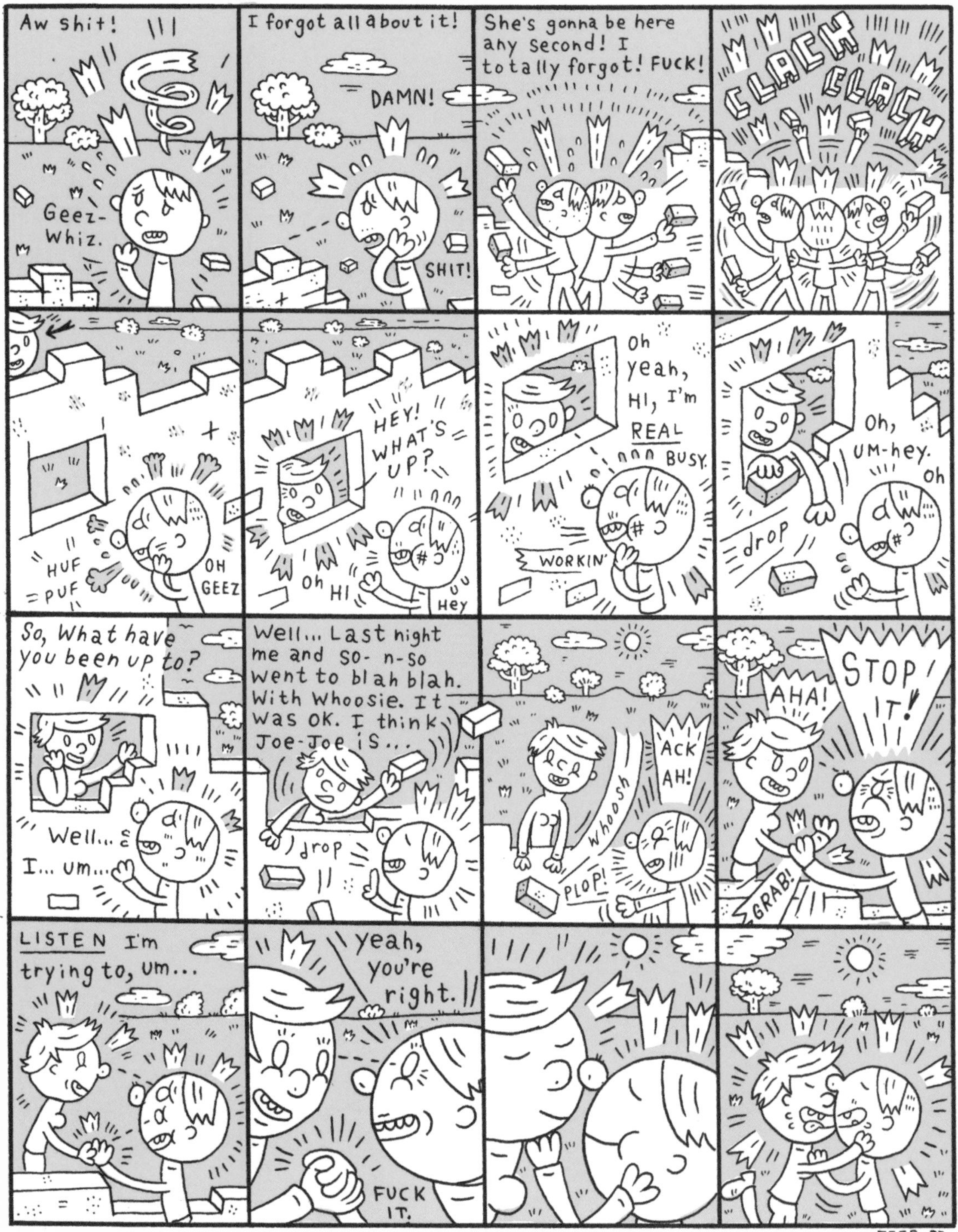
Aw shit!
Geez-Whiz.
I forgot all about it!
DAMN!
SHIT!
She's gonna be here any second! I totally forgot! FUCK!
CLACK CLACK
HUF PUF
OH GEEZ
HEY! WHAT'S UP?
Oh HI
Hey
Oh yeah, HI, I'm REAL BUSY.
WORKIN'
Oh, UM-hey.
Oh
drop
So, What have you been up to?
Well... I... um...
Well... Last night me and so-n-so went to blah blah. With Whoosie. It was OK. I think Joe-Joe is...
drop
Whoosh
ACK AH!
PLOP!
AHA!
STOP IT!
GRAB!
LISTEN I'm trying to, um...
yeah, you're right.
FUCK IT.
REGE-97

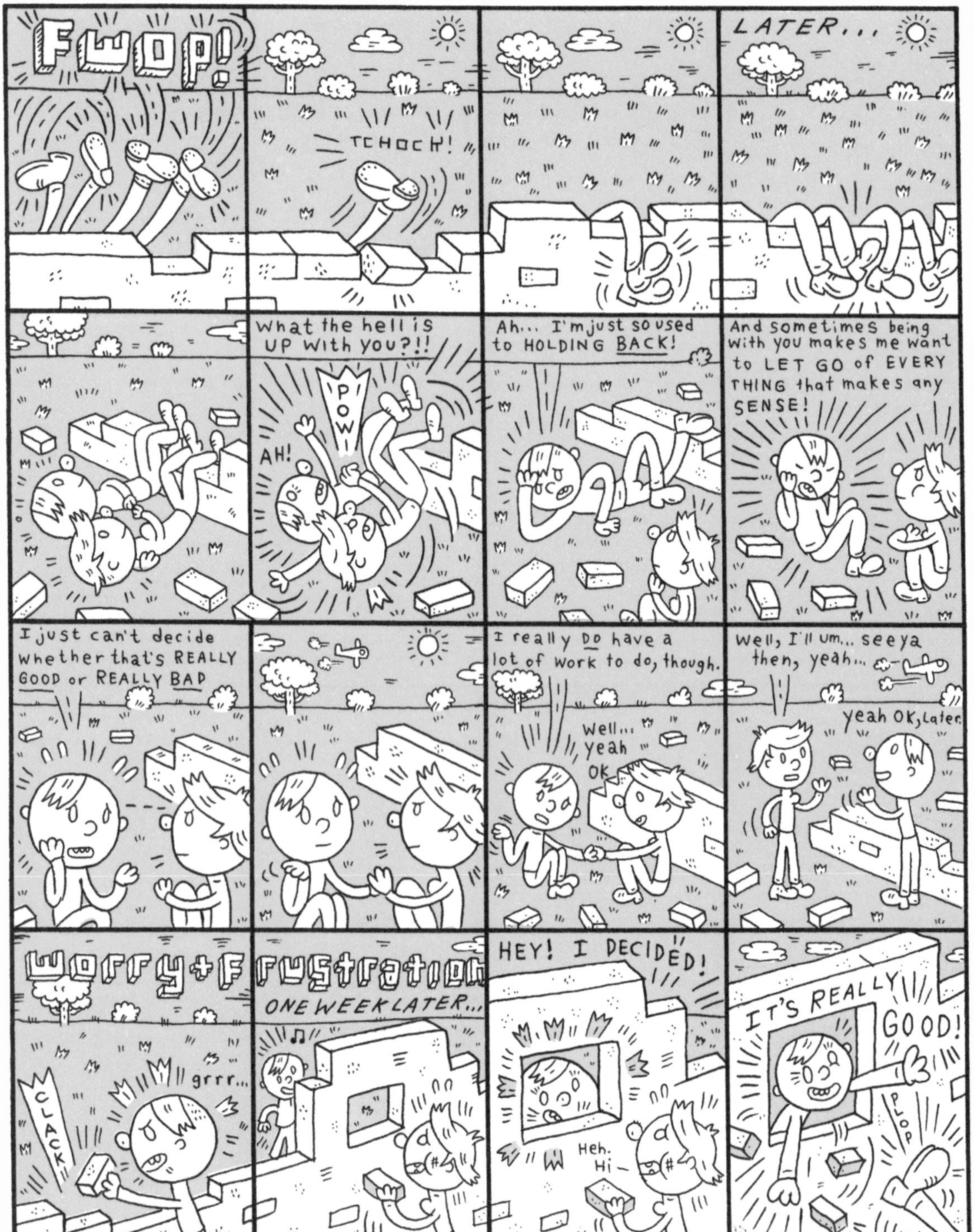
FWOP!
TCHOCK!
LATER...
What the hell is UP with you?!!
POW
AH!
Ah... I'm just so used to HOLDING BACK!
And sometimes being with you makes me want to LET GO of EVERY THING that makes any SENSE!
I just can't decide whether that's REALLY GOOD or REALLY BAD
I really DO have a lot of work to do, though.
Well... yeah OK
Well, I'll um... seeya then, yeah...
yeah OK, Later.
Worry + Frustration
CLACK
grrr...
ONE WEEK LATER...
HEY! I DECIDED!
Heh. Hi—
IT'S REALLY GOOD!
PLOP
REGE-97

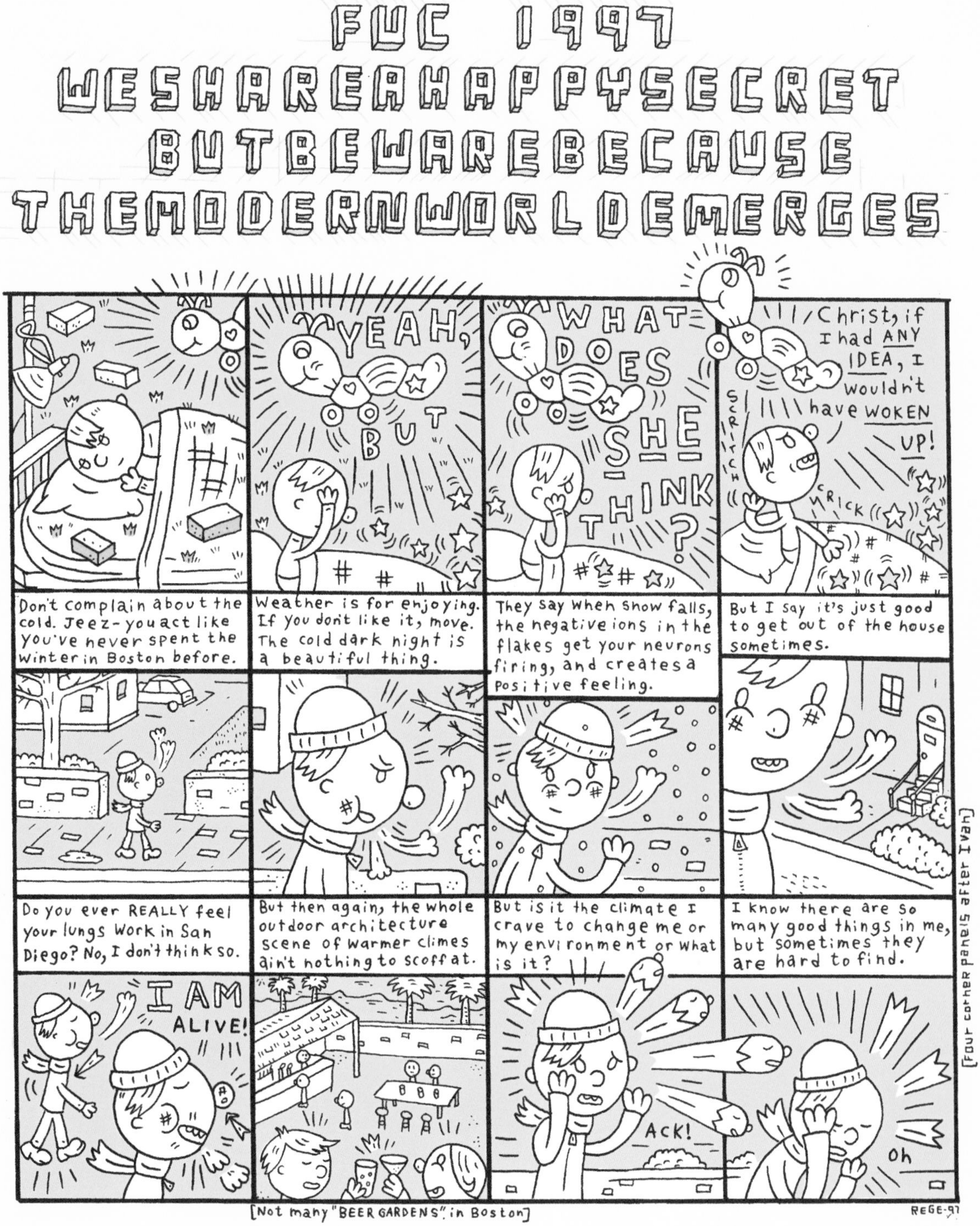
FUC 1997
WESHAREAHAPPYSECRET
BUTBEWAREBECAUSE
THEMODERNWORLDEMERGES
YEAH, BUT
WHAT DOES SHE THINK?
Christ, if I had ANY IDEA, I wouldn't have WOKEN UP!
SCRITCH
CRICK
Don't complain about the cold. Jeez-you act like you've never spent the winter in Boston before.
Weather is for enjoying. If you don't like it, move. The cold dark night is a beautiful thing.
They say when snow falls, the negative ions in the flakes get your neurons firing, and creates a positive feeling.
But I say it's just good to get out of the house sometimes.
Do you ever REALLY feel your lungs work in San Diego? No, I don't think so.
But then again, the whole outdoor architecture scene of warmer climes ain't nothing to scoff at.
But is it the climate I crave to change me or my environment or what is it?
I know there are so many good things in me, but sometimes they are hard to find.
I AM ALIVE!
ACK!
Oh
[Four corner panels after Ivan]
[Not many "BEER GARDENS" in Boston]
REGE-97

MARCH 13 1997

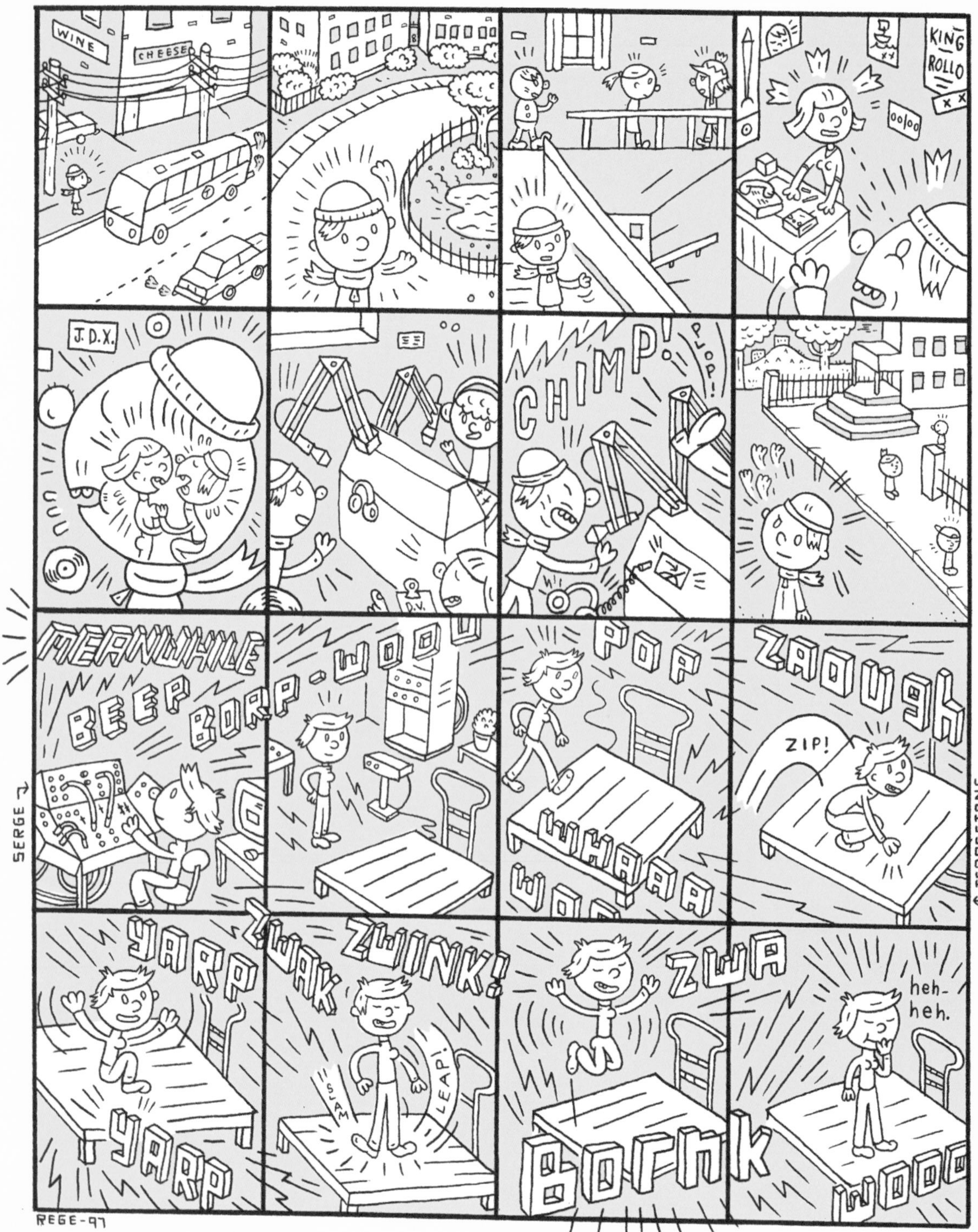
WINE
CHEESE
KING ROLLO
J.D.X.
D.V.
CHIMP!
PLOP!
MEANWHILE
BEEP
BORP-WOOO
POP
WHAAAA
ZAOUGH
ZIP!
YARP
YARP
ZWAK
ZWINK!
SLAM
LEAP!
ZWA
BORNK
heh-heh.
WOOO
SERGE
TERPSETONE

REGE-97

[WILL WONDERS NEVER CEASE?]

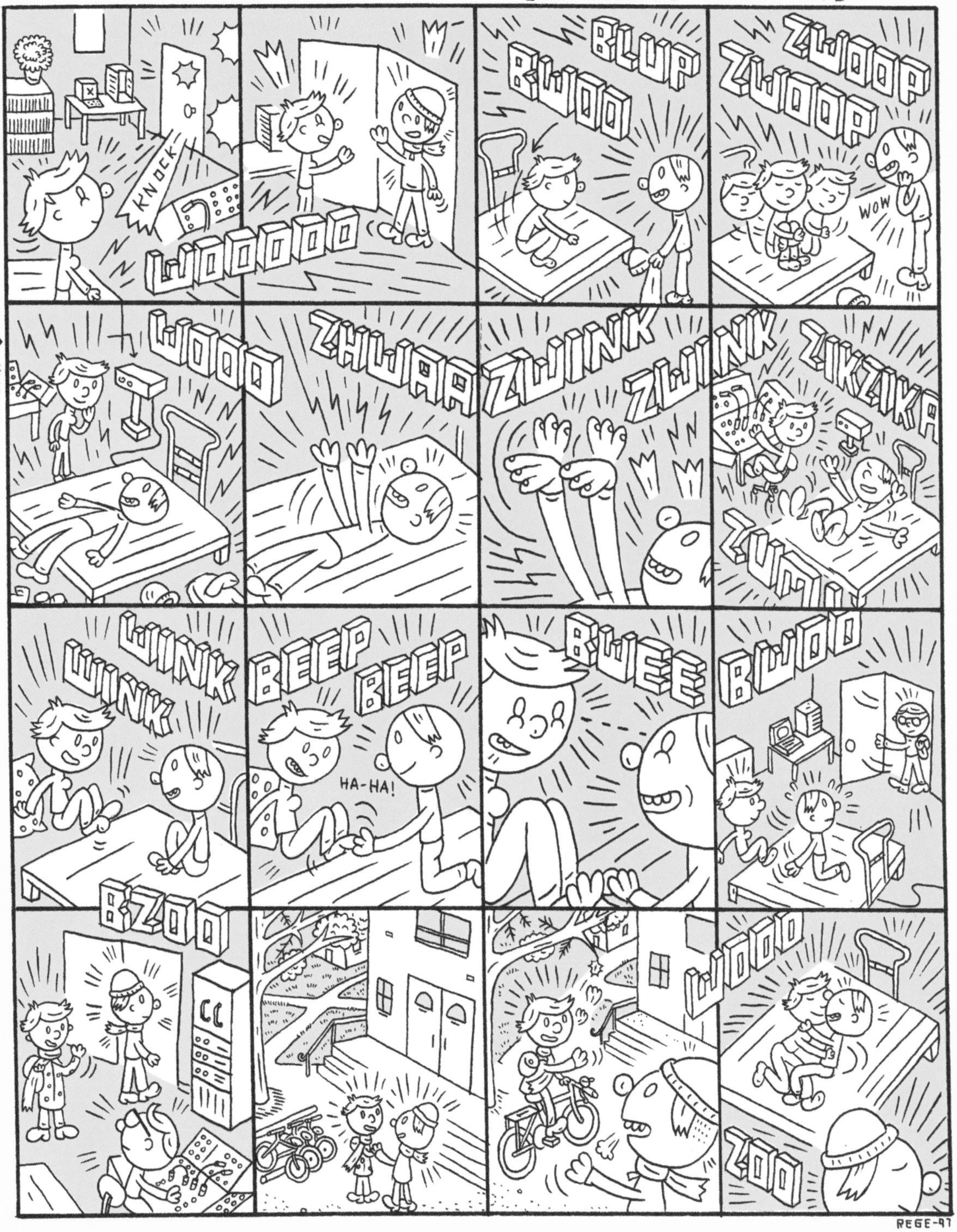
KNOCK
WOOOOOO
BLUP
BWOO
ZWOOP
ZWOOP
WOW
THEREMIN
WOOO
ZHWAA
ZWINK
ZWINK
ZIKZIKA
ZWIN
WINK
WINK
BEEP
BEEP
HA-HA!
BWEE
BWOO
BZOO
CC
WOOO
ZOO
REGE-97

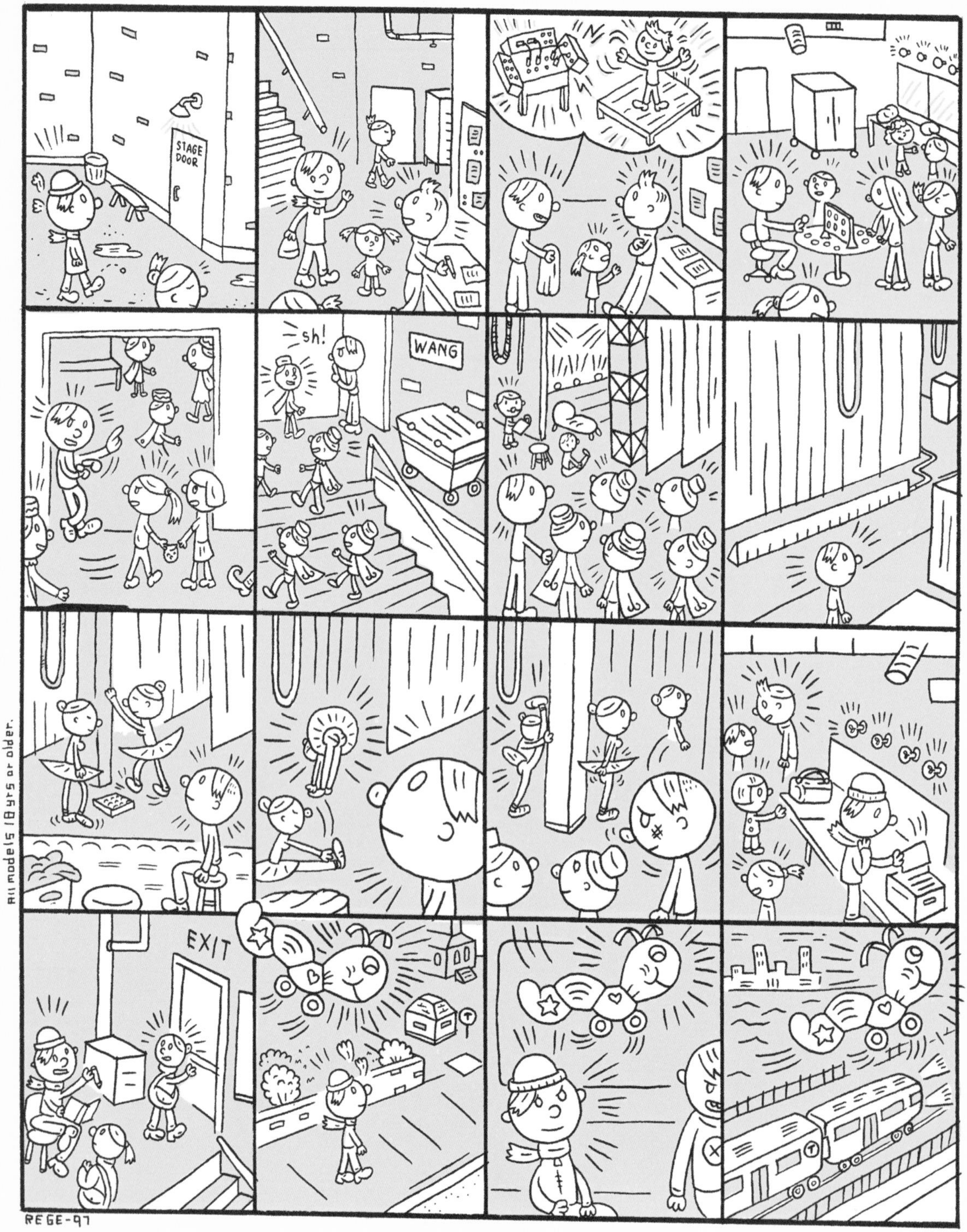
STAGE DOOR
sh!
WANG
EXIT
All models 18 yrs or older.
REGE-97

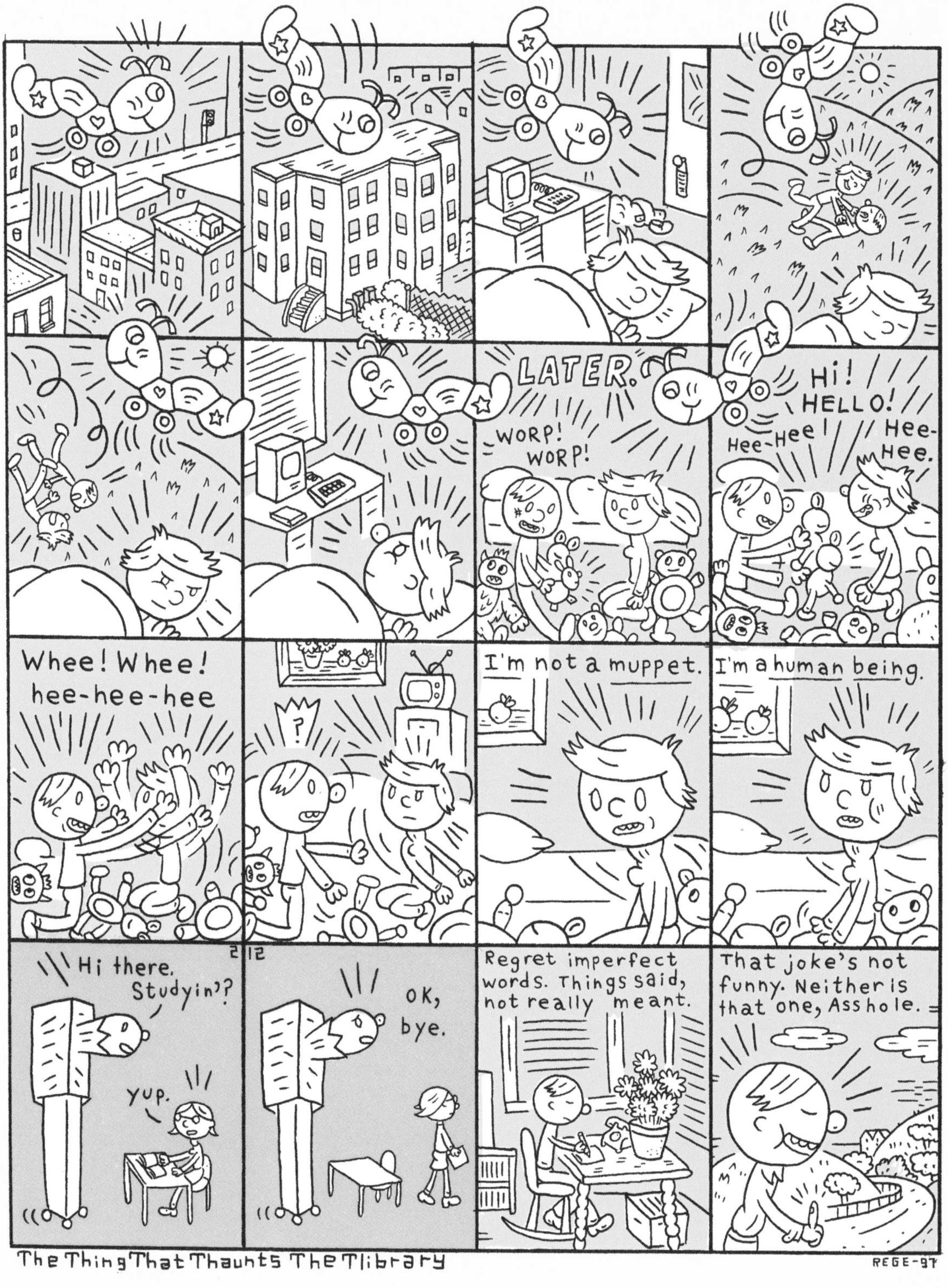
LATER.
WORP! WORP!
Hi! HELLO!
Hee-Hee! Hee-Hee.
Whee! Whee! hee-hee-hee
?
I'm not a muppet.
I'm a human being.
Hi there. Studyin'?
yup.
OK, bye.
Regret imperfect words. Things said, not really meant.
That joke's not funny. Neither is that one, Asshole.

The Thing That Thaunts The Tlibrary

REGE-97

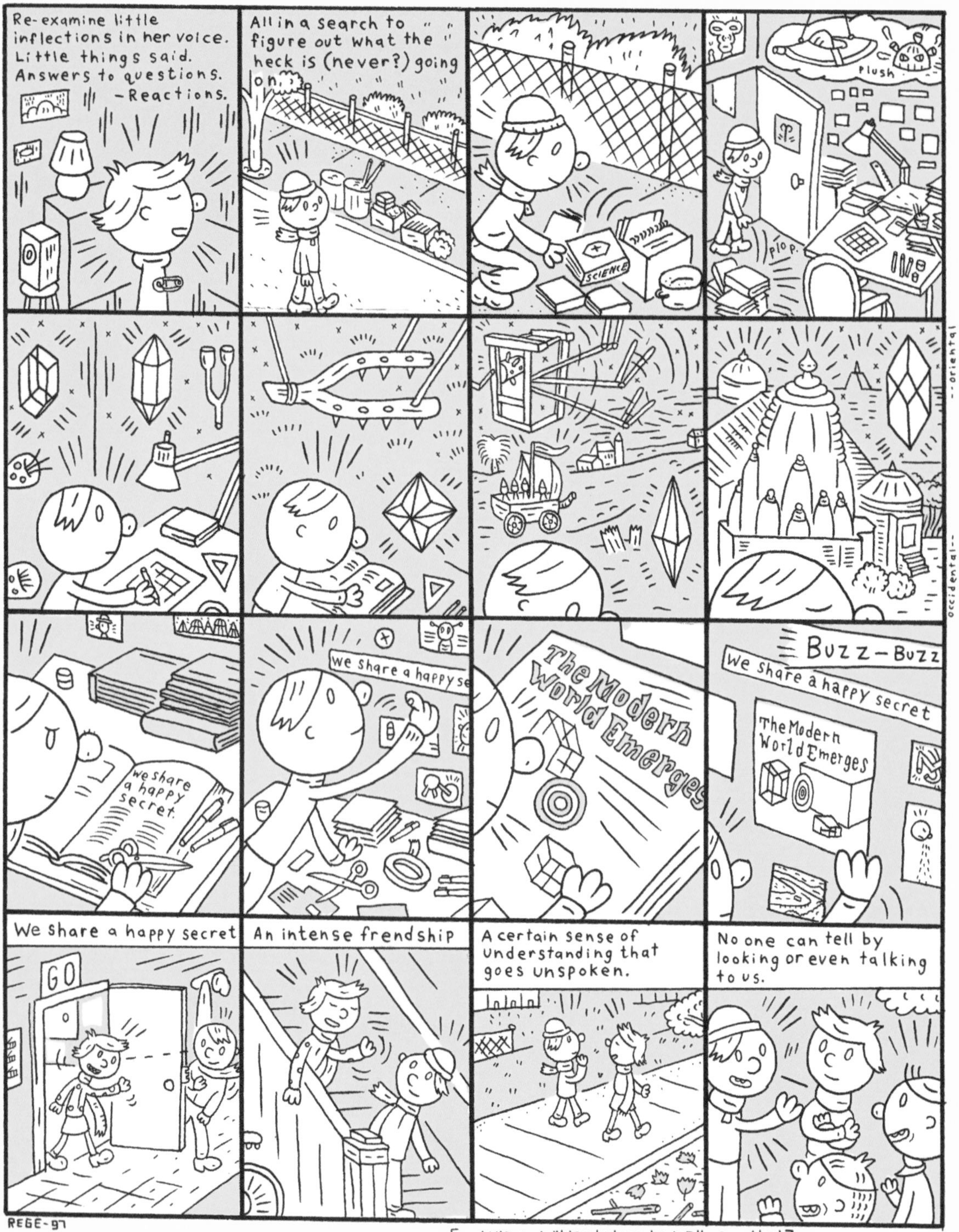
Re-examine little inflections in her voice. Little things said. Answers to questions. —Reactions.
All in a search to figure out what the heck is (never?) going on.
Plush
PloP.
SCIENCE
--oriental--
occidental--
we share a happy secret.
we share a happy se
The Modern World Emerges
BUZZ-BUZZ
We share a happy secret
The Modern World Emerges
We share a happy secret
GO
An intense frendship
A certain sense of understanding that goes unspoken.
No one can tell by looking or even talking to us.
REGE-97
[and it's not "You belong to me"- Fuc that]

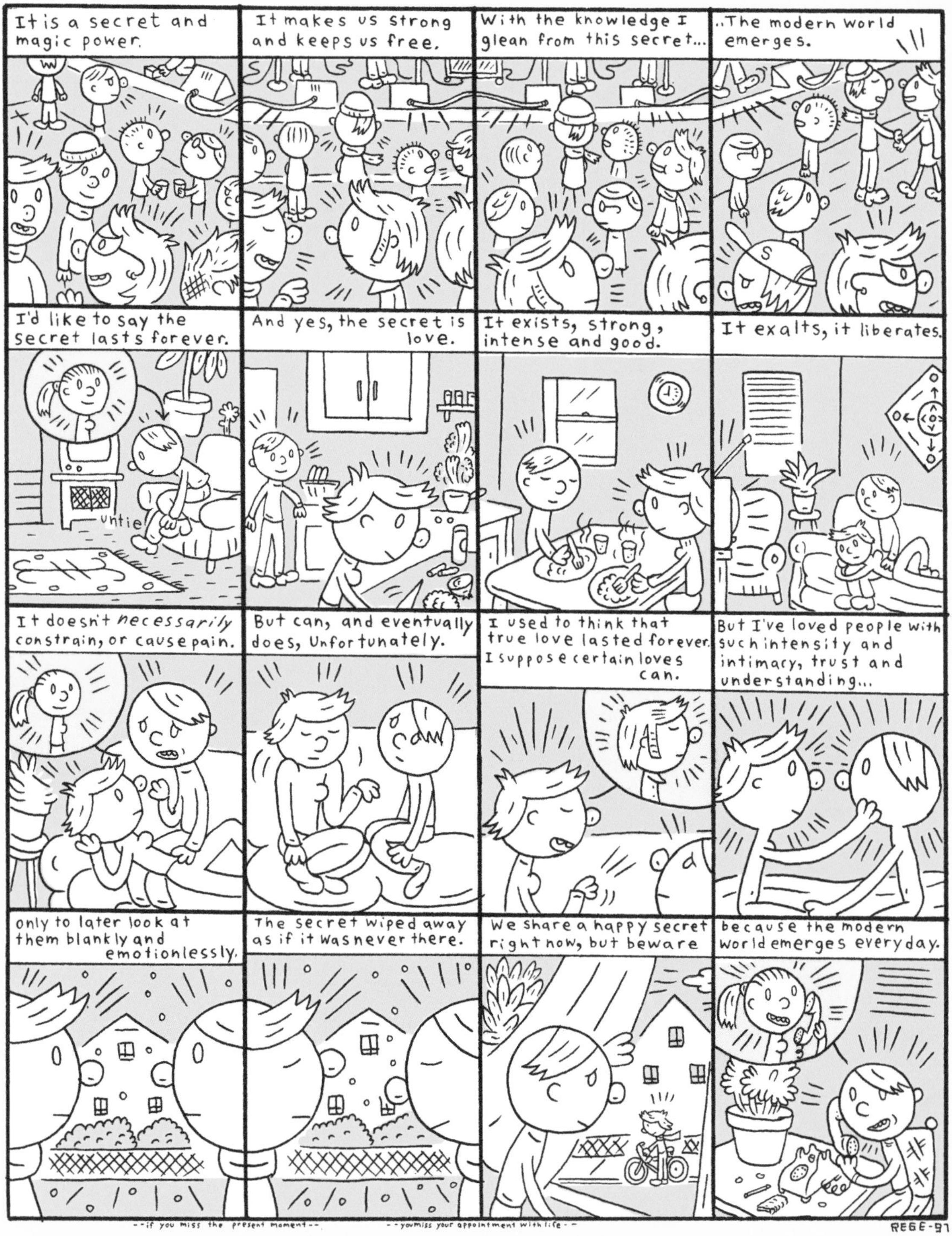
It is a secret and magic power.
It makes us strong and keeps us free.
With the knowledge I glean from this secret...
..The modern world emerges.
I'd like to say the secret lasts forever.
untie!
And yes, the secret is love.
It exists, strong, intense and good.
It exalts, it liberates.
It doesn't *necessarily* constrain, or cause pain.
But can, and eventually does, Unfortunately.
I used to think that true love lasted forever. I suppose certain loves can.
But I've loved people with such intensity and intimacy, trust and understanding...
only to later look at them blankly and emotionlessly.
The secret wiped away as if it was never there.
We share a happy secret right now, but beware
because the modern world emerges everyday.

--if you miss the present moment-- --you miss your appointment with life--

REGE-97

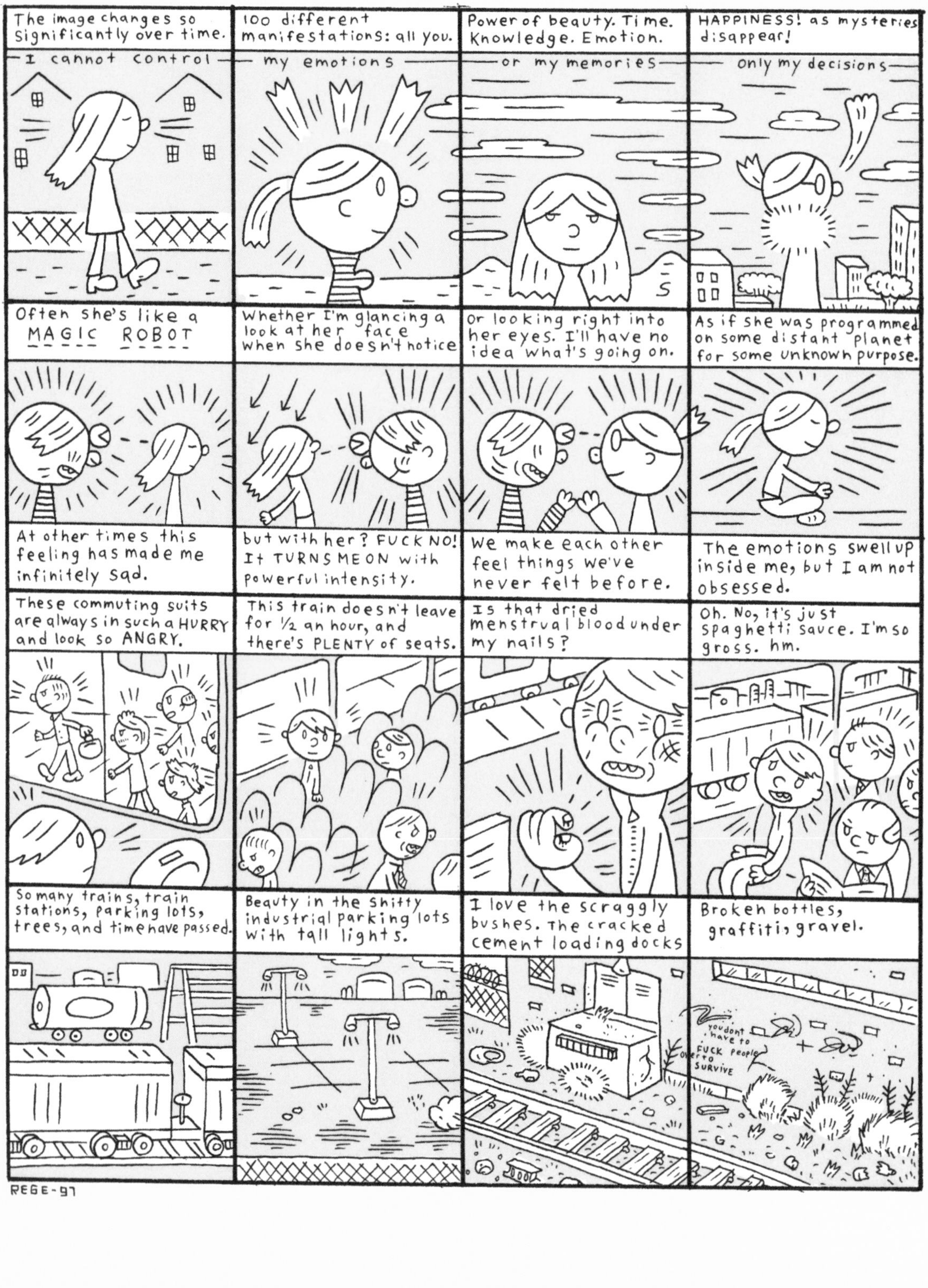

The image changes so significantly over time.
I cannot control
100 different manifestations: all you.
my emotions
Power of beauty. Time. Knowledge. Emotion.
or my memories
HAPPINESS! as mysteries disappear!
only my decisions
Often she's like a MAGIC ROBOT
Whether I'm glancing a look at her face when she doesn't notice
Or looking right into her eyes. I'll have no idea what's going on.
As if she was programmed on some distant planet for some unknown purpose.
At other times this feeling has made me infinitely sad.
but with her? FUCK NO! It TURNS ME ON with powerful intensity.
We make each other feel things we've never felt before.
The emotions swell up inside me, but I am not obsessed.
These commuting suits are always in such a HURRY and look so ANGRY.
This train doesn't leave for ½ an hour, and there's PLENTY of seats.
Is that dried menstrual blood under my nails?
Oh. No, it's just spaghetti sauce. I'm so gross. hm.
So many trains, train stations, parking lots, trees, and time have passed.
Beauty in the shitty industrial parking lots with tall lights.
I love the scraggly bushes. The cracked cement loading docks
Broken bottles, graffiti, gravel.
you dont have to FUCK people over to SURVIVE
REGE-97

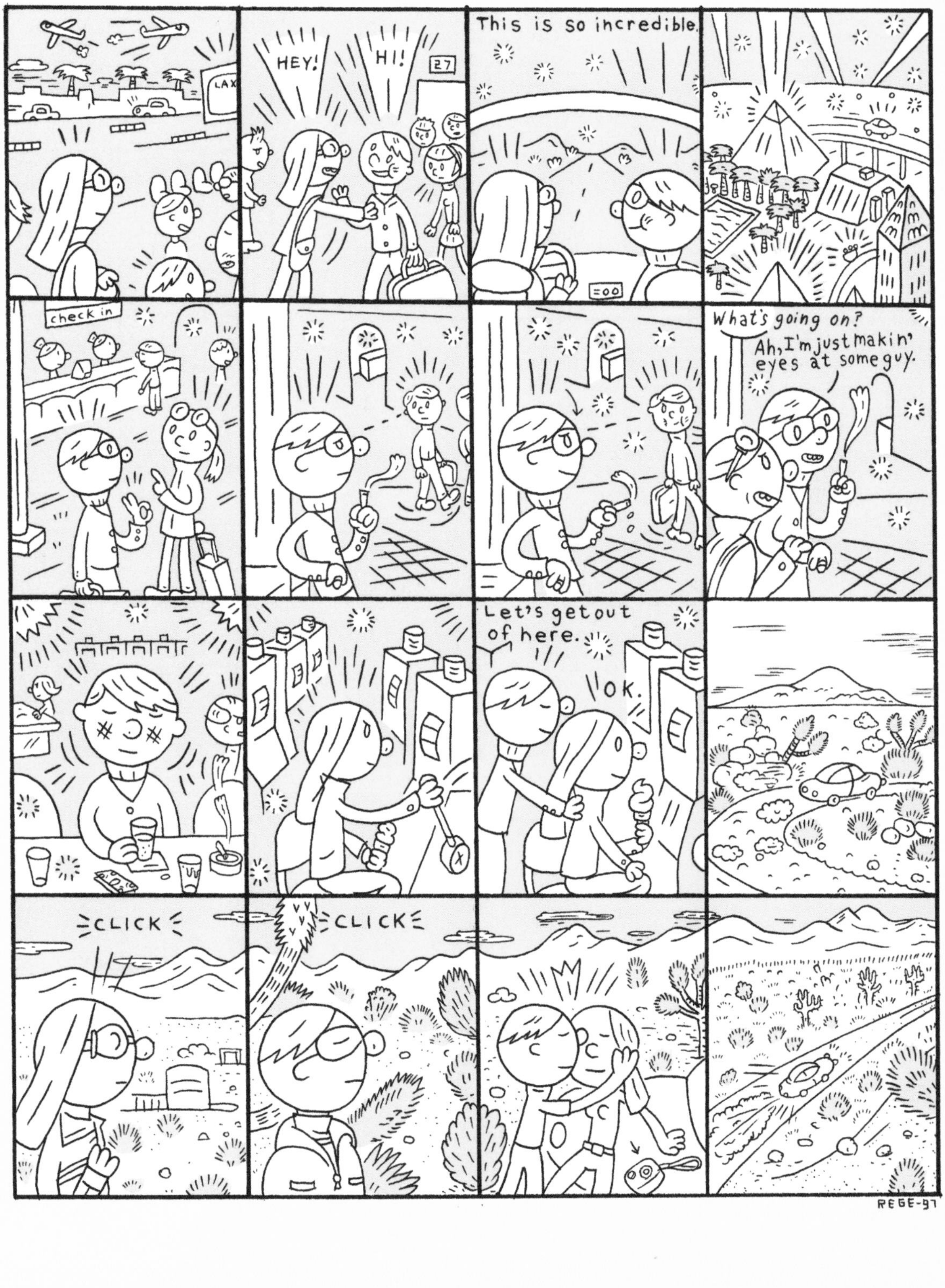
LAX
HEY!
HI!
27
This is so incredible.
check in
What's going on?
Ah, I'm just makin' eyes at some guy.
Let's get out of here.
OK.
CLICK
CLICK
REGE-97

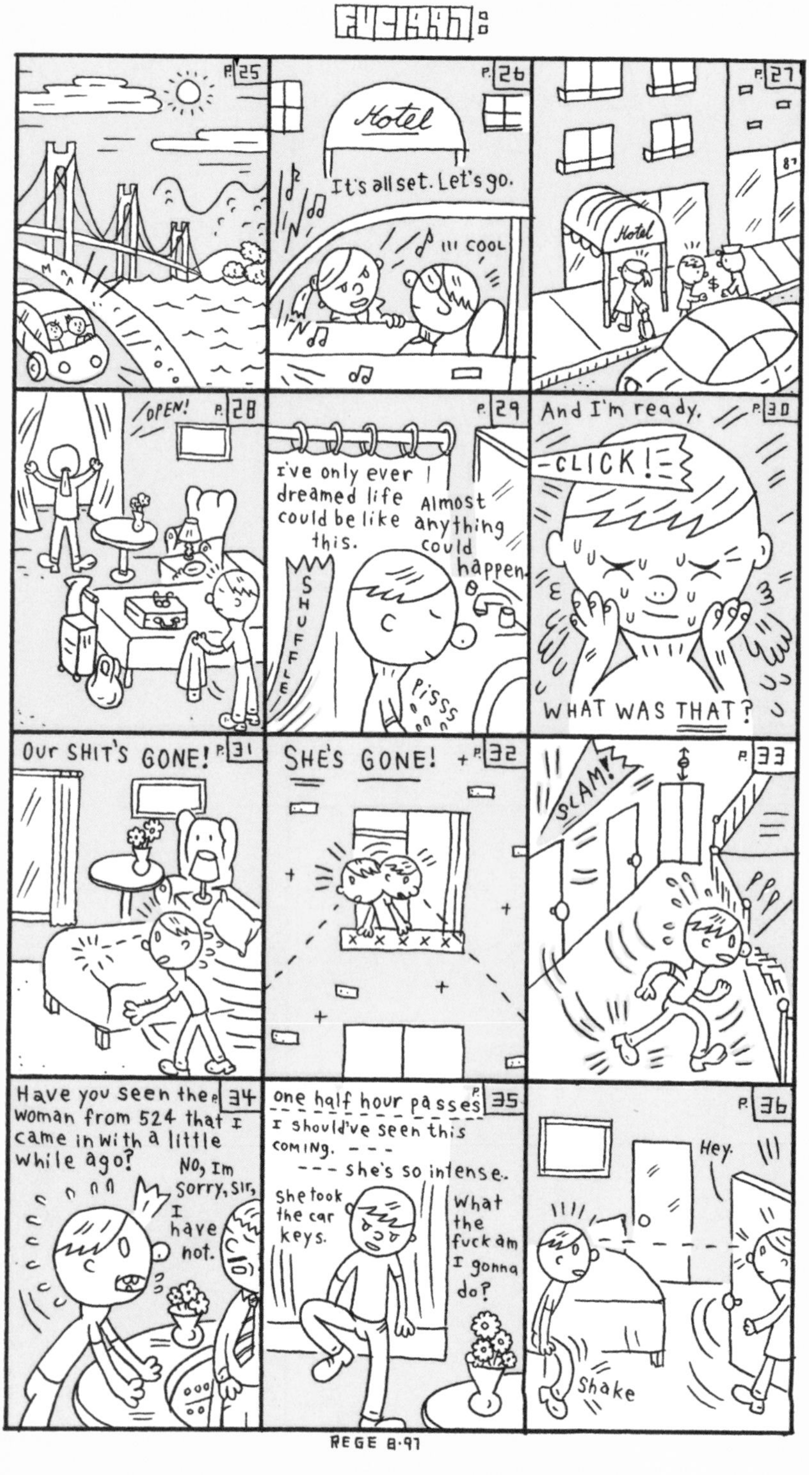
P. 25
P. 26
Motel
It's all set. Let's go.
COOL
P. 27
Motel
87
OPEN!
P. 28
P. 29
I've only ever dreamed life could be like this.
Almost anything could happen.
SHUFFLE
PISSS
And I'm ready.
P. 30
CLICK!
WHAT WAS THAT?
Our SHIT'S GONE!
P. 31
SHE'S GONE!
P. 32
SLAM!
P. 33
Have you seen the woman from 524 that I came in with a little while ago?
P. 34
No, Im sorry, sir, I have not.
one half hour passes
P. 35
I should've seen this coming. --- --- she's so intense.
She took the car keys.
What the fuck am I gonna do?
P. 36
Hey.
Shake
REGE 8·97

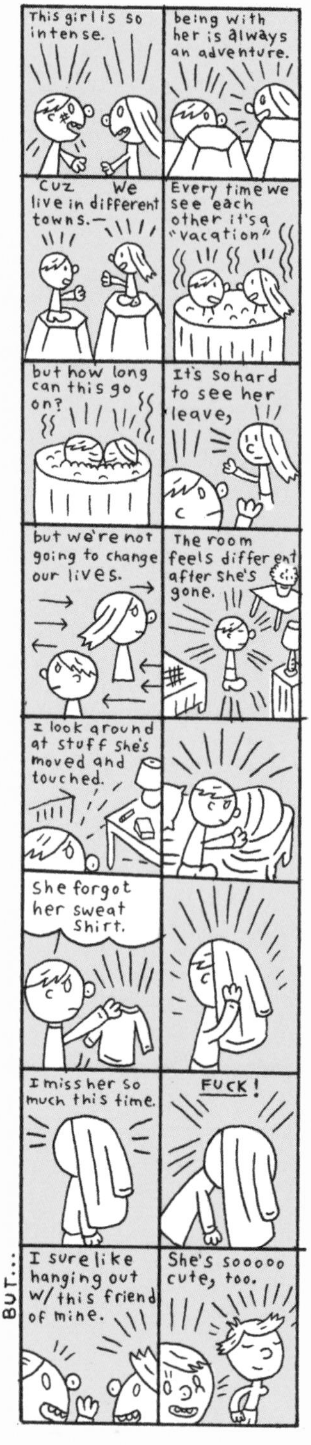
This girl is so intense.
being with her is always an adventure.
Cuz we live in different towns.—
Every time we see each other it's a "vacation"
but how long can this go on?
It's so hard to see her leave,
but we're not going to change our lives.
The room feels different after she's gone.
I look around at stuff she's moved and touched.
She forgot her sweat shirt.
I miss her so much this time.
FUCK!
BUT...
I sure like hanging out w/ this friend of mine.
She's sooooo cute, too.

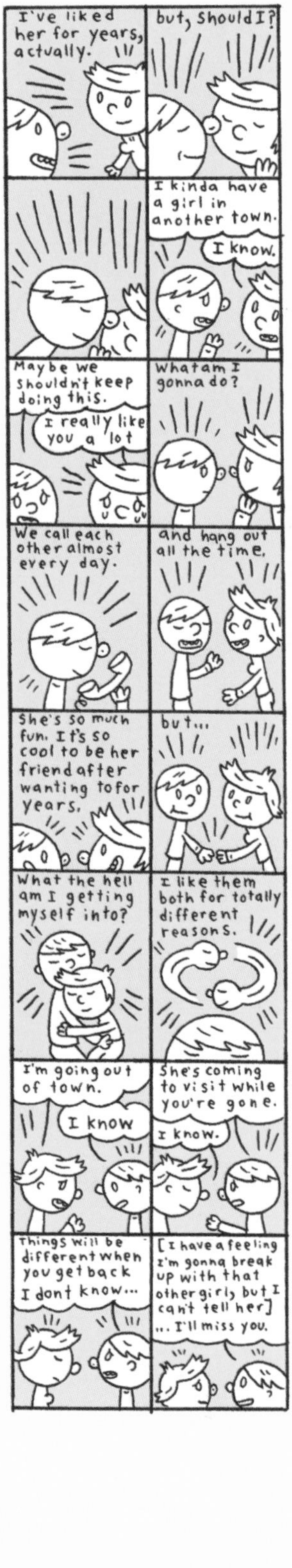
I've liked her for years, actually.
but, Should I?
I kinda have a girl in another town.
I know.
Maybe we shouldn't keep doing this.
I really like you a lot
What am I gonna do?
We call each other almost every day.
and hang out all the time.
She's so much fun. It's so cool to be her friend after wanting to for years.
but...
What the hell am I getting myself into?
I like them both for totally different reasons.
I'm going out of town.
I know
She's coming to visit while you're gone.
I know.
Things will be different when you get back
I dont know...
[I have a feeling I'm gonna break up with that other girl, but I can't tell her]
... I'll miss you.

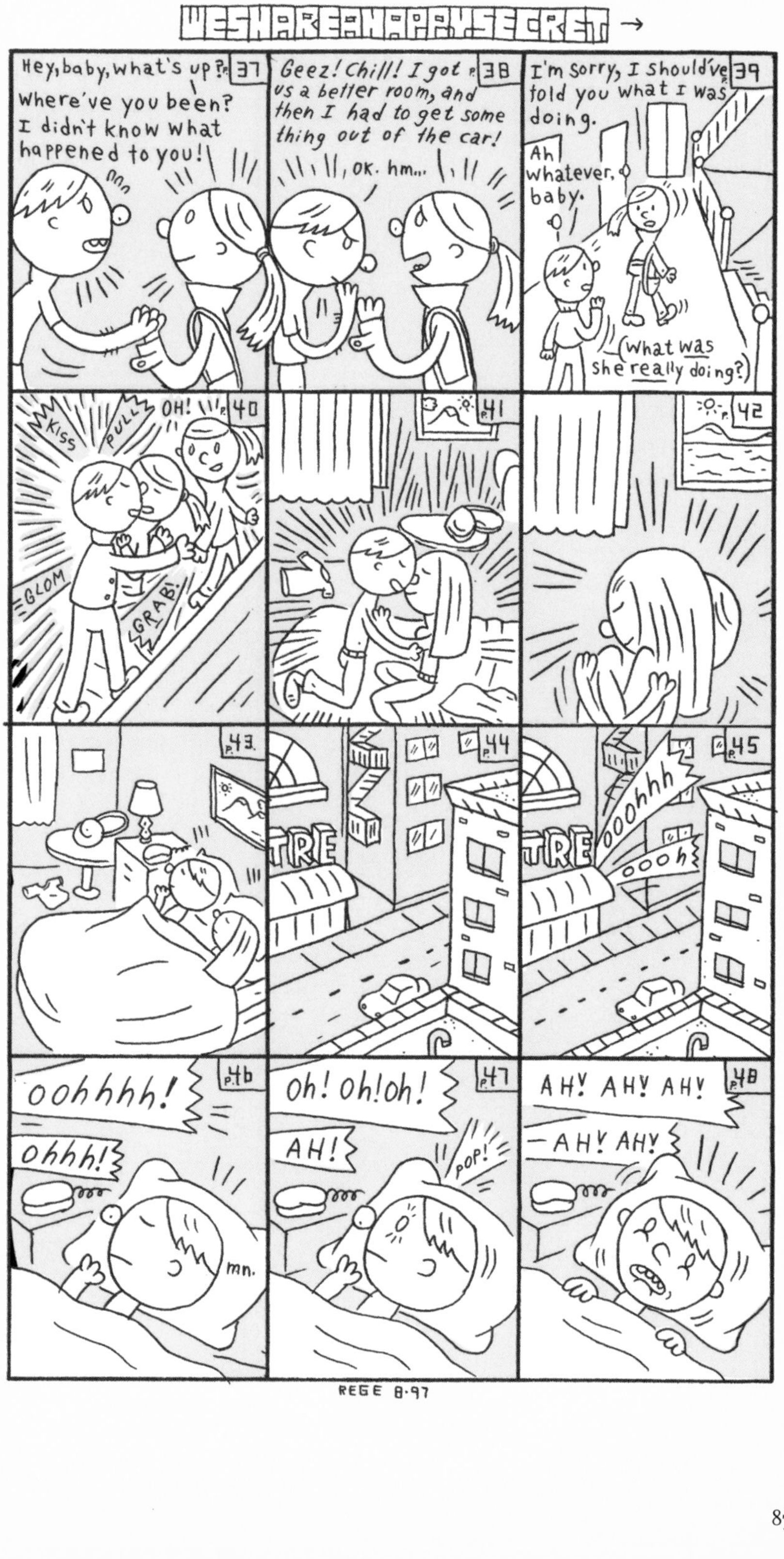
WE SHARE A HAPPY SECRET →
P. 37
Hey, baby, what's up?
Where've you been? I didn't know what happened to you!
P. 38
Geez! Chill! I got us a better room, and then I had to get some thing out of the car!
OK. hm...
P. 39
I'm sorry, I should've told you what I was doing.
Ah whatever, baby.
(What was she really doing?)
P. 40
KISS
PULL
OH!
GLOM
GRAB!
P. 41
P. 42
P. 43
P. 44
TRE
P. 45
TRE
ooohhh
oooh
P. 46
oohhhh!
ohhh!
mn.
P. 47
Oh! Oh! Oh!
AH!
POP!
P. 48
AH! AH! AH!
AH! AH!
REGE 8·97

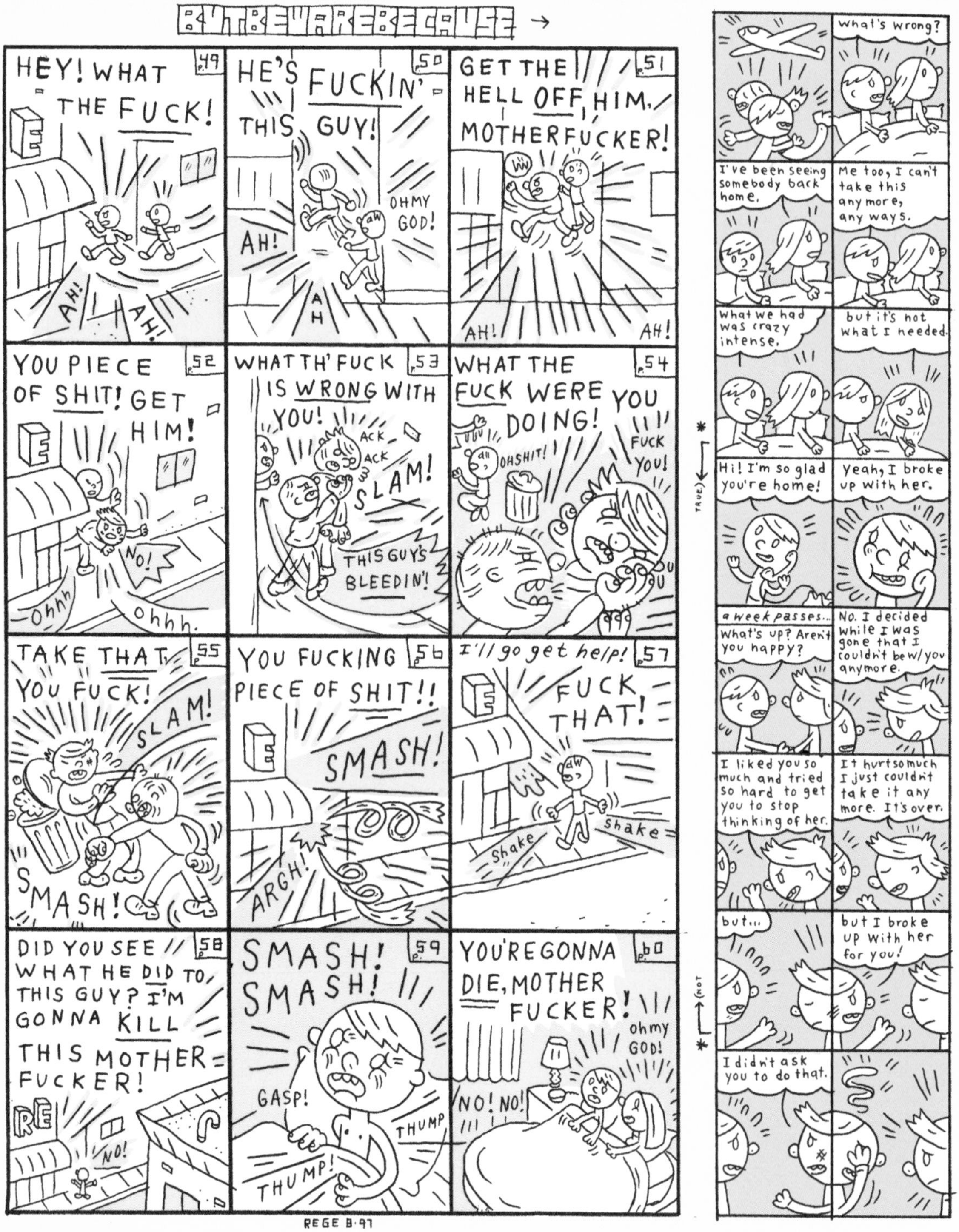
BUTBEWAREBECAUSE →
HEY! WHAT THE FUCK!
49
AH!
AH!
HE'S FUCKIN' THIS GUY!
50
OHMY GOD!
AH!
AH
GET THE HELL OFF HIM, MOTHERFUCKER!
51
AH!
AH!
YOU PIECE OF SHIT! GET HIM!
52
NO!
Ohhh
Ohhh.
WHAT TH' FUCK IS WRONG WITH YOU!
53
ACK ACK
SLAM!
THIS GUY'S BLEEDIN'!
WHAT THE FUCK WERE YOU DOING!
54
OHSHIT!
FUCK YOU!
TAKE THAT YOU FUCK!
55
SLAM!
SMASH!
YOU FUCKING PIECE OF SHIT!!
56
SMASH!
ARGH!
I'll go get help!
57
FUCK THAT!
shake
shake
DID YOU SEE WHAT HE DID TO THIS GUY? I'M GONNA KILL THIS MOTHER FUCKER!
58
NO!
SMASH! SMASH!
59
GASP!
THUMP
THUMP!
YOU'RE GONNA DIE, MOTHER FUCKER!
60
ohmy GOD!
NO! NO!
REGE B·97
What's wrong?
I've been seeing somebody back home.
Me too, I can't take this anymore, any ways.
What we had was crazy intense.
but it's not what I needed.
Hi! I'm so glad you're home!
Yeah, I broke up with her.
a week passes...
What's up? Aren't you happy?
No. I decided while I was gone that I couldn't be w/you anymore.
I liked you so much and tried so hard to get you to stop thinking of her.
It hurts so much I just couldn't take it any more. It's over.
but...
but I broke up with her for you!
I didn't ask you to do that.

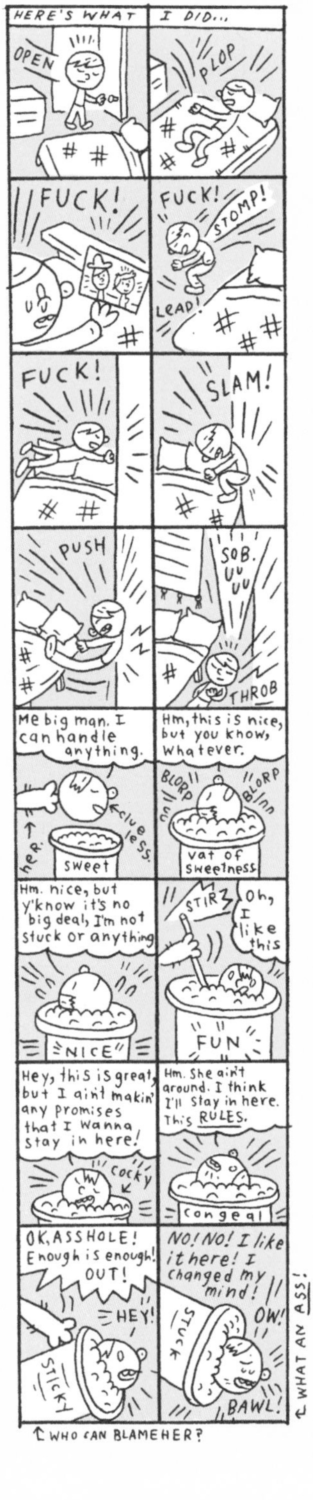
HERE'S WHAT I DID...
OPEN
PLOP
FUCK!
FUCK!
STOMP!
LEAD!
FUCK!
SLAM!
PUSH
SOB.
THROB
Me big man. I can handle anything.
clueless
her
sweet
Hm, this is nice, but you know, whatever.
BLORP
BLORP
vat of sweetness
Hm. nice, but y'know it's no big deal, I'm not stuck or anything
NICE
STIR
Oh, I like this
FUN
Hey, this is great, but I ain't makin' any promises that I wanna stay in here!
COCKY
Hm. She ain't around. I think I'll stay in here. This RULES.
congeal
OK, ASSHOLE! Enough is enough! OUT!
HEY!
STICKY
NO! NO! I like it here! I changed my mind!
OW!
STUCK
BAWL!
WHAT AN ASS!
WHO CAN BLAME HER?

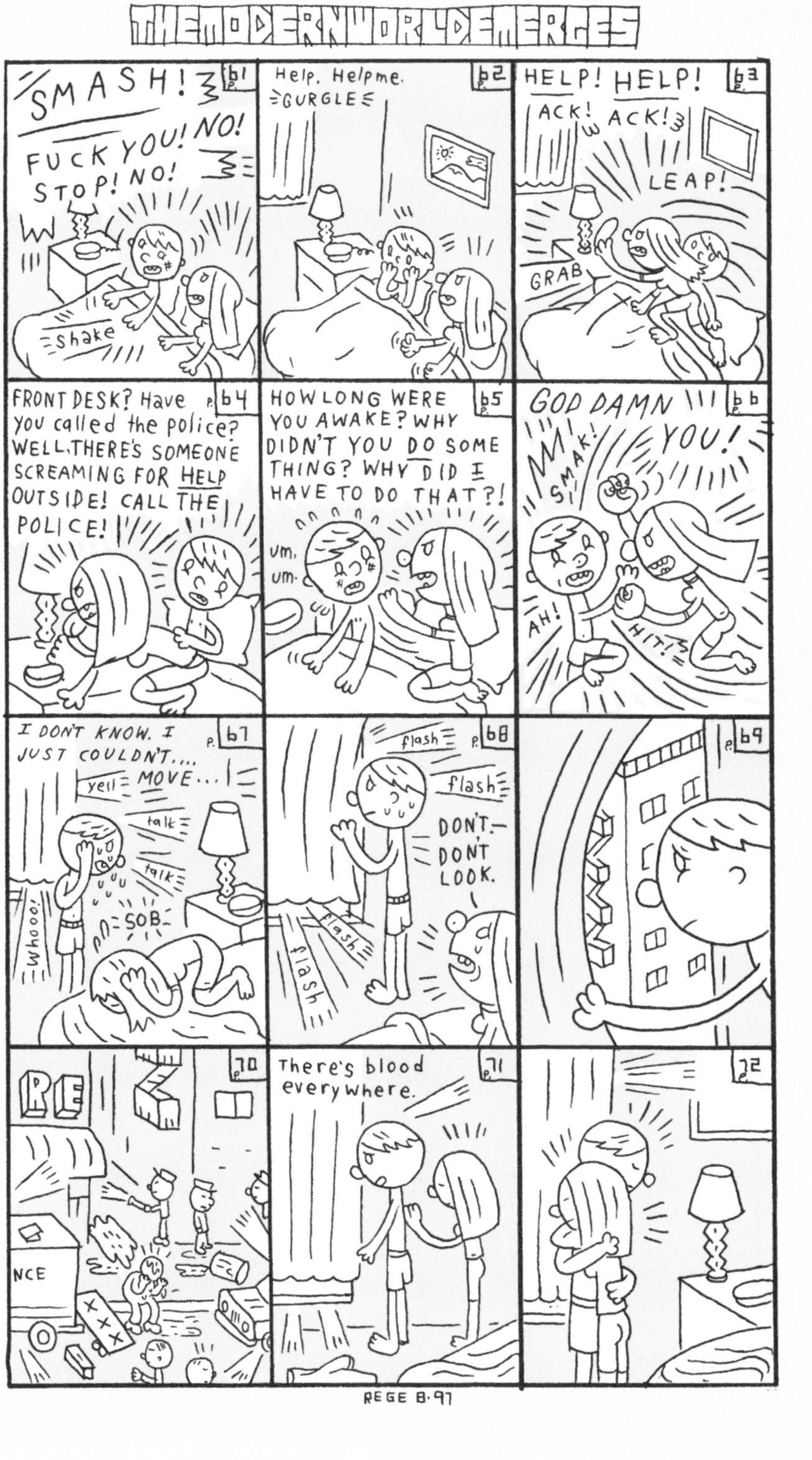
THE MODERN WORLD EMERGES
SMASH!
FUCK YOU! NO! STOP! NO!
shake
Help. Helpme.
GURGLE
HELP! HELP!
ACK! ACK!
LEAP!
GRAB
FRONT DESK? Have you called the police? WELL, THERE'S SOMEONE SCREAMING FOR HELP OUTSIDE! CALL THE POLICE!
HOW LONG WERE YOU AWAKE? WHY DIDN'T YOU DO SOMETHING? WHY DID I HAVE TO DO THAT?!
um. um.
GOD DAMN YOU!
SMAK!
AH!
HIT!
I DON'T KNOW. I JUST COULDN'T.... MOVE...
yell
talk
talk
SOB
whooo!
flash
flash
DON'T. DON'T LOOK.
flash
flash
RE
NCE
There's blood everywhere.
REGE 8·97

--EPILOGUE--

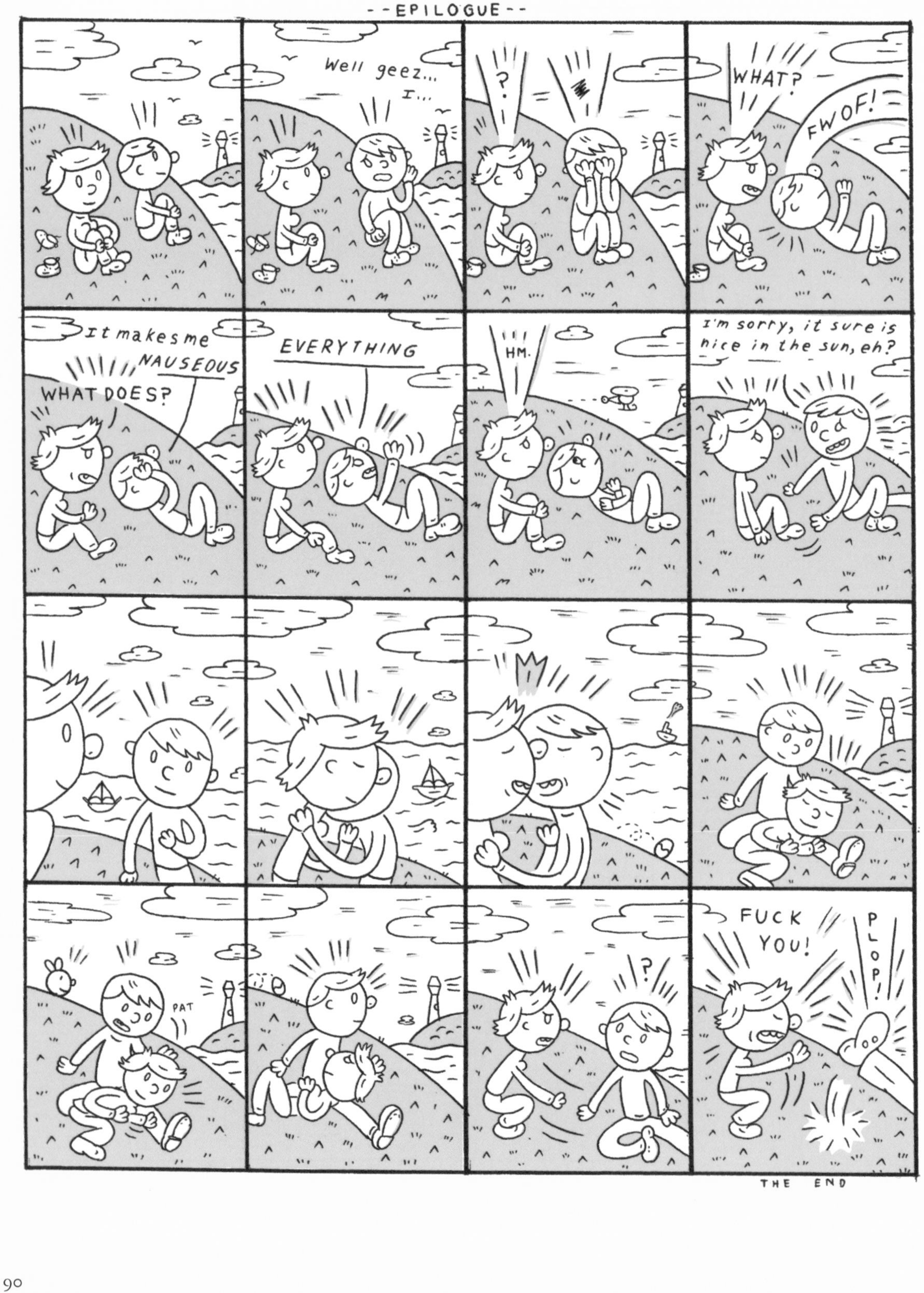
Well geez... I...
?
WHAT?
FWOF!
It makes me NAUSEOUS
WHAT DOES?
EVERYTHING
HM.
I'm sorry, it sure is nice in the sun, eh?
PAT
?
FUCK YOU!
PLOP!

THE END

COUNTRY ROADS - BRIGHTON

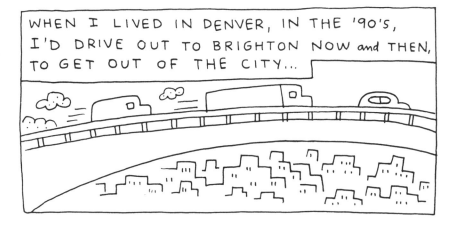

WHEN I LIVED IN DENVER, IN THE '90'S, I'D DRIVE OUT TO BRIGHTON NOW and THEN, TO GET OUT OF THE CITY...

DOWN URBAN STREETS, EMPTY INDUSTRIAL STREETS — TO COUNTRY ROADS, and THE WIDE SKY

PAST THE FARMS and FIELDS, and THE GUY SELLING HONEY OUT OF HIS PICKUP TRUCK ON THE SIDE OF THE ROAD...

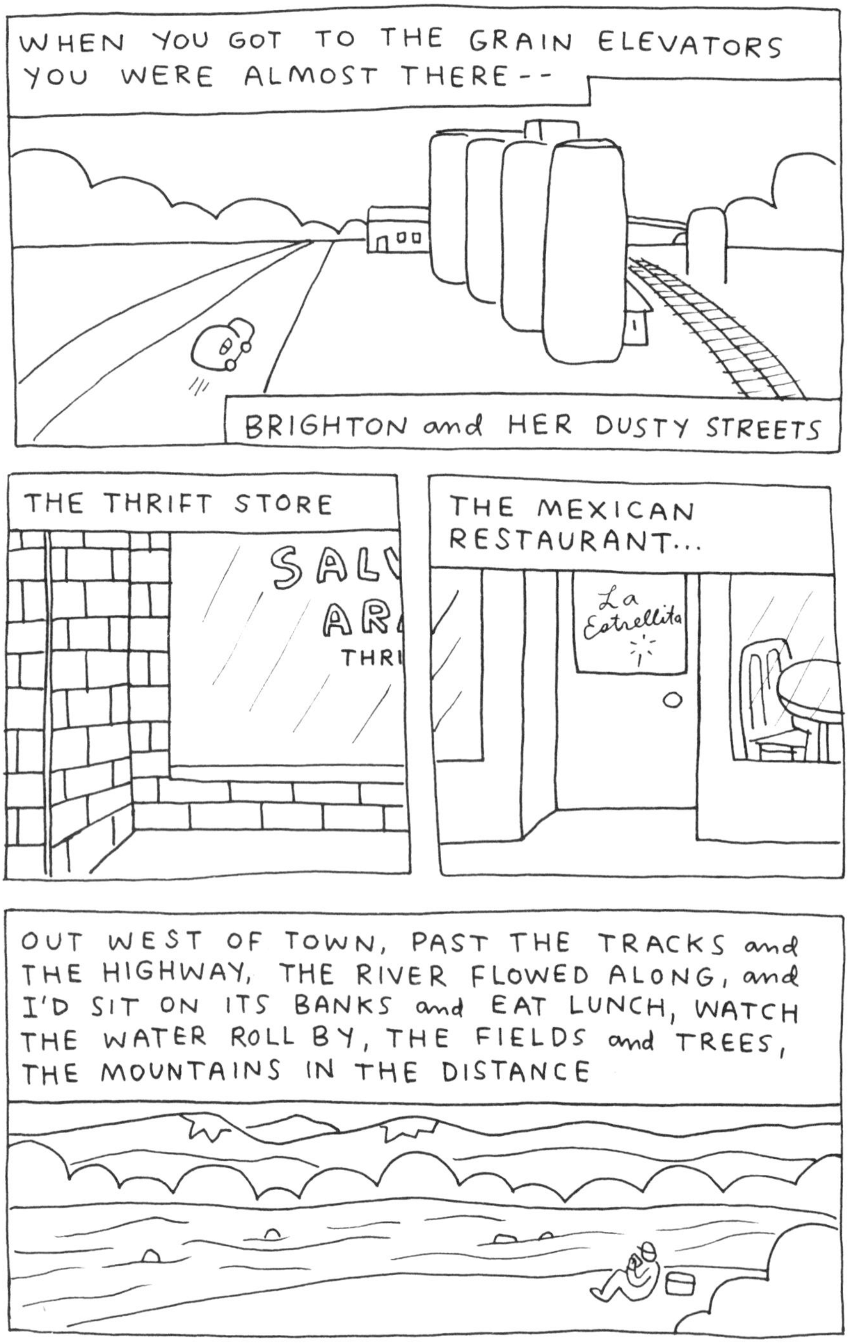
WHEN YOU GOT TO THE GRAIN ELEVATORS YOU WERE ALMOST THERE--
BRIGHTON and HER DUSTY STREETS
THE THRIFT STORE
SAL
AR
THR
THE MEXICAN RESTAURANT...
La Estrellita
OUT WEST OF TOWN, PAST THE TRACKS and THE HIGHWAY, THE RIVER FLOWED ALONG, and I'D SIT ON ITS BANKS and EAT LUNCH, WATCH THE WATER ROLL BY, THE FIELDS and TREES, THE MOUNTAINS IN THE DISTANCE

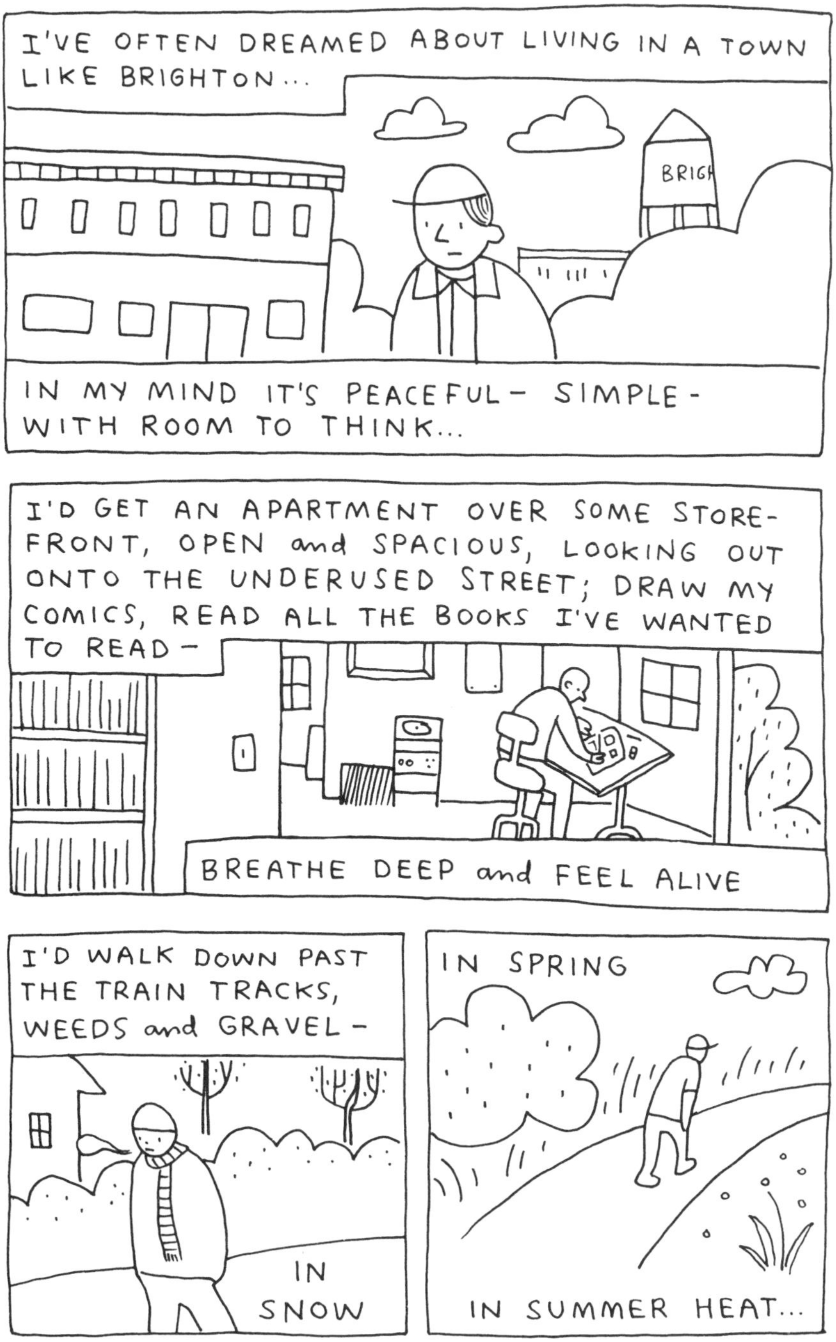
I'VE OFTEN DREAMED ABOUT LIVING IN A TOWN LIKE BRIGHTON...
BRIGH
IN MY MIND IT'S PEACEFUL- SIMPLE- WITH ROOM TO THINK...
I'D GET AN APARTMENT OVER SOME STORE-FRONT, OPEN and SPACIOUS, LOOKING OUT ONTO THE UNDERUSED STREET; DRAW MY COMICS, READ ALL THE BOOKS I'VE WANTED TO READ-
BREATHE DEEP and FEEL ALIVE
I'D WALK DOWN PAST THE TRAIN TRACKS, WEEDS and GRAVEL-
IN SNOW
IN SPRING
IN SUMMER HEAT...

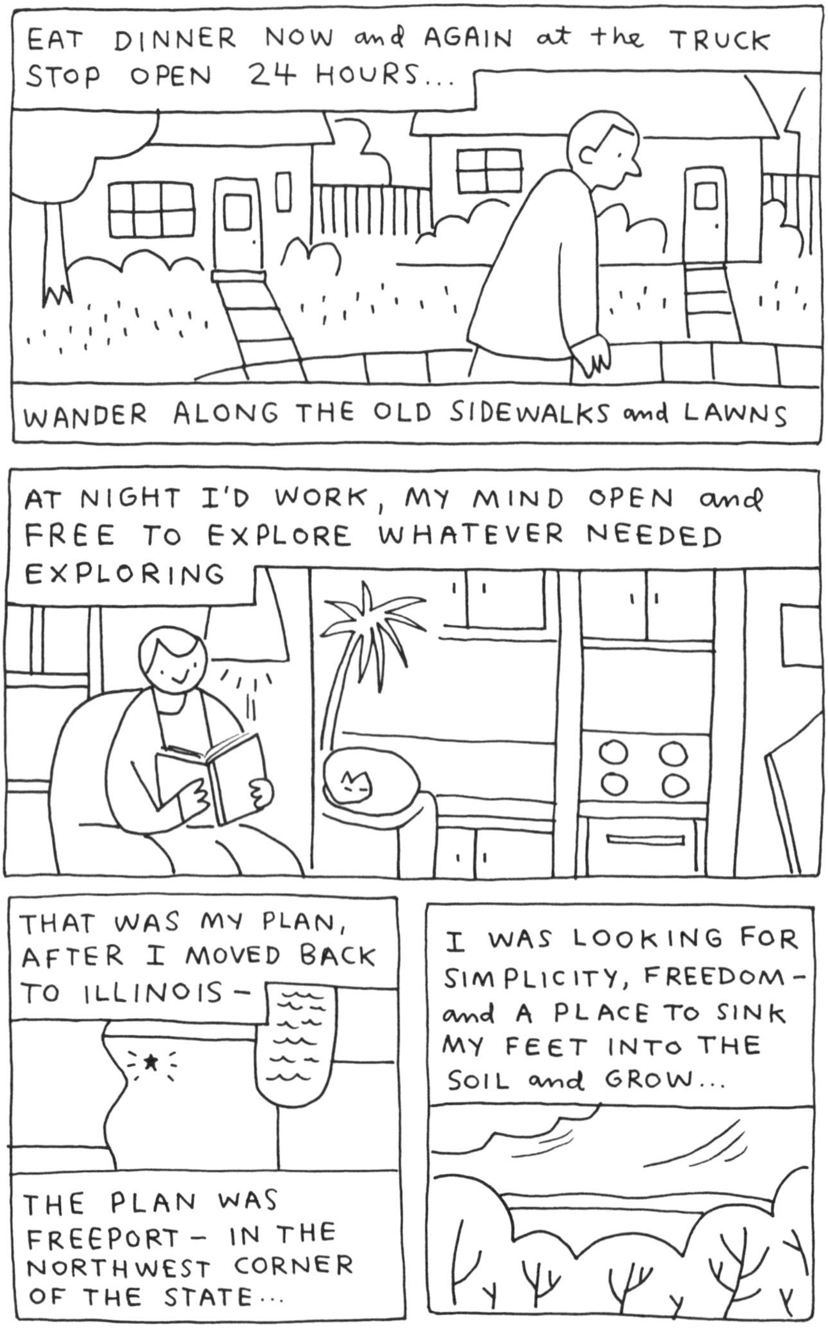
EAT DINNER NOW and AGAIN at the TRUCK STOP OPEN 24 HOURS...
WANDER ALONG THE OLD SIDEWALKS and LAWNS
AT NIGHT I'D WORK, MY MIND OPEN and FREE TO EXPLORE WHATEVER NEEDED EXPLORING
THAT WAS MY PLAN, AFTER I MOVED BACK TO ILLINOIS –
THE PLAN WAS FREEPORT – IN THE NORTHWEST CORNER OF THE STATE...
I WAS LOOKING FOR SIMPLICITY, FREEDOM – and A PLACE TO SINK MY FEET INTO THE SOIL and GROW...

SOME CHEAP, QUIET PLACE WHERE I COULD LIVE, SIMPLY, and WORK; DO THE THINGS THAT REALLY MATTERED TO ME

FEEL FREE and EASY

IT DIDN'T WORK OUT THAT WAY...

2/25/05
8/7/05 J.P.

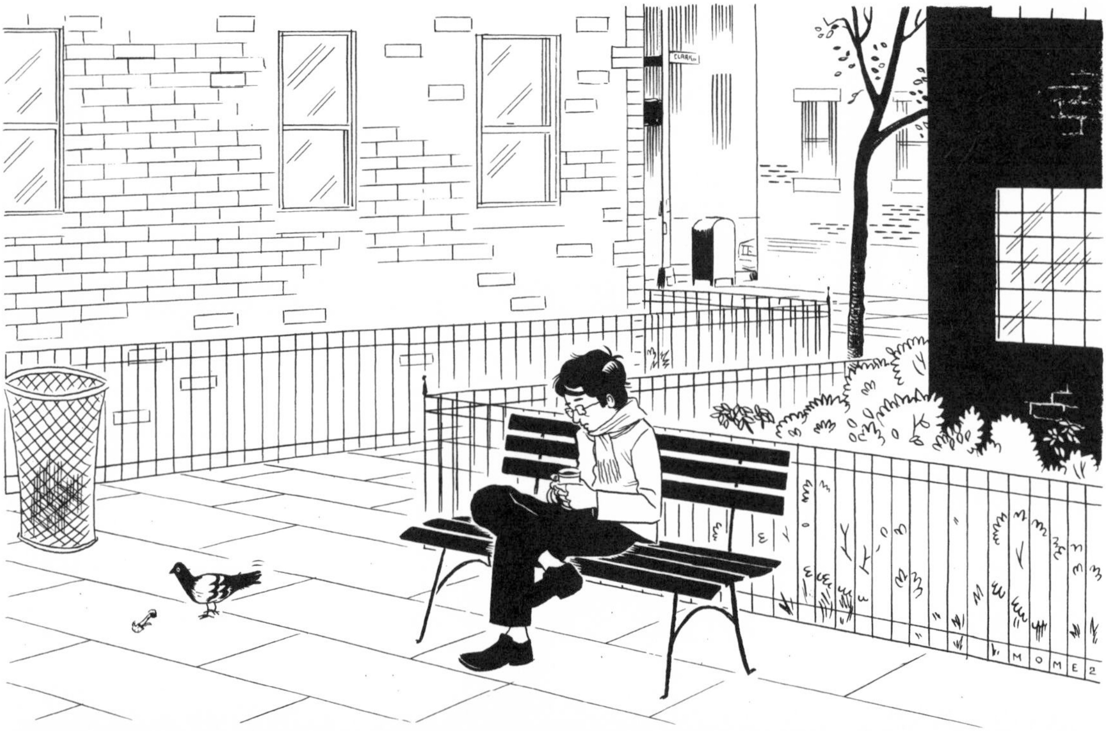
CLARK
MOME 2

needles and pins

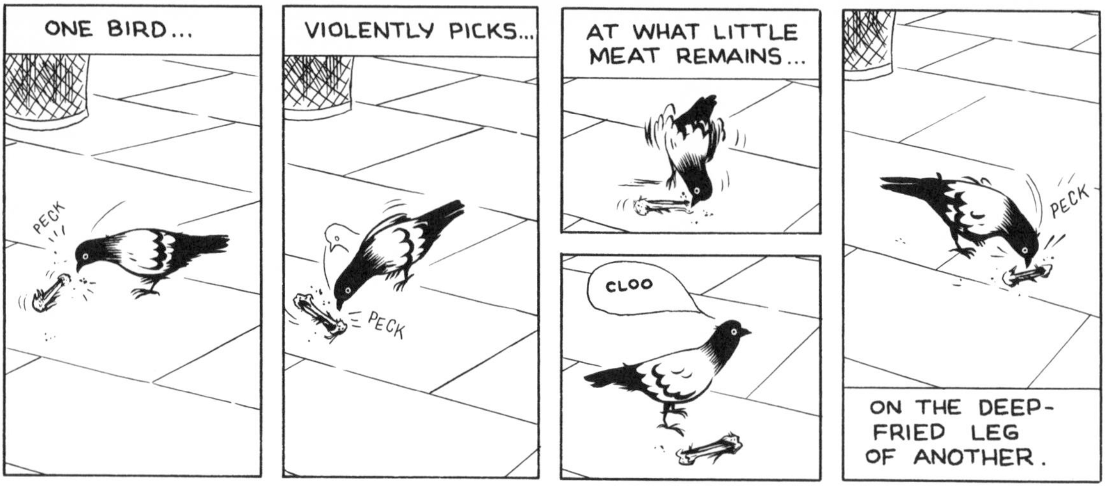
ONE BIRD...
PECK
VIOLENTLY PICKS...
PECK
AT WHAT LITTLE MEAT REMAINS...
CLOO
PECK
ON THE DEEP-FRIED LEG OF ANOTHER.

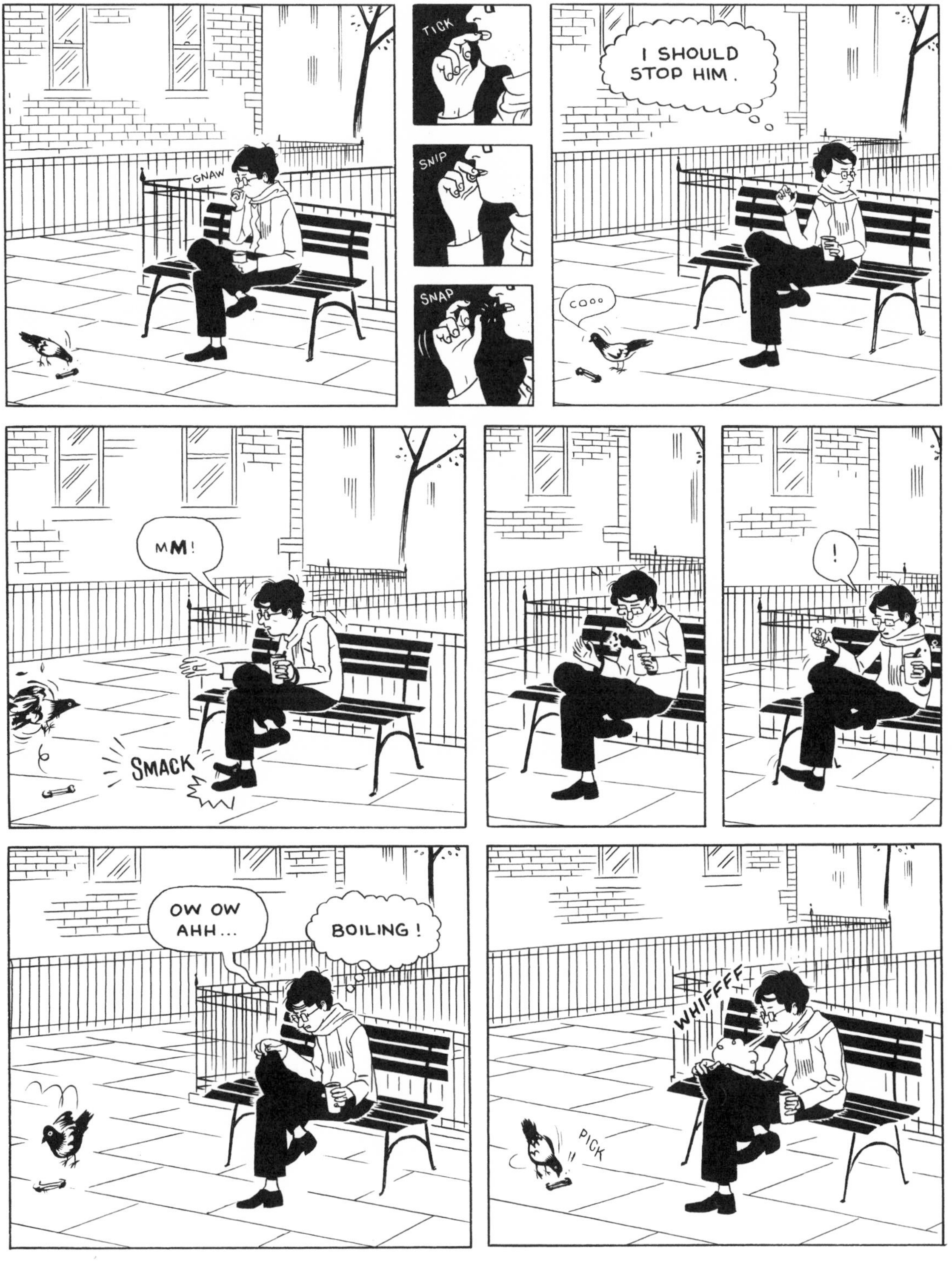
GNAW
TICK
SNIP
SNAP
I SHOULD STOP HIM.
COOO
MM!
SMACK
!
OW OW AHH...
BOILING!
WHIFFFF
PICK

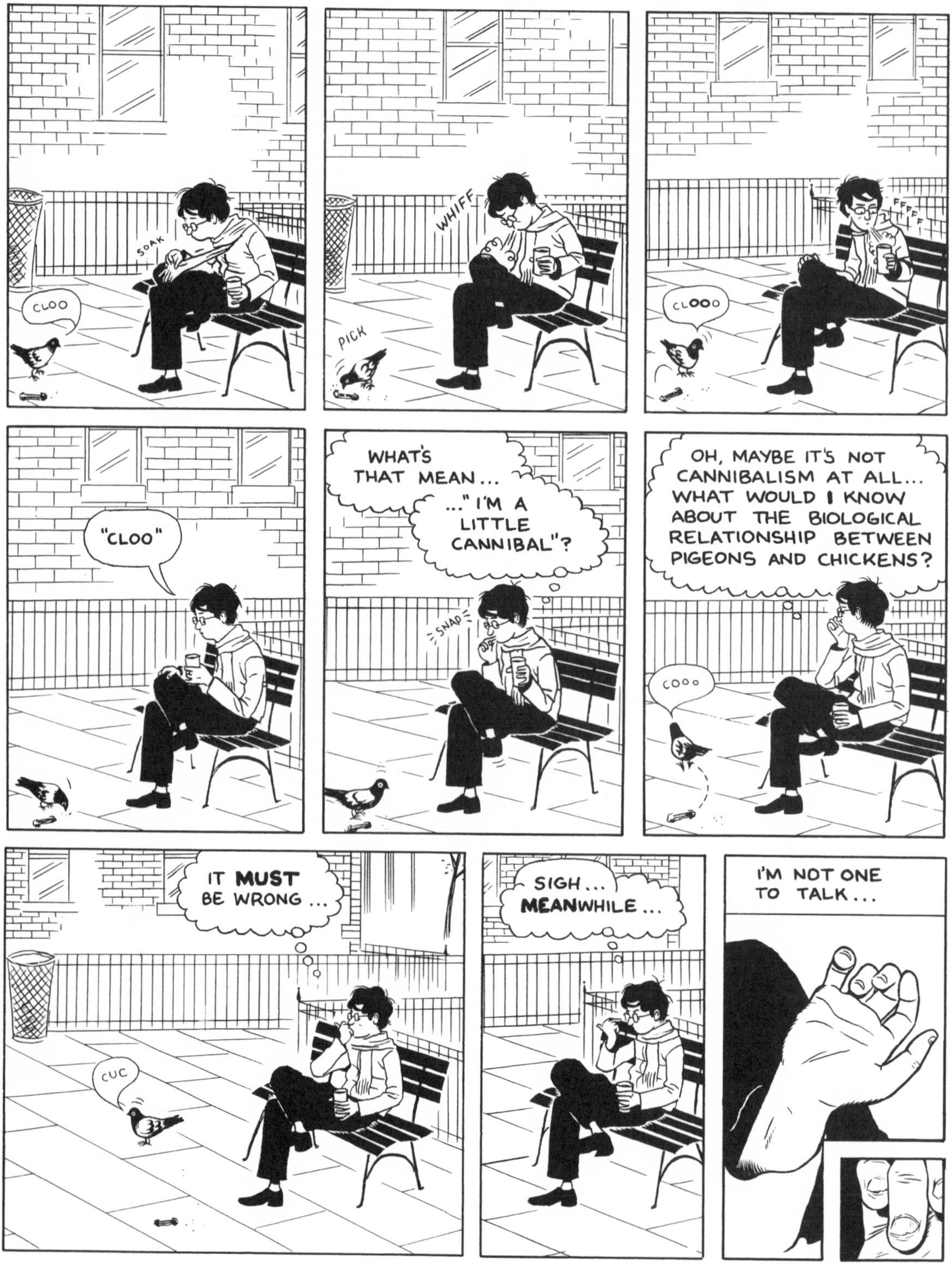
SOAK
CLOO
WHIFF
PICK
FFFFF
CLOOO
"CLOO"
WHAT'S THAT MEAN...
..." I'M A LITTLE CANNIBAL"?
SNAP
OH, MAYBE IT'S NOT CANNIBALISM AT ALL... WHAT WOULD I KNOW ABOUT THE BIOLOGICAL RELATIONSHIP BETWEEN PIGEONS AND CHICKENS?
COOO
IT MUST BE WRONG...
CUC
SIGH... MEANWHILE...
I'M NOT ONE TO TALK...

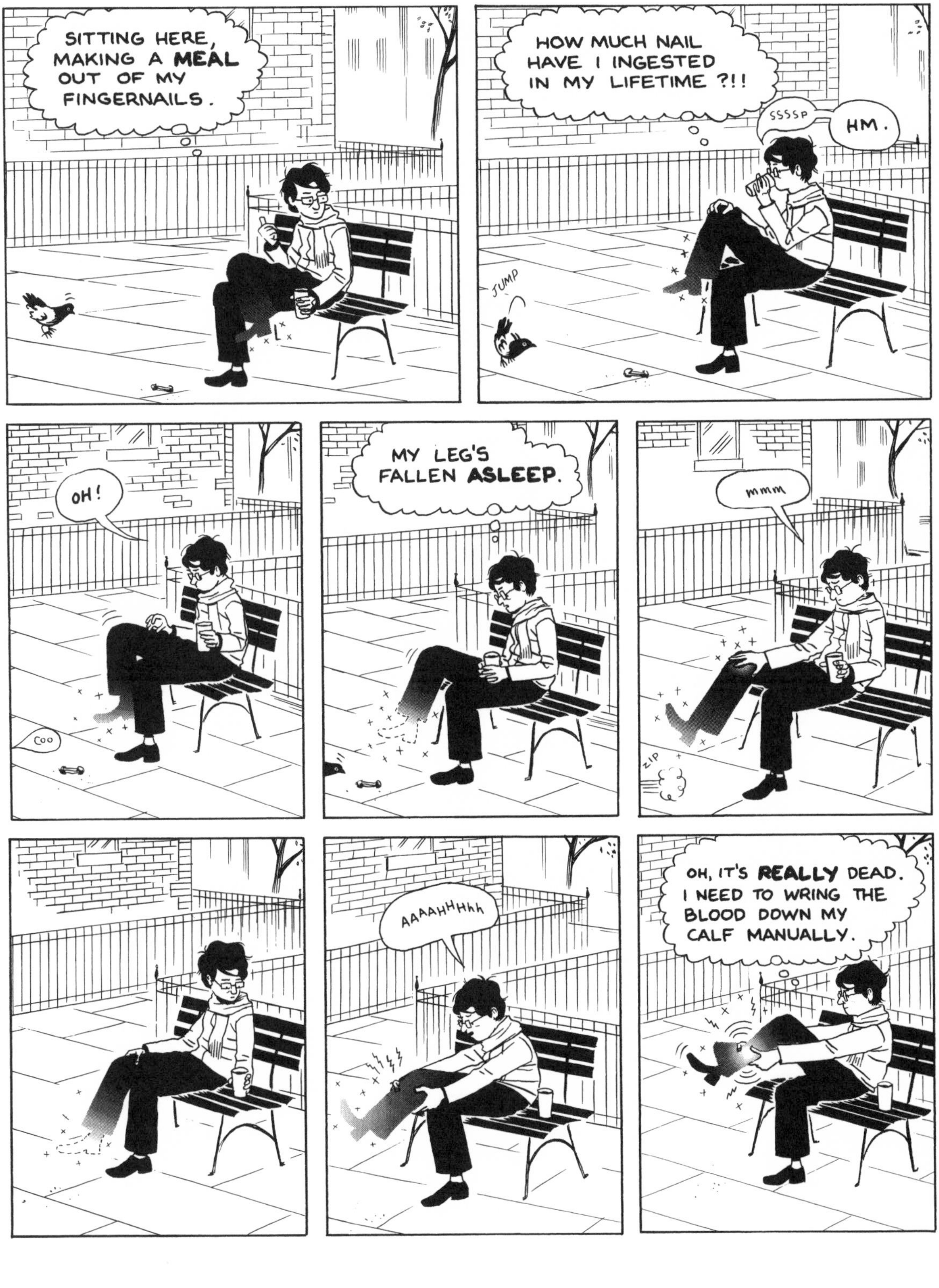
SITTING HERE, MAKING A **MEAL** OUT OF MY FINGERNAILS.
HOW MUCH NAIL HAVE I INGESTED IN MY LIFETIME ?!!
SSSSP
HM.
JUMP
OH!
COO
MY LEG'S FALLEN **ASLEEP**.
mmm
ZIP
AAAAHHhhh
OH, IT'S **REALLY** DEAD. I NEED TO WRING THE BLOOD DOWN MY CALF MANUALLY.

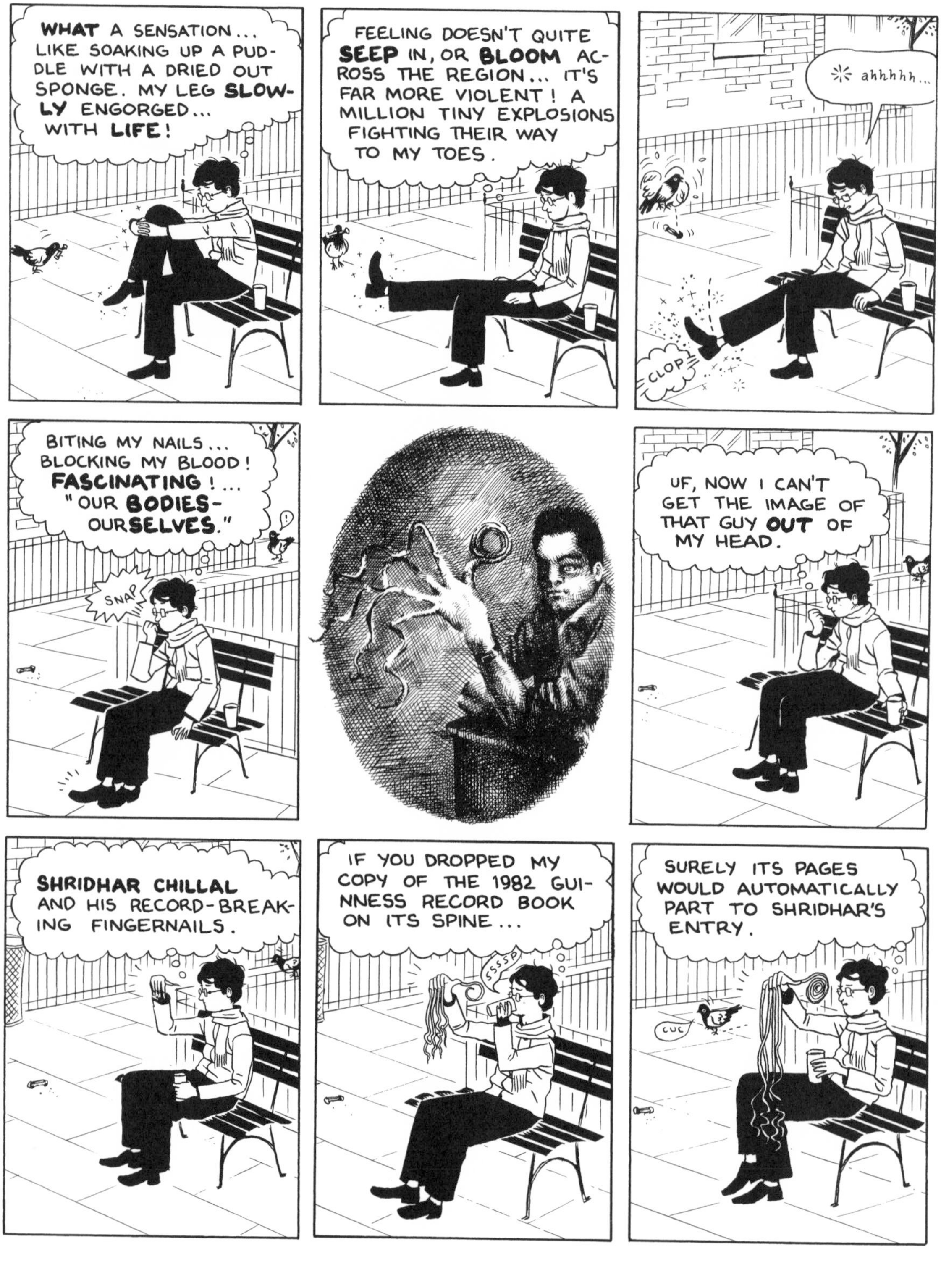
WHAT A SENSATION... LIKE SOAKING UP A PUDDLE WITH A DRIED OUT SPONGE. MY LEG SLOWLY ENGORGED... WITH LIFE!
FEELING DOESN'T QUITE SEEP IN, OR BLOOM ACROSS THE REGION... IT'S FAR MORE VIOLENT! A MILLION TINY EXPLOSIONS FIGHTING THEIR WAY TO MY TOES.
ahhhhh...
CLOP
BITING MY NAILS... BLOCKING MY BLOOD! FASCINATING!... "OUR BODIES-OURSELVES."
SNAP
UF, NOW I CAN'T GET THE IMAGE OF THAT GUY OUT OF MY HEAD.
SHRIDHAR CHILLAL AND HIS RECORD-BREAKING FINGERNAILS.
IF YOU DROPPED MY COPY OF THE 1982 GUINNESS RECORD BOOK ON ITS SPINE...
SSSSP
SURELY ITS PAGES WOULD AUTOMATICALLY PART TO SHRIDHAR'S ENTRY.
CUC

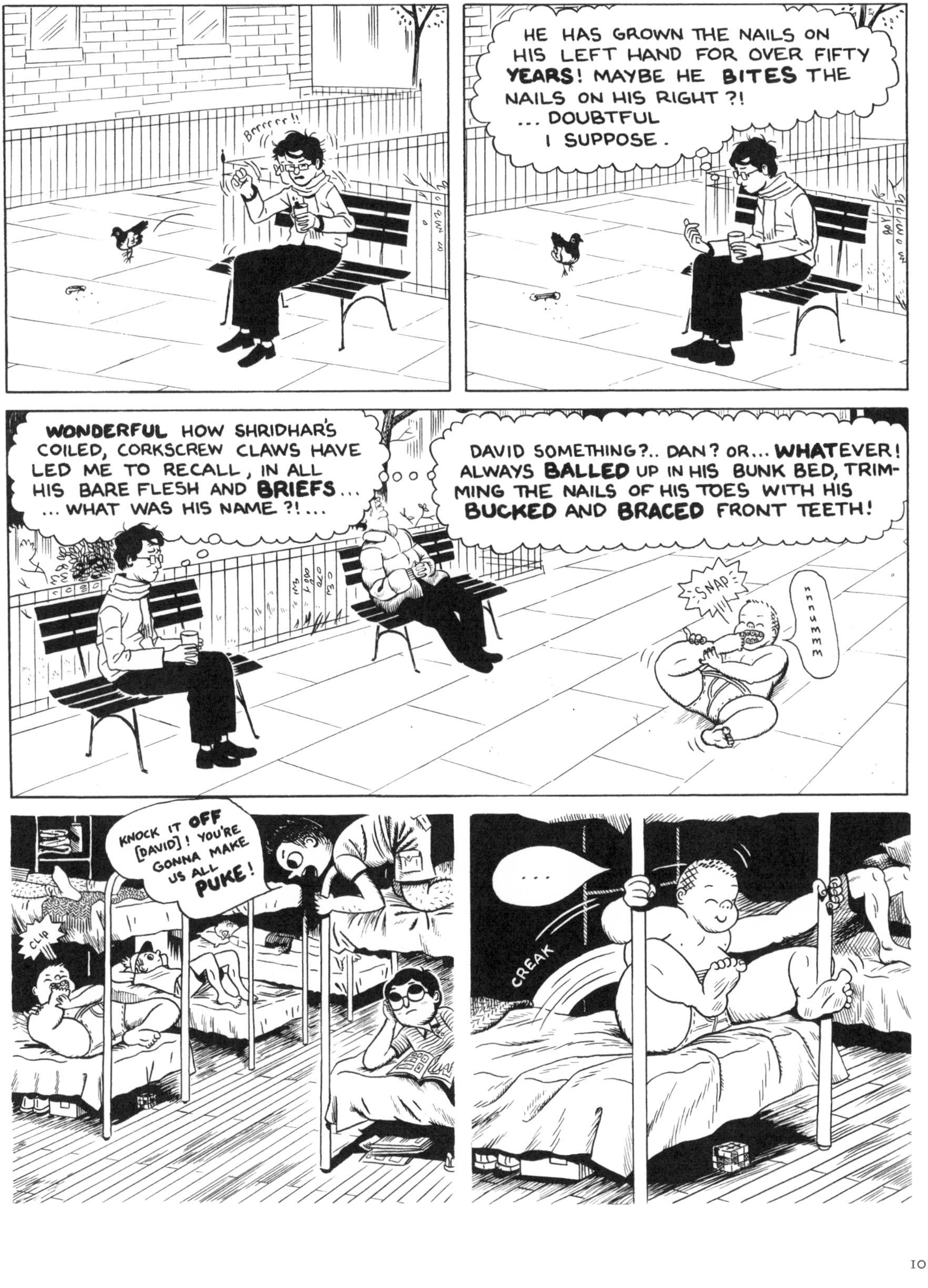
Brrrrrr!!
HE HAS GROWN THE NAILS ON HIS LEFT HAND FOR OVER FIFTY YEARS! MAYBE HE BITES THE NAILS ON HIS RIGHT ?! ... DOUBTFUL I SUPPOSE.
WONDERFUL HOW SHRIDHAR'S COILED, CORKSCREW CLAWS HAVE LED ME TO RECALL, IN ALL HIS BARE FLESH AND BRIEFS... ... WHAT WAS HIS NAME ?!...
DAVID SOMETHING?.. DAN? OR... WHATEVER! ALWAYS BALLED UP IN HIS BUNK BED, TRIMMING THE NAILS OF HIS TOES WITH HIS BUCKED AND BRACED FRONT TEETH!
SNAP
nnnummm
KNOCK IT OFF [DAVID]! YOU'RE GONNA MAKE US ALL PUKE!
CLIP
...
CREAK

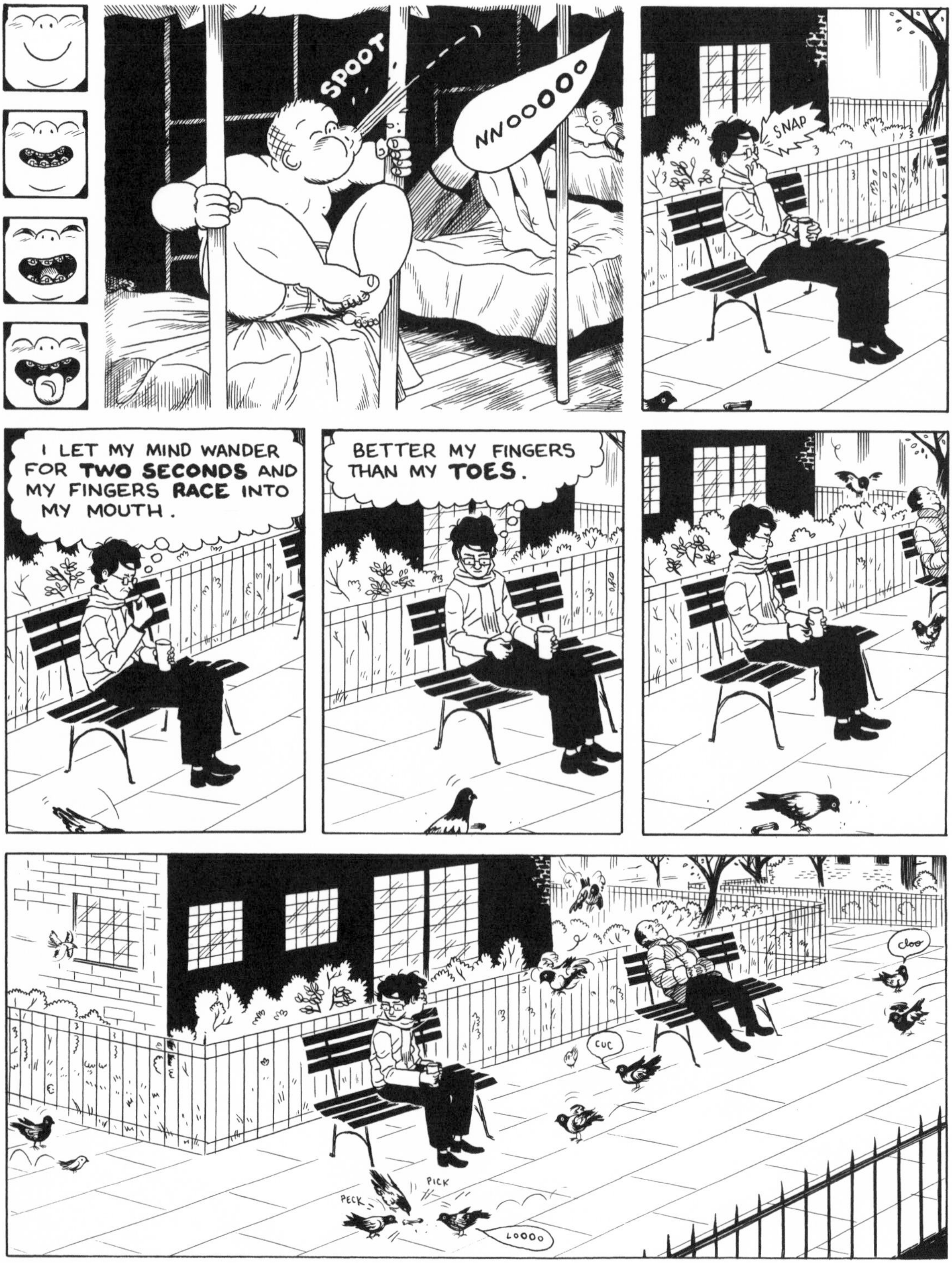
SPOOT
NNOOOOOO
SNAP
I LET MY MIND WANDER FOR TWO SECONDS AND MY FINGERS RACE INTO MY MOUTH.
BETTER MY FINGERS THAN MY TOES.
CUC
cloo
PICK
PECK
LOOOO

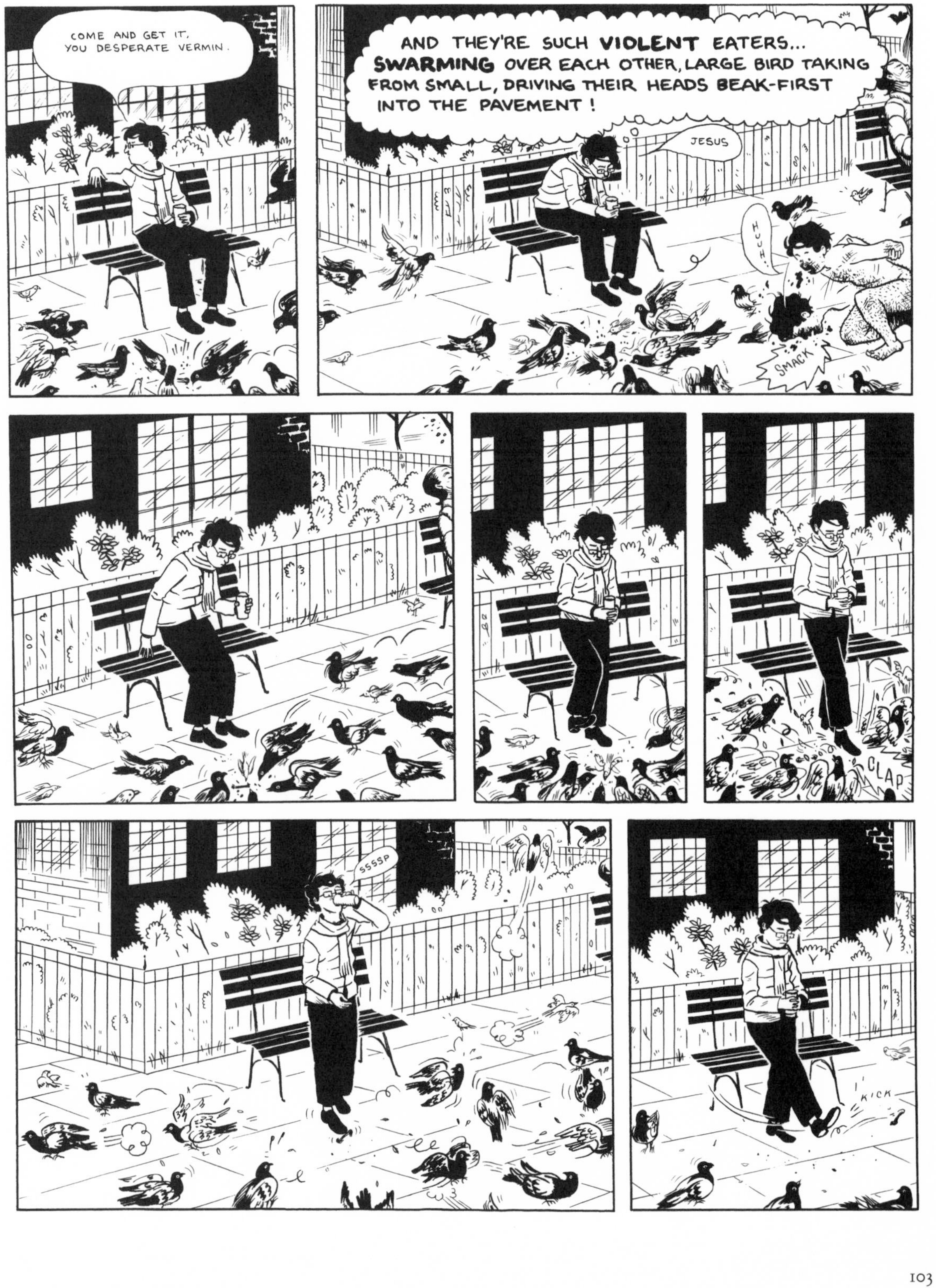
COME AND GET IT, YOU DESPERATE VERMIN.
AND THEY'RE SUCH VIOLENT EATERS... SWARMING OVER EACH OTHER, LARGE BIRD TAKING FROM SMALL, DRIVING THEIR HEADS BEAK-FIRST INTO THE PAVEMENT!
JESUS
HUUH...
SMACK
CLAP
SSSSP
KICK

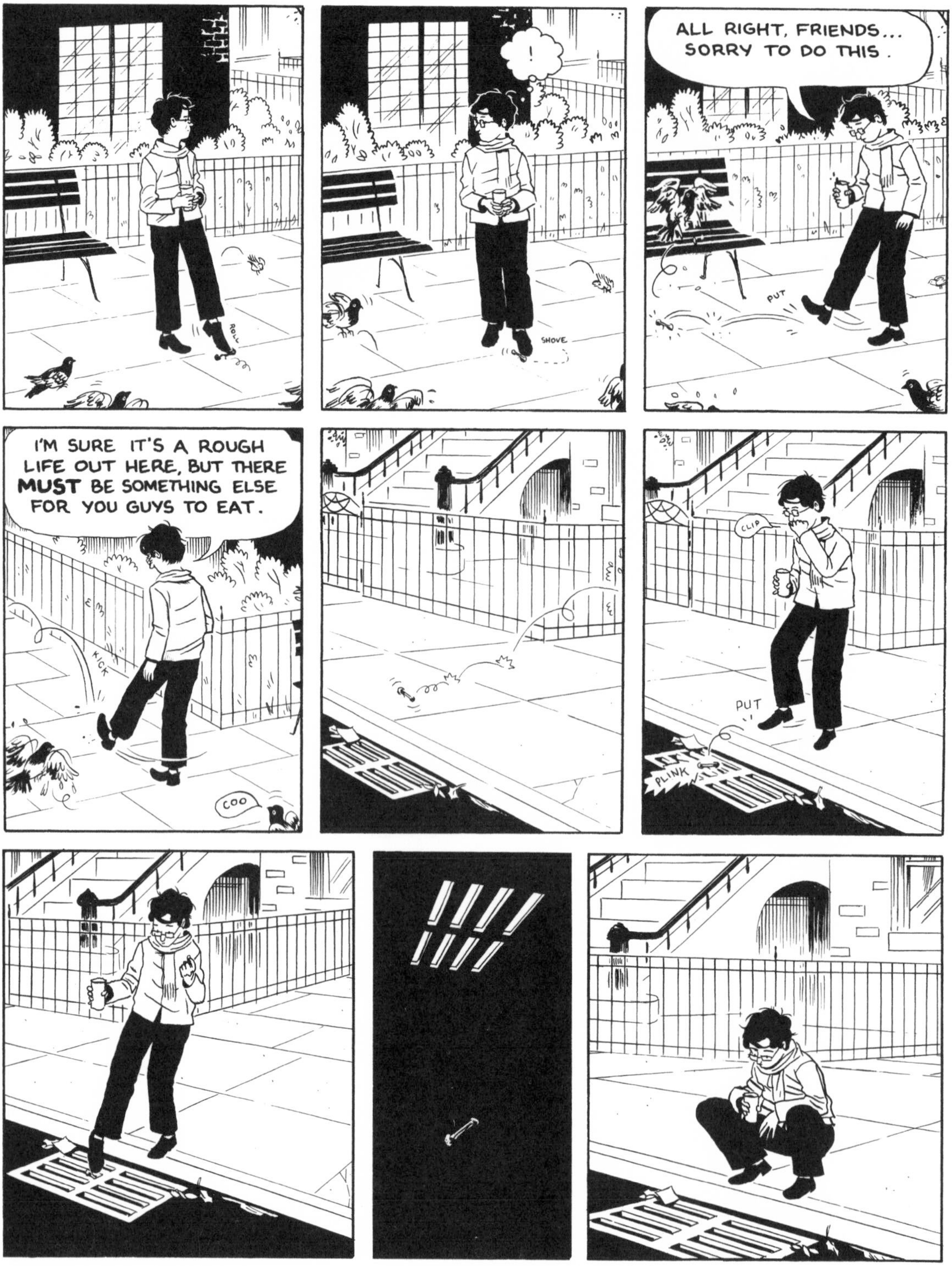
ROLL
!
SHOVE
ALL RIGHT, FRIENDS... SORRY TO DO THIS.
PUT
I'M SURE IT'S A ROUGH LIFE OUT HERE, BUT THERE MUST BE SOMETHING ELSE FOR YOU GUYS TO EAT.
KICK
COO
CLIP
PUT
PLINK

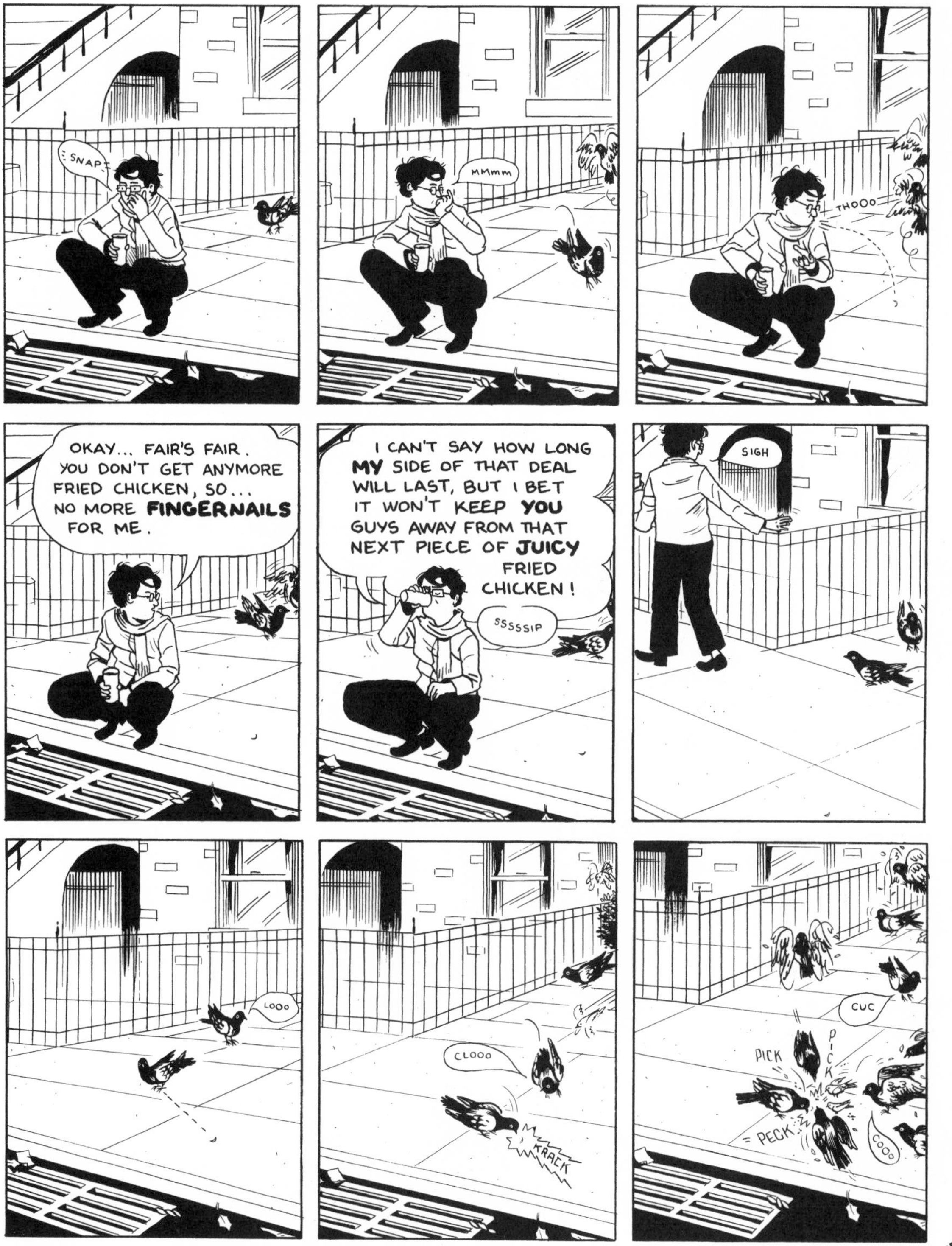
SNAP
MMmm
THOOO
OKAY... FAIR'S FAIR. YOU DON'T GET ANYMORE FRIED CHICKEN, SO... NO MORE FINGERNAILS FOR ME.
I CAN'T SAY HOW LONG MY SIDE OF THAT DEAL WILL LAST, BUT I BET IT WON'T KEEP YOU GUYS AWAY FROM THAT NEXT PIECE OF JUICY FRIED CHICKEN!
SSSSSIP
SIGH
LOOO
CLOOO
KRACK
CUC
PICK
PICK
PECK
COOO

THE END

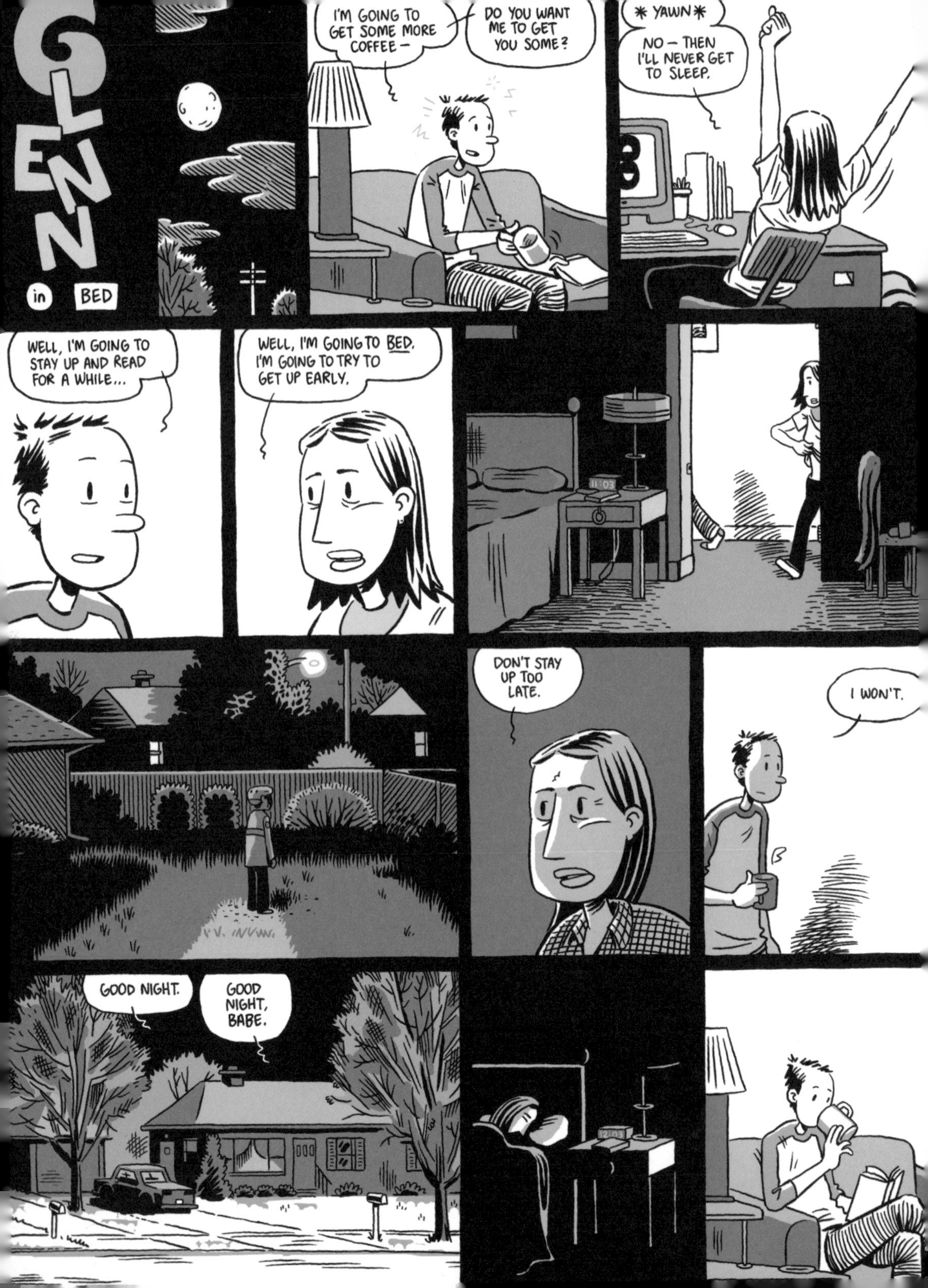
GLENN
in BED
I'M GOING TO GET SOME MORE COFFEE –
DO YOU WANT ME TO GET YOU SOME?
* YAWN *
NO – THEN I'LL NEVER GET TO SLEEP.
WELL, I'M GOING TO STAY UP AND READ FOR A WHILE...
WELL, I'M GOING TO BED. I'M GOING TO TRY TO GET UP EARLY.
11:03
DON'T STAY UP TOO LATE.
I WON'T.
GOOD NIGHT.
GOOD NIGHT, BABE.
12:03

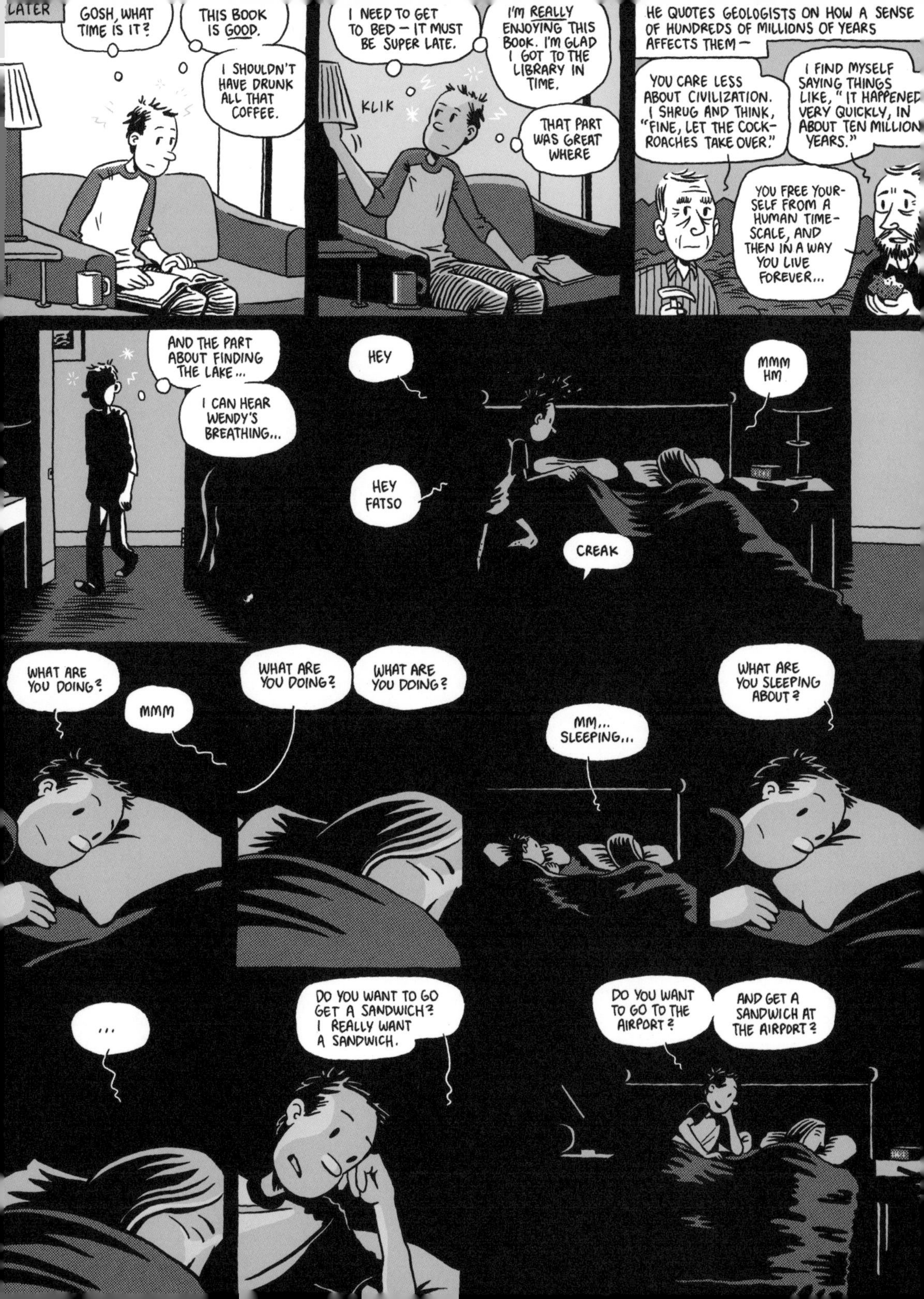
LATER
GOSH, WHAT TIME IS IT?
THIS BOOK IS GOOD.
I SHOULDN'T HAVE DRUNK ALL THAT COFFEE.
I NEED TO GET TO BED — IT MUST BE SUPER LATE.
I'M REALLY ENJOYING THIS BOOK. I'M GLAD I GOT TO THE LIBRARY IN TIME.
KLIK
THAT PART WAS GREAT WHERE
HE QUOTES GEOLOGISTS ON HOW A SENSE OF HUNDREDS OF MILLIONS OF YEARS AFFECTS THEM —
YOU CARE LESS ABOUT CIVILIZATION. I SHRUG AND THINK, "FINE, LET THE COCKROACHES TAKE OVER."
I FIND MYSELF SAYING THINGS LIKE, "IT HAPPENED VERY QUICKLY, IN ABOUT TEN MILLION YEARS."
YOU FREE YOURSELF FROM A HUMAN TIME-SCALE, AND THEN IN A WAY YOU LIVE FOREVER...
AND THE PART ABOUT FINDING THE LAKE...
I CAN HEAR WENDY'S BREATHING...
HEY
HEY FATSO
MMM HM
CREAK
WHAT ARE YOU DOING?
MMM
WHAT ARE YOU DOING?
WHAT ARE YOU DOING?
MM... SLEEPING...
WHAT ARE YOU SLEEPING ABOUT?
...
DO YOU WANT TO GO GET A SANDWICH? I REALLY WANT A SANDWICH.
DO YOU WANT TO GO TO THE AIRPORT?
AND GET A SANDWICH AT THE AIRPORT?

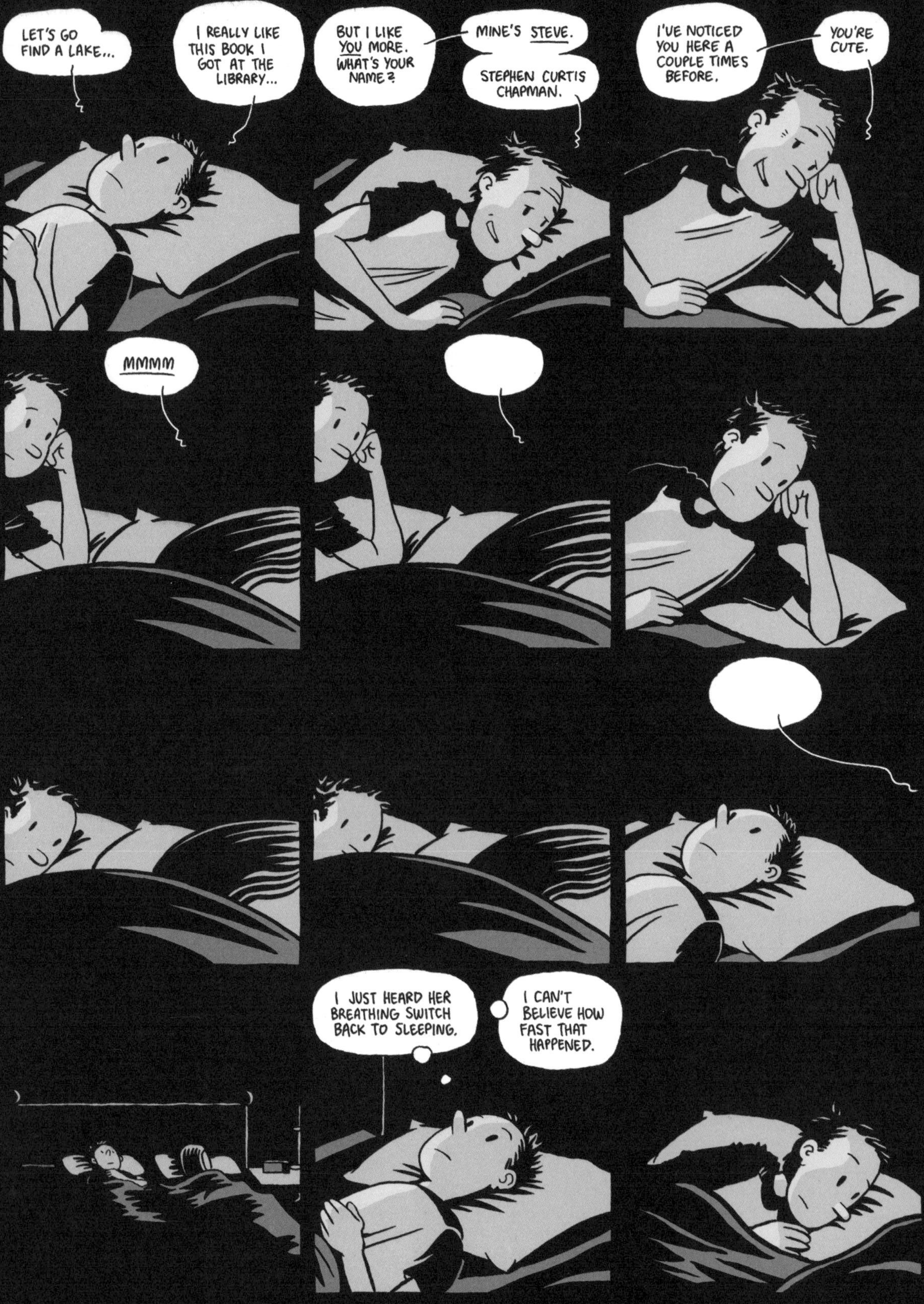
LET'S GO FIND A LAKE...
I REALLY LIKE THIS BOOK I GOT AT THE LIBRARY...
BUT I LIKE YOU MORE. WHAT'S YOUR NAME?
MINE'S STEVE.
STEPHEN CURTIS CHAPMAN.
I'VE NOTICED YOU HERE A COUPLE TIMES BEFORE.
YOU'RE CUTE.
MMMM
I JUST HEARD HER BREATHING SWITCH BACK TO SLEEPING.
I CAN'T BELIEVE HOW FAST THAT HAPPENED.

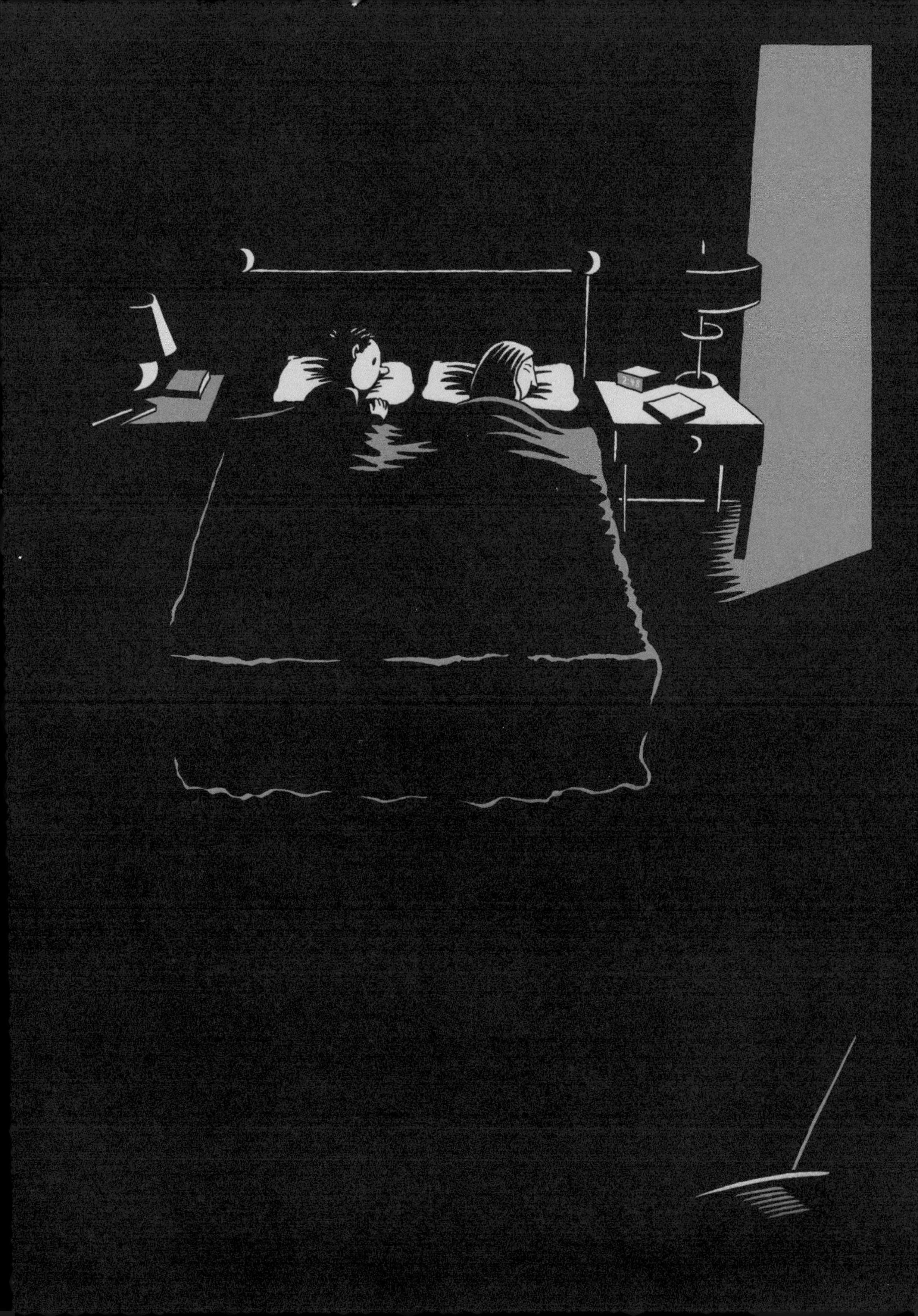
2:48

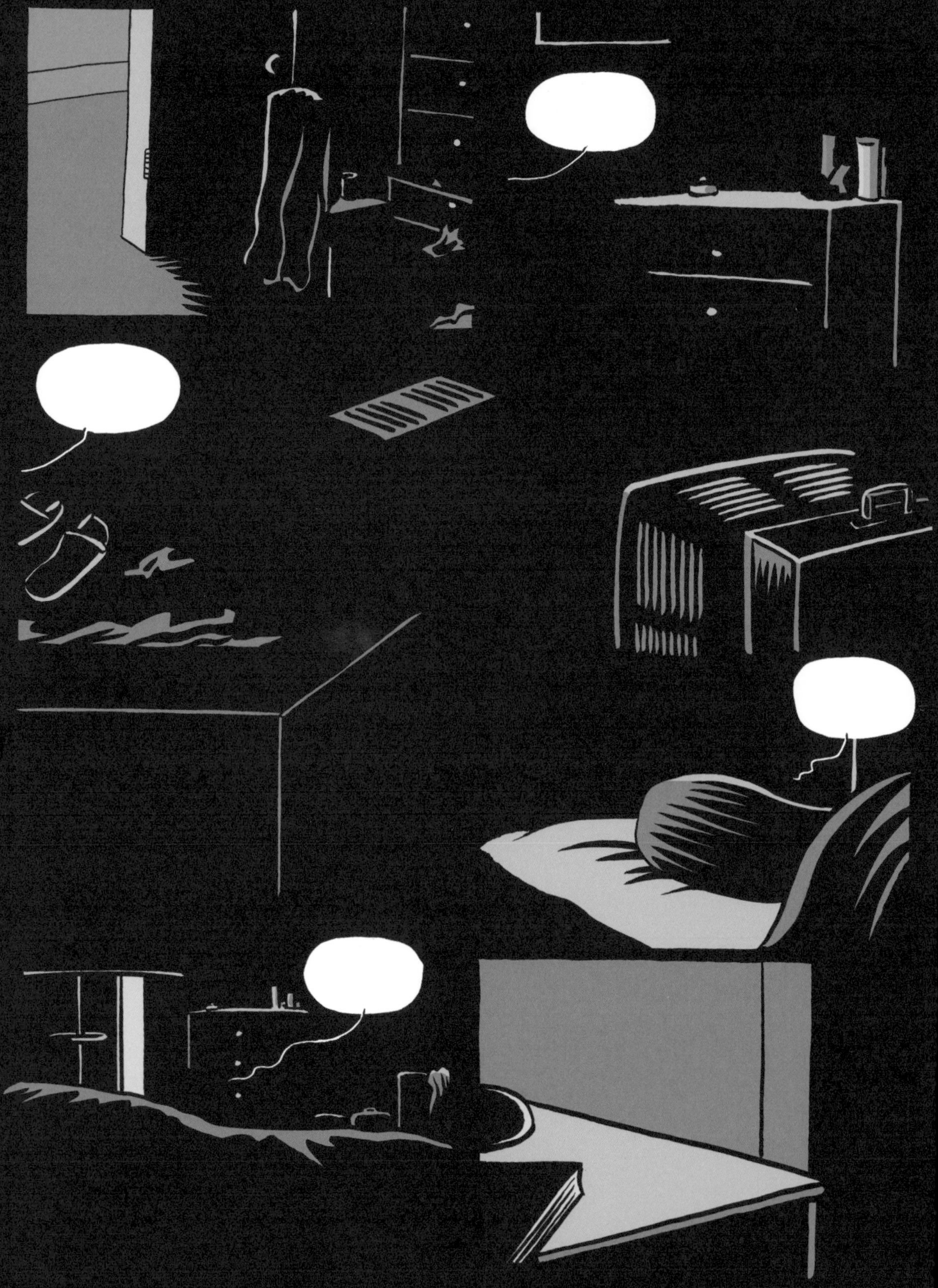

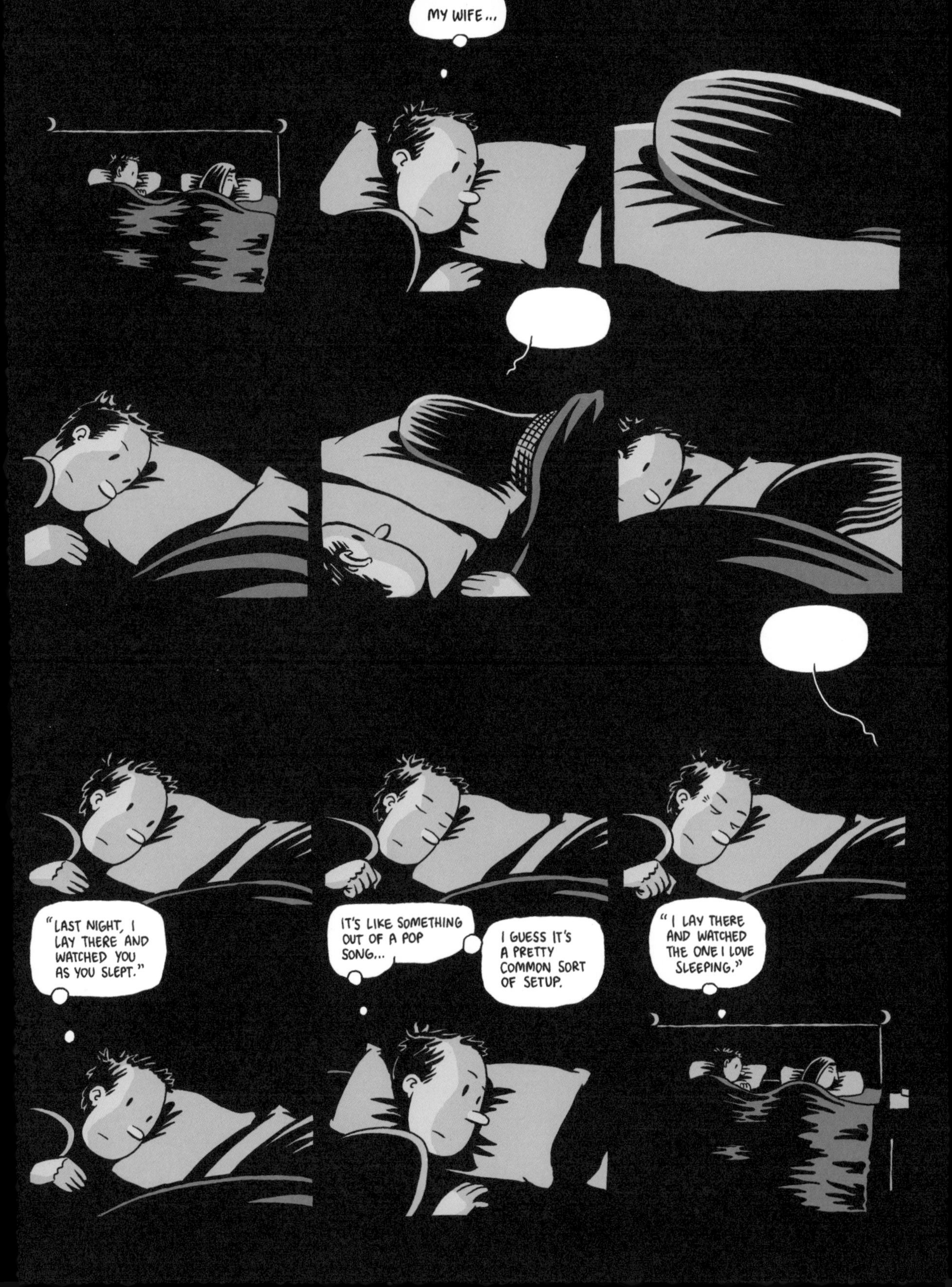
MY WIFE...
"LAST NIGHT, I LAY THERE AND WATCHED YOU AS YOU SLEPT."
IT'S LIKE SOMETHING OUT OF A POP SONG...
I GUESS IT'S A PRETTY COMMON SORT OF SETUP.
"I LAY THERE AND WATCHED THE ONE I LOVE SLEEPING."

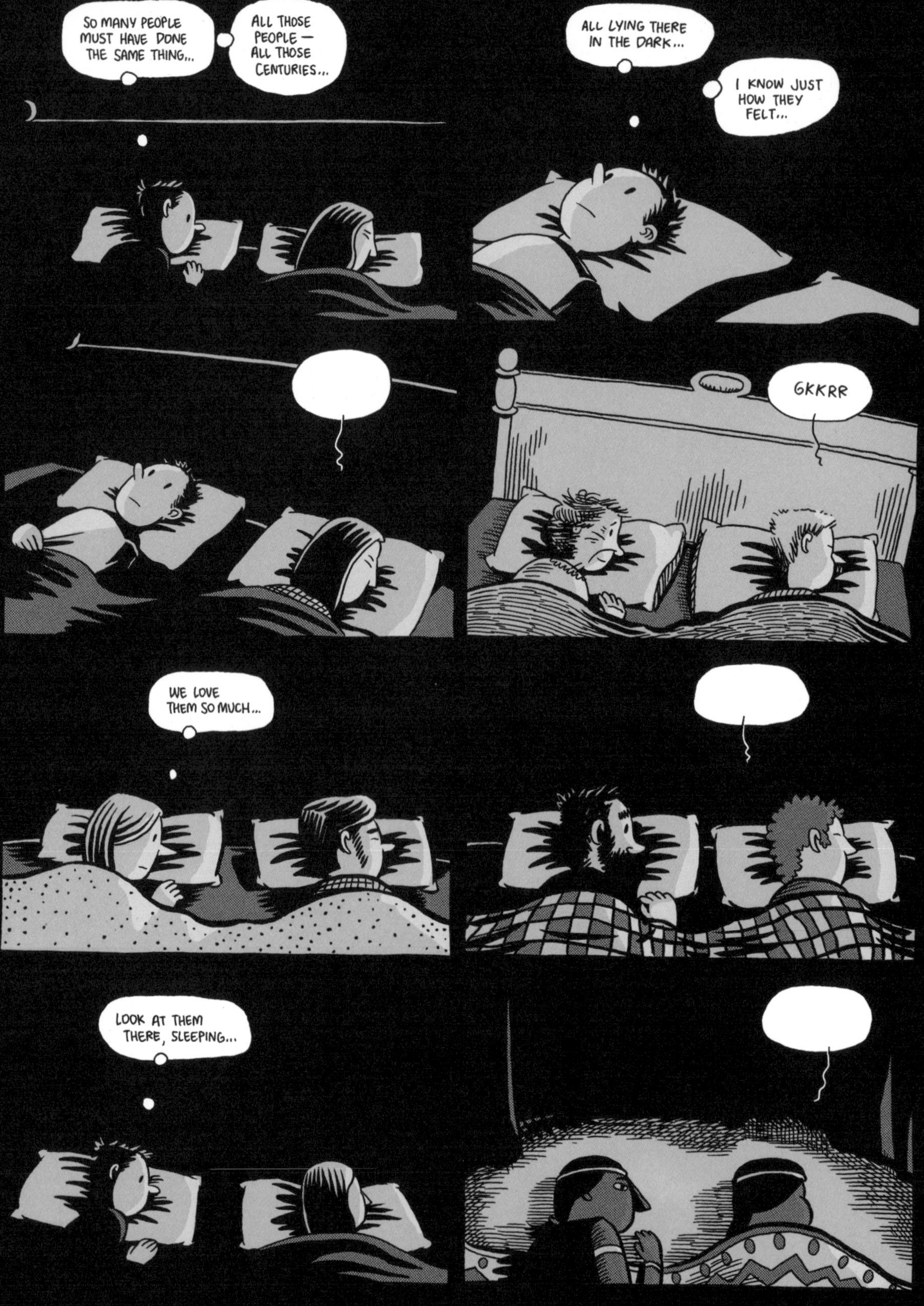
SO MANY PEOPLE MUST HAVE DONE THE SAME THING...
ALL THOSE PEOPLE — ALL THOSE CENTURIES...
ALL LYING THERE IN THE DARK...
I KNOW JUST HOW THEY FELT...
GKKRR
WE LOVE THEM SO MUCH...
LOOK AT THEM THERE, SLEEPING...

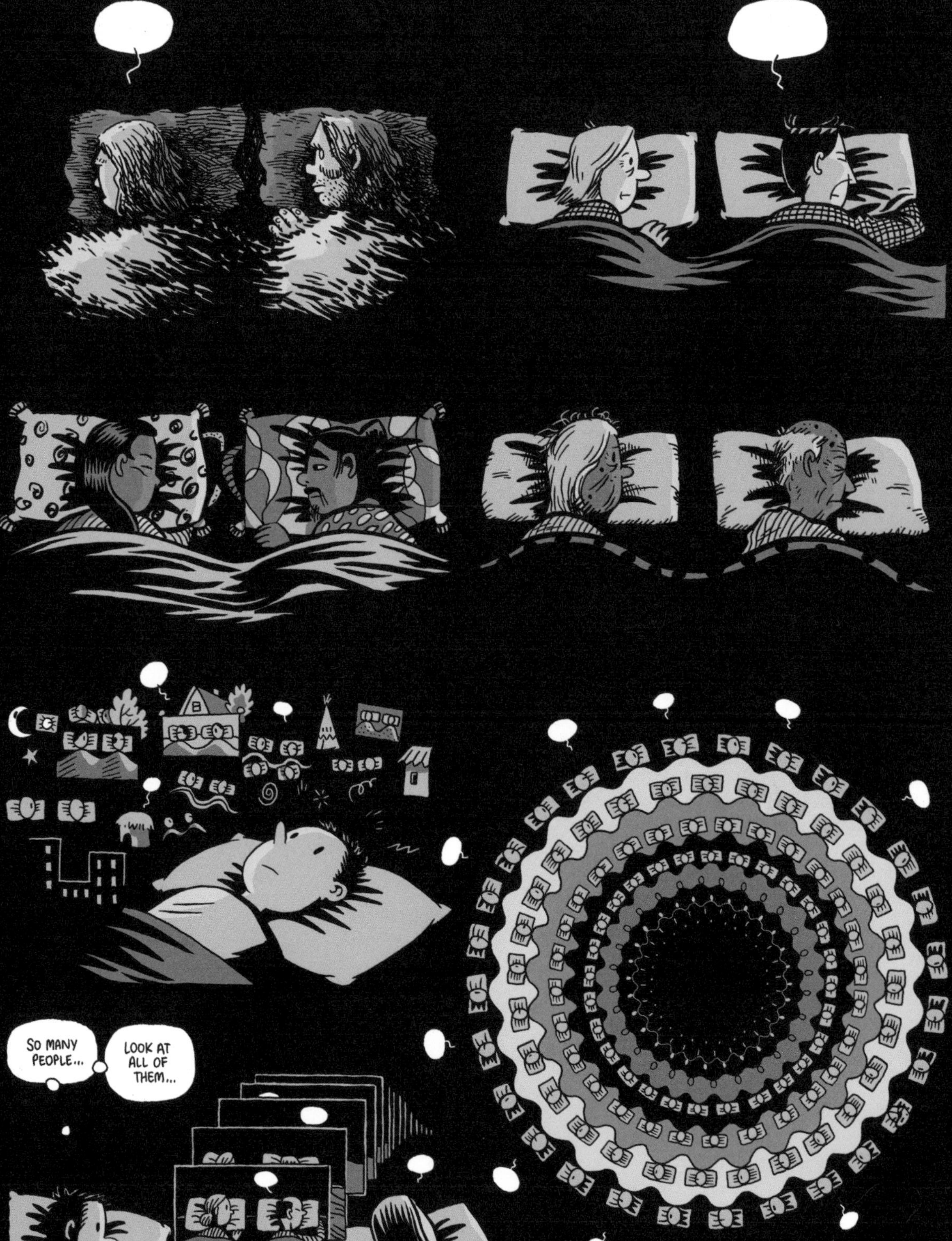
SO MANY PEOPLE...
LOOK AT ALL OF THEM...

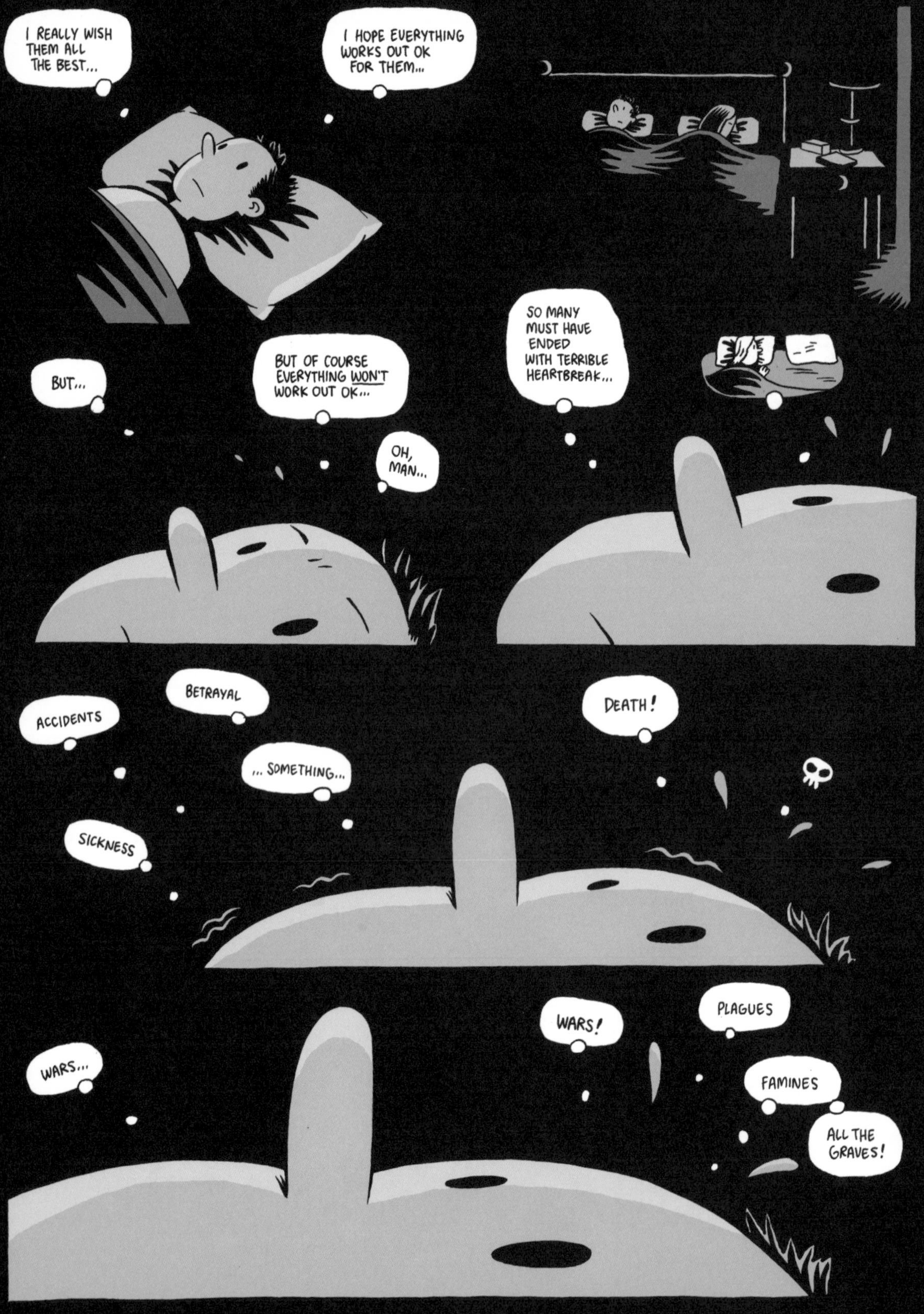
I REALLY WISH THEM ALL THE BEST...
I HOPE EVERYTHING WORKS OUT OK FOR THEM...
BUT...
BUT OF COURSE EVERYTHING WON'T WORK OUT OK...
OH, MAN...
SO MANY MUST HAVE ENDED WITH TERRIBLE HEARTBREAK...
ACCIDENTS
BETRAYAL
...SOMETHING...
SICKNESS
DEATH!
WARS...
WARS!
PLAGUES
FAMINES
ALL THE GRAVES!

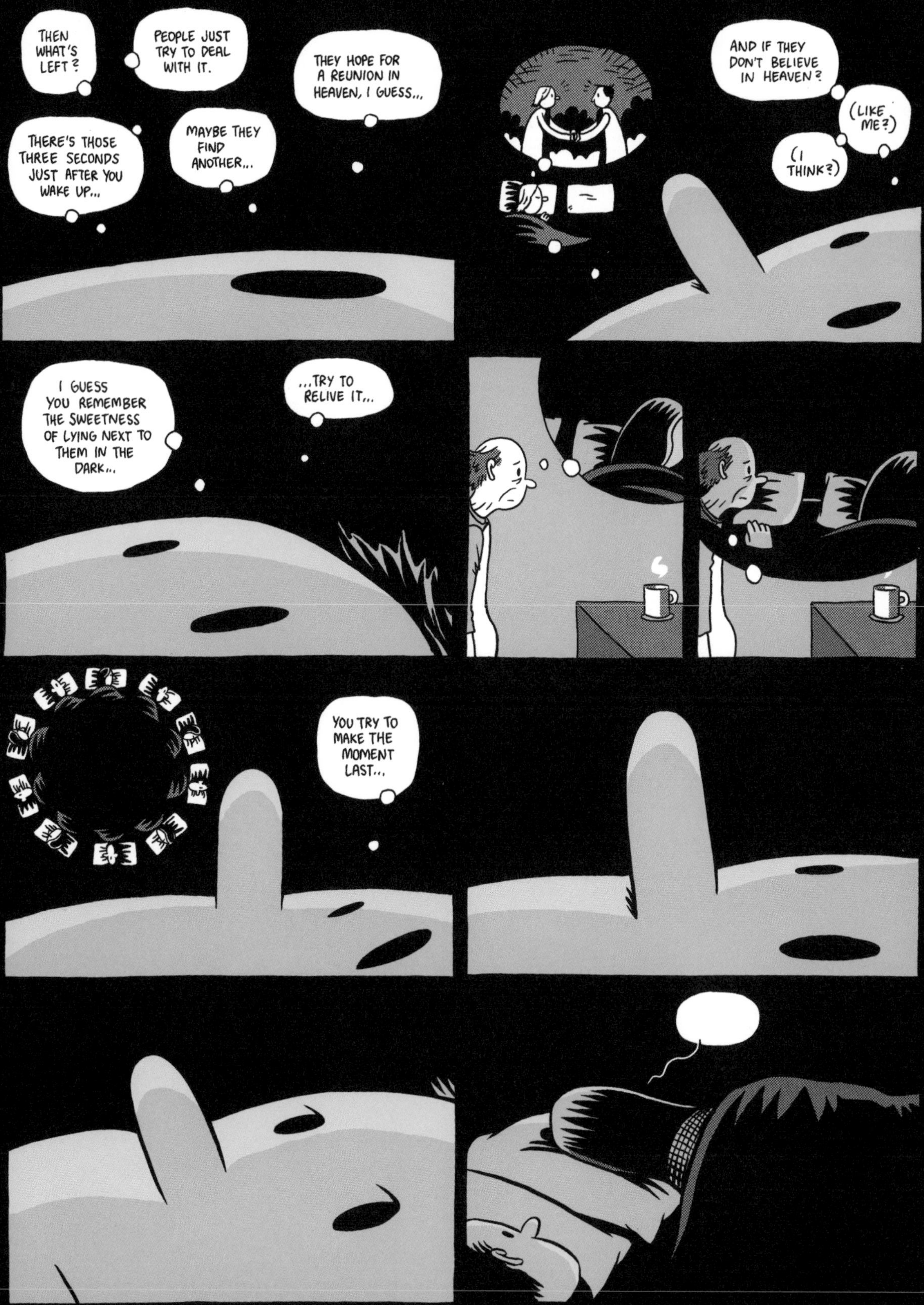
THEN WHAT'S LEFT?
PEOPLE JUST TRY TO DEAL WITH IT.
THERE'S THOSE THREE SECONDS JUST AFTER YOU WAKE UP...
MAYBE THEY FIND ANOTHER...
THEY HOPE FOR A REUNION IN HEAVEN, I GUESS...
AND IF THEY DON'T BELIEVE IN HEAVEN?
(LIKE ME?)
(I THINK?)
I GUESS YOU REMEMBER THE SWEETNESS OF LYING NEXT TO THEM IN THE DARK...
...TRY TO RELIVE IT...
YOU TRY TO MAKE THE MOMENT LAST...

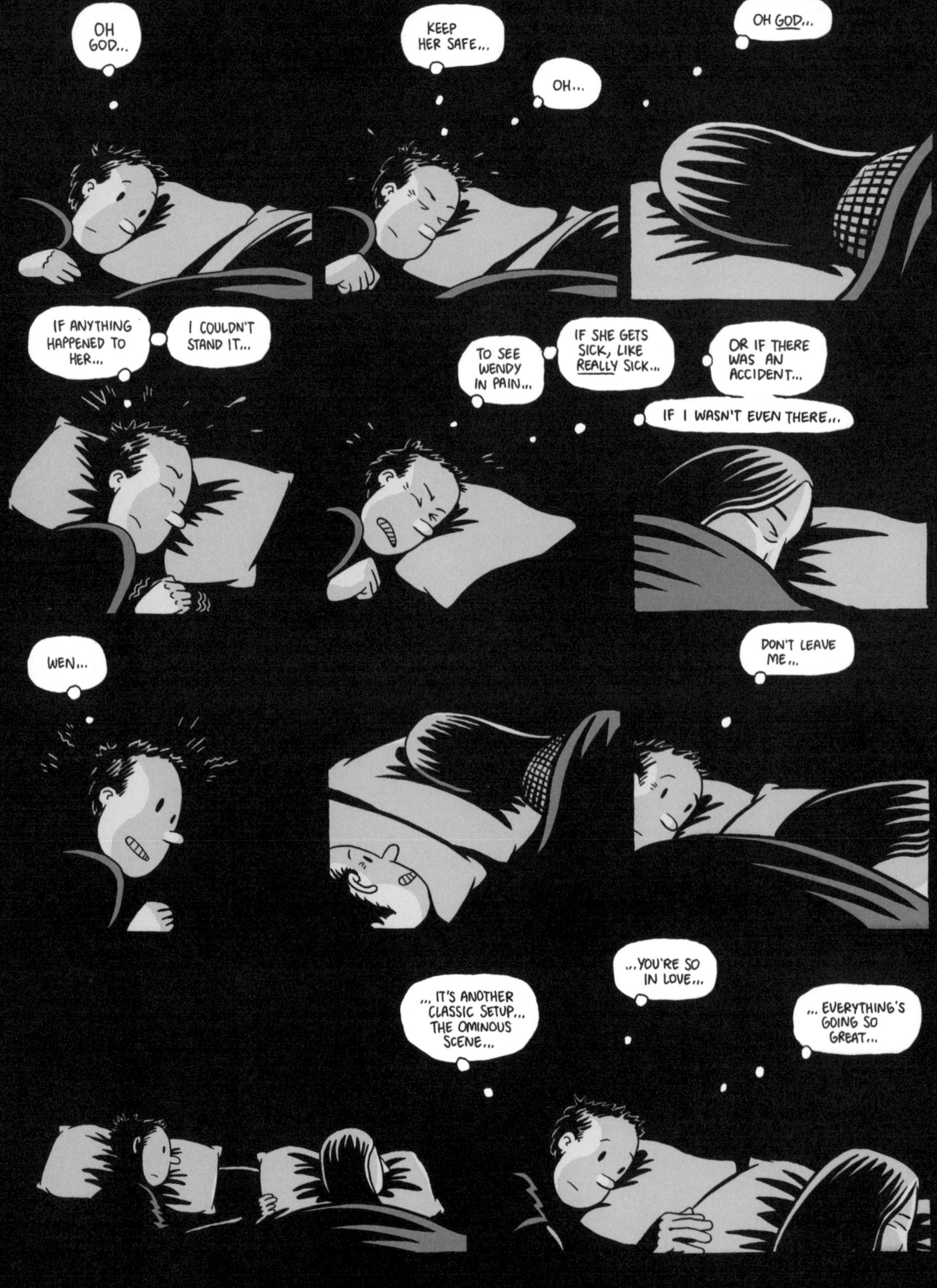
OH GOD...
KEEP HER SAFE...
OH...
OH GOD...
IF ANYTHING HAPPENED TO HER...
I COULDN'T STAND IT...
TO SEE WENDY IN PAIN...
IF SHE GETS SICK, LIKE REALLY SICK...
OR IF THERE WAS AN ACCIDENT...
IF I WASN'T EVEN THERE...
WEN...
DON'T LEAVE ME...
... IT'S ANOTHER CLASSIC SETUP... THE OMINOUS SCENE...
...YOU'RE SO IN LOVE...
... EVERYTHING'S GOING SO GREAT...

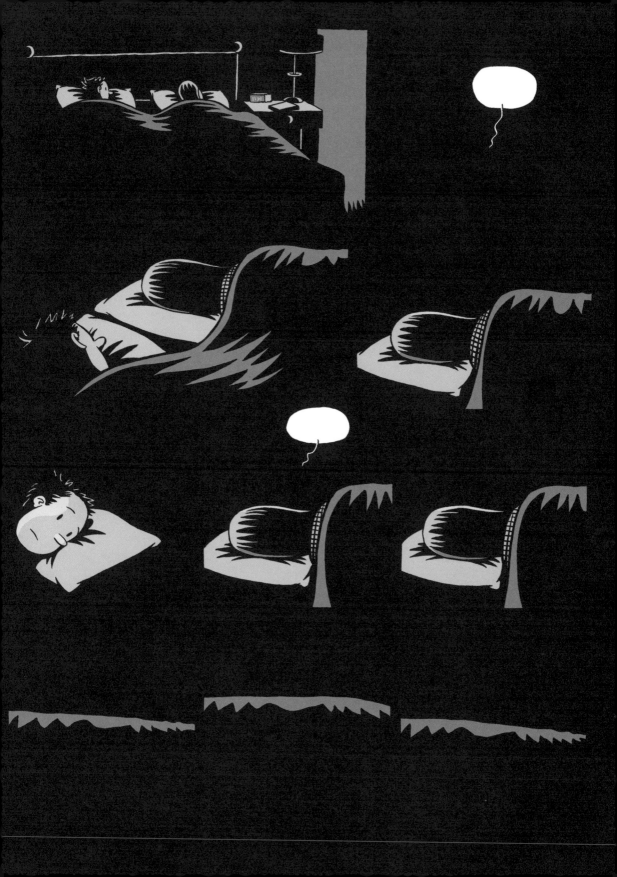

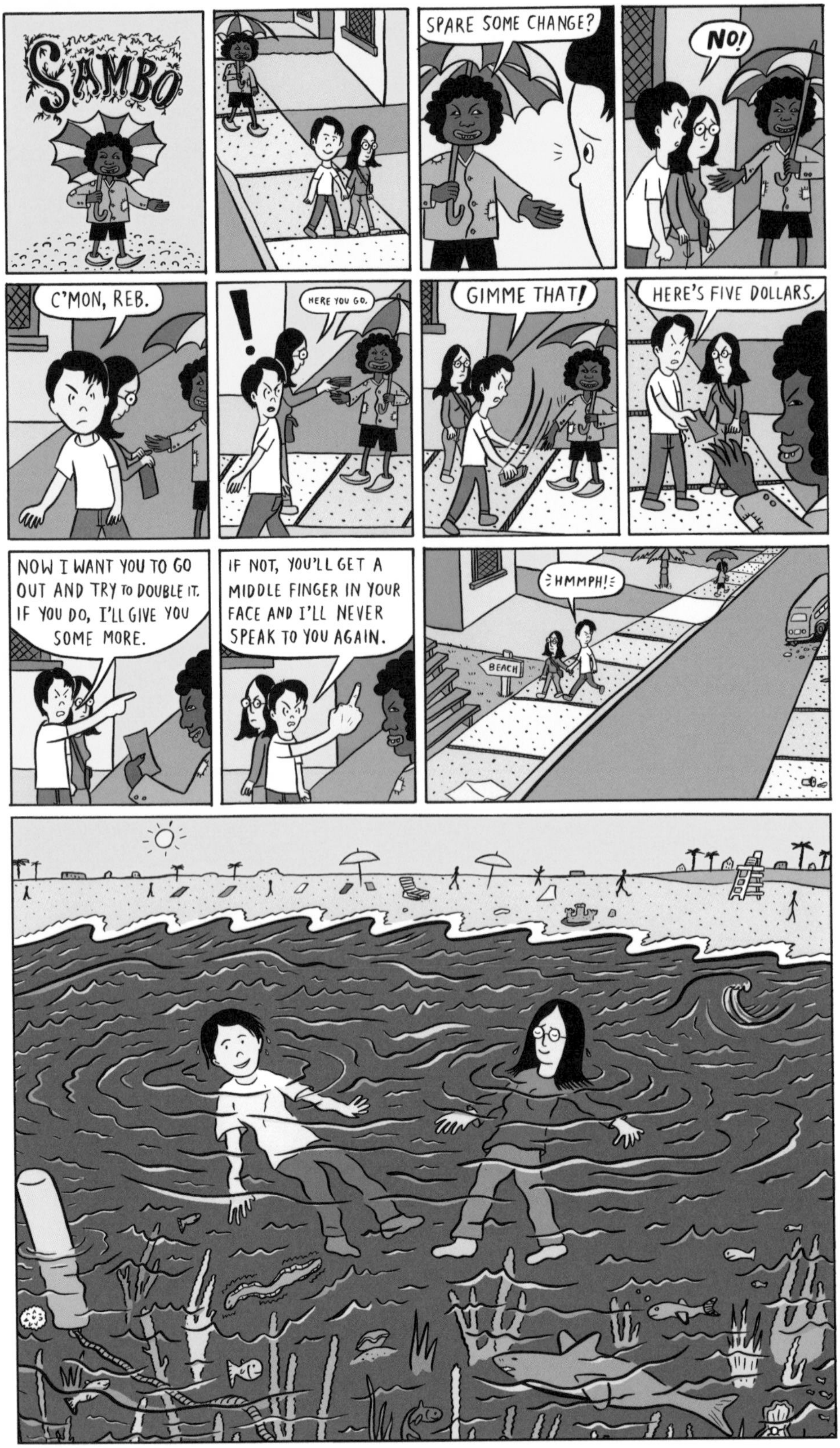
SAMBO
SPARE SOME CHANGE?
NO!
C'MON, REB.
!
HERE YOU GO.
GIMME THAT!
HERE'S FIVE DOLLARS.
NOW I WANT YOU TO GO OUT AND TRY TO DOUBLE IT. IF YOU DO, I'LL GIVE YOU SOME MORE.
IF NOT, YOU'LL GET A MIDDLE FINGER IN YOUR FACE AND I'LL NEVER SPEAK TO YOU AGAIN.
HMMPH!
BEACH

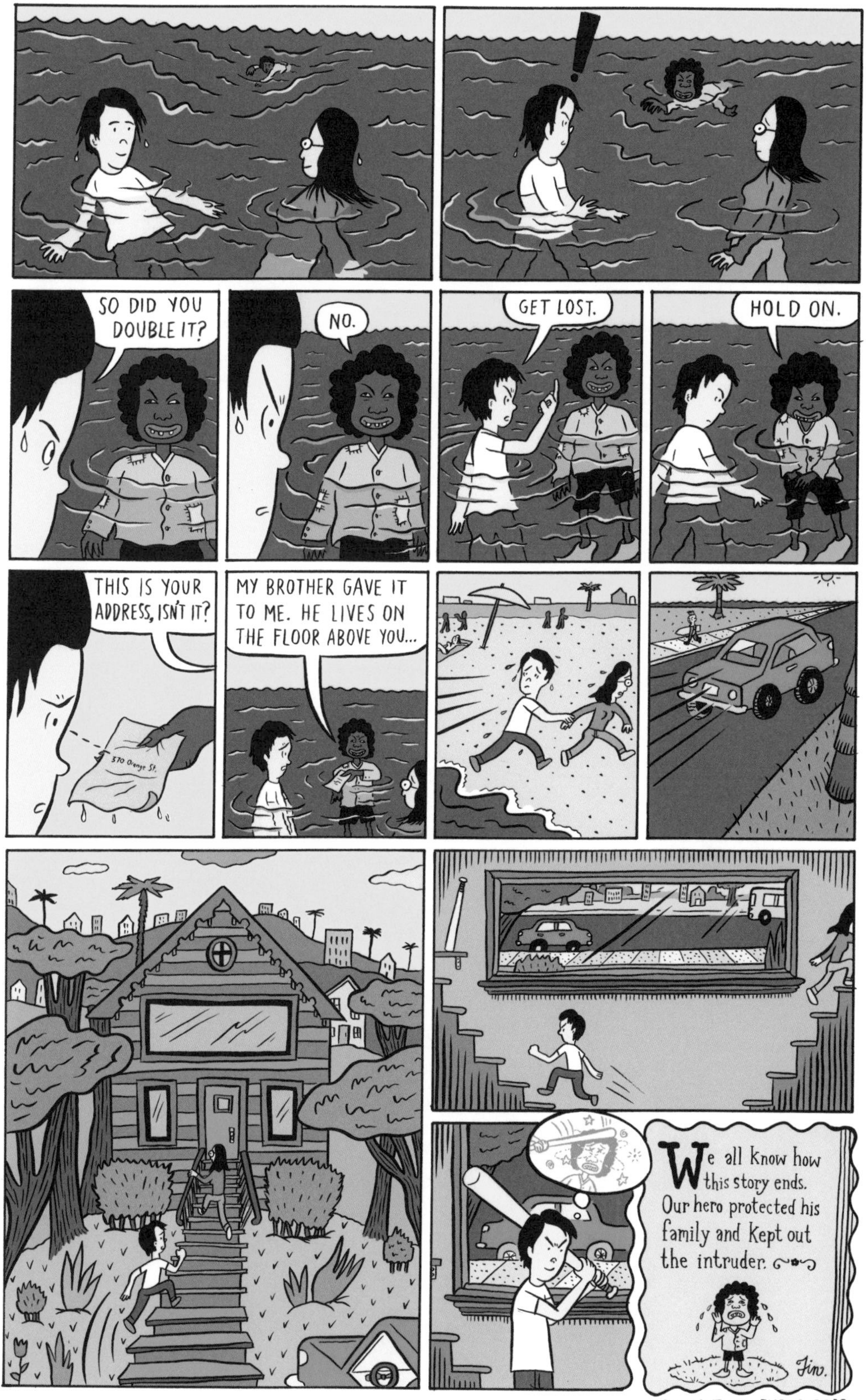
SO DID YOU DOUBLE IT?
NO.
GET LOST.
HOLD ON.
THIS IS YOUR ADDRESS, ISN'T IT?
370 Orange St.
MY BROTHER GAVE IT TO ME. HE LIVES ON THE FLOOR ABOVE YOU...
We all know how this story ends. Our hero protected his family and kept out the intruder.
Jim.

DREAMT NOVEMBER 2002

LUBAVITCH, UKRAINE, 1876

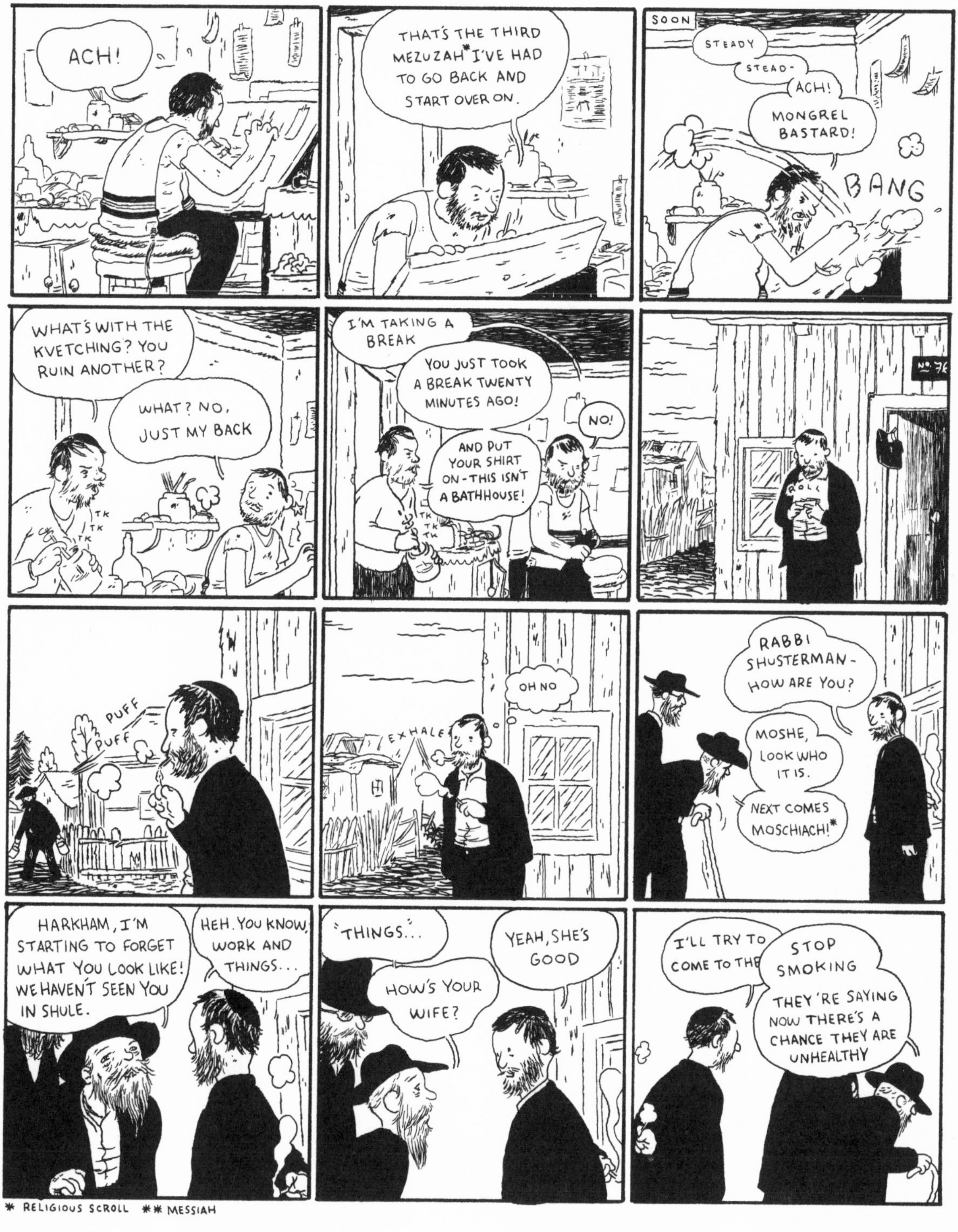
ACH!
THAT'S THE THIRD MEZUZAH* I'VE HAD TO GO BACK AND START OVER ON.
SOON
STEADY
STEAD-
ACH!
MONGREL BASTARD!
BANG
WHAT'S WITH THE KVETCHING? YOU RUIN ANOTHER?
WHAT? NO, JUST MY BACK
TK TK TK
I'M TAKING A BREAK
YOU JUST TOOK A BREAK TWENTY MINUTES AGO!
NO!
AND PUT YOUR SHIRT ON-THIS ISN'T A BATHHOUSE!
TK TK TK
No. 76
ROLL
PUFF PUFF
EXHALE
OH NO
RABBI SHUSTERMAN - HOW ARE YOU?
MOSHE, LOOK WHO IT IS.
NEXT COMES MOSCHIACH!*
HARKHAM, I'M STARTING TO FORGET WHAT YOU LOOK LIKE! WE HAVEN'T SEEN YOU IN SHULE.
HEH. YOU KNOW, WORK AND THINGS...
"THINGS..."
HOW'S YOUR WIFE?
YEAH, SHE'S GOOD
I'LL TRY TO COME TO THE
STOP SMOKING
THEY'RE SAYING NOW THERE'S A CHANCE THEY ARE UNHEALTHY

* RELIGIOUS SCROLL ** MESSIAH

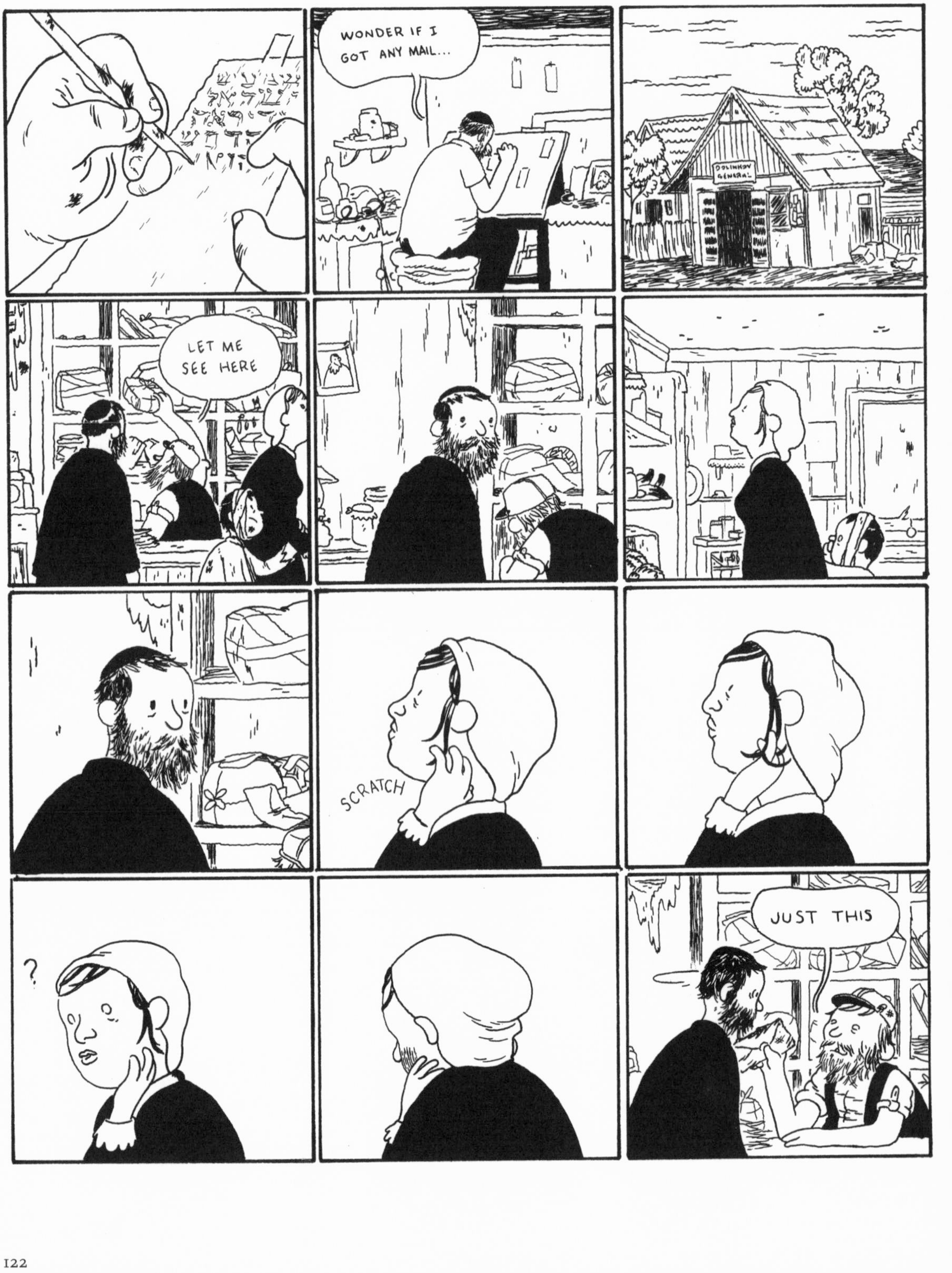
WONDER IF I GOT ANY MAIL...
DOLINKOV GENERAL
LET ME SEE HERE
SCRATCH
?
JUST THIS

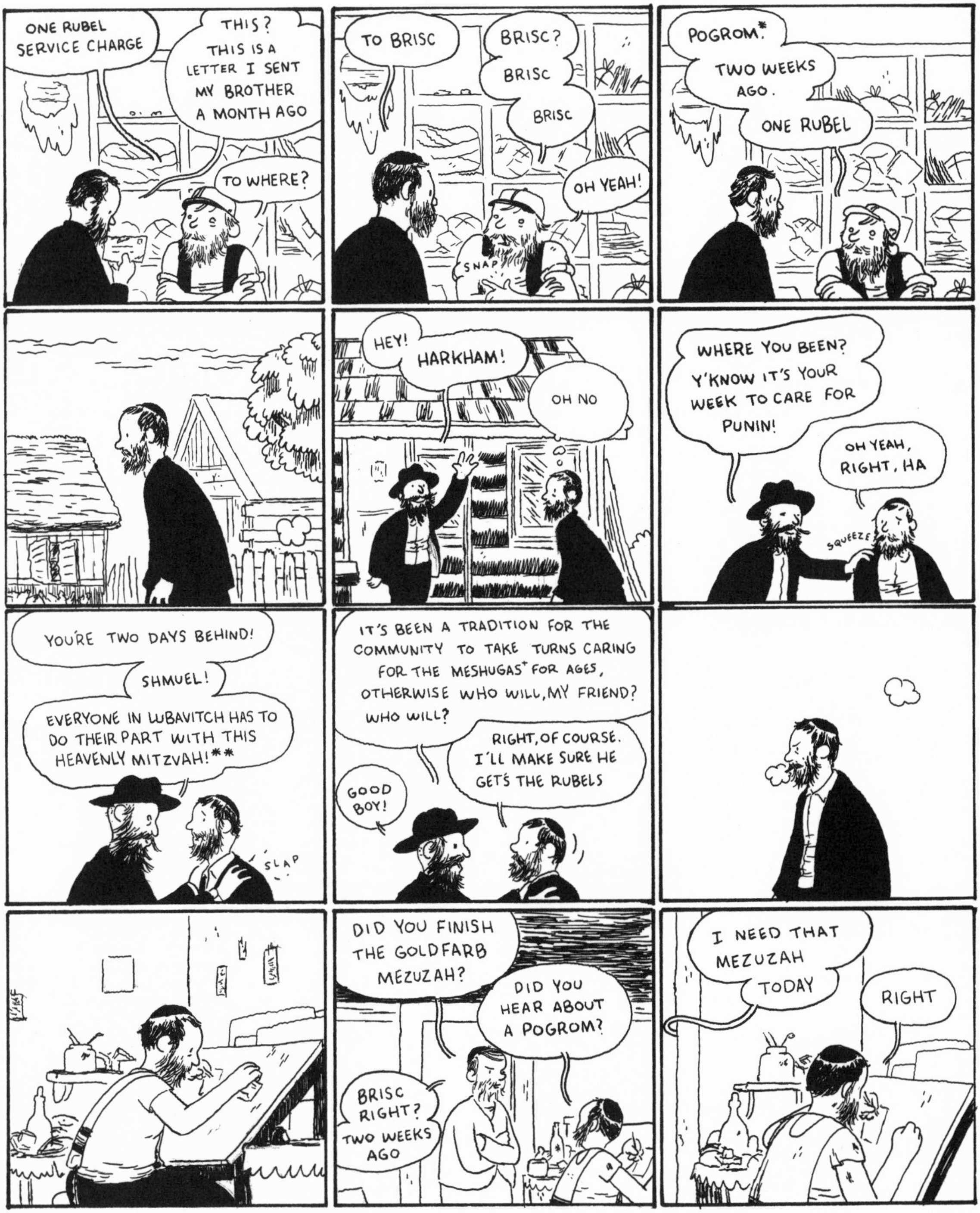
ONE RUBEL SERVICE CHARGE
THIS? THIS IS A LETTER I SENT MY BROTHER A MONTH AGO
TO WHERE?
TO BRISC
BRISC?
BRISC
BRISC
OH YEAH!
SNAP
POGROM*
TWO WEEKS AGO.
ONE RUBEL
HEY!
HARKHAM!
OH NO
WHERE YOU BEEN?
Y'KNOW IT'S YOUR WEEK TO CARE FOR PUNIN!
OH YEAH, RIGHT, HA
SQUEEZE
YOU'RE TWO DAYS BEHIND!
SHMUEL!
EVERYONE IN LUBAVITCH HAS TO DO THEIR PART WITH THIS HEAVENLY MITZVAH!**
SLAP
IT'S BEEN A TRADITION FOR THE COMMUNITY TO TAKE TURNS CARING FOR THE MESHUGAS+ FOR AGES, OTHERWISE WHO WILL, MY FRIEND? WHO WILL?
RIGHT, OF COURSE. I'LL MAKE SURE HE GETS THE RUBELS
GOOD BOY!
DID YOU FINISH THE GOLDFARB MEZUZAH?
DID YOU HEAR ABOUT A POGROM?
BRISC RIGHT? TWO WEEKS AGO
I NEED THAT MEZUZAH TODAY
RIGHT

* ETHNIC MASSACRE ** GOOD DEED + CRAZY PEOPLE

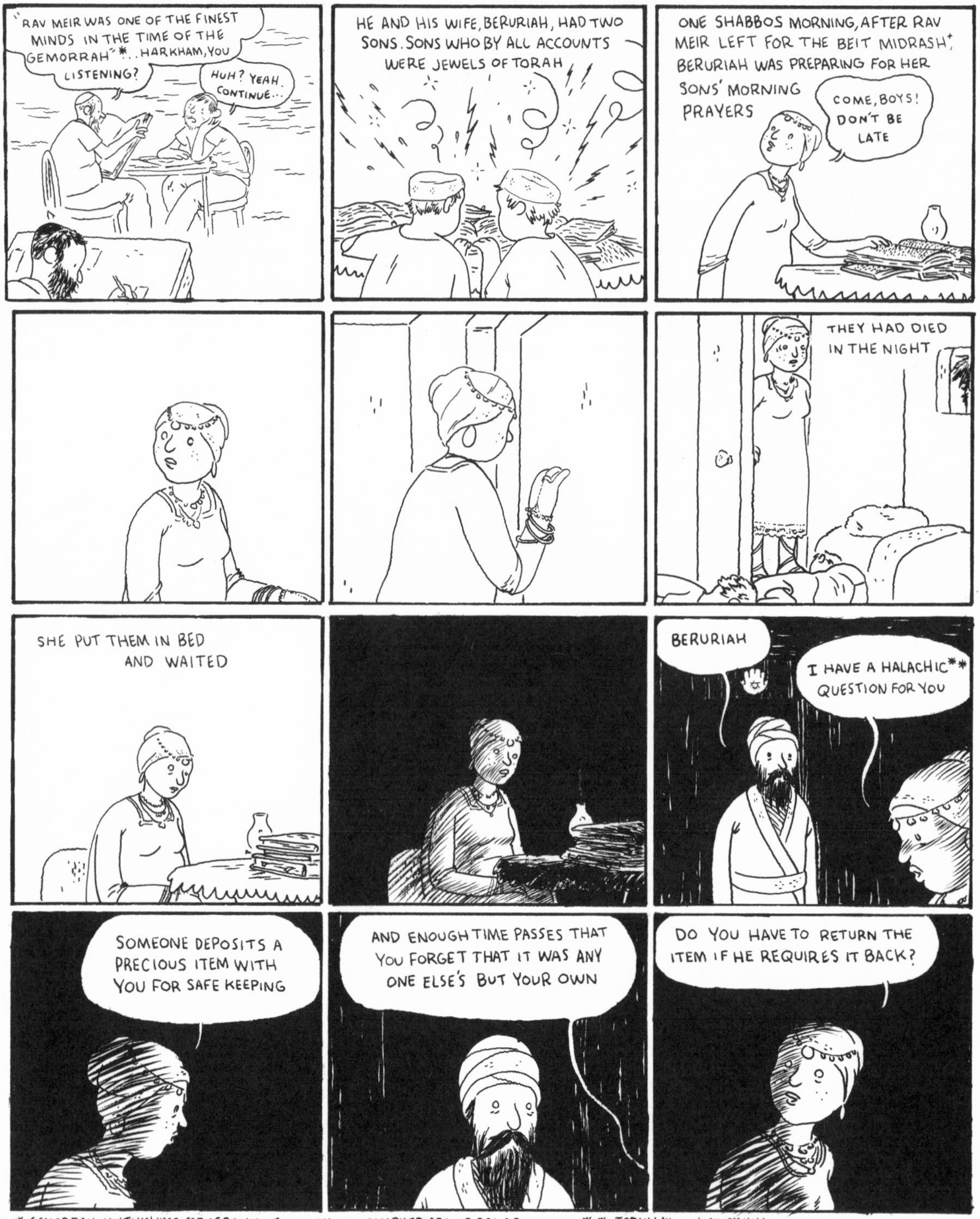
"RAV MEIR WAS ONE OF THE FINEST MINDS IN THE TIME OF THE GEMORRAH"* .. HARKHAM, YOU LISTENING?
HUH? YEAH. CONTINUE...
HE AND HIS WIFE, BERURIAH, HAD TWO SONS. SONS WHO BY ALL ACCOUNTS WERE JEWELS OF TORAH
ONE SHABBOS MORNING, AFTER RAV MEIR LEFT FOR THE BEIT MIDRASH+, BERURIAH WAS PREPARING FOR HER SONS' MORNING PRAYERS
COME, BOYS! DON'T BE LATE
THEY HAD DIED IN THE NIGHT
SHE PUT THEM IN BED AND WAITED
BERURIAH
I HAVE A HALACHIC** QUESTION FOR YOU
SOMEONE DEPOSITS A PRECIOUS ITEM WITH YOU FOR SAFE KEEPING
AND ENOUGH TIME PASSES THAT YOU FORGET THAT IT WAS ANY ONE ELSE'S BUT YOUR OWN
DO YOU HAVE TO RETURN THE ITEM IF HE REQUIRES IT BACK?
* GEMORRAH - MULTI VOLUME SET OF BOOKS OF JEWISH LAW COMPILED AROUND 500 A.D. ** TORAH LAW + STUDY HALL

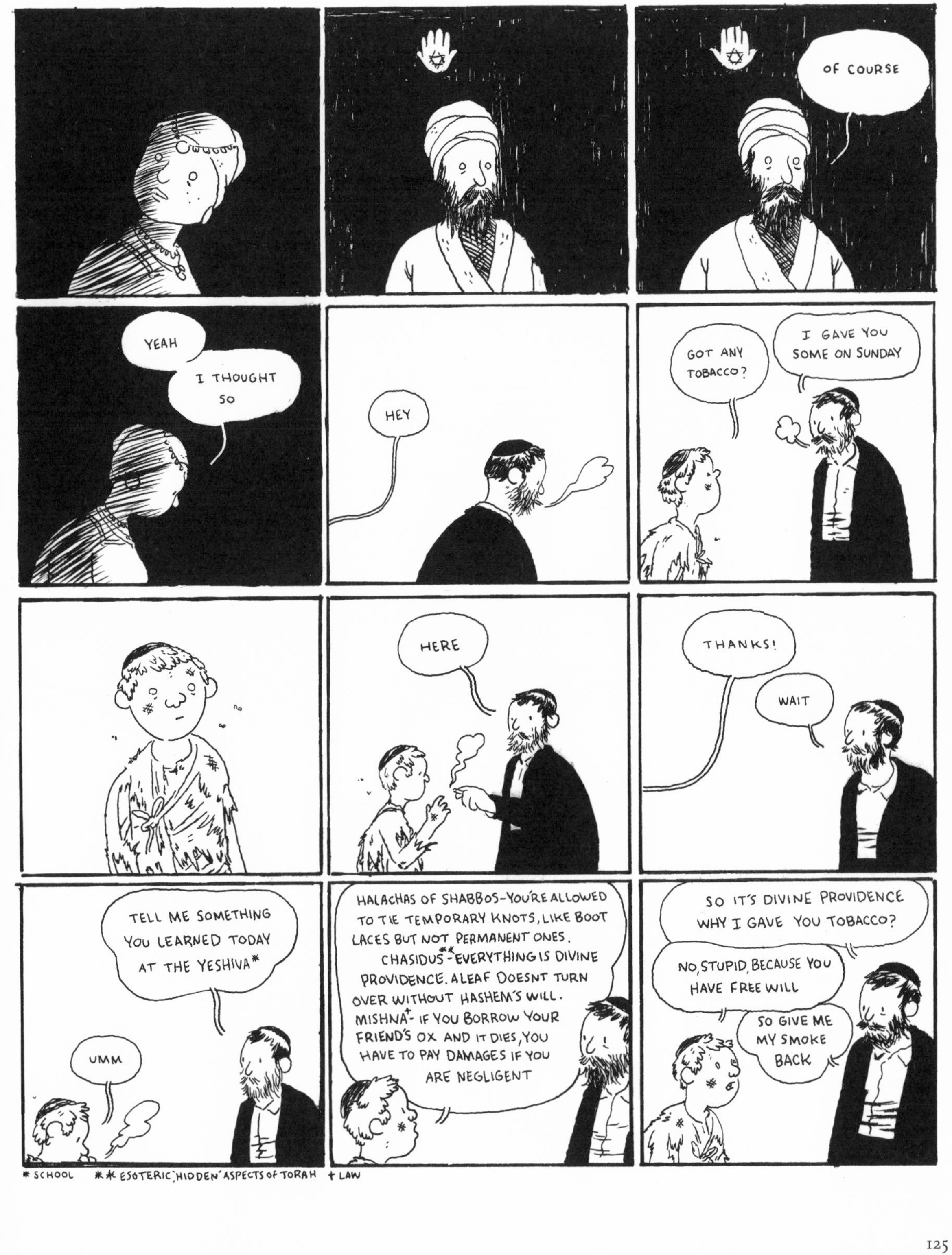
OF COURSE
YEAH
I THOUGHT SO
HEY
GOT ANY TOBACCO?
I GAVE YOU SOME ON SUNDAY
HERE
THANKS!
WAIT
TELL ME SOMETHING YOU LEARNED TODAY AT THE YESHIVA*
UMM
HALACHAS OF SHABBOS-YOU'RE ALLOWED TO TIE TEMPORARY KNOTS, LIKE BOOT LACES BUT NOT PERMANENT ONES.
CHASIDUS**-EVERYTHING IS DIVINE PROVIDENCE. A LEAF DOESNT TURN OVER WITHOUT HASHEM'S WILL.
MISHNA+- IF YOU BORROW YOUR FRIEND'S OX AND IT DIES, YOU HAVE TO PAY DAMAGES IF YOU ARE NEGLIGENT
SO IT'S DIVINE PROVIDENCE WHY I GAVE YOU TOBACCO?
NO, STUPID, BECAUSE YOU HAVE FREE WILL
SO GIVE ME MY SMOKE BACK

* SCHOOL ** ESOTERIC, HIDDEN ASPECTS OF TORAH + LAW

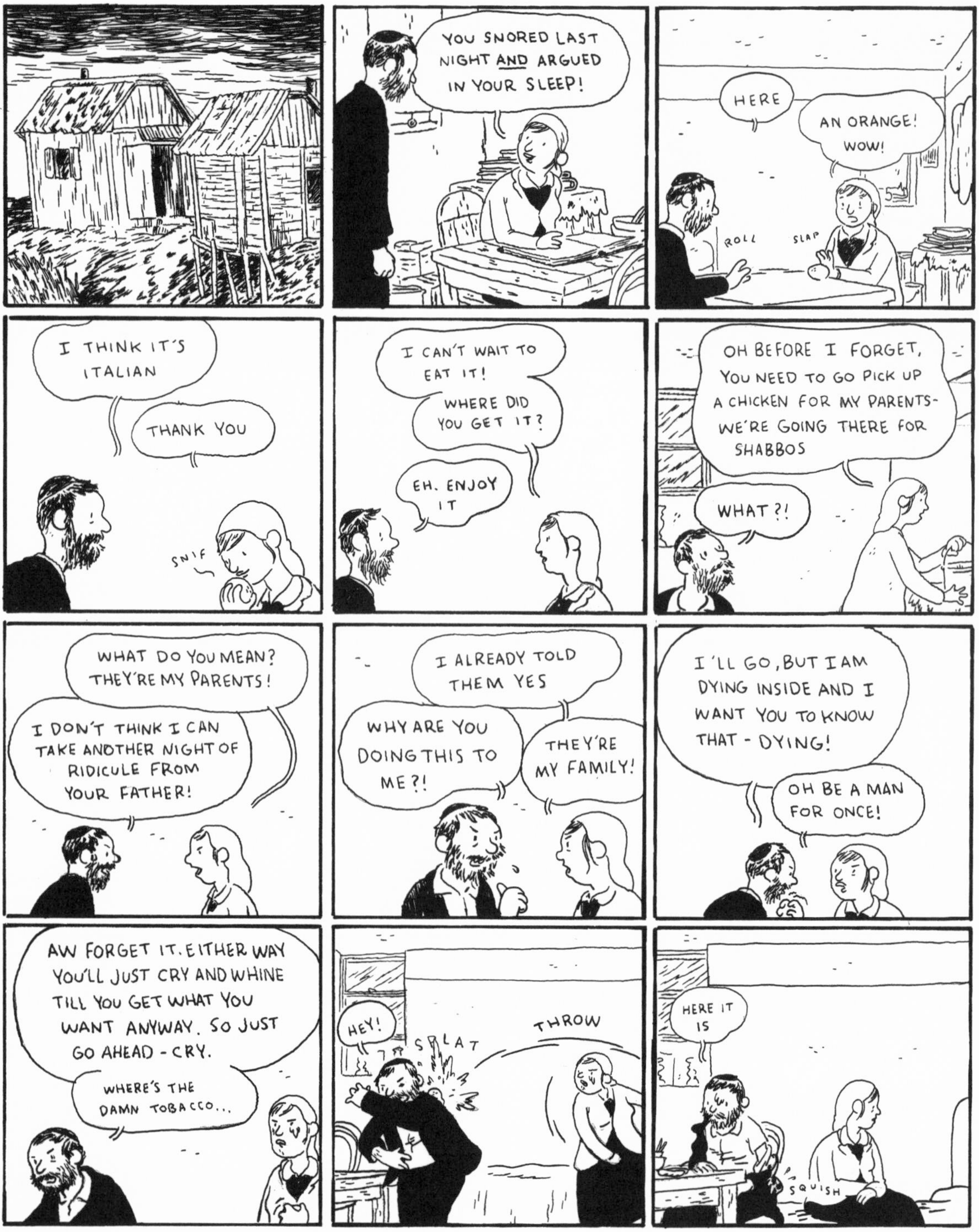
YOU SNORED LAST NIGHT AND ARGUED IN YOUR SLEEP!
HERE
AN ORANGE! WOW!
ROLL
SLAP
I THINK IT'S ITALIAN
THANK YOU
SNIF
I CAN'T WAIT TO EAT IT!
WHERE DID YOU GET IT?
EH. ENJOY IT
OH BEFORE I FORGET, YOU NEED TO GO PICK UP A CHICKEN FOR MY PARENTS- WE'RE GOING THERE FOR SHABBOS
WHAT?!
WHAT DO YOU MEAN? THEY'RE MY PARENTS!
I DON'T THINK I CAN TAKE ANOTHER NIGHT OF RIDICULE FROM YOUR FATHER!
I ALREADY TOLD THEM YES
WHY ARE YOU DOING THIS TO ME?!
THEY'RE MY FAMILY!
I'LL GO, BUT I AM DYING INSIDE AND I WANT YOU TO KNOW THAT - DYING!
OH BE A MAN FOR ONCE!
AW FORGET IT. EITHER WAY YOU'LL JUST CRY AND WHINE TILL YOU GET WHAT YOU WANT ANYWAY. SO JUST GO AHEAD - CRY.
WHERE'S THE DAMN TOBACCO...
HEY!
SPLAT
THROW
HERE IT IS
SQUISH

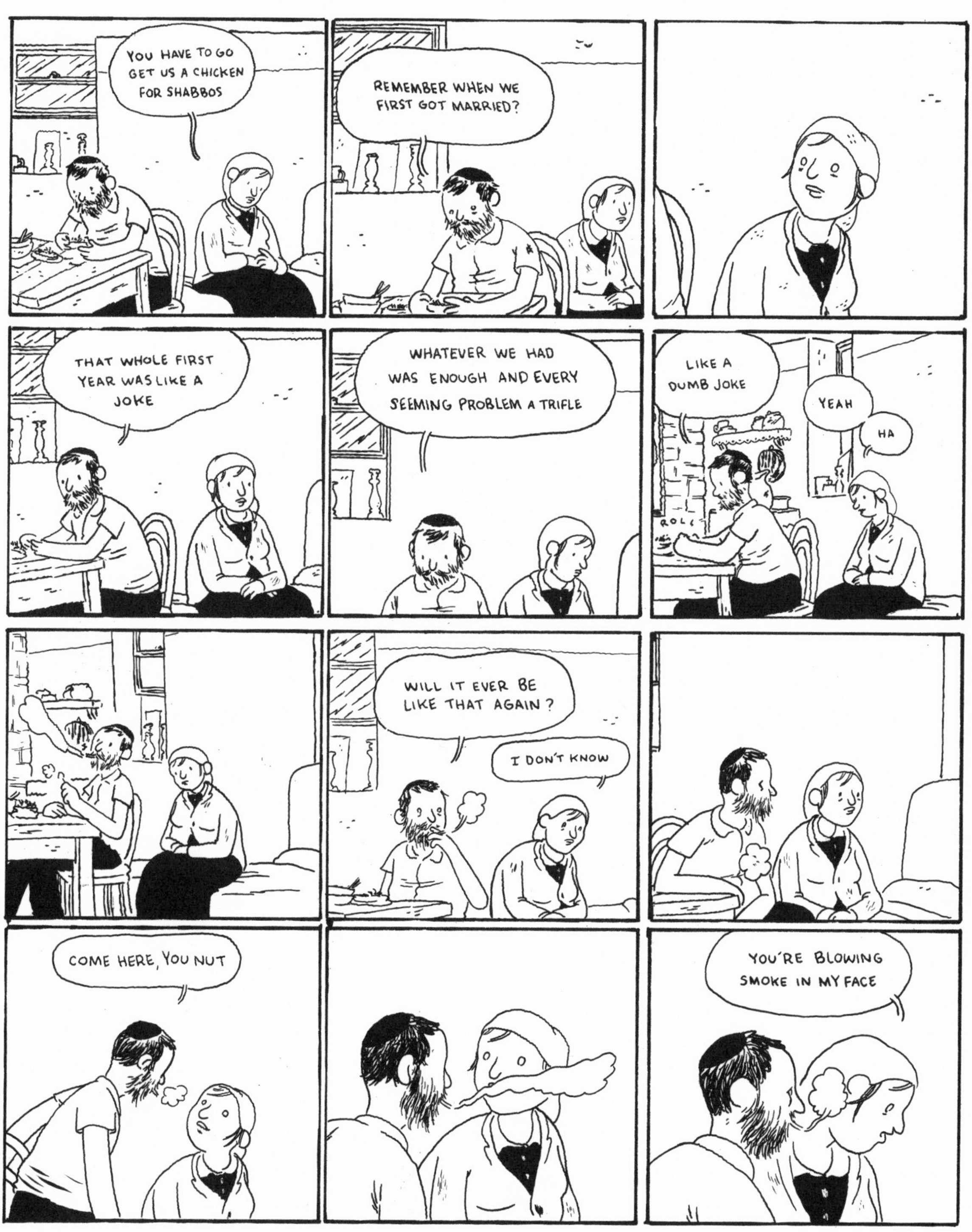

YOU HAVE TO GO GET US A CHICKEN FOR SHABBOS
REMEMBER WHEN WE FIRST GOT MARRIED?
THAT WHOLE FIRST YEAR WAS LIKE A JOKE
WHATEVER WE HAD WAS ENOUGH AND EVERY SEEMING PROBLEM A TRIFLE
LIKE A DUMB JOKE
YEAH
HA
WILL IT EVER BE LIKE THAT AGAIN?
I DON'T KNOW
COME HERE, YOU NUT
YOU'RE BLOWING SMOKE IN MY FACE

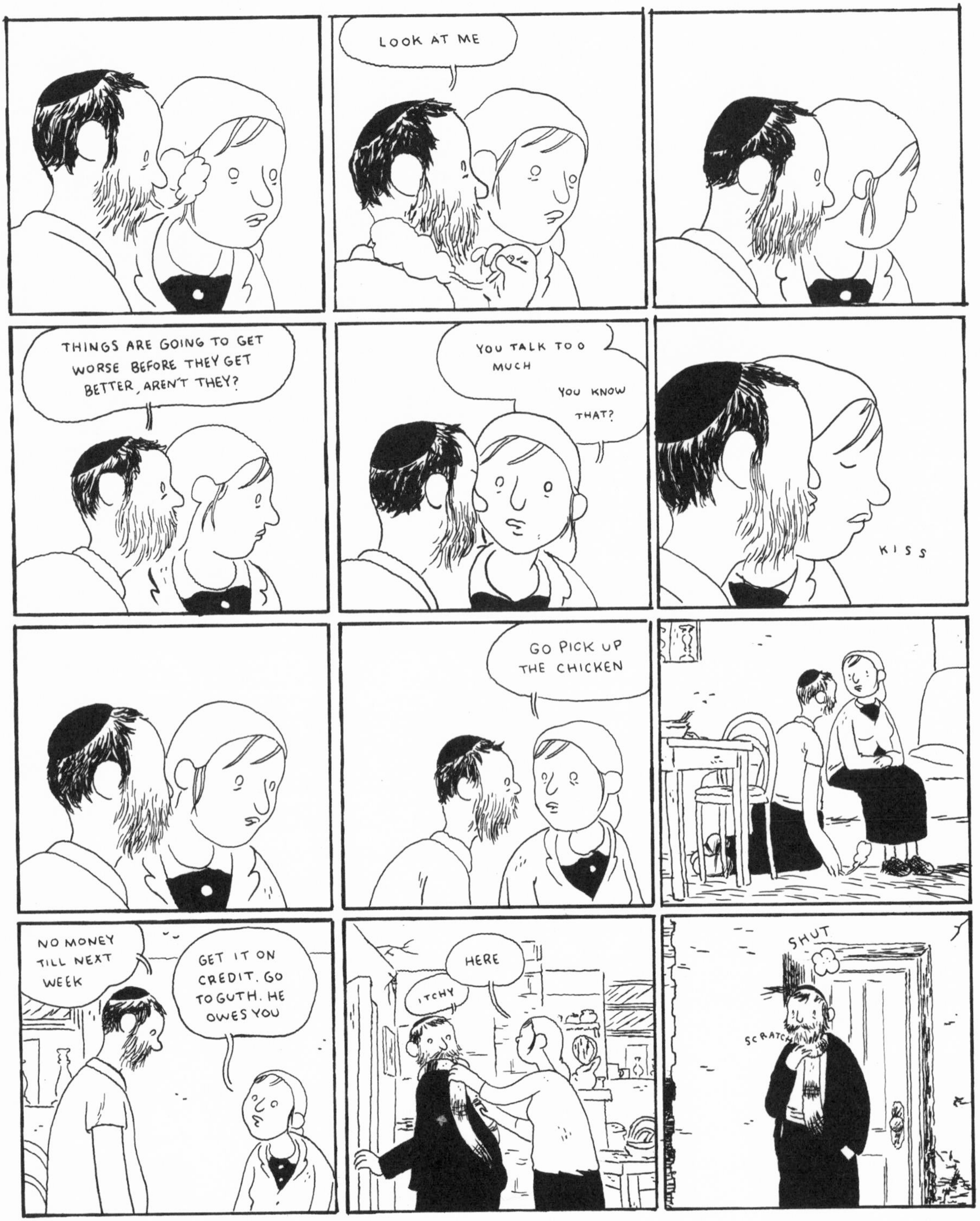
LOOK AT ME
THINGS ARE GOING TO GET WORSE BEFORE THEY GET BETTER, AREN'T THEY?
YOU TALK TOO MUCH
YOU KNOW THAT?
KISS
GO PICK UP THE CHICKEN
NO MONEY TILL NEXT WEEK
GET IT ON CREDIT. GO TO GUTH. HE OWES YOU
ITCHY
HERE
SHUT
SCRATCH

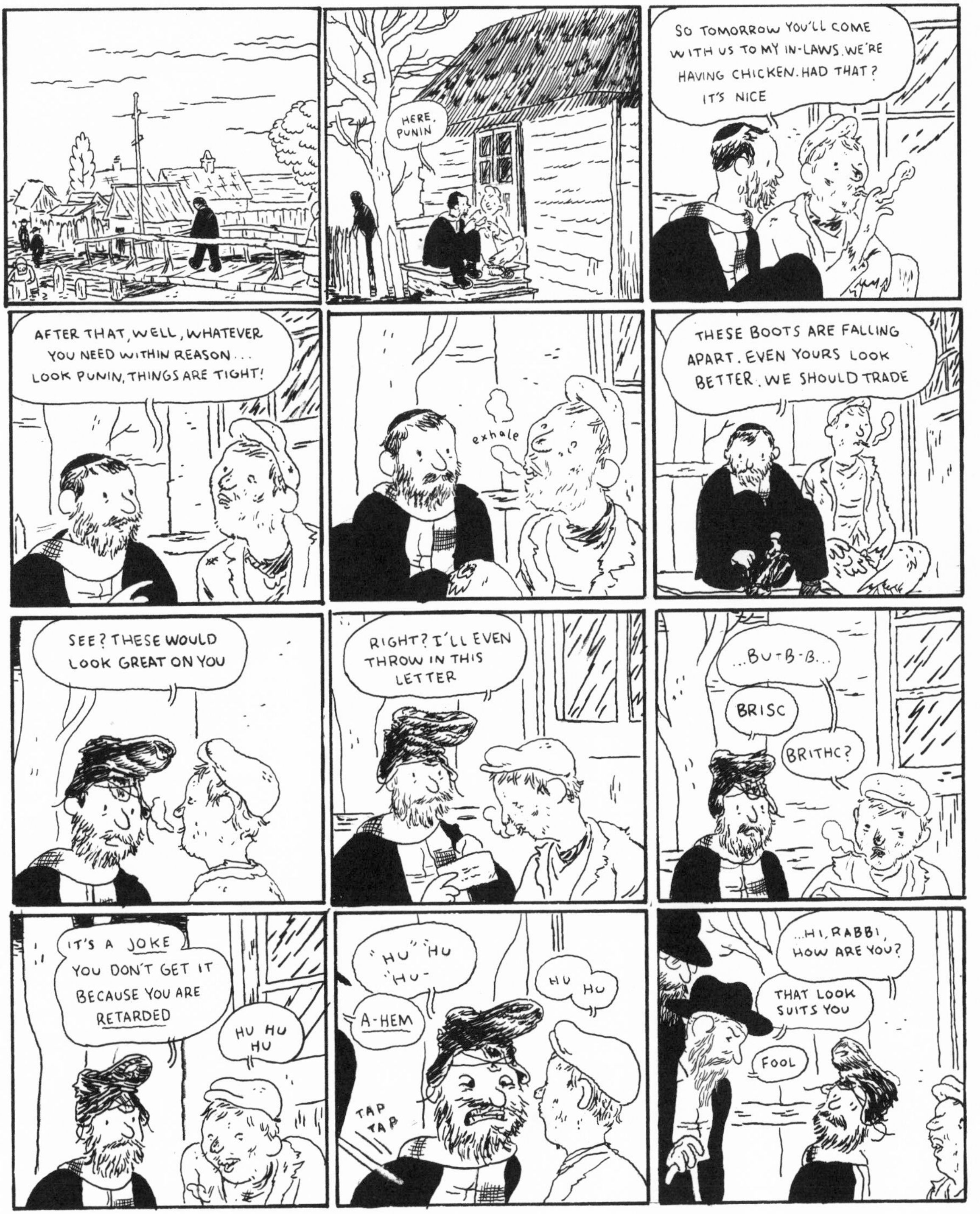
HERE, PUNIN
SO TOMORROW YOU'LL COME WITH US TO MY IN-LAWS. WE'RE HAVING CHICKEN. HAD THAT? IT'S NICE
AFTER THAT, WELL, WHATEVER YOU NEED WITHIN REASON... LOOK PUNIN, THINGS ARE TIGHT!
exhale
THESE BOOTS ARE FALLING APART. EVEN YOURS LOOK BETTER. WE SHOULD TRADE
SEE? THESE WOULD LOOK GREAT ON YOU
RIGHT? I'LL EVEN THROW IN THIS LETTER
...BU-B-B...
BRISC
BRITHC?
IT'S A JOKE
YOU DON'T GET IT BECAUSE YOU ARE RETARDED
HU HU HU
HU HU HU-
HU HU
A-HEM
TAP TAP
...HI, RABBI, HOW ARE YOU?
THAT LOOK SUITS YOU
FOOL

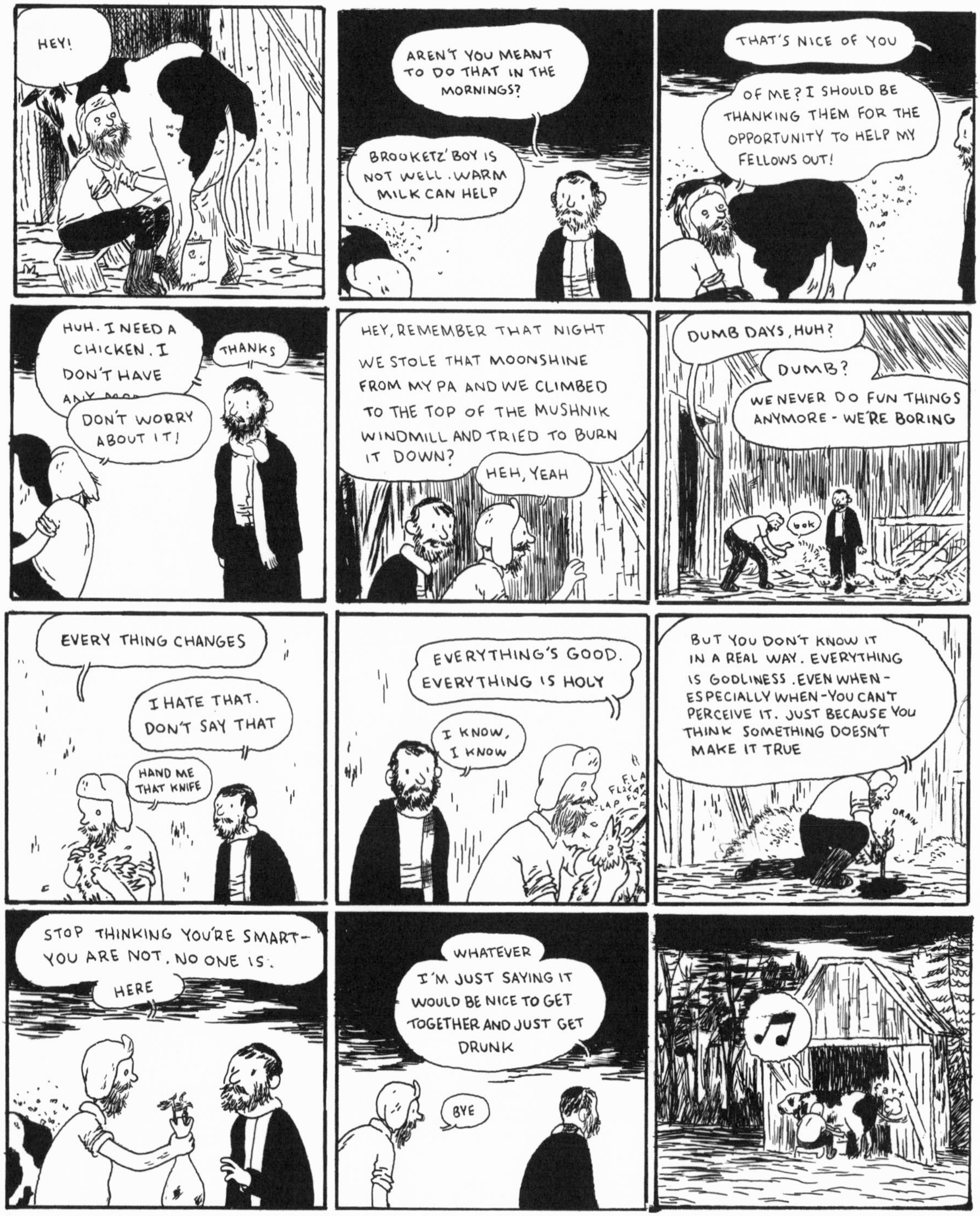

HEY!
AREN'T YOU MEANT TO DO THAT IN THE MORNINGS?
BROOKETZ' BOY IS NOT WELL. WARM MILK CAN HELP
THAT'S NICE OF YOU
OF ME? I SHOULD BE THANKING THEM FOR THE OPPORTUNITY TO HELP MY FELLOWS OUT!
HUH. I NEED A CHICKEN. I DON'T HAVE
THANKS
DON'T WORRY ABOUT IT!
HEY, REMEMBER THAT NIGHT
WE STOLE THAT MOONSHINE FROM MY PA AND WE CLIMBED TO THE TOP OF THE MUSHNIK WINDMILL AND TRIED TO BURN IT DOWN?
HEH, YEAH
DUMB DAYS, HUH?
DUMB?
WE NEVER DO FUN THINGS ANYMORE - WE'RE BORING
bok
EVERY THING CHANGES
I HATE THAT. DON'T SAY THAT
HAND ME THAT KNIFE
EVERYTHING'S GOOD. EVERYTHING IS HOLY
I KNOW, I KNOW
BUT YOU DON'T KNOW IT IN A REAL WAY. EVERYTHING IS GODLINESS. EVEN WHEN - ESPECIALLY WHEN - YOU CAN'T PERCEIVE IT. JUST BECAUSE YOU THINK SOMETHING DOESN'T MAKE IT TRUE
DRAIN
STOP THINKING YOU'RE SMART - YOU ARE NOT. NO ONE IS.
HERE
WHATEVER
I'M JUST SAYING IT WOULD BE NICE TO GET TOGETHER AND JUST GET DRUNK
BYE

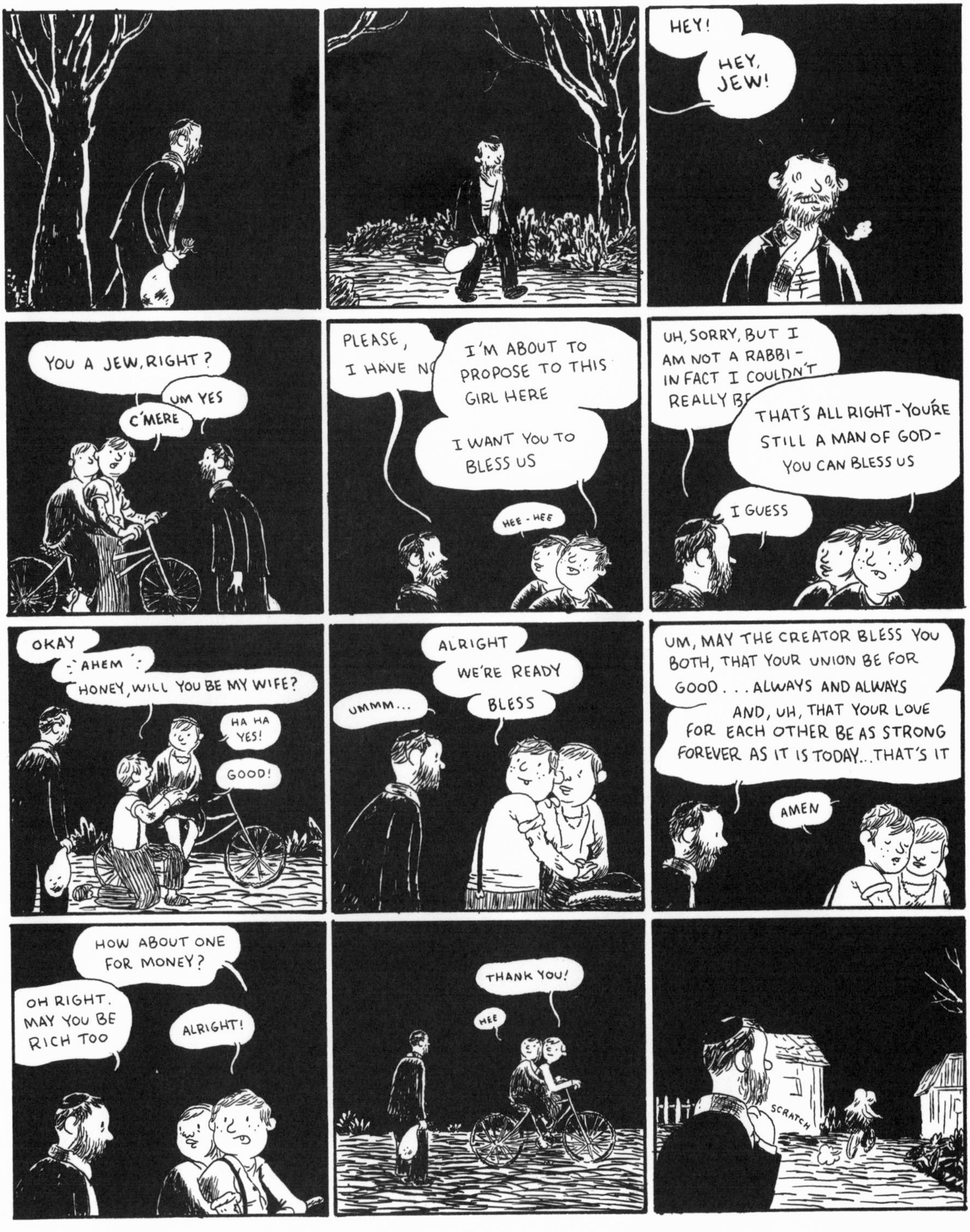
HEY!
HEY, JEW!
YOU A JEW, RIGHT?
UM YES
C'MERE
PLEASE, I HAVE N
I'M ABOUT TO PROPOSE TO THIS GIRL HERE
I WANT YOU TO BLESS US
HEE-HEE
UH, SORRY, BUT I AM NOT A RABBI - IN FACT I COULDN'T REALLY BE
THAT'S ALL RIGHT - YOU'RE STILL A MAN OF GOD - YOU CAN BLESS US
I GUESS
OKAY
AHEM
HONEY, WILL YOU BE MY WIFE?
HA HA YES!
GOOD!
ALRIGHT
WE'RE READY
BLESS
UMMM...
UM, MAY THE CREATOR BLESS YOU BOTH, THAT YOUR UNION BE FOR GOOD . . . ALWAYS AND ALWAYS
AND, UH, THAT YOUR LOVE FOR EACH OTHER BE AS STRONG FOREVER AS IT IS TODAY... THAT'S IT
AMEN
HOW ABOUT ONE FOR MONEY?
OH RIGHT. MAY YOU BE RICH TOO
ALRIGHT!
THANK YOU!
HEE
SCRATCH

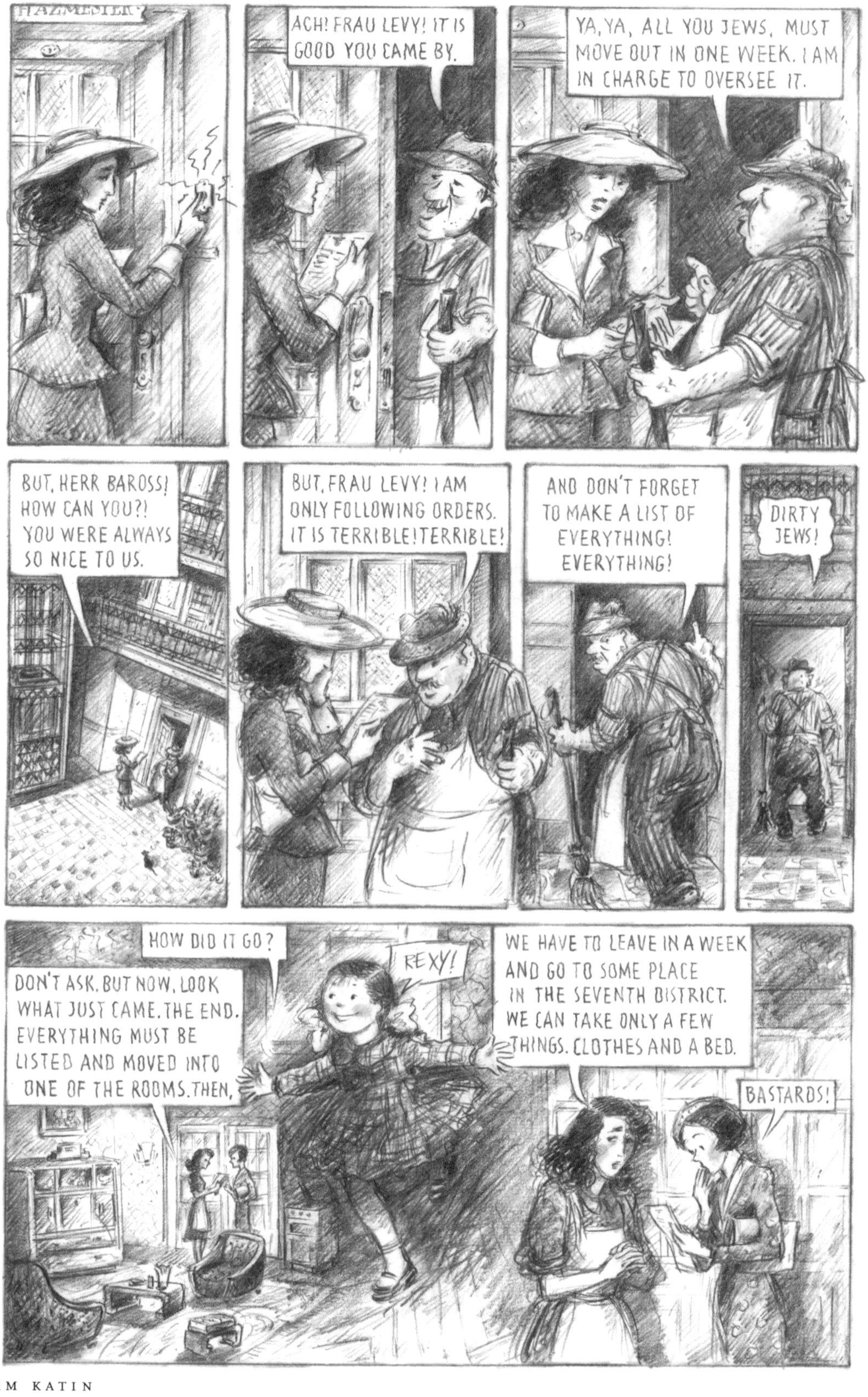
HAZMESTER
ACH! FRAU LEVY! IT IS GOOD YOU CAME BY.
YA, YA, ALL YOU JEWS, MUST MOVE OUT IN ONE WEEK. I AM IN CHARGE TO OVERSEE IT.
BUT, HERR BAROSS! HOW CAN YOU?! YOU WERE ALWAYS SO NICE TO US.
BUT, FRAU LEVY! I AM ONLY FOLLOWING ORDERS. IT IS TERRIBLE! TERRIBLE!
AND DON'T FORGET TO MAKE A LIST OF EVERYTHING! EVERYTHING!
DIRTY JEWS!
HOW DID IT GO?
DON'T ASK. BUT NOW, LOOK WHAT JUST CAME. THE END. EVERYTHING MUST BE LISTED AND MOVED INTO ONE OF THE ROOMS. THEN,
REXY!
WE HAVE TO LEAVE IN A WEEK AND GO TO SOME PLACE IN THE SEVENTH DISTRICT. WE CAN TAKE ONLY A FEW THINGS. CLOTHES AND A BED.
BASTARDS!

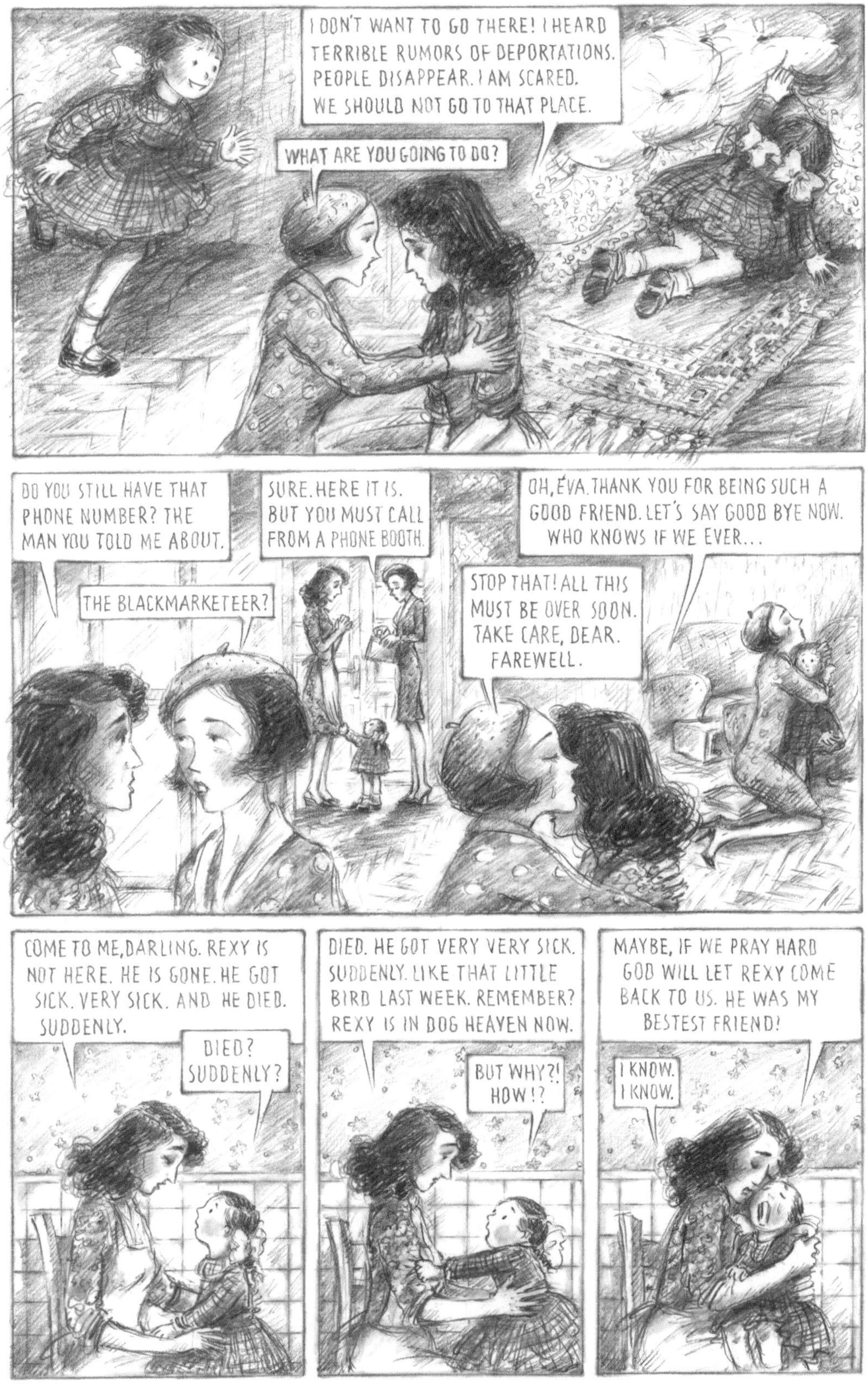
I DON'T WANT TO GO THERE! I HEARD TERRIBLE RUMORS OF DEPORTATIONS. PEOPLE DISAPPEAR. I AM SCARED. WE SHOULD NOT GO TO THAT PLACE.
WHAT ARE YOU GOING TO DO?
DO YOU STILL HAVE THAT PHONE NUMBER? THE MAN YOU TOLD ME ABOUT.
THE BLACKMARKETEER?
SURE. HERE IT IS. BUT YOU MUST CALL FROM A PHONE BOOTH.
OH, ÉVA. THANK YOU FOR BEING SUCH A GOOD FRIEND. LET'S SAY GOOD BYE NOW. WHO KNOWS IF WE EVER...
STOP THAT! ALL THIS MUST BE OVER SOON. TAKE CARE, DEAR. FAREWELL.
COME TO ME, DARLING. REXY IS NOT HERE. HE IS GONE. HE GOT SICK. VERY SICK. AND HE DIED. SUDDENLY.
DIED? SUDDENLY?
DIED. HE GOT VERY VERY SICK. SUDDENLY. LIKE THAT LITTLE BIRD LAST WEEK. REMEMBER? REXY IS IN DOG HEAVEN NOW.
BUT WHY?! HOW!?
MAYBE, IF WE PRAY HARD GOD WILL LET REXY COME BACK TO US. HE WAS MY BESTEST FRIEND!
I KNOW. I KNOW.

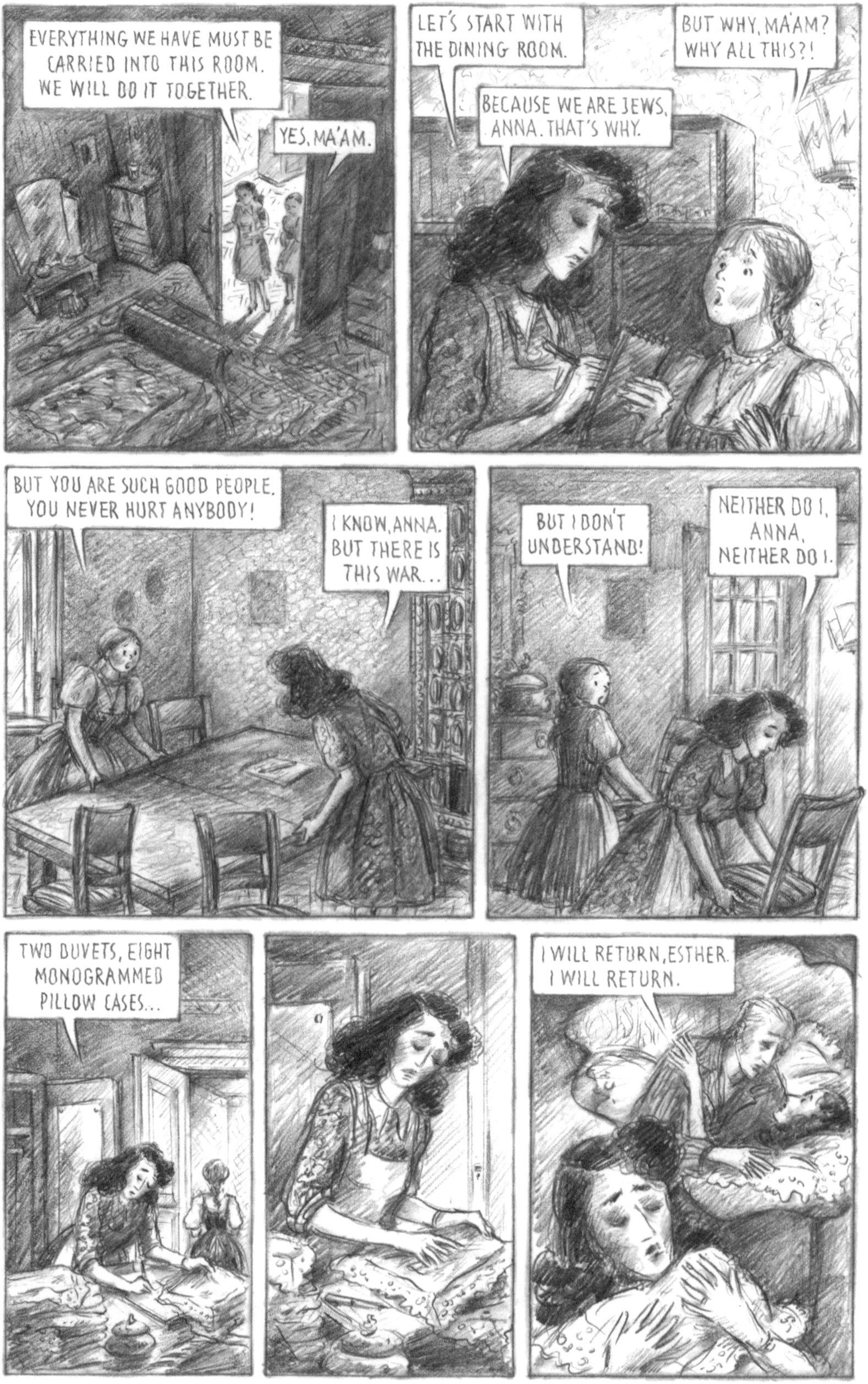
EVERYTHING WE HAVE MUST BE CARRIED INTO THIS ROOM. WE WILL DO IT TOGETHER.
YES, MA'AM.
LET'S START WITH THE DINING ROOM.
BUT WHY, MA'AM? WHY ALL THIS?!
BECAUSE WE ARE JEWS, ANNA. THAT'S WHY.
BUT YOU ARE SUCH GOOD PEOPLE. YOU NEVER HURT ANYBODY!
I KNOW, ANNA. BUT THERE IS THIS WAR...
BUT I DON'T UNDERSTAND!
NEITHER DO I, ANNA, NEITHER DO I.
TWO DUVETS, EIGHT MONOGRAMMED PILLOW CASES...
I WILL RETURN, ESTHER. I WILL RETURN.

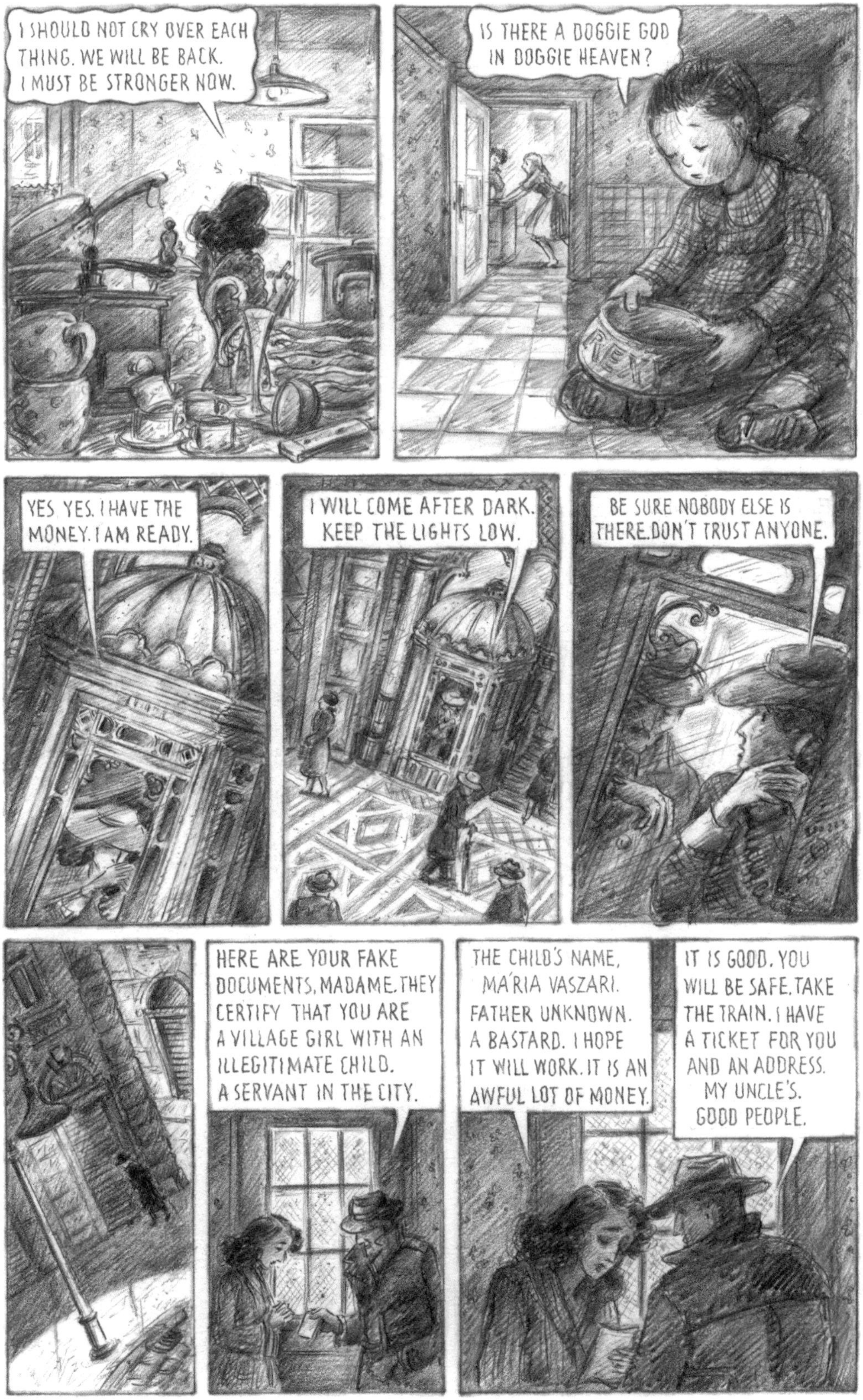
I SHOULD NOT CRY OVER EACH THING. WE WILL BE BACK. I MUST BE STRONGER NOW.
IS THERE A DOGGIE GOD IN DOGGIE HEAVEN?
REX
YES. YES. I HAVE THE MONEY. I AM READY.
I WILL COME AFTER DARK. KEEP THE LIGHTS LOW.
BE SURE NOBODY ELSE IS THERE. DON'T TRUST ANYONE.
HERE ARE YOUR FAKE DOCUMENTS, MADAME. THEY CERTIFY THAT YOU ARE A VILLAGE GIRL WITH AN ILLEGITIMATE CHILD. A SERVANT IN THE CITY.
THE CHILD'S NAME, MÁRIA VASZARI. FATHER UNKNOWN. A BASTARD. I HOPE IT WILL WORK. IT IS AN AWFUL LOT OF MONEY.
IT IS GOOD. YOU WILL BE SAFE. TAKE THE TRAIN. I HAVE A TICKET FOR YOU AND AN ADDRESS. MY UNCLE'S. GOOD PEOPLE.

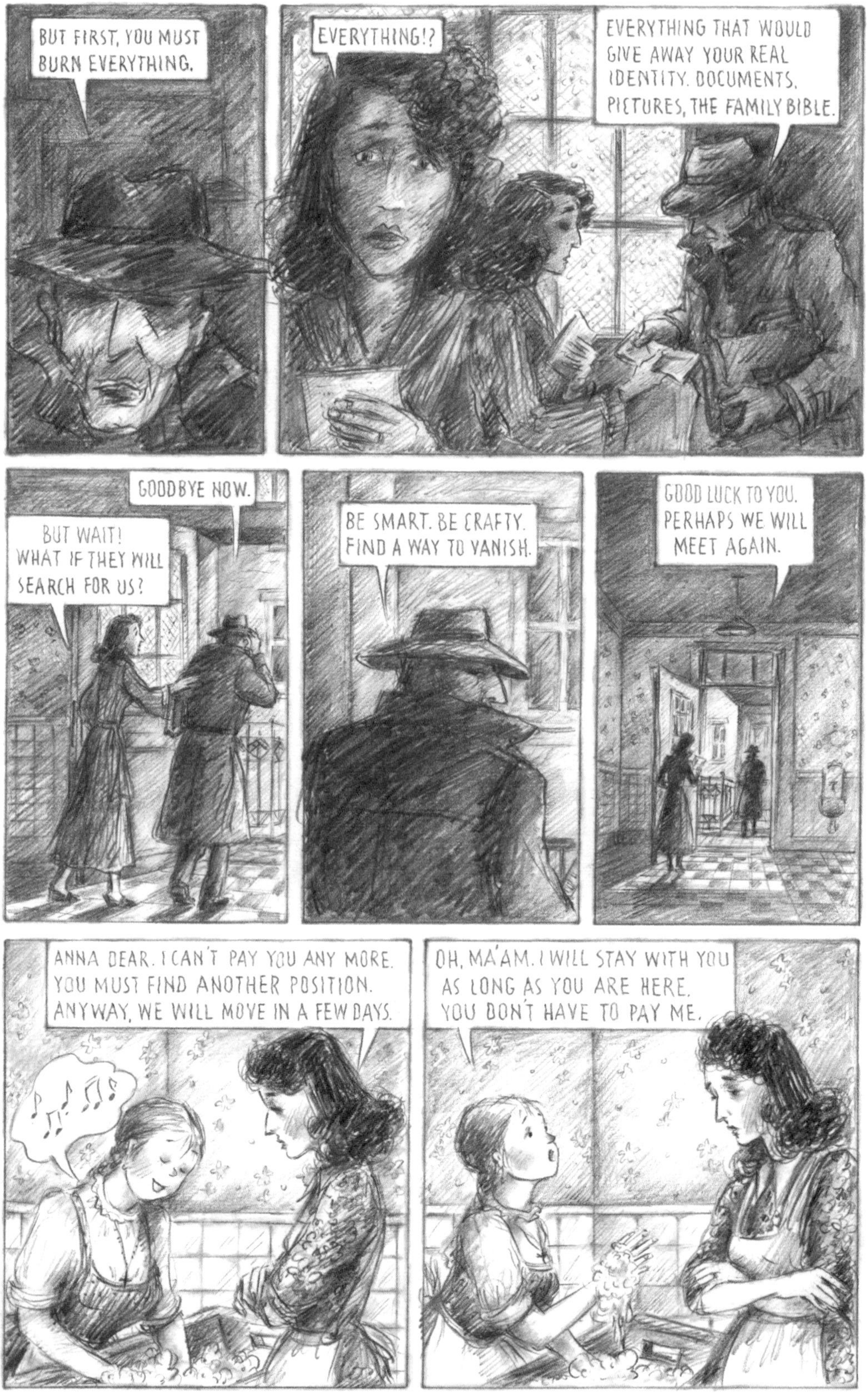
BUT FIRST, YOU MUST BURN EVERYTHING.
EVERYTHING!?
EVERYTHING THAT WOULD GIVE AWAY YOUR REAL IDENTITY. DOCUMENTS, PICTURES, THE FAMILY BIBLE.
GOODBYE NOW.
BUT WAIT! WHAT IF THEY WILL SEARCH FOR US?
BE SMART. BE CRAFTY. FIND A WAY TO VANISH.
GOOD LUCK TO YOU. PERHAPS WE WILL MEET AGAIN.
ANNA DEAR. I CAN'T PAY YOU ANY MORE. YOU MUST FIND ANOTHER POSITION. ANYWAY, WE WILL MOVE IN A FEW DAYS.
OH, MA'AM. I WILL STAY WITH YOU AS LONG AS YOU ARE HERE. YOU DON'T HAVE TO PAY ME.

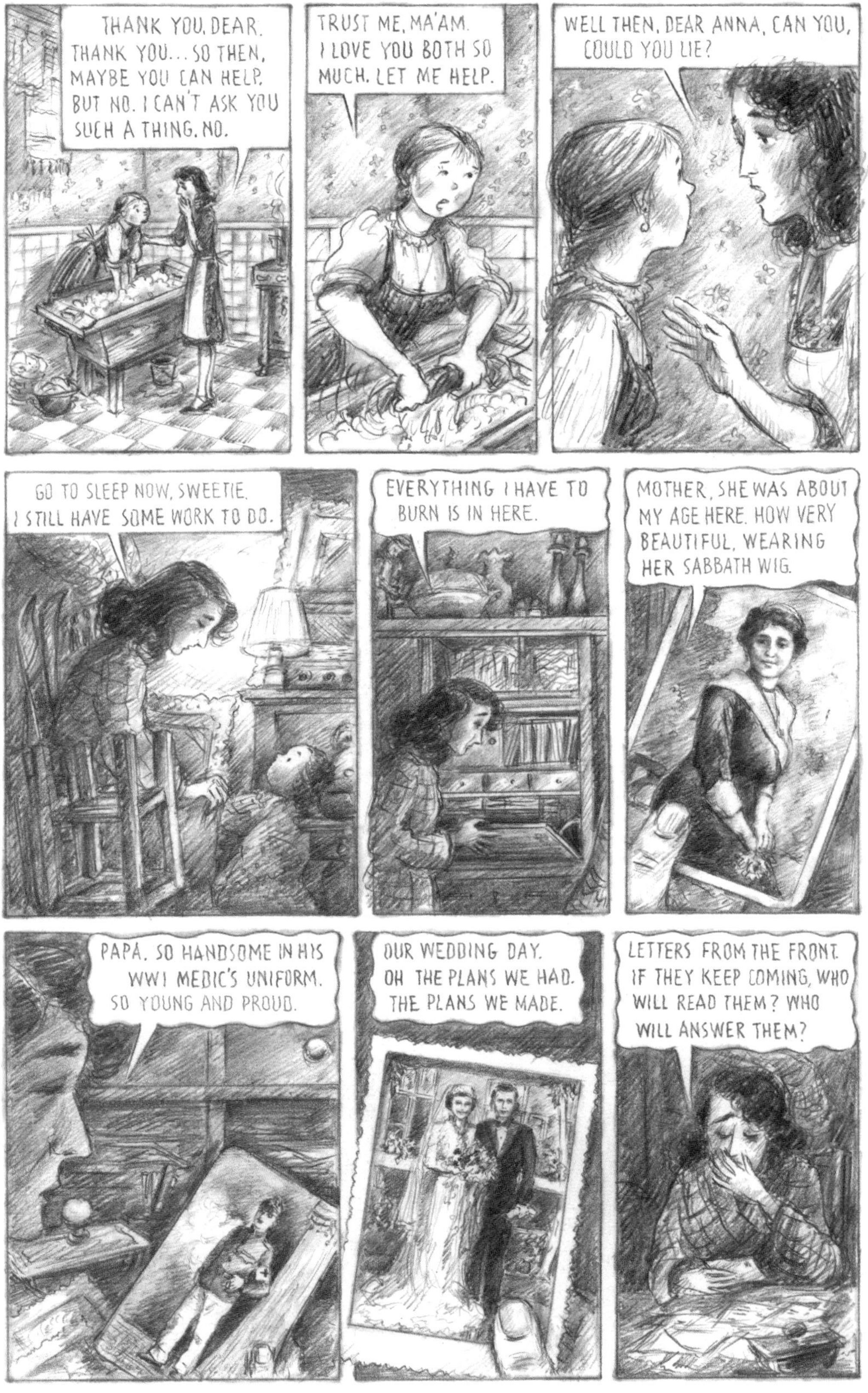
THANK YOU, DEAR. THANK YOU... SO THEN, MAYBE YOU CAN HELP. BUT NO. I CAN'T ASK YOU SUCH A THING. NO.
TRUST ME, MA'AM. I LOVE YOU BOTH SO MUCH. LET ME HELP.
WELL THEN, DEAR ANNA, CAN YOU, COULD YOU LIE?
GO TO SLEEP NOW, SWEETIE. I STILL HAVE SOME WORK TO DO.
EVERYTHING I HAVE TO BURN IS IN HERE.
MOTHER, SHE WAS ABOUT MY AGE HERE. HOW VERY BEAUTIFUL, WEARING HER SABBATH WIG.
PAPA. SO HANDSOME IN HIS WWI MEDIC'S UNIFORM. SO YOUNG AND PROUD.
OUR WEDDING DAY. OH THE PLANS WE HAD. THE PLANS WE MADE.
LETTERS FROM THE FRONT. IF THEY KEEP COMING, WHO WILL READ THEM? WHO WILL ANSWER THEM?

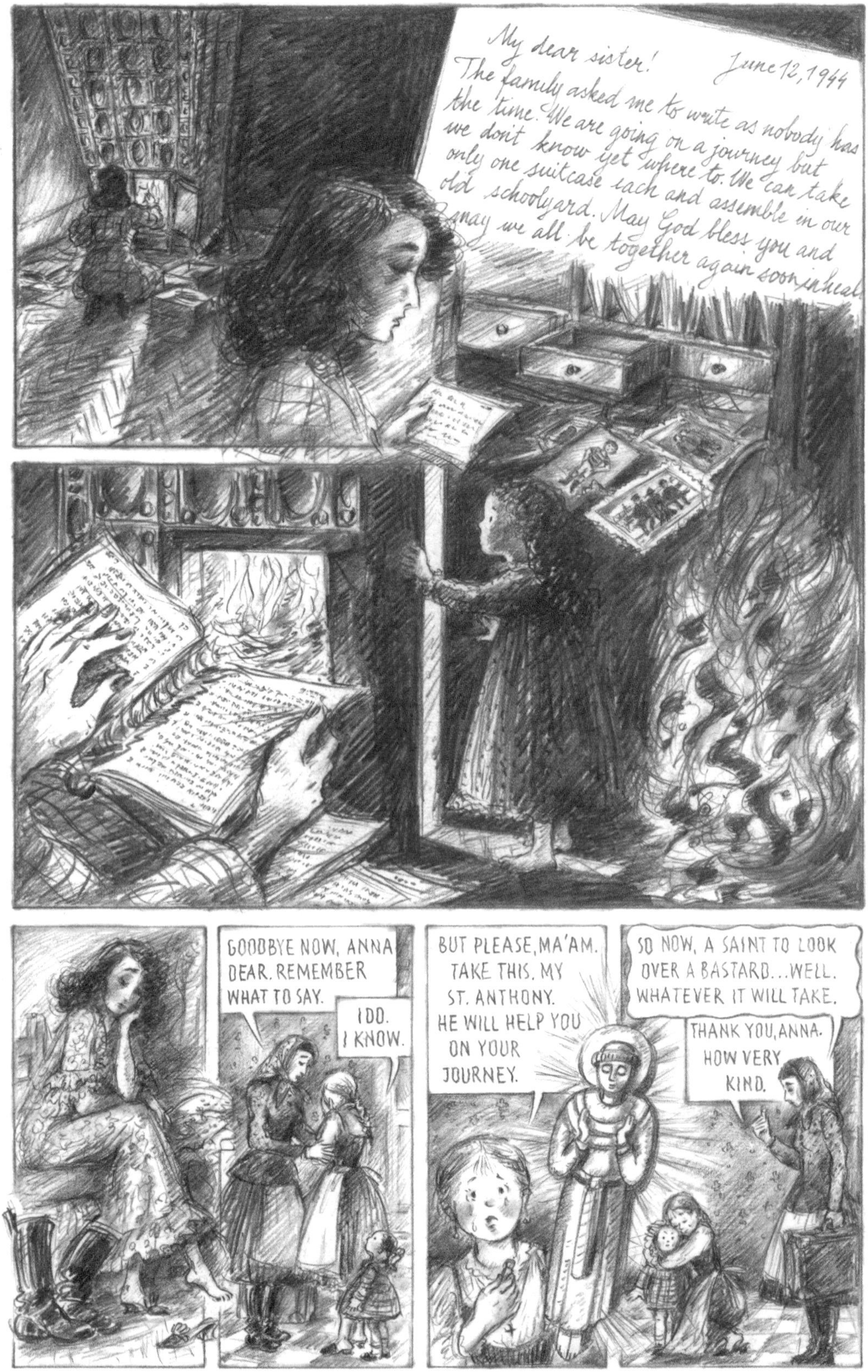
My dear sister! June 12, 1944
The family asked me to write as nobody has the time. We are going on a journey but we don't know yet where to. We can take only one suitcase each and assemble in our old schoolyard. May God bless you and may we all be together again soon in heal
GOODBYE NOW, ANNA DEAR. REMEMBER WHAT TO SAY.
I DO. I KNOW.
BUT PLEASE, MA'AM. TAKE THIS. MY ST. ANTHONY. HE WILL HELP YOU ON YOUR JOURNEY.
SO NOW, A SAINT TO LOOK OVER A BASTARD... WELL. WHATEVER IT WILL TAKE.
THANK YOU, ANNA. HOW VERY KIND.

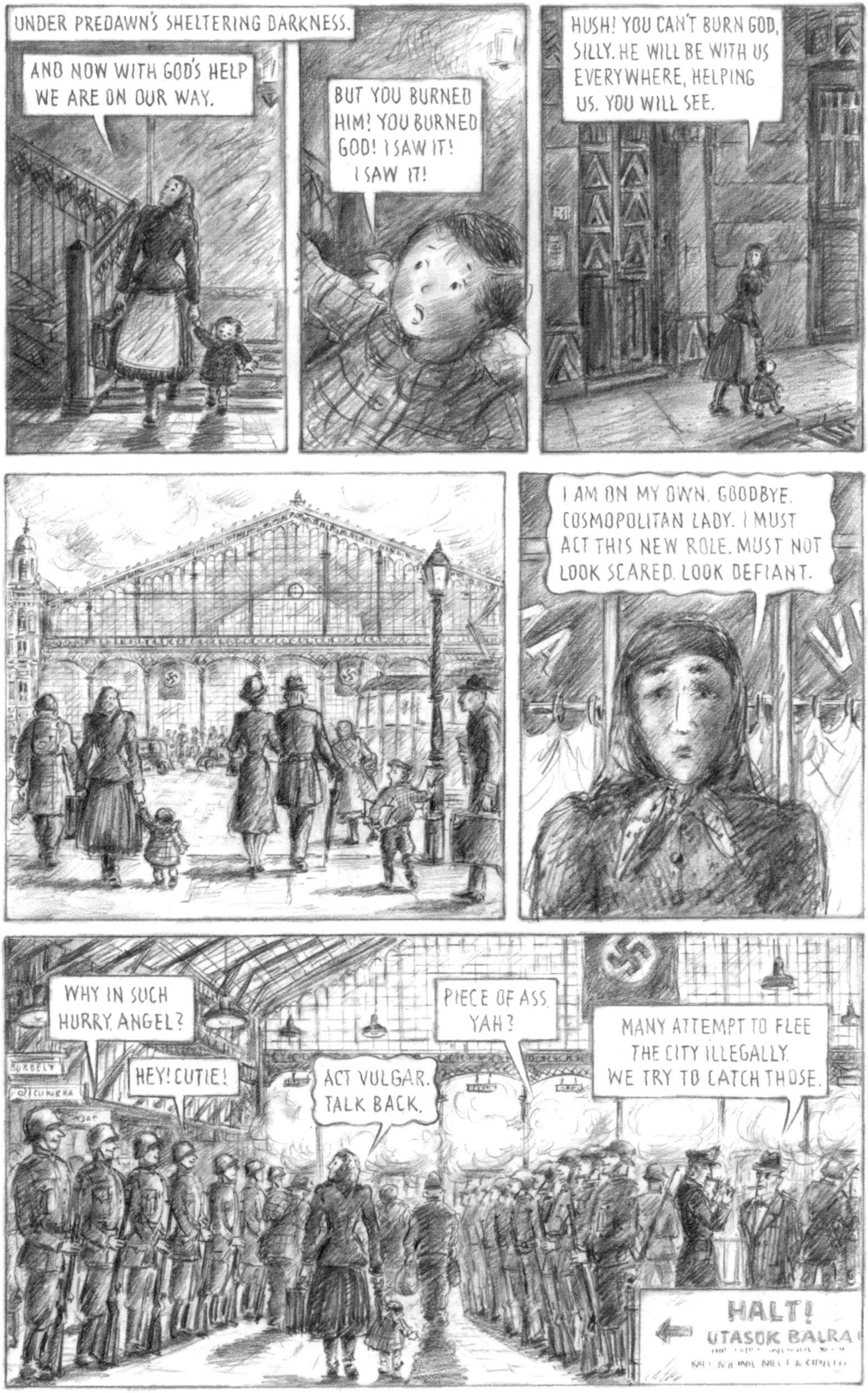
UNDER PREDAWN'S SHELTERING DARKNESS.
AND NOW WITH GOD'S HELP WE ARE ON OUR WAY.
BUT YOU BURNED HIM! YOU BURNED GOD! I SAW IT! I SAW IT!
HUSH! YOU CAN'T BURN GOD, SILLY. HE WILL BE WITH US EVERYWHERE, HELPING US. YOU WILL SEE.
I AM ON MY OWN. GOODBYE. COSMOPOLITAN LADY. I MUST ACT THIS NEW ROLE. MUST NOT LOOK SCARED. LOOK DEFIANT.
WHY IN SUCH HURRY, ANGEL?
HEY! CUTIE!
ACT VULGAR. TALK BACK.
PIECE OF ASS, YAH?
MANY ATTEMPT TO FLEE THE CITY ILLEGALLY. WE TRY TO CATCH THOSE.
HALT!
UTASOK BALRA

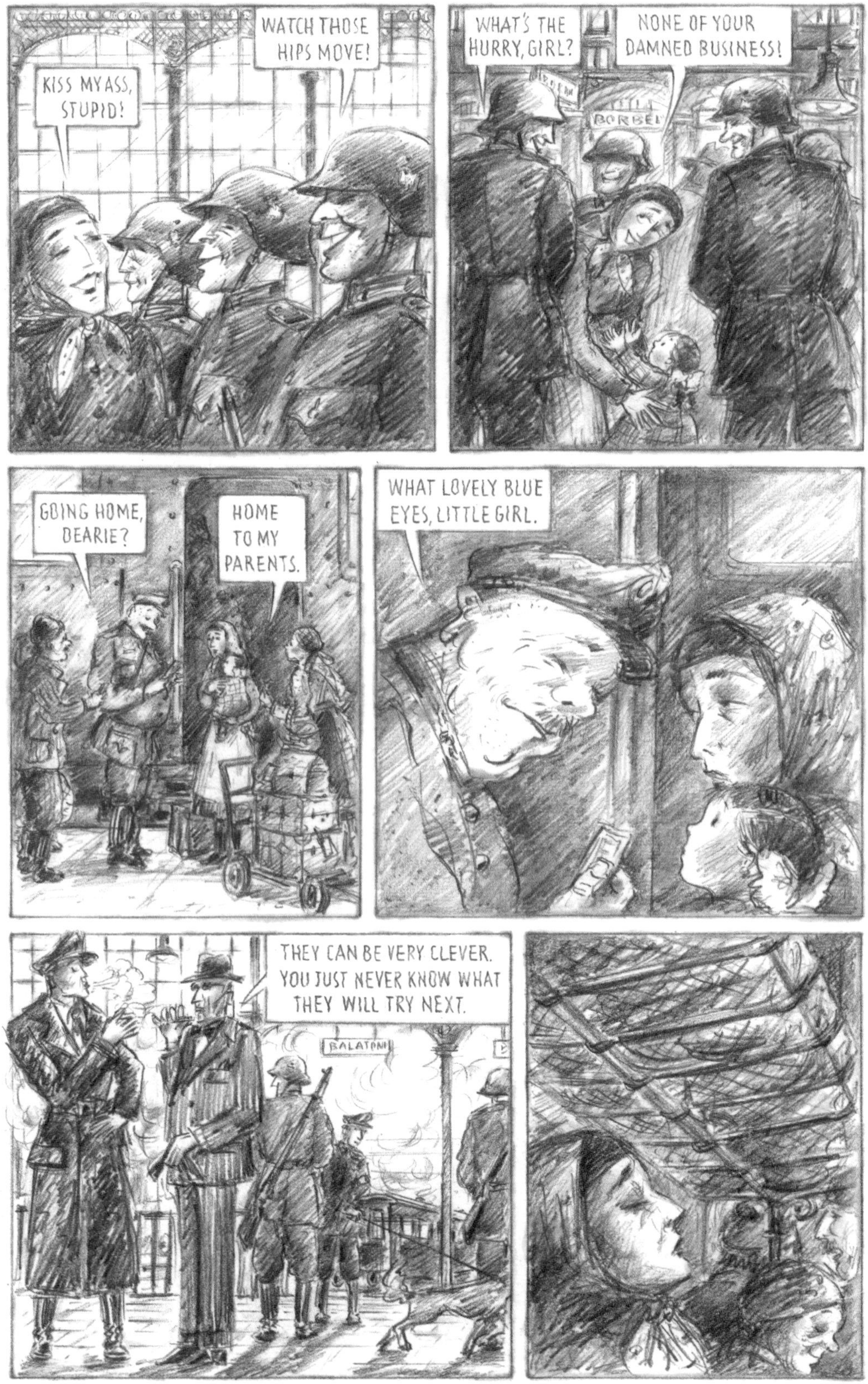
WATCH THOSE HIPS MOVE!
KISS MY ASS, STUPID!
WHAT'S THE HURRY, GIRL?
NONE OF YOUR DAMNED BUSINESS!
GOING HOME, DEARIE?
HOME TO MY PARENTS.
WHAT LOVELY BLUE EYES, LITTLE GIRL.
THEY CAN BE VERY CLEVER. YOU JUST NEVER KNOW WHAT THEY WILL TRY NEXT.
BALATON

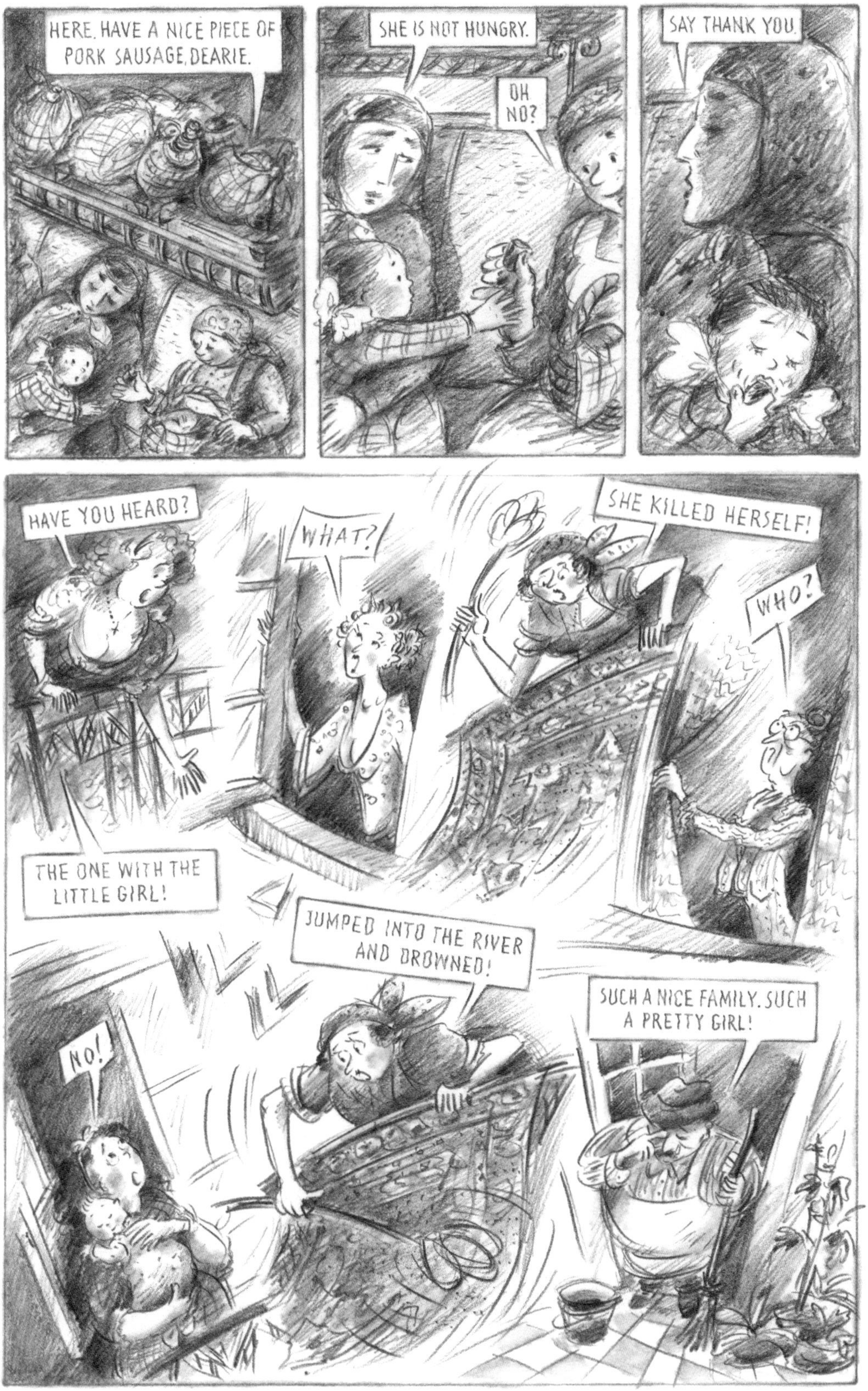
HERE. HAVE A NICE PIECE OF PORK SAUSAGE, DEARIE.
SHE IS NOT HUNGRY.
OH NO?
SAY THANK YOU.
HAVE YOU HEARD?
WHAT?
SHE KILLED HERSELF!
WHO?
THE ONE WITH THE LITTLE GIRL!
JUMPED INTO THE RIVER AND DROWNED!
NO!
SUCH A NICE FAMILY. SUCH A PRETTY GIRL!

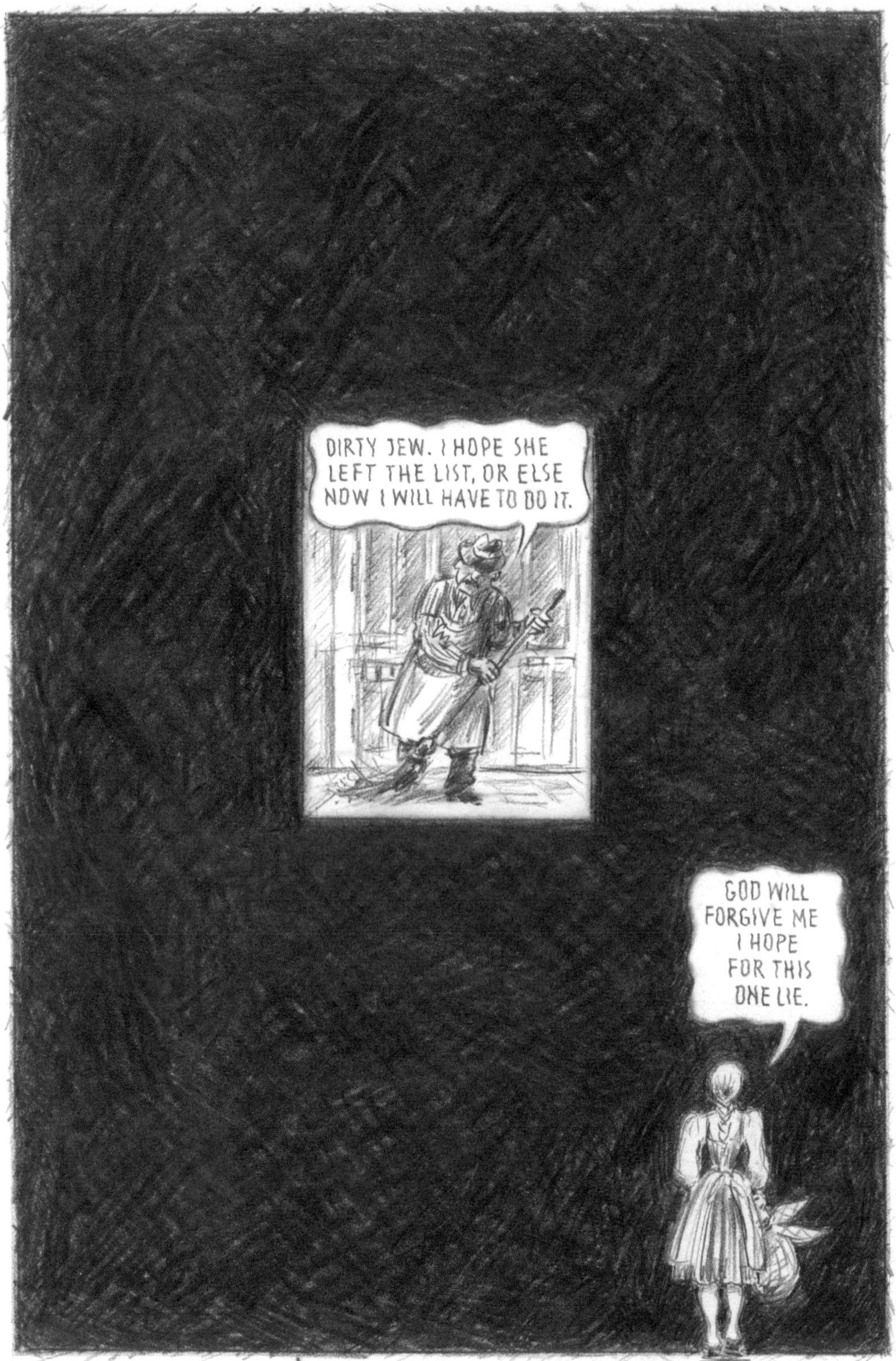
DIRTY JEW. I HOPE SHE LEFT THE LIST, OR ELSE NOW I WILL HAVE TO DO IT.
GOD WILL FORGIVE ME I HOPE FOR THIS ONE LIE.

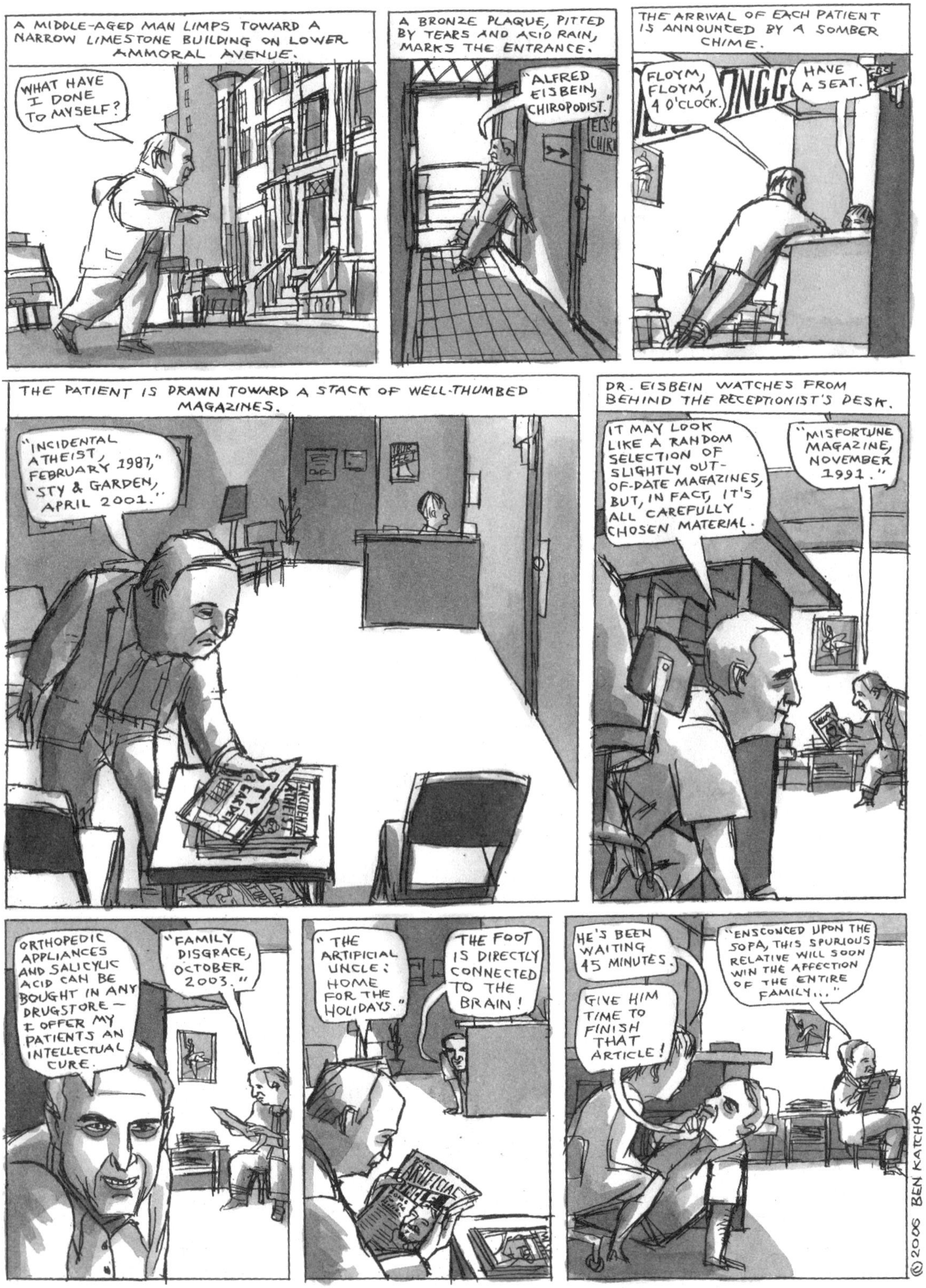

A MIDDLE-AGED MAN LIMPS TOWARD A NARROW LIMESTONE BUILDING ON LOWER AMMORAL AVENUE.
WHAT HAVE I DONE TO MYSELF?
A BRONZE PLAQUE, PITTED BY TEARS AND ACID RAIN, MARKS THE ENTRANCE.
"ALFRED EISBEIN, CHIROPODIST."
THE ARRIVAL OF EACH PATIENT IS ANNOUNCED BY A SOMBER CHIME.
FLOYM, FLOYM, 4 O'CLOCK.
HAVE A SEAT.
THE PATIENT IS DRAWN TOWARD A STACK OF WELL-THUMBED MAGAZINES.
"INCIDENTAL ATHEIST, FEBRUARY 1987," "STY & GARDEN, APRIL 2001."
DR. EISBEIN WATCHES FROM BEHIND THE RECEPTIONIST'S DESK.
IT MAY LOOK LIKE A RANDOM SELECTION OF SLIGHTLY OUT-OF-DATE MAGAZINES, BUT, IN FACT, IT'S ALL CAREFULLY CHOSEN MATERIAL.
"MISFORTUNE MAGAZINE, NOVEMBER 1991."
ORTHOPEDIC APPLIANCES AND SALICYLIC ACID CAN BE BOUGHT IN ANY DRUGSTORE — I OFFER MY PATIENTS AN INTELLECTUAL CURE.
"FAMILY DISGRACE, OCTOBER 2003."
"THE ARTIFICIAL UNCLE: HOME FOR THE HOLIDAYS."
THE FOOT IS DIRECTLY CONNECTED TO THE BRAIN!
HE'S BEEN WAITING 45 MINUTES.
GIVE HIM TIME TO FINISH THAT ARTICLE!
"ENSCONCED UPON THE SOFA, THIS SPURIOUS RELATIVE WILL SOON WIN THE AFFECTION OF THE ENTIRE FAMILY..."
© 2006 BEN KATCHOR

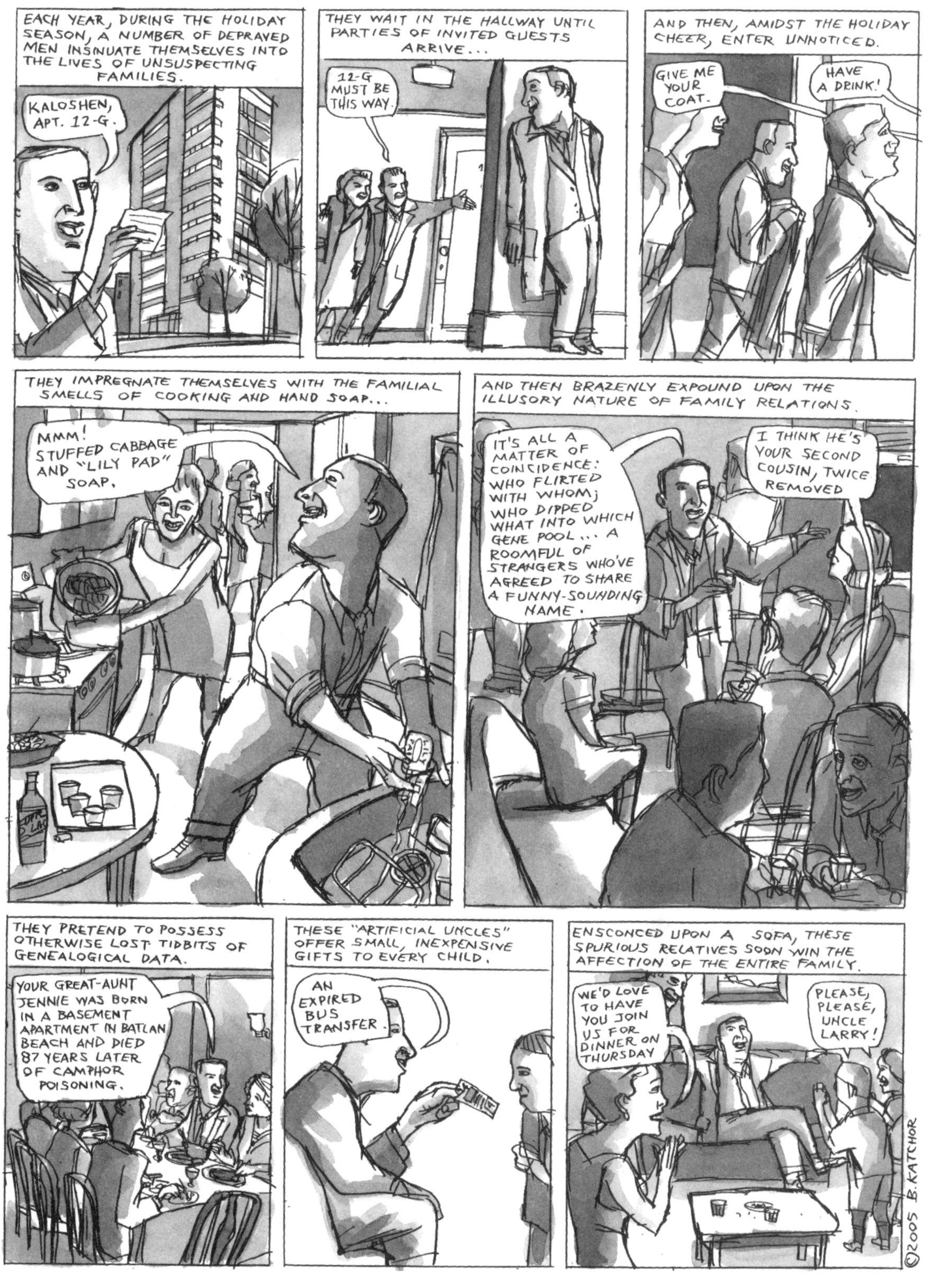
EACH YEAR, DURING THE HOLIDAY SEASON, A NUMBER OF DEPRAVED MEN INSINUATE THEMSELVES INTO THE LIVES OF UNSUSPECTING FAMILIES.
KALOSHEN, APT. 12-G.
THEY WAIT IN THE HALLWAY UNTIL PARTIES OF INVITED GUESTS ARRIVE...
12-G MUST BE THIS WAY.
AND THEN, AMIDST THE HOLIDAY CHEER, ENTER UNNOTICED.
GIVE ME YOUR COAT.
HAVE A DRINK!
THEY IMPREGNATE THEMSELVES WITH THE FAMILIAL SMELLS OF COOKING AND HAND SOAP...
MMM! STUFFED CABBAGE AND "LILY PAD" SOAP.
AND THEN BRAZENLY EXPOUND UPON THE ILLUSORY NATURE OF FAMILY RELATIONS.
IT'S ALL A MATTER OF COINCIDENCE: WHO FLIRTED WITH WHOM; WHO DIPPED WHAT INTO WHICH GENE POOL... A ROOMFUL OF STRANGERS WHO'VE AGREED TO SHARE A FUNNY-SOUNDING NAME.
I THINK HE'S YOUR SECOND COUSIN, TWICE REMOVED
THEY PRETEND TO POSSESS OTHERWISE LOST TIDBITS OF GENEALOGICAL DATA.
YOUR GREAT-AUNT JENNIE WAS BORN IN A BASEMENT APARTMENT IN BATLAN BEACH AND DIED 87 YEARS LATER OF CAMPHOR POISONING.
THESE "ARTIFICIAL UNCLES" OFFER SMALL, INEXPENSIVE GIFTS TO EVERY CHILD.
AN EXPIRED BUS TRANSFER.
ENSCONCED UPON A SOFA, THESE SPURIOUS RELATIVES SOON WIN THE AFFECTION OF THE ENTIRE FAMILY.
WE'D LOVE TO HAVE YOU JOIN US FOR DINNER ON THURSDAY
PLEASE, PLEASE, UNCLE LARRY!
©2005 B. KATCHOR

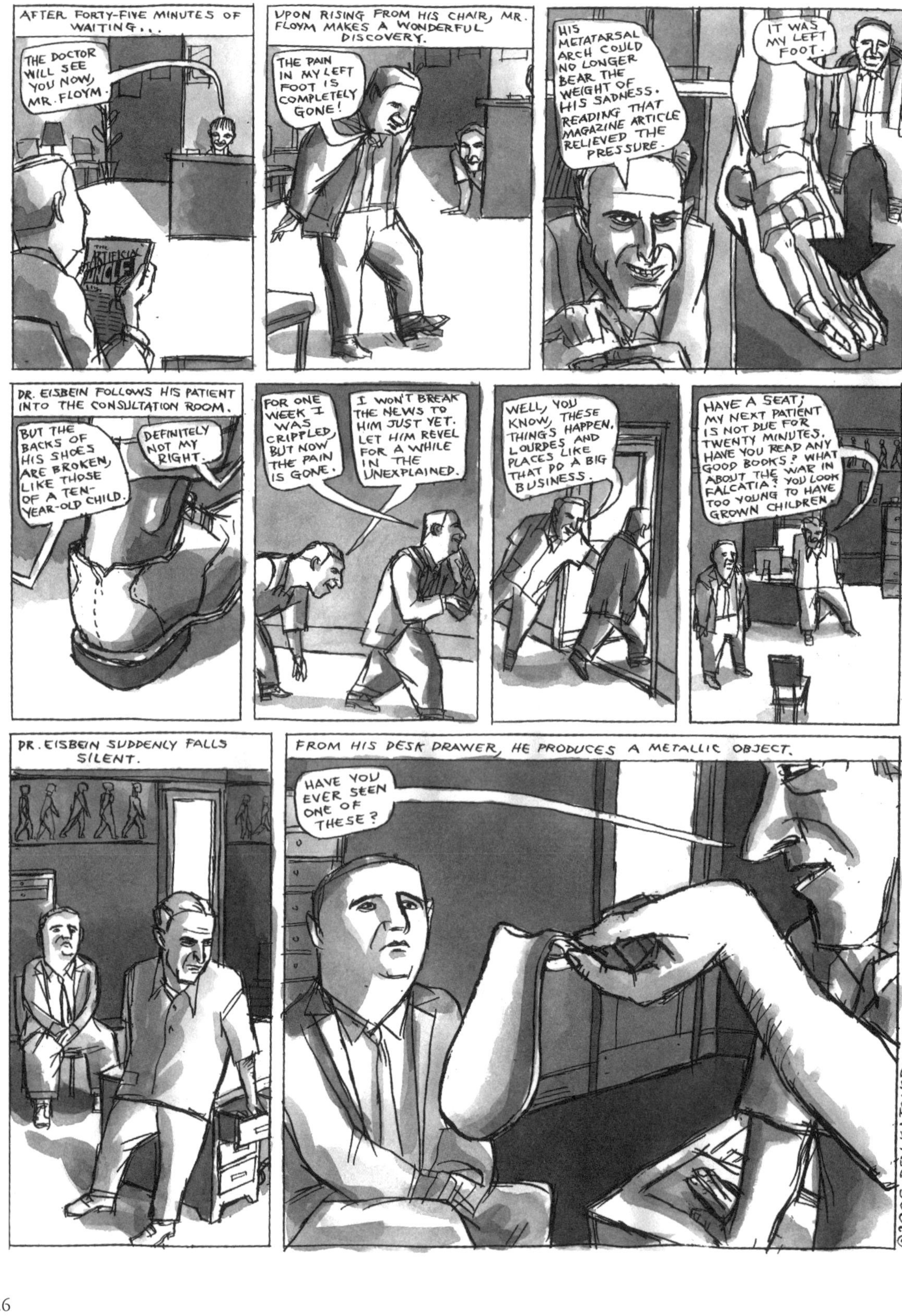
AFTER FORTY-FIVE MINUTES OF WAITING...
THE DOCTOR WILL SEE YOU NOW, MR. FLOYM.
UPON RISING FROM HIS CHAIR, MR. FLOYM MAKES A WONDERFUL DISCOVERY.
THE PAIN IN MY LEFT FOOT IS COMPLETELY GONE!
HIS METATARSAL ARCH COULD NO LONGER BEAR THE WEIGHT OF HIS SADNESS. READING THAT MAGAZINE ARTICLE RELIEVED THE PRESSURE.
IT WAS MY LEFT FOOT.
DR. EISBEIN FOLLOWS HIS PATIENT INTO THE CONSULTATION ROOM.
BUT THE BACKS OF HIS SHOES ARE BROKEN, LIKE THOSE OF A TEN-YEAR-OLD CHILD.
DEFINITELY NOT MY RIGHT.
FOR ONE WEEK I WAS CRIPPLED, BUT NOW THE PAIN IS GONE.
I WON'T BREAK THE NEWS TO HIM JUST YET. LET HIM REVEL FOR A WHILE IN THE UNEXPLAINED.
WELL, YOU KNOW, THESE THINGS HAPPEN. LOURDES AND PLACES LIKE THAT DO A BIG BUSINESS.
HAVE A SEAT; MY NEXT PATIENT IS NOT DUE FOR TWENTY MINUTES. HAVE YOU READ ANY GOOD BOOKS? WHAT ABOUT THE WAR IN FALCATIA? YOU LOOK TOO YOUNG TO HAVE GROWN CHILDREN.
DR. EISBEIN SUDDENLY FALLS SILENT.
FROM HIS DESK DRAWER, HE PRODUCES A METALLIC OBJECT.
HAVE YOU EVER SEEN ONE OF THESE?
©2005 BEN KATCHOR

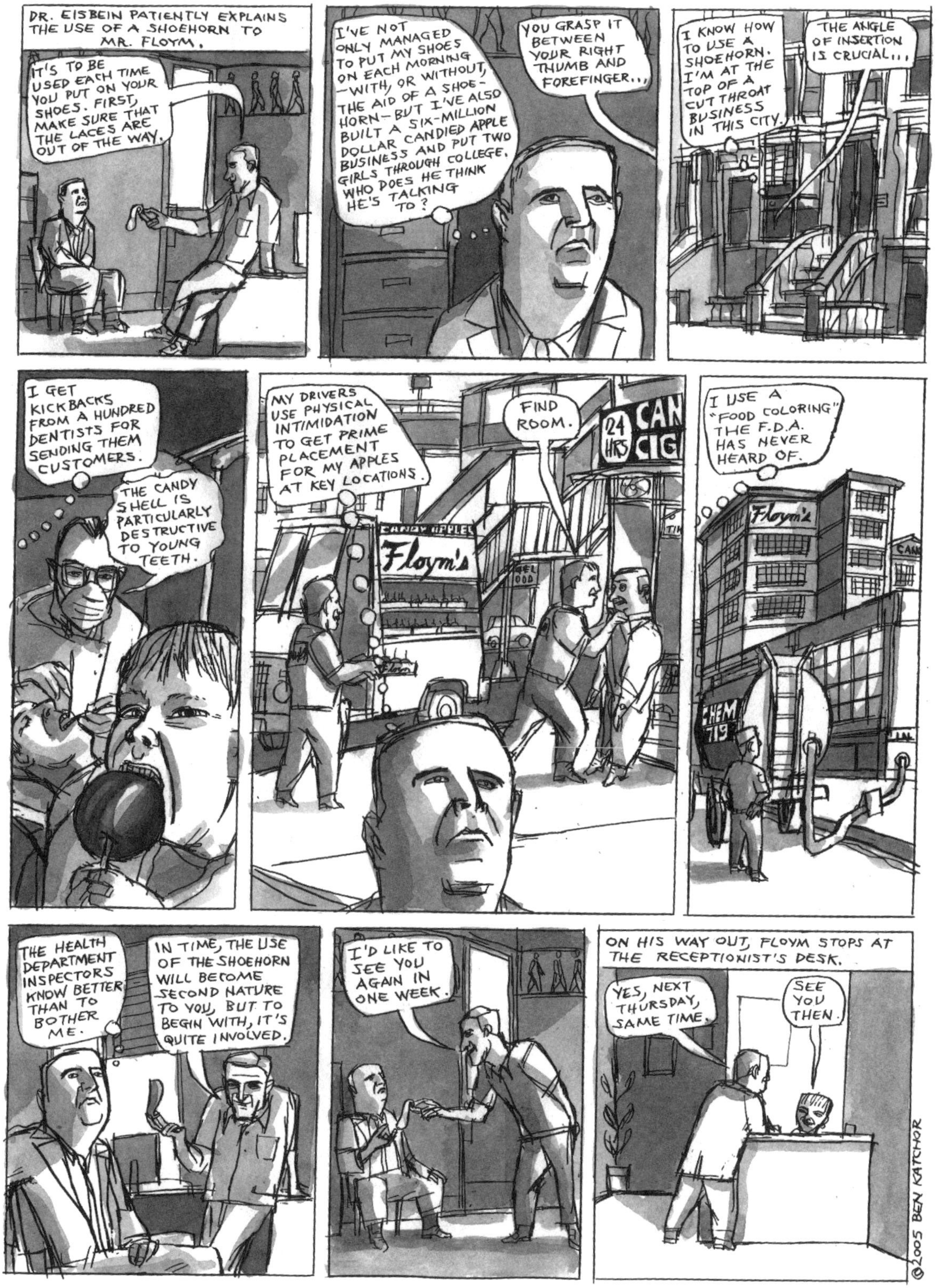
DR. EISBEIN PATIENTLY EXPLAINS THE USE OF A SHOEHORN TO MR. FLOYM.
IT'S TO BE USED EACH TIME YOU PUT ON YOUR SHOES. FIRST, MAKE SURE THAT THE LACES ARE OUT OF THE WAY.
I'VE NOT ONLY MANAGED TO PUT MY SHOES ON EACH MORNING —WITH, OR WITHOUT, THE AID OF A SHOE-HORN—BUT I'VE ALSO BUILT A SIX-MILLION DOLLAR CANDIED APPLE BUSINESS AND PUT TWO GIRLS THROUGH COLLEGE. WHO DOES HE THINK HE'S TALKING TO?
YOU GRASP IT BETWEEN YOUR RIGHT THUMB AND FOREFINGER...
I KNOW HOW TO USE A SHOEHORN. I'M AT THE TOP OF A CUT THROAT BUSINESS IN THIS CITY.
THE ANGLE OF INSERTION IS CRUCIAL...
I GET KICKBACKS FROM A HUNDRED DENTISTS FOR SENDING THEM CUSTOMERS.
THE CANDY SHELL IS PARTICULARLY DESTRUCTIVE TO YOUNG TEETH.
MY DRIVERS USE PHYSICAL INTIMIDATION TO GET PRIME PLACEMENT FOR MY APPLES AT KEY LOCATIONS.
FIND ROOM.
CANDY APPLES
Floym's
24 HRS
I USE A "FOOD COLORING" THE F.D.A. HAS NEVER HEARD OF.
Floym's
THE HEALTH DEPARTMENT INSPECTORS KNOW BETTER THAN TO BOTHER ME.
IN TIME, THE USE OF THE SHOEHORN WILL BECOME SECOND NATURE TO YOU, BUT TO BEGIN WITH, IT'S QUITE INVOLVED.
I'D LIKE TO SEE YOU AGAIN IN ONE WEEK.
ON HIS WAY OUT, FLOYM STOPS AT THE RECEPTIONIST'S DESK.
YES, NEXT THURSDAY, SAME TIME.
SEE YOU THEN.
©2005 BEN KATCHOR

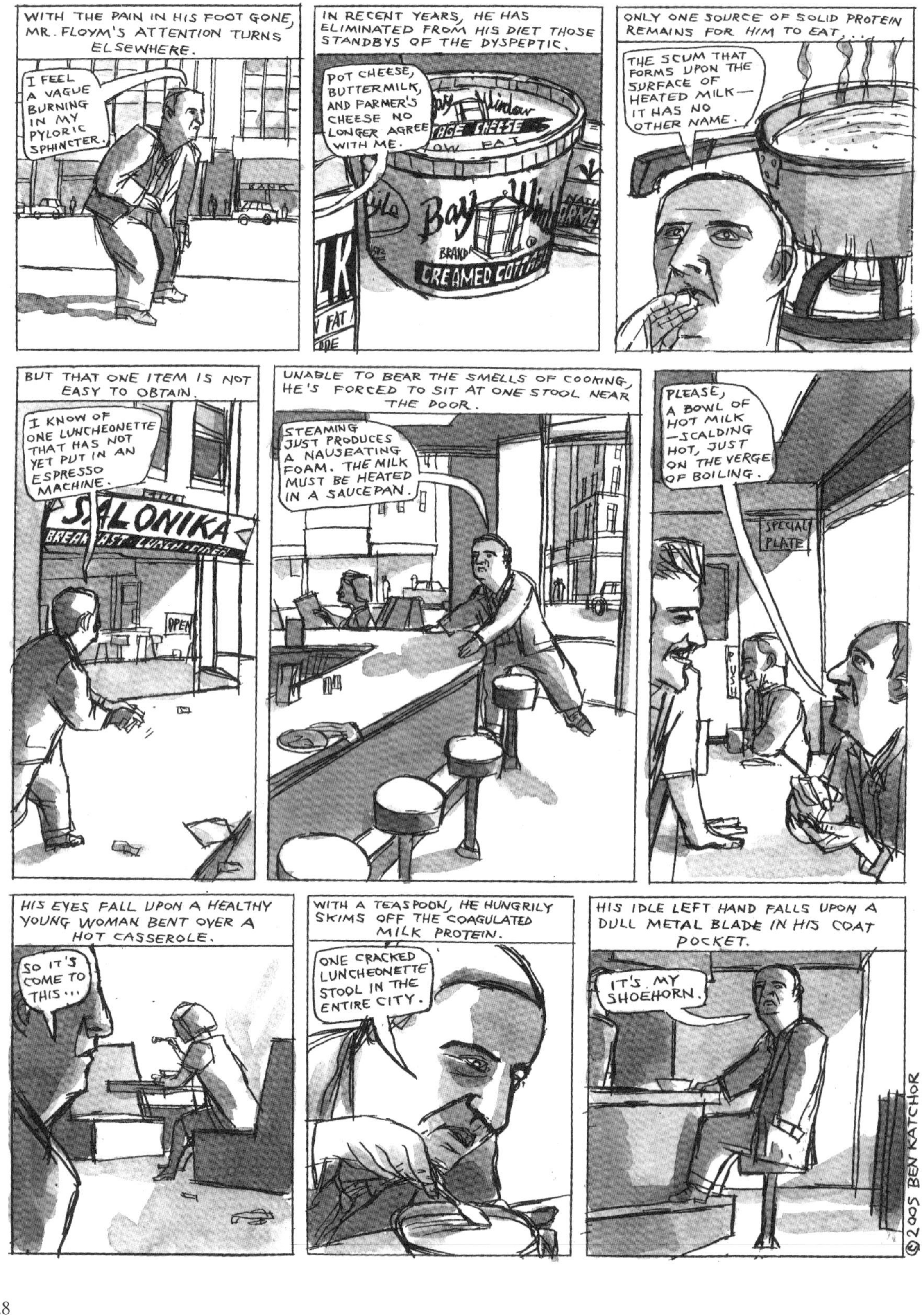

WITH THE PAIN IN HIS FOOT GONE, MR. FLOYM'S ATTENTION TURNS ELSEWHERE.
I FEEL A VAGUE BURNING IN MY PYLORIC SPHINCTER.
IN RECENT YEARS, HE HAS ELIMINATED FROM HIS DIET THOSE STANDBYS OF THE DYSPEPTIC.
POT CHEESE, BUTTERMILK, AND FARMER'S CHEESE NO LONGER AGREE WITH ME.
Bay Window
BRAND
CREAMED COTTAGE
ONLY ONE SOURCE OF SOLID PROTEIN REMAINS FOR HIM TO EAT...
THE SCUM THAT FORMS UPON THE SURFACE OF HEATED MILK— IT HAS NO OTHER NAME.
BUT THAT ONE ITEM IS NOT EASY TO OBTAIN.
I KNOW OF ONE LUNCHEONETTE THAT HAS NOT YET PUT IN AN ESPRESSO MACHINE.
SALONIKA
OPEN
UNABLE TO BEAR THE SMELLS OF COOKING, HE'S FORCED TO SIT AT ONE STOOL NEAR THE DOOR.
STEAMING JUST PRODUCES A NAUSEATING FOAM. THE MILK MUST BE HEATED IN A SAUCEPAN.
PLEASE, A BOWL OF HOT MILK —SCALDING HOT, JUST ON THE VERGE OF BOILING.
SPECIAL PLATE
PUSH
HIS EYES FALL UPON A HEALTHY YOUNG WOMAN BENT OVER A HOT CASSEROLE.
SO IT'S COME TO THIS...
WITH A TEASPOON, HE HUNGRILY SKIMS OFF THE COAGULATED MILK PROTEIN.
ONE CRACKED LUNCHEONETTE STOOL IN THE ENTIRE CITY.
HIS IDLE LEFT HAND FALLS UPON A DULL METAL BLADE IN HIS COAT POCKET.
IT'S MY SHOEHORN.
©2005 BEN KATCHOR

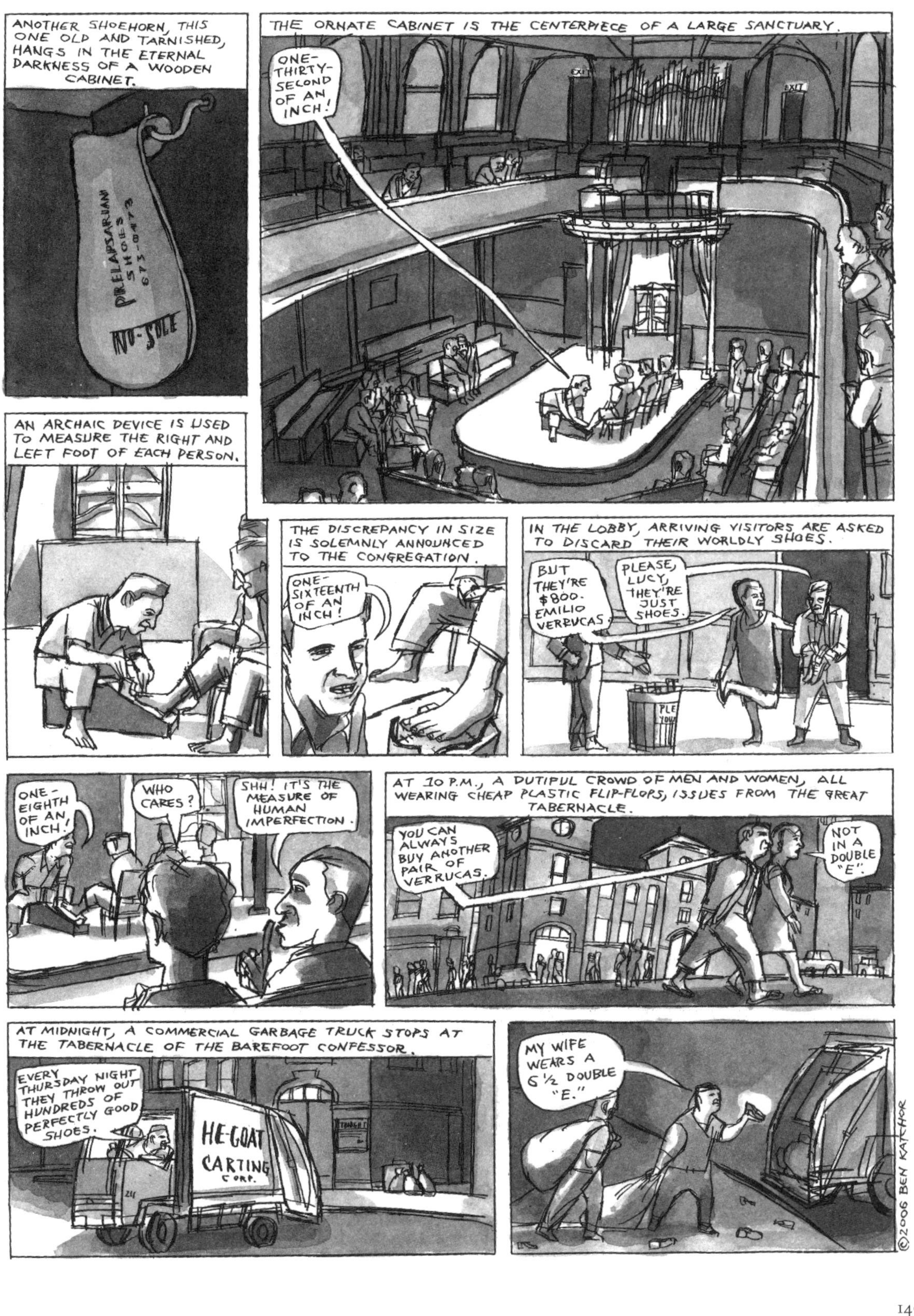
ANOTHER SHOEHORN, THIS ONE OLD AND TARNISHED, HANGS IN THE ETERNAL DARKNESS OF A WOODEN CABINET.
PRELAPSARIAN SHOES 673-0473
NO-SOLE
THE ORNATE CABINET IS THE CENTERPIECE OF A LARGE SANCTUARY.
ONE-THIRTY-SECOND OF AN INCH!
EXIT
EXIT
AN ARCHAIC DEVICE IS USED TO MEASURE THE RIGHT AND LEFT FOOT OF EACH PERSON.
THE DISCREPANCY IN SIZE IS SOLEMNLY ANNOUNCED TO THE CONGREGATION.
ONE-SIXTEENTH OF AN INCH!
IN THE LOBBY, ARRIVING VISITORS ARE ASKED TO DISCARD THEIR WORLDLY SHOES.
BUT THEY'RE $800. EMILIO VERRUCAS.
PLEASE, LUCY, THEY'RE JUST SHOES.
ONE-EIGHTH OF AN INCH!
WHO CARES?
SHH! IT'S THE MEASURE OF HUMAN IMPERFECTION.
AT 10 P.M., A DUTIFUL CROWD OF MEN AND WOMEN, ALL WEARING CHEAP PLASTIC FLIP-FLOPS, ISSUES FROM THE GREAT TABERNACLE.
YOU CAN ALWAYS BUY ANOTHER PAIR OF VERRUCAS.
NOT IN A DOUBLE "E".
AT MIDNIGHT, A COMMERCIAL GARBAGE TRUCK STOPS AT THE TABERNACLE OF THE BAREFOOT CONFESSOR.
EVERY THURSDAY NIGHT THEY THROW OUT HUNDREDS OF PERFECTLY GOOD SHOES.
HE-GOAT CARTING CORP.
MY WIFE WEARS A 6 1/2 DOUBLE "E."
©2006 BEN KATCHOR

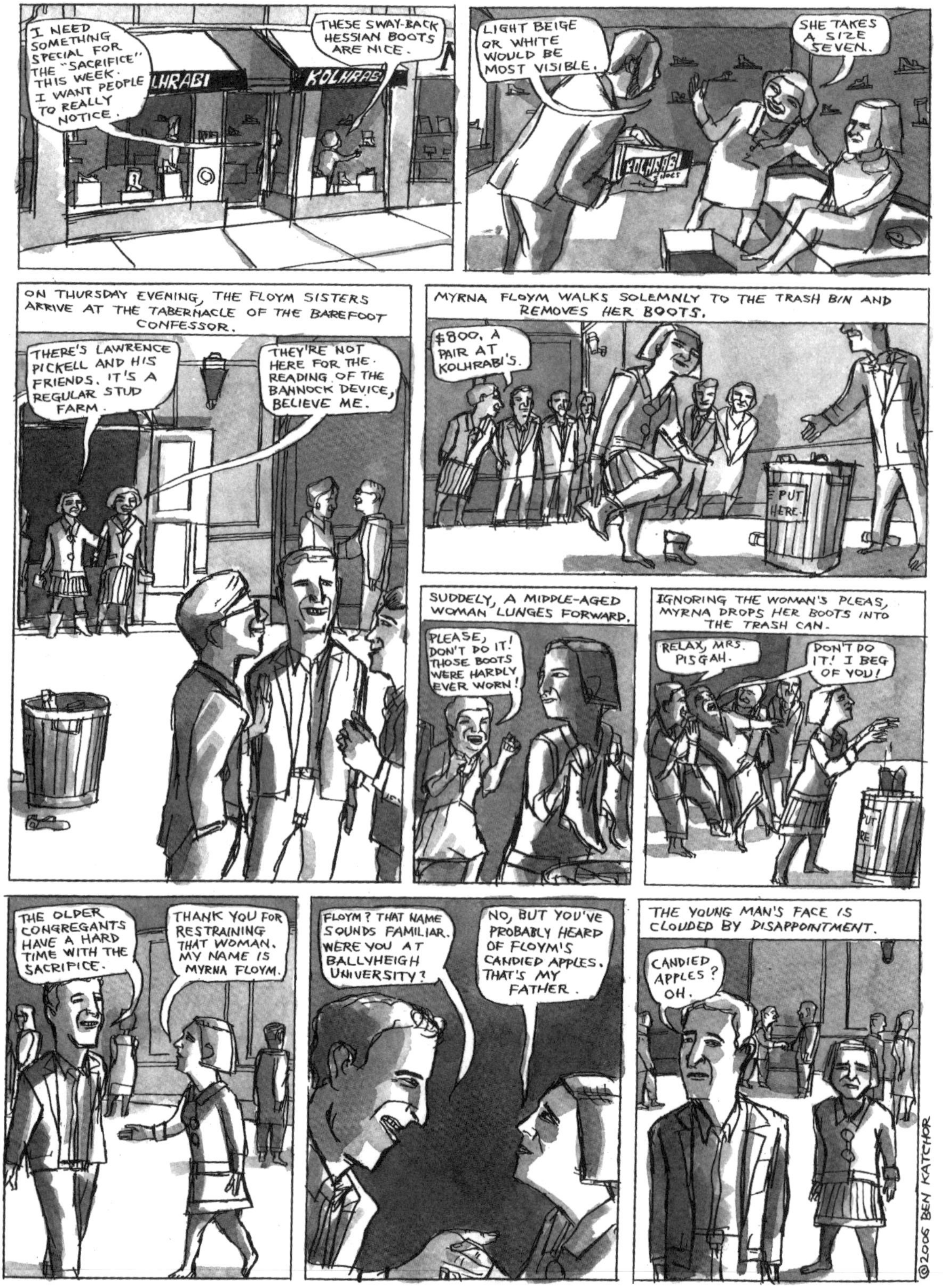
I NEED SOMETHING SPECIAL FOR THE "SACRIFICE" THIS WEEK. I WANT PEOPLE TO REALLY NOTICE.
THESE SWAY-BACK HESSIAN BOOTS ARE NICE.
KOLHRABI
LIGHT BEIGE OR WHITE WOULD BE MOST VISIBLE.
SHE TAKES A SIZE SEVEN.
KOLHRABI SHOES
ON THURSDAY EVENING, THE FLOYM SISTERS ARRIVE AT THE TABERNACLE OF THE BAREFOOT CONFESSOR.
THERE'S LAWRENCE PICKELL AND HIS FRIENDS. IT'S A REGULAR STUD FARM.
THEY'RE NOT HERE FOR THE READING OF THE BANNOCK DEVICE, BELIEVE ME.
MYRNA FLOYM WALKS SOLEMNLY TO THE TRASH BIN AND REMOVES HER BOOTS.
$800, A PAIR AT KOLHRABI'S.
PUT HERE.
SUDDELY, A MIDDLE-AGED WOMAN LUNGES FORWARD.
PLEASE, DON'T DO IT! THOSE BOOTS WERE HARDLY EVER WORN!
IGNORING THE WOMAN'S PLEAS, MYRNA DROPS HER BOOTS INTO THE TRASH CAN.
RELAX, MRS. PISGAH.
DON'T DO IT! I BEG OF YOU!
THE OLDER CONGREGANTS HAVE A HARD TIME WITH THE SACRIFICE.
THANK YOU FOR RESTRAINING THAT WOMAN. MY NAME IS MYRNA FLOYM.
FLOYM? THAT NAME SOUNDS FAMILIAR. WERE YOU AT BALLYHEIGH UNIVERSITY?
NO, BUT YOU'VE PROBABLY HEARD OF FLOYM'S CANDIED APPLES. THAT'S MY FATHER.
THE YOUNG MAN'S FACE IS CLOUDED BY DISAPPOINTMENT.
CANDIED APPLES? OH.
©2005 BEN KATCHOR

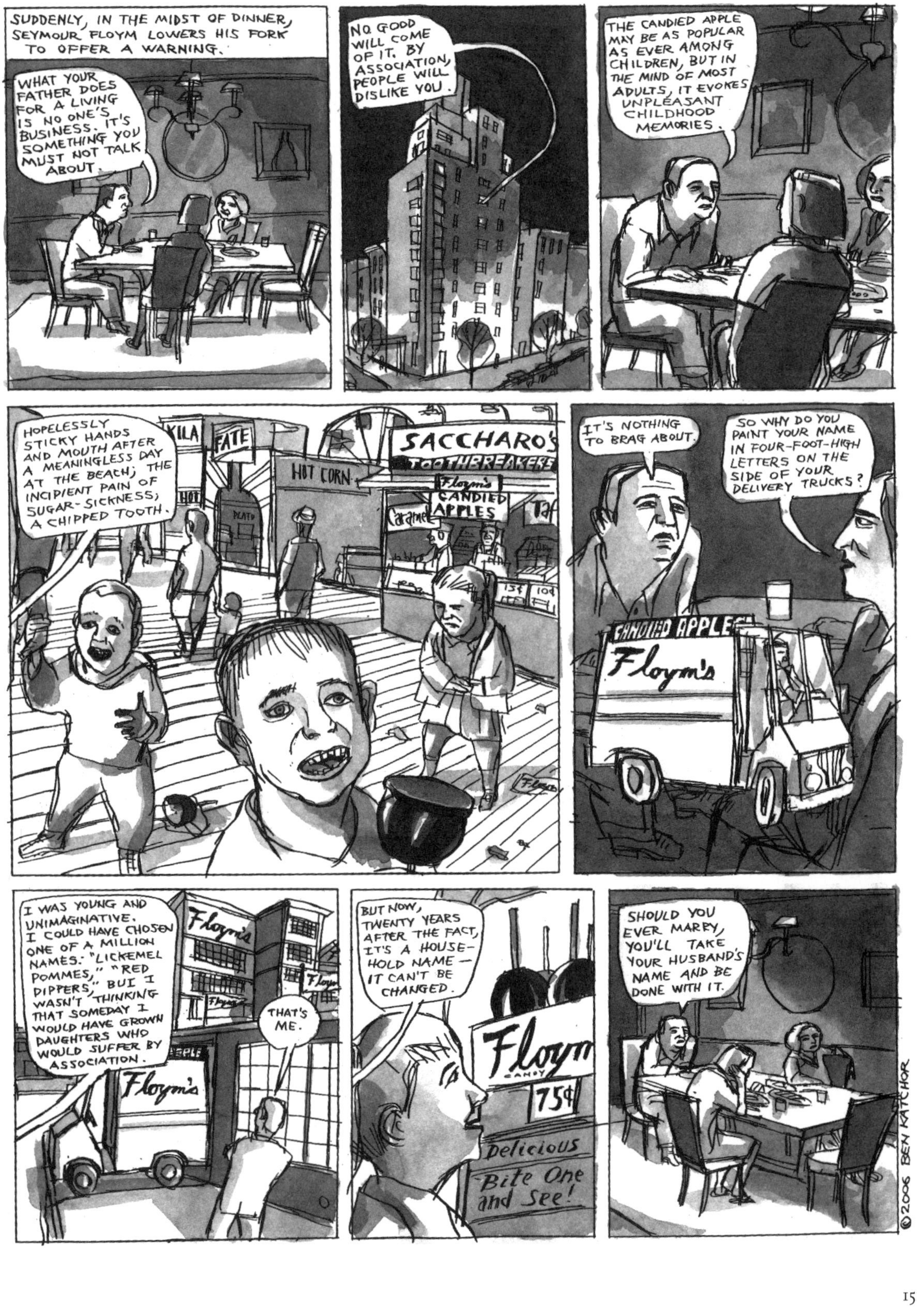
SUDDENLY, IN THE MIDST OF DINNER, SEYMOUR FLOYM LOWERS HIS FORK TO OFFER A WARNING.
WHAT YOUR FATHER DOES FOR A LIVING IS NO ONE'S BUSINESS. IT'S SOMETHING YOU MUST NOT TALK ABOUT.
NO GOOD WILL COME OF IT. BY ASSOCIATION, PEOPLE WILL DISLIKE YOU.
THE CANDIED APPLE MAY BE AS POPULAR AS EVER AMONG CHILDREN, BUT IN THE MIND OF MOST ADULTS, IT EVOKES UNPLEASANT CHILDHOOD MEMORIES.
HOPELESSLY STICKY HANDS AND MOUTH AFTER A MEANINGLESS DAY AT THE BEACH; THE INCIPIENT PAIN OF SUGAR-SICKNESS; A CHIPPED TOOTH.
SACCHARO'S
TOOTHBREAKERS
HOT CORN
FATE
Floym's
CANDIED APPLES
Caramel
IT'S NOTHING TO BRAG ABOUT.
SO WHY DO YOU PAINT YOUR NAME IN FOUR-FOOT-HIGH LETTERS ON THE SIDE OF YOUR DELIVERY TRUCKS?
CANDIED APPLES
Floym's
I WAS YOUNG AND UNIMAGINATIVE. I COULD HAVE CHOSEN ONE OF A MILLION NAMES: "LICKEMEL POMMES," "RED DIPPERS," BUT I WASN'T THINKING THAT SOMEDAY I WOULD HAVE GROWN DAUGHTERS WHO WOULD SUFFER BY ASSOCIATION.
Floym's
THAT'S ME.
BUT NOW, TWENTY YEARS AFTER THE FACT, IT'S A HOUSEHOLD NAME — IT CAN'T BE CHANGED.
Floym
CANDY
75¢
Delicious
Bite One and See!
SHOULD YOU EVER MARRY, YOU'LL TAKE YOUR HUSBAND'S NAME AND BE DONE WITH IT.
©2006 BEN KATCHOR

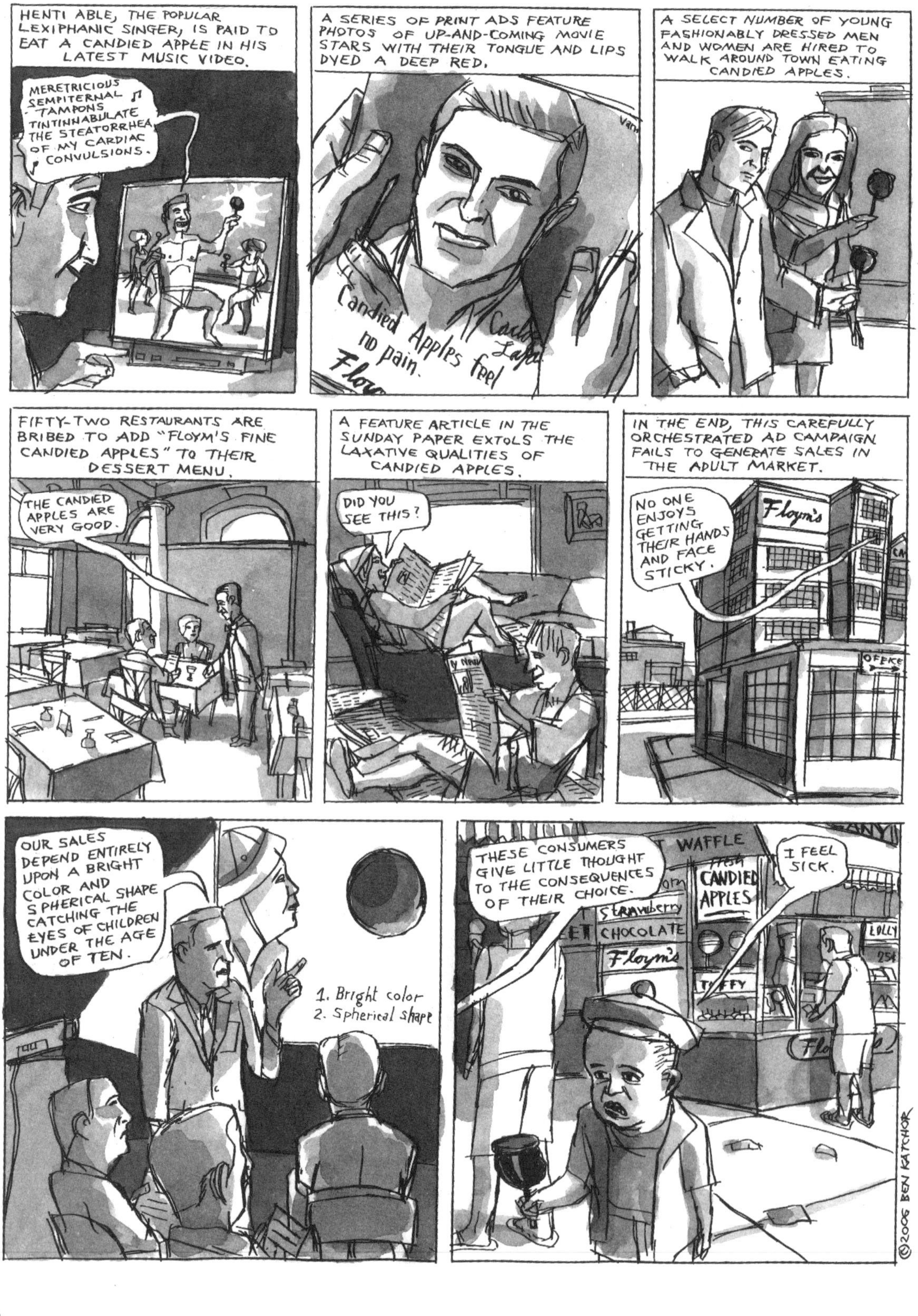
HENTI ABLE, THE POPULAR LEXIPHANIC SINGER, IS PAID TO EAT A CANDIED APPLE IN HIS LATEST MUSIC VIDEO.
MERETRICIOUS SEMPITERNAL TAMPONS TINTINNABULATE THE STEATORRHEA OF MY CARDIAC CONVULSIONS.
A SERIES OF PRINT ADS FEATURE PHOTOS OF UP-AND-COMING MOVIE STARS WITH THEIR TONGUE AND LIPS DYED A DEEP RED.
Candied Apples feel no pain.
A SELECT NUMBER OF YOUNG FASHIONABLY DRESSED MEN AND WOMEN ARE HIRED TO WALK AROUND TOWN EATING CANDIED APPLES.
FIFTY-TWO RESTAURANTS ARE BRIBED TO ADD "FLOYM'S FINE CANDIED APPLES" TO THEIR DESSERT MENU.
THE CANDIED APPLES ARE VERY GOOD.
A FEATURE ARTICLE IN THE SUNDAY PAPER EXTOLS THE LAXATIVE QUALITIES OF CANDIED APPLES.
DID YOU SEE THIS?
IN THE END, THIS CAREFULLY ORCHESTRATED AD CAMPAIGN FAILS TO GENERATE SALES IN THE ADULT MARKET.
NO ONE ENJOYS GETTING THEIR HANDS AND FACE STICKY.
Floym's
OUR SALES DEPEND ENTIRELY UPON A BRIGHT COLOR AND SPHERICAL SHAPE CATCHING THE EYES OF CHILDREN UNDER THE AGE OF TEN.
1. Bright color
2. Spherical shape
THESE CONSUMERS GIVE LITTLE THOUGHT TO THE CONSEQUENCES OF THEIR CHOICE.
I FEEL SICK.
WAFFLE
CANDIED APPLES
Strawberry
CHOCOLATE
Floym's
©2006 BEN KATCHOR

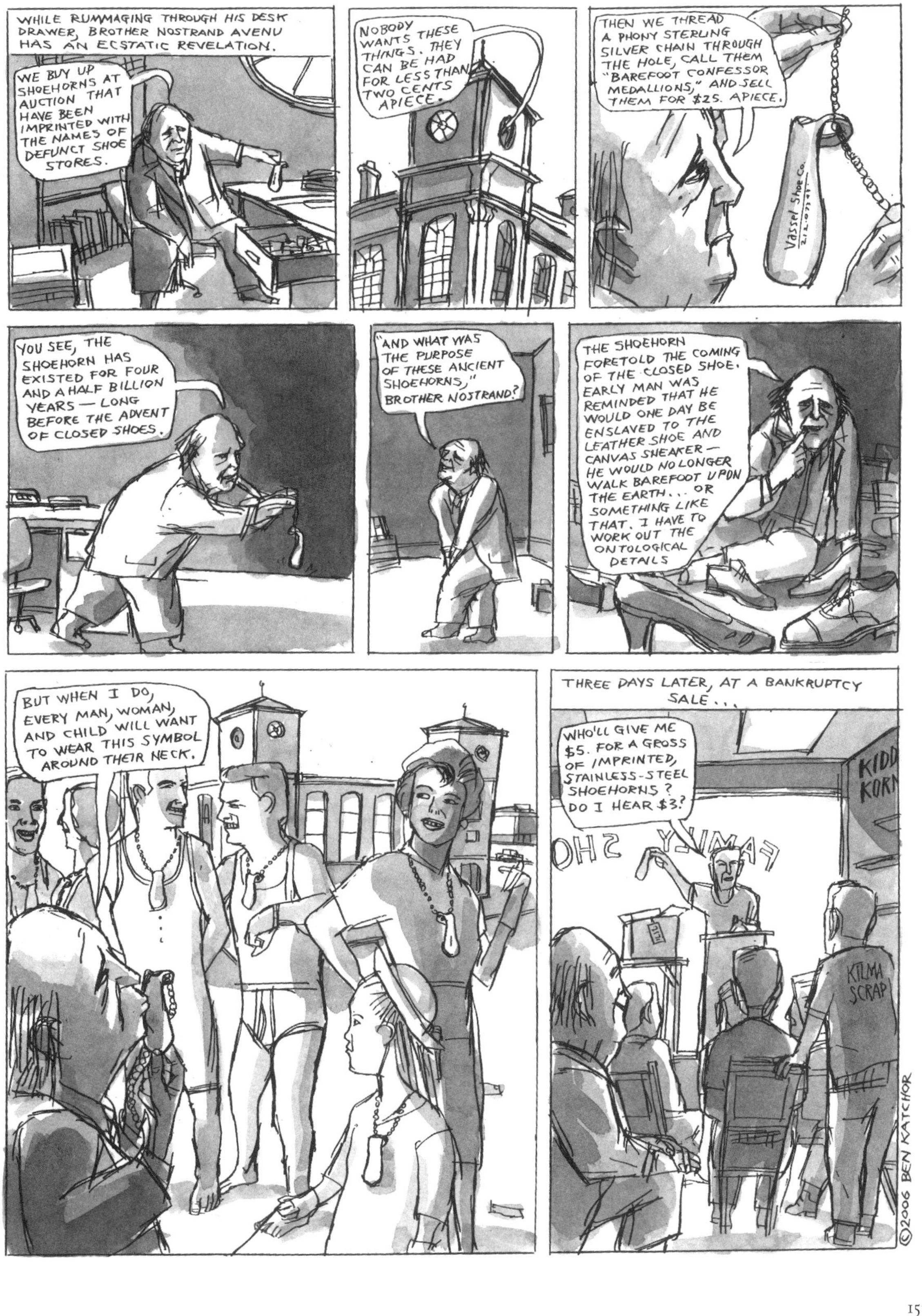
WHILE RUMMAGING THROUGH HIS DESK DRAWER, BROTHER NOSTRAND AVENU HAS AN ECSTATIC REVELATION.
WE BUY UP SHOEHORNS AT AUCTION THAT HAVE BEEN IMPRINTED WITH THE NAMES OF DEFUNCT SHOE STORES.
NOBODY WANTS THESE THINGS. THEY CAN BE HAD FOR LESS THAN TWO CENTS APIECE.
THEN WE THREAD A PHONY STERLING SILVER CHAIN THROUGH THE HOLE, CALL THEM "BAREFOOT CONFESSOR MEDALLIONS," AND SELL THEM FOR $25. APIECE.
Vassel Shoe Co.
YOU SEE, THE SHOEHORN HAS EXISTED FOR FOUR AND A HALF BILLION YEARS — LONG BEFORE THE ADVENT OF CLOSED SHOES.
"AND WHAT WAS THE PURPOSE OF THESE ANCIENT SHOEHORNS," BROTHER NOSTRAND?
THE SHOEHORN FORETOLD THE COMING OF THE CLOSED SHOE. EARLY MAN WAS REMINDED THAT HE WOULD ONE DAY BE ENSLAVED TO THE LEATHER SHOE AND CANVAS SNEAKER — HE WOULD NO LONGER WALK BAREFOOT UPON THE EARTH... OR SOMETHING LIKE THAT. I HAVE TO WORK OUT THE ONTOLOGICAL DETAILS
BUT WHEN I DO, EVERY MAN, WOMAN, AND CHILD WILL WANT TO WEAR THIS SYMBOL AROUND THEIR NECK.
THREE DAYS LATER, AT A BANKRUPTCY SALE...
WHO'LL GIVE ME $5. FOR A GROSS OF IMPRINTED, STAINLESS-STEEL SHOEHORNS? DO I HEAR $3?
KIDD KORN
FAMILY SHO
KILMA SCRAP
©2006 BEN KATCHOR

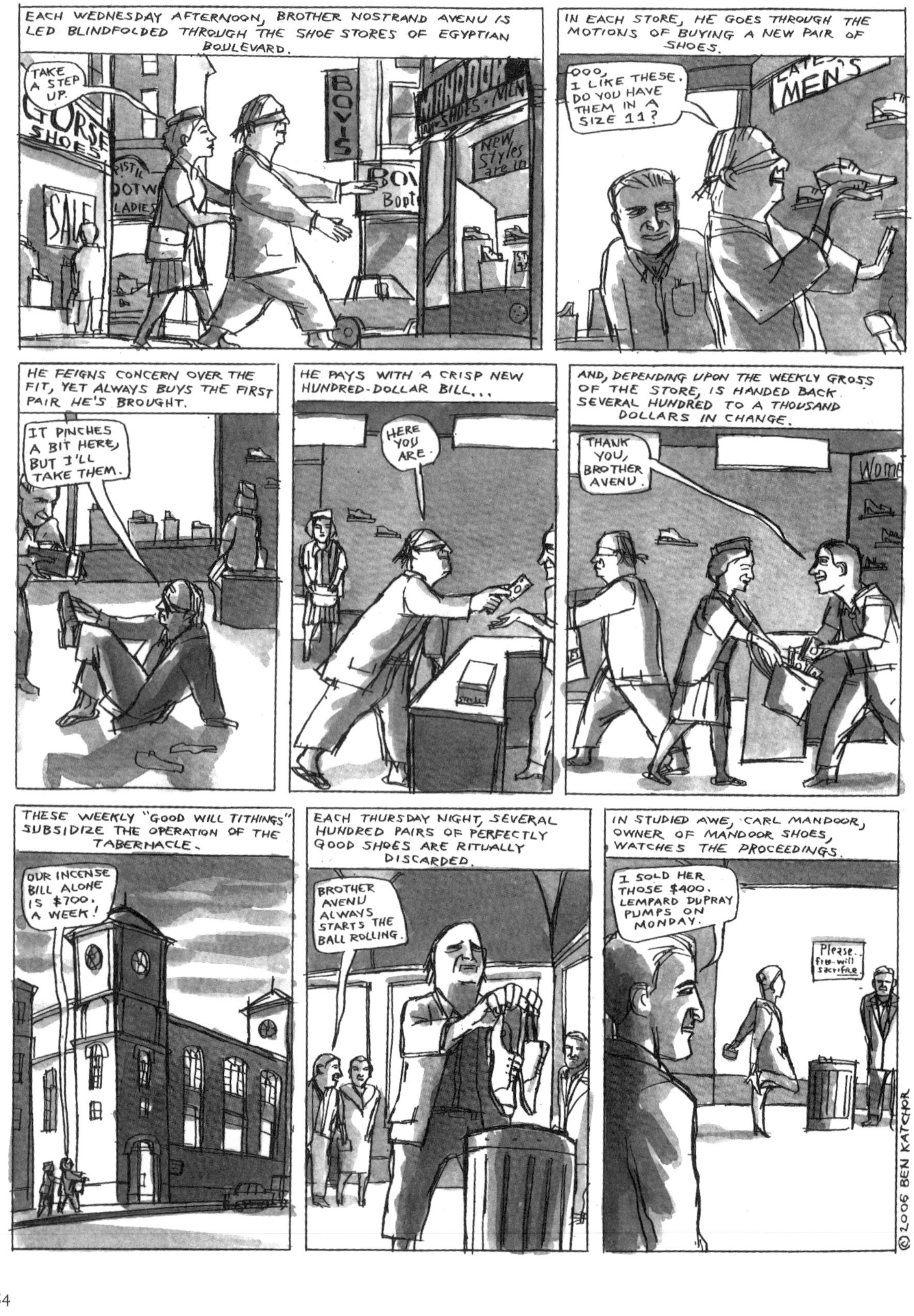

EACH WEDNESDAY AFTERNOON, BROTHER NOSTRAND AVENU IS LED BLINDFOLDED THROUGH THE SHOE STORES OF EGYPTIAN BOULEVARD.
TAKE A STEP UP.
GORSE SHOES
SALE
BOVIS
MANDOOR SHOES - MEN
New Styles are in
IN EACH STORE, HE GOES THROUGH THE MOTIONS OF BUYING A NEW PAIR OF SHOES.
OOO, I LIKE THESE. DO YOU HAVE THEM IN A SIZE 11?
MEN'S
HE FEIGNS CONCERN OVER THE FIT, YET ALWAYS BUYS THE FIRST PAIR HE'S BROUGHT.
IT PINCHES A BIT HERE, BUT I'LL TAKE THEM.
HE PAYS WITH A CRISP NEW HUNDRED-DOLLAR BILL...
HERE YOU ARE.
AND, DEPENDING UPON THE WEEKLY GROSS OF THE STORE, IS HANDED BACK SEVERAL HUNDRED TO A THOUSAND DOLLARS IN CHANGE.
THANK YOU, BROTHER AVENU.
THESE WEEKLY "GOOD WILL TITHINGS" SUBSIDIZE THE OPERATION OF THE TABERNACLE.
OUR INCENSE BILL ALONE IS $700. A WEEK!
EACH THURSDAY NIGHT, SEVERAL HUNDRED PAIRS OF PERFECTLY GOOD SHOES ARE RITUALLY DISCARDED.
BROTHER AVENU ALWAYS STARTS THE BALL ROLLING.
IN STUDIED AWE, CARL MANDOOR, OWNER OF MANDOOR SHOES, WATCHES THE PROCEEDINGS.
I SOLD HER THOSE $400. LEMPARD DUPRAY PUMPS ON MONDAY.
Please. free-will sacrifice
©2006 BEN KATCHOR

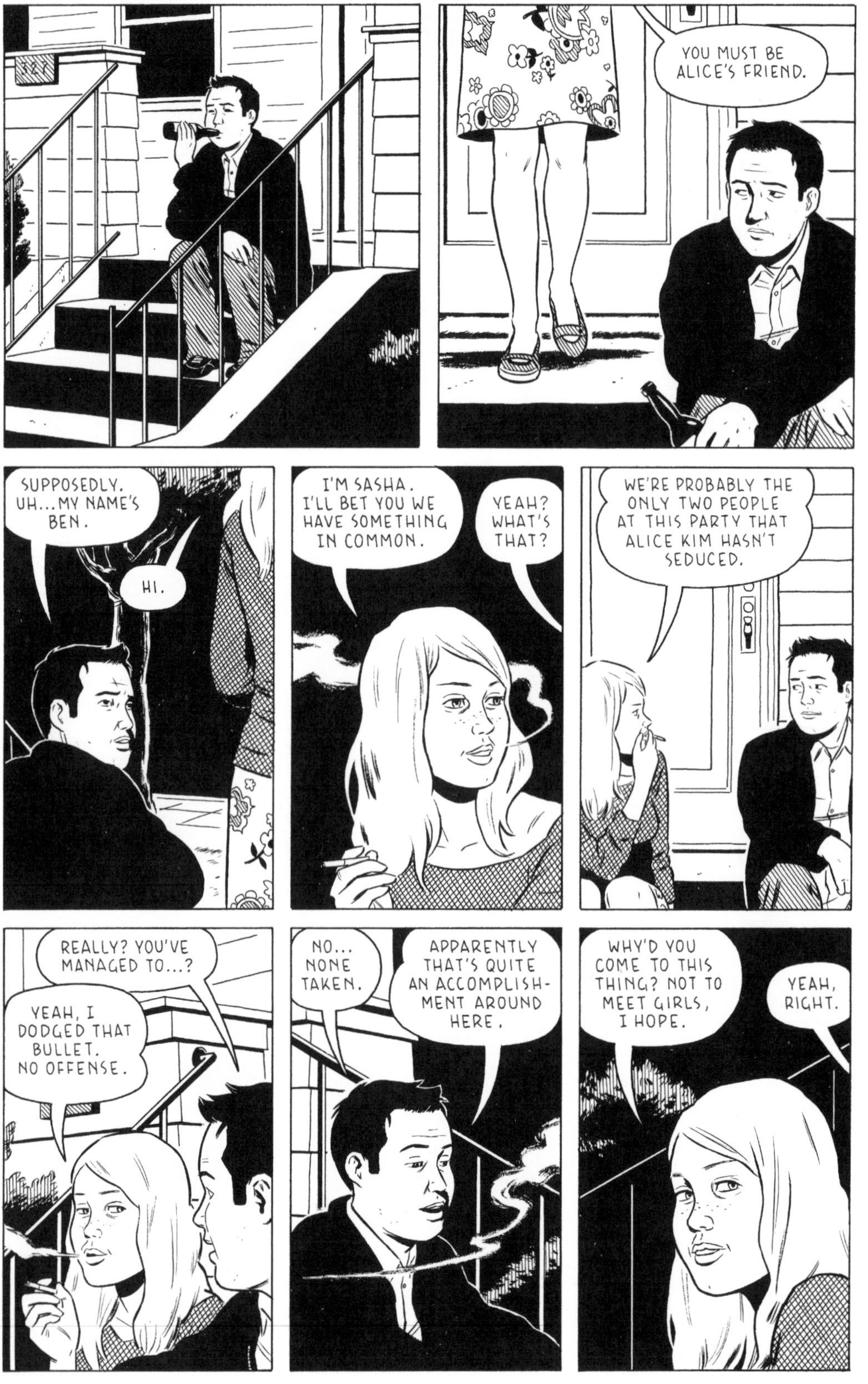
YOU MUST BE ALICE'S FRIEND.
SUPPOSEDLY. UH... MY NAME'S BEN.
HI.
I'M SASHA. I'LL BET YOU WE HAVE SOMETHING IN COMMON.
YEAH? WHAT'S THAT?
WE'RE PROBABLY THE ONLY TWO PEOPLE AT THIS PARTY THAT ALICE KIM HASN'T SEDUCED.
REALLY? YOU'VE MANAGED TO...?
YEAH, I DODGED THAT BULLET. NO OFFENSE.
NO... NONE TAKEN.
APPARENTLY THAT'S QUITE AN ACCOMPLISHMENT AROUND HERE.
WHY'D YOU COME TO THIS THING? NOT TO MEET GIRLS, I HOPE.
YEAH, RIGHT.

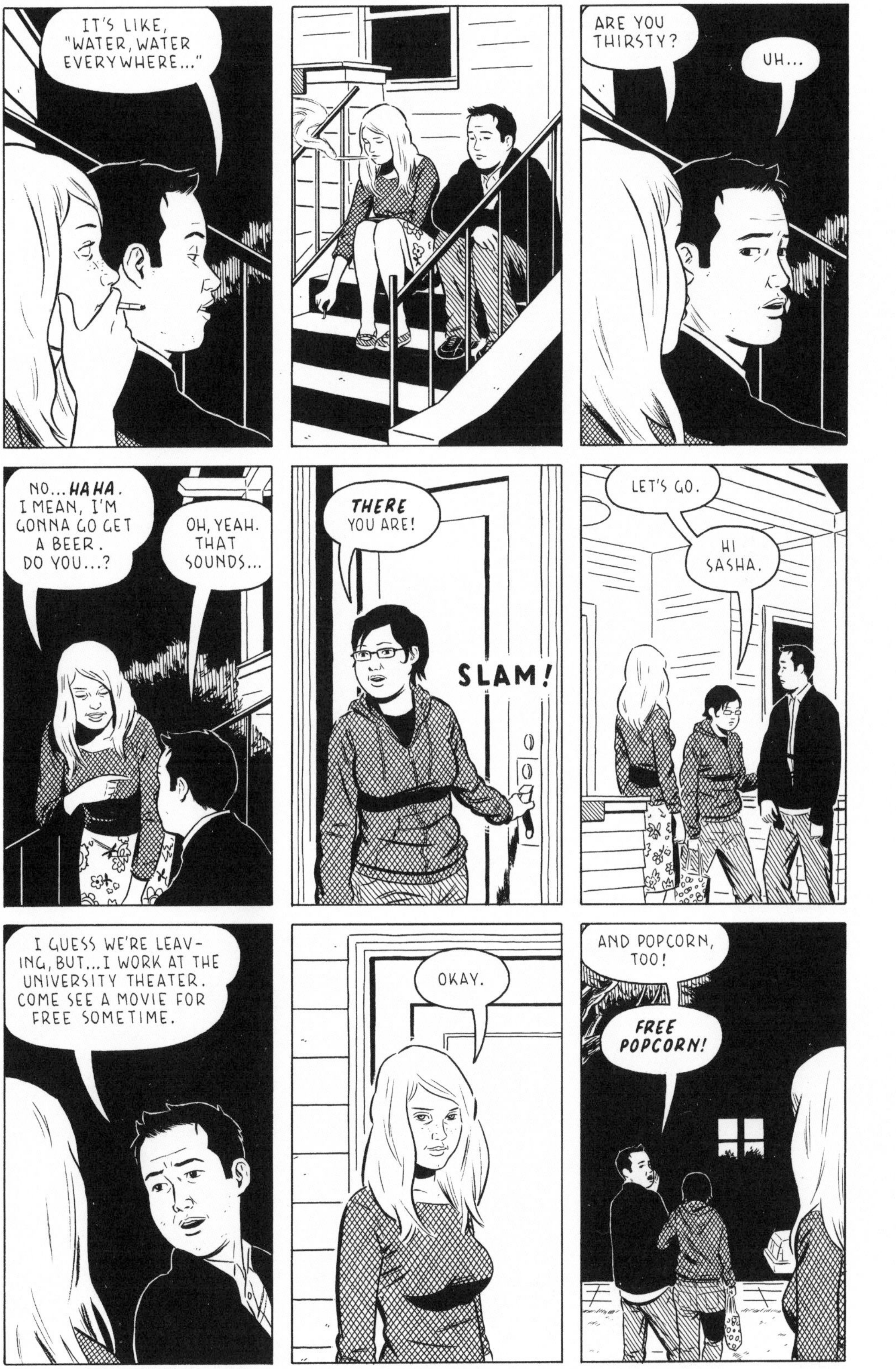
IT'S LIKE, "WATER, WATER EVERYWHERE..."
ARE YOU THIRSTY?
UH...
NO... HAHA. I MEAN, I'M GONNA GO GET A BEER. DO YOU...?
OH, YEAH. THAT SOUNDS...
THERE YOU ARE!
SLAM!
LET'S GO.
HI SASHA.
I GUESS WE'RE LEAVING, BUT... I WORK AT THE UNIVERSITY THEATER. COME SEE A MOVIE FOR FREE SOMETIME.
OKAY.
AND POPCORN, TOO!
FREE POPCORN!

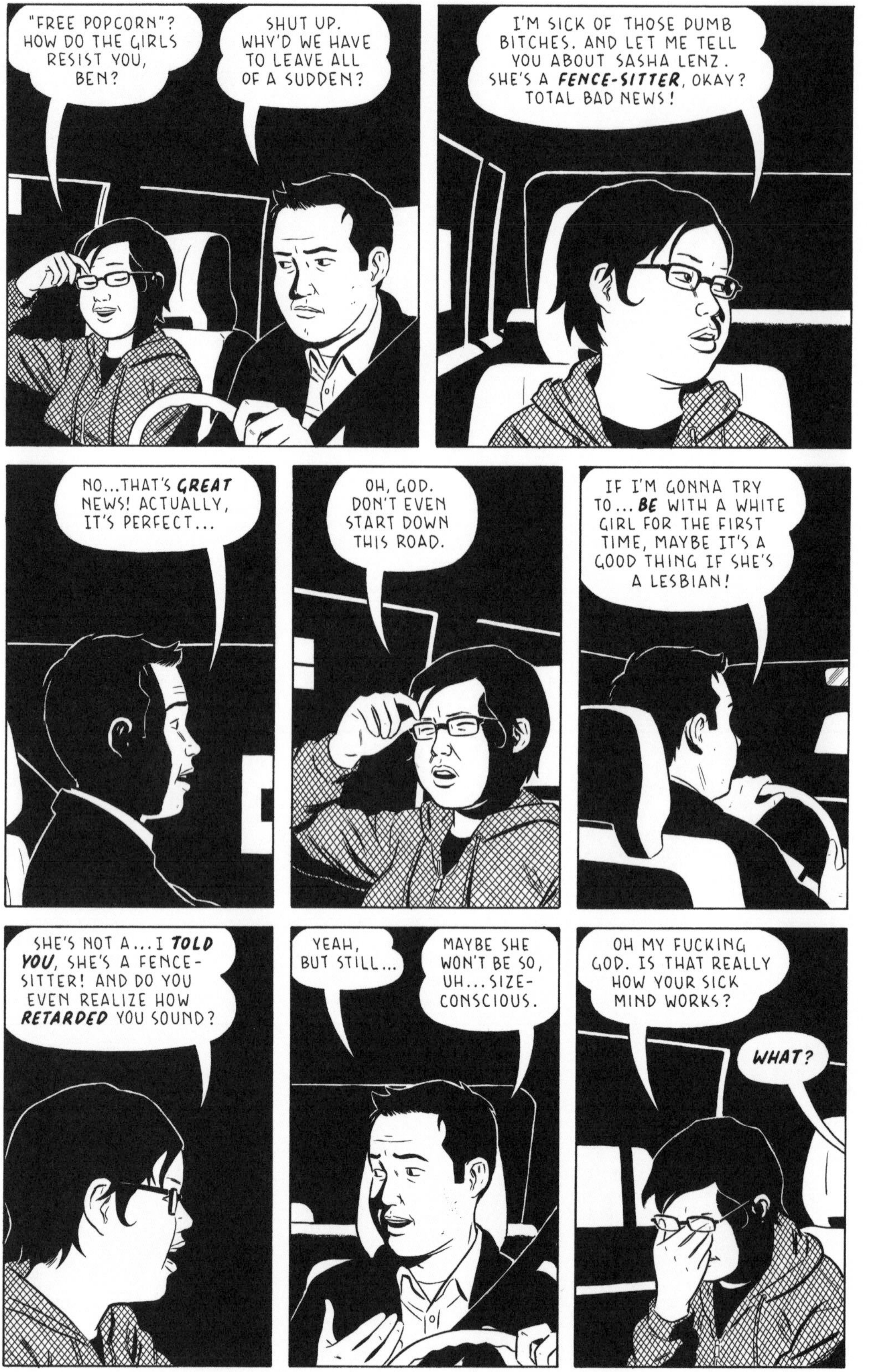
"FREE POPCORN"? HOW DO THE GIRLS RESIST YOU, BEN?
SHUT UP. WHY'D WE HAVE TO LEAVE ALL OF A SUDDEN?
I'M SICK OF THOSE DUMB BITCHES. AND LET ME TELL YOU ABOUT SASHA LENZ. SHE'S A FENCE-SITTER, OKAY? TOTAL BAD NEWS!
NO...THAT'S GREAT NEWS! ACTUALLY, IT'S PERFECT...
OH, GOD. DON'T EVEN START DOWN THIS ROAD.
IF I'M GONNA TRY TO... BE WITH A WHITE GIRL FOR THE FIRST TIME, MAYBE IT'S A GOOD THING IF SHE'S A LESBIAN!
SHE'S NOT A...I TOLD YOU, SHE'S A FENCE-SITTER! AND DO YOU EVEN REALIZE HOW RETARDED YOU SOUND?
YEAH, BUT STILL...
MAYBE SHE WON'T BE SO, UH...SIZE-CONSCIOUS.
OH MY FUCKING GOD. IS THAT REALLY HOW YOUR SICK MIND WORKS?
WHAT?

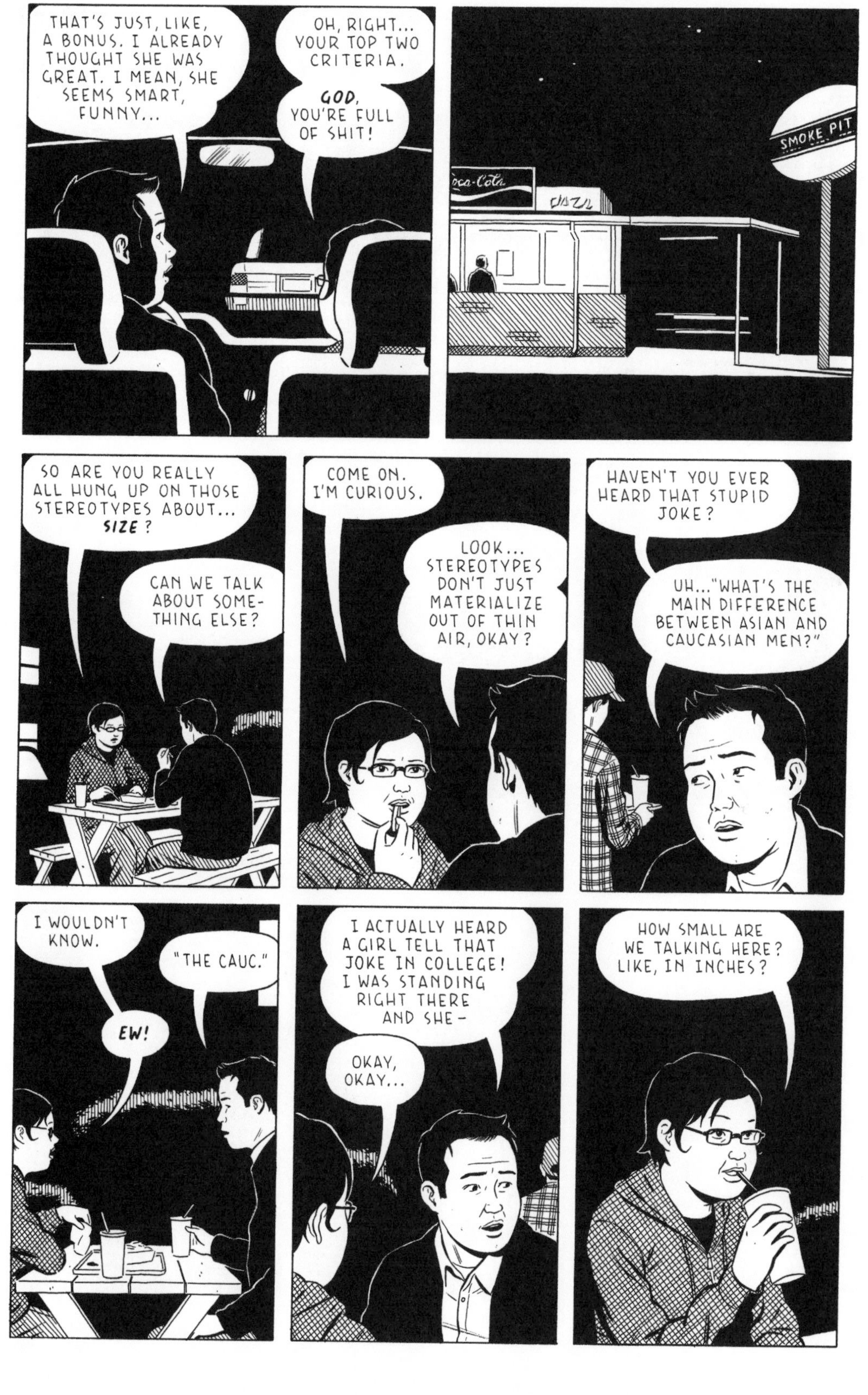
THAT'S JUST, LIKE, A BONUS. I ALREADY THOUGHT SHE WAS GREAT. I MEAN, SHE SEEMS SMART, FUNNY...
OH, RIGHT... YOUR TOP TWO CRITERIA.
GOD, YOU'RE FULL OF SHIT!
Coca-Cola
SMOKE PIT
SO ARE YOU REALLY ALL HUNG UP ON THOSE STEREOTYPES ABOUT... **SIZE**?
CAN WE TALK ABOUT SOME-THING ELSE?
COME ON. I'M CURIOUS.
LOOK... STEREOTYPES DON'T JUST MATERIALIZE OUT OF THIN AIR, OKAY?
HAVEN'T YOU EVER HEARD THAT STUPID JOKE?
UH..."WHAT'S THE MAIN DIFFERENCE BETWEEN ASIAN AND CAUCASIAN MEN?"
I WOULDN'T KNOW.
"THE CAUC."
EW!
I ACTUALLY HEARD A GIRL TELL THAT JOKE IN COLLEGE! I WAS STANDING RIGHT THERE AND SHE-
OKAY, OKAY...
HOW SMALL ARE WE TALKING HERE? LIKE, IN INCHES?

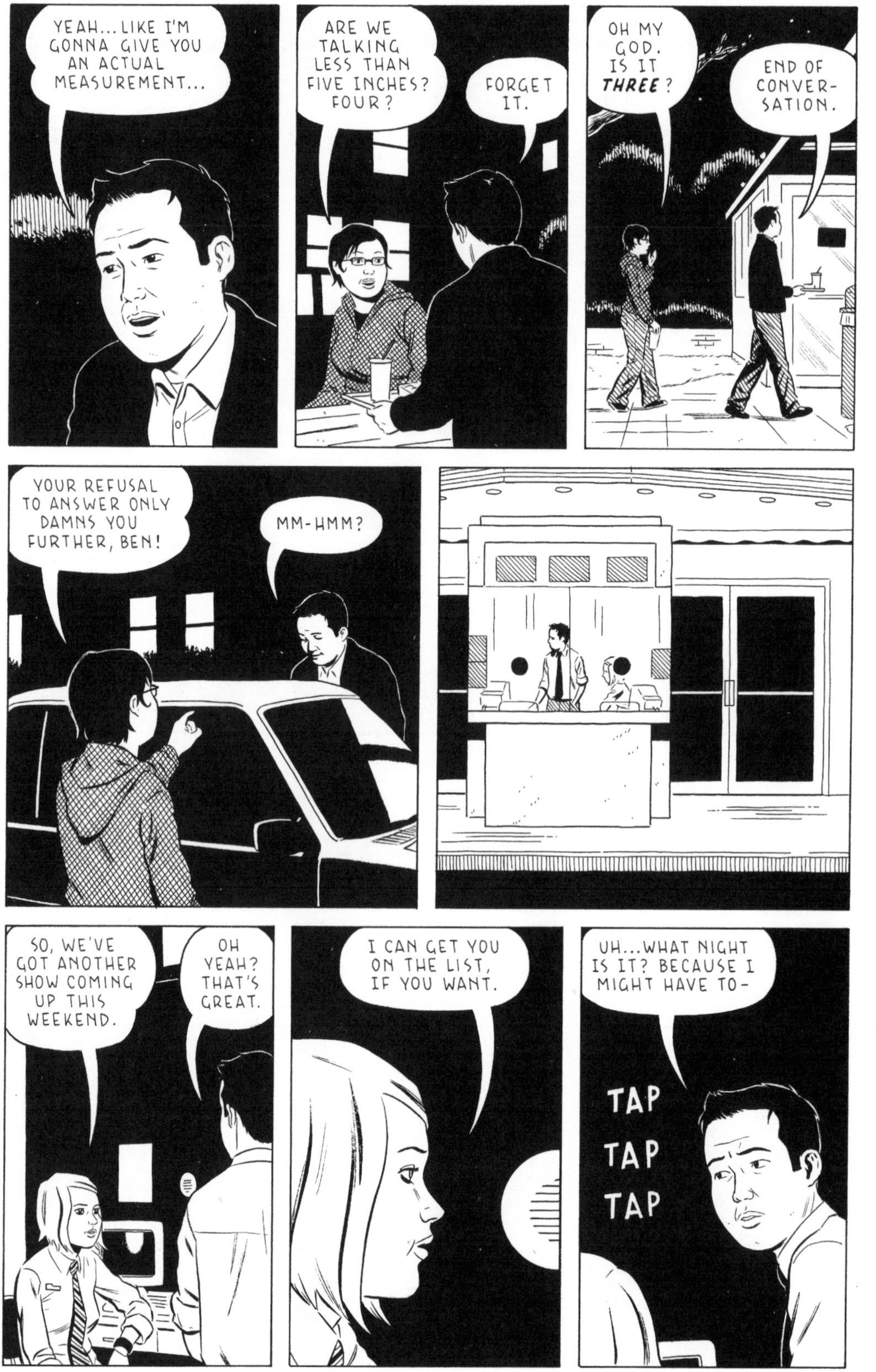
YEAH... LIKE I'M GONNA GIVE YOU AN ACTUAL MEASUREMENT...
ARE WE TALKING LESS THAN FIVE INCHES? FOUR?
FORGET IT.
OH MY GOD. IS IT **THREE**?
END OF CONVER-SATION.
YOUR REFUSAL TO ANSWER ONLY DAMNS YOU FURTHER, BEN!
MM-HMM?
SO, WE'VE GOT ANOTHER SHOW COMING UP THIS WEEKEND.
OH YEAH? THAT'S GREAT.
I CAN GET YOU ON THE LIST, IF YOU WANT.
UH... WHAT NIGHT IS IT? BECAUSE I MIGHT HAVE TO-
TAP
TAP
TAP

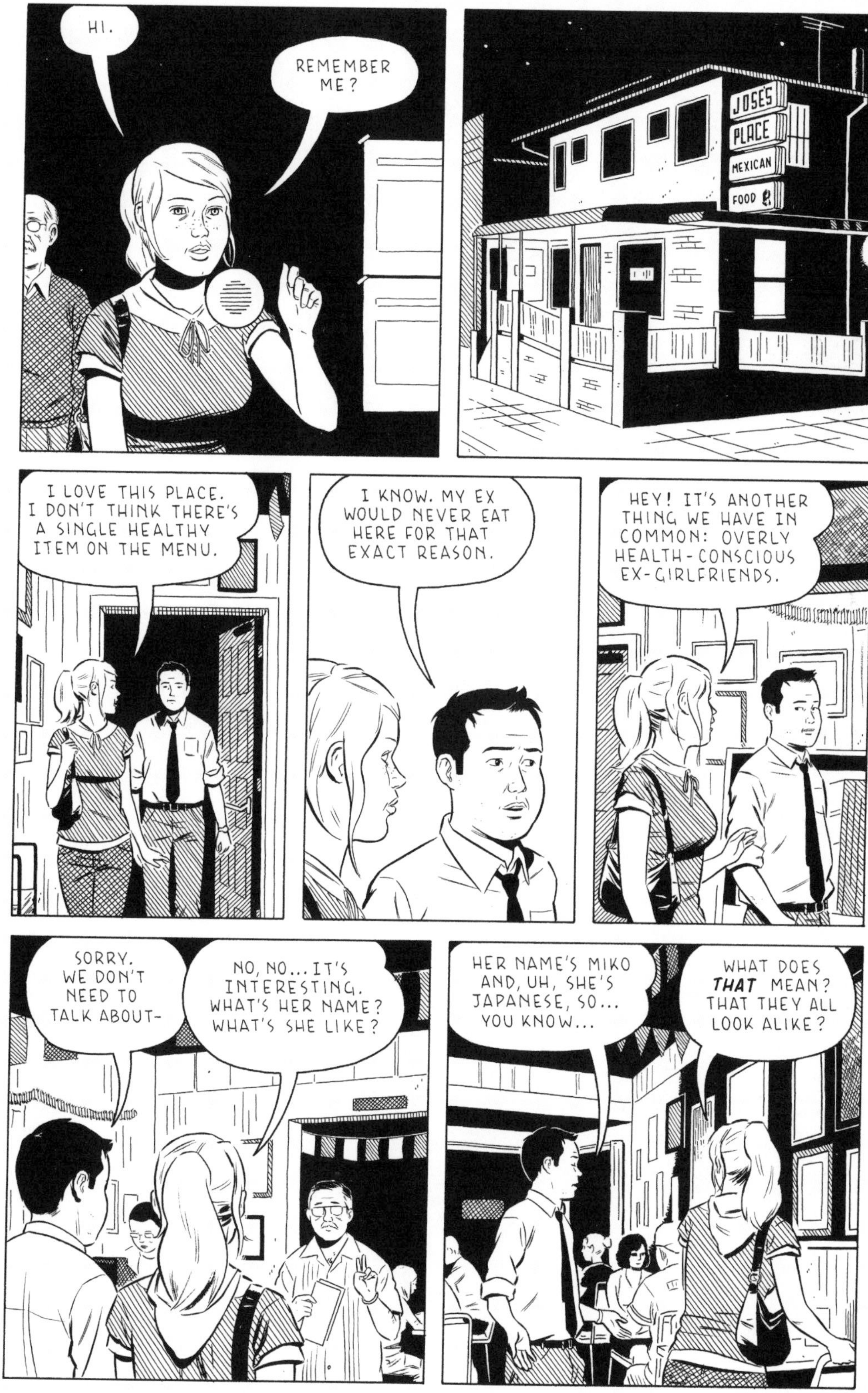
HI.
REMEMBER ME?
JOSE'S PLACE MEXICAN FOOD
I LOVE THIS PLACE. I DON'T THINK THERE'S A SINGLE HEALTHY ITEM ON THE MENU.
I KNOW. MY EX WOULD NEVER EAT HERE FOR THAT EXACT REASON.
HEY! IT'S ANOTHER THING WE HAVE IN COMMON: OVERLY HEALTH-CONSCIOUS EX-GIRLFRIENDS.
SORRY. WE DON'T NEED TO TALK ABOUT-
NO, NO... IT'S INTERESTING. WHAT'S HER NAME? WHAT'S SHE LIKE?
HER NAME'S MIKO AND, UH, SHE'S JAPANESE, SO... YOU KNOW...
WHAT DOES **THAT** MEAN? THAT THEY ALL LOOK ALIKE?

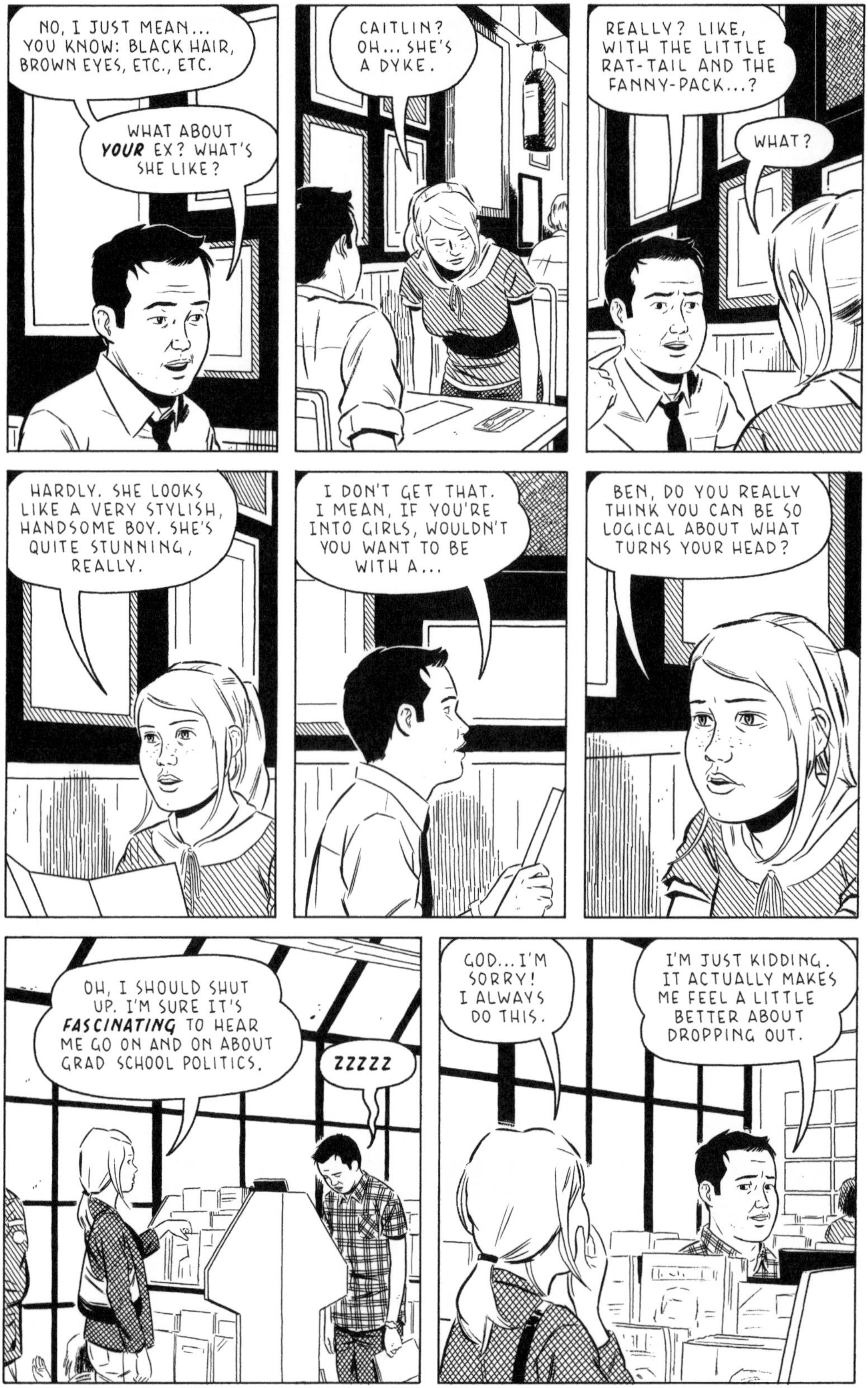
NO, I JUST MEAN... YOU KNOW: BLACK HAIR, BROWN EYES, ETC., ETC.
WHAT ABOUT **YOUR** EX? WHAT'S SHE LIKE?
CAITLIN? OH... SHE'S A DYKE.
REALLY? LIKE, WITH THE LITTLE RAT-TAIL AND THE FANNY-PACK...?
WHAT?
HARDLY. SHE LOOKS LIKE A VERY STYLISH, HANDSOME BOY. SHE'S QUITE STUNNING, REALLY.
I DON'T GET THAT. I MEAN, IF YOU'RE INTO GIRLS, WOULDN'T YOU WANT TO BE WITH A...
BEN, DO YOU REALLY THINK YOU CAN BE SO LOGICAL ABOUT WHAT TURNS YOUR HEAD?
OH, I SHOULD SHUT UP. I'M SURE IT'S **FASCINATING** TO HEAR ME GO ON AND ON ABOUT GRAD SCHOOL POLITICS.
ZZZZZ
GOD... I'M SORRY! I ALWAYS DO THIS.
I'M JUST KIDDING. IT ACTUALLY MAKES ME FEEL A LITTLE BETTER ABOUT DROPPING OUT.

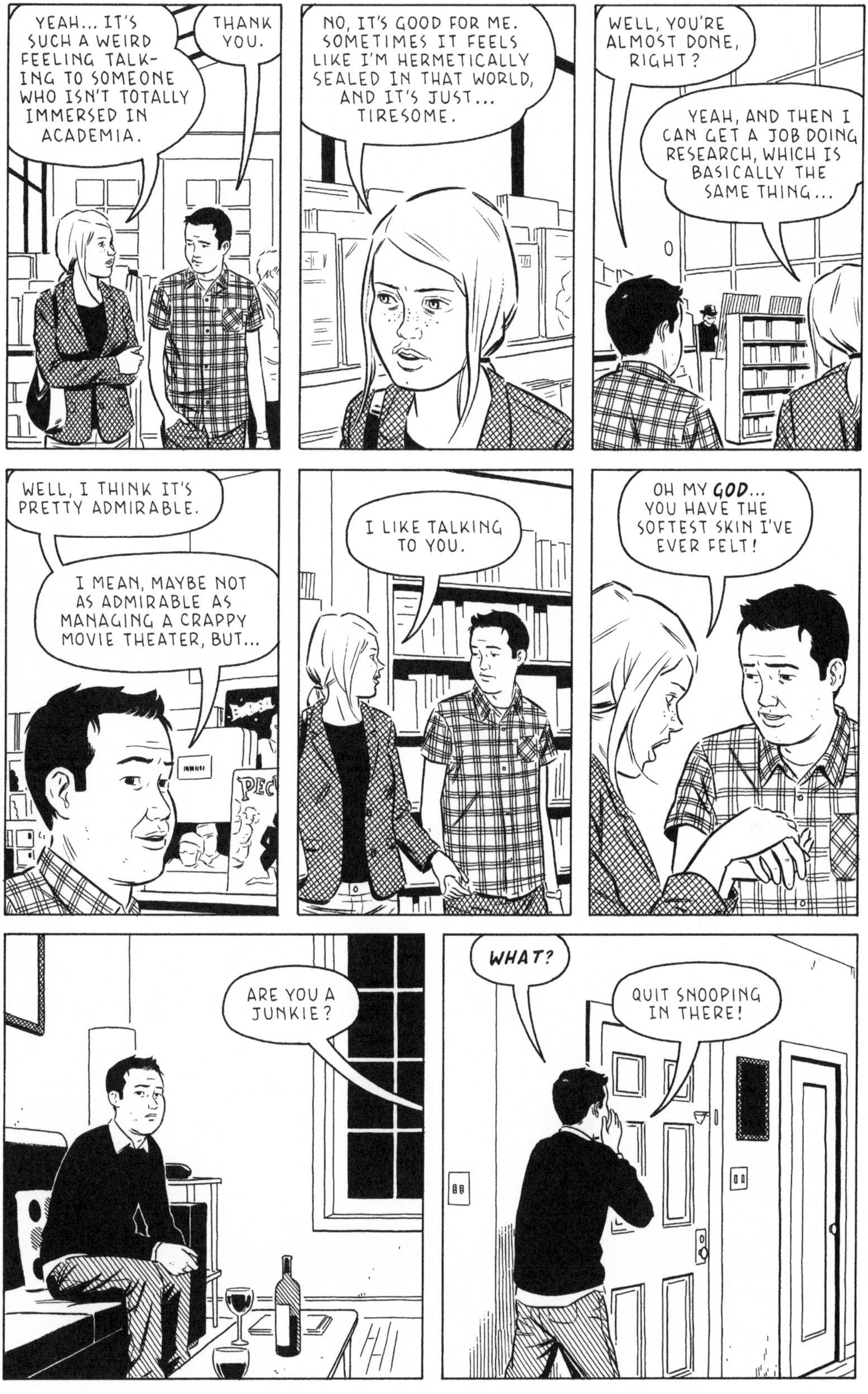
YEAH... IT'S SUCH A WEIRD FEELING TALKING TO SOMEONE WHO ISN'T TOTALLY IMMERSED IN ACADEMIA.
THANK YOU.
NO, IT'S GOOD FOR ME. SOMETIMES IT FEELS LIKE I'M HERMETICALLY SEALED IN THAT WORLD, AND IT'S JUST... TIRESOME.
WELL, YOU'RE ALMOST DONE, RIGHT?
YEAH, AND THEN I CAN GET A JOB DOING RESEARCH, WHICH IS BASICALLY THE SAME THING...
WELL, I THINK IT'S PRETTY ADMIRABLE.
I MEAN, MAYBE NOT AS ADMIRABLE AS MANAGING A CRAPPY MOVIE THEATER, BUT...
I LIKE TALKING TO YOU.
OH MY GOD... YOU HAVE THE SOFTEST SKIN I'VE EVER FELT!
ARE YOU A JUNKIE?
WHAT?
QUIT SNOOPING IN THERE!

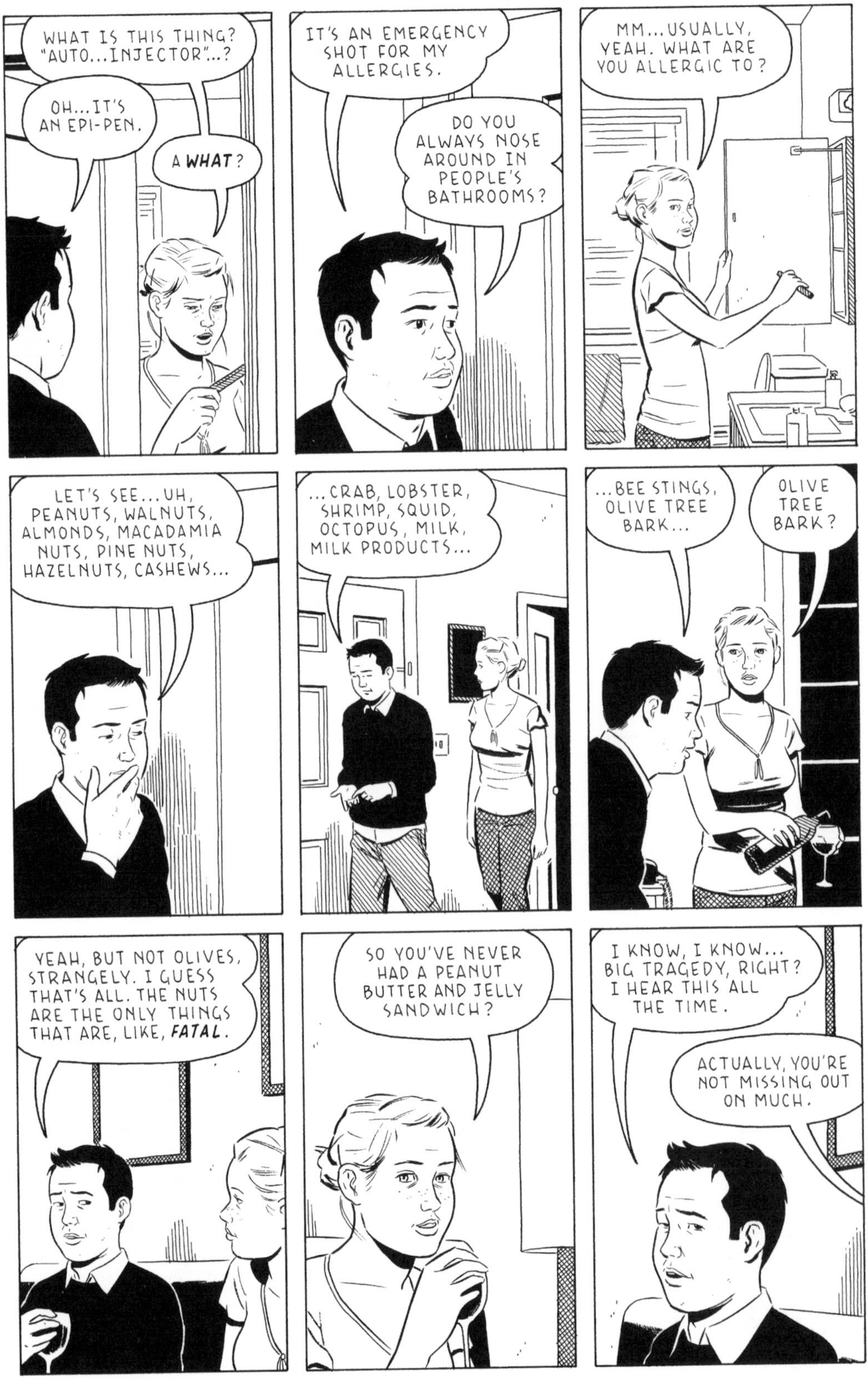
WHAT IS THIS THING? "AUTO...INJECTOR"...?
OH...IT'S AN EPI-PEN.
A WHAT?
IT'S AN EMERGENCY SHOT FOR MY ALLERGIES.
DO YOU ALWAYS NOSE AROUND IN PEOPLE'S BATHROOMS?
MM...USUALLY, YEAH. WHAT ARE YOU ALLERGIC TO?
LET'S SEE...UH, PEANUTS, WALNUTS, ALMONDS, MACADAMIA NUTS, PINE NUTS, HAZELNUTS, CASHEWS...
...CRAB, LOBSTER, SHRIMP, SQUID, OCTOPUS, MILK, MILK PRODUCTS...
...BEE STINGS, OLIVE TREE BARK...
OLIVE TREE BARK?
YEAH, BUT NOT OLIVES, STRANGELY. I GUESS THAT'S ALL. THE NUTS ARE THE ONLY THINGS THAT ARE, LIKE, FATAL.
SO YOU'VE NEVER HAD A PEANUT BUTTER AND JELLY SANDWICH?
I KNOW, I KNOW... BIG TRAGEDY, RIGHT? I HEAR THIS ALL THE TIME.
ACTUALLY, YOU'RE NOT MISSING OUT ON MUCH.

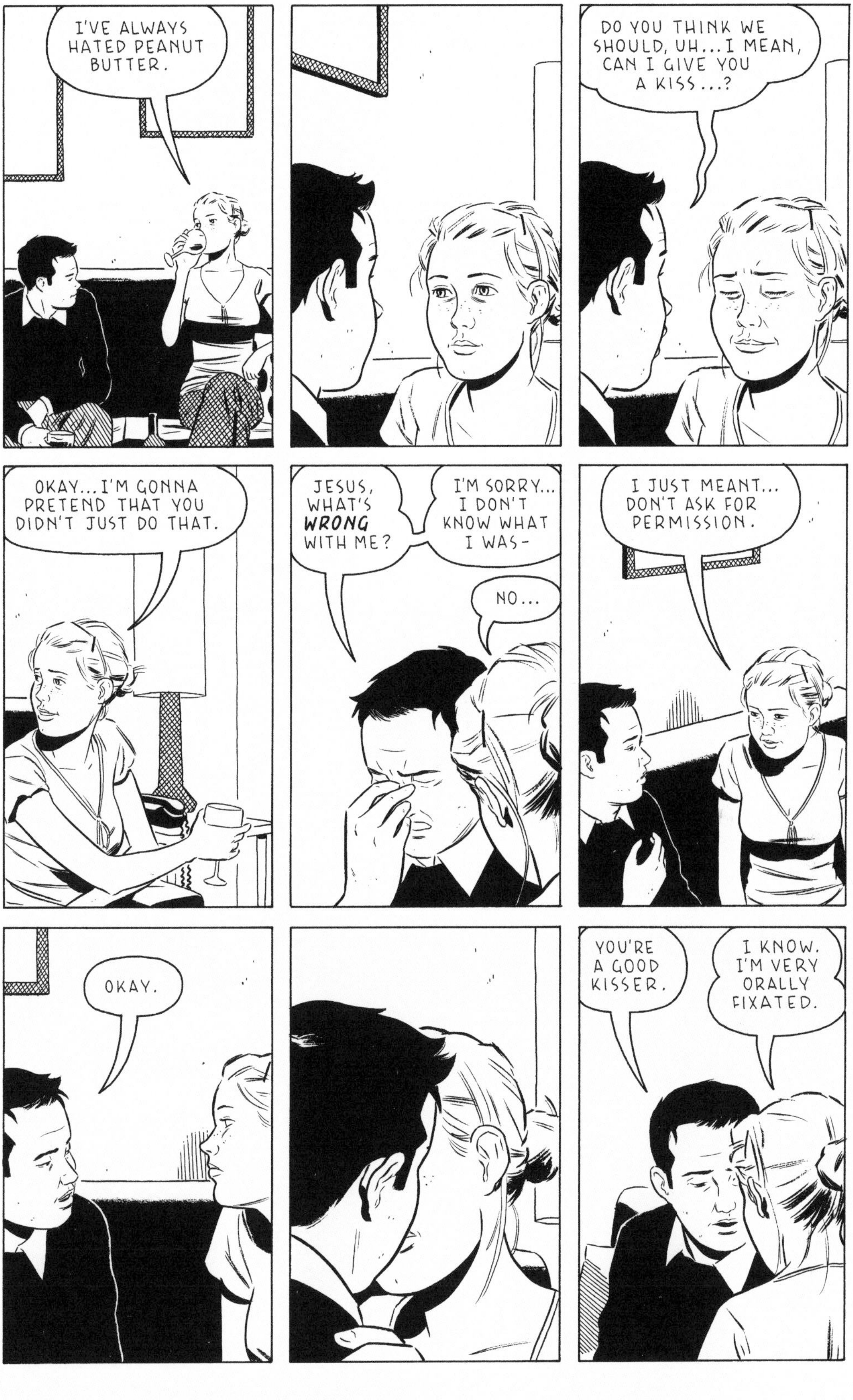
I'VE ALWAYS HATED PEANUT BUTTER.
DO YOU THINK WE SHOULD, UH... I MEAN, CAN I GIVE YOU A KISS...?
OKAY... I'M GONNA PRETEND THAT YOU DIDN'T JUST DO THAT.
JESUS, WHAT'S WRONG WITH ME?
I'M SORRY... I DON'T KNOW WHAT I WAS-
NO...
I JUST MEANT... DON'T ASK FOR PERMISSION.
OKAY.
YOU'RE A GOOD KISSER.
I KNOW. I'M VERY ORALLY FIXATED.

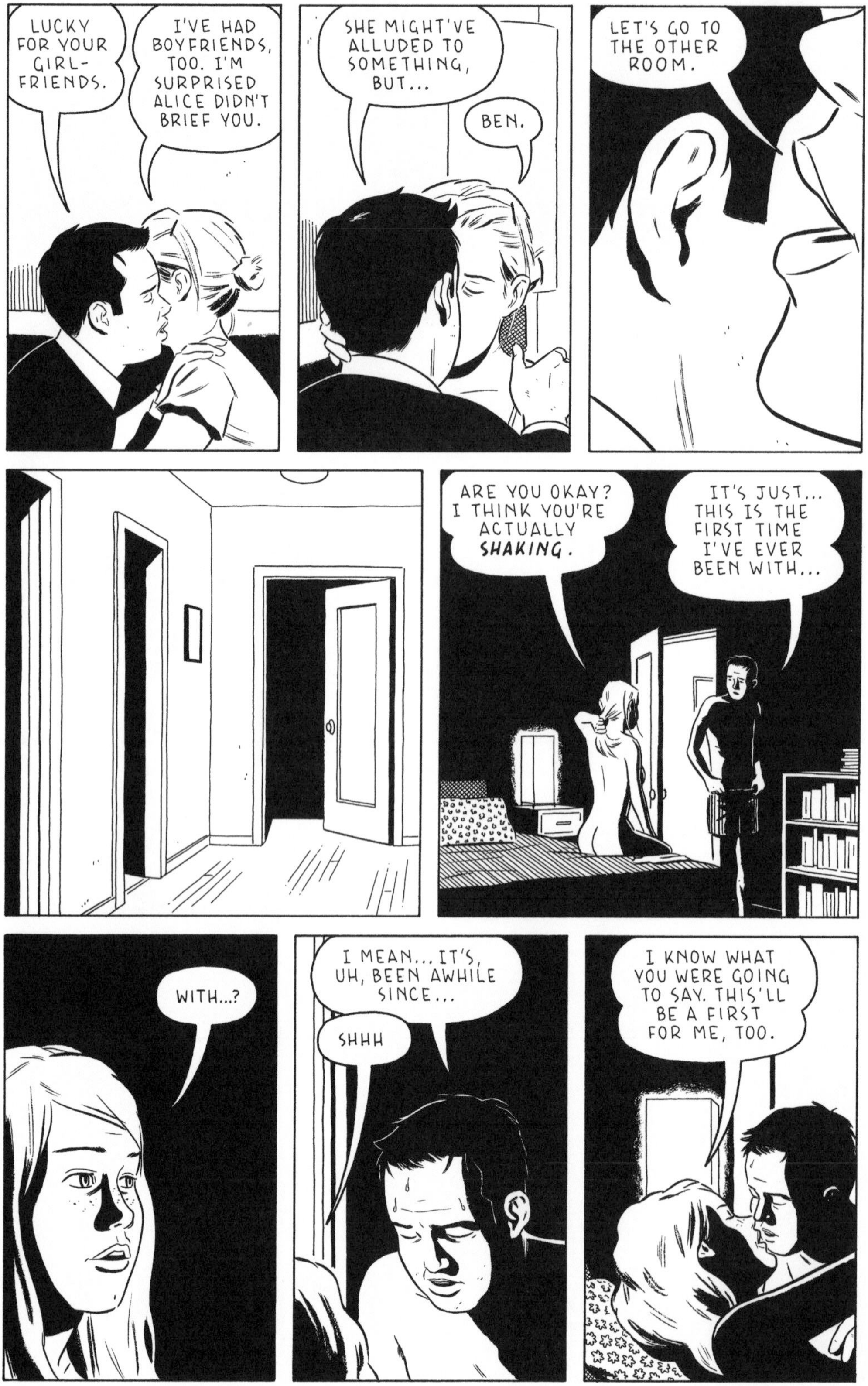
LUCKY FOR YOUR GIRL-FRIENDS.
I'VE HAD BOYFRIENDS, TOO. I'M SURPRISED ALICE DIDN'T BRIEF YOU.
SHE MIGHT'VE ALLUDED TO SOMETHING, BUT...
BEN.
LET'S GO TO THE OTHER ROOM.
ARE YOU OKAY? I THINK YOU'RE ACTUALLY SHAKING.
IT'S JUST... THIS IS THE FIRST TIME I'VE EVER BEEN WITH...
WITH...?
I MEAN... IT'S, UH, BEEN AWHILE SINCE...
SHHH
I KNOW WHAT YOU WERE GOING TO SAY. THIS'LL BE A FIRST FOR ME, TOO.

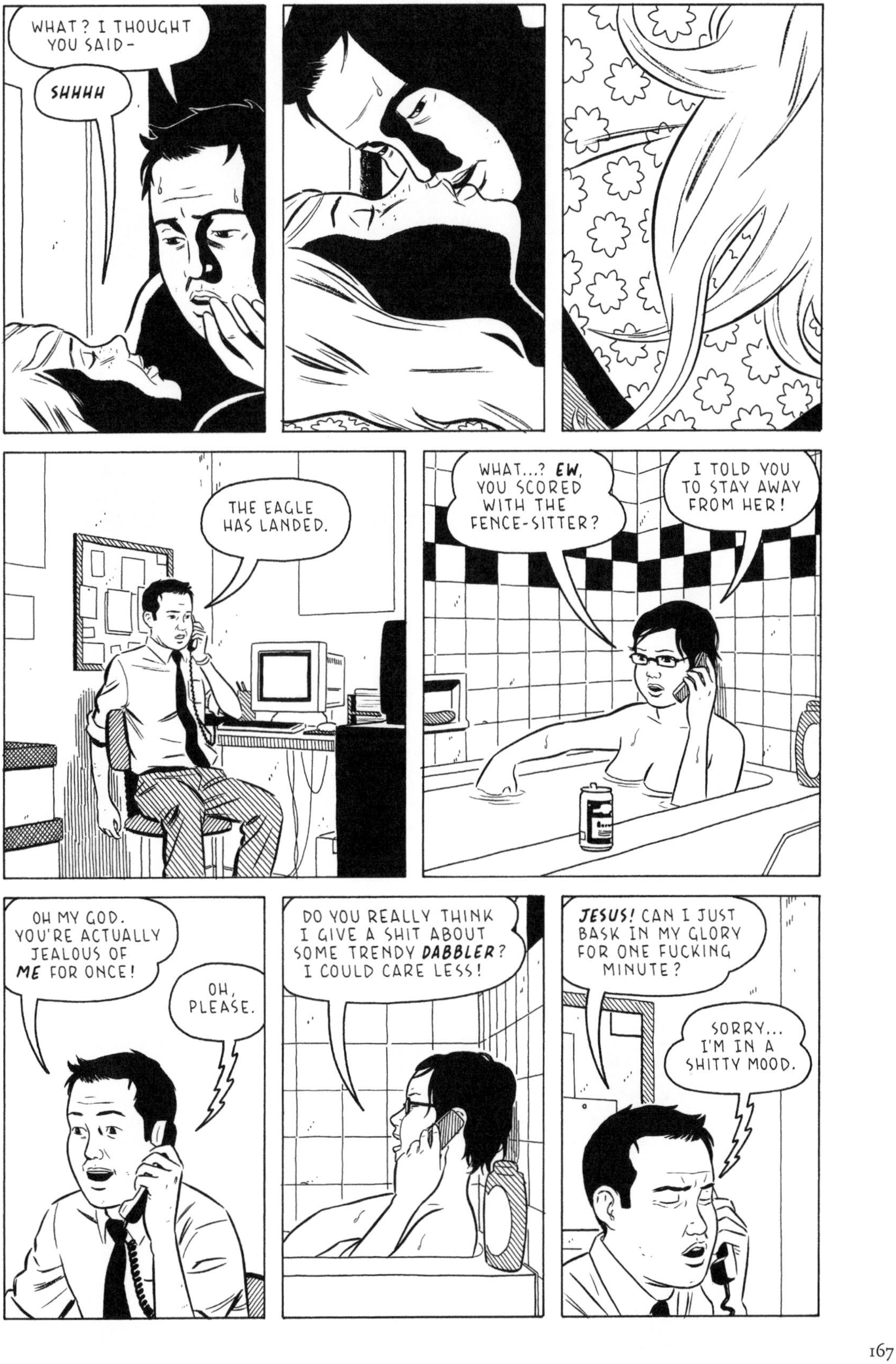
WHAT? I THOUGHT YOU SAID-
SHHHH
THE EAGLE HAS LANDED.
WHAT...? EW, YOU SCORED WITH THE FENCE-SITTER?
I TOLD YOU TO STAY AWAY FROM HER!
OH MY GOD. YOU'RE ACTUALLY JEALOUS OF ME FOR ONCE!
OH, PLEASE.
DO YOU REALLY THINK I GIVE A SHIT ABOUT SOME TRENDY DABBLER? I COULD CARE LESS!
JESUS! CAN I JUST BASK IN MY GLORY FOR ONE FUCKING MINUTE?
SORRY... I'M IN A SHITTY MOOD.

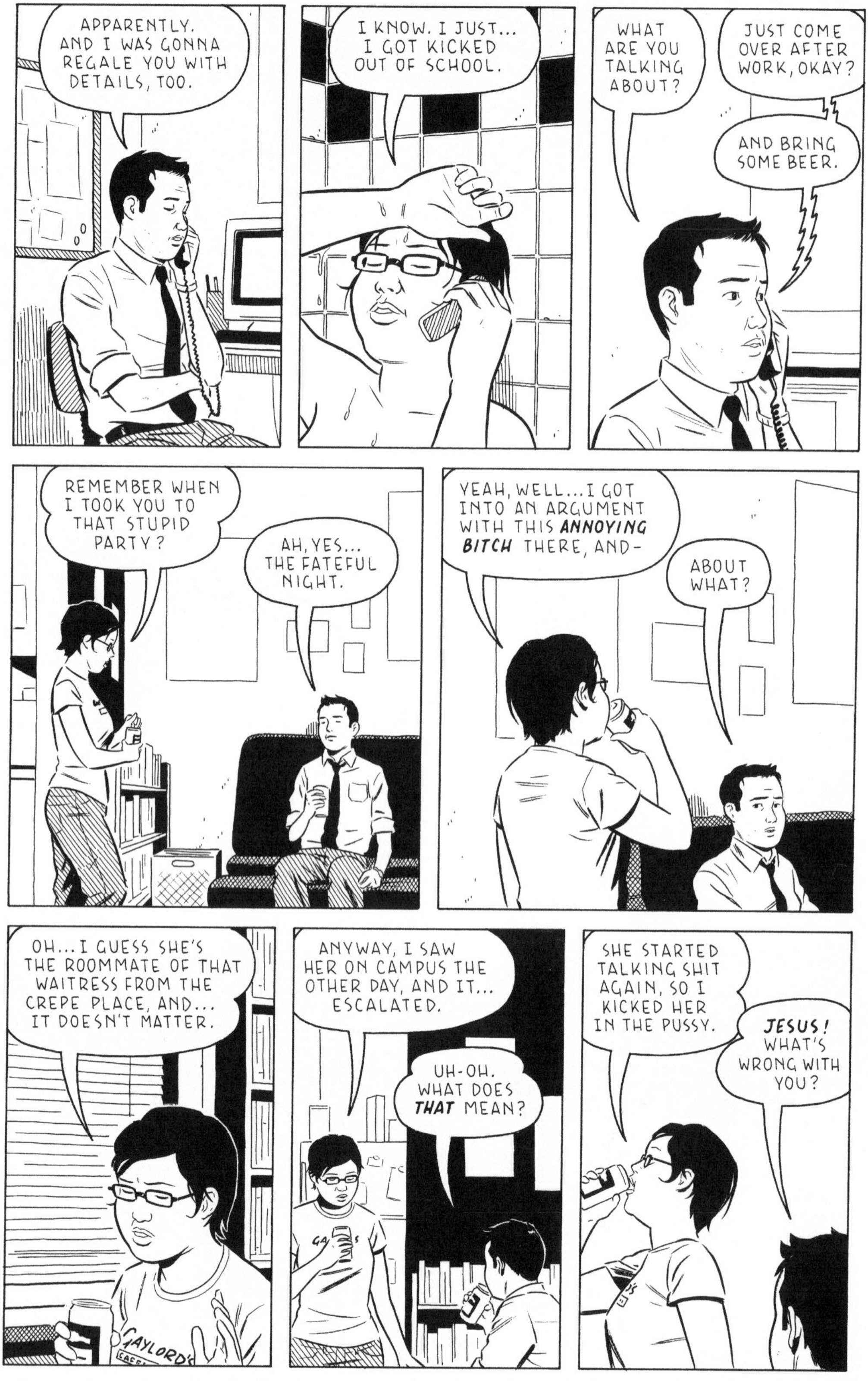
APPARENTLY. AND I WAS GONNA REGALE YOU WITH DETAILS, TOO.
I KNOW. I JUST... I GOT KICKED OUT OF SCHOOL.
WHAT ARE YOU TALKING ABOUT?
JUST COME OVER AFTER WORK, OKAY?
AND BRING SOME BEER.
REMEMBER WHEN I TOOK YOU TO THAT STUPID PARTY?
AH, YES... THE FATEFUL NIGHT.
YEAH, WELL... I GOT INTO AN ARGUMENT WITH THIS **ANNOYING BITCH** THERE, AND-
ABOUT WHAT?
OH... I GUESS SHE'S THE ROOMMATE OF THAT WAITRESS FROM THE CREPE PLACE, AND... IT DOESN'T MATTER.
ANYWAY, I SAW HER ON CAMPUS THE OTHER DAY, AND IT... ESCALATED.
UH-OH. WHAT DOES **THAT** MEAN?
SHE STARTED TALKING SHIT AGAIN, SO I KICKED HER IN THE PUSSY.
JESUS! WHAT'S WRONG WITH YOU?

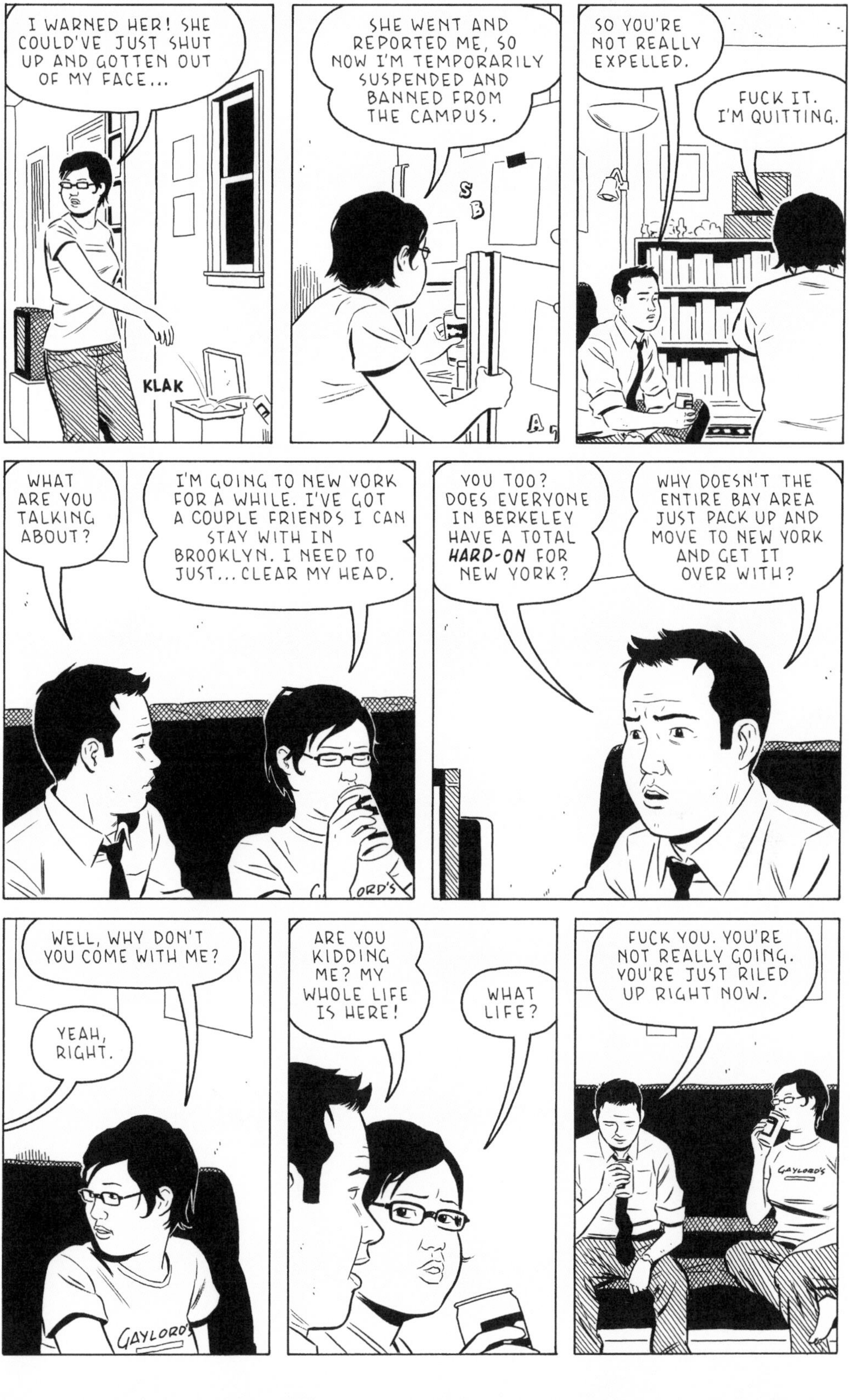
I WARNED HER! SHE COULD'VE JUST SHUT UP AND GOTTEN OUT OF MY FACE...
KLAK
SHE WENT AND REPORTED ME, SO NOW I'M TEMPORARILY SUSPENDED AND BANNED FROM THE CAMPUS.
SO YOU'RE NOT REALLY EXPELLED.
FUCK IT. I'M QUITTING.
WHAT ARE YOU TALKING ABOUT?
I'M GOING TO NEW YORK FOR A WHILE. I'VE GOT A COUPLE FRIENDS I CAN STAY WITH IN BROOKLYN. I NEED TO JUST... CLEAR MY HEAD.
YOU TOO? DOES EVERYONE IN BERKELEY HAVE A TOTAL HARD-ON FOR NEW YORK?
WHY DOESN'T THE ENTIRE BAY AREA JUST PACK UP AND MOVE TO NEW YORK AND GET IT OVER WITH?
WELL, WHY DON'T YOU COME WITH ME?
YEAH, RIGHT.
GAYLORD'S
ARE YOU KIDDING ME? MY WHOLE LIFE IS HERE!
WHAT LIFE?
FUCK YOU. YOU'RE NOT REALLY GOING. YOU'RE JUST RILED UP RIGHT NOW.
GAYLORD'S

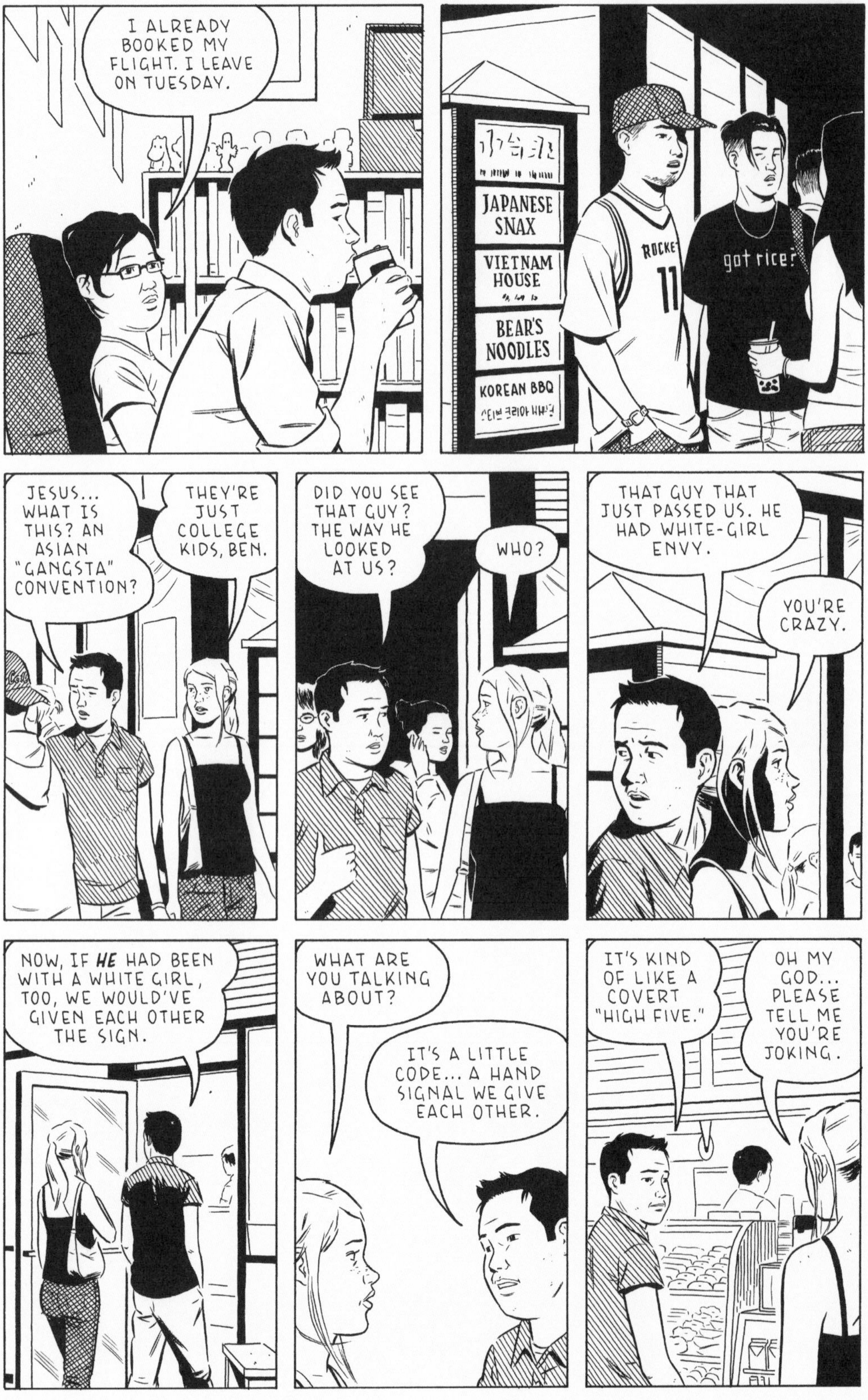
I ALREADY BOOKED MY FLIGHT. I LEAVE ON TUESDAY.
JAPANESE SNAX
VIETNAM HOUSE
BEAR'S NOODLES
KOREAN BBQ
ROCKETS
11
got rice?
JESUS... WHAT IS THIS? AN ASIAN "GANGSTA" CONVENTION?
THEY'RE JUST COLLEGE KIDS, BEN.
DID YOU SEE THAT GUY? THE WAY HE LOOKED AT US?
WHO?
THAT GUY THAT JUST PASSED US. HE HAD WHITE-GIRL ENVY.
YOU'RE CRAZY.
NOW, IF HE HAD BEEN WITH A WHITE GIRL, TOO, WE WOULD'VE GIVEN EACH OTHER THE SIGN.
WHAT ARE YOU TALKING ABOUT?
IT'S A LITTLE CODE... A HAND SIGNAL WE GIVE EACH OTHER.
IT'S KIND OF LIKE A COVERT "HIGH FIVE."
OH MY GOD... PLEASE TELL ME YOU'RE JOKING.

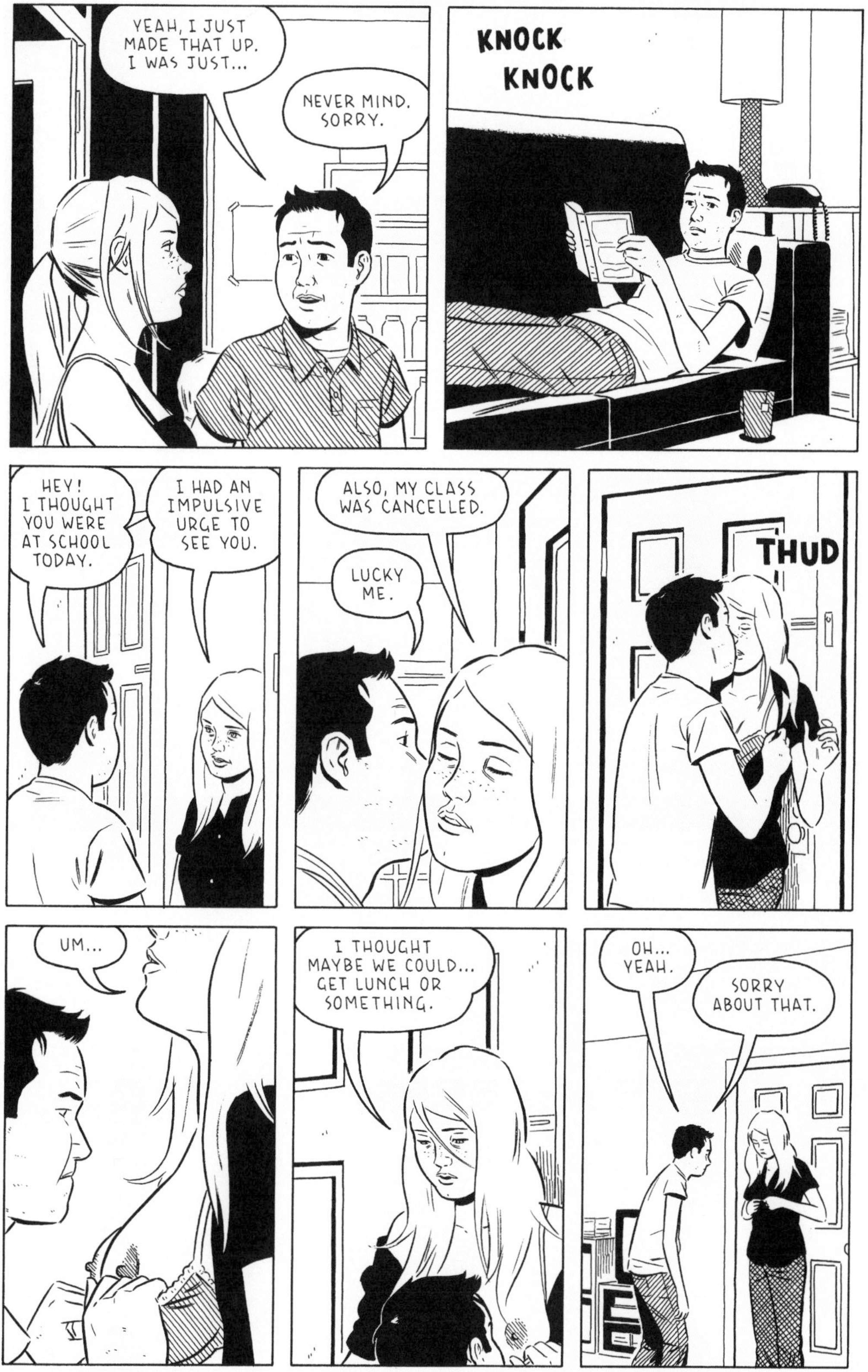
YEAH, I JUST MADE THAT UP. I WAS JUST...
NEVER MIND. SORRY.
KNOCK
KNOCK
HEY! I THOUGHT YOU WERE AT SCHOOL TODAY.
I HAD AN IMPULSIVE URGE TO SEE YOU.
ALSO, MY CLASS WAS CANCELLED.
LUCKY ME.
THUD
UM...
I THOUGHT MAYBE WE COULD... GET LUNCH OR SOMETHING.
OH... YEAH.
SORRY ABOUT THAT.

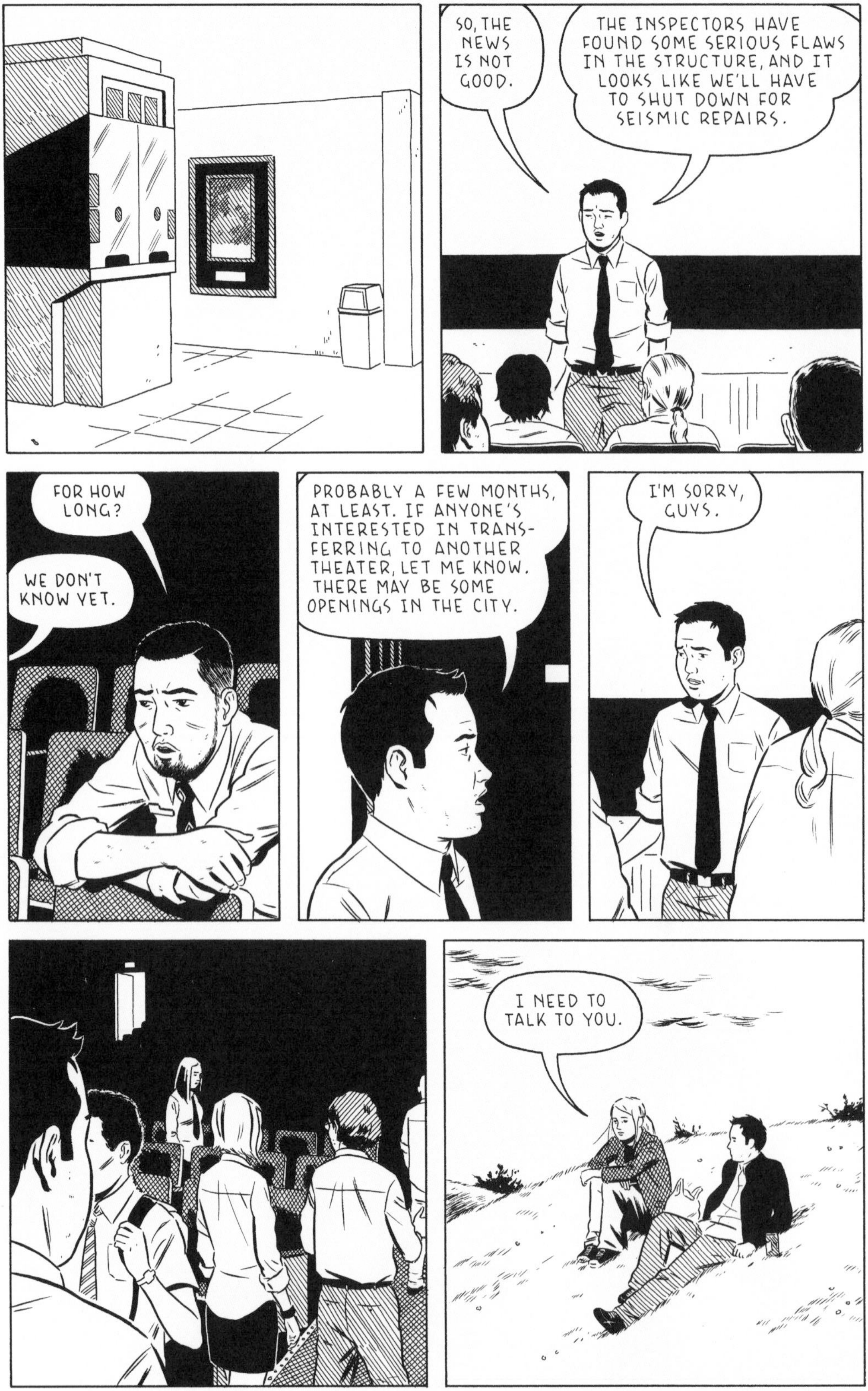
SO, THE NEWS IS NOT GOOD.
THE INSPECTORS HAVE FOUND SOME SERIOUS FLAWS IN THE STRUCTURE, AND IT LOOKS LIKE WE'LL HAVE TO SHUT DOWN FOR SEISMIC REPAIRS.
FOR HOW LONG?
WE DON'T KNOW YET.
PROBABLY A FEW MONTHS, AT LEAST. IF ANYONE'S INTERESTED IN TRANSFERRING TO ANOTHER THEATER, LET ME KNOW. THERE MAY BE SOME OPENINGS IN THE CITY.
I'M SORRY, GUYS.
I NEED TO TALK TO YOU.

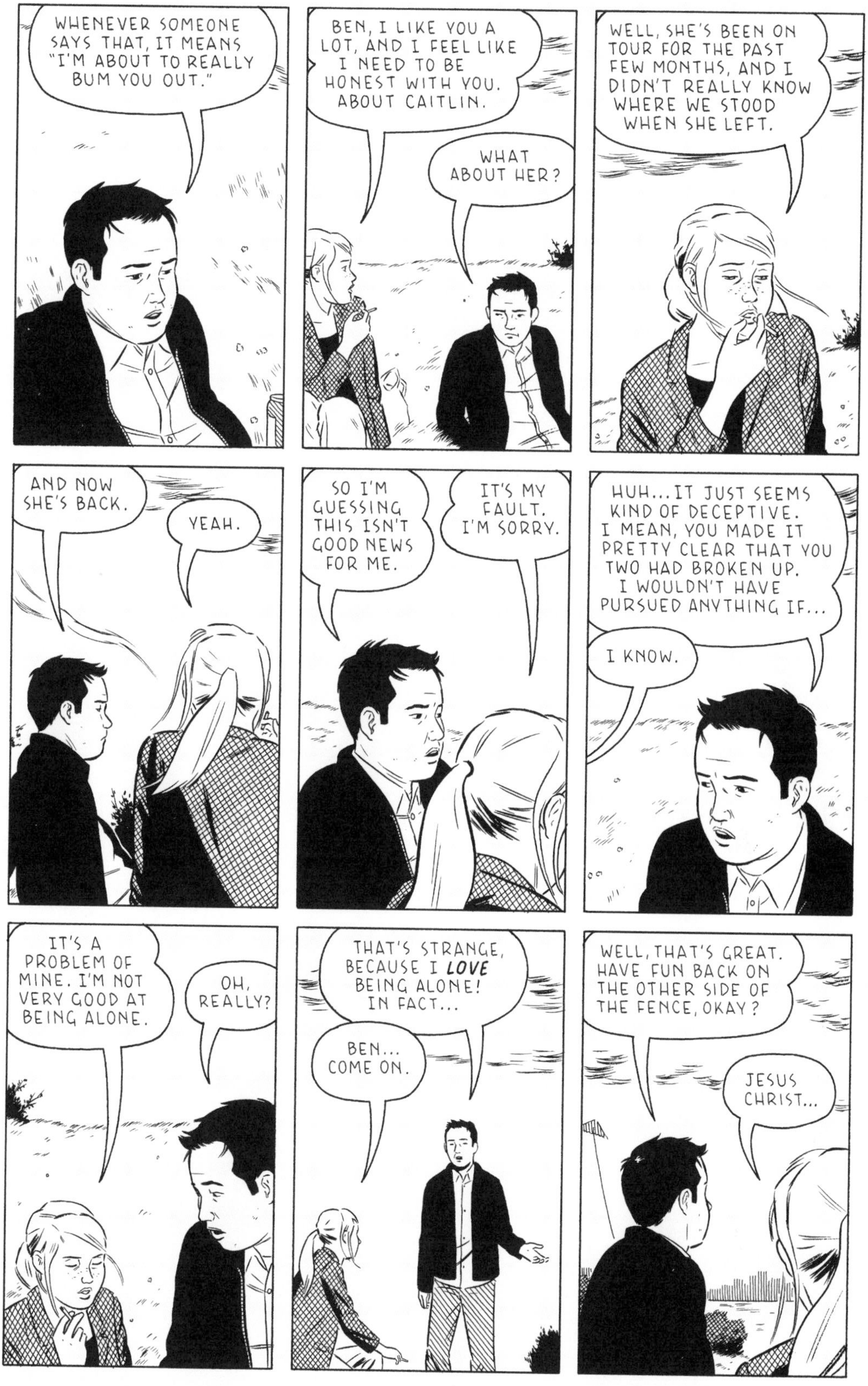
WHENEVER SOMEONE SAYS THAT, IT MEANS "I'M ABOUT TO REALLY BUM YOU OUT."
BEN, I LIKE YOU A LOT, AND I FEEL LIKE I NEED TO BE HONEST WITH YOU. ABOUT CAITLIN.
WHAT ABOUT HER?
WELL, SHE'S BEEN ON TOUR FOR THE PAST FEW MONTHS, AND I DIDN'T REALLY KNOW WHERE WE STOOD WHEN SHE LEFT.
AND NOW SHE'S BACK.
YEAH.
SO I'M GUESSING THIS ISN'T GOOD NEWS FOR ME.
IT'S MY FAULT. I'M SORRY.
HUH... IT JUST SEEMS KIND OF DECEPTIVE. I MEAN, YOU MADE IT PRETTY CLEAR THAT YOU TWO HAD BROKEN UP. I WOULDN'T HAVE PURSUED ANYTHING IF...
I KNOW.
IT'S A PROBLEM OF MINE. I'M NOT VERY GOOD AT BEING ALONE.
OH, REALLY?
THAT'S STRANGE, BECAUSE I LOVE BEING ALONE! IN FACT...
BEN... COME ON.
WELL, THAT'S GREAT. HAVE FUN BACK ON THE OTHER SIDE OF THE FENCE, OKAY?
JESUS CHRIST...

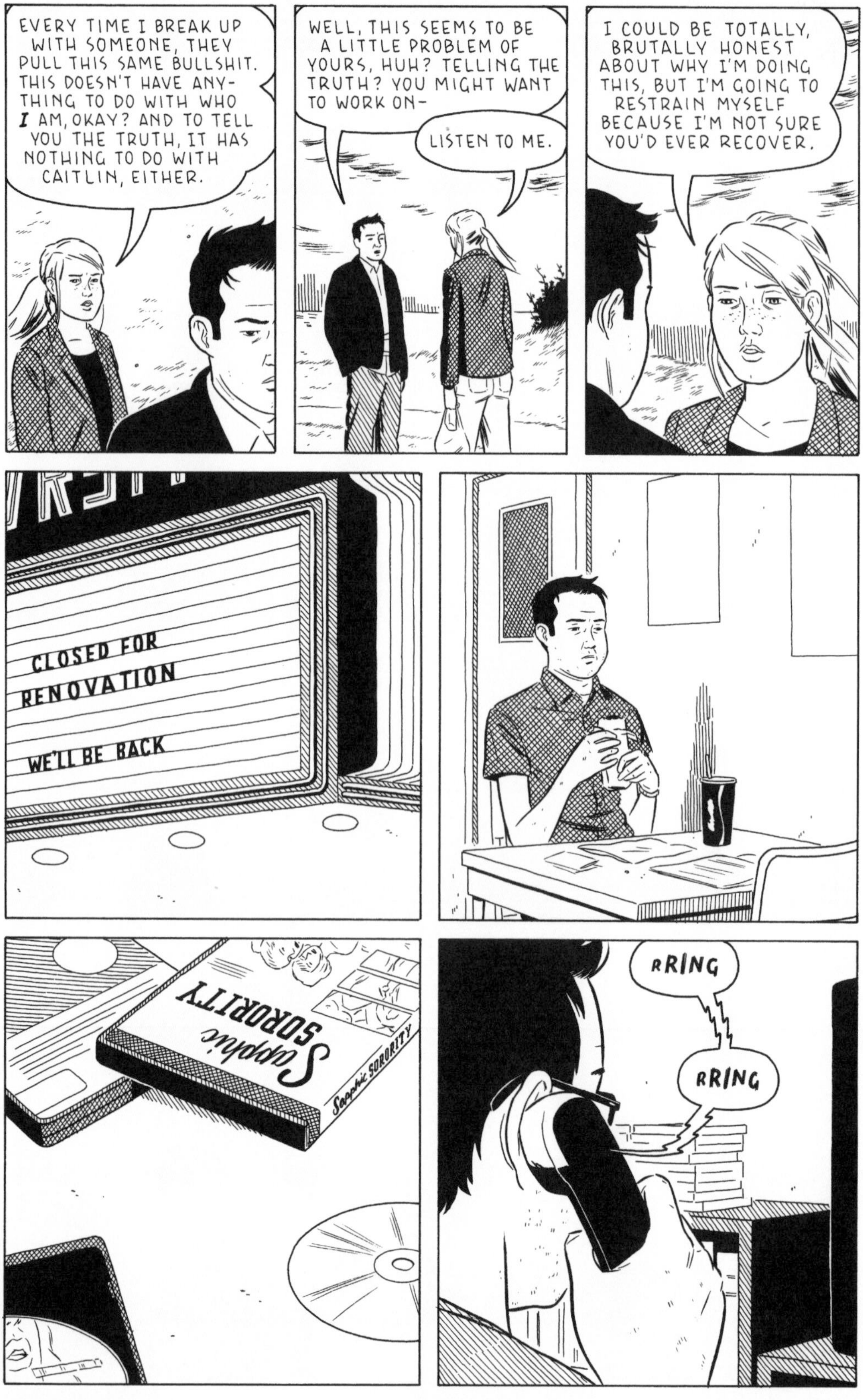
EVERY TIME I BREAK UP WITH SOMEONE, THEY PULL THIS SAME BULLSHIT. THIS DOESN'T HAVE ANYTHING TO DO WITH WHO I AM, OKAY? AND TO TELL YOU THE TRUTH, IT HAS NOTHING TO DO WITH CAITLIN, EITHER.
WELL, THIS SEEMS TO BE A LITTLE PROBLEM OF YOURS, HUH? TELLING THE TRUTH? YOU MIGHT WANT TO WORK ON-
LISTEN TO ME.
I COULD BE TOTALLY, BRUTALLY HONEST ABOUT WHY I'M DOING THIS, BUT I'M GOING TO RESTRAIN MYSELF BECAUSE I'M NOT SURE YOU'D EVER RECOVER.
CLOSED FOR RENOVATION
WE'LL BE BACK
Sapphic SORORITY
Sapphic SORORITY
RRING
RRING

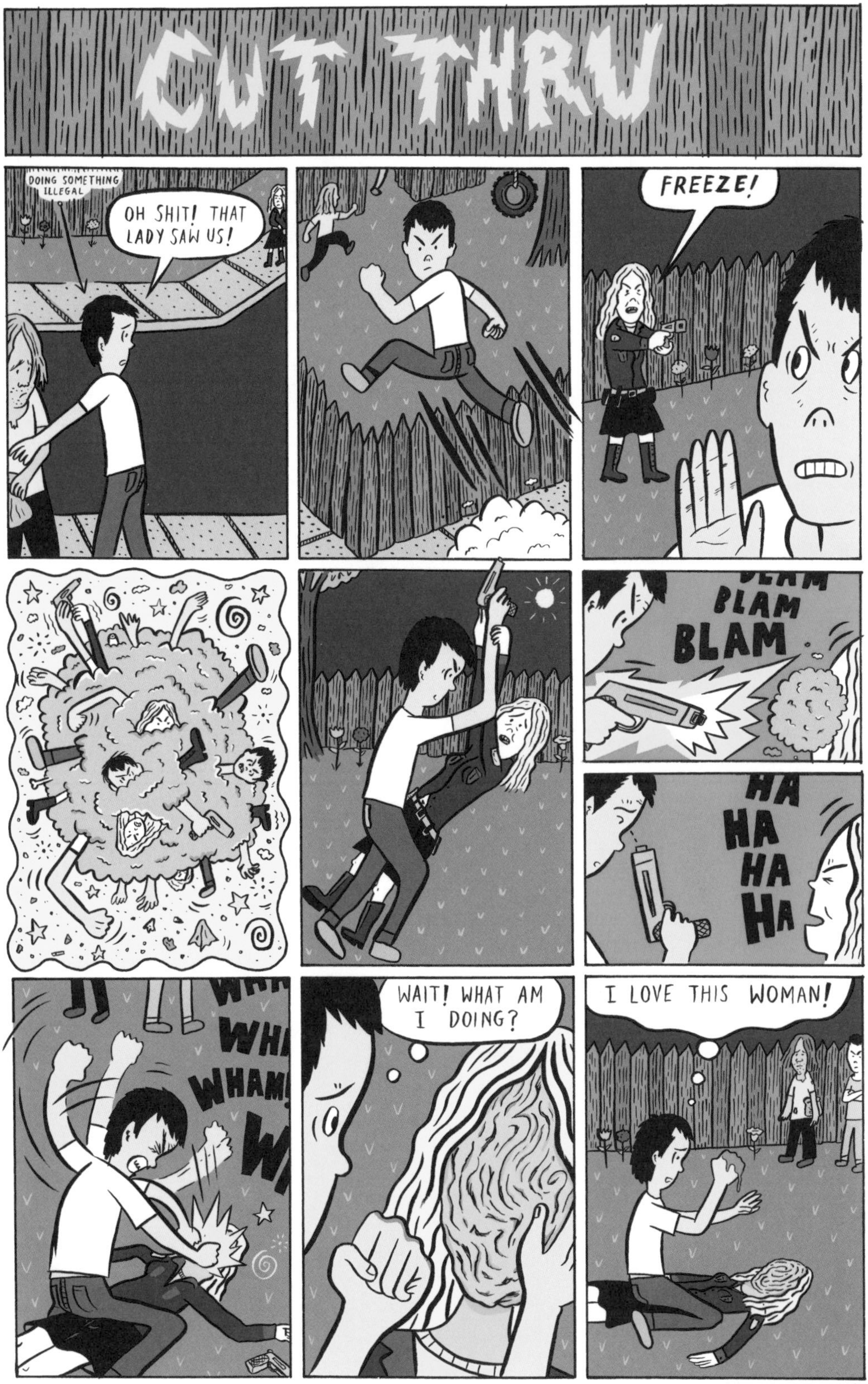
CUT THRU
DOING SOMETHING ILLEGAL
OH SHIT! THAT LADY SAW US!
FREEZE!
BLAM
BLAM
BLAM
HA
HA
HA
HA
WAIT! WHAT AM I DOING?
I LOVE THIS WOMAN!
DREAMT MARCH 1996

DAVID HEATLEY

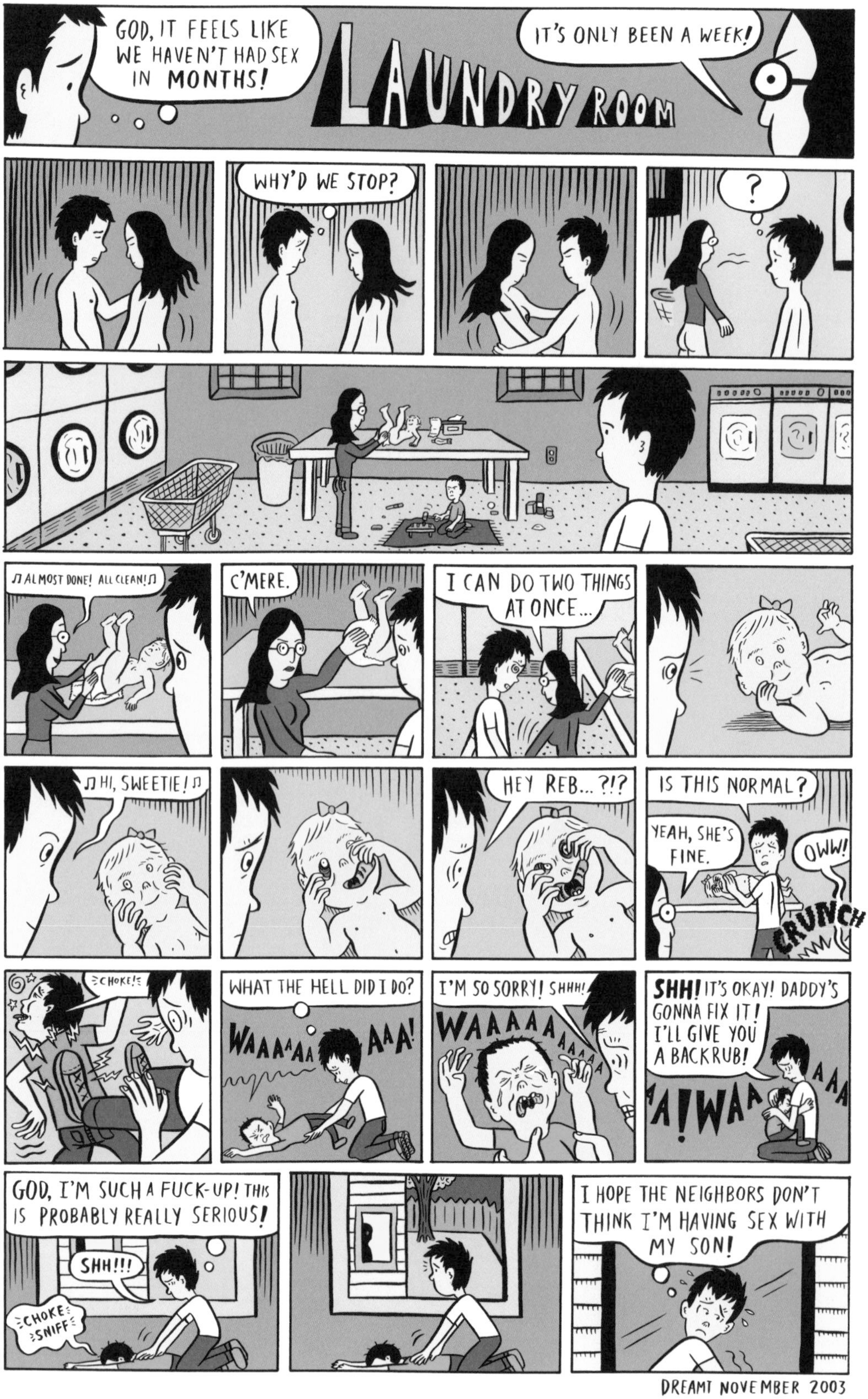
GOD, IT FEELS LIKE WE HAVEN'T HAD SEX IN MONTHS!
LAUNDRY ROOM
IT'S ONLY BEEN A WEEK!
WHY'D WE STOP?
?
♫ ALMOST DONE! ALL CLEAN! ♫
C'MERE.
I CAN DO TWO THINGS AT ONCE...
♫ HI, SWEETIE! ♫
HEY REB...?!?
IS THIS NORMAL?
YEAH, SHE'S FINE.
OWW!
CRUNCH
CHOKE!
WHAT THE HELL DID I DO?
WAAAAAA AAA!
I'M SO SORRY! SHHH!
WAAAAAAAAAA
SHH! IT'S OKAY! DADDY'S GONNA FIX IT! I'LL GIVE YOU A BACKRUB!
AA! WAA AAA
GOD, I'M SUCH A FUCK-UP! THIS IS PROBABLY REALLY SERIOUS!
SHH!!!
CHOKE SNIFF
I HOPE THE NEIGHBORS DON'T THINK I'M HAVING SEX WITH MY SON!

DREAMT NOVEMBER 2003

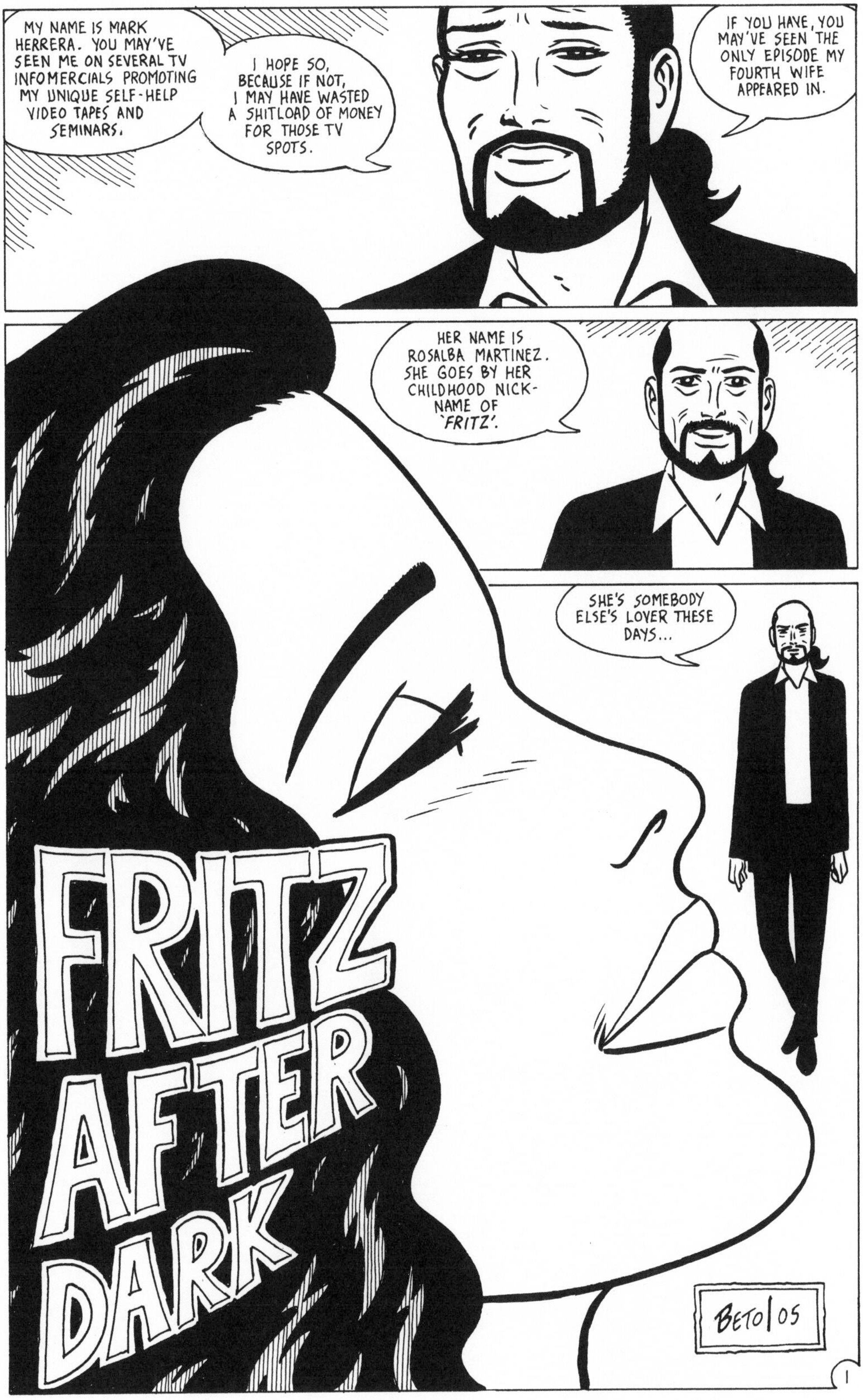
MY NAME IS MARK HERRERA. YOU MAY'VE SEEN ME ON SEVERAL TV INFOMERCIALS PROMOTING MY UNIQUE SELF-HELP VIDEO TAPES AND SEMINARS.
I HOPE SO, BECAUSE IF NOT, I MAY HAVE WASTED A SHITLOAD OF MONEY FOR THOSE TV SPOTS.
IF YOU HAVE, YOU MAY'VE SEEN THE ONLY EPISODE MY FOURTH WIFE APPEARED IN.
HER NAME IS ROSALBA MARTINEZ. SHE GOES BY HER CHILDHOOD NICK-NAME OF 'FRITZ'.
SHE'S SOMEBODY ELSE'S LOVER THESE DAYS...
FRITZ AFTER DARK
BETO | 05
1

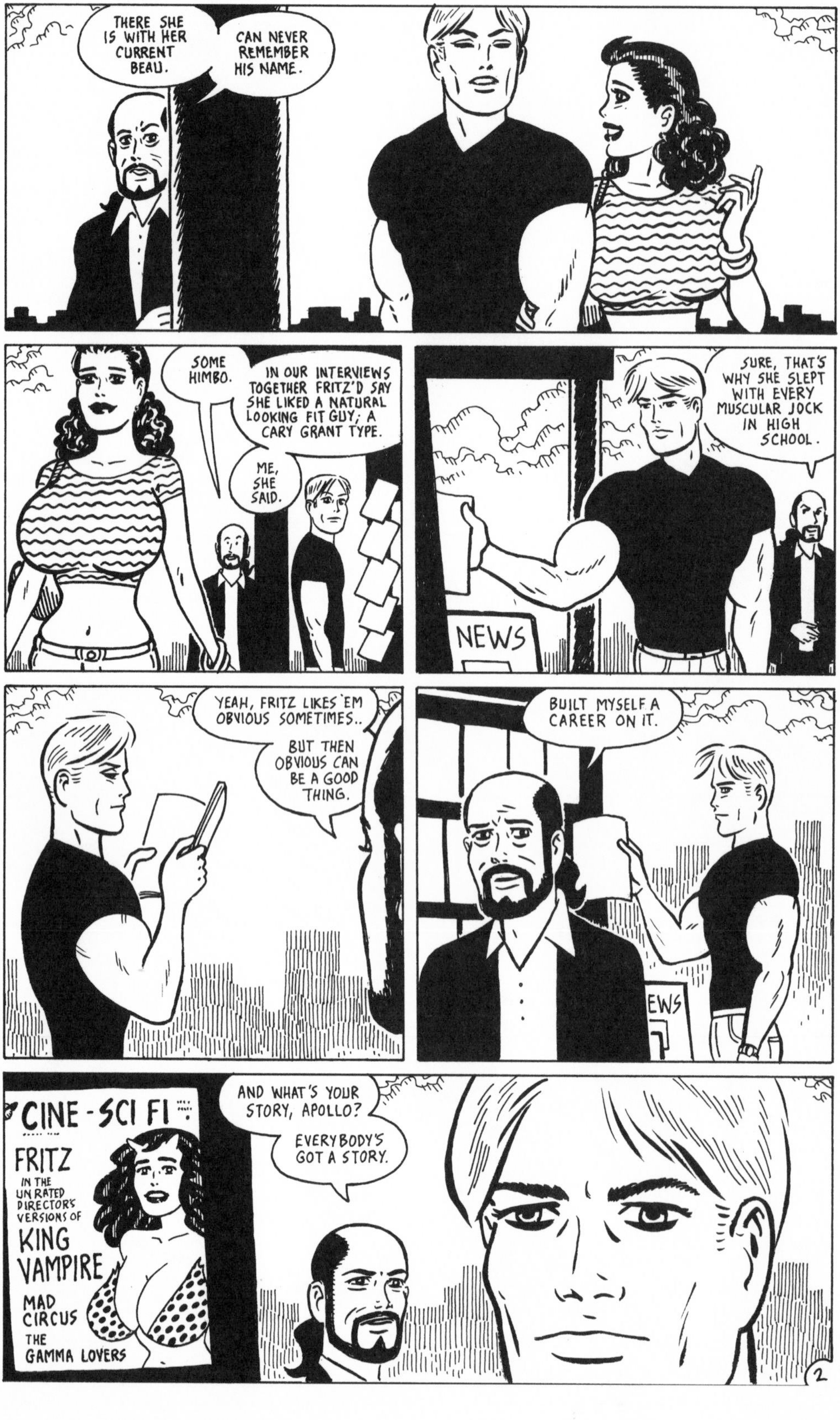
THERE SHE IS WITH HER CURRENT BEAU.
CAN NEVER REMEMBER HIS NAME.
SOME HIMBO.
IN OUR INTERVIEWS TOGETHER FRITZ'D SAY SHE LIKED A NATURAL LOOKING FIT GUY; A CARY GRANT TYPE.
ME, SHE SAID.
SURE, THAT'S WHY SHE SLEPT WITH EVERY MUSCULAR JOCK IN HIGH SCHOOL.
NEWS
YEAH, FRITZ LIKES 'EM OBVIOUS SOMETIMES..
BUT THEN OBVIOUS CAN BE A GOOD THING.
BUILT MYSELF A CAREER ON IT.
CINE-SCI FI
FRITZ IN THE UNRATED DIRECTOR'S VERSIONS OF
KING VAMPIRE
MAD CIRCUS
THE GAMMA LOVERS
AND WHAT'S YOUR STORY, APOLLO?
EVERYBODY'S GOT A STORY.
2

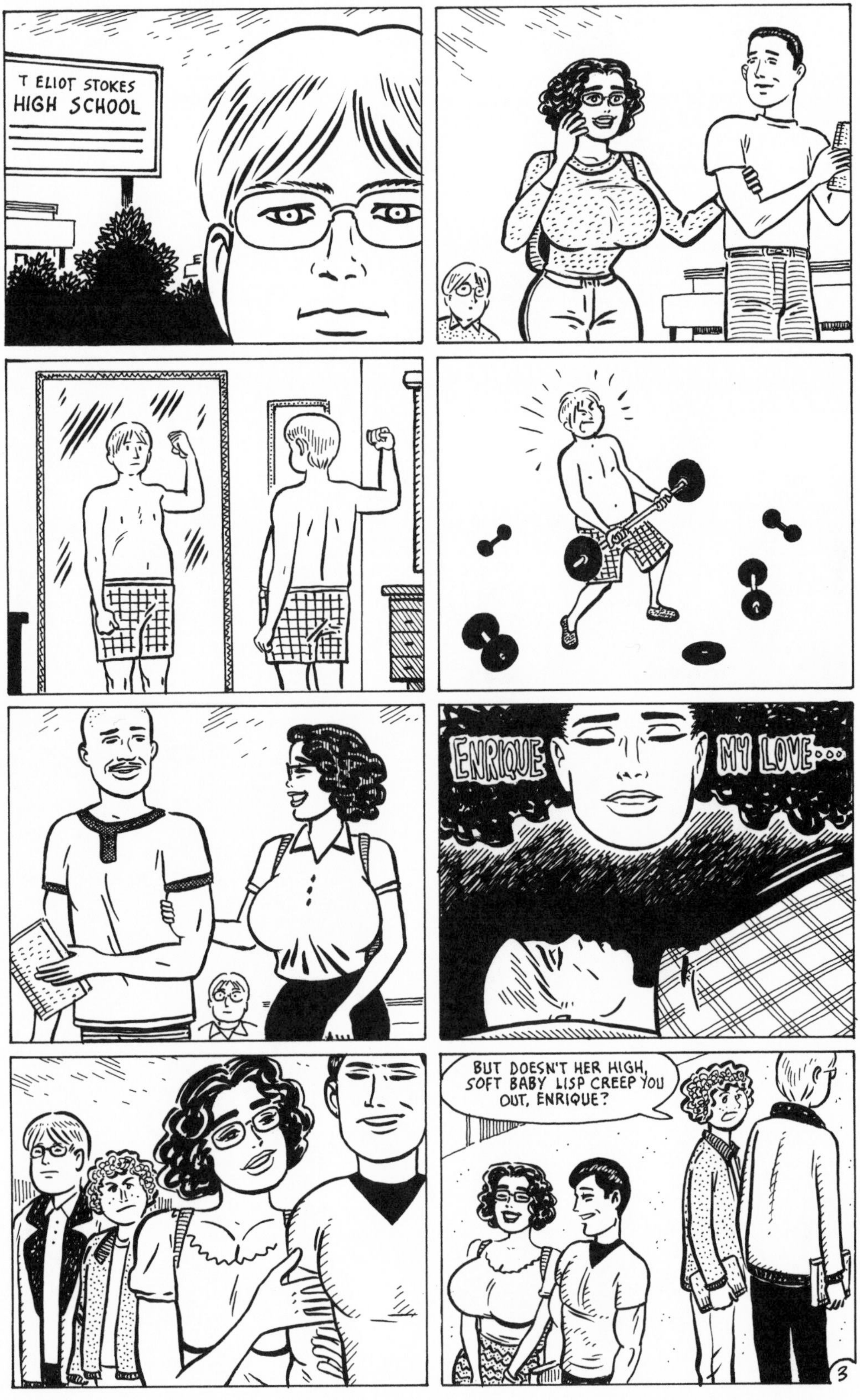
T ELIOT STOKES
HIGH SCHOOL
ENRIQUE
MY LOVE...
BUT DOESN'T HER HIGH, SOFT BABY LISP CREEP YOU OUT, ENRIQUE?
3

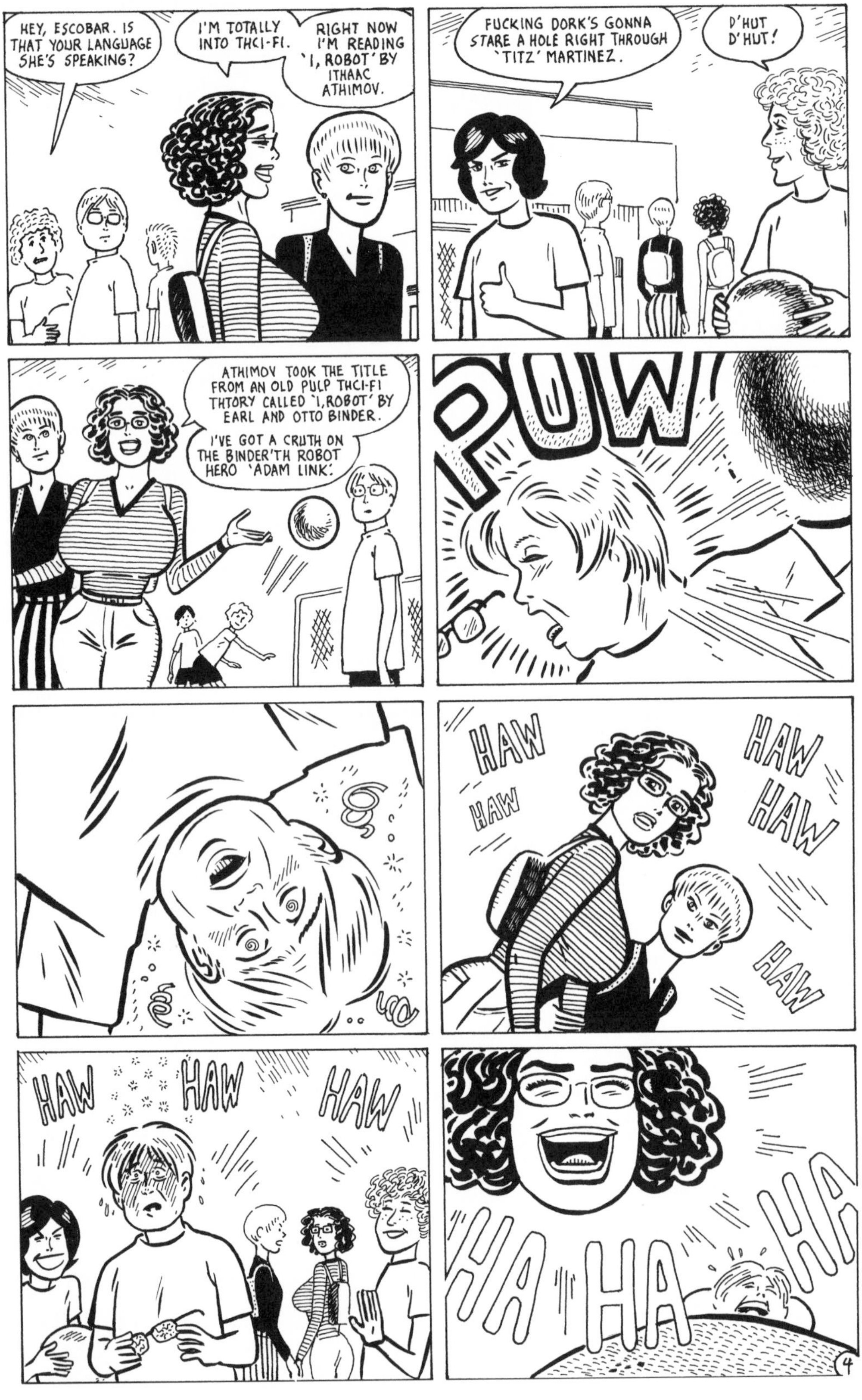
HEY, ESCOBAR. IS THAT YOUR LANGUAGE SHE'S SPEAKING?
I'M TOTALLY INTO THCI-FI.
RIGHT NOW I'M READING 'I, ROBOT' BY ITHAAC ATHIMOV.
FUCKING DORK'S GONNA STARE A HOLE RIGHT THROUGH 'TITZ' MARTINEZ.
D'HUT D'HUT!
ATHIMOV TOOK THE TITLE FROM AN OLD PULP THCI-FI THTORY CALLED 'I, ROBOT' BY EARL AND OTTO BINDER.
I'VE GOT A CRUTH ON THE BINDER'TH ROBOT HERO 'ADAM LINK'.
POW
HAW
HAW
HAW
HAW
HAW
HAW
HAW
HAW
HAW
HA HA HA HA
4

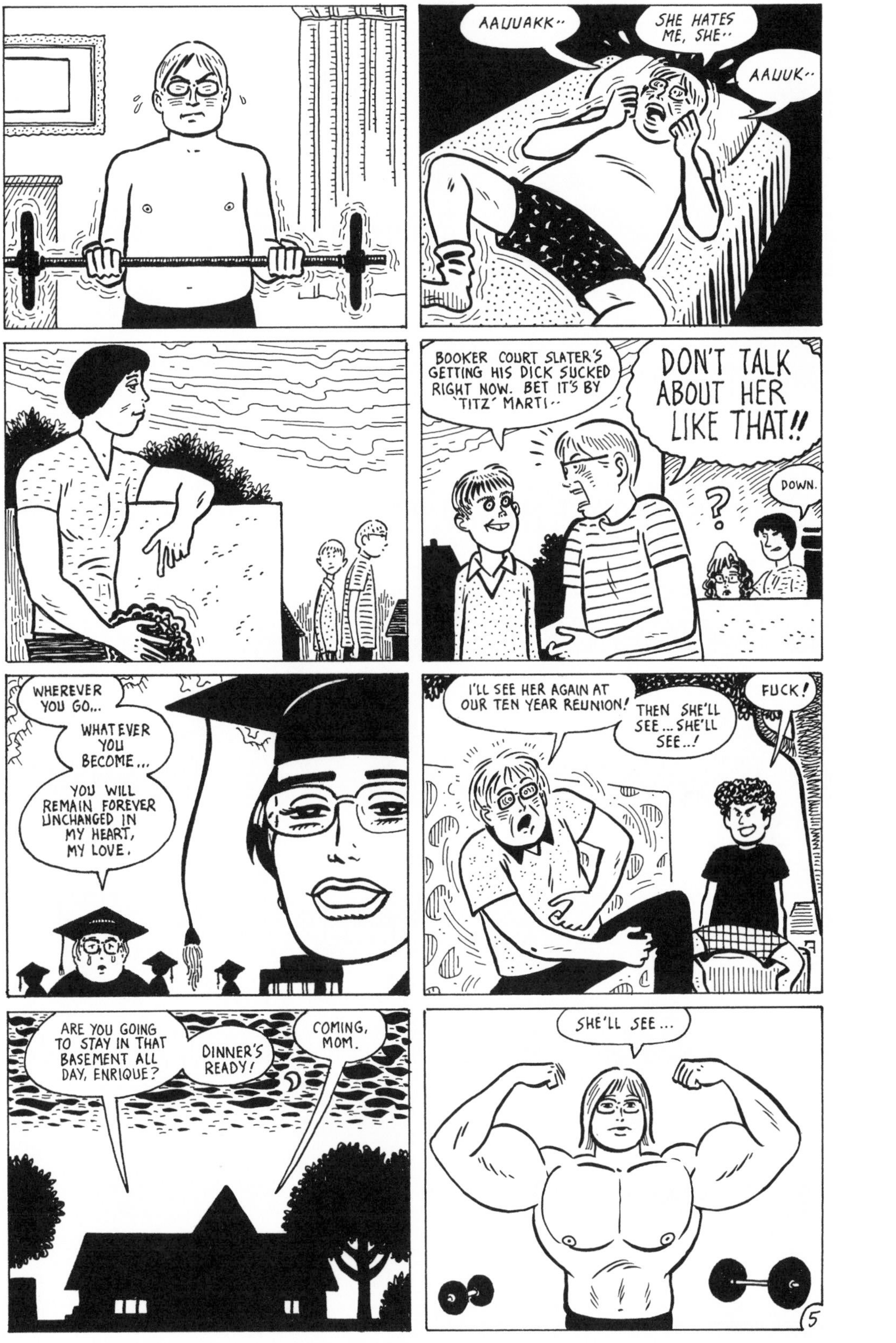
AAUUAKK..
SHE HATES ME, SHE..
AAUUK..
BOOKER COURT SLATER'S GETTING HIS DICK SUCKED RIGHT NOW. BET IT'S BY 'TITZ' MARTI..
DON'T TALK ABOUT HER LIKE THAT!!
?
DOWN.
WHEREVER YOU GO...
WHATEVER YOU BECOME...
YOU WILL REMAIN FOREVER UNCHANGED IN MY HEART, MY LOVE.
I'LL SEE HER AGAIN AT OUR TEN YEAR REUNION!
THEN SHE'LL SEE... SHE'LL SEE...!
FUCK!
ARE YOU GOING TO STAY IN THAT BASEMENT ALL DAY, ENRIQUE?
DINNER'S READY!
COMING, MOM.
SHE'LL SEE...
5

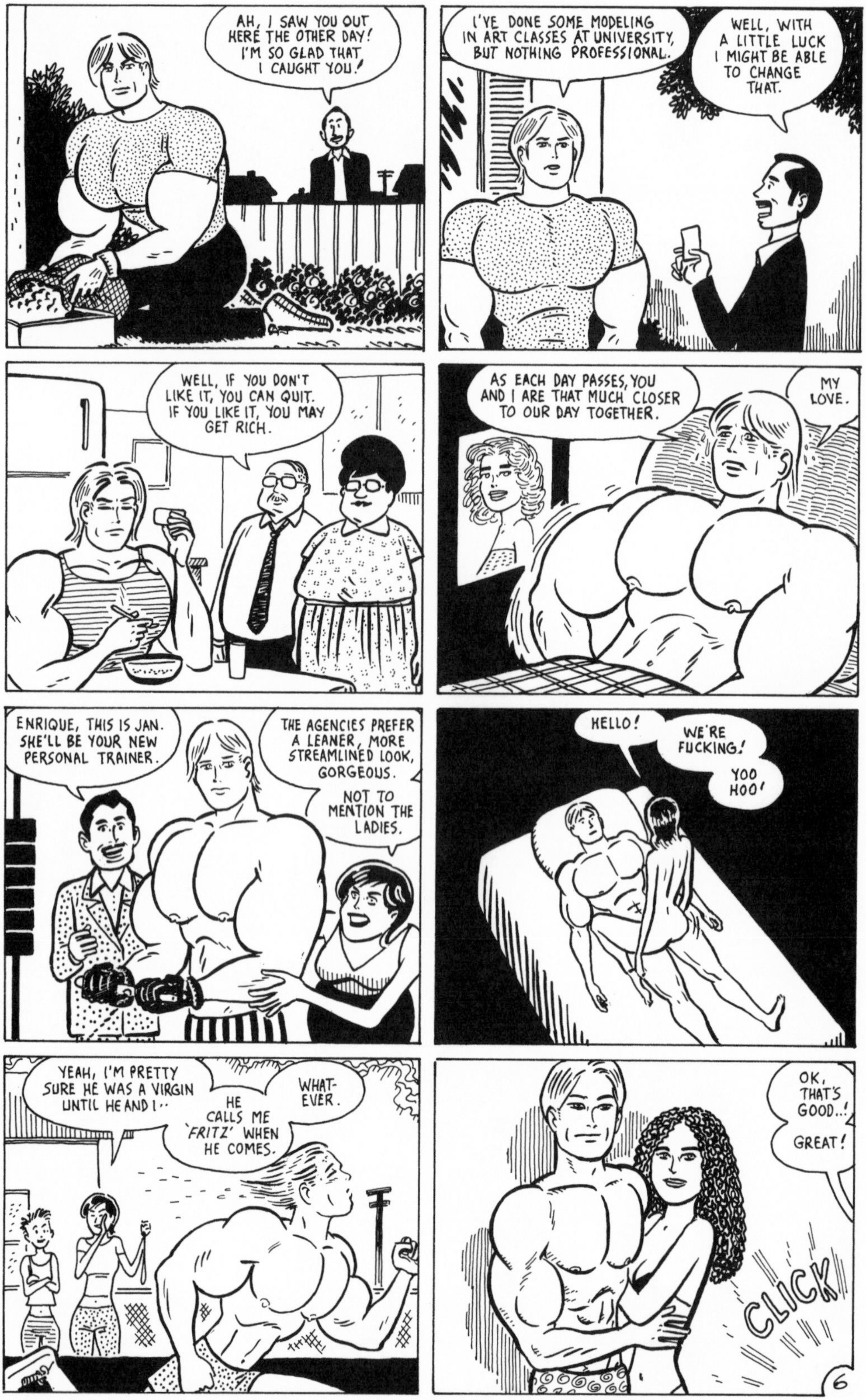
AH, I SAW YOU OUT HERE THE OTHER DAY! I'M SO GLAD THAT I CAUGHT YOU!
I'VE DONE SOME MODELING IN ART CLASSES AT UNIVERSITY, BUT NOTHING PROFESSIONAL.
WELL, WITH A LITTLE LUCK I MIGHT BE ABLE TO CHANGE THAT.
WELL, IF YOU DON'T LIKE IT, YOU CAN QUIT. IF YOU LIKE IT, YOU MAY GET RICH.
AS EACH DAY PASSES, YOU AND I ARE THAT MUCH CLOSER TO OUR DAY TOGETHER.
MY LOVE.
ENRIQUE, THIS IS JAN. SHE'LL BE YOUR NEW PERSONAL TRAINER.
THE AGENCIES PREFER A LEANER, MORE STREAMLINED LOOK, GORGEOUS.
NOT TO MENTION THE LADIES.
HELLO!
WE'RE FUCKING!
YOO HOO!
YEAH, I'M PRETTY SURE HE WAS A VIRGIN UNTIL HE AND I..
HE CALLS ME 'FRITZ' WHEN HE COMES.
WHAT-EVER.
OK, THAT'S GOOD..!
GREAT!
CLICK
6

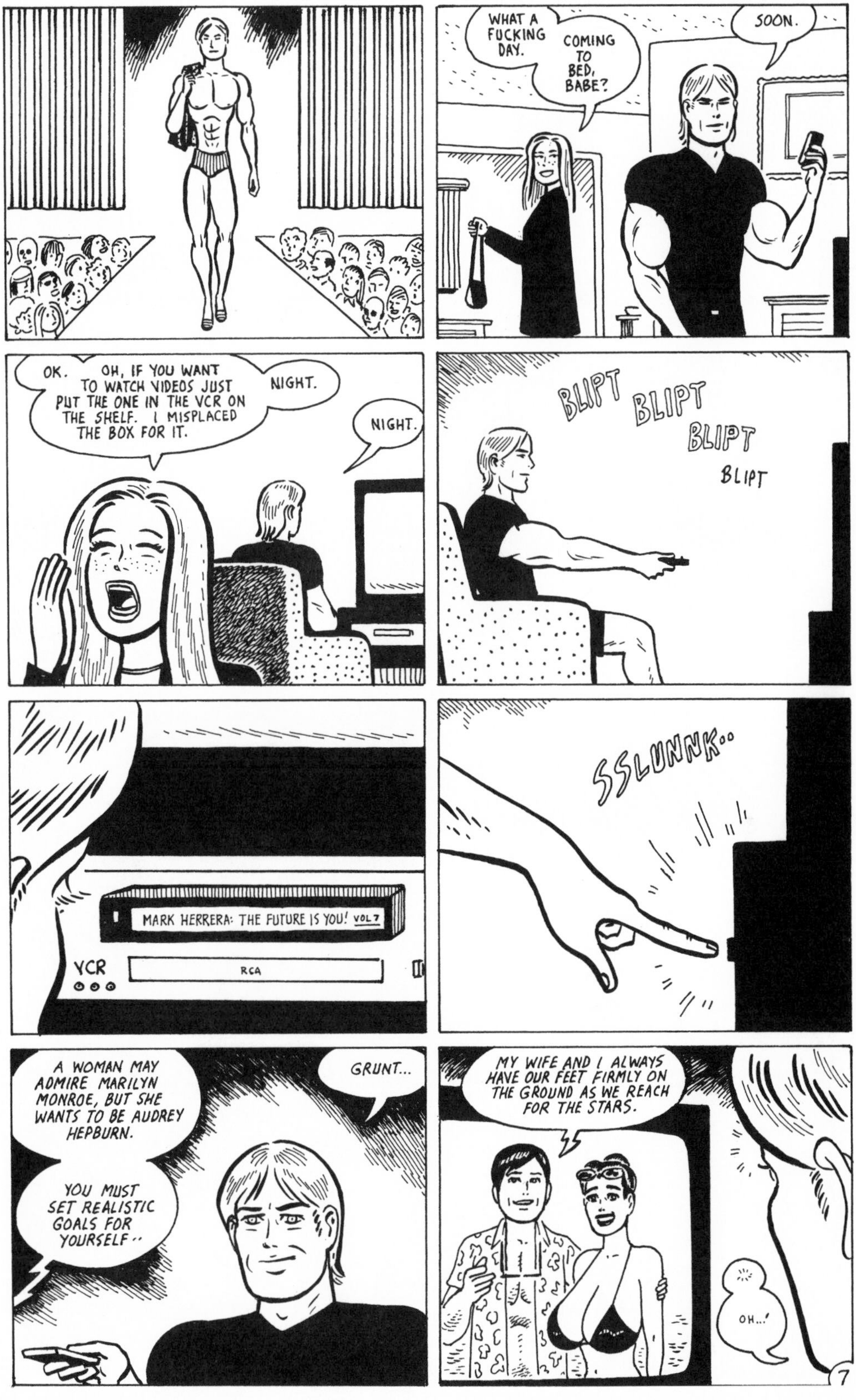
WHAT A FUCKING DAY.
COMING TO BED, BABE?
SOON.
OK. OH, IF YOU WANT TO WATCH VIDEOS JUST PUT THE ONE IN THE VCR ON THE SHELF. I MISPLACED THE BOX FOR IT.
NIGHT.
NIGHT.
BLIPT
BLIPT
BLIPT
BLIPT
MARK HERRERA: THE FUTURE IS YOU! VOL 7
VCR
RCA
SSLUNNK..
A WOMAN MAY ADMIRE MARILYN MONROE, BUT SHE WANTS TO BE AUDREY HEPBURN.
GRUNT...
YOU MUST SET REALISTIC GOALS FOR YOURSELF..
MY WIFE AND I ALWAYS HAVE OUR FEET FIRMLY ON THE GROUND AS WE REACH FOR THE STARS.
OH...!
7

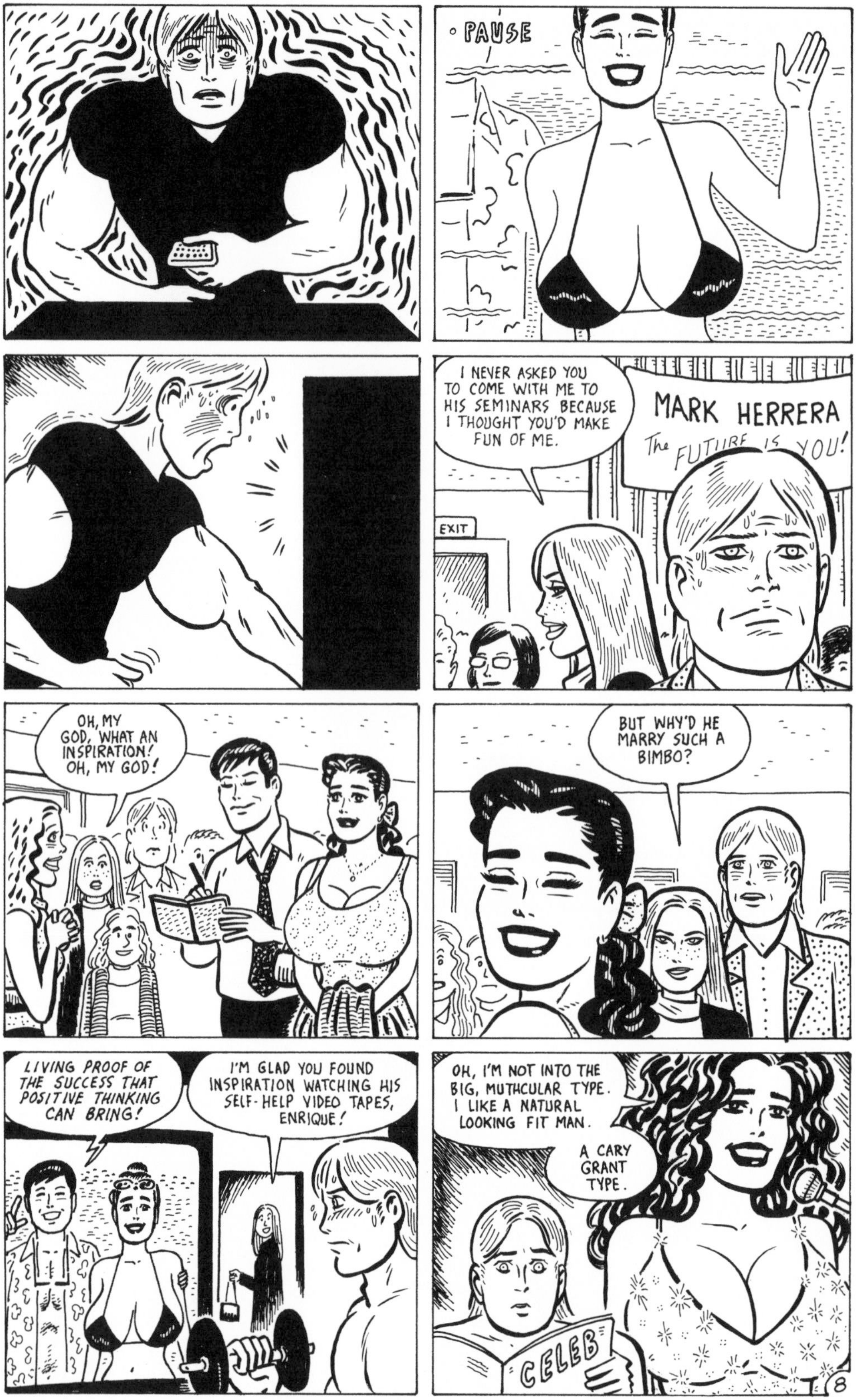
PAUSE
I NEVER ASKED YOU TO COME WITH ME TO HIS SEMINARS BECAUSE I THOUGHT YOU'D MAKE FUN OF ME.
MARK HERRERA
EXIT
OH, MY GOD, WHAT AN INSPIRATION! OH, MY GOD!
BUT WHY'D HE MARRY SUCH A BIMBO?
LIVING PROOF OF THE SUCCESS THAT POSITIVE THINKING CAN BRING!
I'M GLAD YOU FOUND INSPIRATION WATCHING HIS SELF-HELP VIDEO TAPES, ENRIQUE!
OH, I'M NOT INTO THE BIG, MUTHCULAR TYPE. I LIKE A NATURAL LOOKING FIT MAN.
A CARY GRANT TYPE.
CELEB
8

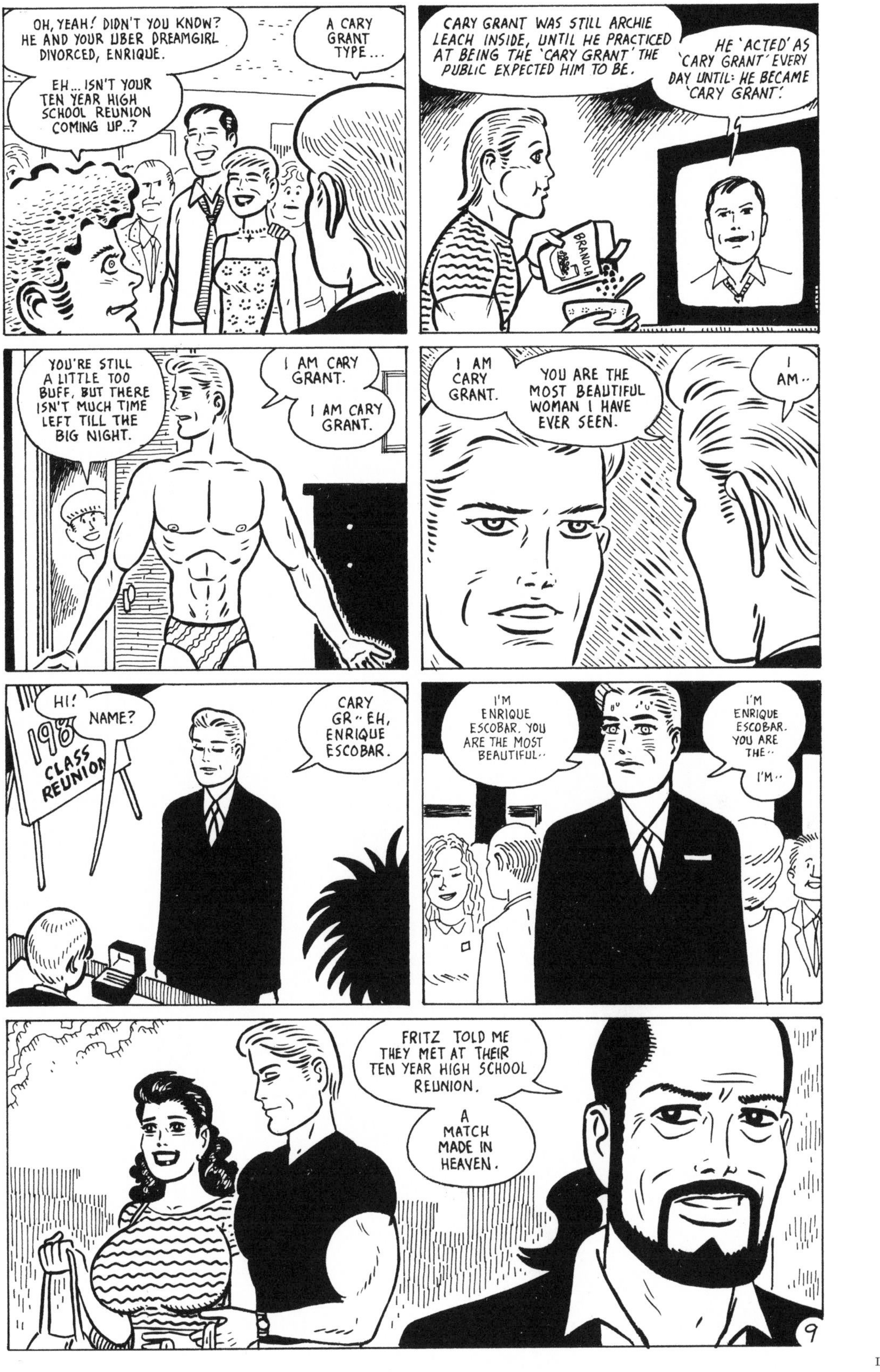
OH, YEAH! DIDN'T YOU KNOW? HE AND YOUR UBER DREAMGIRL DIVORCED, ENRIQUE.
EH... ISN'T YOUR TEN YEAR HIGH SCHOOL REUNION COMING UP..?
A CARY GRANT TYPE...
CARY GRANT WAS STILL ARCHIE LEACH INSIDE, UNTIL HE PRACTICED AT BEING THE 'CARY GRANT' THE PUBLIC EXPECTED HIM TO BE.
HE 'ACTED' AS 'CARY GRANT' EVERY DAY UNTIL: HE BECAME 'CARY GRANT'.
YOU'RE STILL A LITTLE TOO BUFF, BUT THERE ISN'T MUCH TIME LEFT TILL THE BIG NIGHT.
I AM CARY GRANT.
I AM CARY GRANT.
I AM CARY GRANT.
YOU ARE THE MOST BEAUTIFUL WOMAN I HAVE EVER SEEN.
I AM..
HI!
NAME?
CARY GR.. EH, ENRIQUE ESCOBAR.
CLASS REUNION
I'M ENRIQUE ESCOBAR. YOU ARE THE MOST BEAUTIFUL..
I'M ENRIQUE ESCOBAR. YOU ARE THE..
I'M..
FRITZ TOLD ME THEY MET AT THEIR TEN YEAR HIGH SCHOOL REUNION.
A MATCH MADE IN HEAVEN.
9

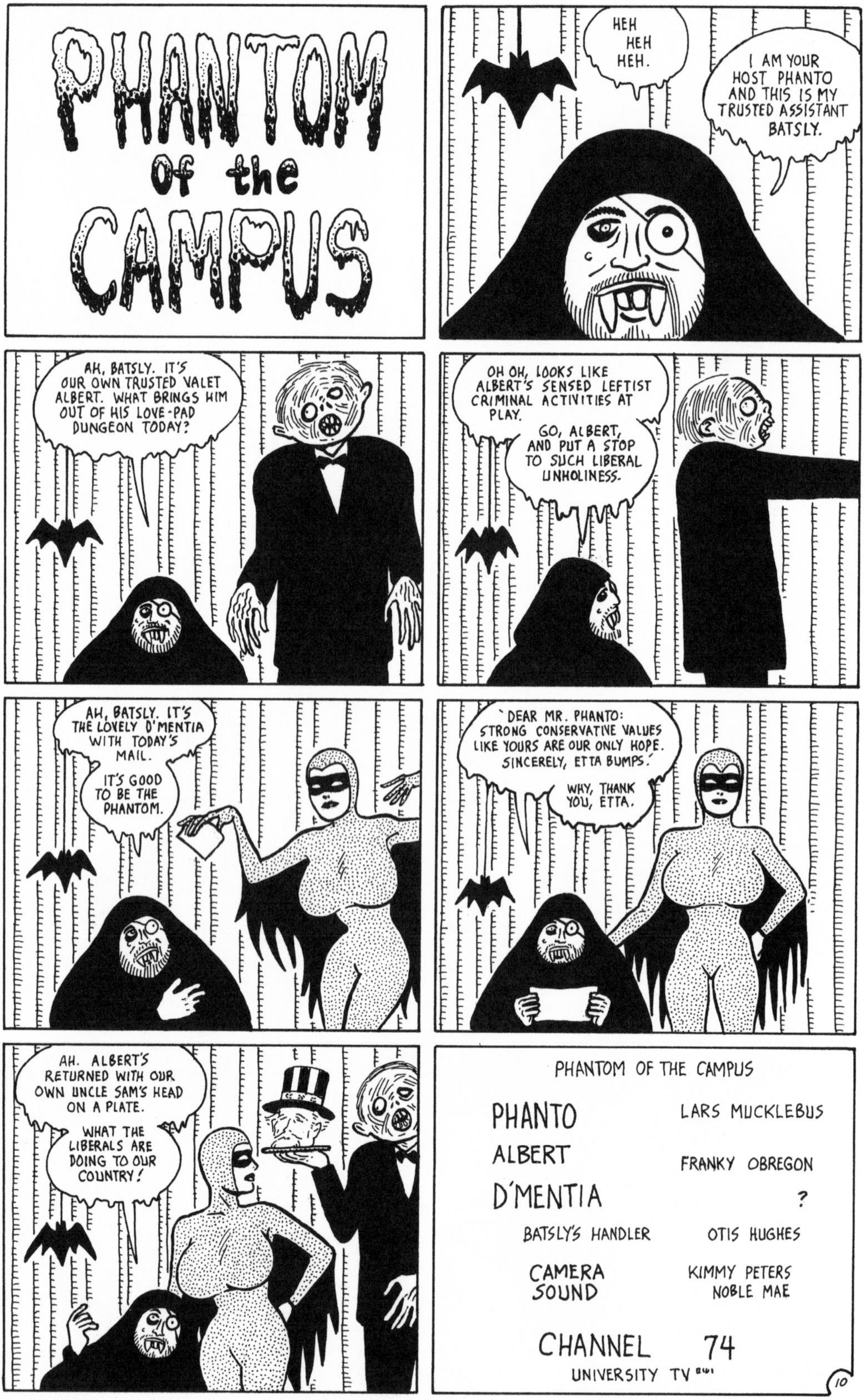
PHANTOM of the CAMPUS
HEH HEH HEH.
I AM YOUR HOST PHANTO AND THIS IS MY TRUSTED ASSISTANT BATSLY.
AH, BATSLY. IT'S OUR OWN TRUSTED VALET ALBERT. WHAT BRINGS HIM OUT OF HIS LOVE-PAD DUNGEON TODAY?
OH OH, LOOKS LIKE ALBERT'S SENSED LEFTIST CRIMINAL ACTIVITIES AT PLAY.
GO, ALBERT, AND PUT A STOP TO SUCH LIBERAL UNHOLINESS.
AH, BATSLY. IT'S THE LOVELY D'MENTIA WITH TODAY'S MAIL.
IT'S GOOD TO BE THE PHANTOM.
'DEAR MR. PHANTO: STRONG CONSERVATIVE VALUES LIKE YOURS ARE OUR ONLY HOPE. SINCERELY, ETTA BUMPS.'
WHY, THANK YOU, ETTA.
AH. ALBERT'S RETURNED WITH OUR OWN UNCLE SAM'S HEAD ON A PLATE.
WHAT THE LIBERALS ARE DOING TO OUR COUNTRY!
PHANTOM OF THE CAMPUS
PHANTO LARS MUCKLEBUS
ALBERT FRANKY OBREGON
D'MENTIA ?
BATSLY'S HANDLER OTIS HUGHES
CAMERA KIMMY PETERS
SOUND NOBLE MAE
CHANNEL 74
UNIVERSITY TV
10

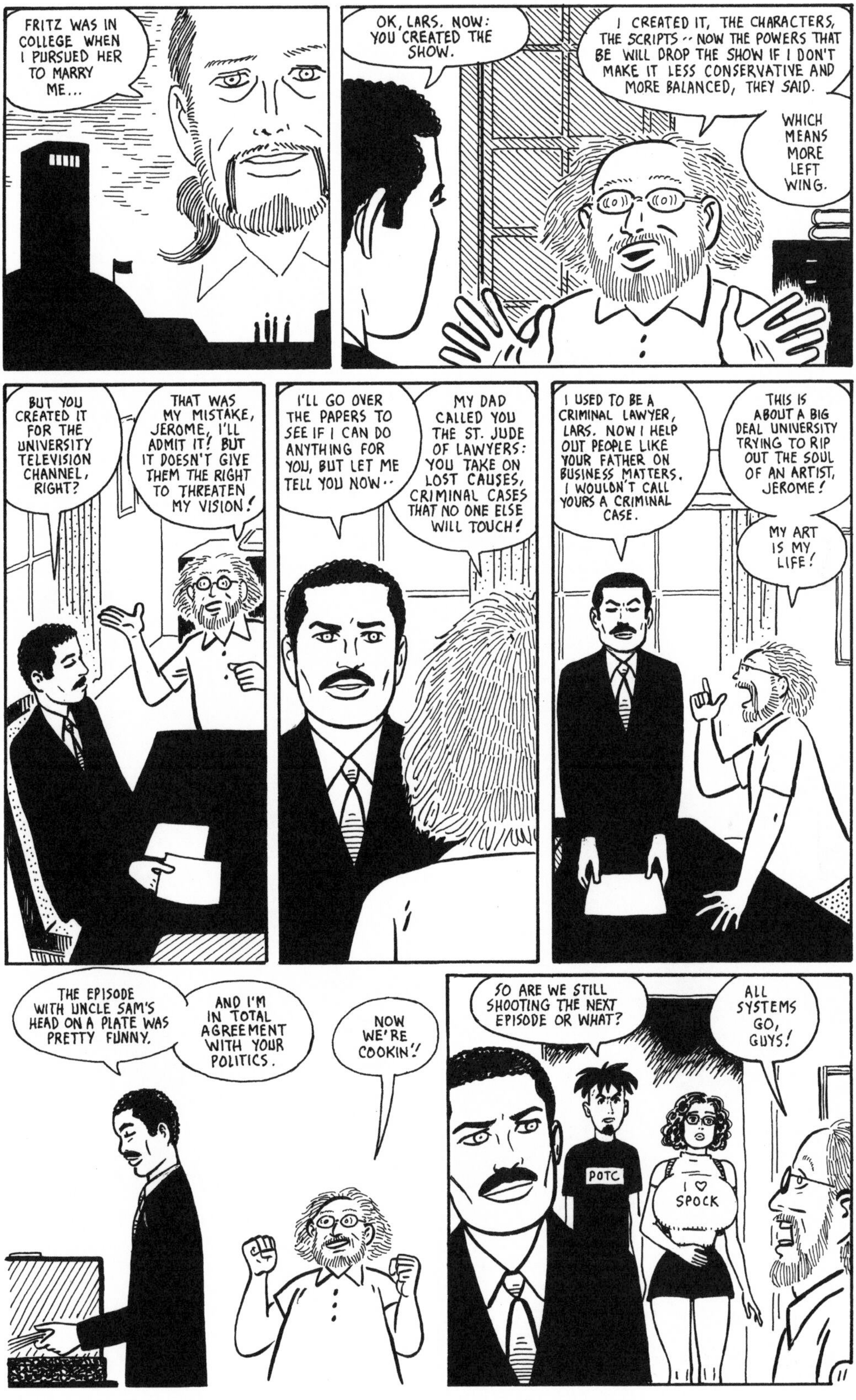

FRITZ WAS IN COLLEGE WHEN I PURSUED HER TO MARRY ME...
OK, LARS. NOW: YOU CREATED THE SHOW.
I CREATED IT, THE CHARACTERS, THE SCRIPTS -- NOW THE POWERS THAT BE WILL DROP THE SHOW IF I DON'T MAKE IT LESS CONSERVATIVE AND MORE BALANCED, THEY SAID.
WHICH MEANS MORE LEFT WING.
BUT YOU CREATED IT FOR THE UNIVERSITY TELEVISION CHANNEL, RIGHT?
THAT WAS MY MISTAKE, JEROME, I'LL ADMIT IT! BUT IT DOESN'T GIVE THEM THE RIGHT TO THREATEN MY VISION!
I'LL GO OVER THE PAPERS TO SEE IF I CAN DO ANYTHING FOR YOU, BUT LET ME TELL YOU NOW..
MY DAD CALLED YOU THE ST. JUDE OF LAWYERS: YOU TAKE ON LOST CAUSES, CRIMINAL CASES THAT NO ONE ELSE WILL TOUCH!
I USED TO BE A CRIMINAL LAWYER, LARS. NOW I HELP OUT PEOPLE LIKE YOUR FATHER ON BUSINESS MATTERS. I WOULDN'T CALL YOURS A CRIMINAL CASE.
THIS IS ABOUT A BIG DEAL UNIVERSITY TRYING TO RIP OUT THE SOUL OF AN ARTIST, JEROME!
MY ART IS MY LIFE!
THE EPISODE WITH UNCLE SAM'S HEAD ON A PLATE WAS PRETTY FUNNY.
AND I'M IN TOTAL AGREEMENT WITH YOUR POLITICS.
NOW WE'RE COOKIN'!
SO ARE WE STILL SHOOTING THE NEXT EPISODE OR WHAT?
ALL SYSTEMS GO, GUYS!
POTC
I ♡ SPOCK

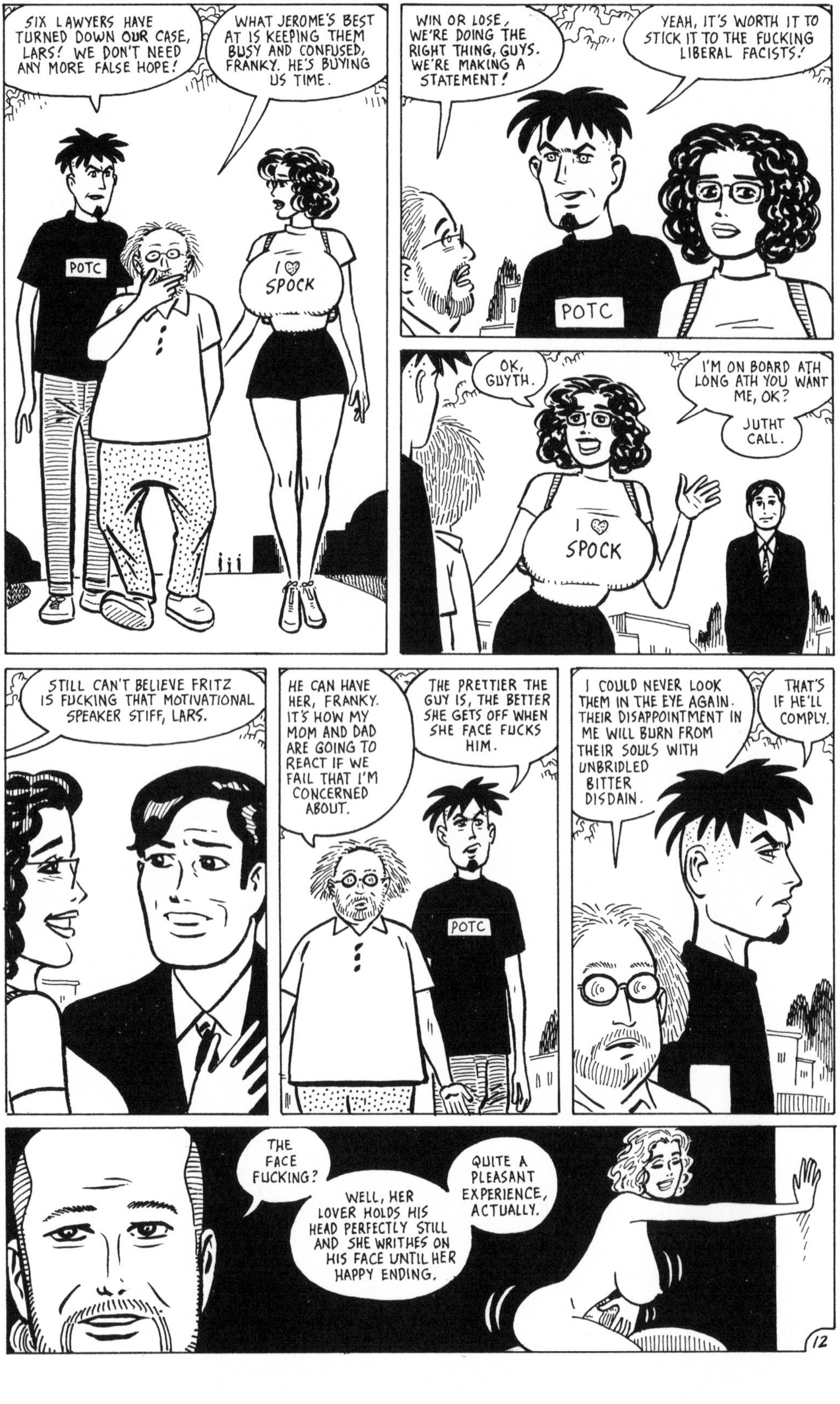
SIX LAWYERS HAVE TURNED DOWN OUR CASE, LARS! WE DON'T NEED ANY MORE FALSE HOPE!
WHAT JEROME'S BEST AT IS KEEPING THEM BUSY AND CONFUSED, FRANKY. HE'S BUYING US TIME.
POTC
I ♡ SPOCK
WIN OR LOSE, WE'RE DOING THE RIGHT THING, GUYS. WE'RE MAKING A STATEMENT!
YEAH, IT'S WORTH IT TO STICK IT TO THE FUCKING LIBERAL FACISTS!
POTC
OK, GUYTH.
I'M ON BOARD ATH LONG ATH YOU WANT ME, OK?
JUTHT CALL.
I ♡ SPOCK
STILL CAN'T BELIEVE FRITZ IS FUCKING THAT MOTIVATIONAL SPEAKER STIFF, LARS.
HE CAN HAVE HER, FRANKY. IT'S HOW MY MOM AND DAD ARE GOING TO REACT IF WE FAIL THAT I'M CONCERNED ABOUT.
THE PRETTIER THE GUY IS, THE BETTER SHE GETS OFF WHEN SHE FACE FUCKS HIM.
POTC
I COULD NEVER LOOK THEM IN THE EYE AGAIN. THEIR DISAPPOINTMENT IN ME WILL BURN FROM THEIR SOULS WITH UNBRIDLED BITTER DISDAIN.
THAT'S IF HE'LL COMPLY.
THE FACE FUCKING?
WELL, HER LOVER HOLDS HIS HEAD PERFECTLY STILL AND SHE WRITHES ON HIS FACE UNTIL HER HAPPY ENDING.
QUITE A PLEASANT EXPERIENCE, ACTUALLY.
12

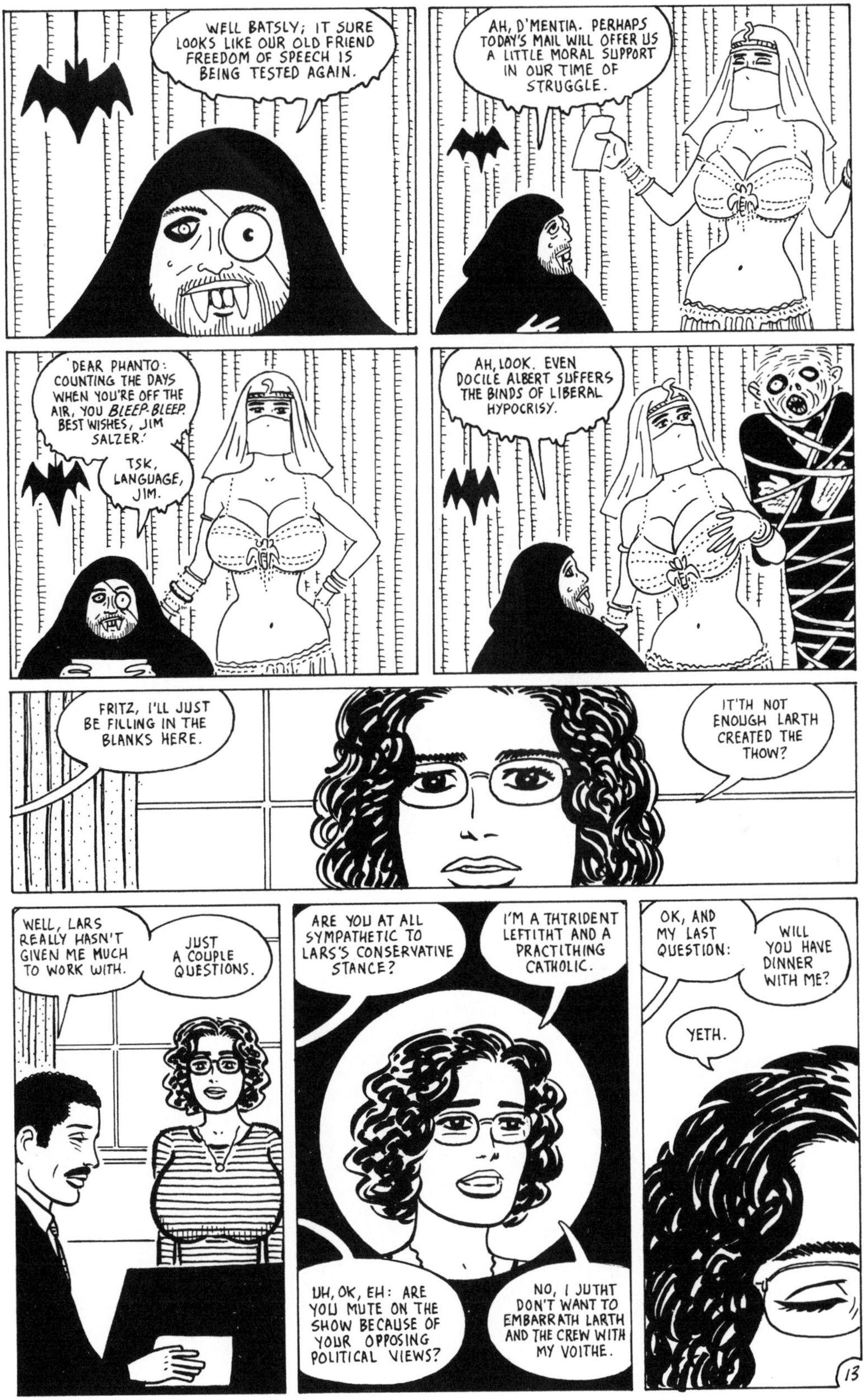
WELL BATSLY; IT SURE LOOKS LIKE OUR OLD FRIEND FREEDOM OF SPEECH IS BEING TESTED AGAIN.
AH, D'MENTIA. PERHAPS TODAY'S MAIL WILL OFFER US A LITTLE MORAL SUPPORT IN OUR TIME OF STRUGGLE.
'DEAR PHANTO: COUNTING THE DAYS WHEN YOU'RE OFF THE AIR, YOU BLEEP-BLEEP. BEST WISHES, JIM SALZER.'
TSK, LANGUAGE, JIM.
AH, LOOK. EVEN DOCILE ALBERT SUFFERS THE BINDS OF LIBERAL HYPOCRISY.
FRITZ, I'LL JUST BE FILLING IN THE BLANKS HERE.
IT'TH NOT ENOUGH LARTH CREATED THE THOW?
WELL, LARS REALLY HASN'T GIVEN ME MUCH TO WORK WITH.
JUST A COUPLE QUESTIONS.
ARE YOU AT ALL SYMPATHETIC TO LARS'S CONSERVATIVE STANCE?
I'M A THTRIDENT LEFTITHT AND A PRACTITHING CATHOLIC.
UH, OK, EH: ARE YOU MUTE ON THE SHOW BECAUSE OF YOUR OPPOSING POLITICAL VIEWS?
NO, I JUTHT DON'T WANT TO EMBARRATH LARTH AND THE CREW WITH MY VOITHE.
OK, AND MY LAST QUESTION:
WILL YOU HAVE DINNER WITH ME?
YETH.
13

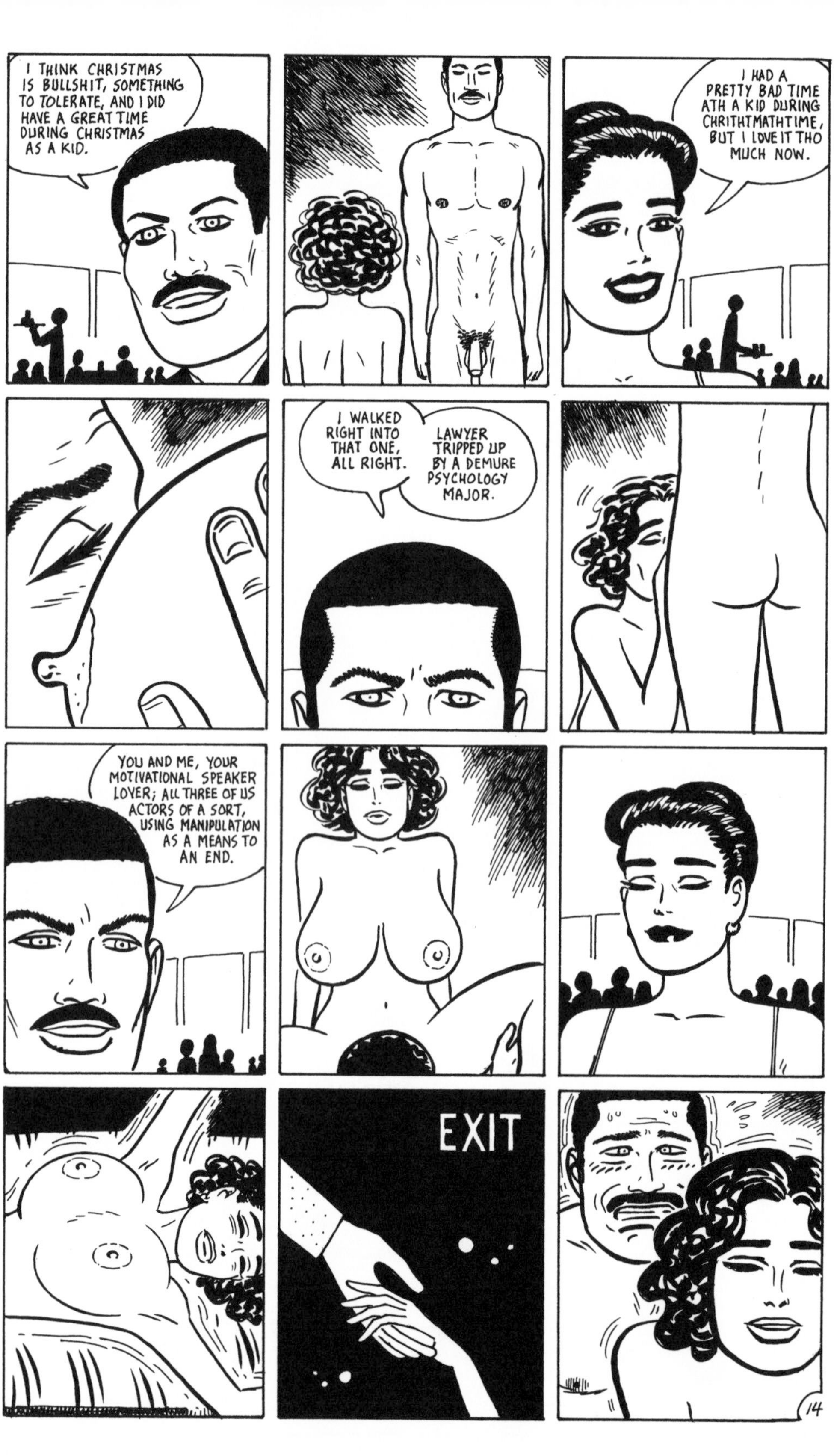
I THINK CHRISTMAS IS BULLSHIT, SOMETHING TO TOLERATE, AND I DID HAVE A GREAT TIME DURING CHRISTMAS AS A KID.
I HAD A PRETTY BAD TIME ATH A KID DURING CHRITHTMATHTIME, BUT I LOVE IT THO MUCH NOW.
I WALKED RIGHT INTO THAT ONE, ALL RIGHT.
LAWYER TRIPPED UP BY A DEMURE PSYCHOLOGY MAJOR.
YOU AND ME, YOUR MOTIVATIONAL SPEAKER LOVER; ALL THREE OF US ACTORS OF A SORT, USING MANIPULATION AS A MEANS TO AN END.
EXIT
14

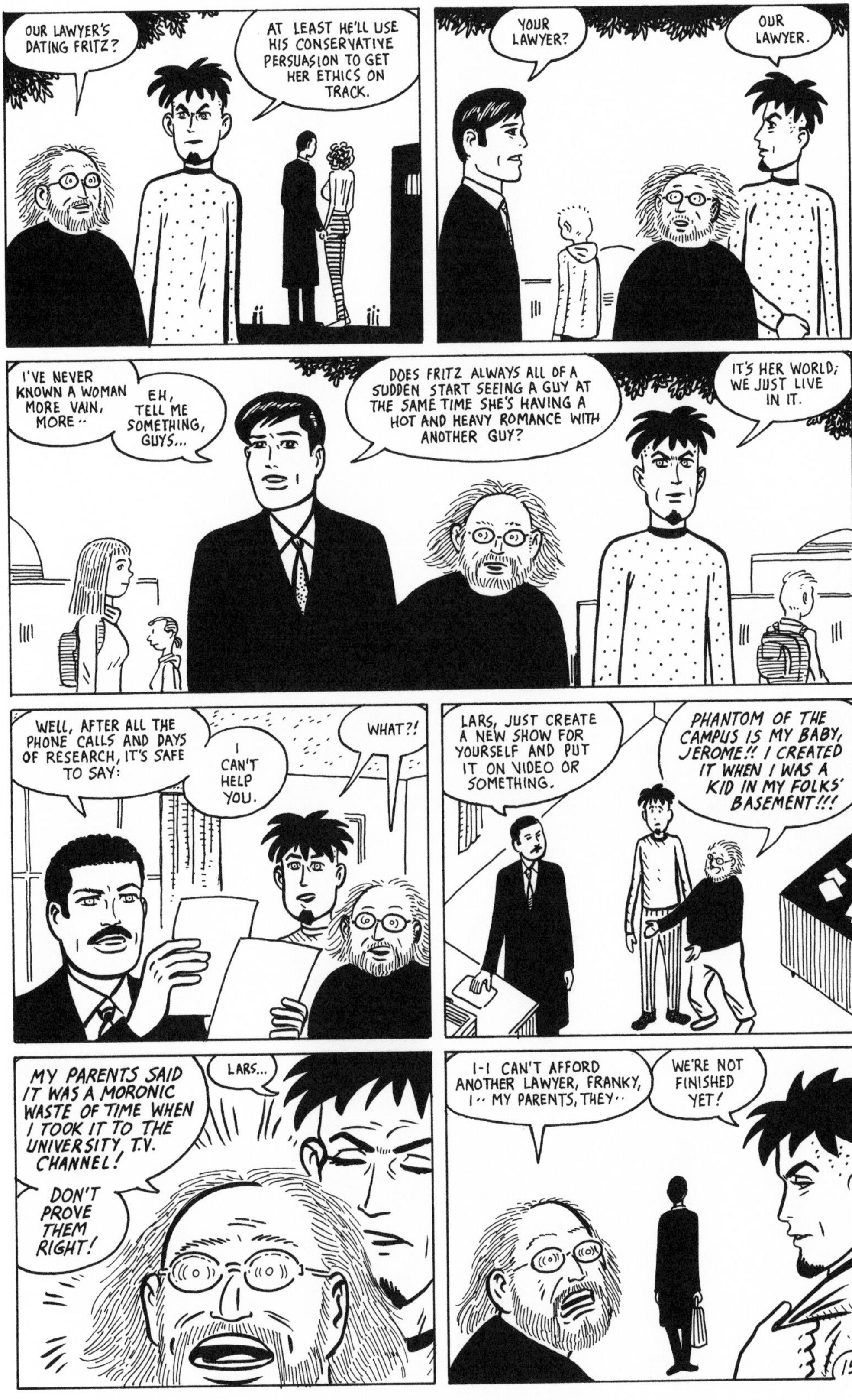
OUR LAWYER'S DATING FRITZ?
AT LEAST HE'LL USE HIS CONSERVATIVE PERSUASION TO GET HER ETHICS ON TRACK.
YOUR LAWYER?
OUR LAWYER.
I'VE NEVER KNOWN A WOMAN MORE VAIN, MORE··
EH, TELL ME SOMETHING, GUYS...
DOES FRITZ ALWAYS ALL OF A SUDDEN START SEEING A GUY AT THE SAME TIME SHE'S HAVING A HOT AND HEAVY ROMANCE WITH ANOTHER GUY?
IT'S HER WORLD; WE JUST LIVE IN IT.
WELL, AFTER ALL THE PHONE CALLS AND DAYS OF RESEARCH, IT'S SAFE TO SAY:
I CAN'T HELP YOU.
WHAT?!
LARS, JUST CREATE A NEW SHOW FOR YOURSELF AND PUT IT ON VIDEO OR SOMETHING.
PHANTOM OF THE CAMPUS IS MY BABY, JEROME!! I CREATED IT WHEN I WAS A KID IN MY FOLKS' BASEMENT!!!
MY PARENTS SAID IT WAS A MORONIC WASTE OF TIME WHEN I TOOK IT TO THE UNIVERSITY T.V. CHANNEL!
LARS...
DON'T PROVE THEM RIGHT!
I-I CAN'T AFFORD ANOTHER LAWYER, FRANKY, I·· MY PARENTS, THEY··
WE'RE NOT FINISHED YET!
15

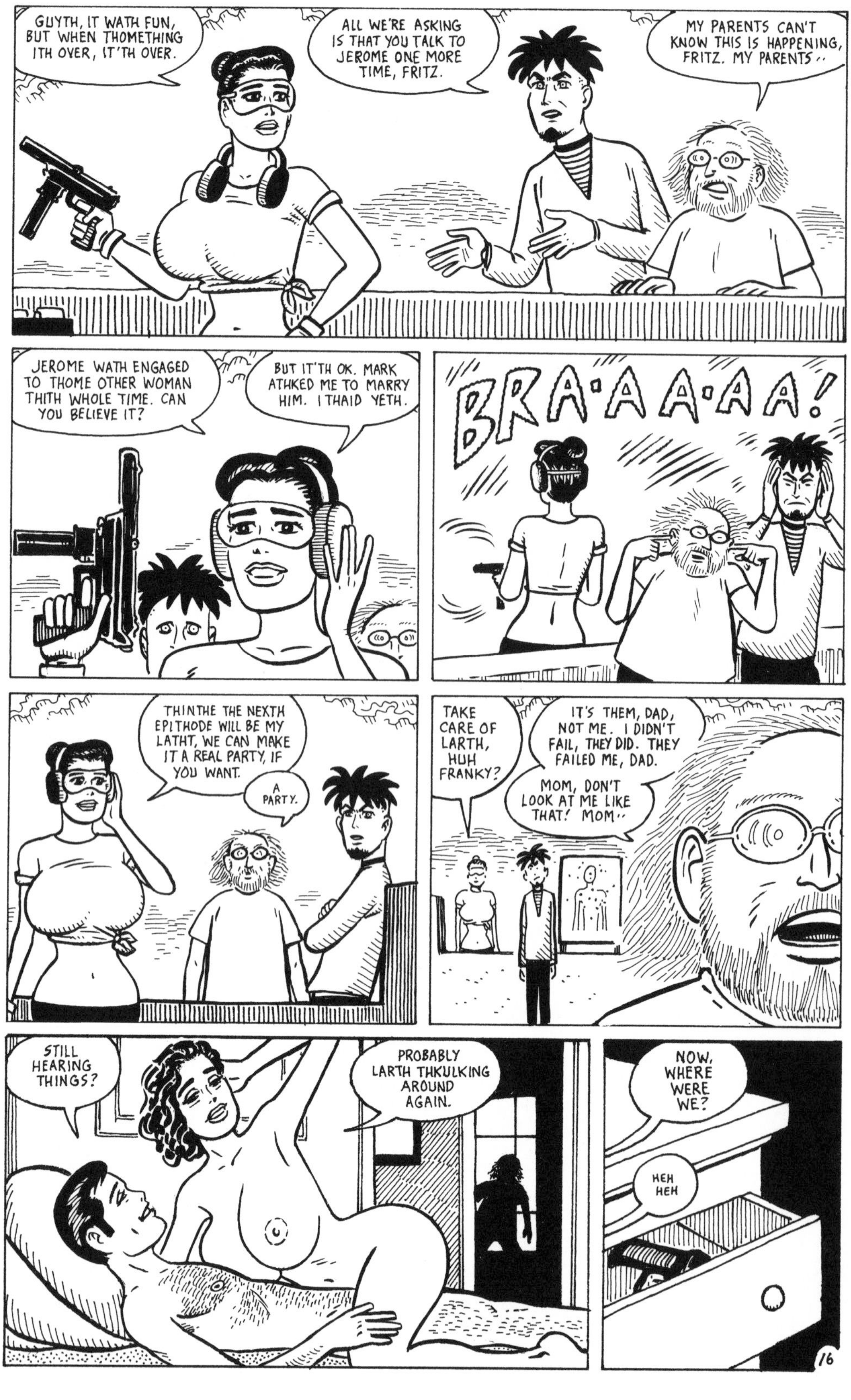
GUYTH, IT WATH FUN, BUT WHEN THOMETHING ITH OVER, IT'TH OVER.
ALL WE'RE ASKING IS THAT YOU TALK TO JEROME ONE MORE TIME, FRITZ.
MY PARENTS CAN'T KNOW THIS IS HAPPENING, FRITZ. MY PARENTS..
JEROME WATH ENGAGED TO THOME OTHER WOMAN THITH WHOLE TIME. CAN YOU BELIEVE IT?
BUT IT'TH OK. MARK ATHKED ME TO MARRY HIM. I THAID YETH.
BRA-A-A-AA!
THINTHE THE NEXTH EPITHODE WILL BE MY LATHT, WE CAN MAKE IT A REAL PARTY, IF YOU WANT.
A PARTY.
TAKE CARE OF LARTH, HUH FRANKY?
IT'S THEM, DAD, NOT ME. I DIDN'T FAIL, THEY DID. THEY FAILED ME, DAD.
MOM, DON'T LOOK AT ME LIKE THAT! MOM..
STILL HEARING THINGS?
PROBABLY LARTH THKULKING AROUND AGAIN.
NOW, WHERE WERE WE?
HEH HEH
16

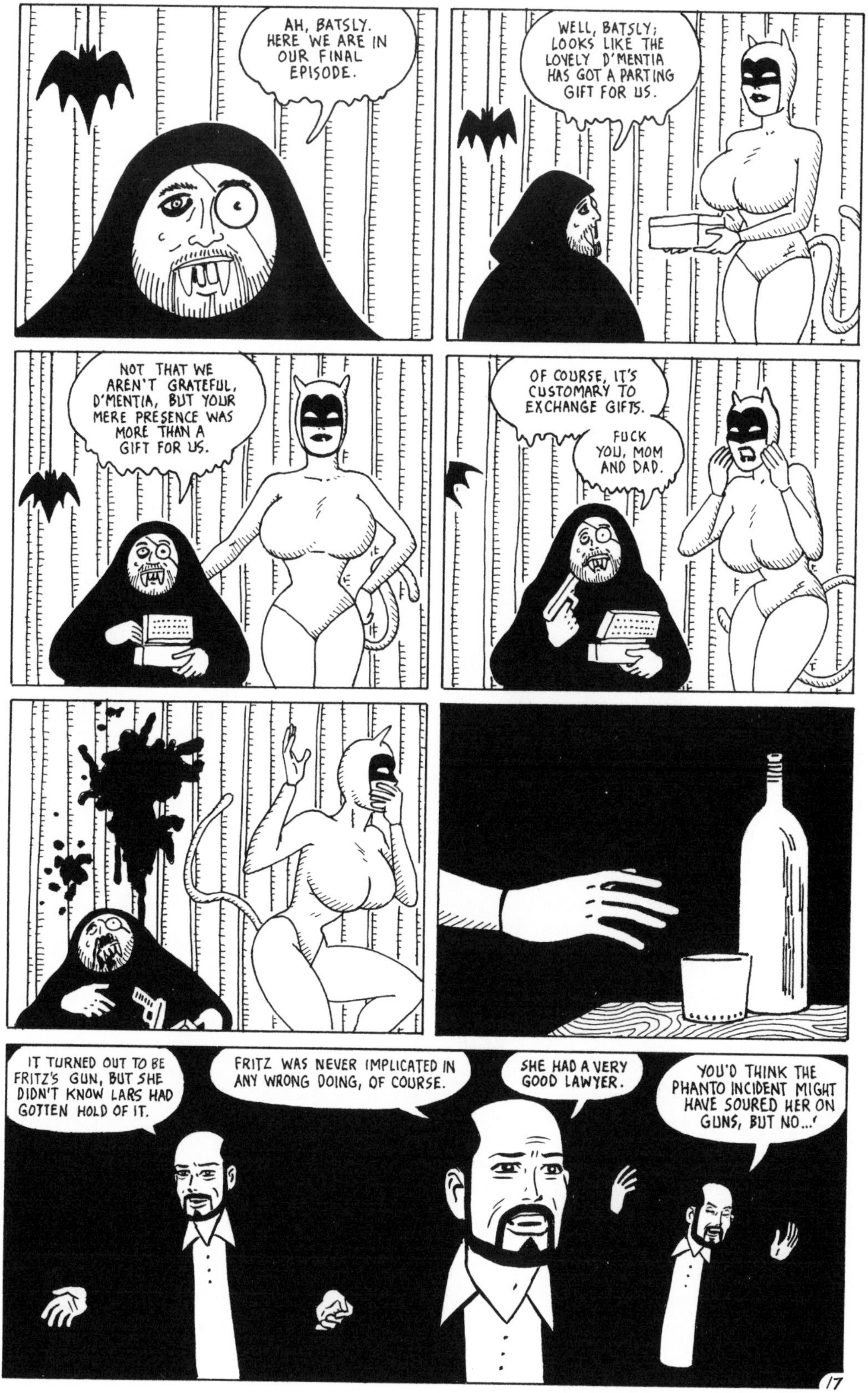
AH, BATSLY. HERE WE ARE IN OUR FINAL EPISODE.
WELL, BATSLY; LOOKS LIKE THE LOVELY D'MENTIA HAS GOT A PARTING GIFT FOR US.
NOT THAT WE AREN'T GRATEFUL, D'MENTIA, BUT YOUR MERE PRESENCE WAS MORE THAN A GIFT FOR US.
OF COURSE, IT'S CUSTOMARY TO EXCHANGE GIFTS.
FUCK YOU, MOM AND DAD.
IT TURNED OUT TO BE FRITZ'S GUN, BUT SHE DIDN'T KNOW LARS HAD GOTTEN HOLD OF IT.
FRITZ WAS NEVER IMPLICATED IN ANY WRONG DOING, OF COURSE.
SHE HAD A VERY GOOD LAWYER.
YOU'D THINK THE PHANTO INCIDENT MIGHT HAVE SOURED HER ON GUNS, BUT NO...'
17

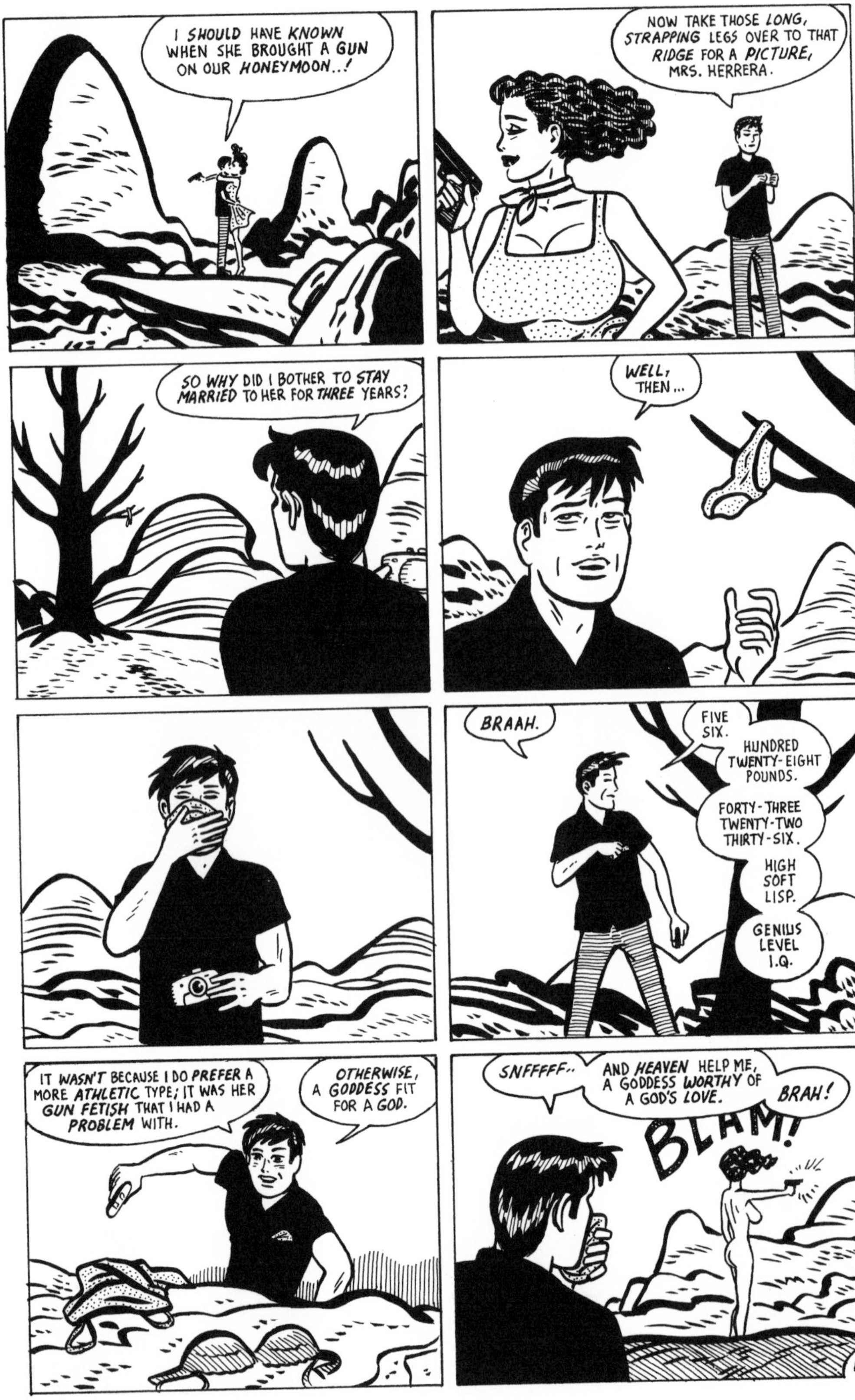
I SHOULD HAVE KNOWN WHEN SHE BROUGHT A GUN ON OUR HONEYMOON..!
NOW TAKE THOSE LONG, STRAPPING LEGS OVER TO THAT RIDGE FOR A PICTURE, MRS. HERRERA.
SO WHY DID I BOTHER TO STAY MARRIED TO HER FOR THREE YEARS?
WELL, THEN...
BRAAH.
FIVE SIX.
HUNDRED TWENTY-EIGHT POUNDS.
FORTY-THREE TWENTY-TWO THIRTY-SIX.
HIGH SOFT LISP.
GENIUS LEVEL I.Q.
IT WASN'T BECAUSE I DO PREFER A MORE ATHLETIC TYPE; IT WAS HER GUN FETISH THAT I HAD A PROBLEM WITH.
OTHERWISE, A GODDESS FIT FOR A GOD.
SNFFFFF..
AND HEAVEN HELP ME, A GODDESS WORTHY OF A GOD'S LOVE.
BRAH!
BLAM!
18

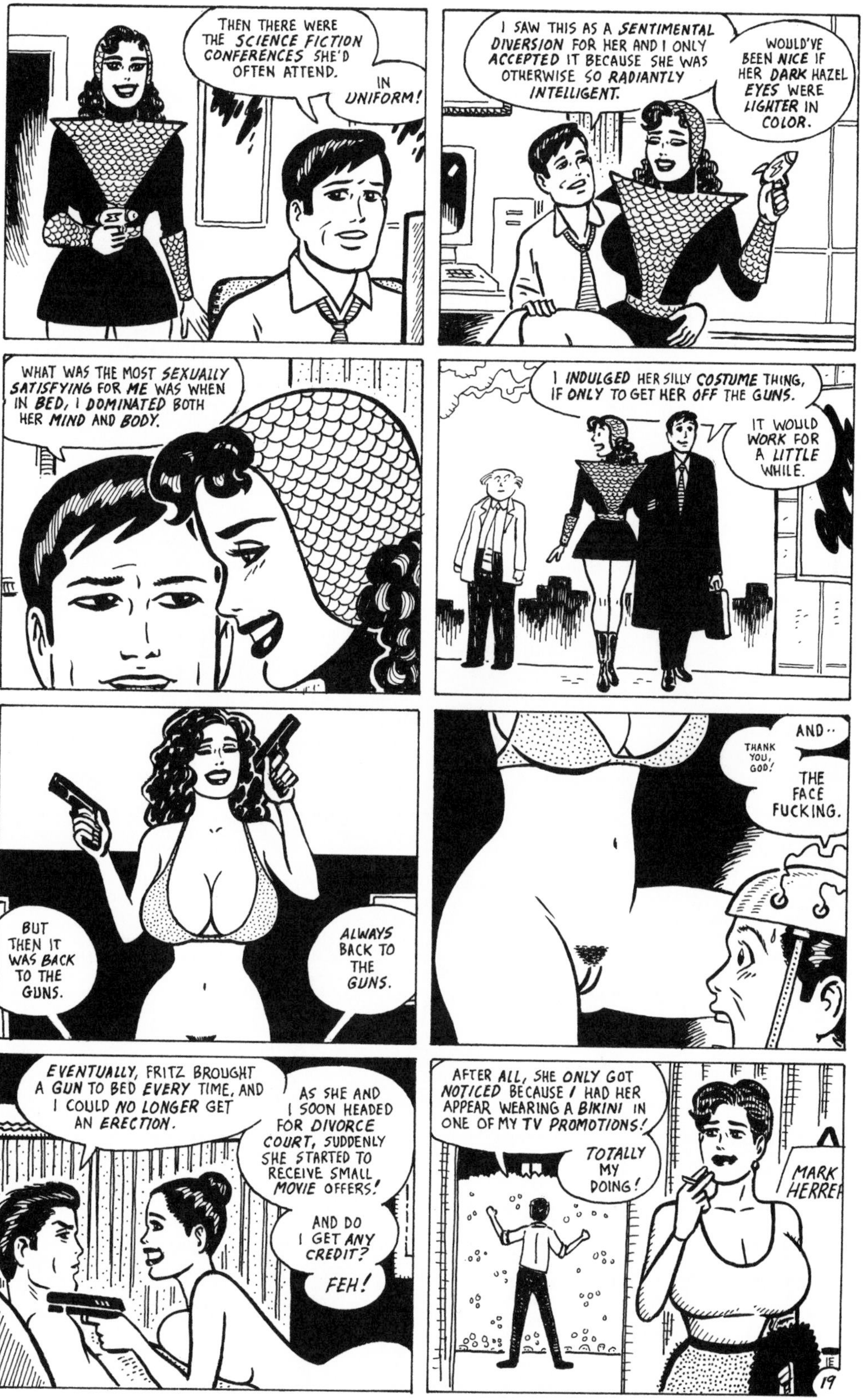

THEN THERE WERE THE SCIENCE FICTION CONFERENCES SHE'D OFTEN ATTEND.
IN UNIFORM!
I SAW THIS AS A SENTIMENTAL DIVERSION FOR HER AND I ONLY ACCEPTED IT BECAUSE SHE WAS OTHERWISE SO RADIANTLY INTELLIGENT.
WOULD'VE BEEN NICE IF HER DARK HAZEL EYES WERE LIGHTER IN COLOR.
WHAT WAS THE MOST SEXUALLY SATISFYING FOR ME WAS WHEN IN BED, I DOMINATED BOTH HER MIND AND BODY.
I INDULGED HER SILLY COSTUME THING, IF ONLY TO GET HER OFF THE GUNS.
IT WOULD WORK FOR A LITTLE WHILE.
BUT THEN IT WAS BACK TO THE GUNS.
ALWAYS BACK TO THE GUNS.
AND..
THANK YOU, GOD!
THE FACE FUCKING.
EVENTUALLY, FRITZ BROUGHT A GUN TO BED EVERY TIME, AND I COULD NO LONGER GET AN ERECTION.
AS SHE AND I SOON HEADED FOR DIVORCE COURT, SUDDENLY SHE STARTED TO RECEIVE SMALL MOVIE OFFERS!
AND DO I GET ANY CREDIT?
FEH!
AFTER ALL, SHE ONLY GOT NOTICED BECAUSE I HAD HER APPEAR WEARING A BIKINI IN ONE OF MY TV PROMOTIONS!
TOTALLY MY DOING!
MARK HERRE
19

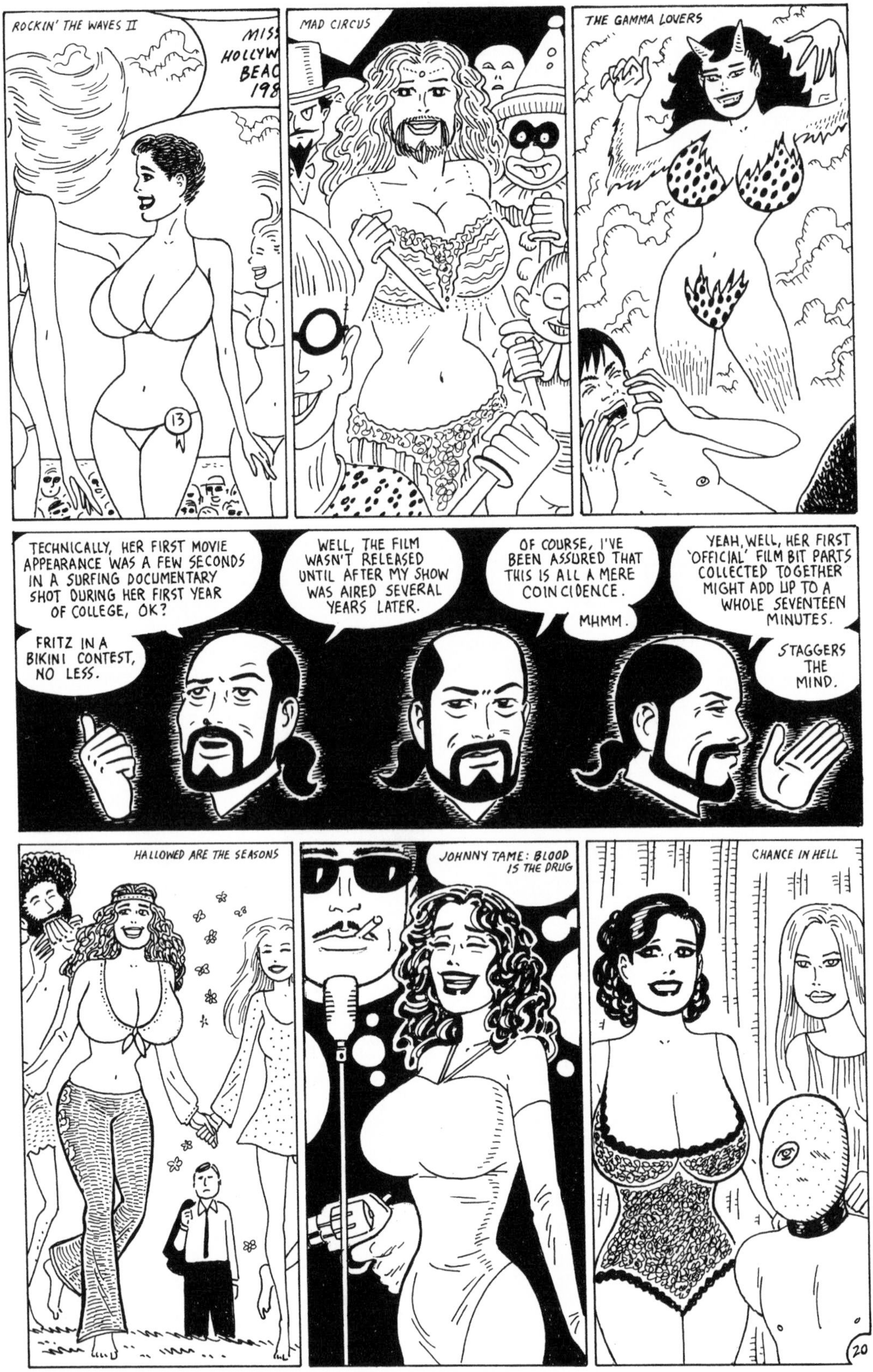
ROCKIN' THE WAVES II
MISS HOLLYW BEAC 198
13
MAD CIRCUS
THE GAMMA LOVERS
TECHNICALLY, HER FIRST MOVIE APPEARANCE WAS A FEW SECONDS IN A SURFING DOCUMENTARY SHOT DURING HER FIRST YEAR OF COLLEGE, OK?
FRITZ IN A BIKINI CONTEST, NO LESS.
WELL, THE FILM WASN'T RELEASED UNTIL AFTER MY SHOW WAS AIRED SEVERAL YEARS LATER.
OF COURSE, I'VE BEEN ASSURED THAT THIS IS ALL A MERE COINCIDENCE.
MHMM.
YEAH, WELL, HER FIRST 'OFFICIAL' FILM BIT PARTS COLLECTED TOGETHER MIGHT ADD UP TO A WHOLE SEVENTEEN MINUTES.
STAGGERS THE MIND.
HALLOWED ARE THE SEASONS
JOHNNY TAME: BLOOD IS THE DRUG
CHANCE IN HELL
20

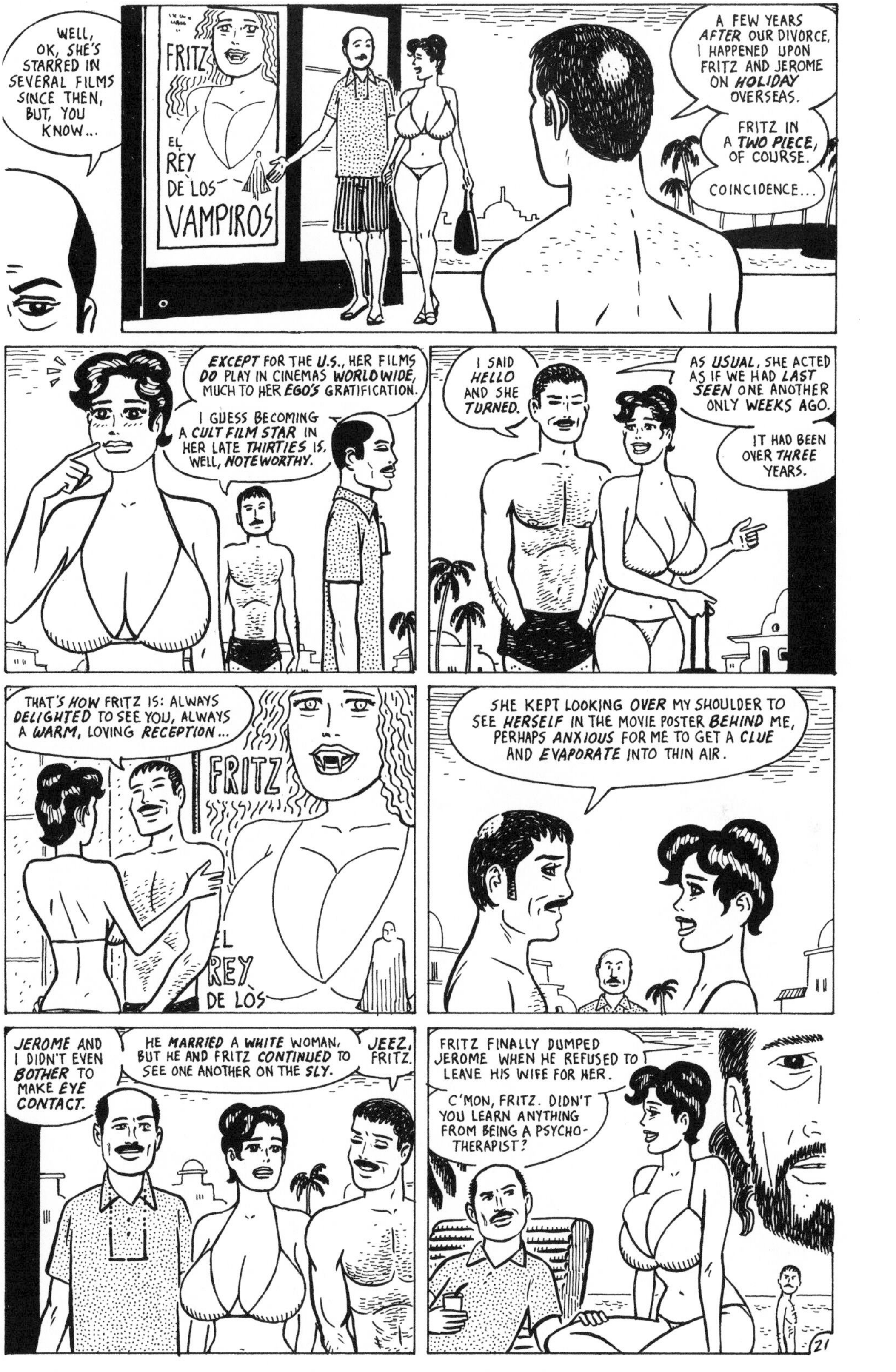
WELL, OK, SHE'S STARRED IN SEVERAL FILMS SINCE THEN, BUT, YOU KNOW...
FRITZ
EL REY DE LOS VAMPIROS
A FEW YEARS AFTER OUR DIVORCE, I HAPPENED UPON FRITZ AND JEROME ON HOLIDAY OVERSEAS.
FRITZ IN A TWO PIECE, OF COURSE.
COINCIDENCE...
EXCEPT FOR THE U.S., HER FILMS DO PLAY IN CINEMAS WORLDWIDE, MUCH TO HER EGO'S GRATIFICATION.
I GUESS BECOMING A CULT FILM STAR IN HER LATE THIRTIES IS, WELL, NOTEWORTHY.
I SAID HELLO AND SHE TURNED.
AS USUAL, SHE ACTED AS IF WE HAD LAST SEEN ONE ANOTHER ONLY WEEKS AGO.
IT HAD BEEN OVER THREE YEARS.
THAT'S HOW FRITZ IS: ALWAYS DELIGHTED TO SEE YOU, ALWAYS A WARM, LOVING RECEPTION...
FRITZ
EL REY DE LOS
SHE KEPT LOOKING OVER MY SHOULDER TO SEE HERSELF IN THE MOVIE POSTER BEHIND ME, PERHAPS ANXIOUS FOR ME TO GET A CLUE AND EVAPORATE INTO THIN AIR.
JEROME AND I DIDN'T EVEN BOTHER TO MAKE EYE CONTACT.
HE MARRIED A WHITE WOMAN, BUT HE AND FRITZ CONTINUED TO SEE ONE ANOTHER ON THE SLY.
JEEZ, FRITZ.
FRITZ FINALLY DUMPED JEROME WHEN HE REFUSED TO LEAVE HIS WIFE FOR HER.
C'MON, FRITZ. DIDN'T YOU LEARN ANYTHING FROM BEING A PSYCHOTHERAPIST?
21

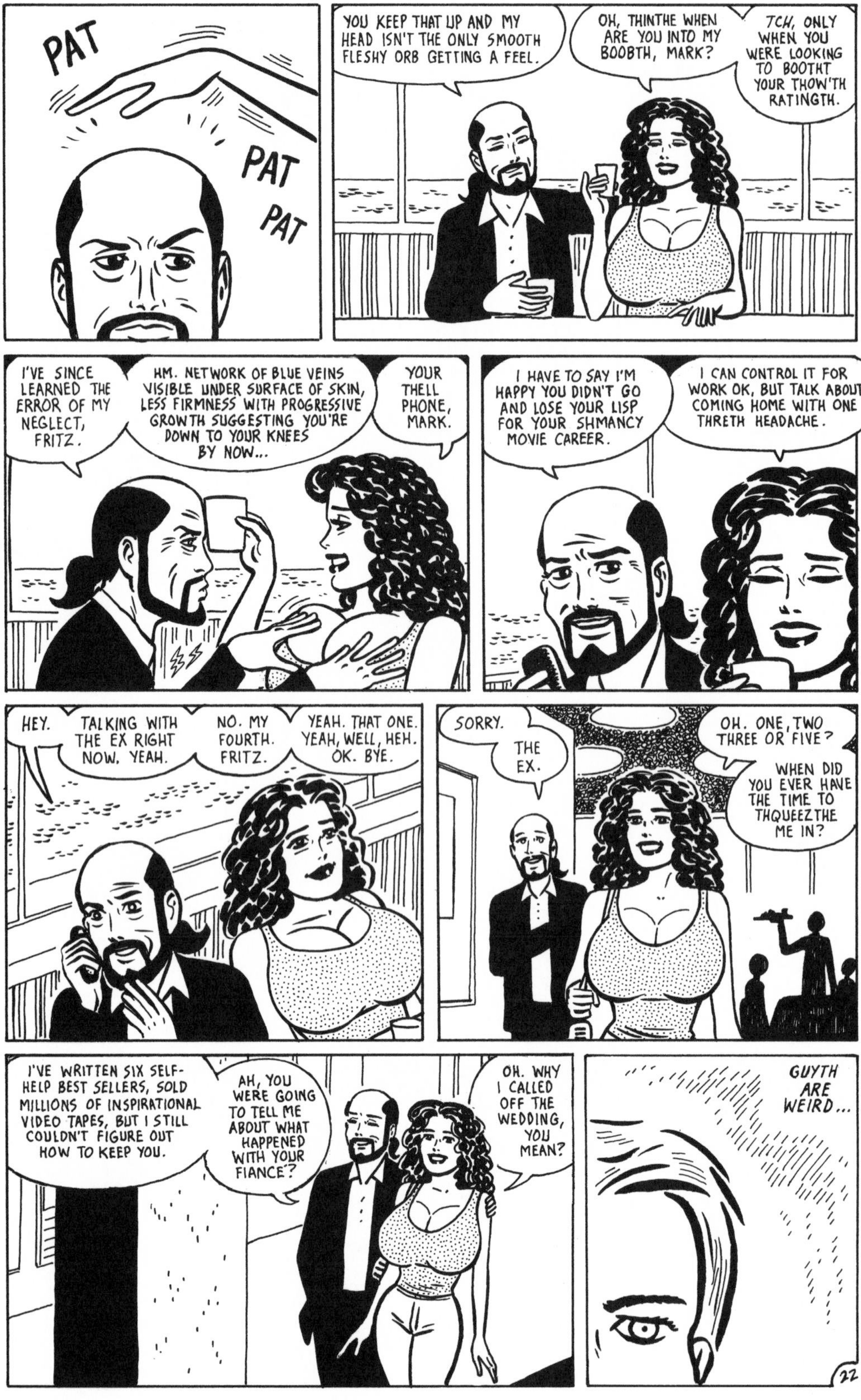
PAT
PAT
PAT
YOU KEEP THAT UP AND MY HEAD ISN'T THE ONLY SMOOTH FLESHY ORB GETTING A FEEL.
OH, THINTHE WHEN ARE YOU INTO MY BOOBTH, MARK?
TCH, ONLY WHEN YOU WERE LOOKING TO BOOTHT YOUR THOW'TH RATINGTH.
I'VE SINCE LEARNED THE ERROR OF MY NEGLECT, FRITZ.
HM. NETWORK OF BLUE VEINS VISIBLE UNDER SURFACE OF SKIN, LESS FIRMNESS WITH PROGRESSIVE GROWTH SUGGESTING YOU'RE DOWN TO YOUR KNEES BY NOW...
YOUR THELL PHONE, MARK.
I HAVE TO SAY I'M HAPPY YOU DIDN'T GO AND LOSE YOUR LISP FOR YOUR SHMANCY MOVIE CAREER.
I CAN CONTROL IT FOR WORK OK, BUT TALK ABOUT COMING HOME WITH ONE THRETH HEADACHE.
HEY.
TALKING WITH THE EX RIGHT NOW. YEAH.
NO. MY FOURTH. FRITZ.
YEAH. THAT ONE. YEAH, WELL, HEH. OK. BYE.
SORRY.
THE EX.
OH. ONE, TWO THREE OR FIVE?
WHEN DID YOU EVER HAVE THE TIME TO THQUEEZTHE ME IN?
I'VE WRITTEN SIX SELF-HELP BEST SELLERS, SOLD MILLIONS OF INSPIRATIONAL VIDEO TAPES, BUT I STILL COULDN'T FIGURE OUT HOW TO KEEP YOU.
AH, YOU WERE GOING TO TELL ME ABOUT WHAT HAPPENED WITH YOUR FIANCÉ?
OH. WHY I CALLED OFF THE WEDDING, YOU MEAN?
GUYTH ARE WEIRD...
22

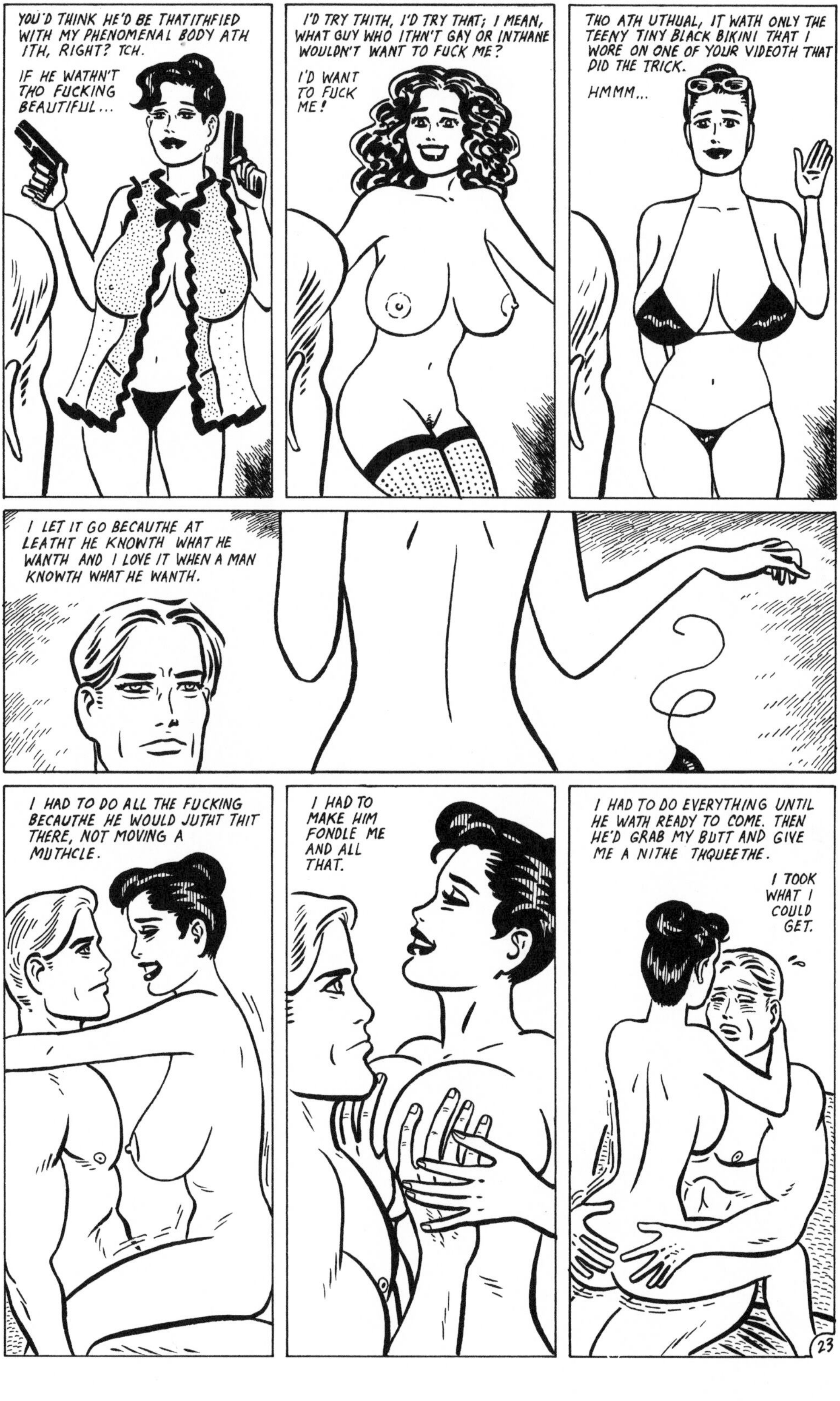
YOU'D THINK HE'D BE THATITHFIED WITH MY PHENOMENAL BODY ATH ITH, RIGHT? TCH.
IF HE WATHN'T THO FUCKING BEAUTIFUL...
I'D TRY THITH, I'D TRY THAT; I MEAN, WHAT GUY WHO ITHN'T GAY OR INTHANE WOULDN'T WANT TO FUCK ME?
I'D WANT TO FUCK ME!
THO ATH UTHUAL, IT WATH ONLY THE TEENY TINY BLACK BIKINI THAT I WORE ON ONE OF YOUR VIDEOTH THAT DID THE TRICK.
HMMM...
I LET IT GO BECAUTHE AT LEATHT HE KNOWTH WHAT HE WANTH AND I LOVE IT WHEN A MAN KNOWTH WHAT HE WANTH.
I HAD TO DO ALL THE FUCKING BECAUTHE HE WOULD JUTHT THIT THERE, NOT MOVING A MUTHCLE.
I HAD TO MAKE HIM FONDLE ME AND ALL THAT.
I HAD TO DO EVERYTHING UNTIL HE WATH READY TO COME. THEN HE'D GRAB MY BUTT AND GIVE ME A NITHE THQUEETHE.
I TOOK WHAT I COULD GET.
23

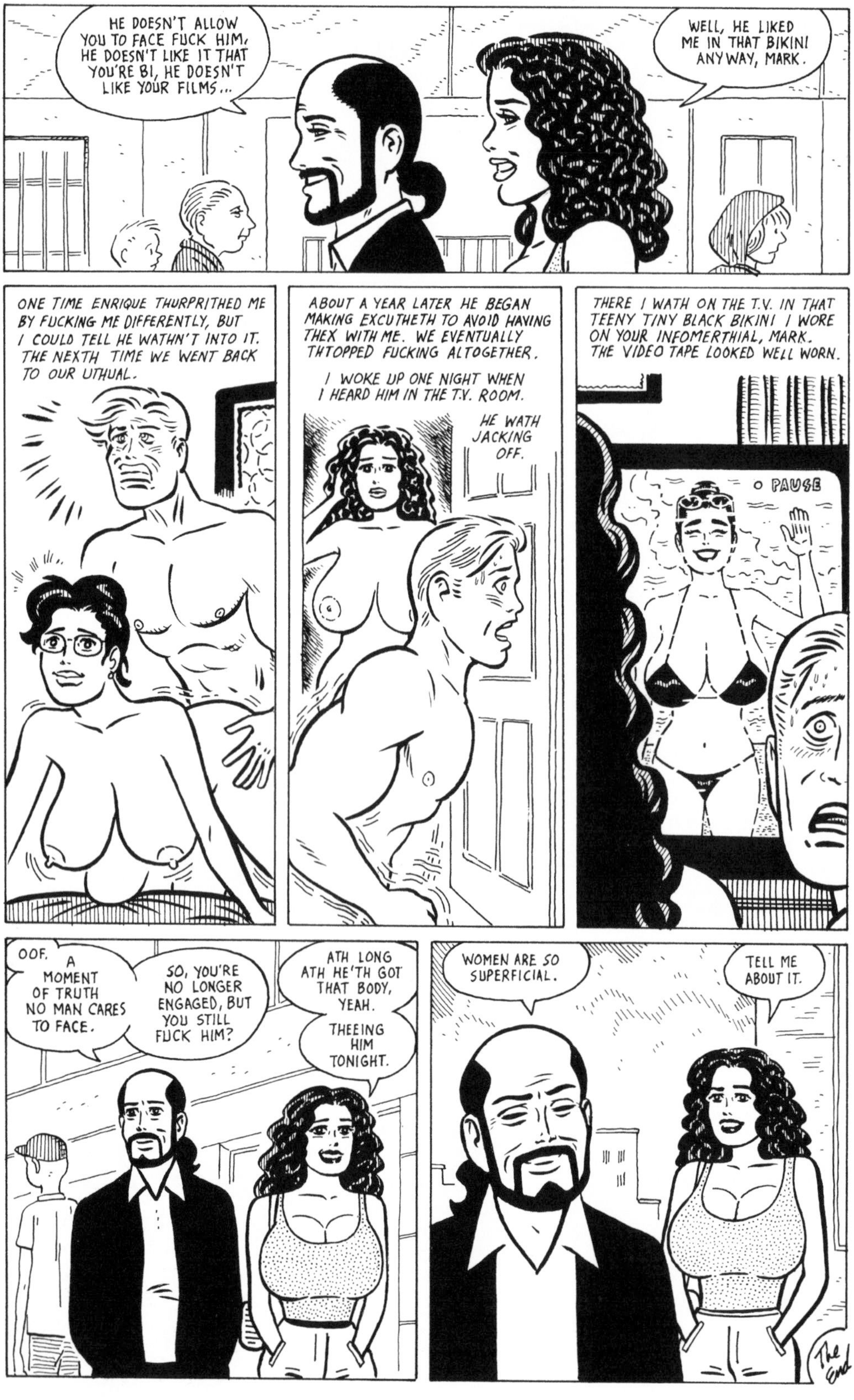
HE DOESN'T ALLOW YOU TO FACE FUCK HIM, HE DOESN'T LIKE IT THAT YOU'RE BI, HE DOESN'T LIKE YOUR FILMS...
WELL, HE LIKED ME IN THAT BIKINI ANYWAY, MARK.
ONE TIME ENRIQUE THURPRITHED ME BY FUCKING ME DIFFERENTLY, BUT I COULD TELL HE WATHN'T INTO IT. THE NEXTH TIME WE WENT BACK TO OUR UTHUAL.
ABOUT A YEAR LATER HE BEGAN MAKING EXCUTHETH TO AVOID HAVING THEX WITH ME. WE EVENTUALLY THTOPPED FUCKING ALTOGETHER.
I WOKE UP ONE NIGHT WHEN I HEARD HIM IN THE T.V. ROOM.
HE WATH JACKING OFF.
THERE I WATH ON THE T.V. IN THAT TEENY TINY BLACK BIKINI I WORE ON YOUR INFOMERTHIAL, MARK. THE VIDEO TAPE LOOKED WELL WORN.
PAUSE
OOF. A MOMENT OF TRUTH NO MAN CARES TO FACE.
SO, YOU'RE NO LONGER ENGAGED, BUT YOU STILL FUCK HIM?
ATH LONG ATH HE'TH GOT THAT BODY, YEAH.
THEEING HIM TONIGHT.
WOMEN ARE SO SUPERFICIAL.
TELL ME ABOUT IT.
The End

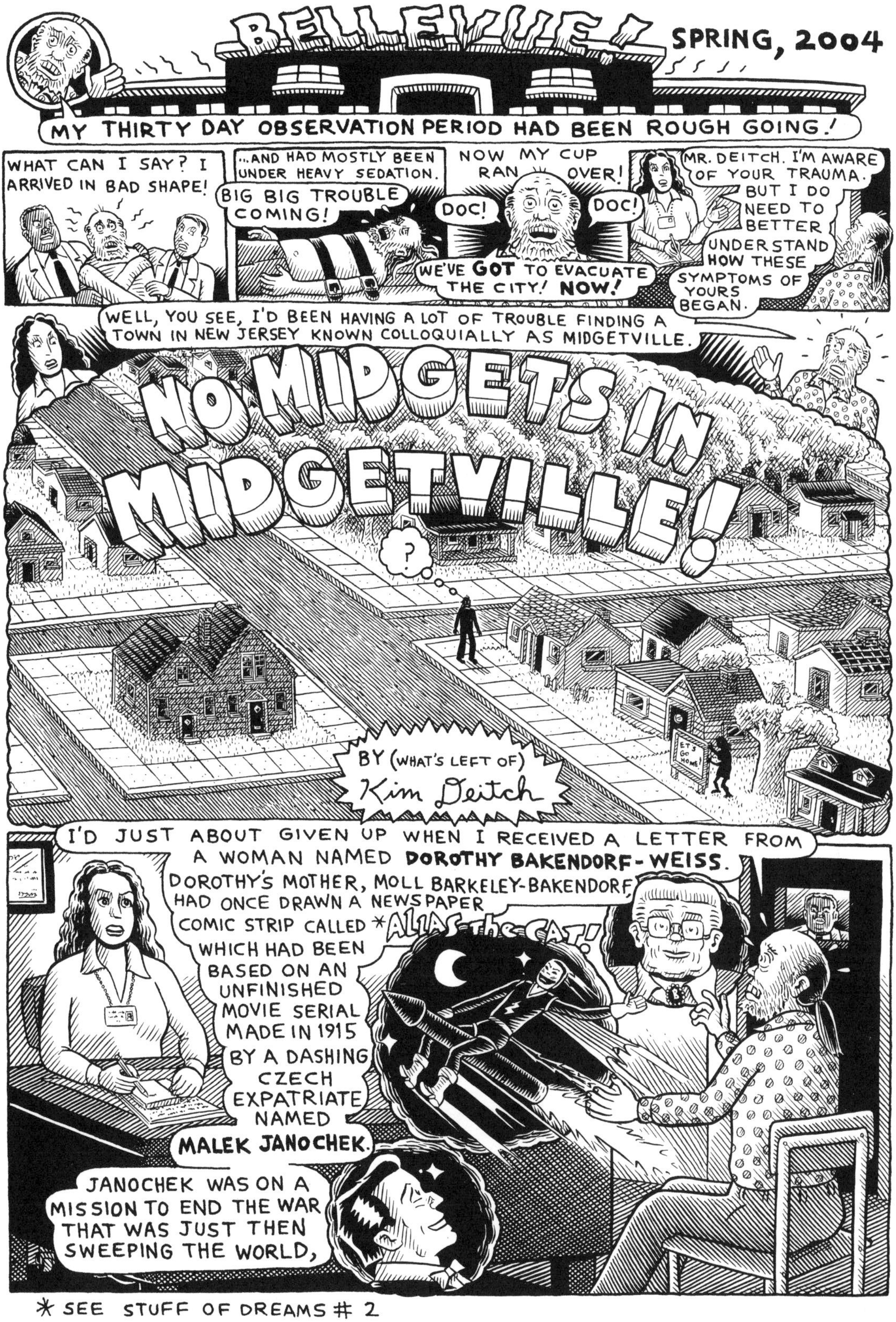
BELLEVUE!
SPRING, 2004
MY THIRTY DAY OBSERVATION PERIOD HAD BEEN ROUGH GOING!
WHAT CAN I SAY? I ARRIVED IN BAD SHAPE!
...AND HAD MOSTLY BEEN UNDER HEAVY SEDATION.
BIG BIG TROUBLE COMING!
NOW MY CUP RAN OVER!
DOC!
DOC!
WE'VE GOT TO EVACUATE THE CITY! NOW!
MR. DEITCH. I'M AWARE OF YOUR TRAUMA. BUT I DO NEED TO BETTER UNDERSTAND HOW THESE SYMPTOMS OF YOURS BEGAN.
WELL, YOU SEE, I'D BEEN HAVING A LOT OF TROUBLE FINDING A TOWN IN NEW JERSEY KNOWN COLLOQUIALLY AS MIDGETVILLE.
NO MIDGETS IN MIDGETVILLE!
?
BY (WHAT'S LEFT OF) Kim Deitch
I'D JUST ABOUT GIVEN UP WHEN I RECEIVED A LETTER FROM A WOMAN NAMED DOROTHY BAKENDORF-WEISS.
DOROTHY'S MOTHER, MOLL BARKELEY-BAKENDORF HAD ONCE DRAWN A NEWSPAPER COMIC STRIP CALLED *ALIAS the CAT! WHICH HAD BEEN BASED ON AN UNFINISHED MOVIE SERIAL MADE IN 1915 BY A DASHING CZECH EXPATRIATE NAMED MALEK JANOCHEK.
JANOCHEK WAS ON A MISSION TO END THE WAR THAT WAS JUST THEN SWEEPING THE WORLD,
* SEE STUFF OF DREAMS # 2

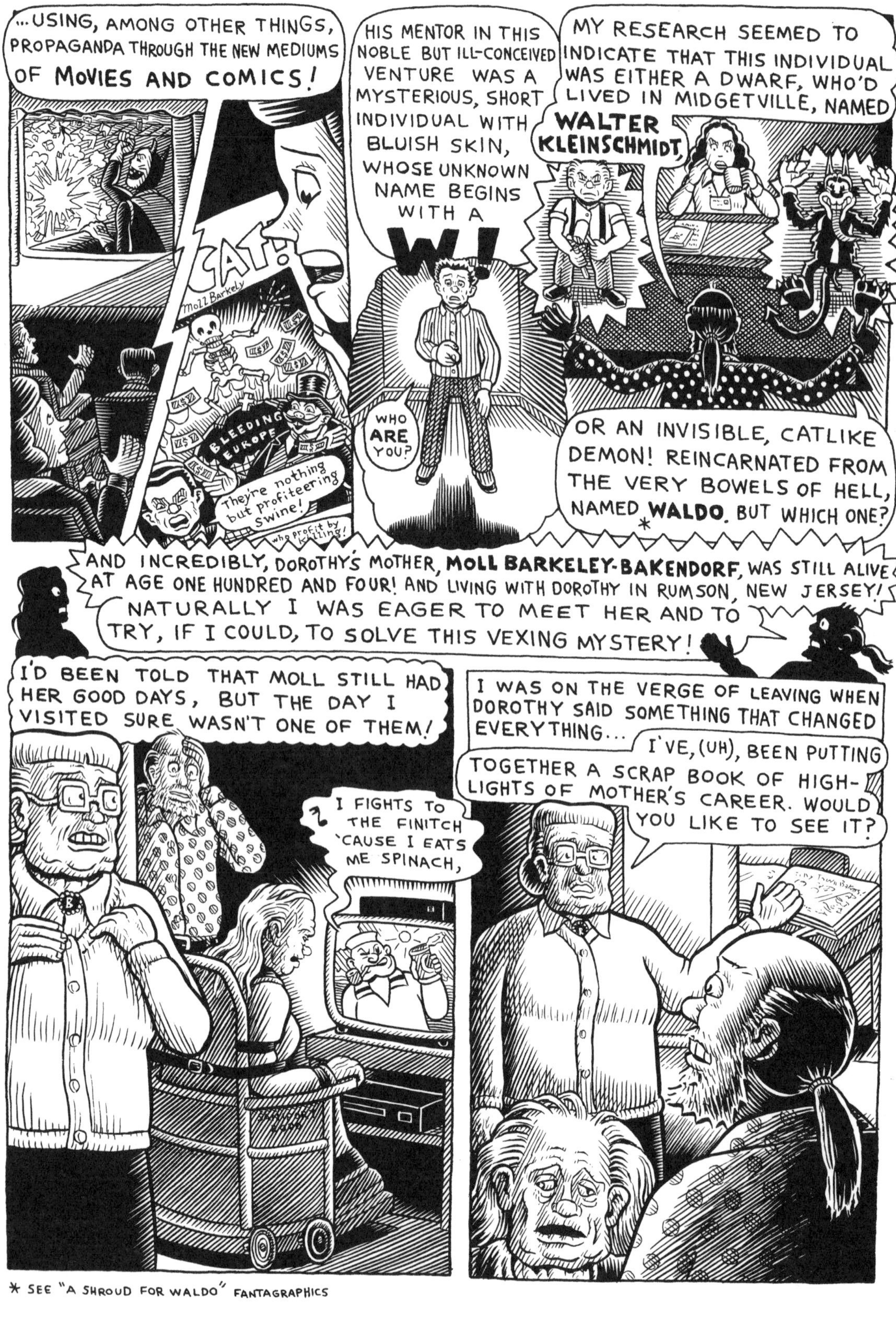
...USING, AMONG OTHER THINGS, PROPAGANDA THROUGH THE NEW MEDIUMS OF MOVIES AND COMICS!
CAT!
Moll Barkely
BLEEDING EUROPE
They're nothing but profiteering swine!
who profit by killing!
HIS MENTOR IN THIS NOBLE BUT ILL-CONCEIVED VENTURE WAS A MYSTERIOUS, SHORT INDIVIDUAL WITH BLUISH SKIN, WHOSE UNKNOWN NAME BEGINS WITH A
W!
WHO ARE YOU?
MY RESEARCH SEEMED TO INDICATE THAT THIS INDIVIDUAL WAS EITHER A DWARF, WHO'D LIVED IN MIDGETVILLE, NAMED
WALTER KLEINSCHMIDT,
OR AN INVISIBLE, CATLIKE DEMON! REINCARNATED FROM THE VERY BOWELS OF HELL, NAMED WALDO. * BUT WHICH ONE?
AND INCREDIBLY, DOROTHY'S MOTHER, MOLL BARKELEY-BAKENDORF, WAS STILL ALIVE AT AGE ONE HUNDRED AND FOUR! AND LIVING WITH DOROTHY IN RUMSON, NEW JERSEY!
NATURALLY I WAS EAGER TO MEET HER AND TO TRY, IF I COULD, TO SOLVE THIS VEXING MYSTERY!
I'D BEEN TOLD THAT MOLL STILL HAD HER GOOD DAYS, BUT THE DAY I VISITED SURE WASN'T ONE OF THEM!
I FIGHTS TO THE FINITCH 'CAUSE I EATS ME SPINACH,
I WAS ON THE VERGE OF LEAVING WHEN DOROTHY SAID SOMETHING THAT CHANGED EVERYTHING...
I'VE, (UH), BEEN PUTTING TOGETHER A SCRAP BOOK OF HIGH-LIGHTS OF MOTHER'S CAREER. WOULD YOU LIKE TO SEE IT?

* SEE "A SHROUD FOR WALDO" FANTAGRAPHICS

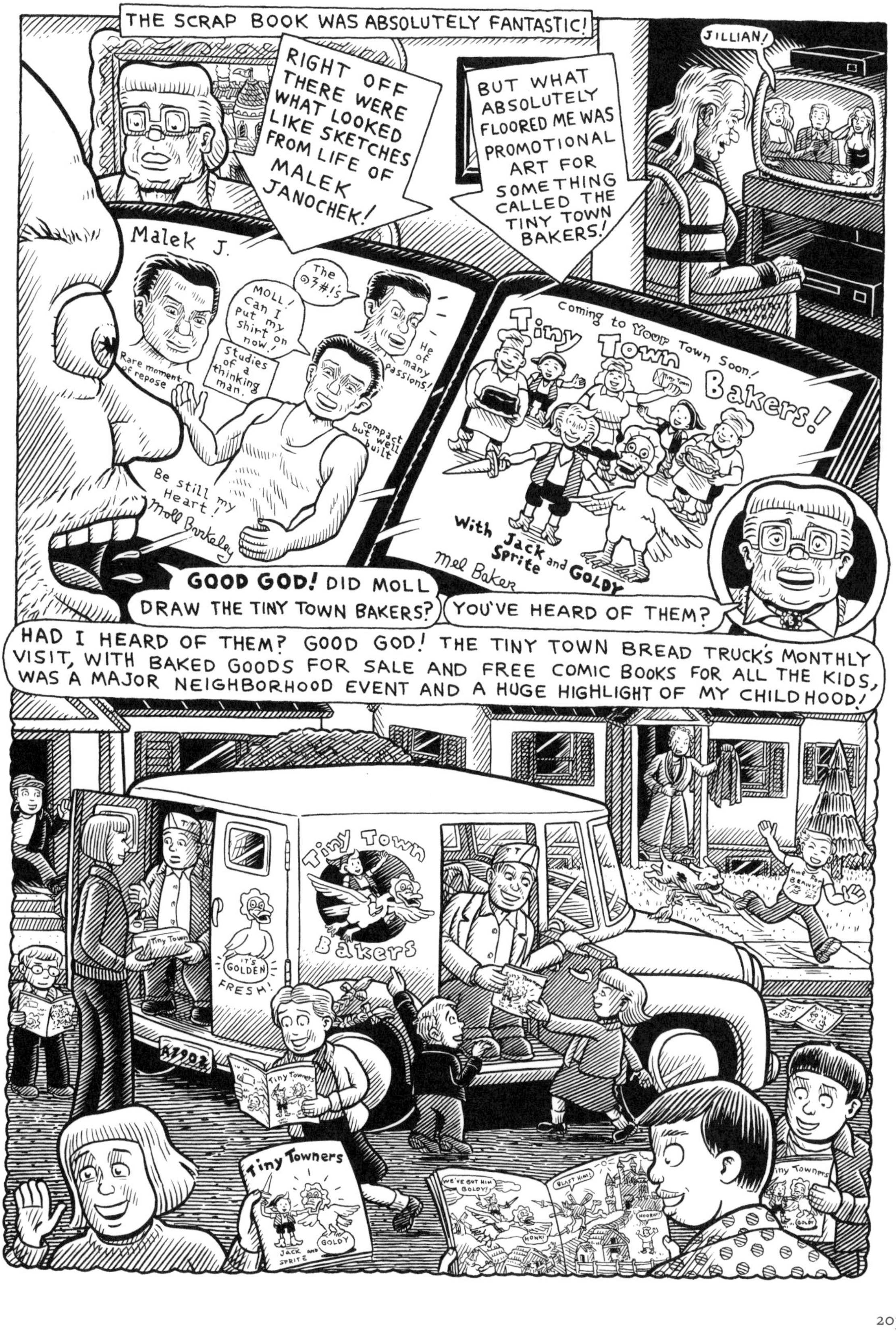

THE SCRAP BOOK WAS ABSOLUTELY FANTASTIC!
RIGHT OFF THERE WERE WHAT LOOKED LIKE SKETCHES FROM LIFE OF MALEK JANOCHEK!
BUT WHAT ABSOLUTELY FLOORED ME WAS PROMOTIONAL ART FOR SOMETHING CALLED THE TINY TOWN BAKERS!
JILLIAN!
Malek J.
Rare moment of repose
MOLL! Can I put my shirt on now!
The @3#!'s
Studies of a thinking man.
He of many passions!
compact but well built
Be still my Heart!
Moll Berkeley
Coming to Your Town Soon!
Tiny Town Bakers!
With Jack Sprite and GOLDY
Mel Baker
GOOD GOD! DID MOLL DRAW THE TINY TOWN BAKERS?
YOU'VE HEARD OF THEM?
HAD I HEARD OF THEM? GOOD GOD! THE TINY TOWN BREAD TRUCK'S MONTHLY VISIT, WITH BAKED GOODS FOR SALE AND FREE COMIC BOOKS FOR ALL THE KIDS, WAS A MAJOR NEIGHBORHOOD EVENT AND A HUGE HIGHLIGHT OF MY CHILDHOOD!
Tiny Town
Tiny Town Bakers
IT'S GOLDEN FRESH!
A1902
Tiny Towners
Tiny Towners
JACK AND SPRITE GOLDY
WE'VE GOT HIM GOLDY!
BLAST HIM!
HONK!
HOORAY!
Tiny Towners

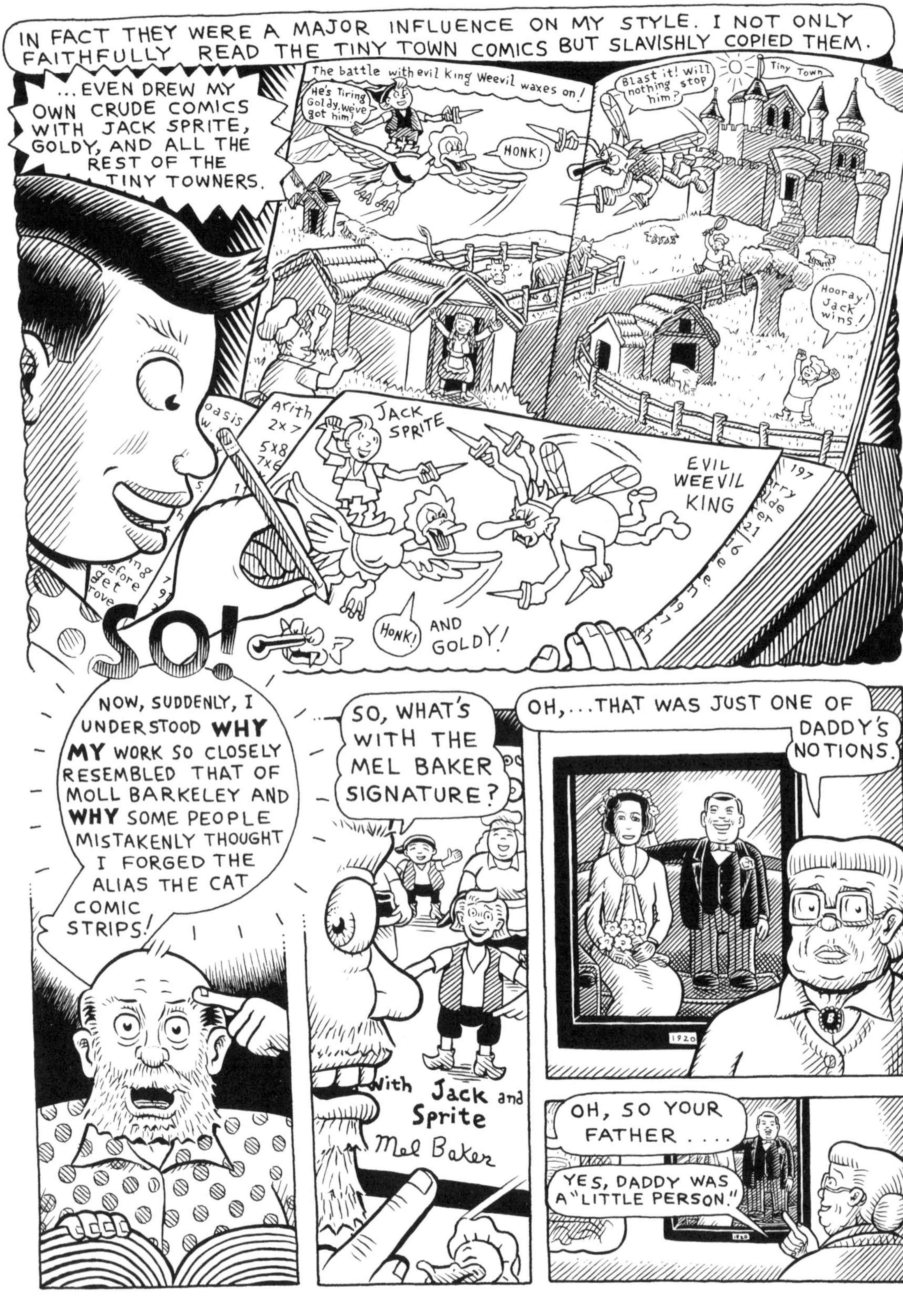
IN FACT THEY WERE A MAJOR INFLUENCE ON MY STYLE. I NOT ONLY FAITHFULLY READ THE TINY TOWN COMICS BUT SLAVISHLY COPIED THEM.
...EVEN DREW MY OWN CRUDE COMICS WITH JACK SPRITE, GOLDY, AND ALL THE REST OF THE TINY TOWNERS.
The battle with evil King Weevil waxes on!
He's Tiring Goldy, we've got him!
HONK!
Blast it! will nothing stop him?
Tiny Town
Hooray! Jack wins!
JACK SPRITE
EVIL WEEVIL KING
HONK!
AND GOLDY!
SO!
NOW, SUDDENLY, I UNDERSTOOD WHY MY WORK SO CLOSELY RESEMBLED THAT OF MOLL BARKELEY AND WHY SOME PEOPLE MISTAKENLY THOUGHT I FORGED THE ALIAS THE CAT COMIC STRIPS!
SO, WHAT'S WITH THE MEL BAKER SIGNATURE?
With Jack and Sprite
Mel Baker
OH,...THAT WAS JUST ONE OF DADDY'S NOTIONS.
1920
OH, SO YOUR FATHER....
YES, DADDY WAS A "LITTLE PERSON."

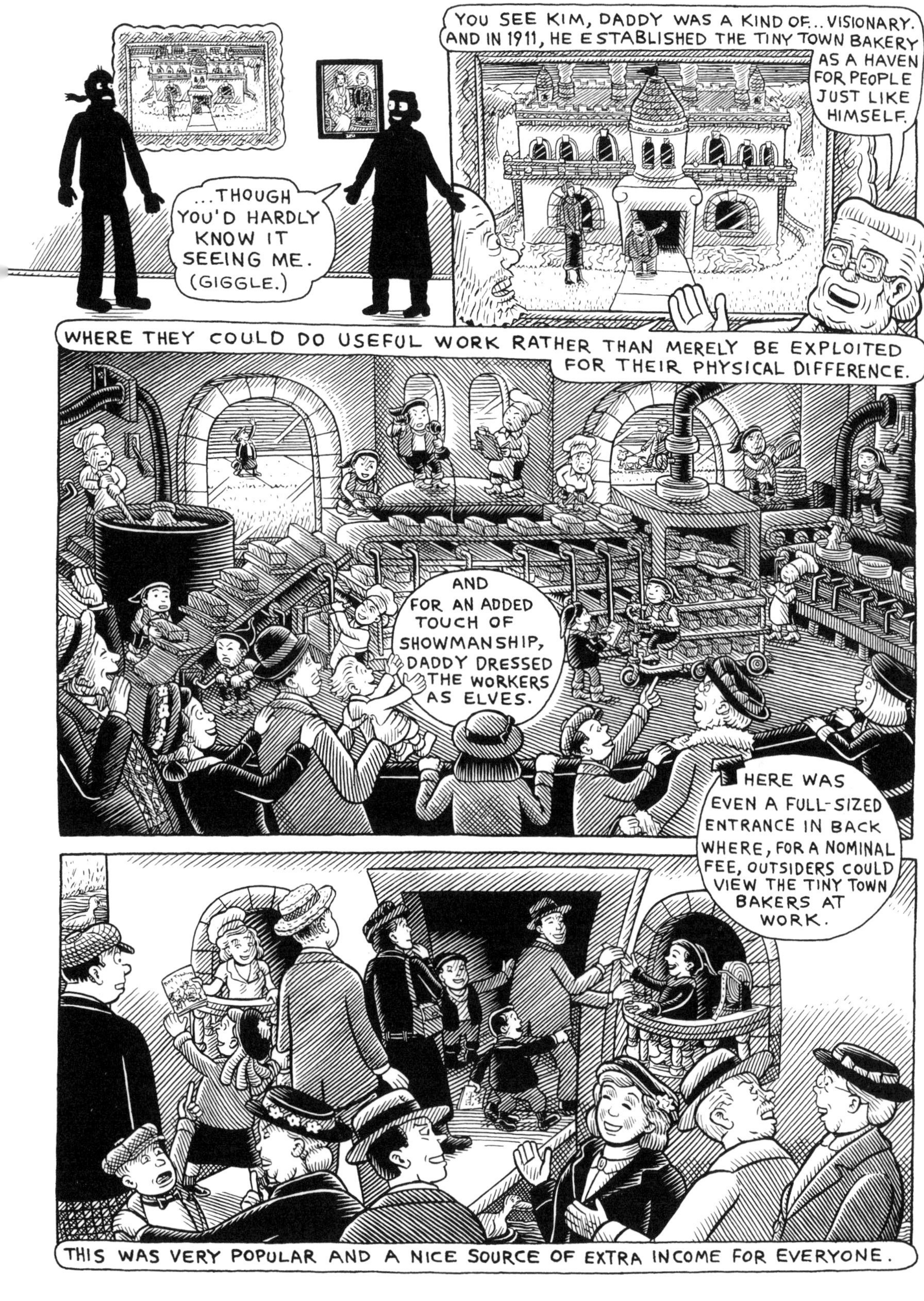
...THOUGH YOU'D HARDLY KNOW IT SEEING ME. (GIGGLE.)
YOU SEE KIM, DADDY WAS A KIND OF... VISIONARY. AND IN 1911, HE ESTABLISHED THE TINY TOWN BAKERY AS A HAVEN FOR PEOPLE JUST LIKE HIMSELF.
WHERE THEY COULD DO USEFUL WORK RATHER THAN MERELY BE EXPLOITED FOR THEIR PHYSICAL DIFFERENCE.
AND FOR AN ADDED TOUCH OF SHOWMANSHIP, DADDY DRESSED THE WORKERS AS ELVES.
THERE WAS EVEN A FULL-SIZED ENTRANCE IN BACK WHERE, FOR A NOMINAL FEE, OUTSIDERS COULD VIEW THE TINY TOWN BAKERS AT WORK.
THIS WAS VERY POPULAR AND A NICE SOURCE OF EXTRA INCOME FOR EVERYONE.

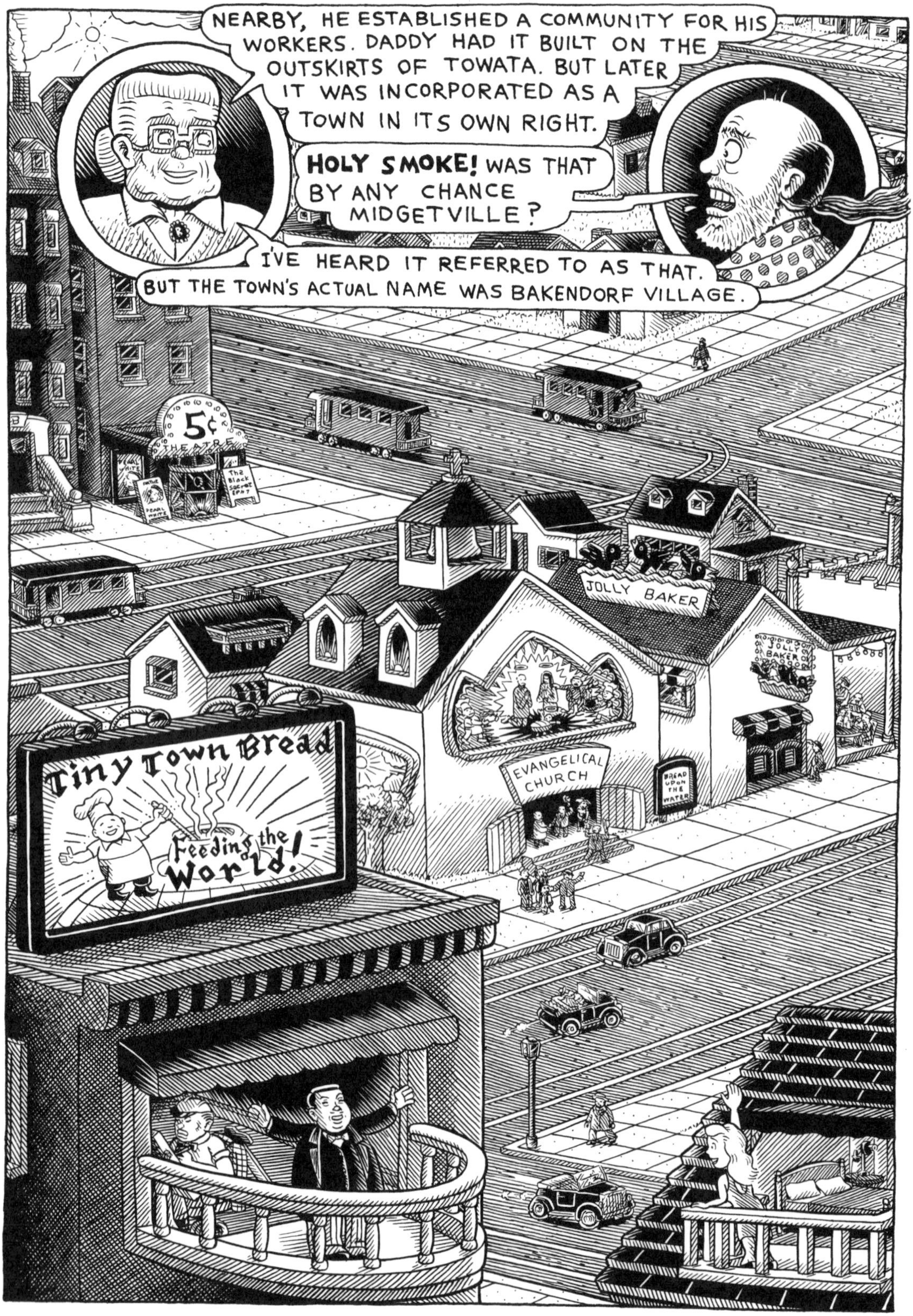
NEARBY, HE ESTABLISHED A COMMUNITY FOR HIS WORKERS. DADDY HAD IT BUILT ON THE OUTSKIRTS OF TOWATA. BUT LATER IT WAS INCORPORATED AS A TOWN IN ITS OWN RIGHT.
HOLY SMOKE! WAS THAT BY ANY CHANCE MIDGETVILLE?
I'VE HEARD IT REFERRED TO AS THAT. BUT THE TOWN'S ACTUAL NAME WAS BAKENDORF VILLAGE.
5¢
THEATRE
JOLLY BAKER
EVANGELICAL CHURCH
BREAD UPON THE WATER
Tiny Town Bread
Feeding the World!

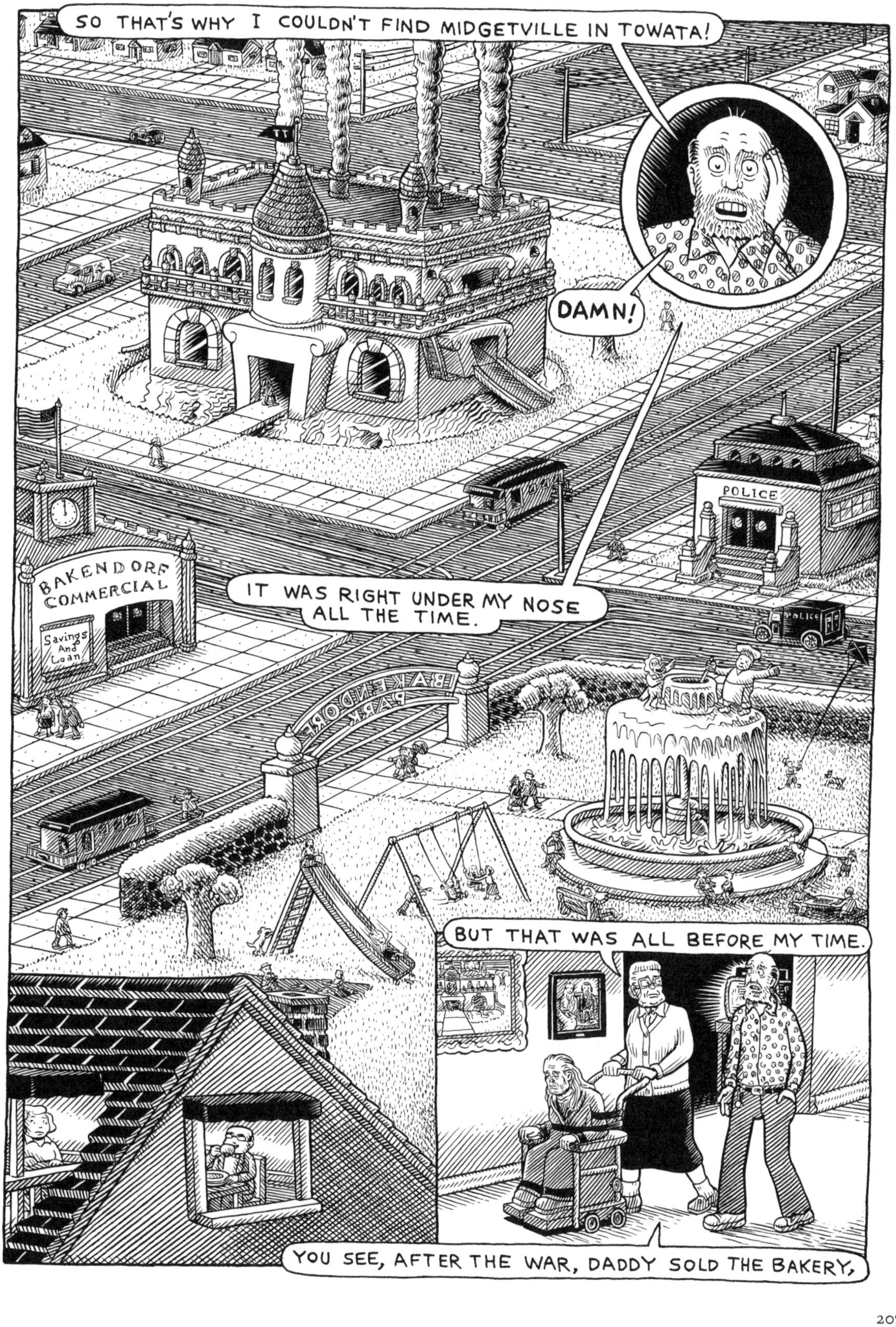
SO THAT'S WHY I COULDN'T FIND MIDGETVILLE IN TOWATA!
DAMN!
IT WAS RIGHT UNDER MY NOSE ALL THE TIME.
POLICE
BAKENDORF COMMERCIAL
Savings And Loan
BAKENDORF PARK
BUT THAT WAS ALL BEFORE MY TIME.
YOU SEE, AFTER THE WAR, DADDY SOLD THE BAKERY,

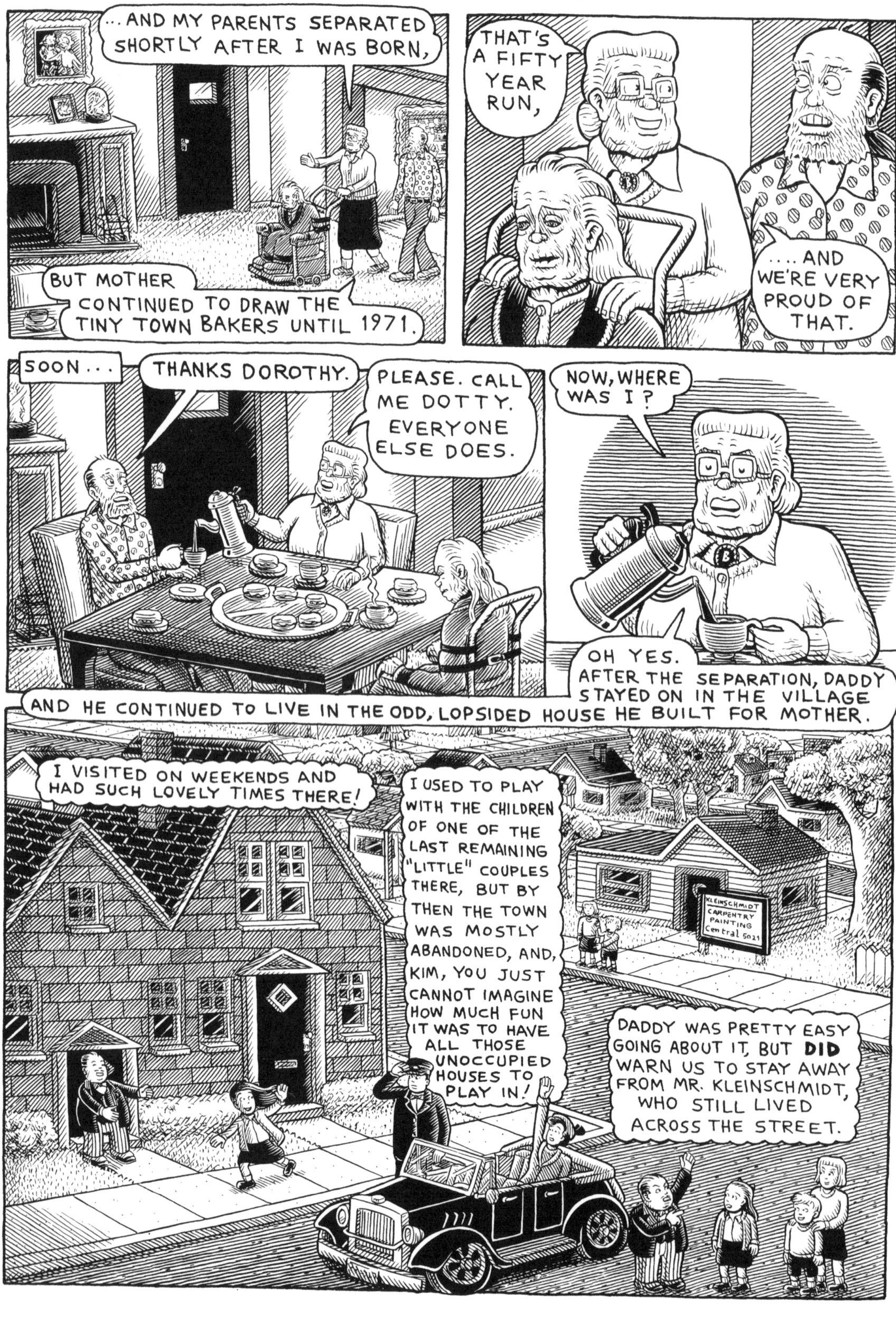
...AND MY PARENTS SEPARATED SHORTLY AFTER I WAS BORN,
BUT MOTHER CONTINUED TO DRAW THE TINY TOWN BAKERS UNTIL 1971.
THAT'S A FIFTY YEAR RUN,
....AND WE'RE VERY PROUD OF THAT.
SOON...
THANKS DOROTHY.
PLEASE. CALL ME DOTTY. EVERYONE ELSE DOES.
NOW, WHERE WAS I?
OH YES. AFTER THE SEPARATION, DADDY STAYED ON IN THE VILLAGE
AND HE CONTINUED TO LIVE IN THE ODD, LOPSIDED HOUSE HE BUILT FOR MOTHER.
I VISITED ON WEEKENDS AND HAD SUCH LOVELY TIMES THERE!
I USED TO PLAY WITH THE CHILDREN OF ONE OF THE LAST REMAINING "LITTLE" COUPLES THERE, BUT BY THEN THE TOWN WAS MOSTLY ABANDONED, AND, KIM, YOU JUST CANNOT IMAGINE HOW MUCH FUN IT WAS TO HAVE ALL THOSE UNOCCUPIED HOUSES TO PLAY IN!
KLEINSCHMIDT CARPENTRY PAINTING Central 5021
DADDY WAS PRETTY EASY GOING ABOUT IT, BUT **DID** WARN US TO STAY AWAY FROM MR. KLEINSCHMIDT, WHO STILL LIVED ACROSS THE STREET.

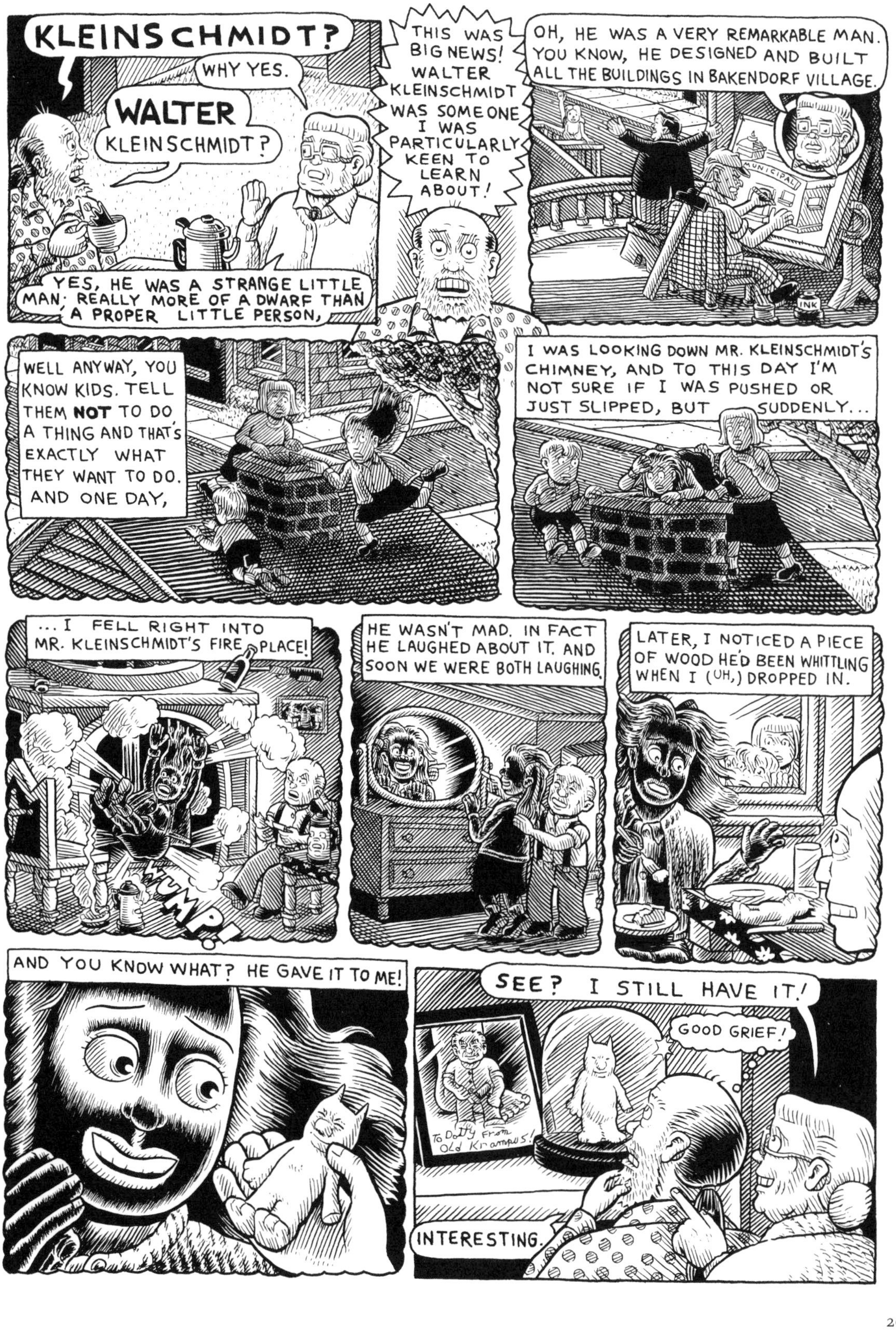

KLEINSCHMIDT?
WHY YES.
WALTER KLEINSCHMIDT?
YES, HE WAS A STRANGE LITTLE MAN. REALLY MORE OF A DWARF THAN A PROPER LITTLE PERSON,
THIS WAS BIG NEWS! WALTER KLEINSCHMIDT WAS SOMEONE I WAS PARTICULARLY KEEN TO LEARN ABOUT!
OH, HE WAS A VERY REMARKABLE MAN. YOU KNOW, HE DESIGNED AND BUILT ALL THE BUILDINGS IN BAKENDORF VILLAGE.
MUNICIPAL
INK
WELL ANYWAY, YOU KNOW KIDS. TELL THEM **NOT** TO DO A THING AND THAT'S EXACTLY WHAT THEY WANT TO DO. AND ONE DAY,
I WAS LOOKING DOWN MR. KLEINSCHMIDT'S CHIMNEY, AND TO THIS DAY I'M NOT SURE IF I WAS PUSHED OR JUST SLIPPED, BUT SUDDENLY...
...I FELL RIGHT INTO MR. KLEINSCHMIDT'S FIRE PLACE!
WUMP!
HE WASN'T MAD. IN FACT HE LAUGHED ABOUT IT. AND SOON WE WERE BOTH LAUGHING.
LATER, I NOTICED A PIECE OF WOOD HE'D BEEN WHITTLING WHEN I (UH,) DROPPED IN.
AND YOU KNOW WHAT? HE GAVE IT TO ME!
SEE? I STILL HAVE IT!
GOOD GRIEF!
To Dotty From Old Krampus!
INTERESTING.

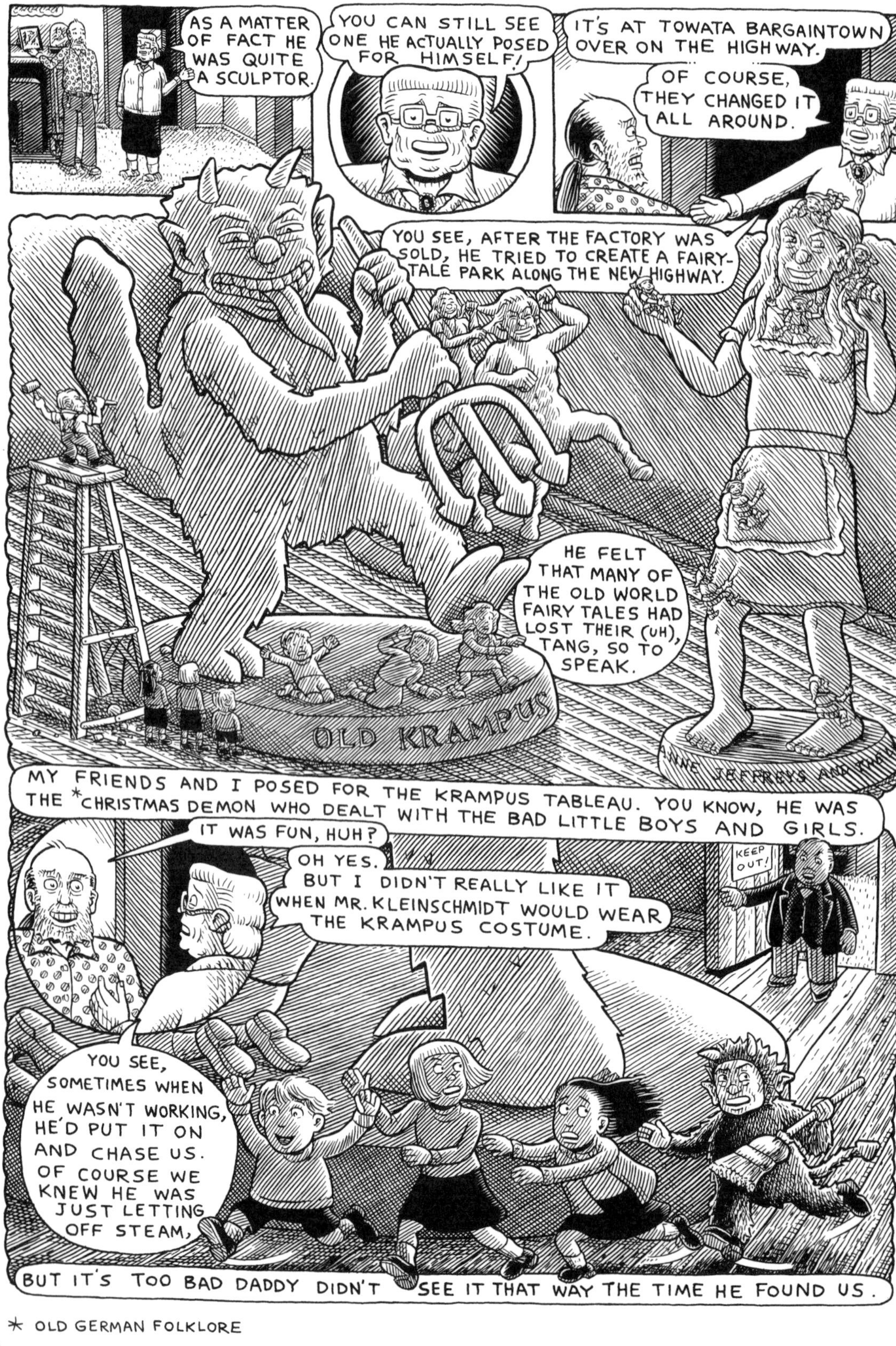

AS A MATTER OF FACT HE WAS QUITE A SCULPTOR.
YOU CAN STILL SEE ONE HE ACTUALLY POSED FOR HIMSELF!
IT'S AT TOWATA BARGAINTOWN OVER ON THE HIGHWAY.
OF COURSE, THEY CHANGED IT ALL AROUND.
YOU SEE, AFTER THE FACTORY WAS SOLD, HE TRIED TO CREATE A FAIRY-TALE PARK ALONG THE NEW HIGHWAY.
HE FELT THAT MANY OF THE OLD WORLD FAIRY TALES HAD LOST THEIR (UH), TANG, SO TO SPEAK.
OLD KRAMPUS
ANNE JEFFREYS AND THE
MY FRIENDS AND I POSED FOR THE KRAMPUS TABLEAU. YOU KNOW, HE WAS THE *CHRISTMAS DEMON WHO DEALT WITH THE BAD LITTLE BOYS AND GIRLS.
IT WAS FUN, HUH?
OH YES. BUT I DIDN'T REALLY LIKE IT WHEN MR. KLEINSCHMIDT WOULD WEAR THE KRAMPUS COSTUME.
KEEP OUT!
YOU SEE, SOMETIMES WHEN HE WASN'T WORKING, HE'D PUT IT ON AND CHASE US. OF COURSE WE KNEW HE WAS JUST LETTING OFF STEAM,
BUT IT'S TOO BAD DADDY DIDN'T SEE IT THAT WAY THE TIME HE FOUND US.

* OLD GERMAN FOLKLORE

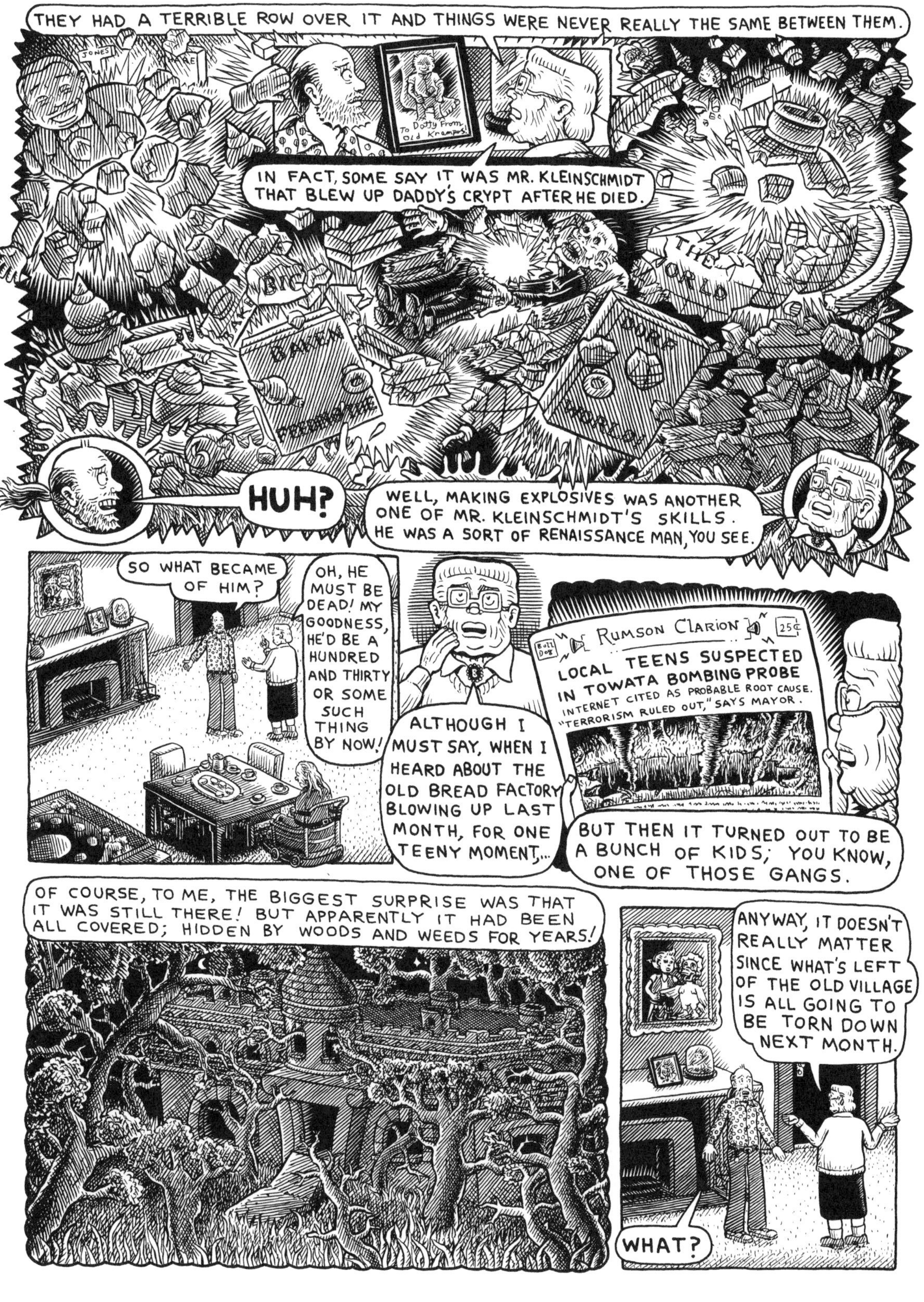
THEY HAD A TERRIBLE ROW OVER IT AND THINGS WERE NEVER REALLY THE SAME BETWEEN THEM.
To Dotty From Old Krampus!
IN FACT, SOME SAY IT WAS MR. KLEINSCHMIDT THAT BLEW UP DADDY'S CRYPT AFTER HE DIED.
HUH?
WELL, MAKING EXPLOSIVES WAS ANOTHER ONE OF MR. KLEINSCHMIDT'S SKILLS. HE WAS A SORT OF RENAISSANCE MAN, YOU SEE.
SO WHAT BECAME OF HIM?
OH, HE MUST BE DEAD! MY GOODNESS, HE'D BE A HUNDRED AND THIRTY OR SOME SUCH THING BY NOW!
ALTHOUGH I MUST SAY, WHEN I HEARD ABOUT THE OLD BREAD FACTORY BLOWING UP LAST MONTH, FOR ONE TEENY MOMENT,...
RUMSON CLARION
25¢
LOCAL TEENS SUSPECTED IN TOWATA BOMBING PROBE
INTERNET CITED AS PROBABLE ROOT CAUSE.
"TERRORISM RULED OUT," SAYS MAYOR.
BUT THEN IT TURNED OUT TO BE A BUNCH OF KIDS; YOU KNOW, ONE OF THOSE GANGS.
OF COURSE, TO ME, THE BIGGEST SURPRISE WAS THAT IT WAS STILL THERE! BUT APPARENTLY IT HAD BEEN ALL COVERED; HIDDEN BY WOODS AND WEEDS FOR YEARS!
ANYWAY, IT DOESN'T REALLY MATTER SINCE WHAT'S LEFT OF THE OLD VILLAGE IS ALL GOING TO BE TORN DOWN NEXT MONTH.
WHAT?

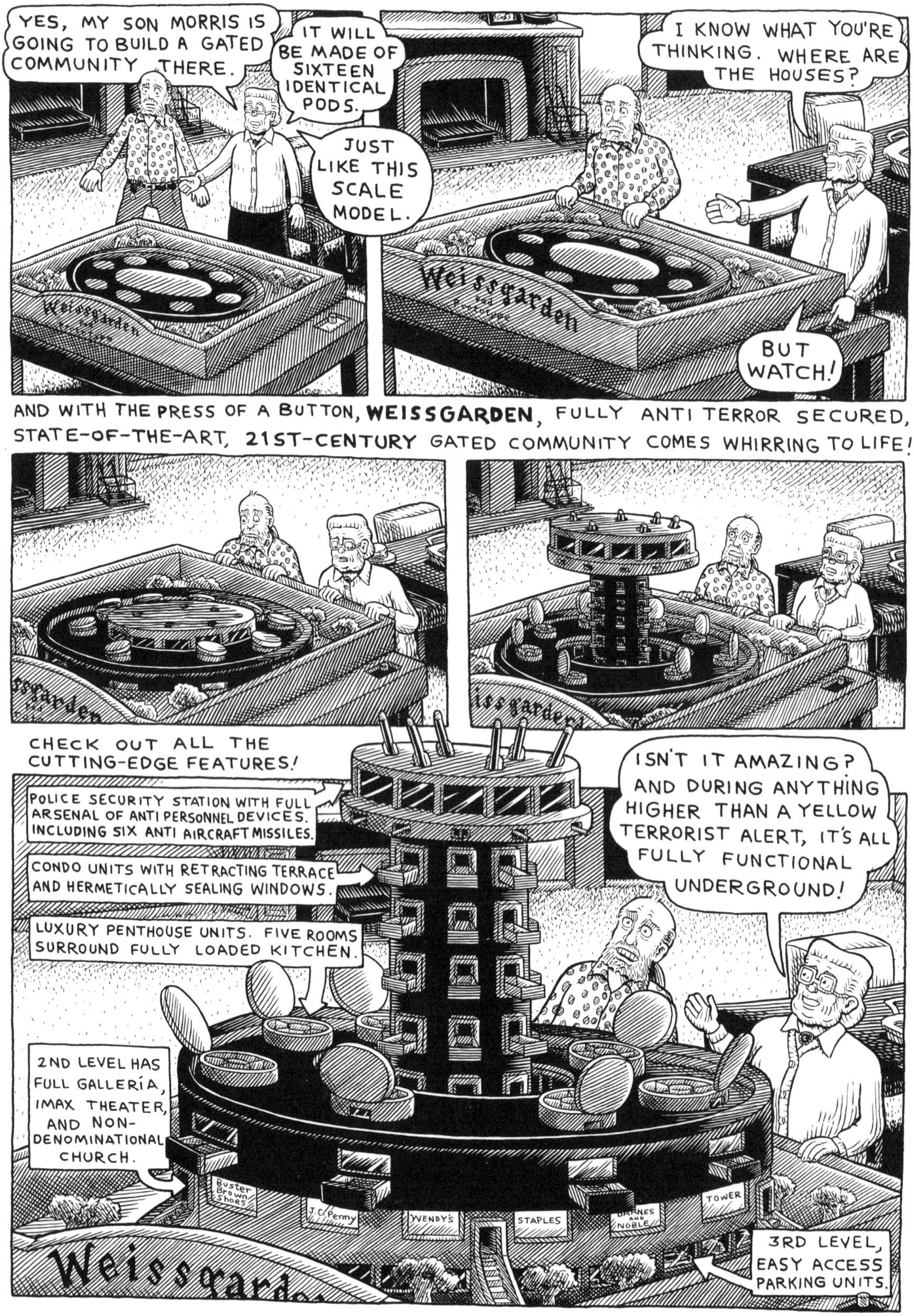
YES, MY SON MORRIS IS GOING TO BUILD A GATED COMMUNITY THERE.
IT WILL BE MADE OF SIXTEEN IDENTICAL PODS.
JUST LIKE THIS SCALE MODEL.
Weissgarden
I KNOW WHAT YOU'RE THINKING. WHERE ARE THE HOUSES?
BUT WATCH!
AND WITH THE PRESS OF A BUTTON, WEISSGARDEN, FULLY ANTI TERROR SECURED, STATE-OF-THE-ART, 21ST-CENTURY GATED COMMUNITY COMES WHIRRING TO LIFE!
CHECK OUT ALL THE CUTTING-EDGE FEATURES!
POLICE SECURITY STATION WITH FULL ARSENAL OF ANTI PERSONNEL DEVICES. INCLUDING SIX ANTI AIRCRAFT MISSILES.
CONDO UNITS WITH RETRACTING TERRACE AND HERMETICALLY SEALING WINDOWS.
LUXURY PENTHOUSE UNITS. FIVE ROOMS SURROUND FULLY LOADED KITCHEN.
ISN'T IT AMAZING? AND DURING ANYTHING HIGHER THAN A YELLOW TERRORIST ALERT, IT'S ALL FULLY FUNCTIONAL UNDERGROUND!
2ND LEVEL HAS FULL GALLERÍA, IMAX THEATER, AND NON-DENOMINATIONAL CHURCH.
Buster Brown Shoes
J.C. Penny
WENDY'S
STAPLES
BARNES AND NOBLE
TOWER
3RD LEVEL, EASY ACCESS PARKING UNITS.
Weissgarden

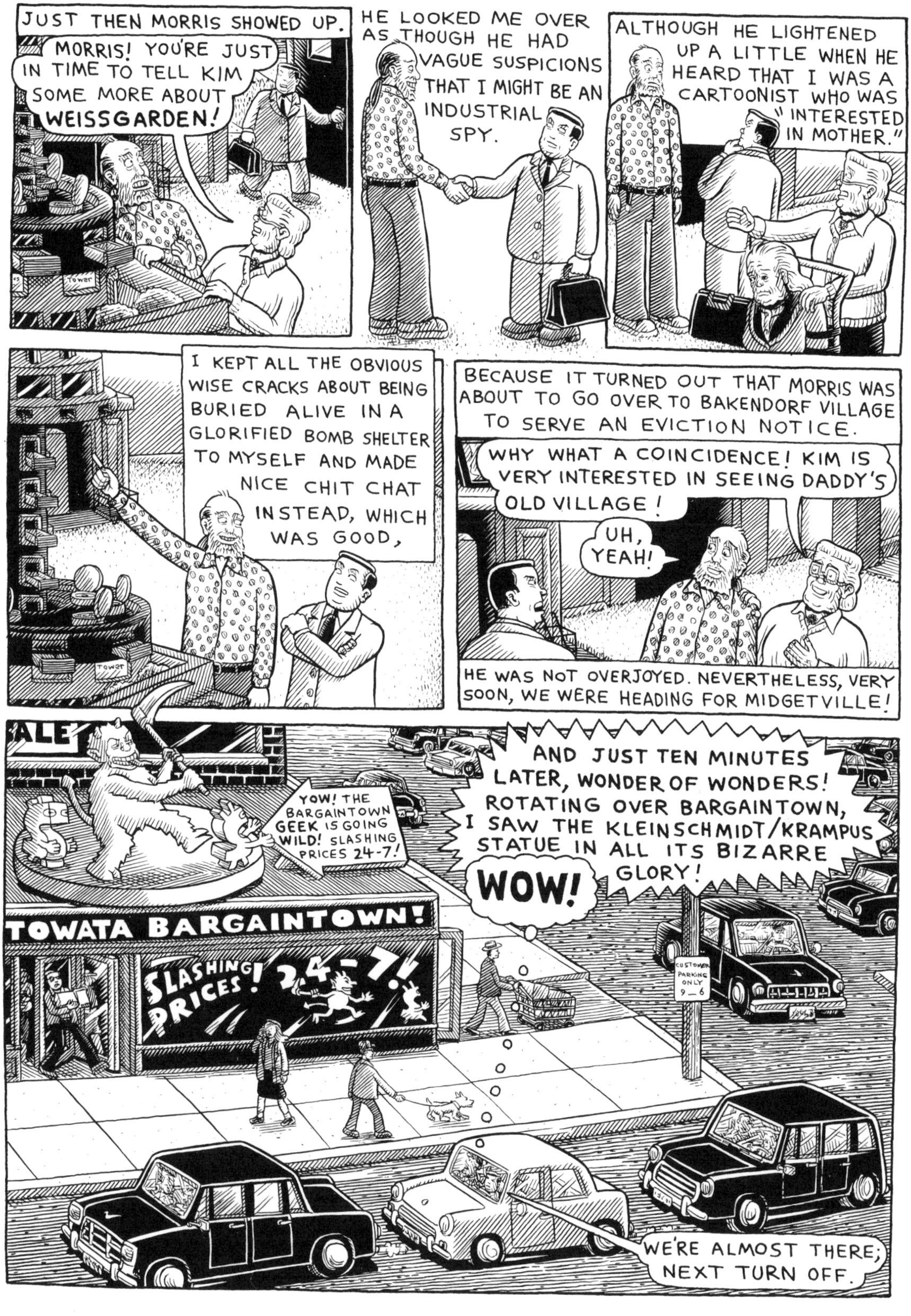

JUST THEN MORRIS SHOWED UP.
MORRIS! YOU'RE JUST IN TIME TO TELL KIM SOME MORE ABOUT WEISSGARDEN!
HE LOOKED ME OVER AS THOUGH HE HAD VAGUE SUSPICIONS THAT I MIGHT BE AN INDUSTRIAL SPY.
ALTHOUGH HE LIGHTENED UP A LITTLE WHEN HE HEARD THAT I WAS A CARTOONIST WHO WAS "INTERESTED IN MOTHER."
I KEPT ALL THE OBVIOUS WISE CRACKS ABOUT BEING BURIED ALIVE IN A GLORIFIED BOMB SHELTER TO MYSELF AND MADE NICE CHIT CHAT INSTEAD, WHICH WAS GOOD,
BECAUSE IT TURNED OUT THAT MORRIS WAS ABOUT TO GO OVER TO BAKENDORF VILLAGE TO SERVE AN EVICTION NOTICE.
WHY WHAT A COINCIDENCE! KIM IS VERY INTERESTED IN SEEING DADDY'S OLD VILLAGE!
UH, YEAH!
HE WAS NOT OVERJOYED. NEVERTHELESS, VERY SOON, WE WERE HEADING FOR MIDGETVILLE!
YOW! THE BARGAINTOWN GEEK IS GOING WILD! SLASHING PRICES 24-7!
AND JUST TEN MINUTES LATER, WONDER OF WONDERS! ROTATING OVER BARGAINTOWN, I SAW THE KLEINSCHMIDT/KRAMPUS STATUE IN ALL ITS BIZARRE GLORY!
WOW!
TOWATA BARGAINTOWN!
SLASHING PRICES! 24-7!
CUSTOMER PARKING ONLY 9—6
WE'RE ALMOST THERE; NEXT TURN OFF.

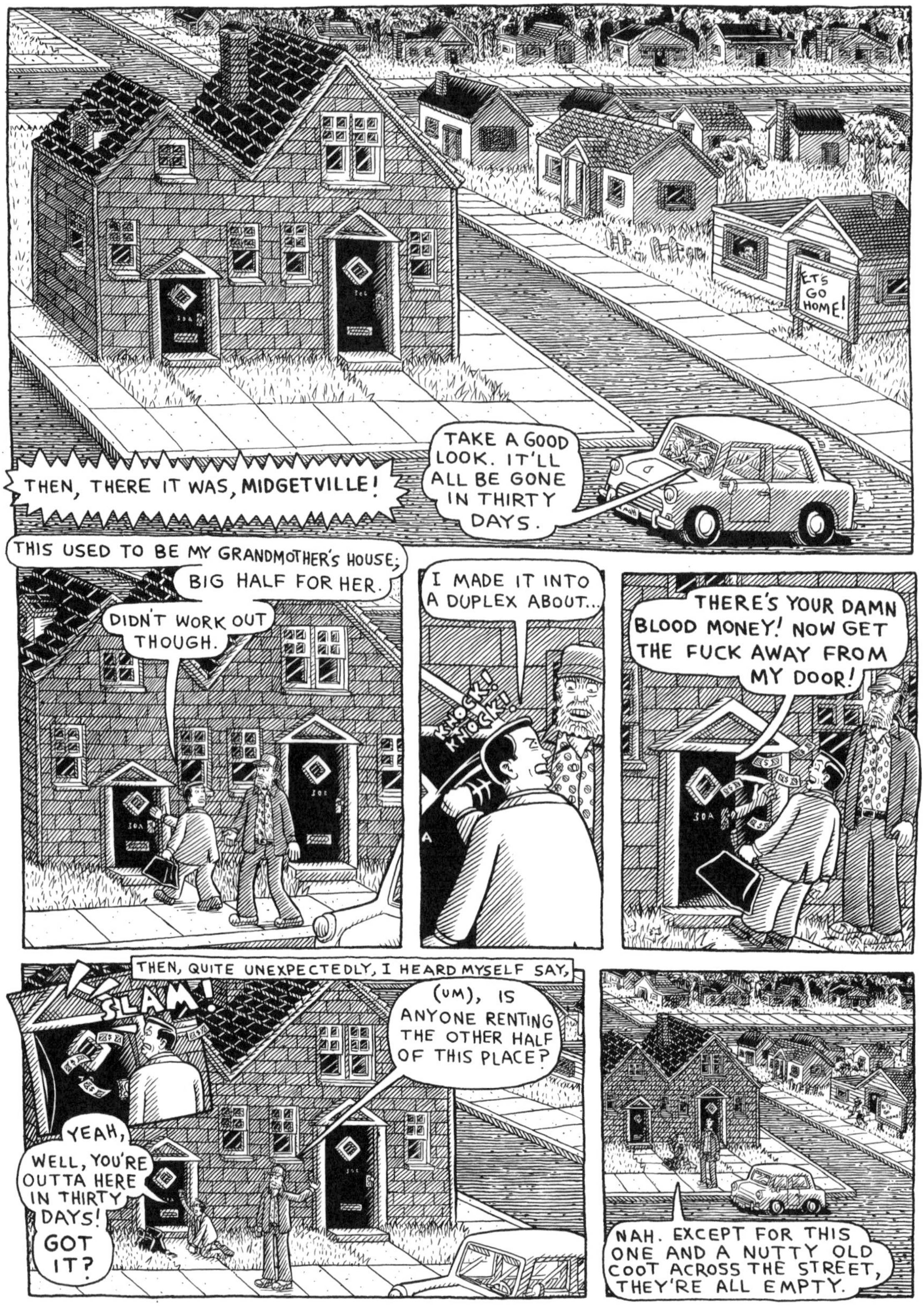

ET'S GO HOME!
THEN, THERE IT WAS, MIDGETVILLE!
TAKE A GOOD LOOK. IT'LL ALL BE GONE IN THIRTY DAYS.
THIS USED TO BE MY GRANDMOTHER'S HOUSE;
BIG HALF FOR HER.
DIDN'T WORK OUT THOUGH.
I MADE IT INTO A DUPLEX ABOUT...
KNOCK! KNOCK!
THERE'S YOUR DAMN BLOOD MONEY! NOW GET THE FUCK AWAY FROM MY DOOR!
THEN, QUITE UNEXPECTEDLY, I HEARD MYSELF SAY,
SLAM!
(UM), IS ANYONE RENTING THE OTHER HALF OF THIS PLACE?
YEAH, WELL, YOU'RE OUTTA HERE IN THIRTY DAYS! GOT IT?
NAH. EXCEPT FOR THIS ONE AND A NUTTY OLD COOT ACROSS THE STREET, THEY'RE ALL EMPTY.

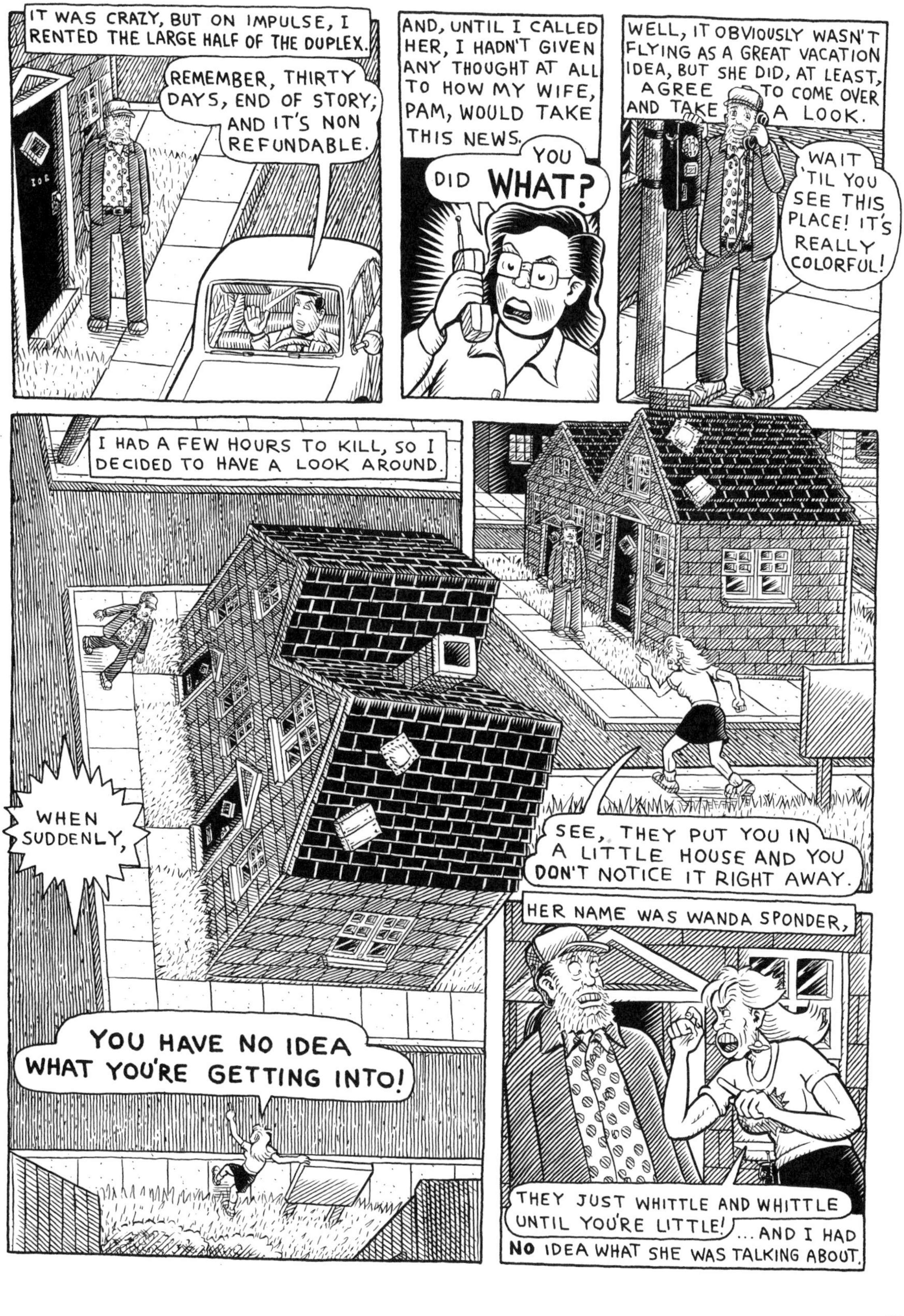

IT WAS CRAZY, BUT ON IMPULSE, I RENTED THE LARGE HALF OF THE DUPLEX.
REMEMBER, THIRTY DAYS, END OF STORY; AND IT'S NON REFUNDABLE.
AND, UNTIL I CALLED HER, I HADN'T GIVEN ANY THOUGHT AT ALL TO HOW MY WIFE, PAM, WOULD TAKE THIS NEWS.
YOU DID WHAT?
WELL, IT OBVIOUSLY WASN'T FLYING AS A GREAT VACATION IDEA, BUT SHE DID, AT LEAST, AGREE TO COME OVER AND TAKE A LOOK.
WAIT 'TIL YOU SEE THIS PLACE! IT'S REALLY COLORFUL!
I HAD A FEW HOURS TO KILL, SO I DECIDED TO HAVE A LOOK AROUND.
WHEN SUDDENLY,
YOU HAVE NO IDEA WHAT YOU'RE GETTING INTO!
SEE, THEY PUT YOU IN A LITTLE HOUSE AND YOU DON'T NOTICE IT RIGHT AWAY.
HER NAME WAS WANDA SPONDER,
THEY JUST WHITTLE AND WHITTLE UNTIL YOU'RE LITTLE!
... AND I HAD NO IDEA WHAT SHE WAS TALKING ABOUT.

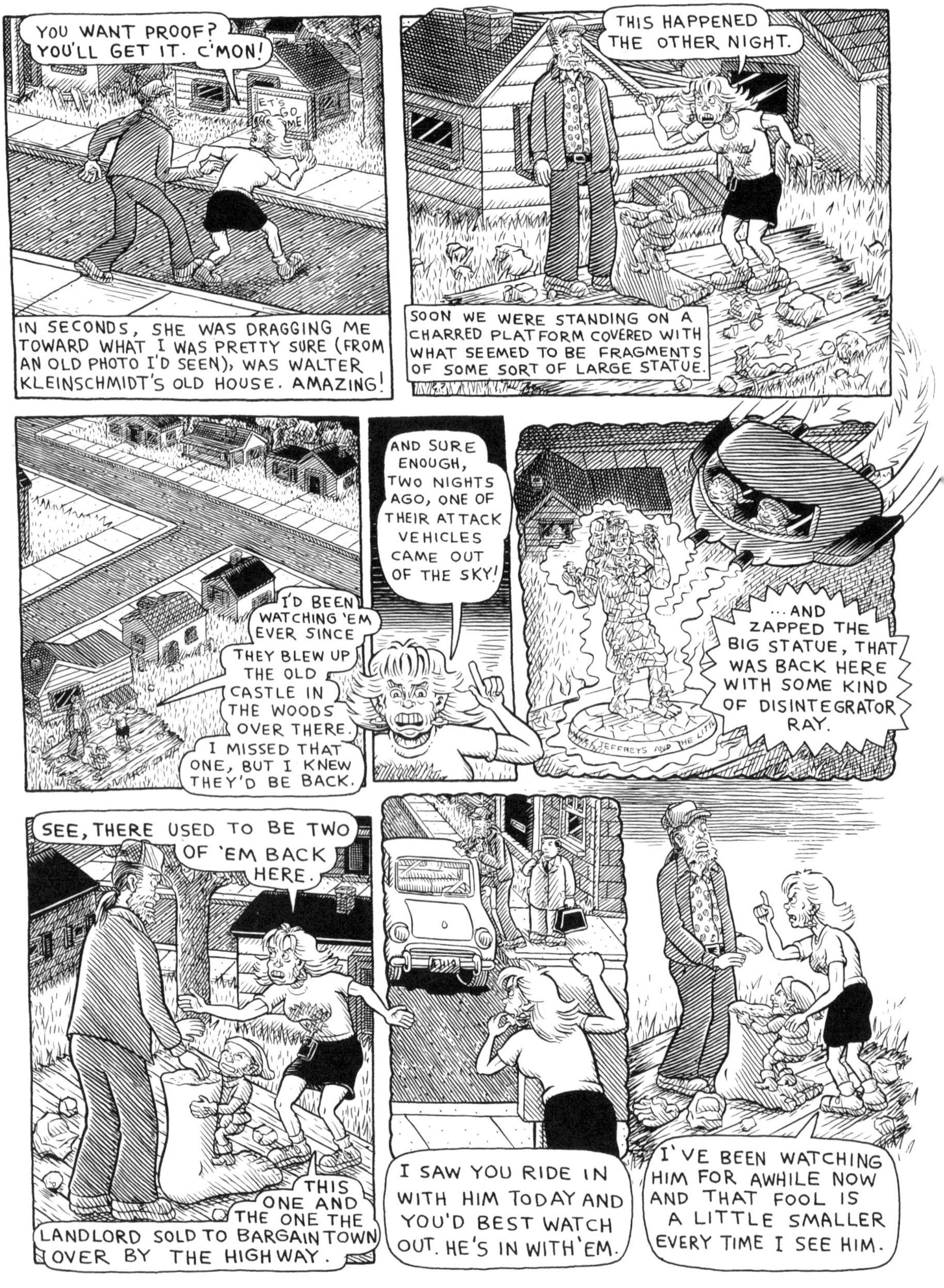
YOU WANT PROOF? YOU'LL GET IT. C'MON!
IN SECONDS, SHE WAS DRAGGING ME TOWARD WHAT I WAS PRETTY SURE (FROM AN OLD PHOTO I'D SEEN), WAS WALTER KLEINSCHMIDT'S OLD HOUSE. AMAZING!
THIS HAPPENED THE OTHER NIGHT.
SOON WE WERE STANDING ON A CHARRED PLATFORM COVERED WITH WHAT SEEMED TO BE FRAGMENTS OF SOME SORT OF LARGE STATUE.
I'D BEEN WATCHING 'EM EVER SINCE
THEY BLEW UP THE OLD CASTLE IN THE WOODS OVER THERE.
I MISSED THAT ONE, BUT I KNEW THEY'D BE BACK.
AND SURE ENOUGH, TWO NIGHTS AGO, ONE OF THEIR ATTACK VEHICLES CAME OUT OF THE SKY!
...AND ZAPPED THE BIG STATUE, THAT WAS BACK HERE WITH SOME KIND OF DISINTEGRATOR RAY.
SEE, THERE USED TO BE TWO OF 'EM BACK HERE.
THIS ONE AND THE ONE THE LANDLORD SOLD TO BARGAIN TOWN OVER BY THE HIGHWAY.
I SAW YOU RIDE IN WITH HIM TODAY AND YOU'D BEST WATCH OUT. HE'S IN WITH 'EM.
I'VE BEEN WATCHING HIM FOR AWHILE NOW AND THAT FOOL IS A LITTLE SMALLER EVERY TIME I SEE HIM.

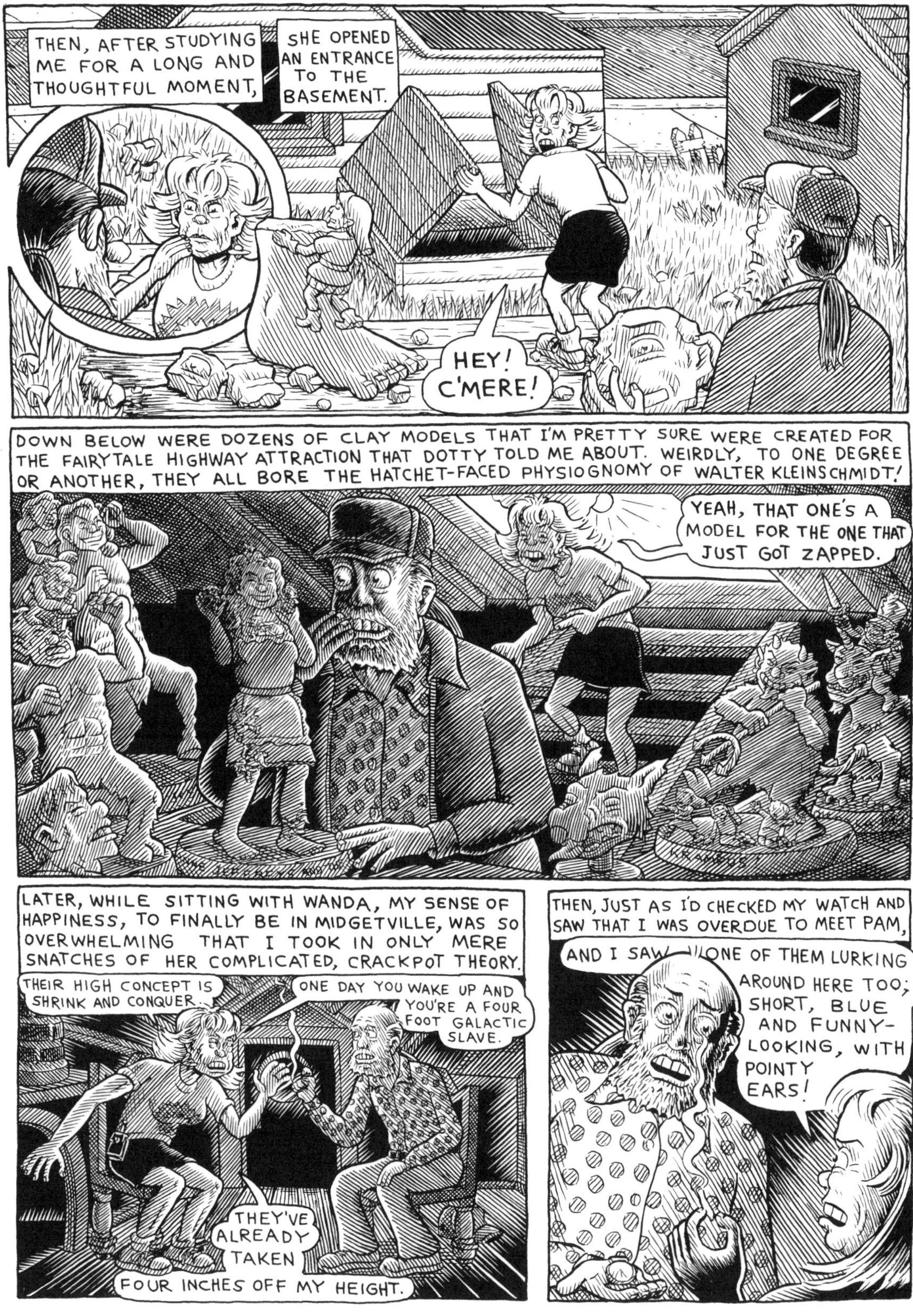
THEN, AFTER STUDYING ME FOR A LONG AND THOUGHTFUL MOMENT,
SHE OPENED AN ENTRANCE TO THE BASEMENT.
HEY! C'MERE!
DOWN BELOW WERE DOZENS OF CLAY MODELS THAT I'M PRETTY SURE WERE CREATED FOR THE FAIRYTALE HIGHWAY ATTRACTION THAT DOTTY TOLD ME ABOUT. WEIRDLY, TO ONE DEGREE OR ANOTHER, THEY ALL BORE THE HATCHET-FACED PHYSIOGNOMY OF WALTER KLEINSCHMIDT!
YEAH, THAT ONE'S A MODEL FOR THE ONE THAT JUST GOT ZAPPED.
LATER, WHILE SITTING WITH WANDA, MY SENSE OF HAPPINESS, TO FINALLY BE IN MIDGETVILLE, WAS SO OVERWHELMING THAT I TOOK IN ONLY MERE SNATCHES OF HER COMPLICATED, CRACKPOT THEORY.
THEIR HIGH CONCEPT IS SHRINK AND CONQUER.
ONE DAY YOU WAKE UP AND YOU'RE A FOUR FOOT GALACTIC SLAVE.
THEY'VE ALREADY TAKEN
FOUR INCHES OFF MY HEIGHT.
THEN, JUST AS I'D CHECKED MY WATCH AND SAW THAT I WAS OVERDUE TO MEET PAM,
AND I SAW ONE OF THEM LURKING AROUND HERE TOO; SHORT, BLUE AND FUNNY-LOOKING, WITH POINTY EARS!

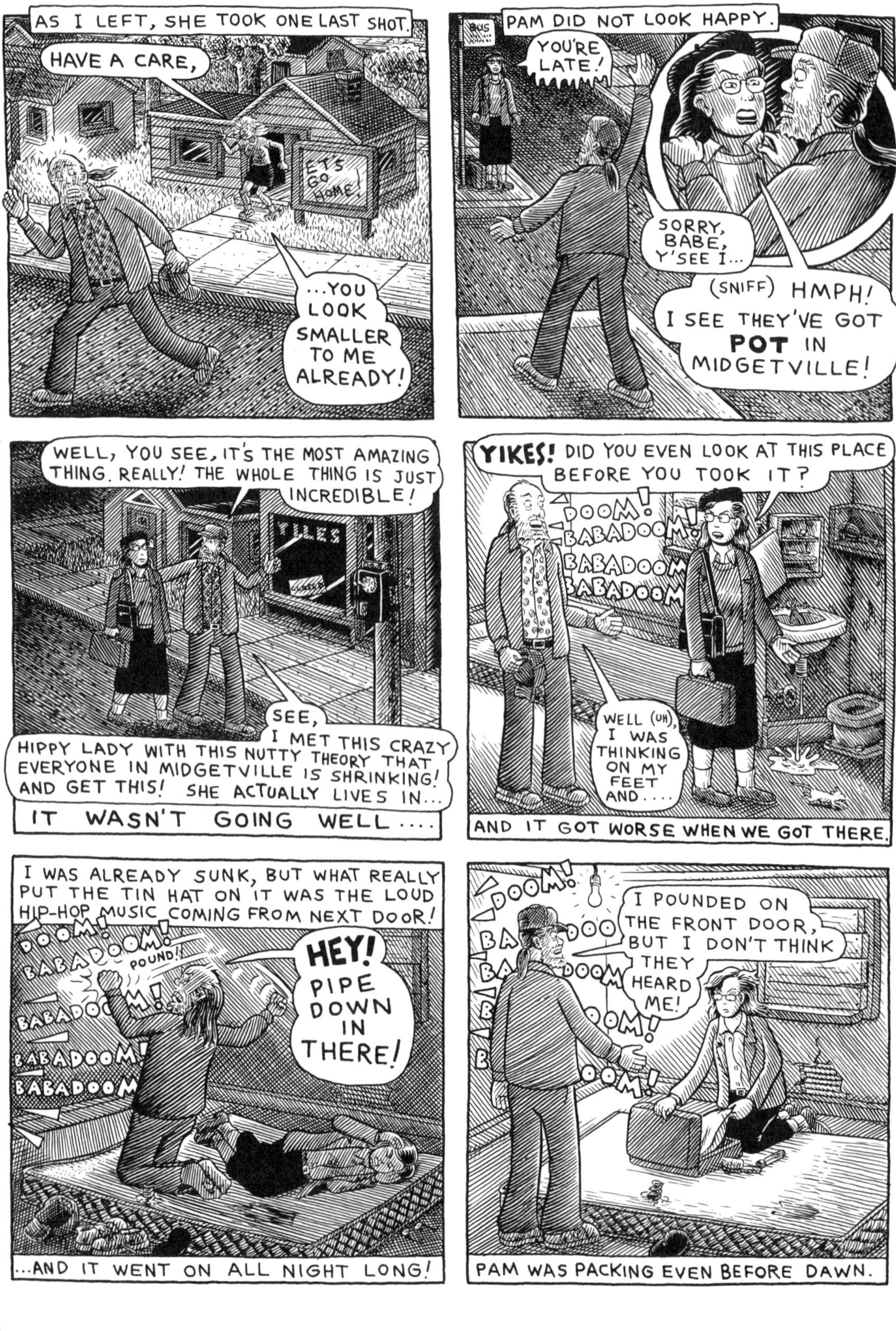
AS I LEFT, SHE TOOK ONE LAST SHOT.
HAVE A CARE,
...YOU LOOK SMALLER TO ME ALREADY!
PAM DID NOT LOOK HAPPY.
YOU'RE LATE!
SORRY, BABE, Y'SEE I...
(SNIFF) HMPH! I SEE THEY'VE GOT POT IN MIDGETVILLE!
WELL, YOU SEE, IT'S THE MOST AMAZING THING. REALLY! THE WHOLE THING IS JUST INCREDIBLE!
SEE, I MET THIS CRAZY HIPPY LADY WITH THIS NUTTY THEORY THAT EVERYONE IN MIDGETVILLE IS SHRINKING! AND GET THIS! SHE ACTUALLY LIVES IN...
IT WASN'T GOING WELL....
YIKES! DID YOU EVEN LOOK AT THIS PLACE BEFORE YOU TOOK IT?
DOOM! BABADOOM! BABADOOM BABADOOM
WELL (UH), I WAS THINKING ON MY FEET AND....
AND IT GOT WORSE WHEN WE GOT THERE.
I WAS ALREADY SUNK, BUT WHAT REALLY PUT THE TIN HAT ON IT WAS THE LOUD HIP-HOP MUSIC COMING FROM NEXT DOOR!
DOOM! BABADOOM! BABADOOM! BABADOOM! BABADOOM
POUND!
HEY! PIPE DOWN IN THERE!
...AND IT WENT ON ALL NIGHT LONG!
DOOM!
I POUNDED ON THE FRONT DOOR, BUT I DON'T THINK THEY HEARD ME!
PAM WAS PACKING EVEN BEFORE DAWN.

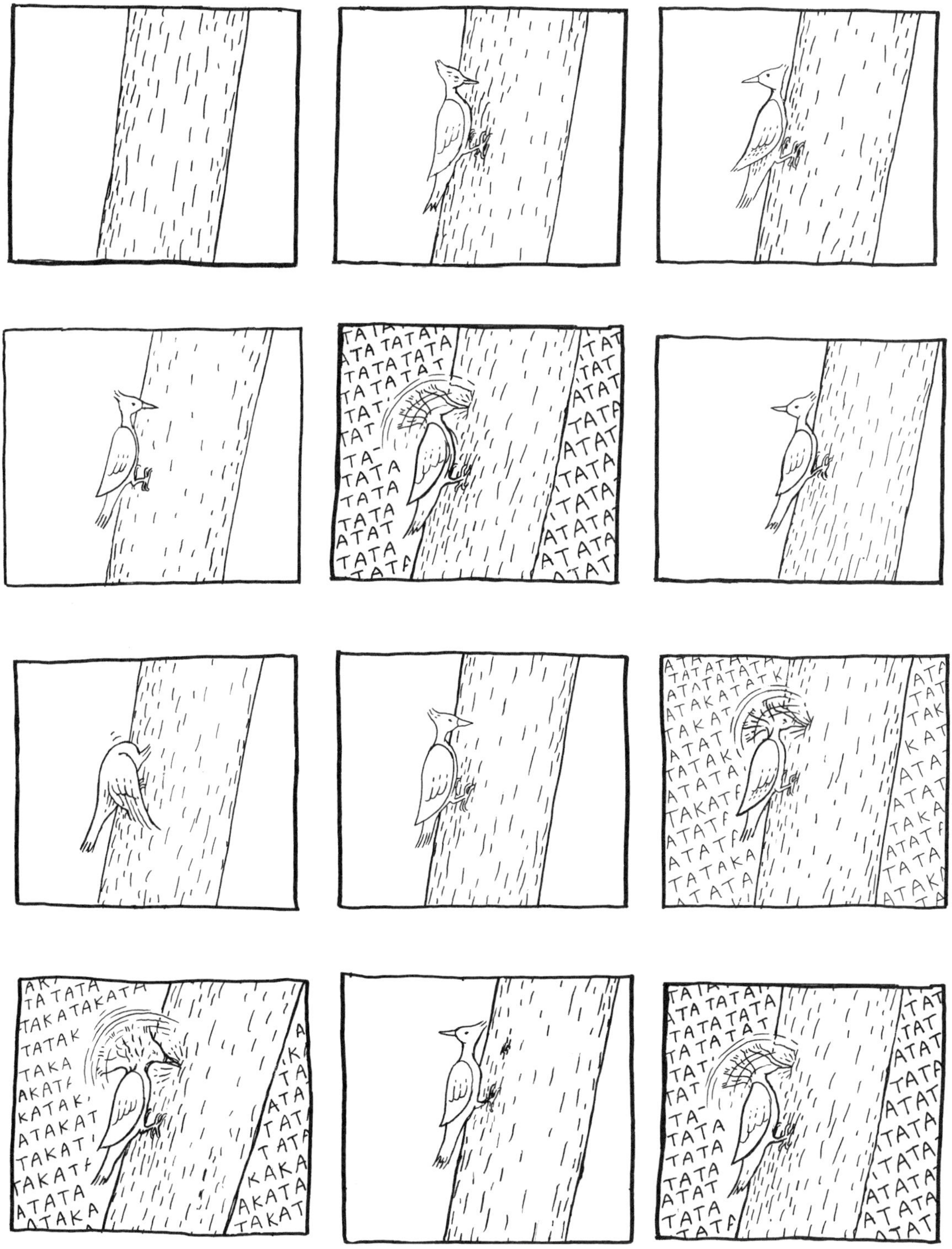
ATATATATA
TATATAT
TATATAT
TAT
TAT
TA-
TATA
TATA
TATA
ATAT
TATA
TAT
TAT
ATAT
TATA
ATAT
ATATA
TATA
TATAT
ATATA
ATATA
ATAT
TATATATA
ATATATATK
ATAKAT
TAKAT
ATAT
TATAK
TATATA
ATATA
TAKAT
ATAT
ATAT
TATAKA
ATATA
ATA
TAT
TAK
KAT
ATA
ATAT
ATAKA
TAKA
ATAT
TATA
ATAK
TA TATA
TAKATAKATA
TATAK
TAKA
AKAT
KATAK
ATAKAT
TAKAT
TAKAT
ATATA
ATAKA
TA
ATA
TAT
TATA
KAKA
AKATA
TAKAT
ATATATATA
TATATAT
TATATAT
TAT
TAT
TA-
TATA
TATA
TATA
ATAT
TATA
TAT
TAT
ATAT
TATA
ATAT
ATATA
TATA
TATAT
ATATA
ATATA
ATAT

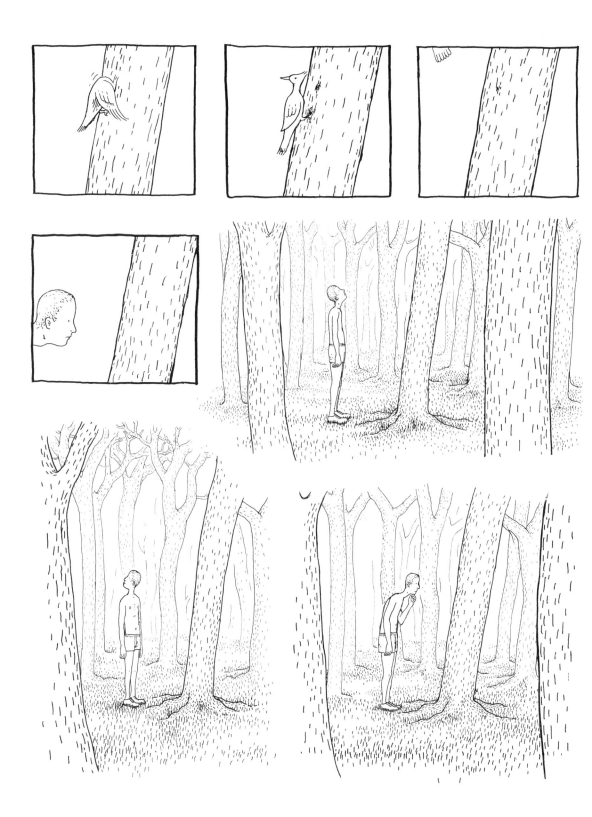

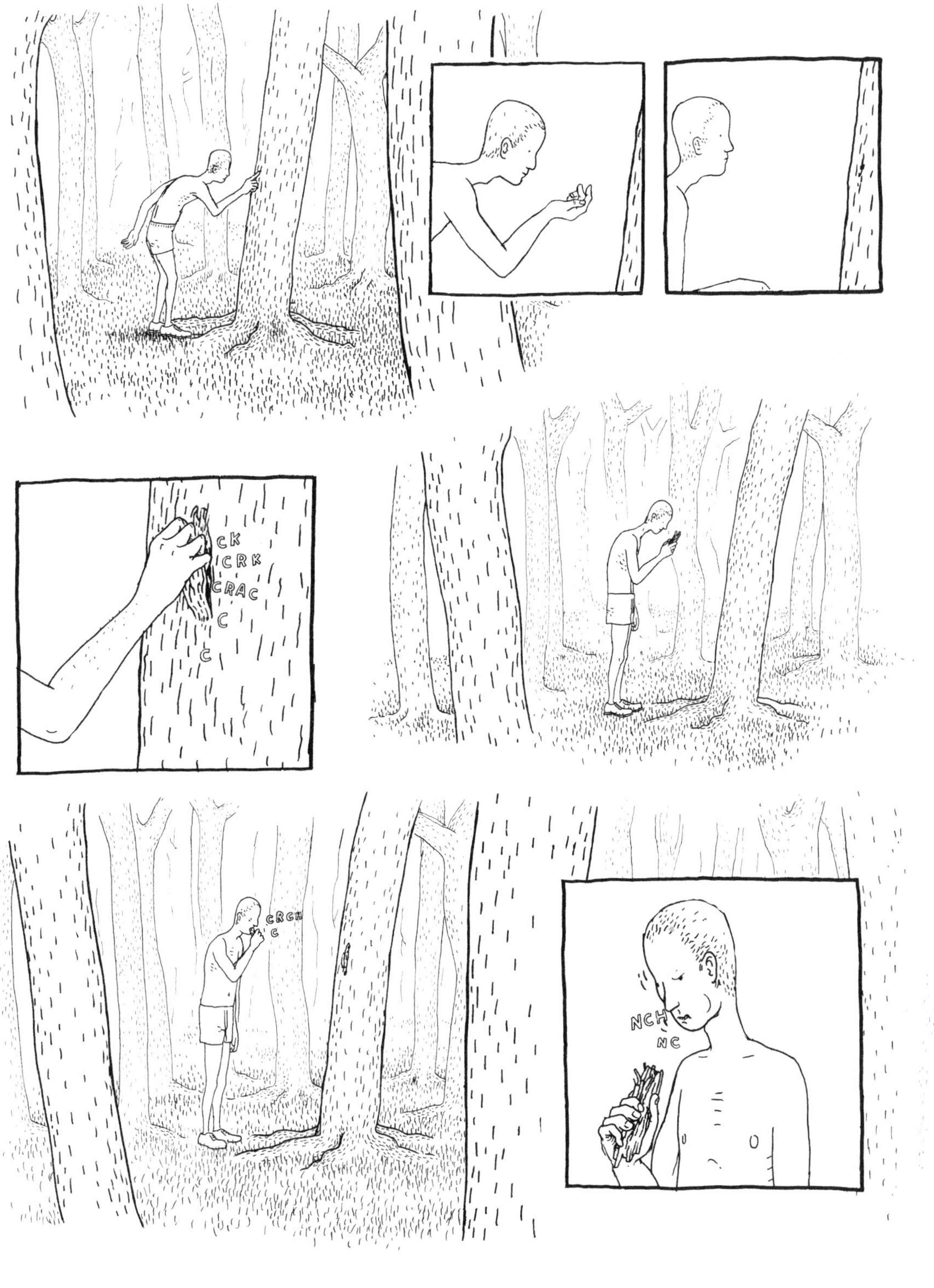
CK
CRK
CRAC
C
C
CRCH
C
NCH
NC

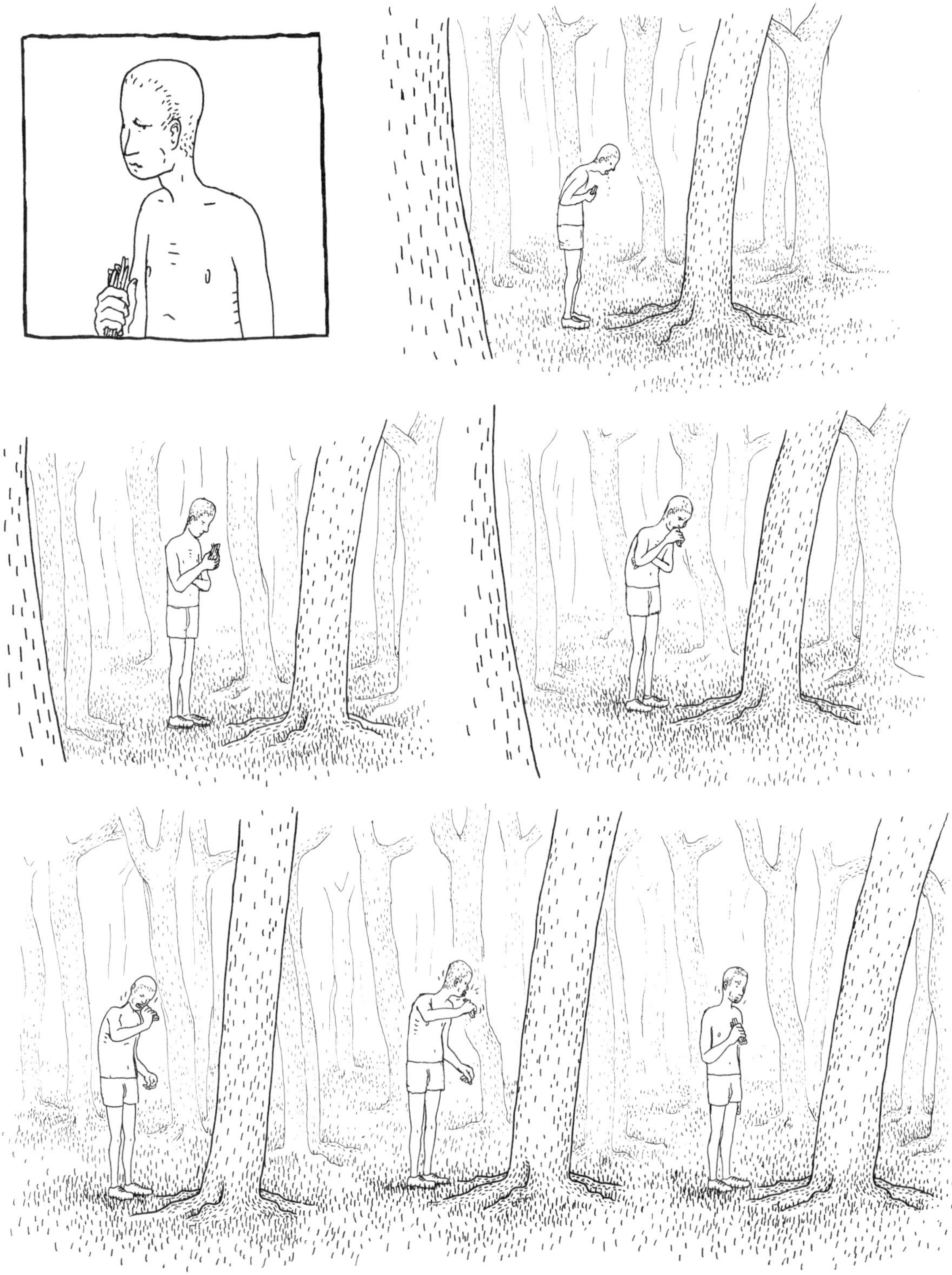

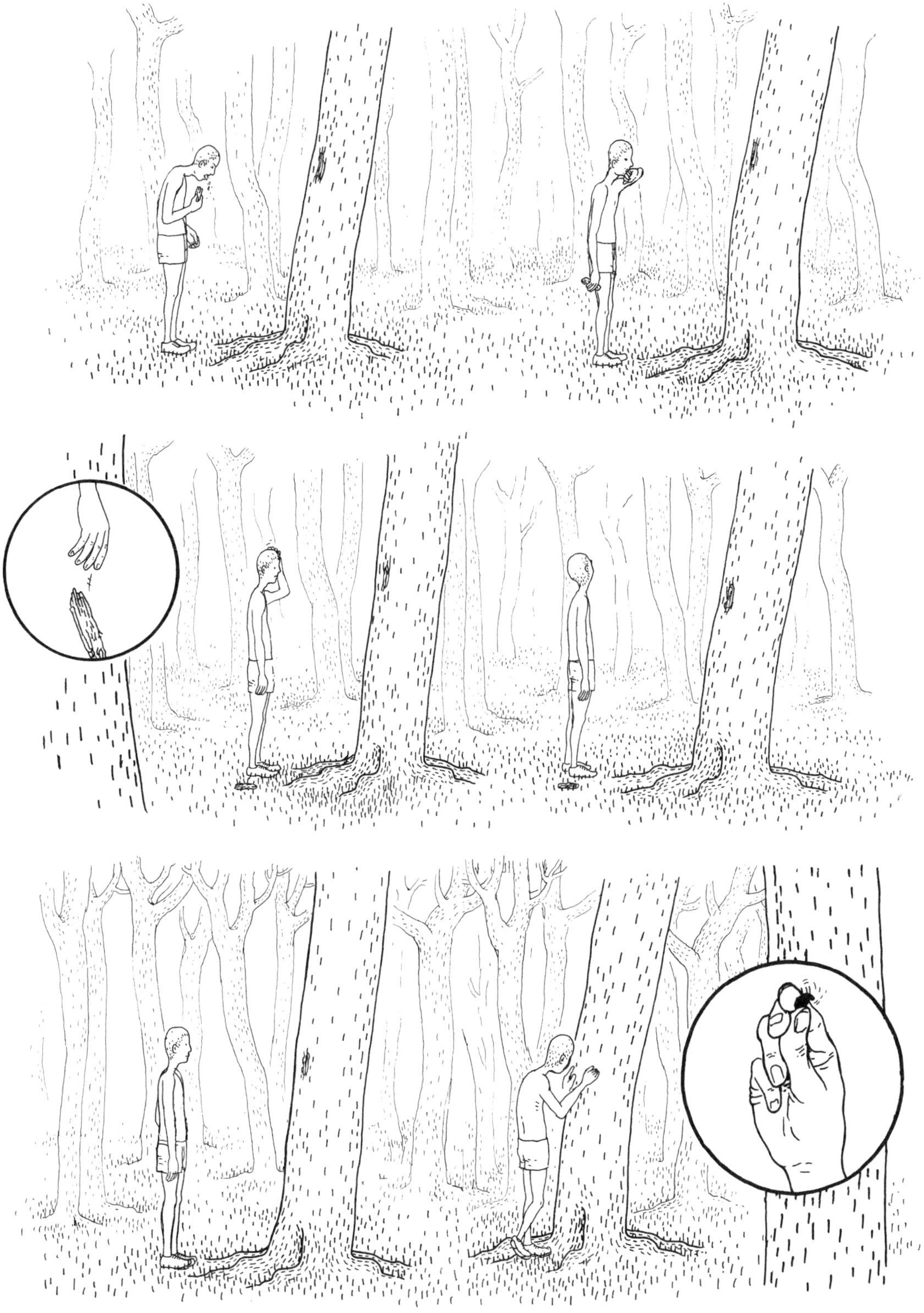

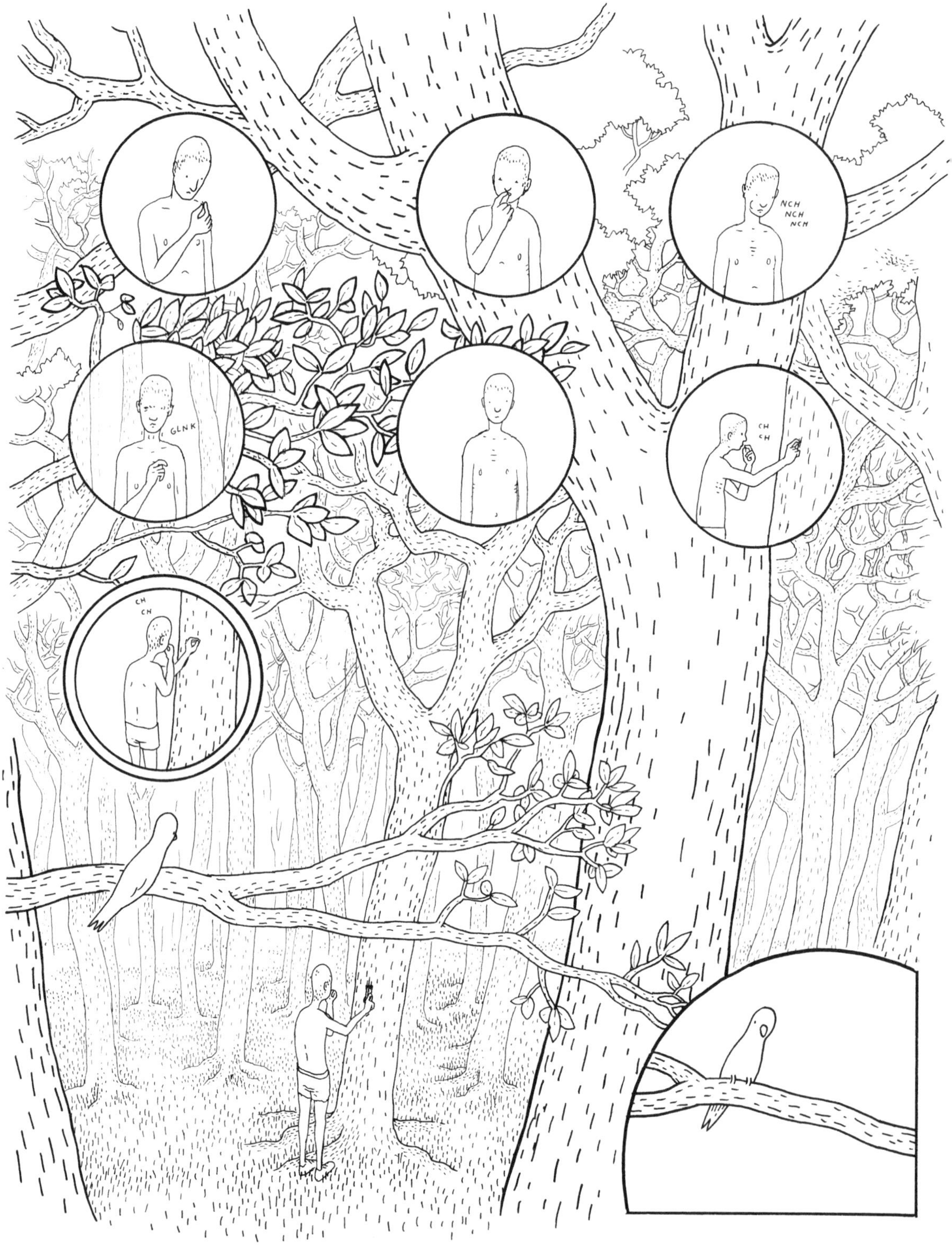
NCH
NCH
NCH
GLNK
CH
CH
CH
CH

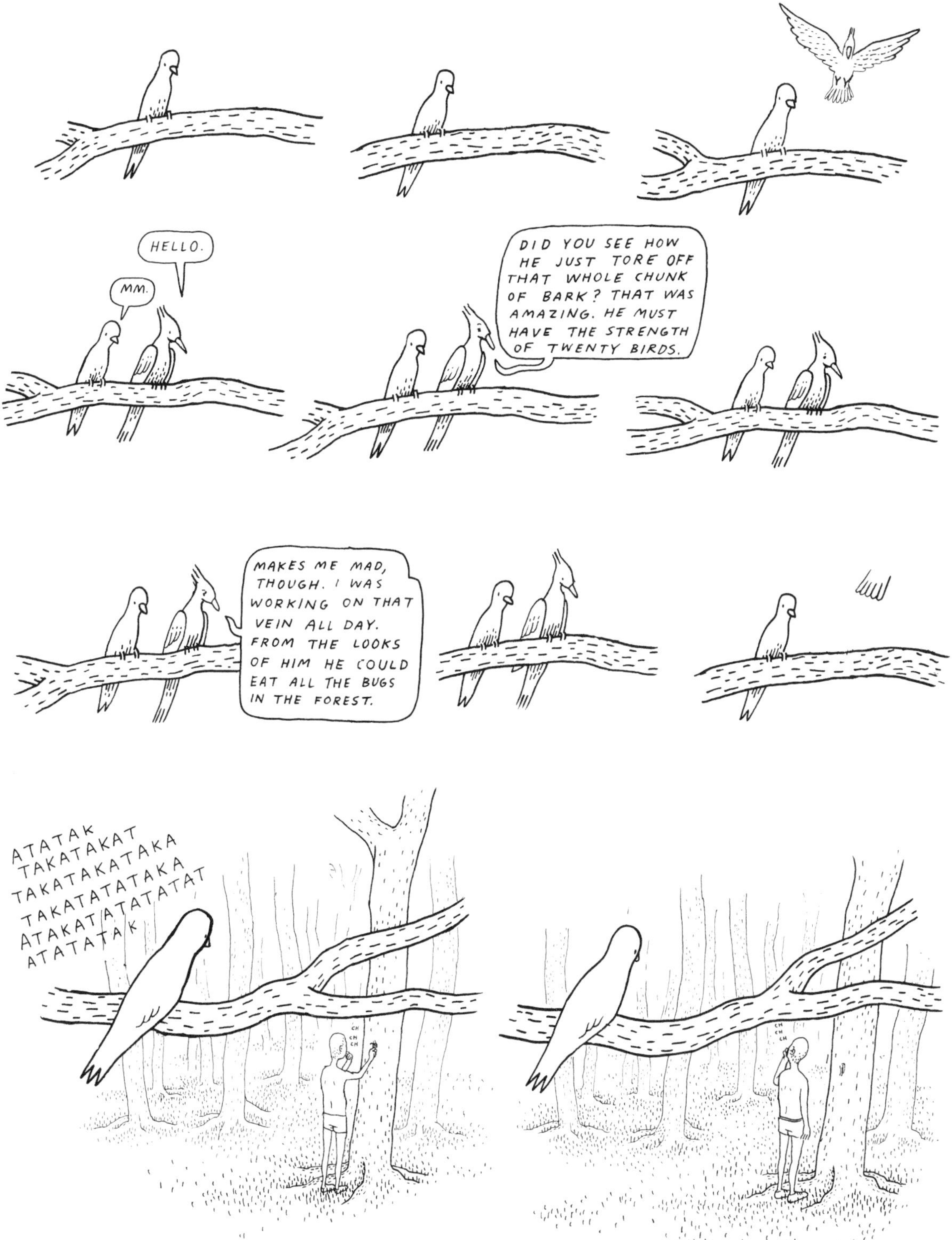
MM.
HELLO.
DID YOU SEE HOW HE JUST TORE OFF THAT WHOLE CHUNK OF BARK? THAT WAS AMAZING. HE MUST HAVE THE STRENGTH OF TWENTY BIRDS.
MAKES ME MAD, THOUGH. I WAS WORKING ON THAT VEIN ALL DAY. FROM THE LOOKS OF HIM HE COULD EAT ALL THE BUGS IN THE FOREST.
ATATAK
TAKATAKAT
TAKATAKATAKA
TAKATATATAKA
TAKATATATATAT
ATAKATATATATAK
ATATATAK

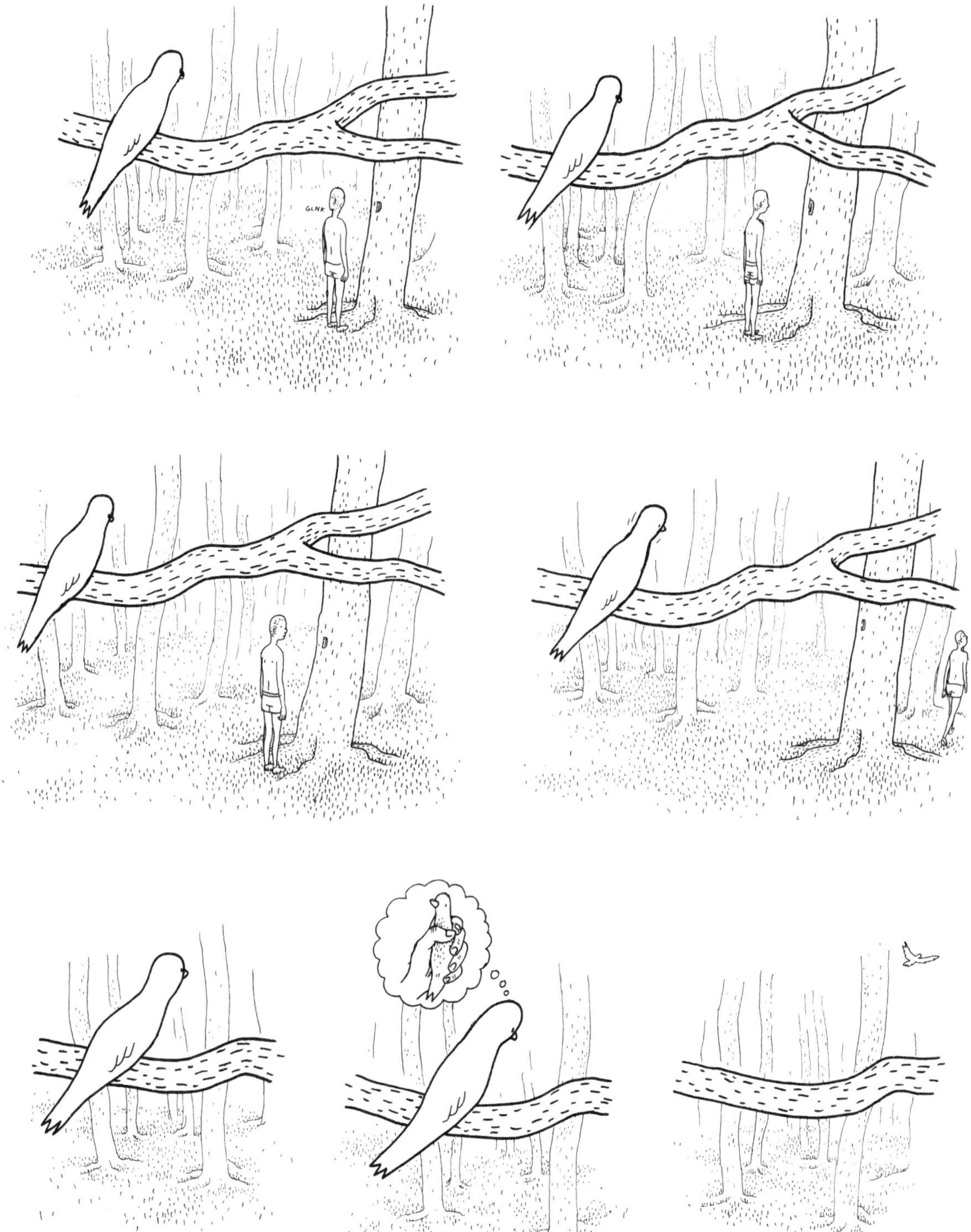
GLNK

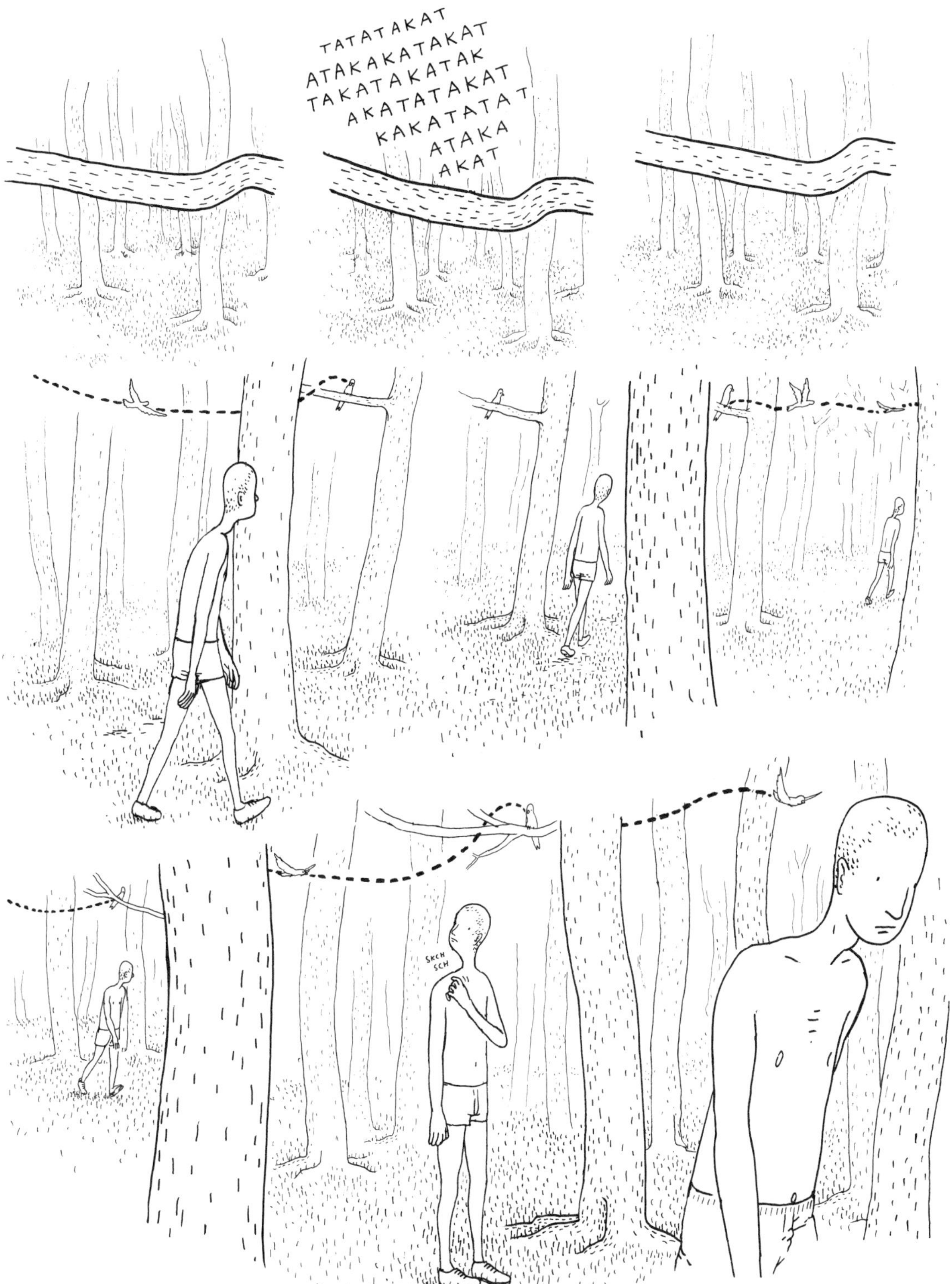
TATATAKAT
ATAKAKATAKAT
TAKATAKATAK
AKATATAKAT
KAKATATAT
ATAKA
AKAT
SKCH
SCH

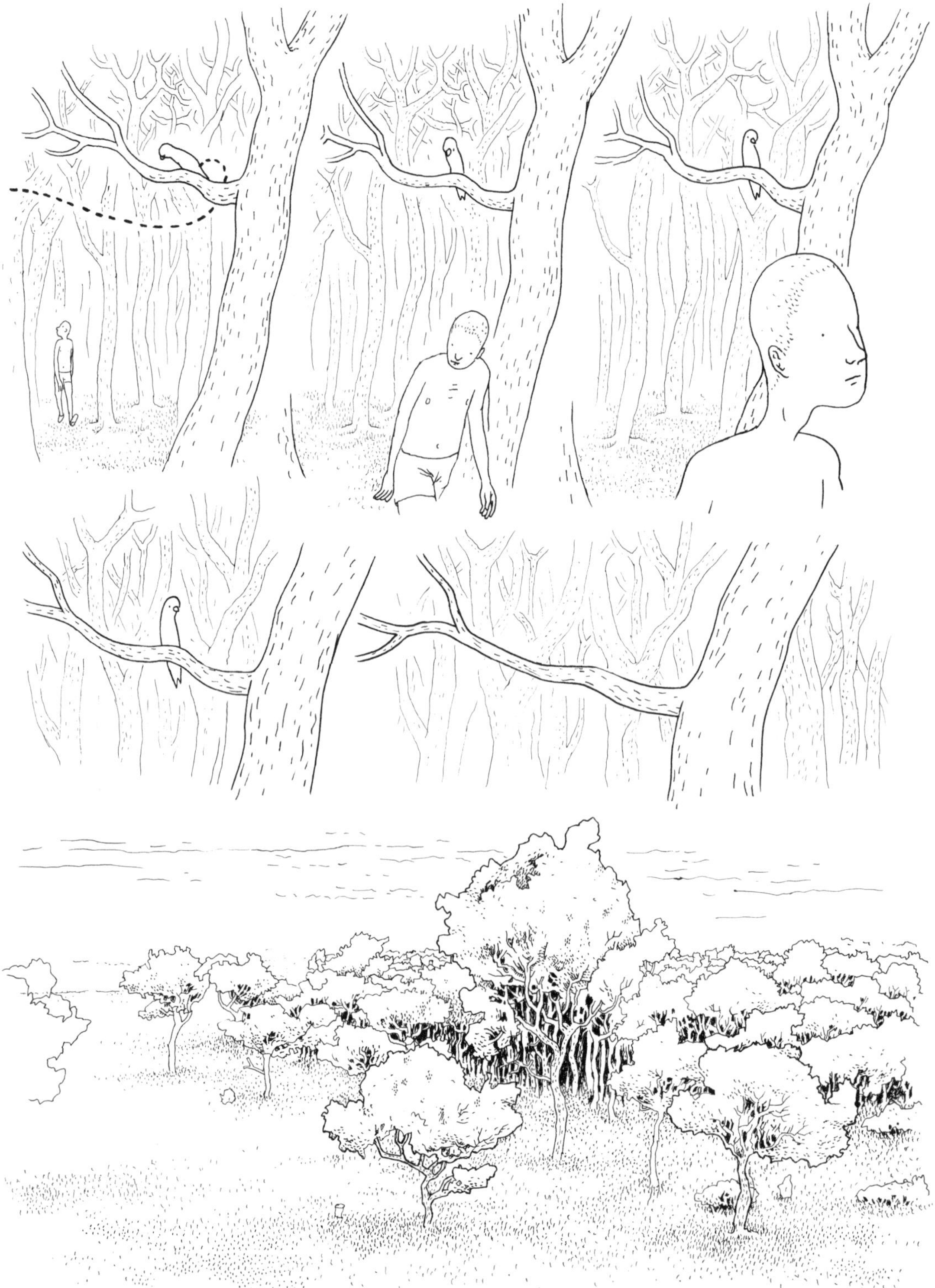

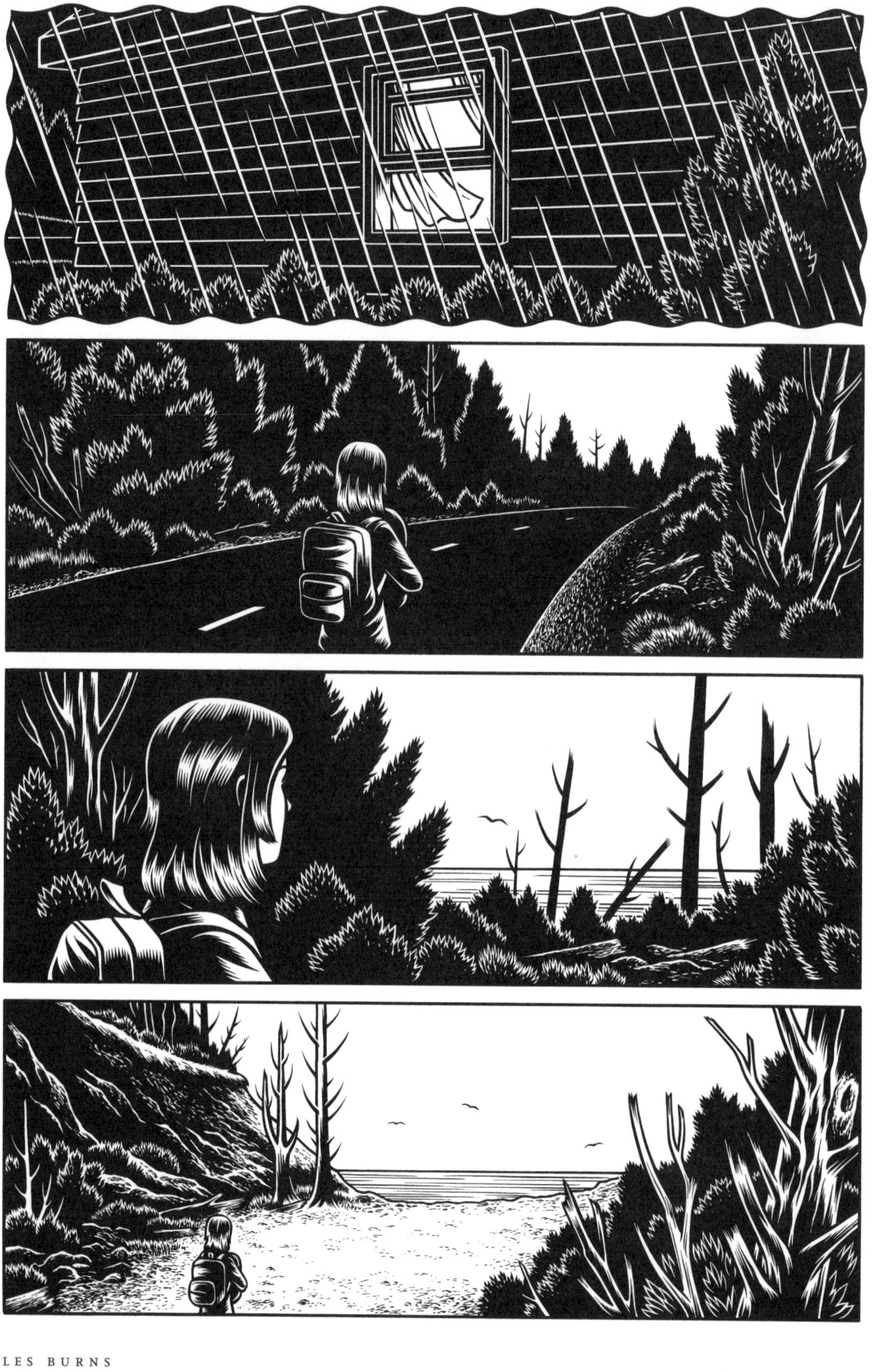

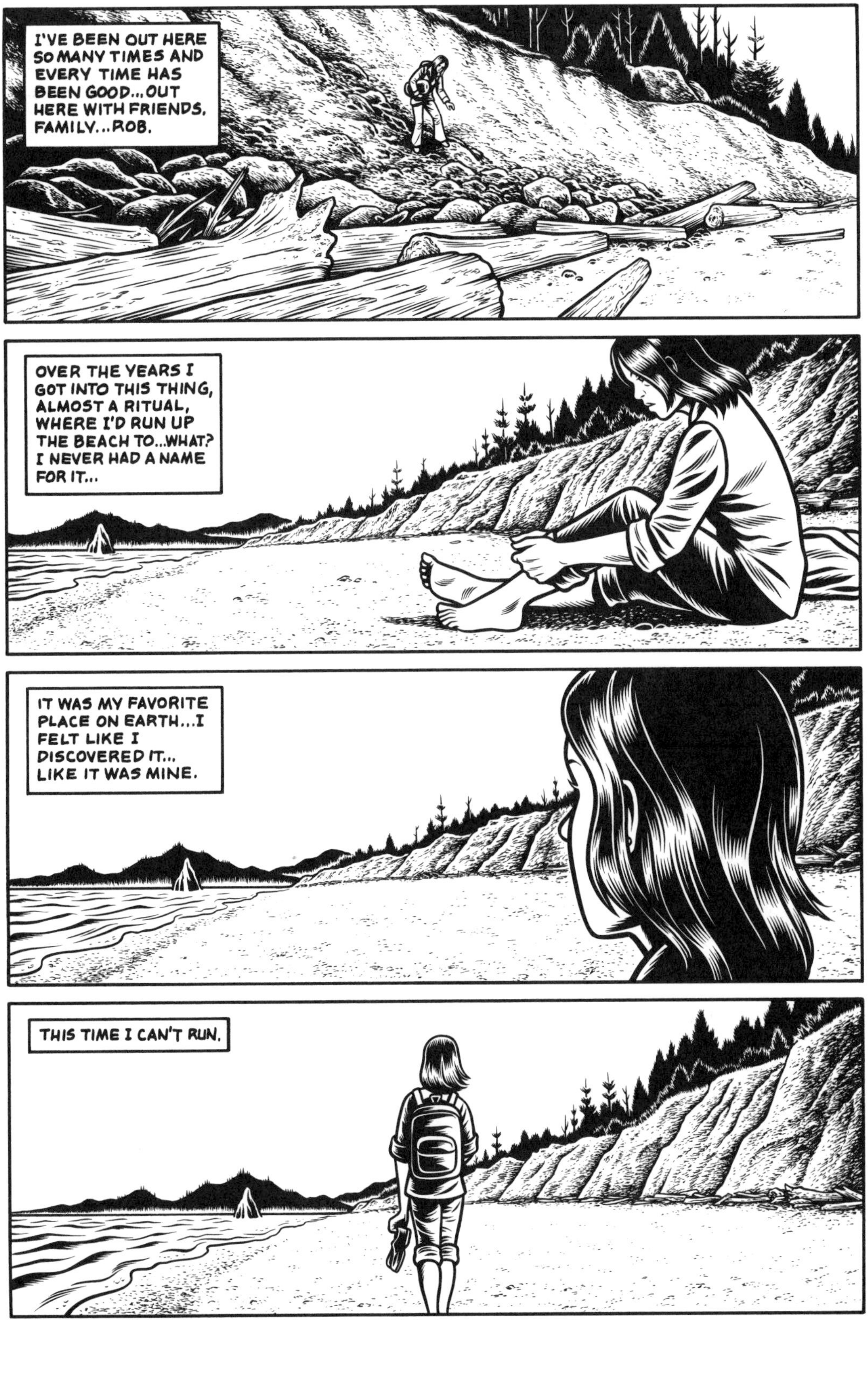
I'VE BEEN OUT HERE SO MANY TIMES AND EVERY TIME HAS BEEN GOOD... OUT HERE WITH FRIENDS, FAMILY... ROB.
OVER THE YEARS I GOT INTO THIS THING, ALMOST A RITUAL, WHERE I'D RUN UP THE BEACH TO... WHAT? I NEVER HAD A NAME FOR IT...
IT WAS MY FAVORITE PLACE ON EARTH... I FELT LIKE I DISCOVERED IT... LIKE IT WAS MINE.
THIS TIME I CAN'T RUN.

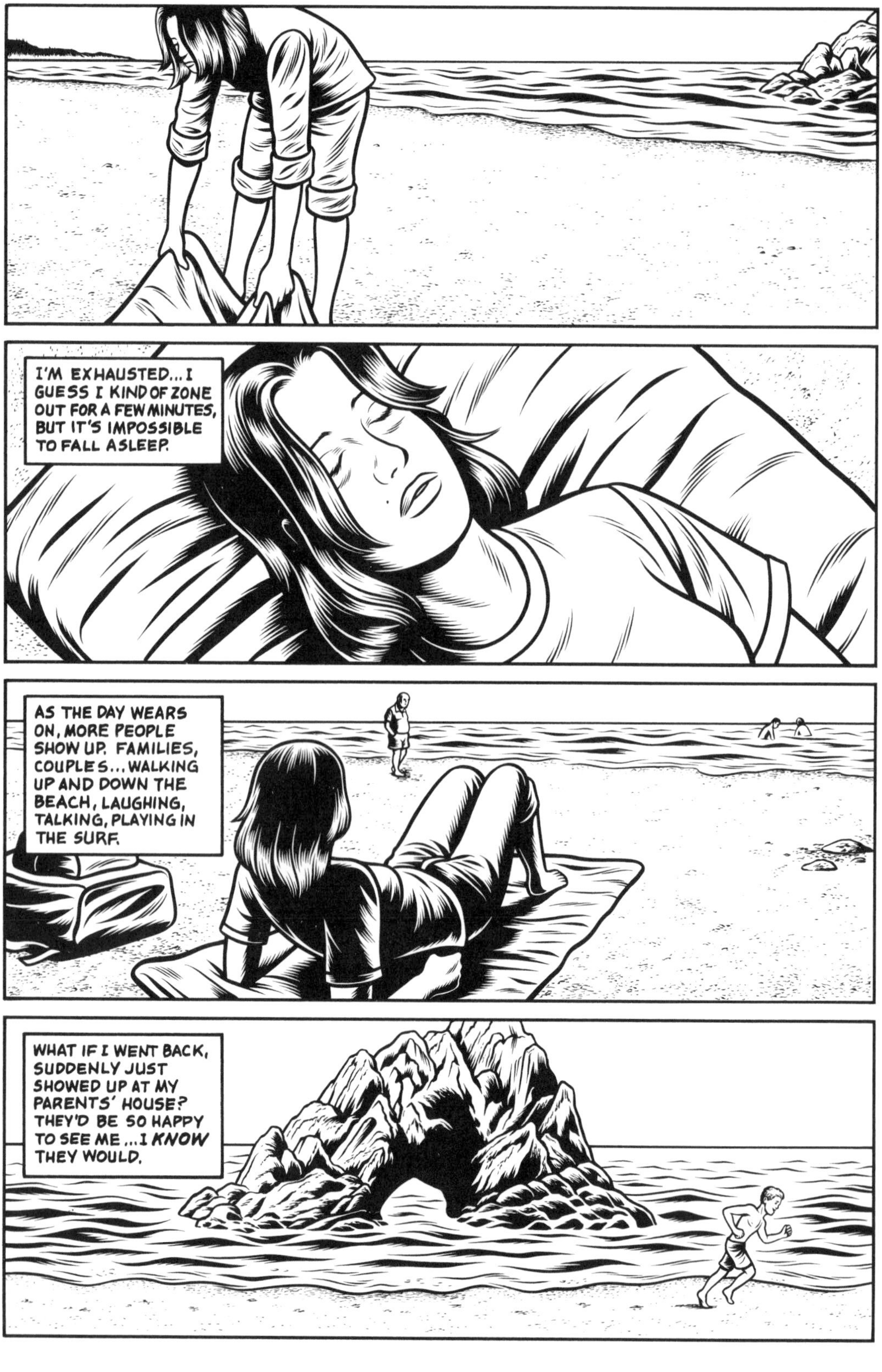
I'M EXHAUSTED... I GUESS I KIND OF ZONE OUT FOR A FEW MINUTES, BUT IT'S IMPOSSIBLE TO FALL ASLEEP.
AS THE DAY WEARS ON, MORE PEOPLE SHOW UP. FAMILIES, COUPLES... WALKING UP AND DOWN THE BEACH, LAUGHING, TALKING, PLAYING IN THE SURF.
WHAT IF I WENT BACK, SUDDENLY JUST SHOWED UP AT MY PARENTS' HOUSE? THEY'D BE SO HAPPY TO SEE ME... I *KNOW* THEY WOULD.

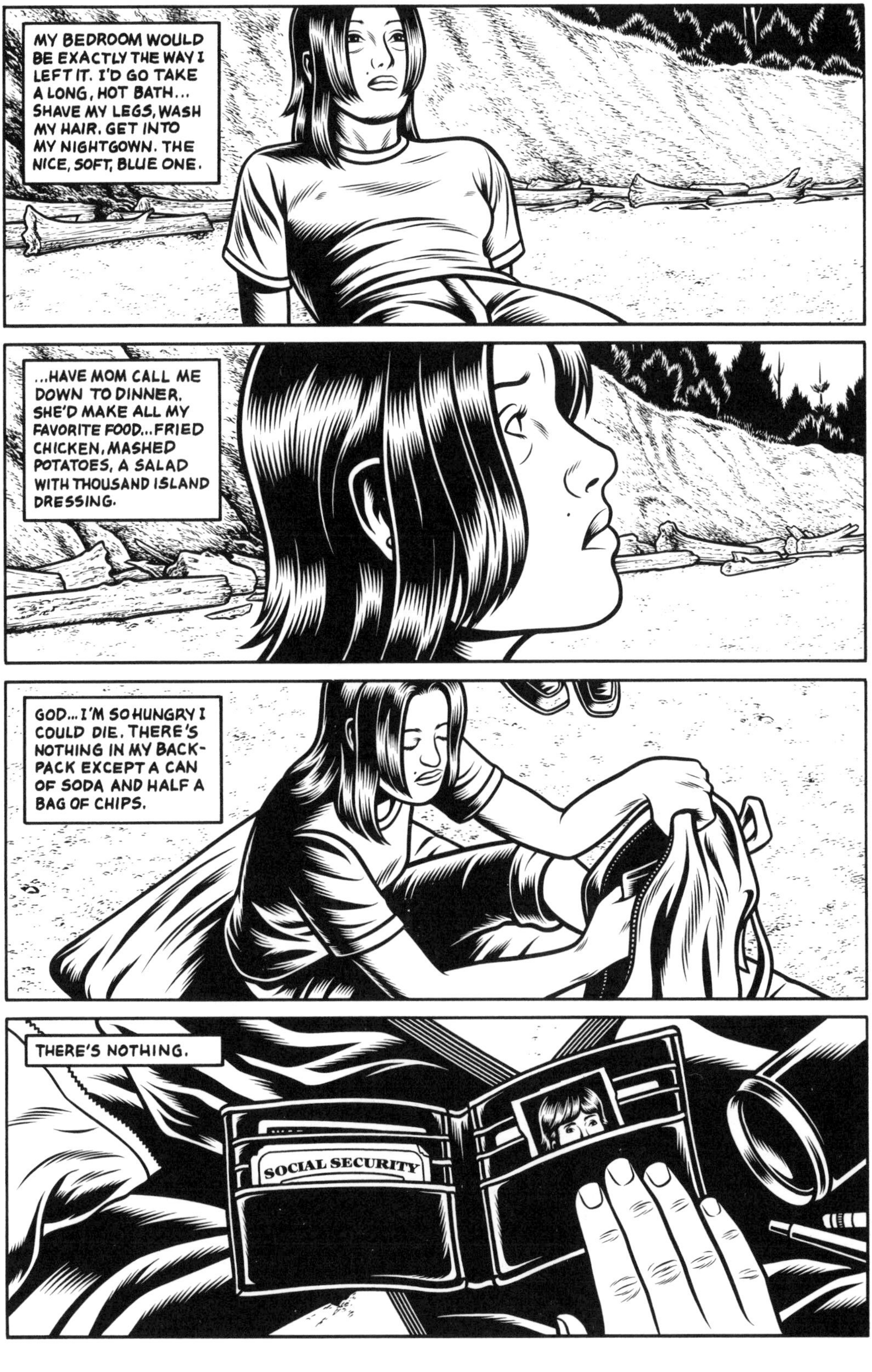
MY BEDROOM WOULD BE EXACTLY THE WAY I LEFT IT. I'D GO TAKE A LONG, HOT BATH... SHAVE MY LEGS, WASH MY HAIR. GET INTO MY NIGHTGOWN. THE NICE, SOFT, BLUE ONE.
...HAVE MOM CALL ME DOWN TO DINNER. SHE'D MAKE ALL MY FAVORITE FOOD... FRIED CHICKEN, MASHED POTATOES, A SALAD WITH THOUSAND ISLAND DRESSING.
GOD... I'M SO HUNGRY I COULD DIE. THERE'S NOTHING IN MY BACK-PACK EXCEPT A CAN OF SODA AND HALF A BAG OF CHIPS.
THERE'S NOTHING.
SOCIAL SECURITY

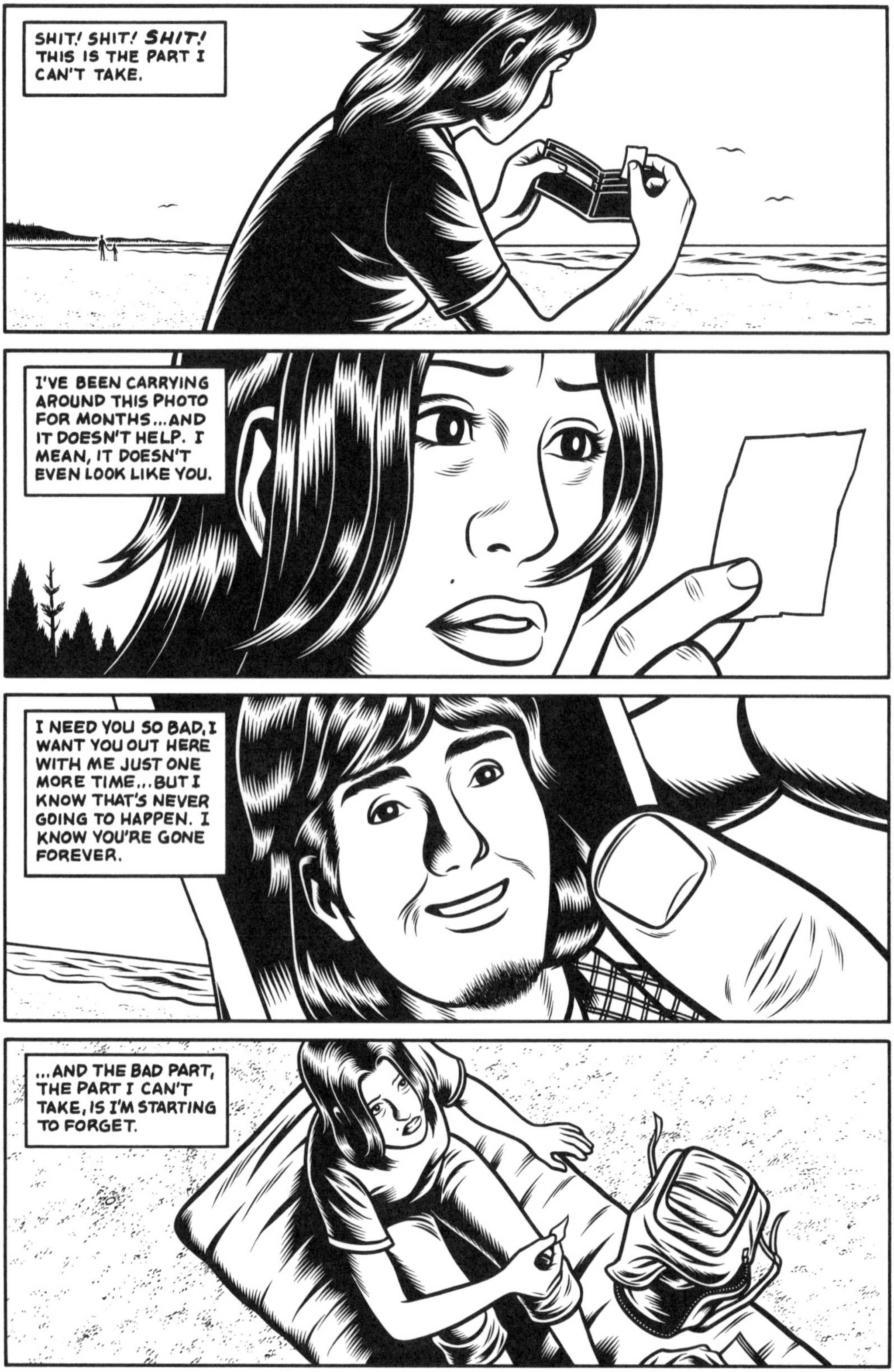
SHIT! SHIT! SHIT! THIS IS THE PART I CAN'T TAKE.
I'VE BEEN CARRYING AROUND THIS PHOTO FOR MONTHS...AND IT DOESN'T HELP. I MEAN, IT DOESN'T EVEN LOOK LIKE YOU.
I NEED YOU SO BAD, I WANT YOU OUT HERE WITH ME JUST ONE MORE TIME...BUT I KNOW THAT'S NEVER GOING TO HAPPEN. I KNOW YOU'RE GONE FOREVER.
...AND THE BAD PART, THE PART I CAN'T TAKE, IS I'M STARTING TO FORGET.

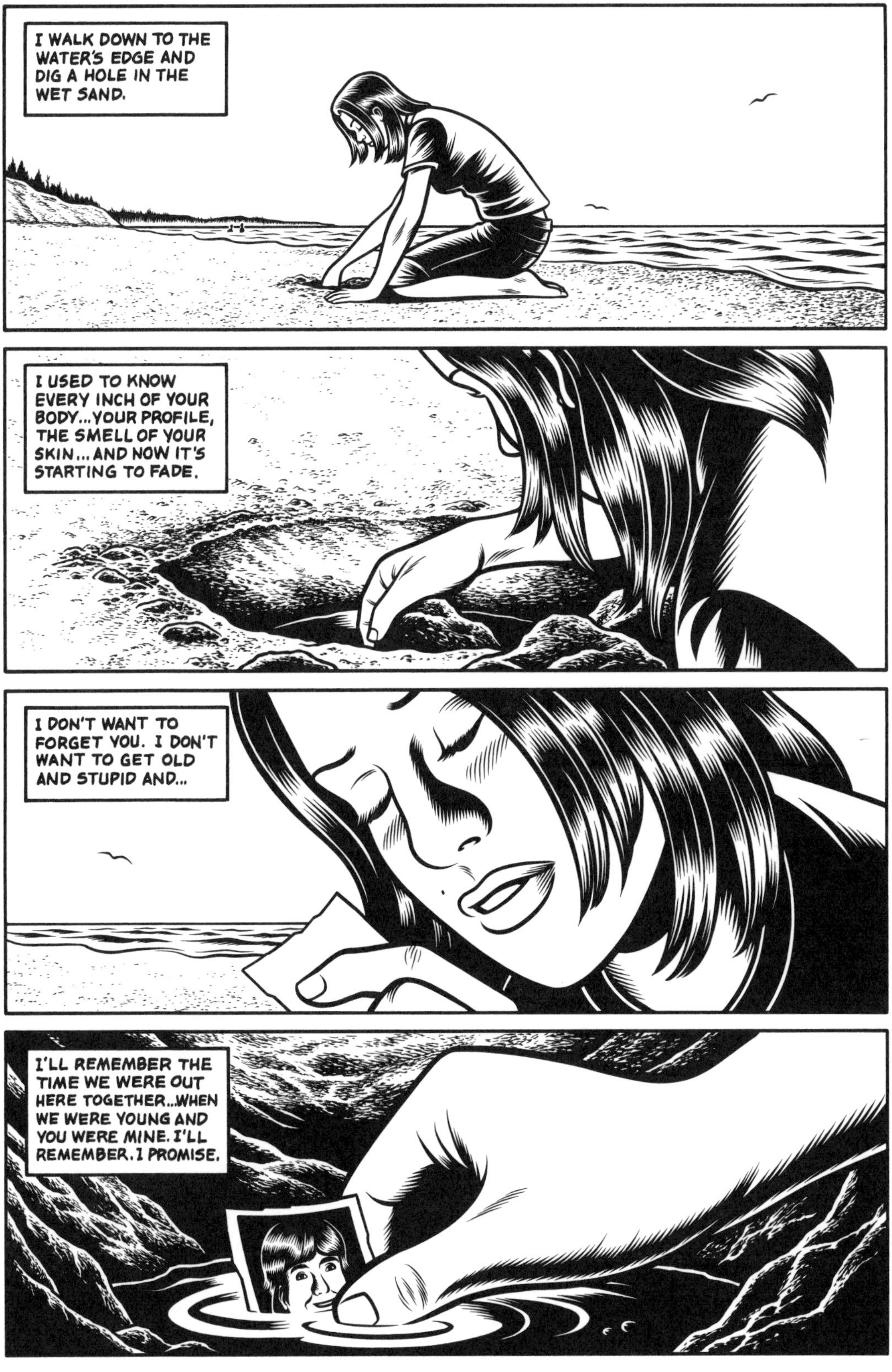
I WALK DOWN TO THE WATER'S EDGE AND DIG A HOLE IN THE WET SAND.
I USED TO KNOW EVERY INCH OF YOUR BODY... YOUR PROFILE, THE SMELL OF YOUR SKIN... AND NOW IT'S STARTING TO FADE.
I DON'T WANT TO FORGET YOU. I DON'T WANT TO GET OLD AND STUPID AND...
I'LL REMEMBER THE TIME WE WERE OUT HERE TOGETHER... WHEN WE WERE YOUNG AND YOU WERE MINE. I'LL REMEMBER. I PROMISE.

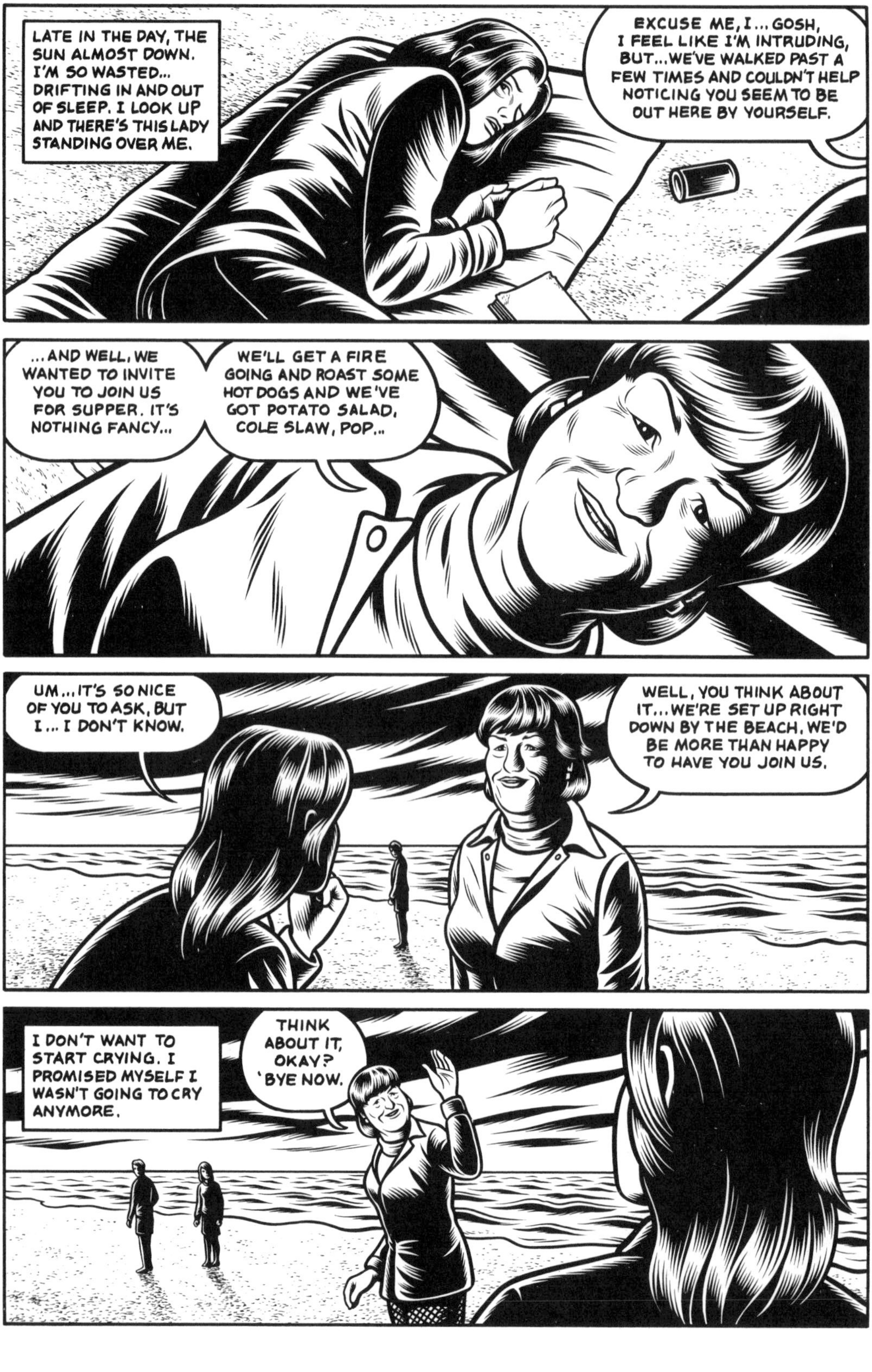
LATE IN THE DAY, THE SUN ALMOST DOWN. I'M SO WASTED... DRIFTING IN AND OUT OF SLEEP. I LOOK UP AND THERE'S THIS LADY STANDING OVER ME.
EXCUSE ME, I... GOSH, I FEEL LIKE I'M INTRUDING, BUT... WE'VE WALKED PAST A FEW TIMES AND COULDN'T HELP NOTICING YOU SEEM TO BE OUT HERE BY YOURSELF.
...AND WELL, WE WANTED TO INVITE YOU TO JOIN US FOR SUPPER. IT'S NOTHING FANCY...
WE'LL GET A FIRE GOING AND ROAST SOME HOT DOGS AND WE'VE GOT POTATO SALAD, COLE SLAW, POP...
UM... IT'S SO NICE OF YOU TO ASK, BUT I... I DON'T KNOW.
WELL, YOU THINK ABOUT IT... WE'RE SET UP RIGHT DOWN BY THE BEACH, WE'D BE MORE THAN HAPPY TO HAVE YOU JOIN US.
I DON'T WANT TO START CRYING. I PROMISED MYSELF I WASN'T GOING TO CRY ANYMORE.
THINK ABOUT IT, OKAY? 'BYE NOW.

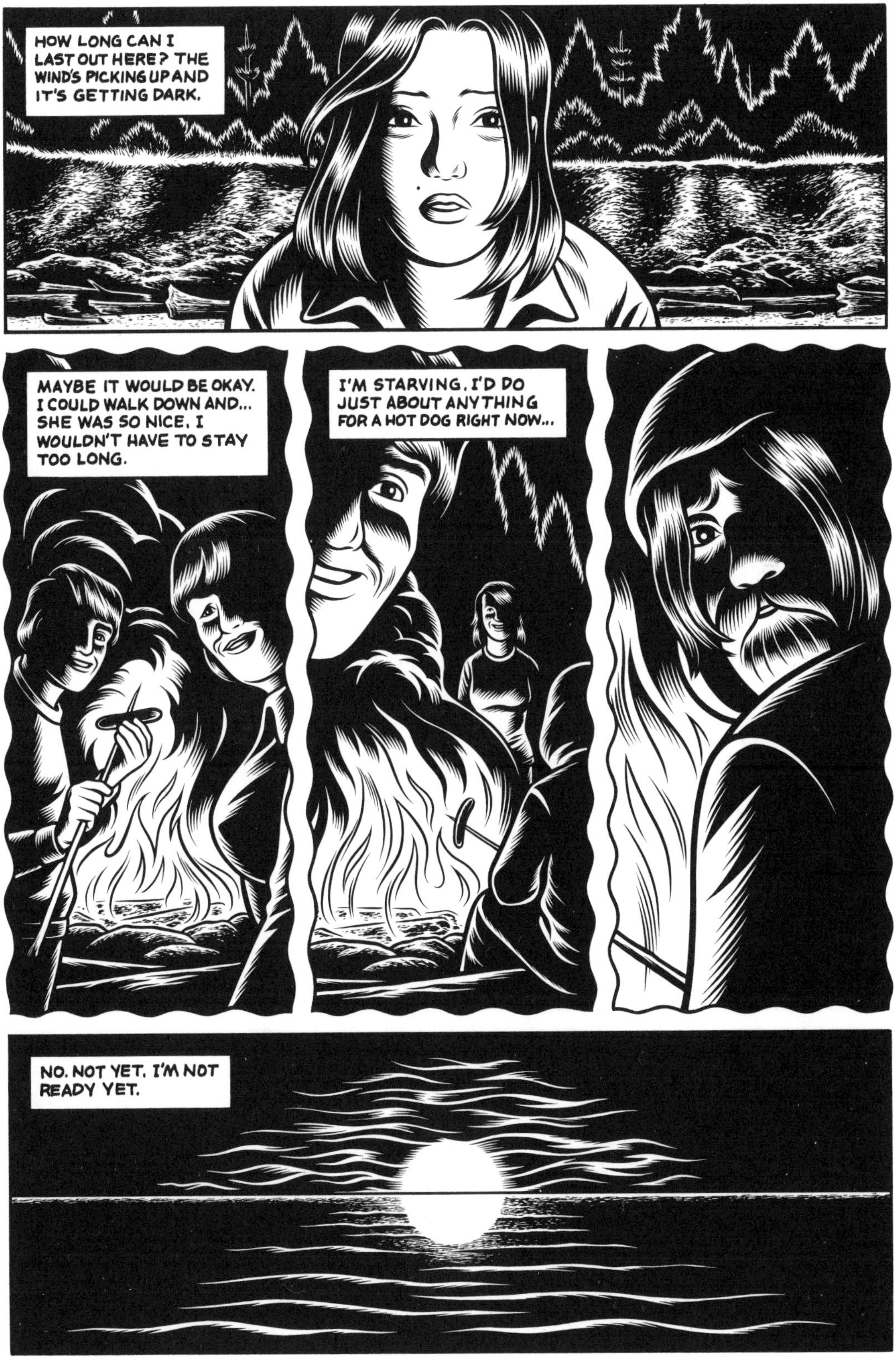
HOW LONG CAN I LAST OUT HERE? THE WIND'S PICKING UP AND IT'S GETTING DARK.
MAYBE IT WOULD BE OKAY. I COULD WALK DOWN AND... SHE WAS SO NICE. I WOULDN'T HAVE TO STAY TOO LONG.
I'M STARVING. I'D DO JUST ABOUT ANYTHING FOR A HOT DOG RIGHT NOW...
NO. NOT YET. I'M NOT READY YET.

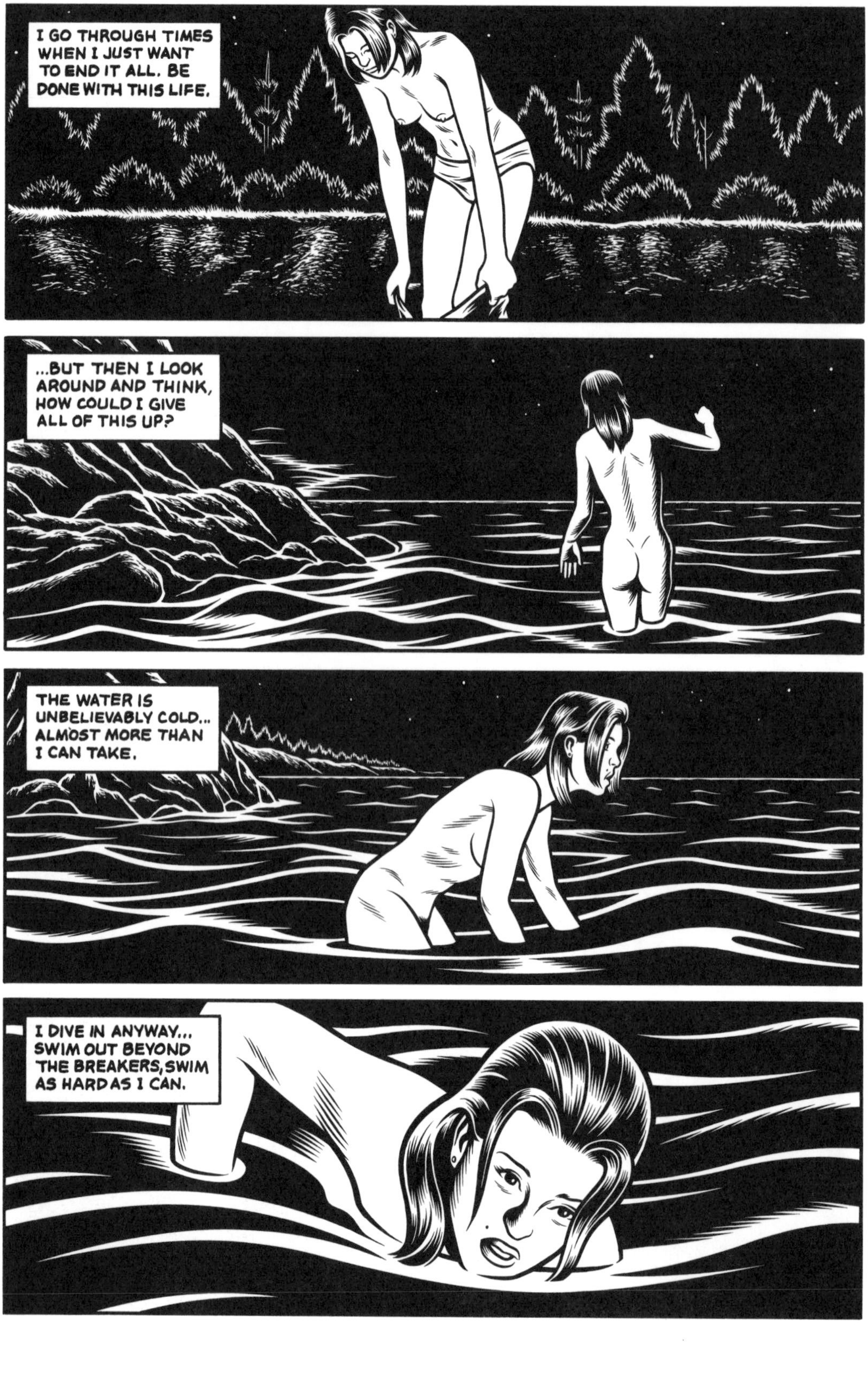
I GO THROUGH TIMES WHEN I JUST WANT TO END IT ALL. BE DONE WITH THIS LIFE.
...BUT THEN I LOOK AROUND AND THINK, HOW COULD I GIVE ALL OF THIS UP?
THE WATER IS UNBELIEVABLY COLD... ALMOST MORE THAN I CAN TAKE.
I DIVE IN ANYWAY... SWIM OUT BEYOND THE BREAKERS, SWIM AS HARD AS I CAN.

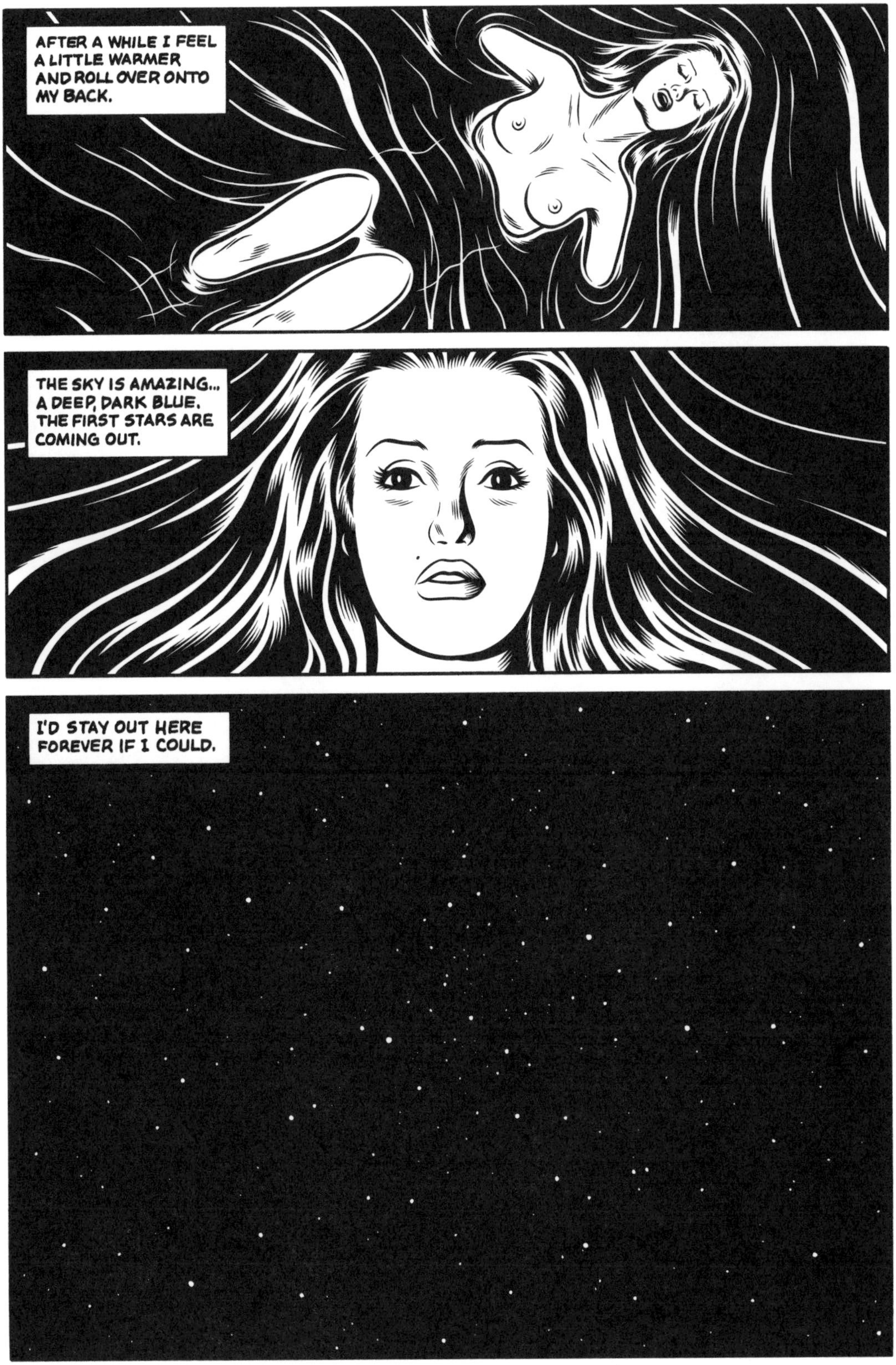
AFTER A WHILE I FEEL A LITTLE WARMER AND ROLL OVER ONTO MY BACK.
THE SKY IS AMAZING... A DEEP, DARK BLUE. THE FIRST STARS ARE COMING OUT.
I'D STAY OUT HERE FOREVER IF I COULD.

RANK NATIVE WEED

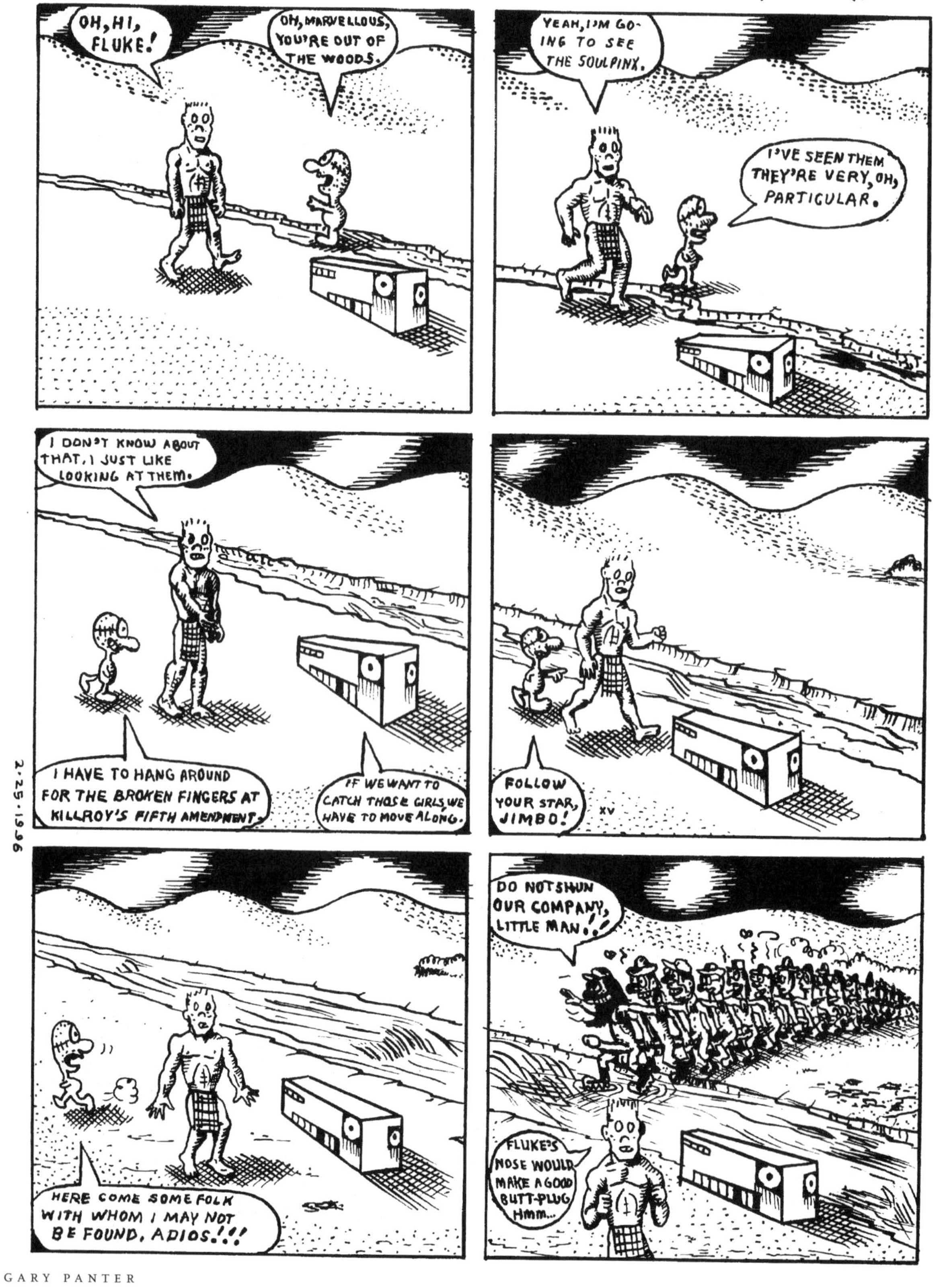
OH, HI, FLUKE!
OH, MARVELLOUS, YOU'RE OUT OF THE WOODS.
YEAH, I'M GOING TO SEE THE SOULPINX.
I'VE SEEN THEM THEY'RE VERY, OH, PARTICULAR.
I DON'T KNOW ABOUT THAT, I JUST LIKE LOOKING AT THEM.
I HAVE TO HANG AROUND FOR THE BROKEN FINGERS AT KILLROY'S FIFTH AMENDMENT.
IF WE WANT TO CATCH THOSE GIRLS, WE HAVE TO MOVE ALONG.
FOLLOW YOUR STAR, JIMBO!
XV
HERE COME SOME FOLK WITH WHOM I MAY NOT BE FOUND, ADIOS.!.!!
DO NOT SHUN OUR COMPANY, LITTLE MAN.!.!
FLUKE'S NOSE WOULD MAKE A GOOD BUTT-PLUG HMM...
2.25.1996

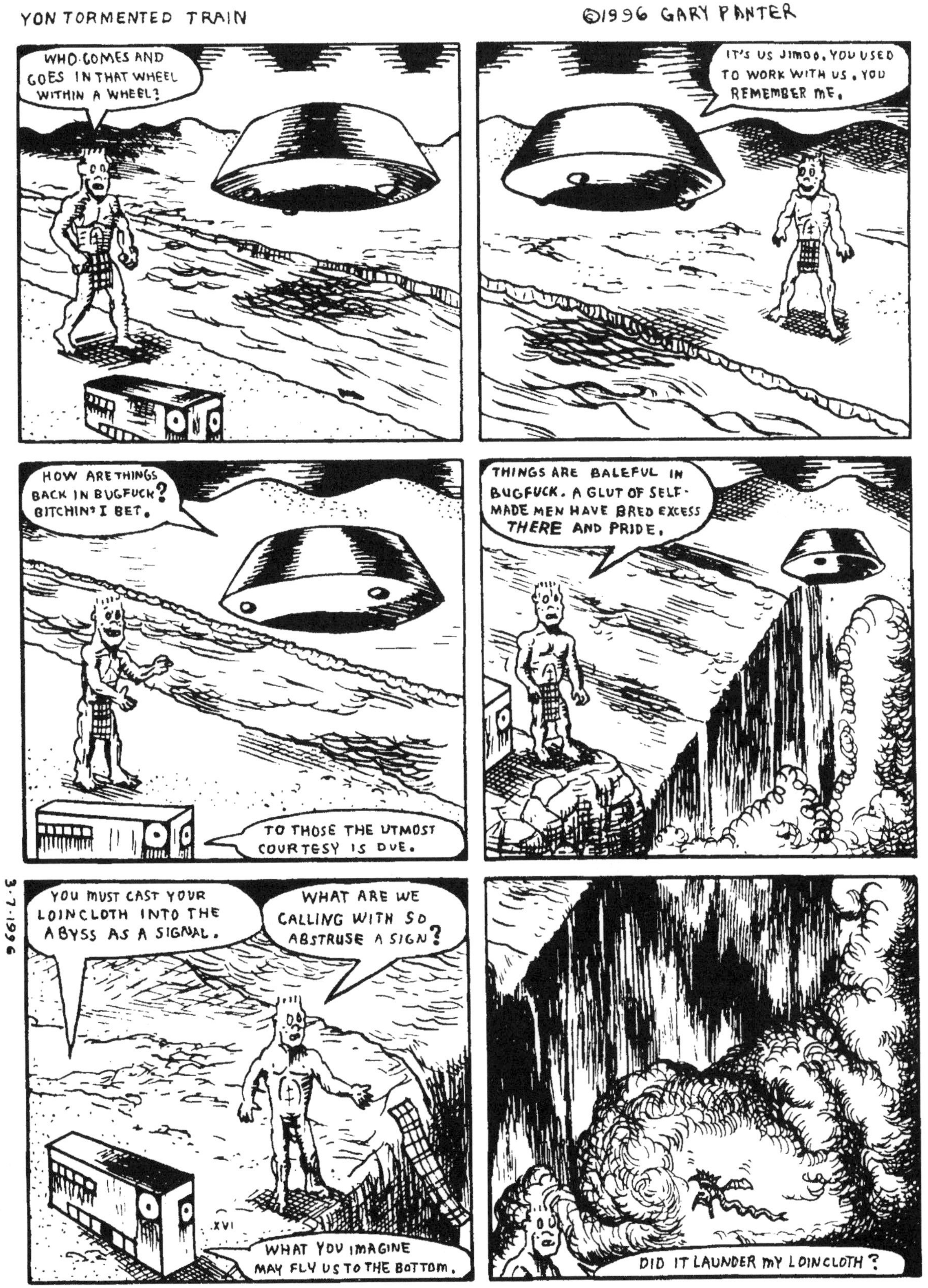
YON TORMENTED TRAIN
©1996 GARY PANTER
WHO COMES AND GOES IN THAT WHEEL WITHIN A WHEEL?
IT'S US JIMBO. YOU USED TO WORK WITH US. YOU REMEMBER ME.
HOW ARE THINGS BACK IN BUGFUCK? BITCHIN' I BET.
TO THOSE THE UTMOST COURTESY IS DUE.
THINGS ARE BALEFUL IN BUGFUCK. A GLUT OF SELF-MADE MEN HAVE BRED EXCESS THERE AND PRIDE.
3-7-1996
YOU MUST CAST YOUR LOINCLOTH INTO THE ABYSS AS A SIGNAL.
WHAT ARE WE CALLING WITH SO ABSTRUSE A SIGN?
XVI
WHAT YOU IMAGINE MAY FLY US TO THE BOTTOM.
DID IT LAUNDER MY LOINCLOTH?

NOW MOVE THEE, GERYON!

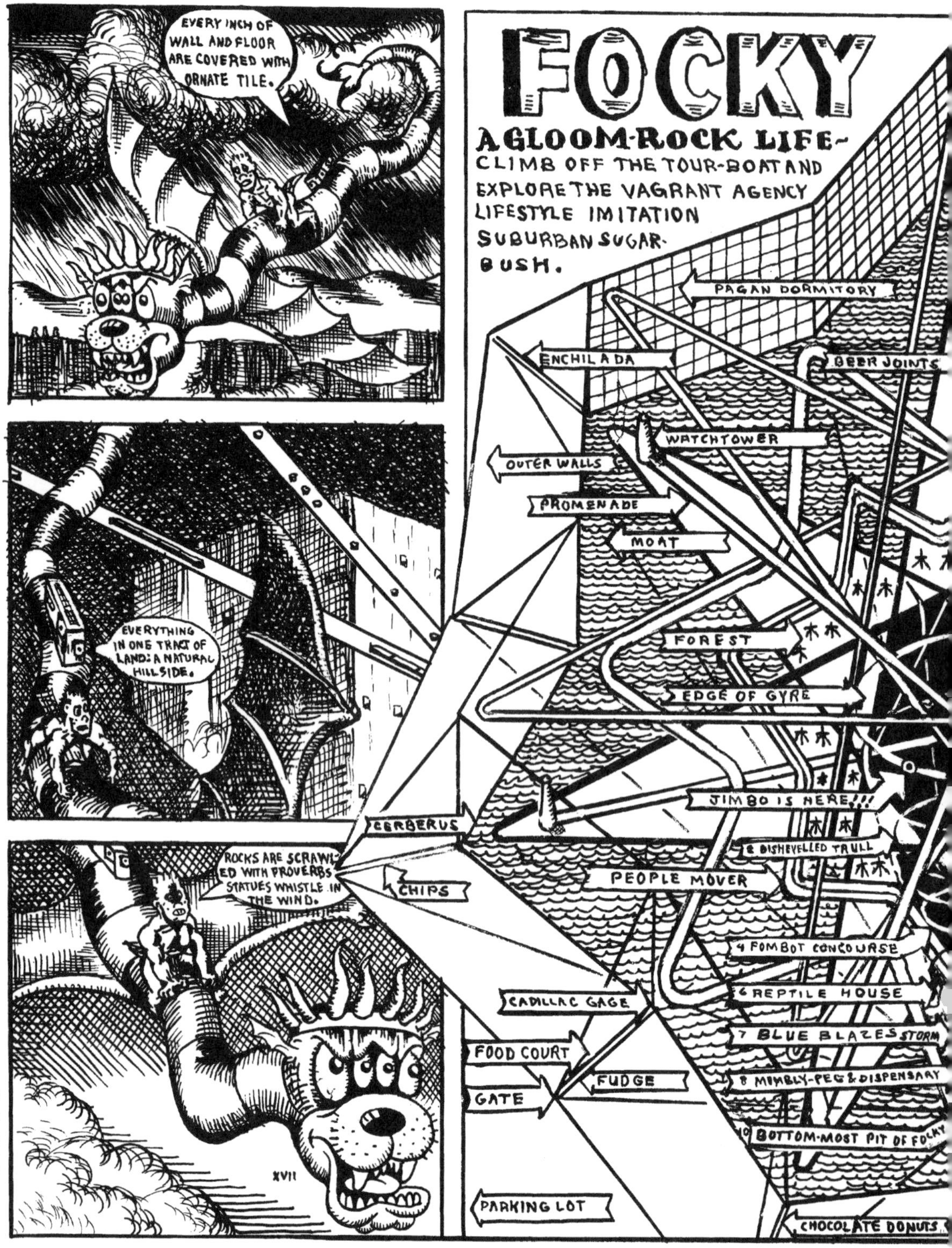
EVERY INCH OF WALL AND FLOOR ARE COVERED WITH ORNATE TILE.
EVERYTHING IN ONE TRACT OF LAND: A NATURAL HILLSIDE.
ROCKS ARE SCRAWLED WITH PROVERBS STATUES WHISTLE IN THE WIND.
XVII
FOCKY
A GLOOM-ROCK LIFE-
CLIMB OFF THE TOUR-BOAT AND EXPLORE THE VAGRANT AGENCY LIFESTYLE IMITATION SUBURBAN SUGAR-BUSH.
PAGAN DORMITORY
ENCHILADA
BEER JOINTS
WATCHTOWER
OUTER WALLS
PROMENADE
MOAT
FOREST
EDGE OF GYRE
JIMBO IS HERE!!!
CERBERUS
2 DISHEVELLED TRULL
CHIPS
PEOPLE MOVER
4 FOMBOT CONCOURSE
6 REPTILE HOUSE
CADILLAC GAGE
7 BLUE BLAZES STORM
FOOD COURT
FUDGE
8 MUMBLY-PEG & DISPENSARY
GATE
10 BOTTOM-MOST PIT OF FOCKY
PARKING LOT
CHOCOLATE DONUTS

3-11-1996

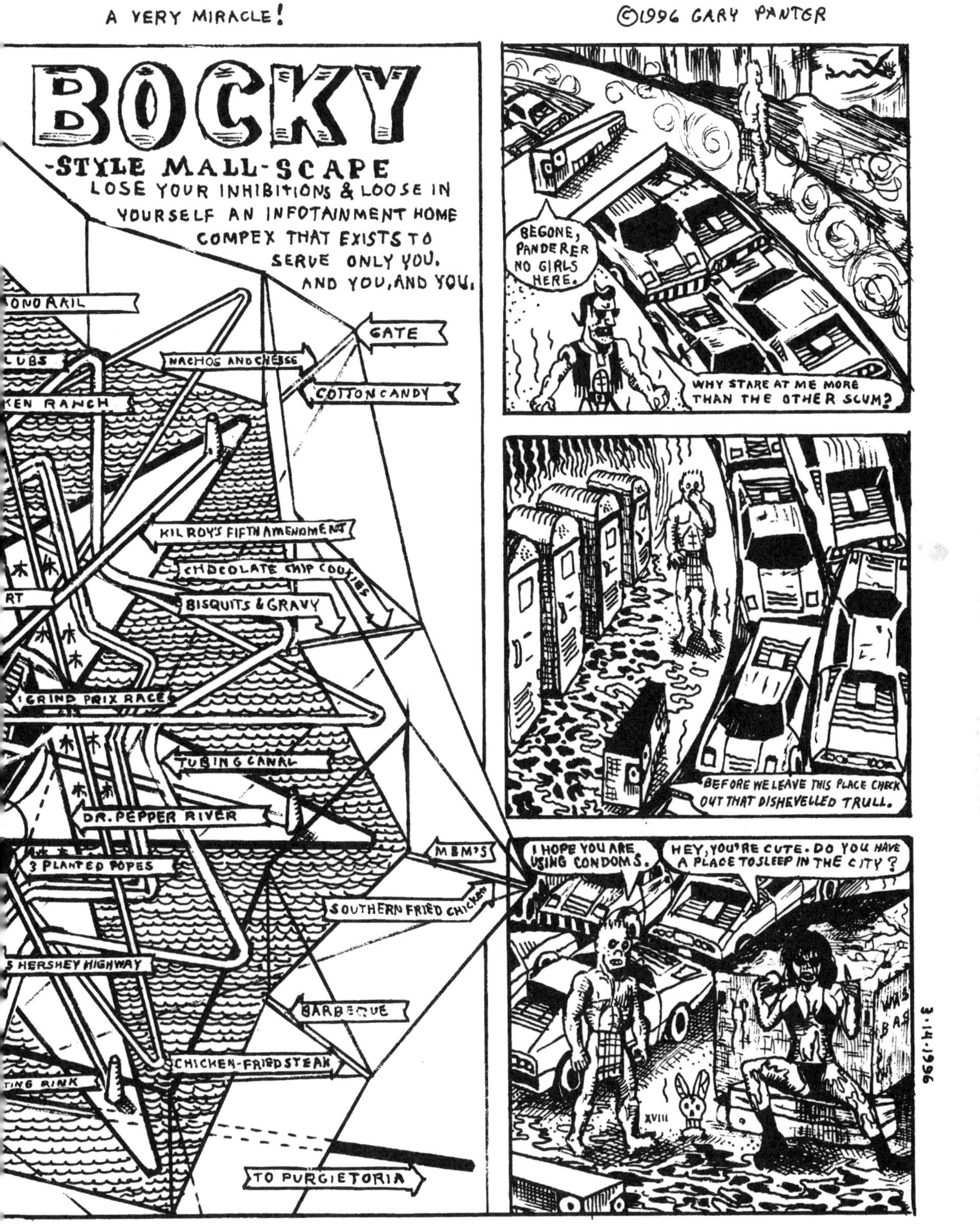
A VERY MIRACLE!
©1996 GARY PANTER
BOCKY
-STYLE MALL-SCAPE
LOSE YOUR INHIBITIONS & LOOSE IN YOURSELF AN INFOTAINMENT HOME COMPEX THAT EXISTS TO SERVE ONLY YOU. AND YOU, AND YOU.
GATE
NACHOS AND CHEESE
COTTON CANDY
KILROY'S FIFTH AMENDMENT
CHOCOLATE CHIP COOKIES
BISQUITS & GRAVY
GRAND PRIX RACE
TUBING CANAL
DR. PEPPER RIVER
M&M'S
3 PLANTED POPES
SOUTHERN FRIED CHICKEN
HERSHEY HIGHWAY
BARBECUE
CHICKEN-FRIED STEAK
TO PURGIETORIA
BEGONE, PANDERER NO GIRLS HERE.
WHY STARE AT ME MORE THAN THE OTHER SCUM?
BEFORE WE LEAVE THIS PLACE CHECK OUT THAT DISHEVELLED TRULL.
I HOPE YOU ARE USING CONDOMS.
HEY, YOU'RE CUTE. DO YOU HAVE A PLACE TO SLEEP IN THE CITY?
XVIII
3-14-1996

SNAPPED WITHIES

3-14-1996

3-15-1996

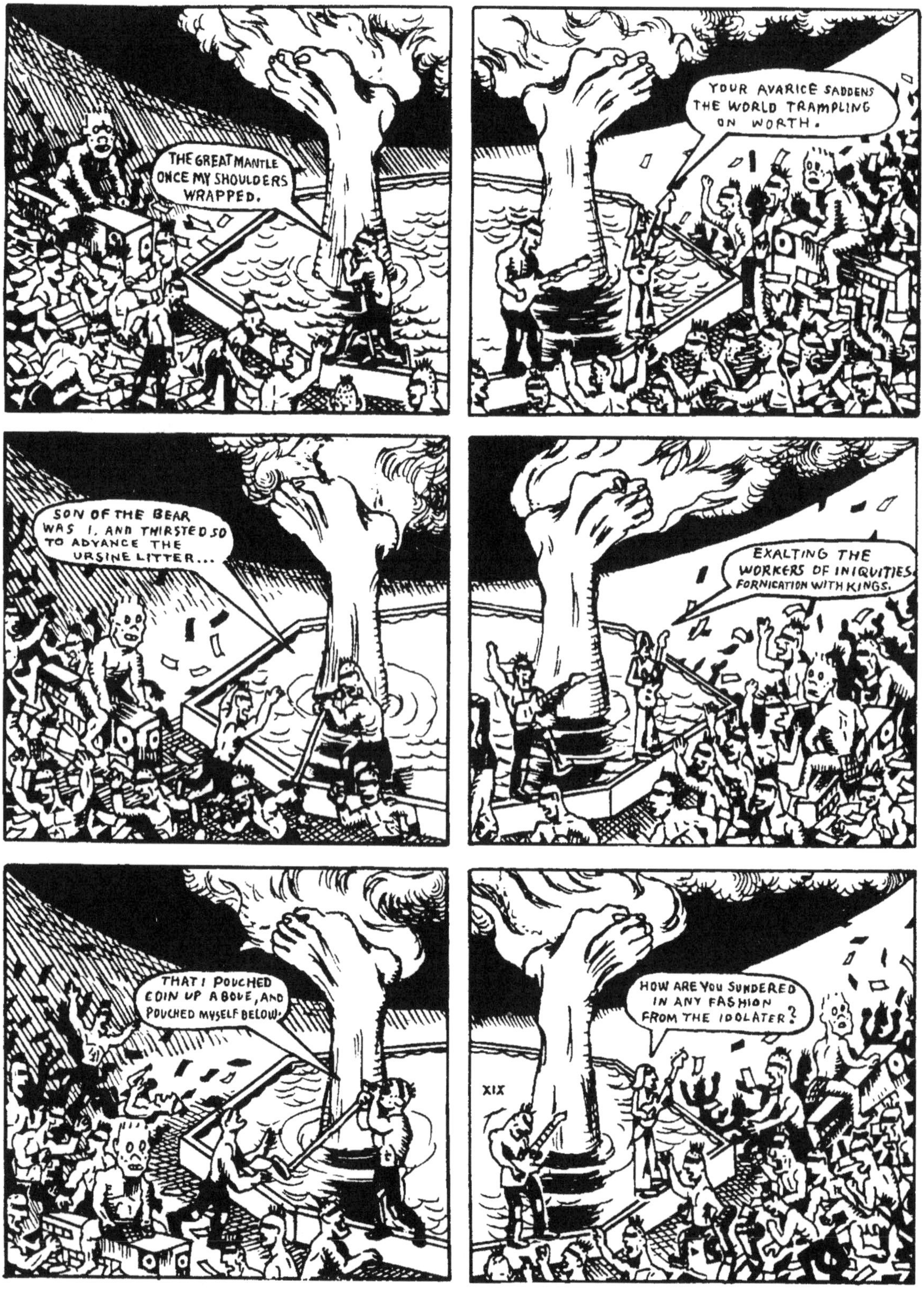
THE GREAT MANTLE ONCE MY SHOULDERS WRAPPED.
YOUR AVARICE SADDENS THE WORLD TRAMPLING ON WORTH.
SON OF THE BEAR WAS I, AND THIRSTED SO TO ADVANCE THE URSINE LITTER...
EXALTING THE WORKERS OF INIQUITIES. FORNICATION WITH KINGS.
THAT I POUCHED COIN UP ABOVE, AND POUCHED MYSELF BELOW.
HOW ARE YOU SUNDERED IN ANY FASHION FROM THE IDOLATER?
XIX

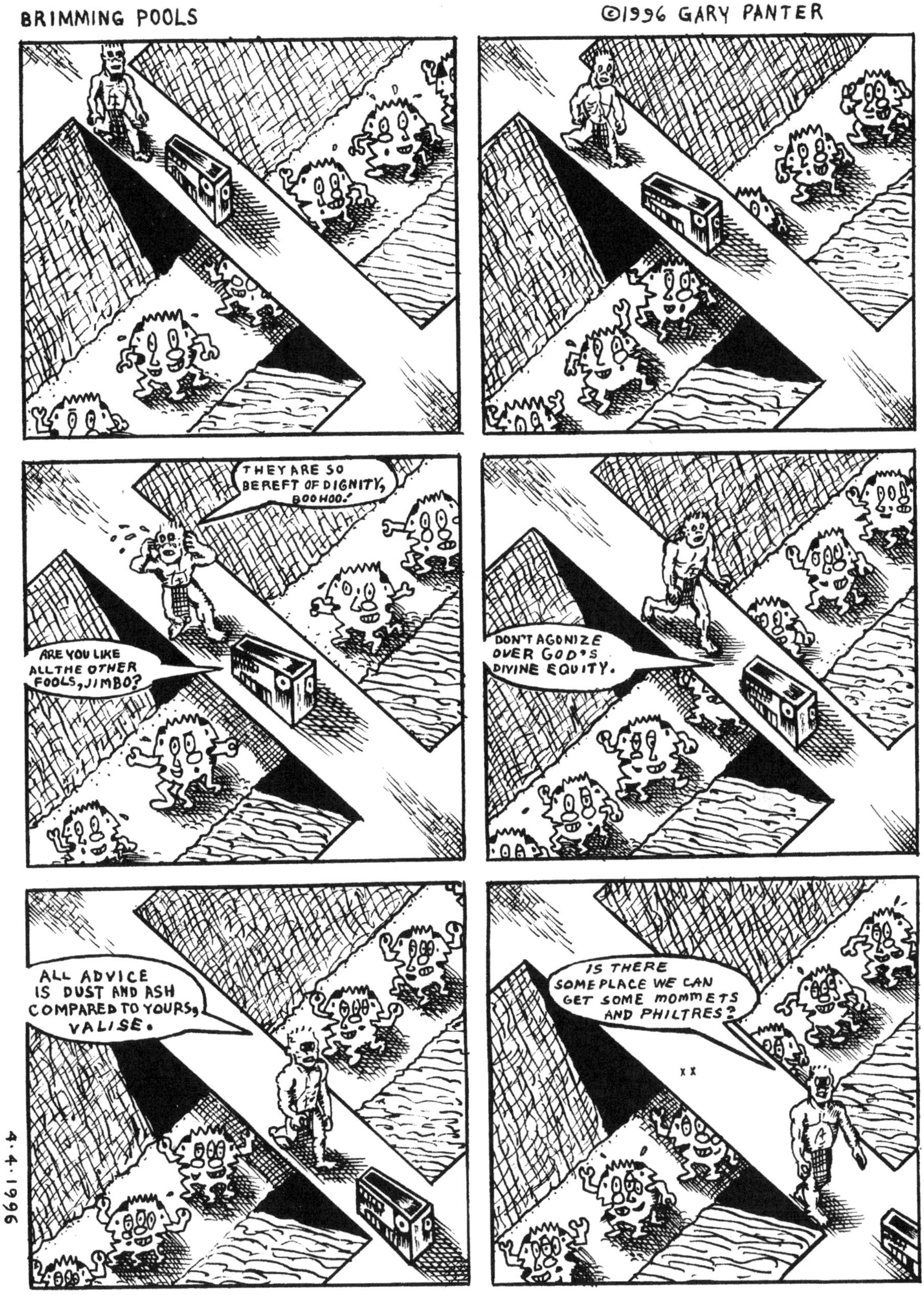
BRIMMING POOLS
©1996 GARY PANTER
THEY ARE SO BEREFT OF DIGNITY, BOOHOO!
ARE YOU LIKE ALL THE OTHER FOOLS, JIMBO?
DON'T AGONIZE OVER GOD'S DIVINE EQUITY.
ALL ADVICE IS DUST AND ASH COMPARED TO YOURS, VALISE.
IS THERE SOME PLACE WE CAN GET SOME MOMMETS AND PHILTRES?
4·4·1996

SPATTERING THE BRINK ©1996 GARY PANTER

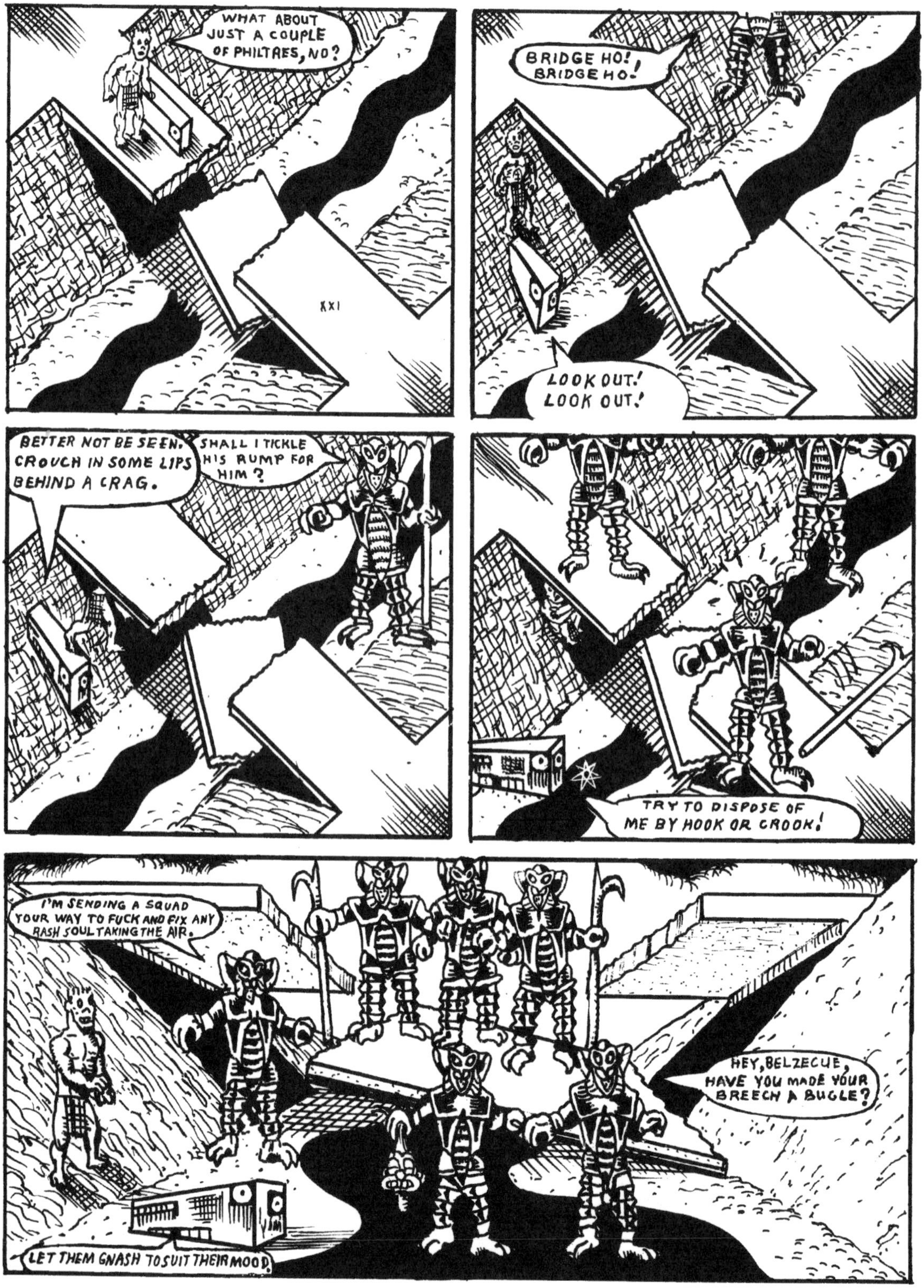
WHAT ABOUT JUST A COUPLE OF PHILTRES, NO?
XXI
BRIDGE HO! BRIDGE HO!
LOOK OUT! LOOK OUT!
BETTER NOT BE SEEN. CROUCH IN SOME LIPS BEHIND A CRAG.
SHALL I TICKLE HIS RUMP FOR HIM?
TRY TO DISPOSE OF ME BY HOOK OR CROOK!
I'M SENDING A SQUAD YOUR WAY TO FUCK AND FIX ANY RASH SOUL TAKING THE AIR.
HEY, BELZECUE, HAVE YOU MADE YOUR BREECH A BUGLE?
LET THEM GNASH TO SUIT THEIR MOOD.
4-10-1996

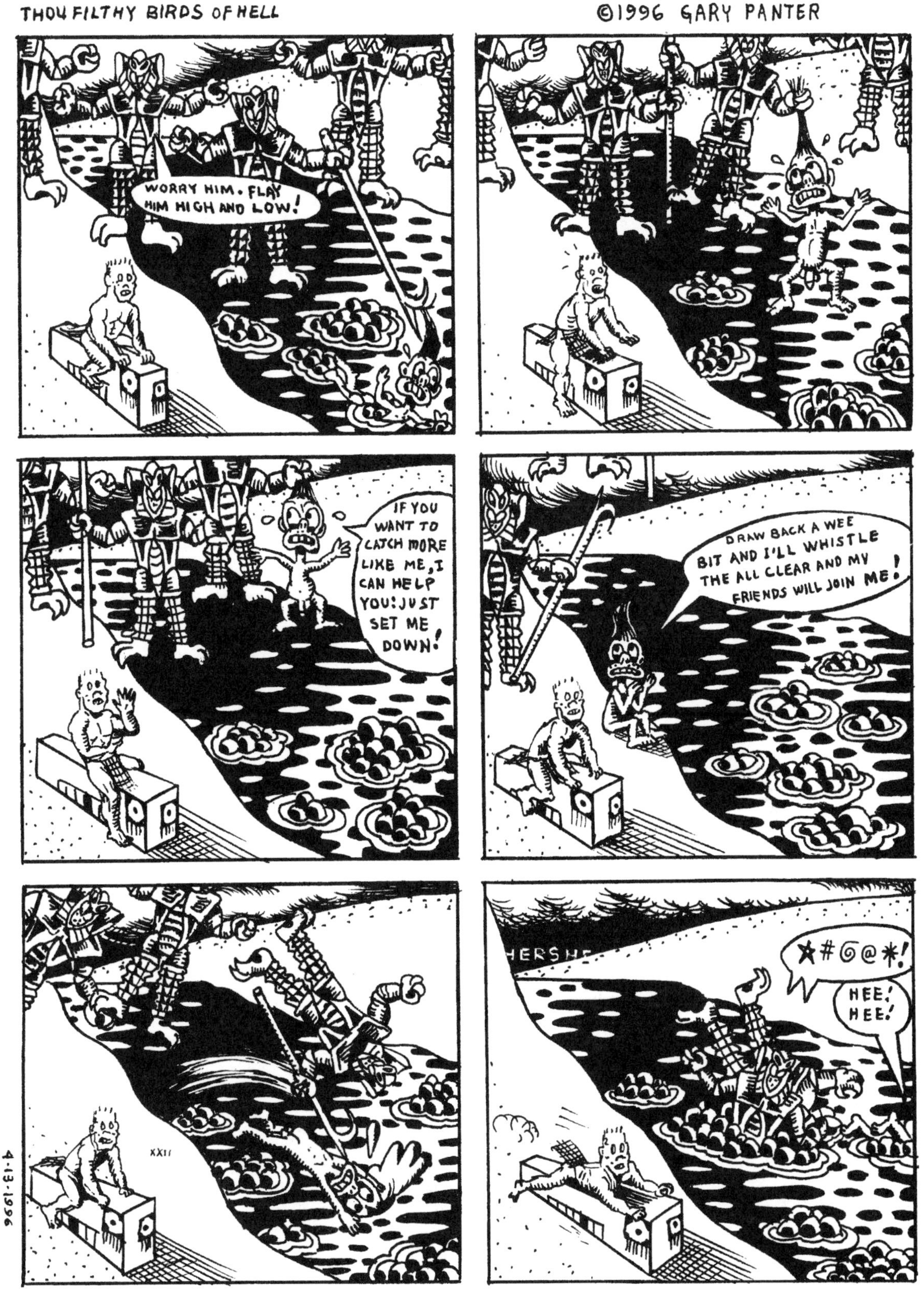
THOU FILTHY BIRDS OF HELL
©1996 GARY PANTER
WORRY HIM. FLAY HIM HIGH AND LOW!
IF YOU WANT TO CATCH MORE LIKE ME, I CAN HELP YOU! JUST SET ME DOWN!
DRAW BACK A WEE BIT AND I'LL WHISTLE THE ALL CLEAR AND MY FRIENDS WILL JOIN ME!
XXII
4-13-1996
HERSHE
#@@!
HEE! HEE!

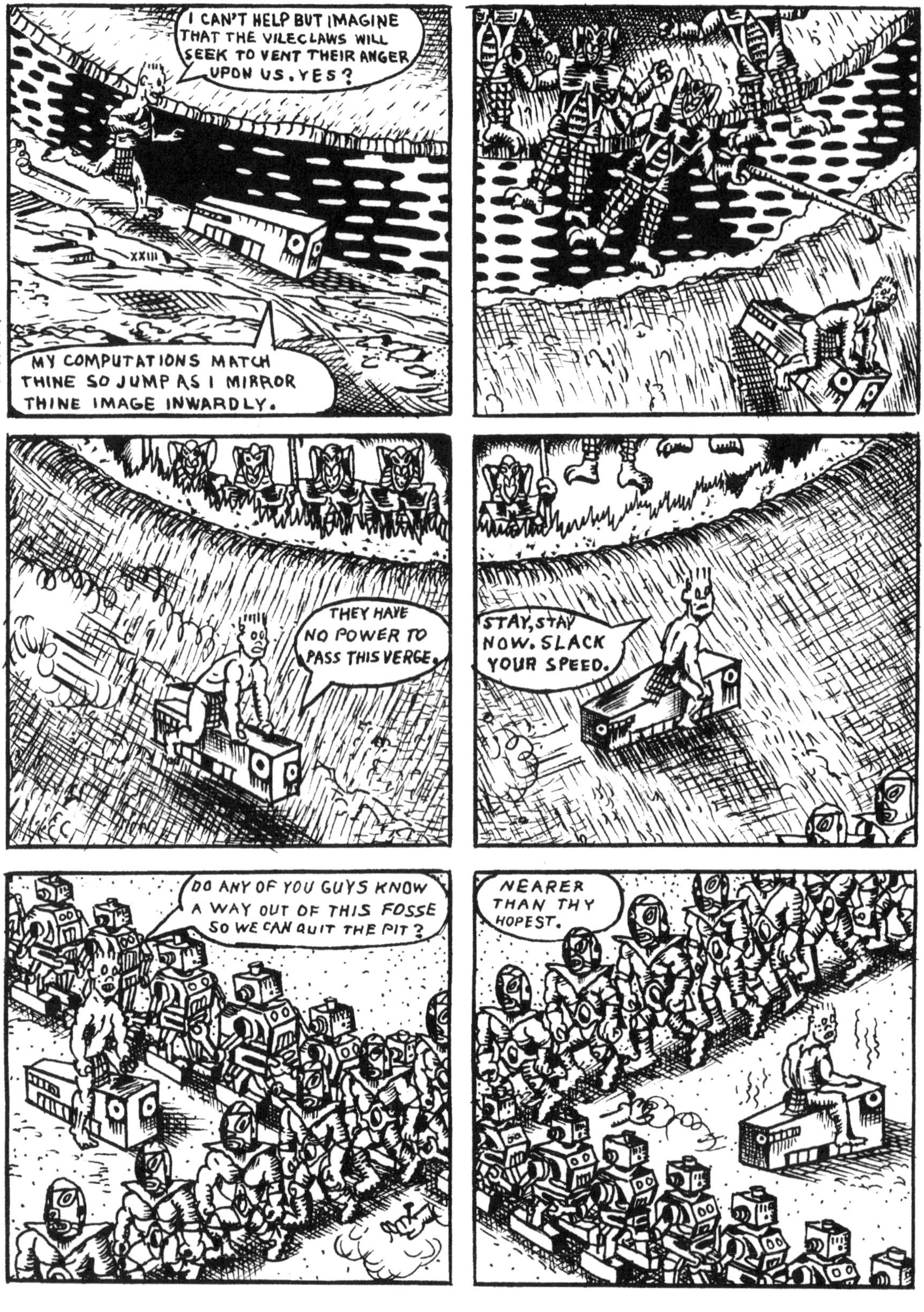
I CAN'T HELP BUT IMAGINE THAT THE VILECLAWS WILL SEEK TO VENT THEIR ANGER UPON US. YES?
XXIII
MY COMPUTATIONS MATCH THINE SO JUMP AS I MIRROR THINE IMAGE INWARDLY.
THEY HAVE NO POWER TO PASS THIS VERGE.
STAY, STAY NOW. SLACK YOUR SPEED.
DO ANY OF YOU GUYS KNOW A WAY OUT OF THIS FOSSE SO WE CAN QUIT THE PIT?
NEARER THAN THY HOPEST.

4-14-1996

4-26-1996

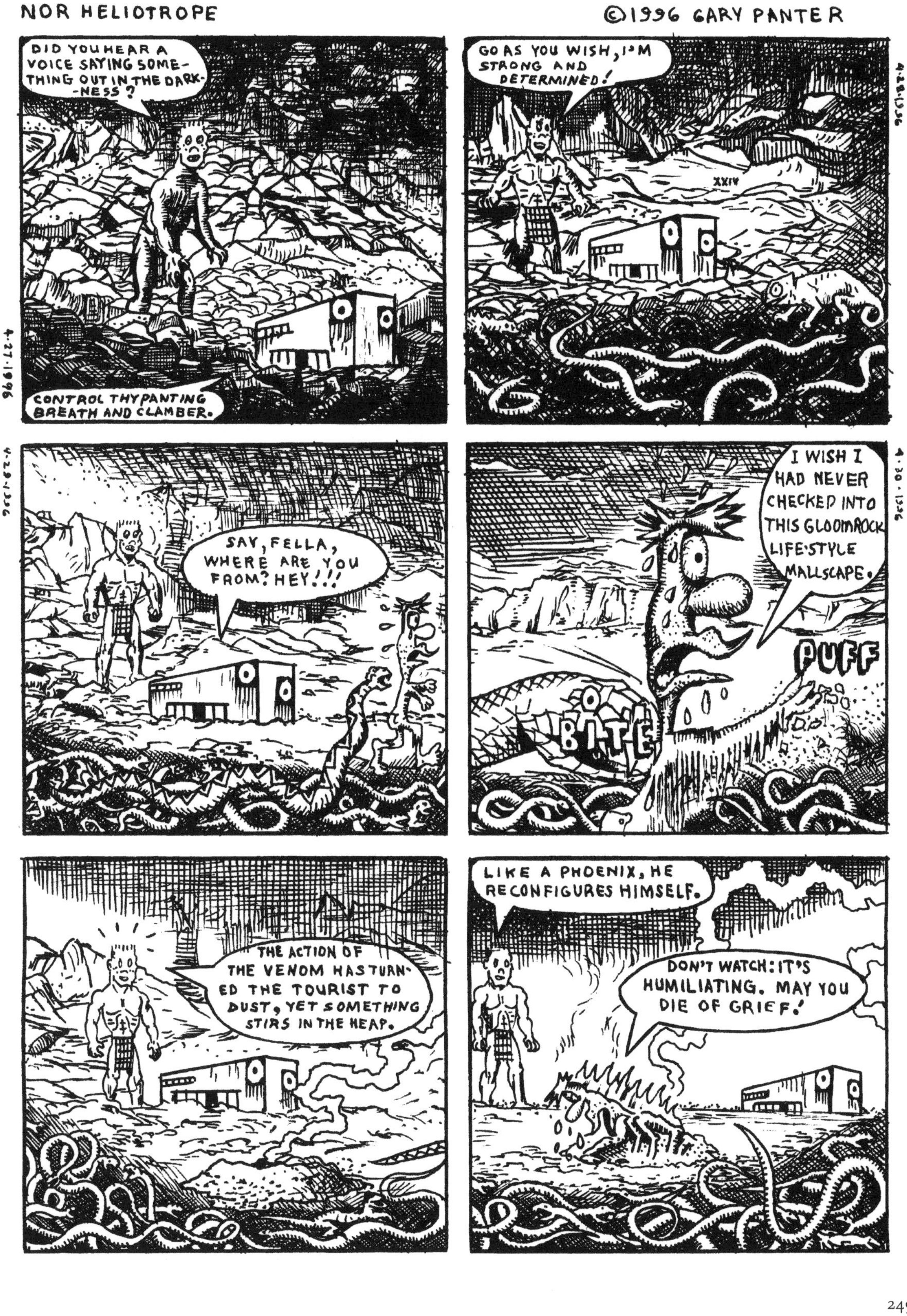
NOR HELIOTROPE
©1996 GARY PANTER
DID YOU HEAR A VOICE SAYING SOME-THING OUT IN THE DARK-NESS?
CONTROL THY PANTING BREATH AND CLAMBER.
4-27-1996
GO AS YOU WISH, I'M STRONG AND DETERMINED!
XXIV
4-28-1996
SAY, FELLA, WHERE ARE YOU FROM? HEY!!!
4-29-1996
I WISH I HAD NEVER CHECKED INTO THIS GLOOMROCK LIFE-STYLE MALLSCAPE.
PUFF
BITE
4-30-1996
THE ACTION OF THE VENOM HAS TURN-ED THE TOURIST TO DUST, YET SOMETHING STIRS IN THE HEAP.
LIKE A PHOENIX, HE RECONFIGURES HIMSELF.
DON'T WATCH: IT'S HUMILIATING. MAY YOU DIE OF GRIEF!

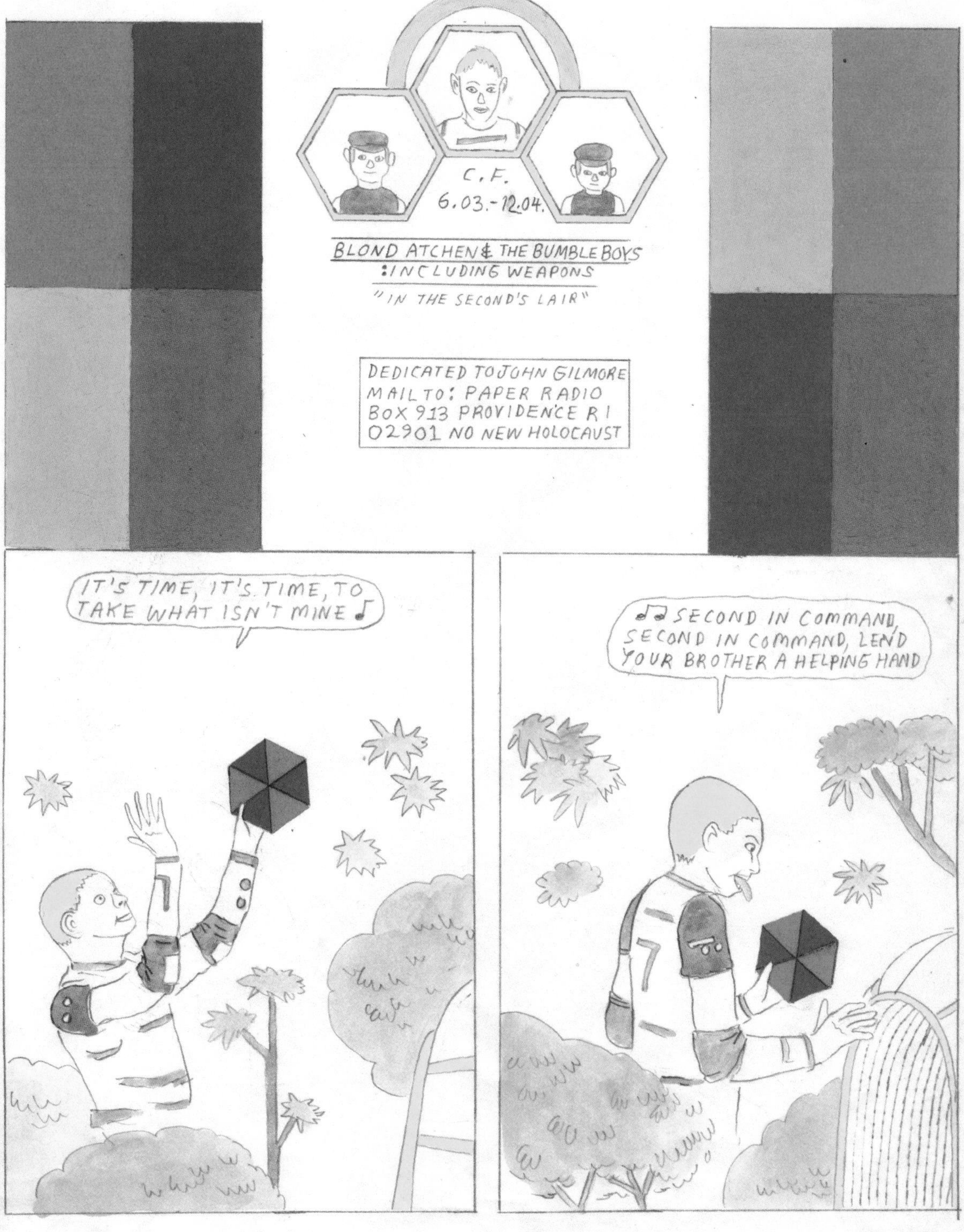
C.F.
6.03.-12.04.
BLOND ATCHEN & THE BUMBLE BOYS
:INCLUDING WEAPONS
"IN THE SECOND'S LAIR"
DEDICATED TO JOHN GILMORE MAIL TO: PAPER RADIO BOX 913 PROVIDENCE RI 02901 NO NEW HOLOCAUST
IT'S TIME, IT'S TIME, TO TAKE WHAT ISN'T MINE
SECOND IN COMMAND, SECOND IN COMMAND, LEND YOUR BROTHER A HELPING HAND

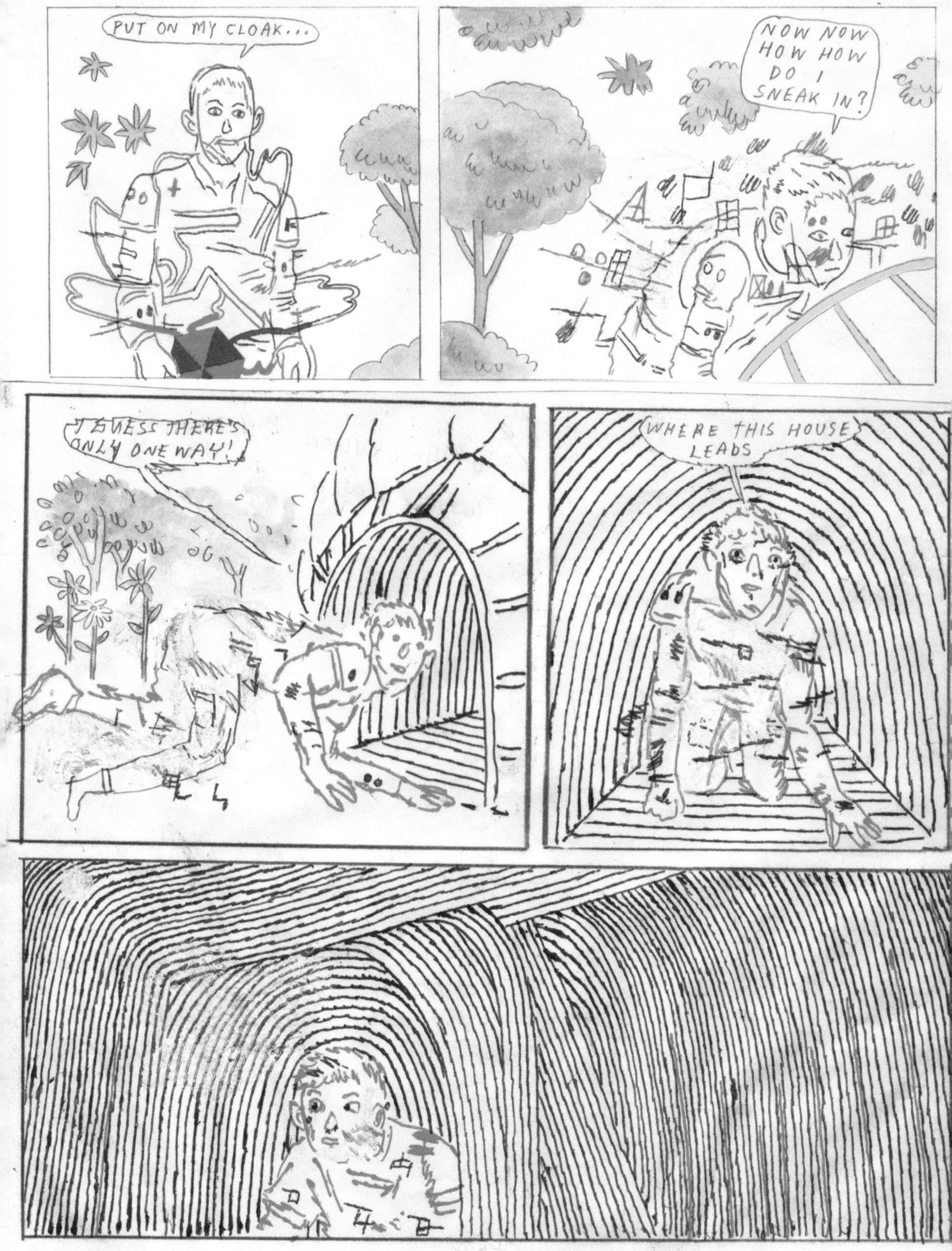
PUT ON MY CLOAK...
NOW NOW HOW HOW DO I SNEAK IN?
I GUESS THERE'S ONLY ONE WAY!
WHERE THIS HOUSE LEADS

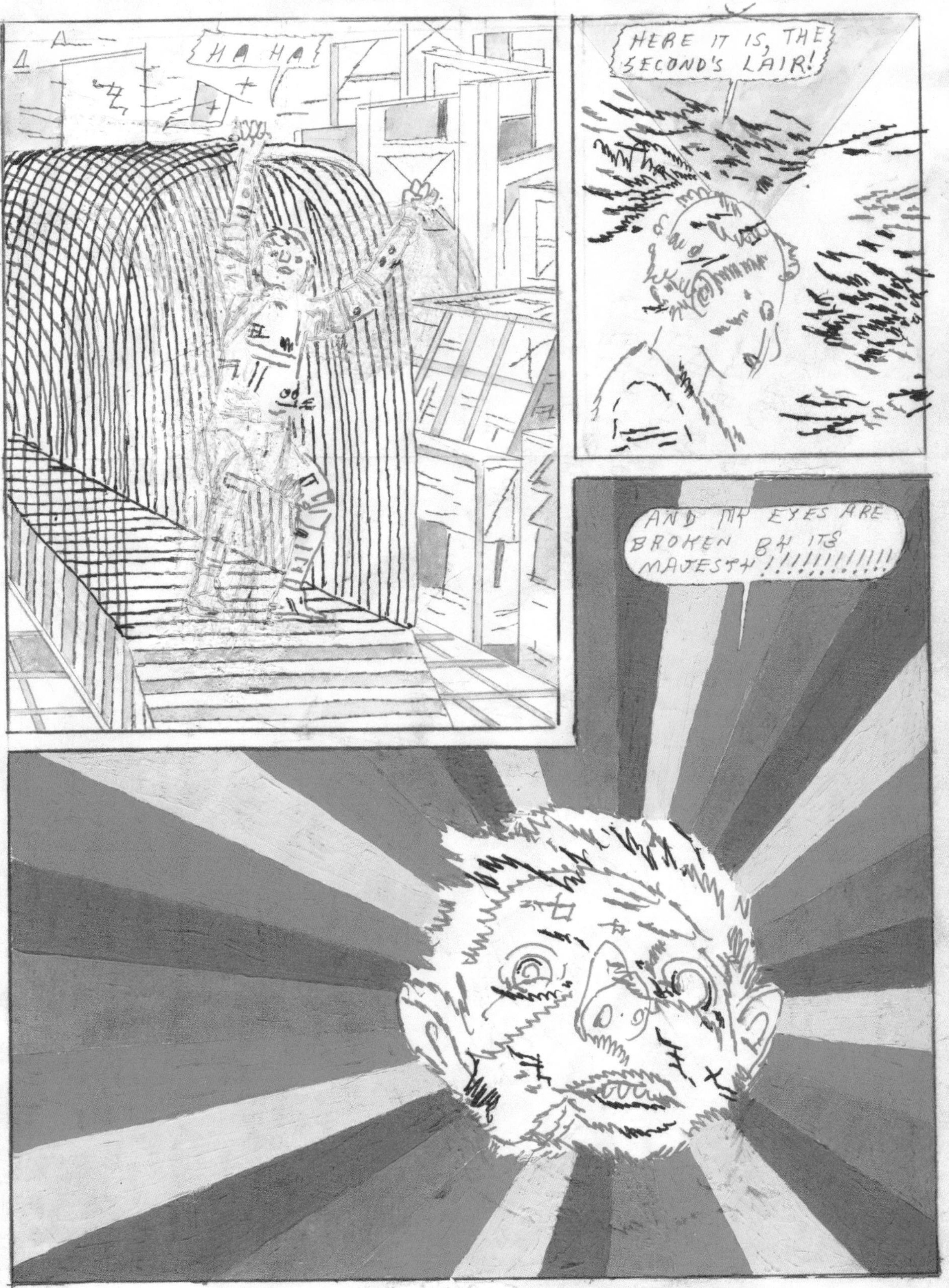
HA HA!
HERE IT IS, THE SECOND'S LAIR!
AND MY EYES ARE BROKEN BY ITS MAJESTY!!!!!!!!!!!!

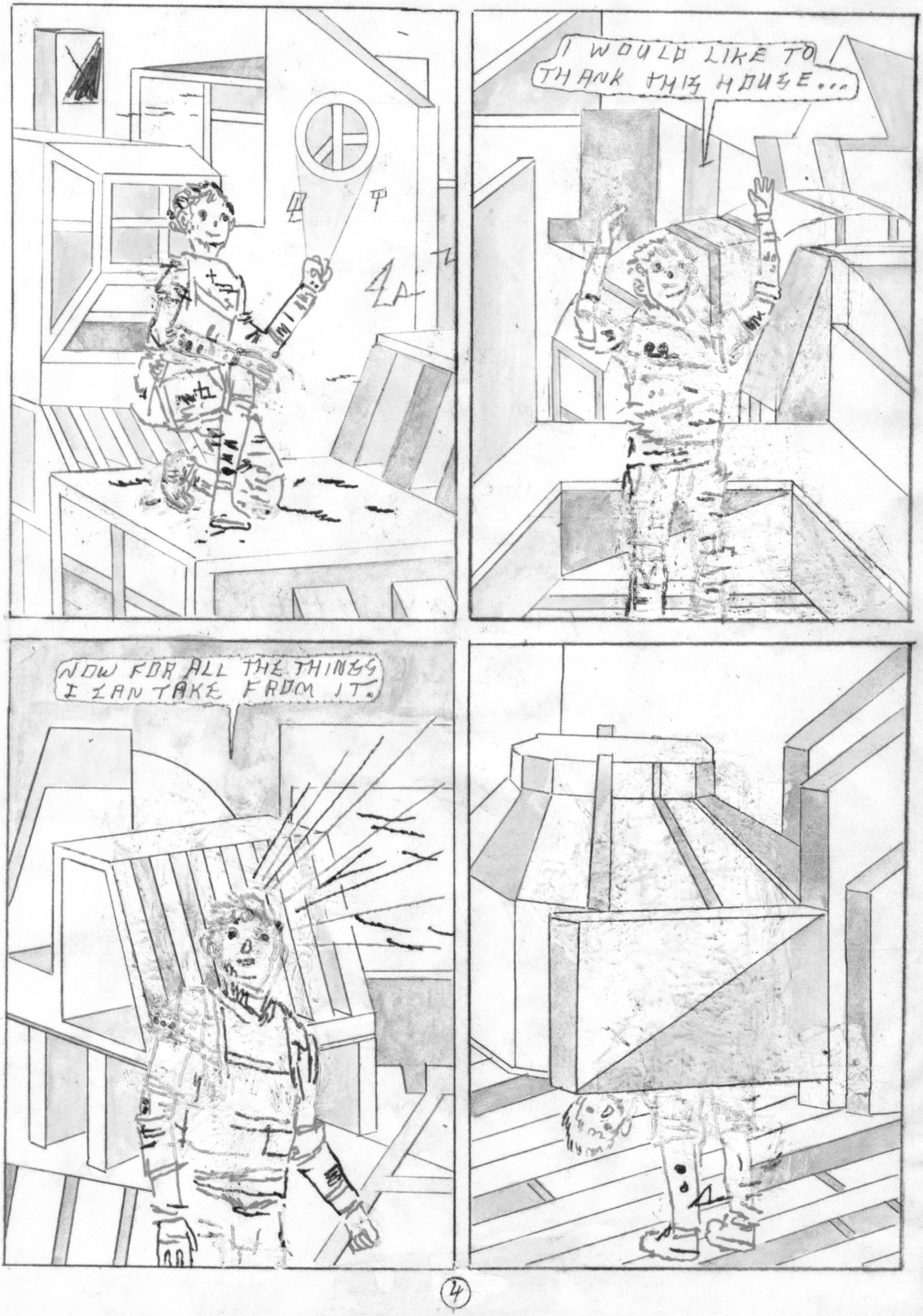
I WOULD LIKE TO THANK THIS HOUSE...
NOW FOR ALL THE THINGS I CAN TAKE FROM IT.

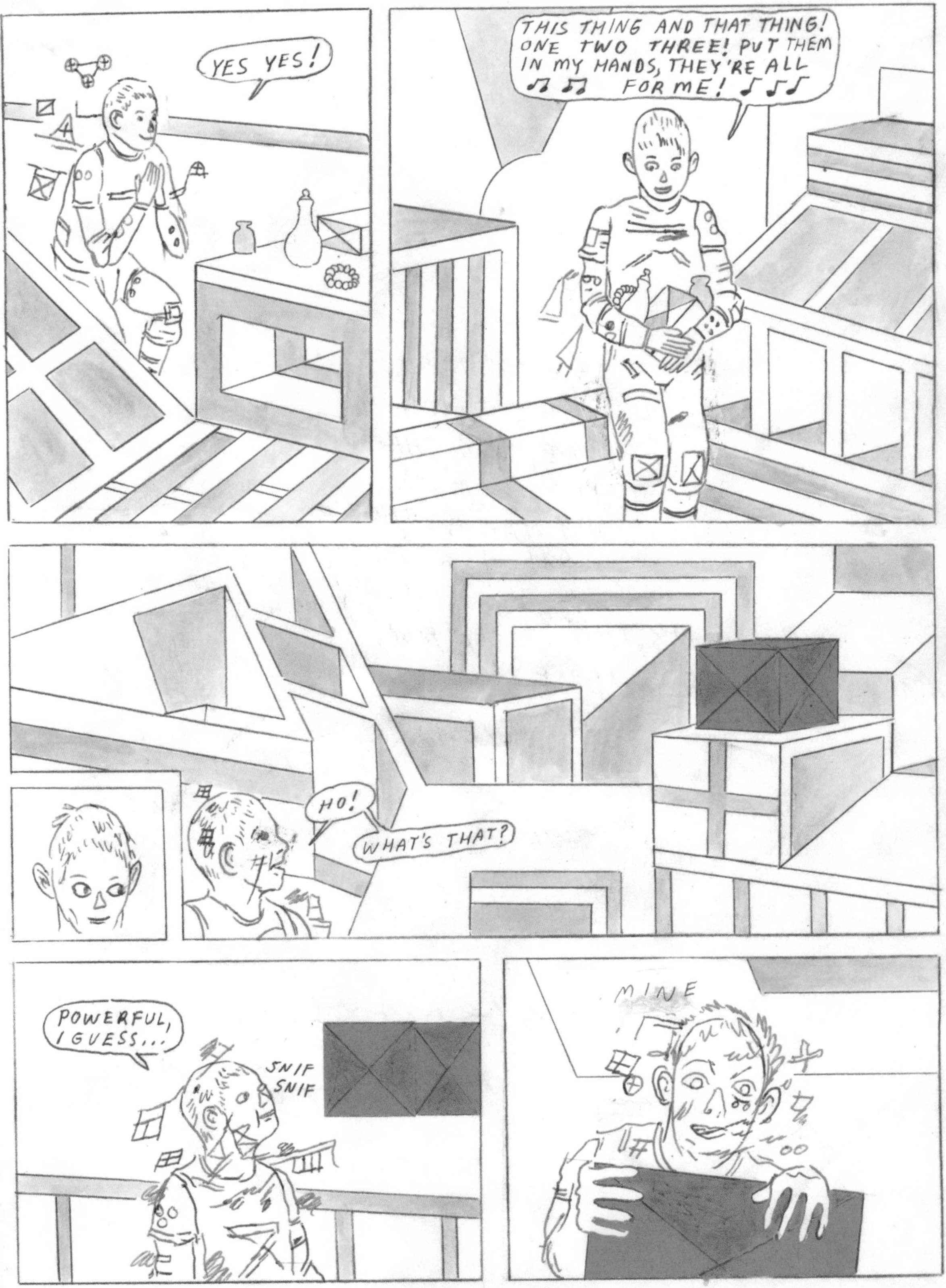
YES YES!
THIS THING AND THAT THING! ONE TWO THREE! PUT THEM IN MY HANDS, THEY'RE ALL ♫ ♫ FOR ME! ♩♩♩
HO!
WHAT'S THAT?
POWERFUL, I GUESS...
SNIF SNIF
MINE

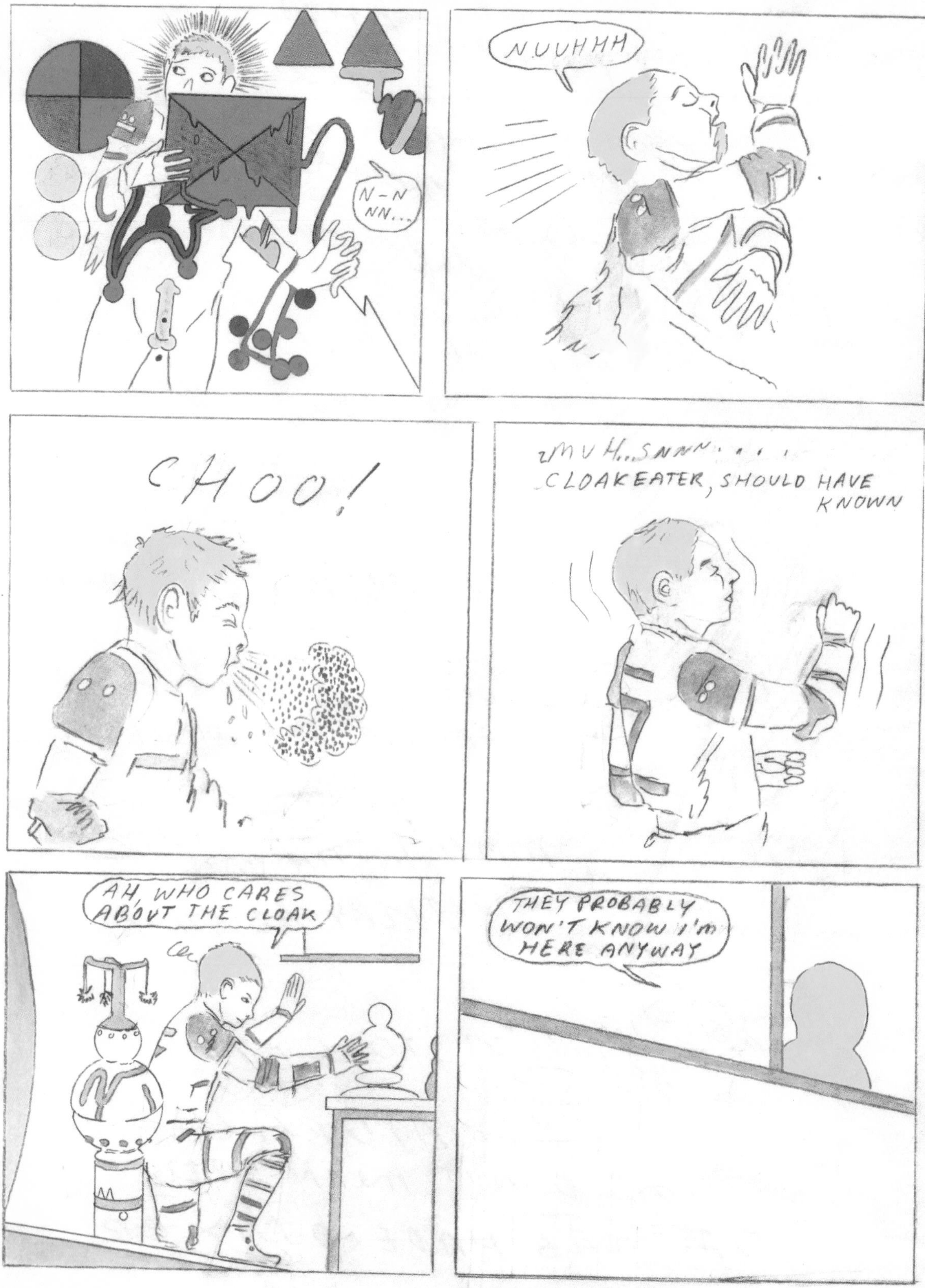
N-N NN...
N.UUHHH
CHOO!
MUH...SNNN......
CLOAKEATER, SHOULD HAVE KNOWN
AH, WHO CARES ABOUT THE CLOAK
THEY PROBABLY WON'T KNOW I'M HERE ANYWAY

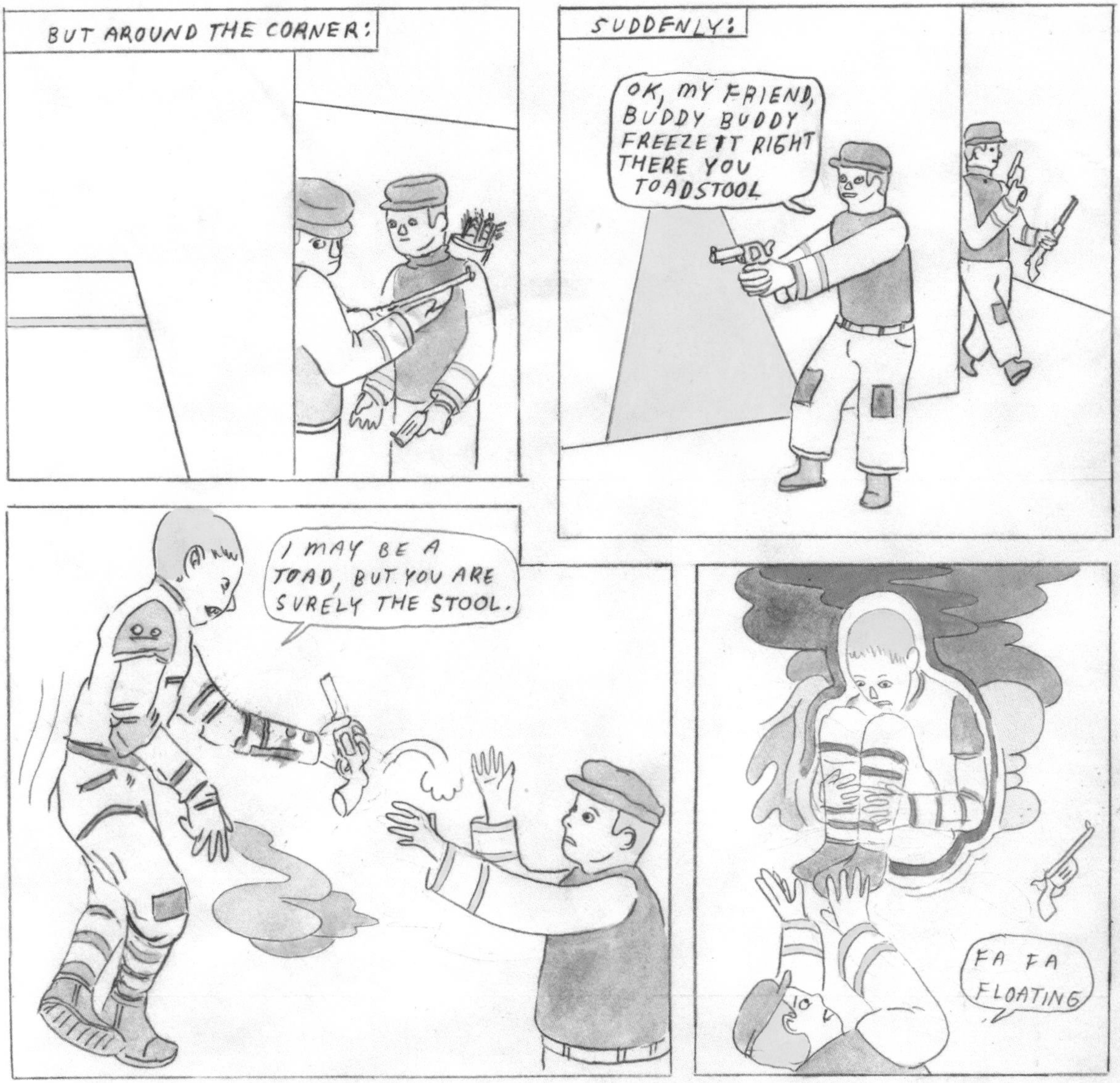
BUT AROUND THE CORNER:
SUDDENLY:
OK, MY FRIEND, BUDDY BUDDY FREEZE IT RIGHT THERE YOU TOADSTOOL
I MAY BE A TOAD, BUT YOU ARE SURELY THE STOOL.
FA FA FLOATING
S'OKAY
I'LL GET HIM, SEE? HEY

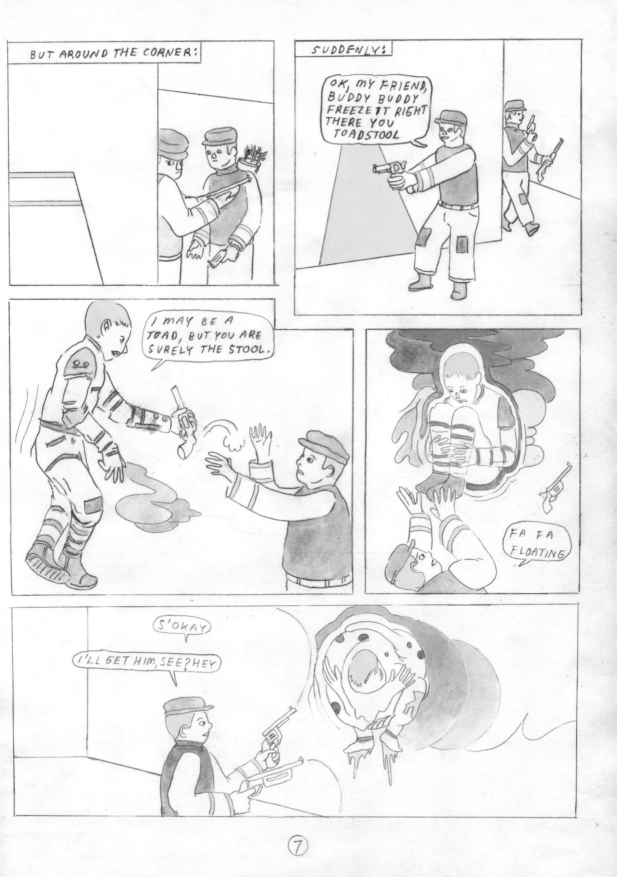

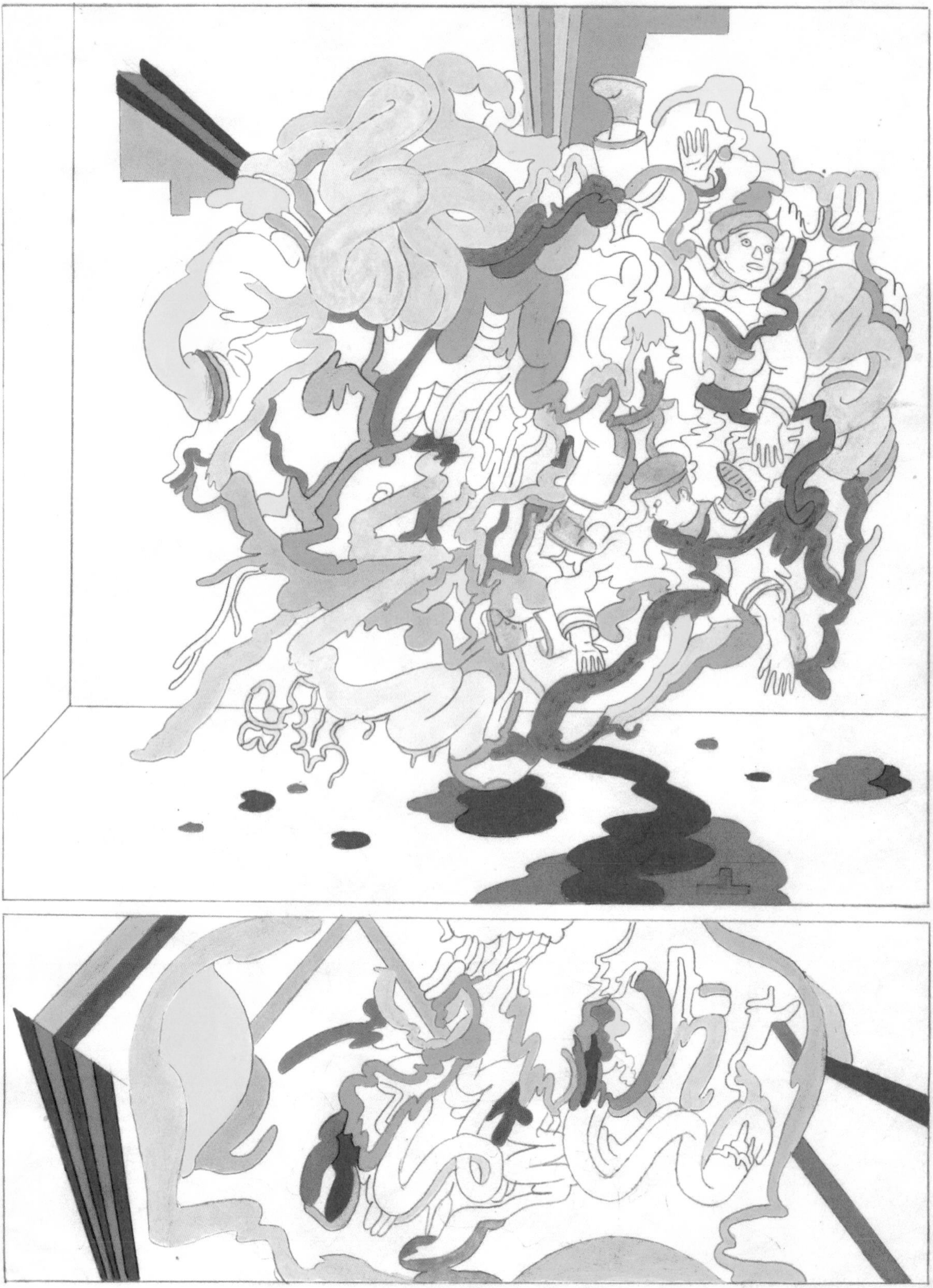

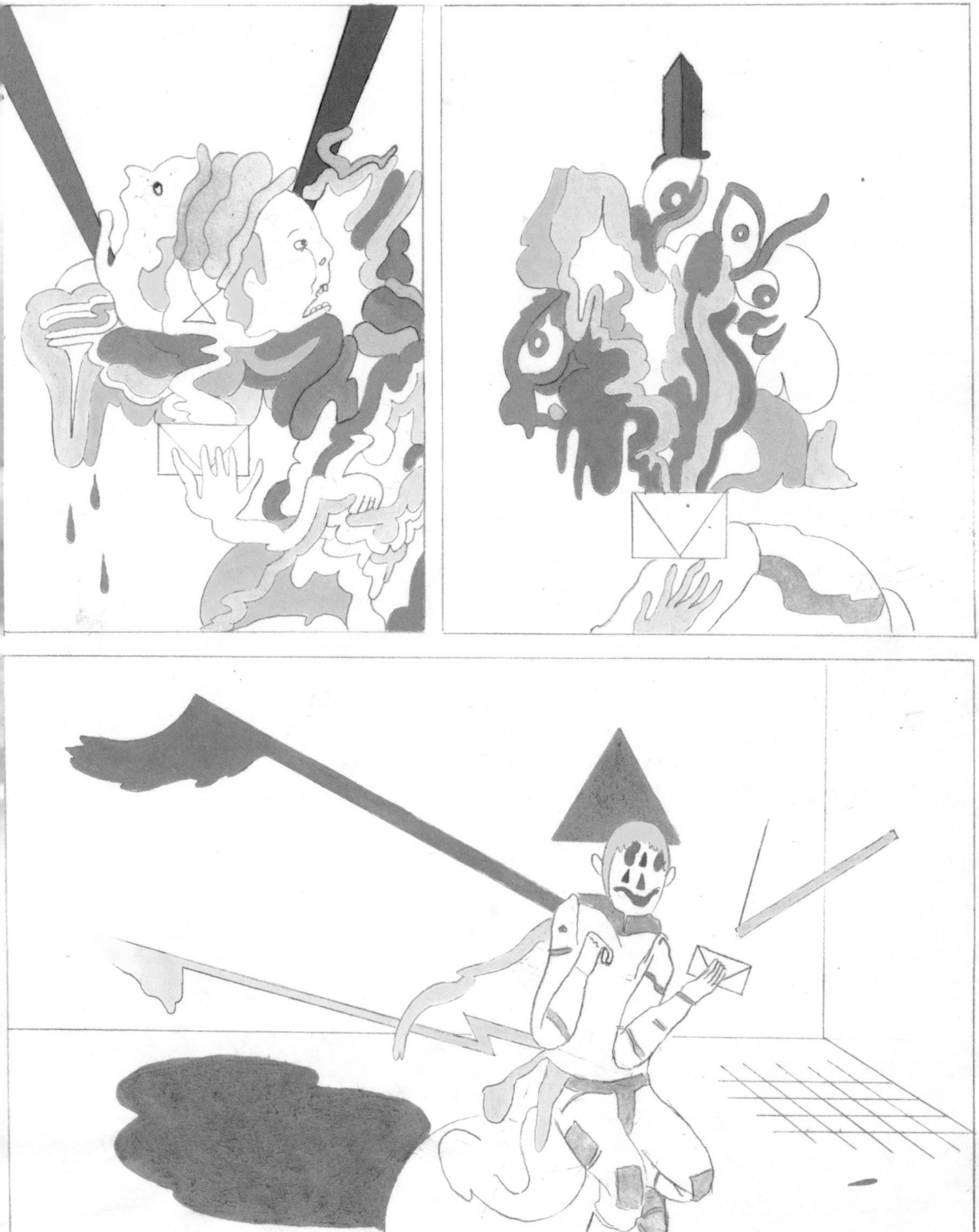

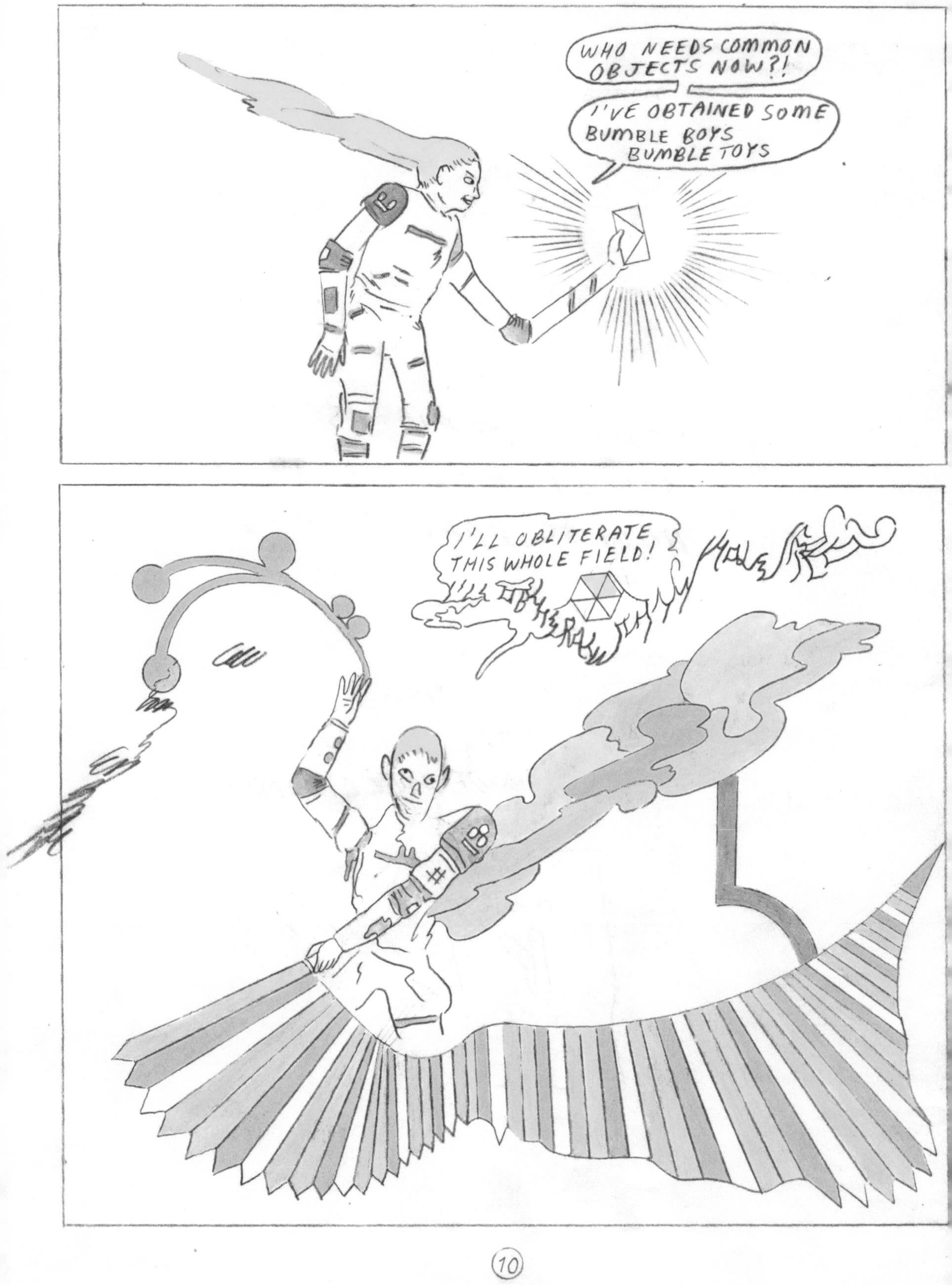
WHO NEEDS COMMON OBJECTS NOW?!
I'VE OBTAINED SOME BUMBLE BOYS BUMBLE TOYS
I'LL OBLITERATE THIS WHOLE FIELD!

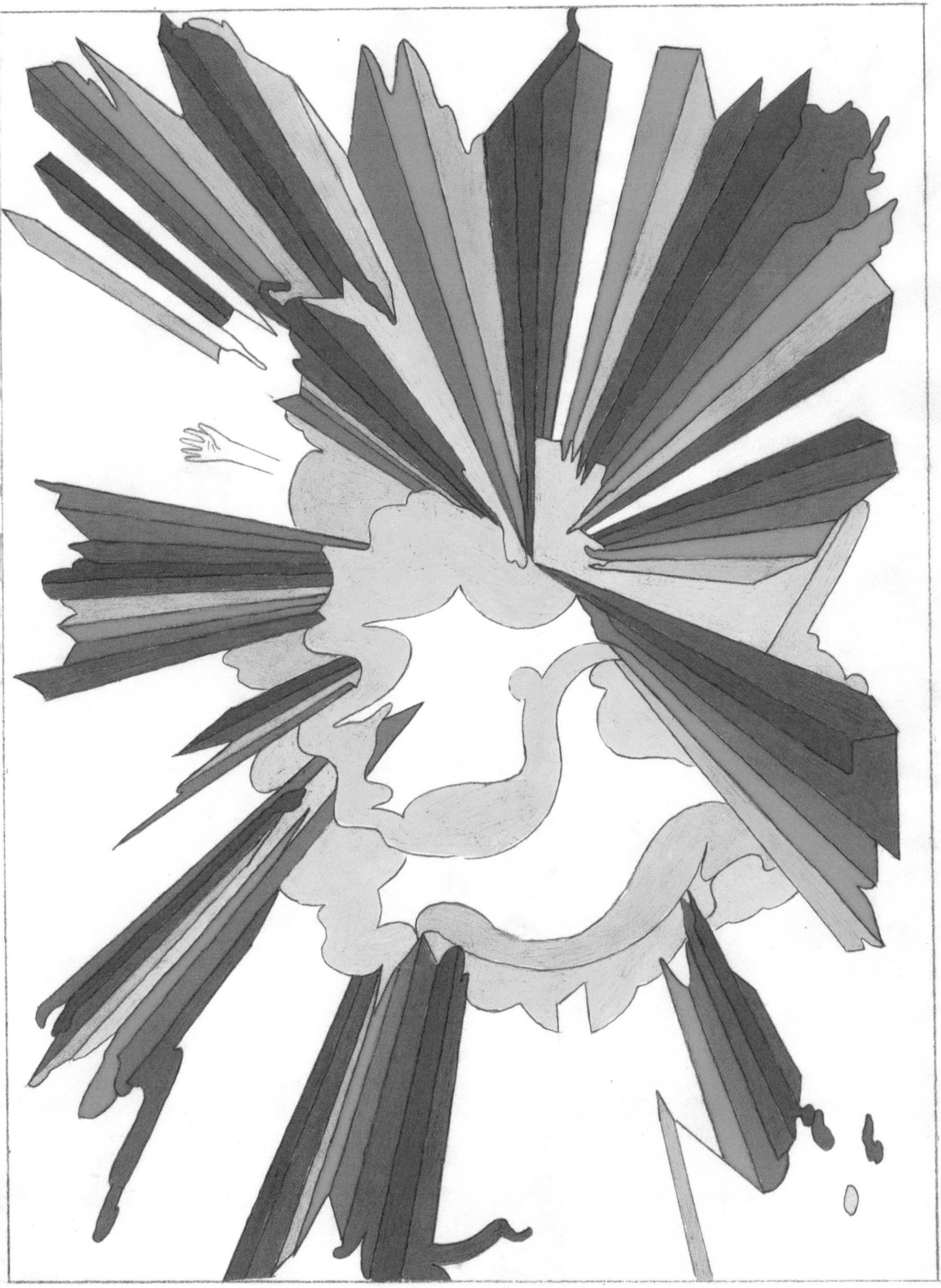

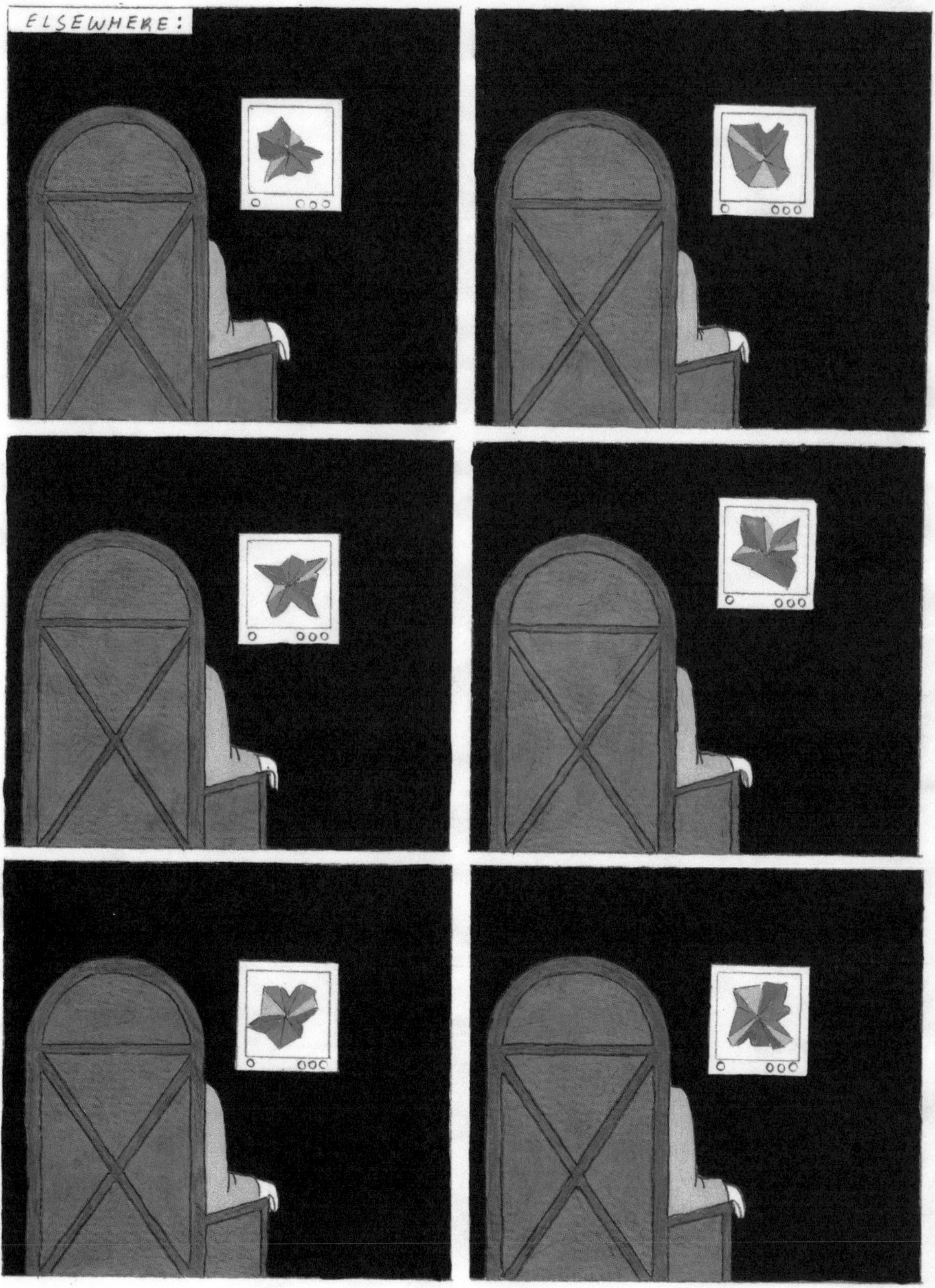
ELSEWHERE:

MY BUMBLING, CORPULENT MASS

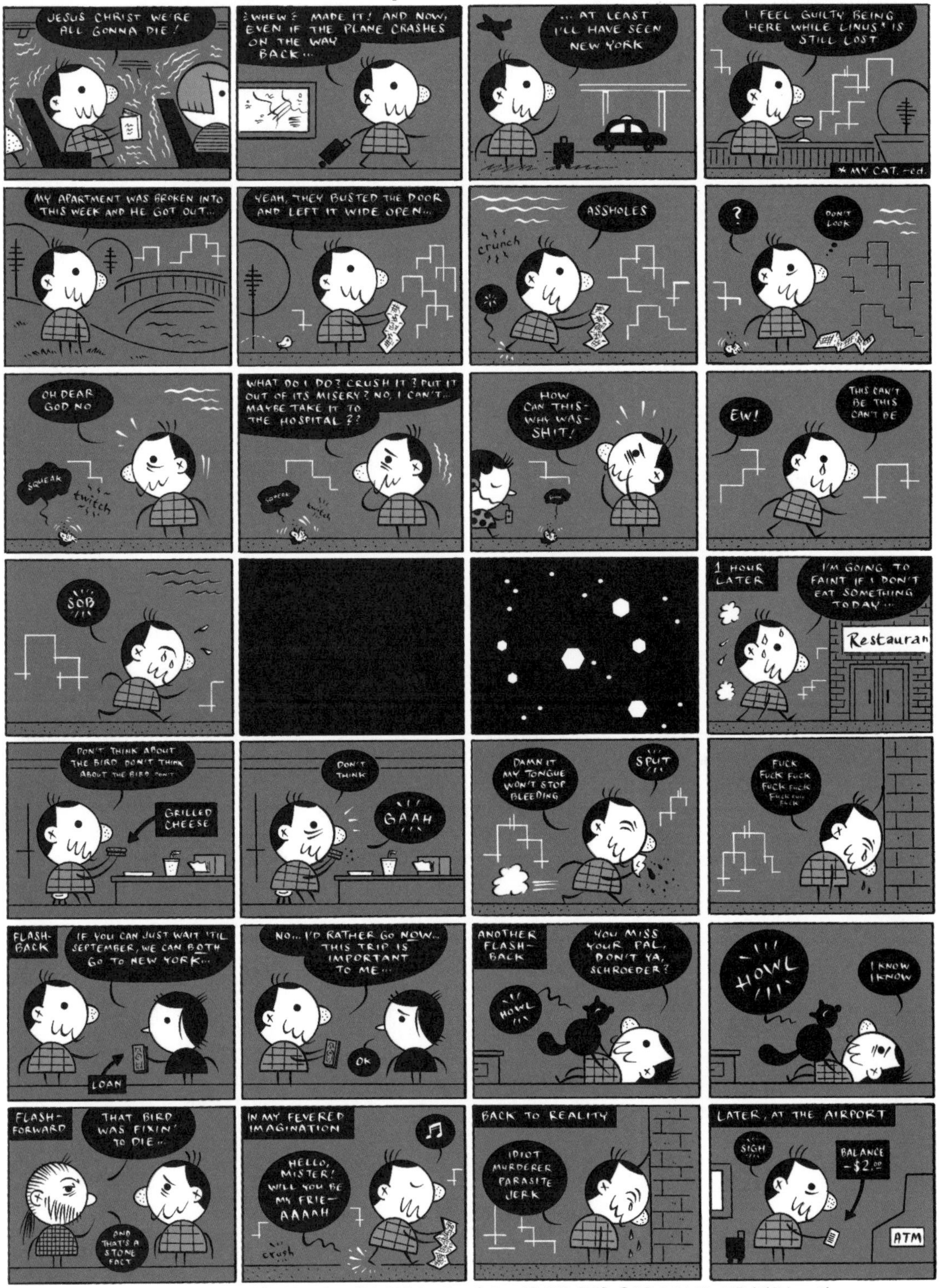
JESUS CHRIST WE'RE ALL GONNA DIE!
≈WHEW≈ MADE IT! AND NOW, EVEN IF THE PLANE CRASHES ON THE WAY BACK...
... AT LEAST I'LL HAVE SEEN NEW YORK
I FEEL GUILTY BEING HERE WHILE LINUS* IS STILL LOST
* MY CAT. —ed.
MY APARTMENT WAS BROKEN INTO THIS WEEK AND HE GOT OUT...
YEAH, THEY BUSTED THE DOOR AND LEFT IT WIDE OPEN...
crunch
ASSHOLES
?
DON'T LOOK
OH DEAR GOD NO
SQUEAK
twitch
WHAT DO I DO? CRUSH IT? PUT IT OUT OF ITS MISERY? NO, I CAN'T... MAYBE TAKE IT TO THE HOSPITAL??
twitch
HOW CAN THIS- WHY WAS- SHIT!
EW!
THIS CAN'T BE THIS CAN'T BE
SOB
1 HOUR LATER
I'M GOING TO FAINT IF I DON'T EAT SOMETHING TODAY...
Restauran
DON'T THINK ABOUT THE BIRD DON'T THINK ABOUT THE BIRD DON'T
GRILLED CHEESE
DON'T THINK
GAAH
DAMN IT MY TONGUE WON'T STOP BLEEDING
SPUT
FUCK FUCK FUCK FUCK FUCK
FLASH-BACK
IF YOU CAN JUST WAIT 'TIL SEPTEMBER, WE CAN BOTH GO TO NEW YORK...
LOAN
NO... I'D RATHER GO NOW... THIS TRIP IS IMPORTANT TO ME...
OK
ANOTHER FLASH-BACK
YOU MISS YOUR PAL, DON'T YA, SCHROEDER?
HOWL
HOWL
I KNOW I KNOW
FLASH-FORWARD
THAT BIRD WAS FIXIN' TO DIE...
AND THAT'S A STONE FACT
IN MY FEVERED IMAGINATION
HELLO, MISTER! WILL YOU BE MY FRIE-AAAAH
crush
BACK TO REALITY
IDIOT MURDERER PARASITE JERK
LATER, AT THE AIRPORT
SIGH
BALANCE -$2.00
ATM

POSTSCRIPT: EVENTUALLY I GOT MY CAT BACK (A NEIGHBOR FOUND HIM), BUT AT THE TIME, THIS I COULD NOT KNOW. —ed.

IVAN BRUNETTI

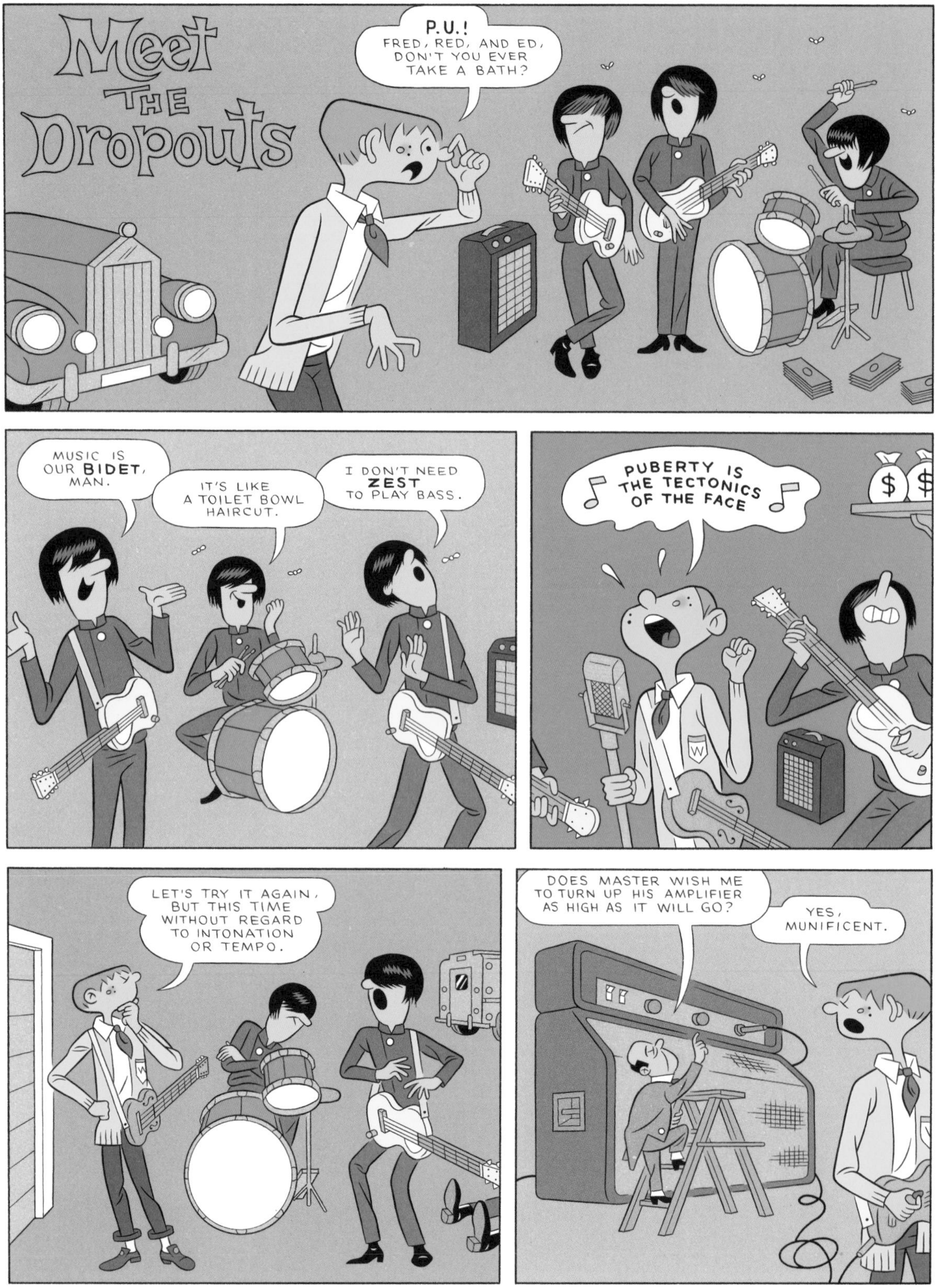
Meet THE Dropouts
P.U.! FRED, RED, AND ED, DON'T YOU EVER TAKE A BATH?
MUSIC IS OUR BIDET, MAN.
IT'S LIKE A TOILET BOWL HAIRCUT.
I DON'T NEED ZEST TO PLAY BASS.
PUBERTY IS THE TECTONICS OF THE FACE
LET'S TRY IT AGAIN, BUT THIS TIME WITHOUT REGARD TO INTONATION OR TEMPO.
DOES MASTER WISH ME TO TURN UP HIS AMPLIFIER AS HIGH AS IT WILL GO?
YES, MUNIFICENT.

TIM HENSLEY

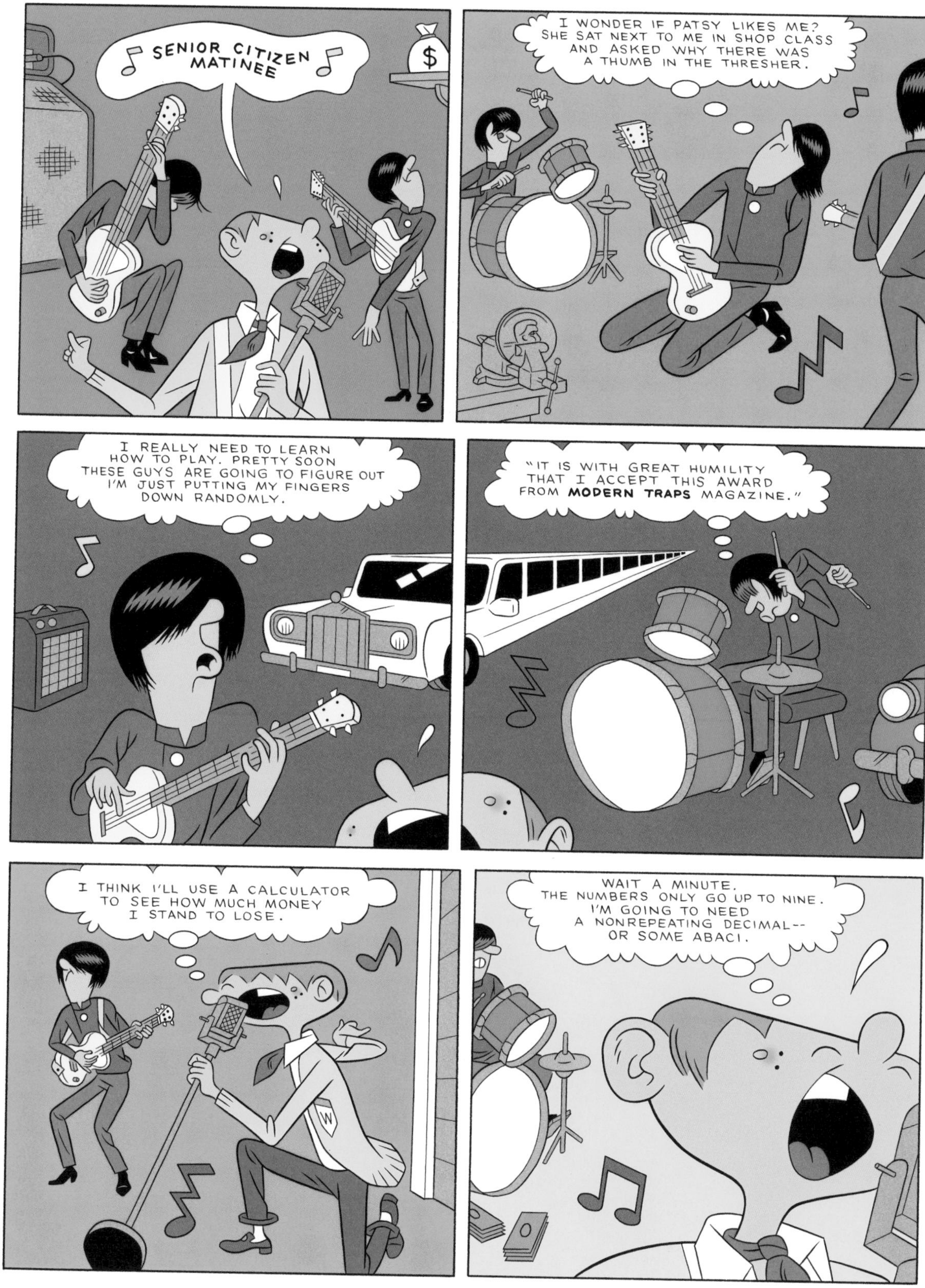
SENIOR CITIZEN MATINEE
I WONDER IF PATSY LIKES ME? SHE SAT NEXT TO ME IN SHOP CLASS AND ASKED WHY THERE WAS A THUMB IN THE THRESHER.
I REALLY NEED TO LEARN HOW TO PLAY. PRETTY SOON THESE GUYS ARE GOING TO FIGURE OUT I'M JUST PUTTING MY FINGERS DOWN RANDOMLY.
"IT IS WITH GREAT HUMILITY THAT I ACCEPT THIS AWARD FROM MODERN TRAPS MAGAZINE."
I THINK I'LL USE A CALCULATOR TO SEE HOW MUCH MONEY I STAND TO LOSE.
WAIT A MINUTE. THE NUMBERS ONLY GO UP TO NINE. I'M GOING TO NEED A NONREPEATING DECIMAL-- OR SOME ABACI.

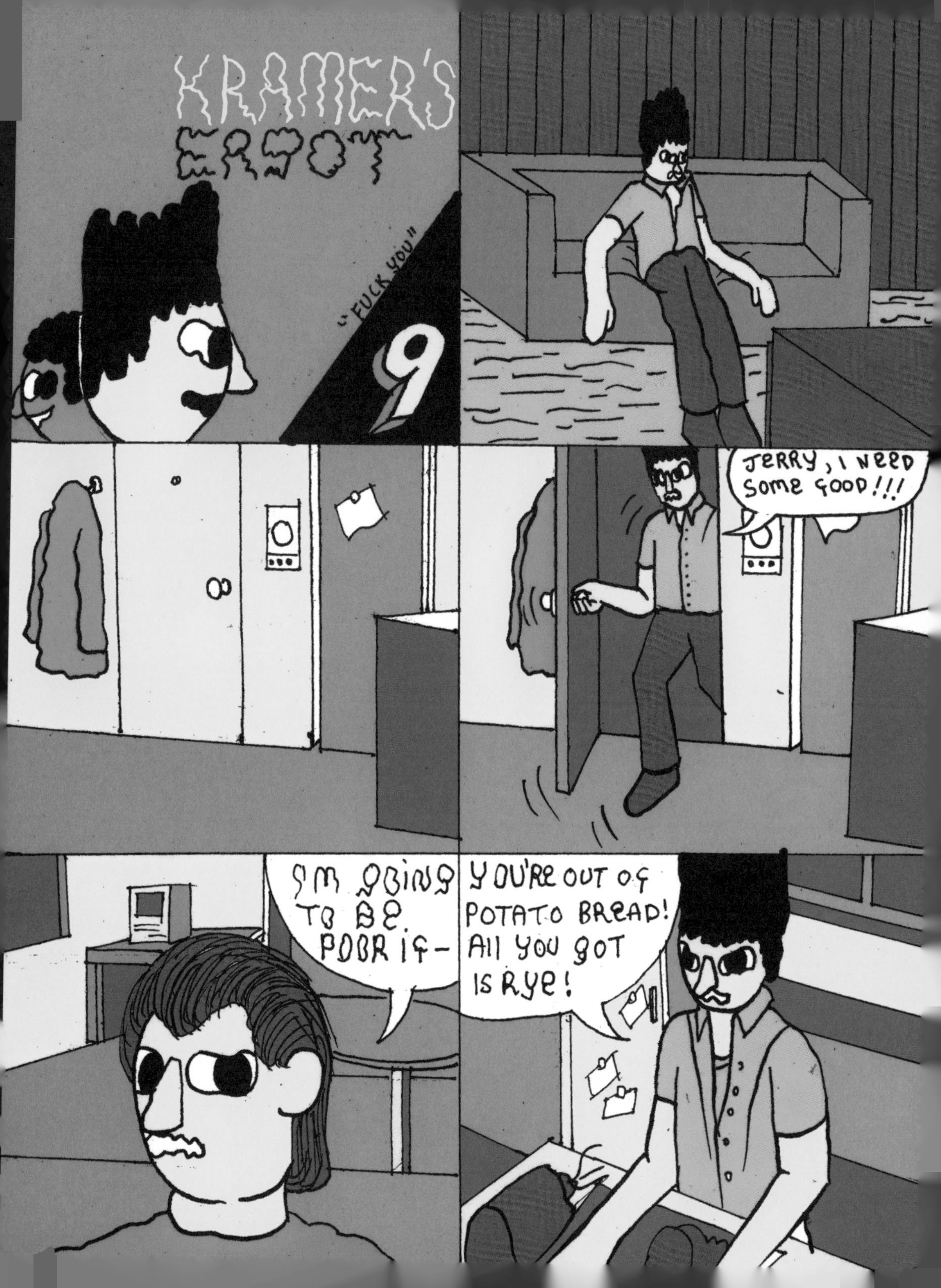
KRAMER'S
ERGOT
"FUCK YOU"
9
JERRY, I NEED SOME FOOD!!!
I'M GOING TO BE POOR IF-
YOU'RE OUT OF POTATO BREAD! All YOU GOT IS RYE!

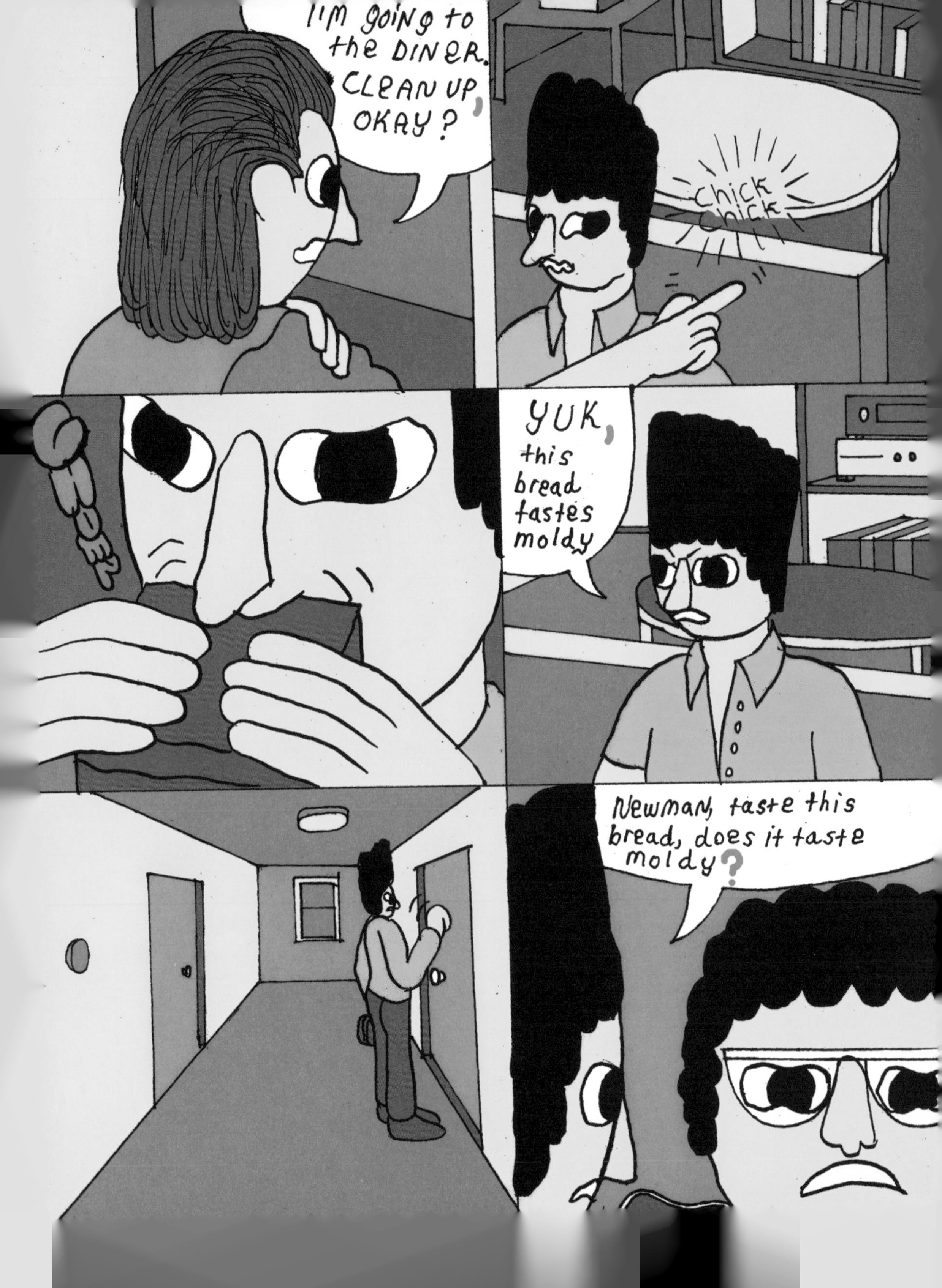
I'M going to the DINER. CLEAN UP, OKAY?
chick chick
YUK, this bread tastes moldy
Newman, taste this bread, does it taste moldy?

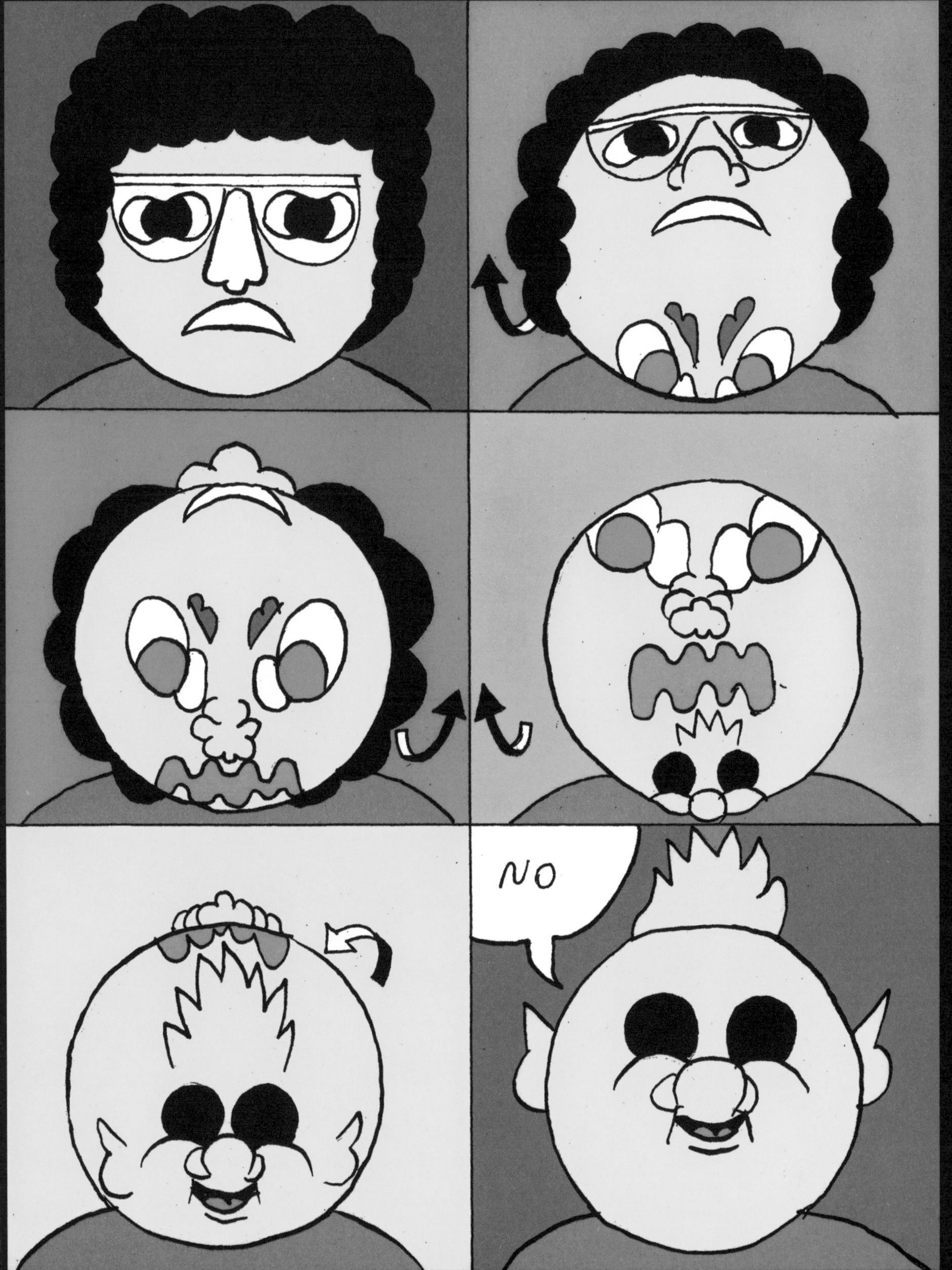
NO

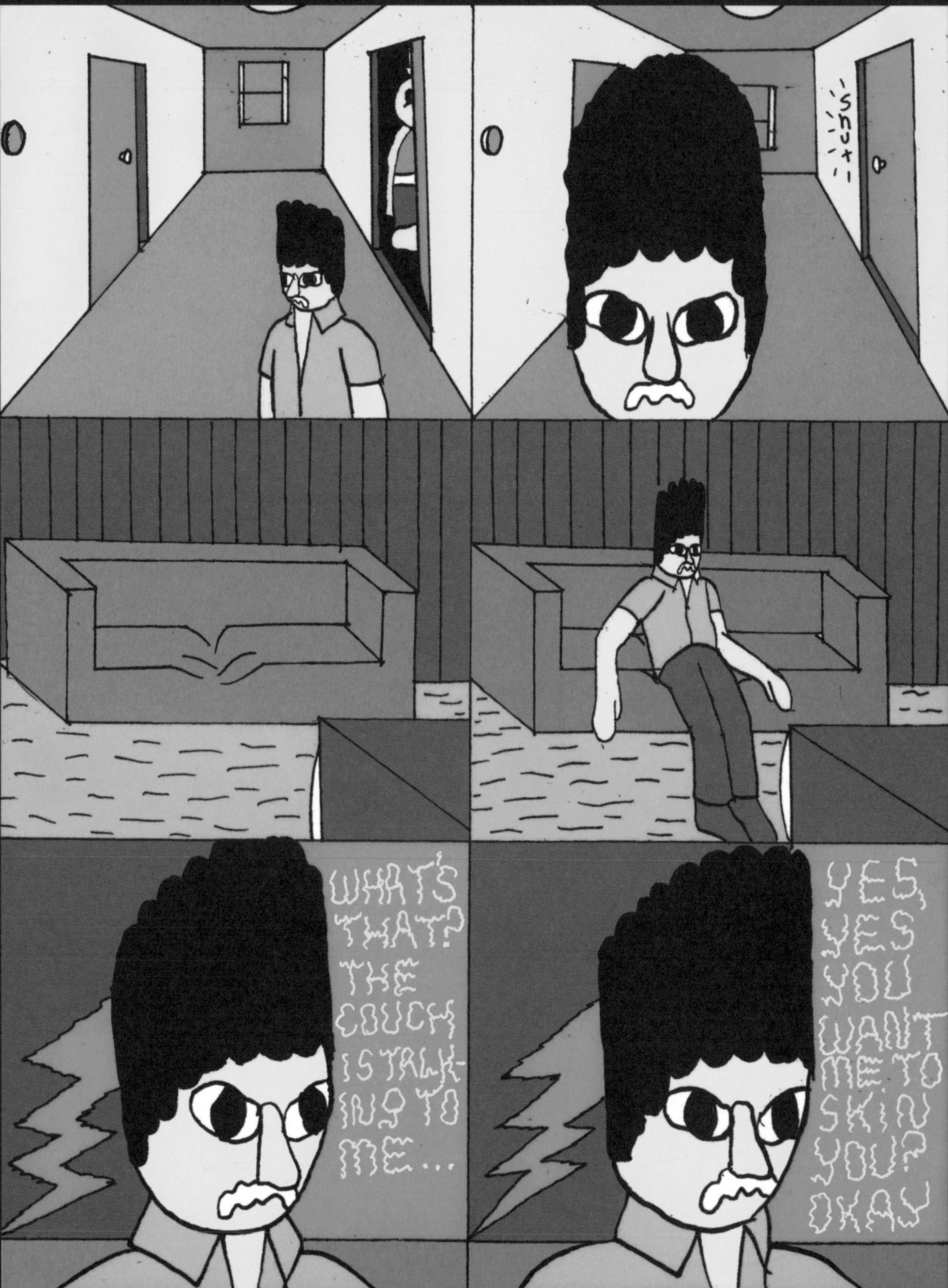
SNUT
WHAT'S THAT? THE COUCH IS TALKING TO ME...
YES, YES YOU WANT ME TO SKIN YOU? OKAY

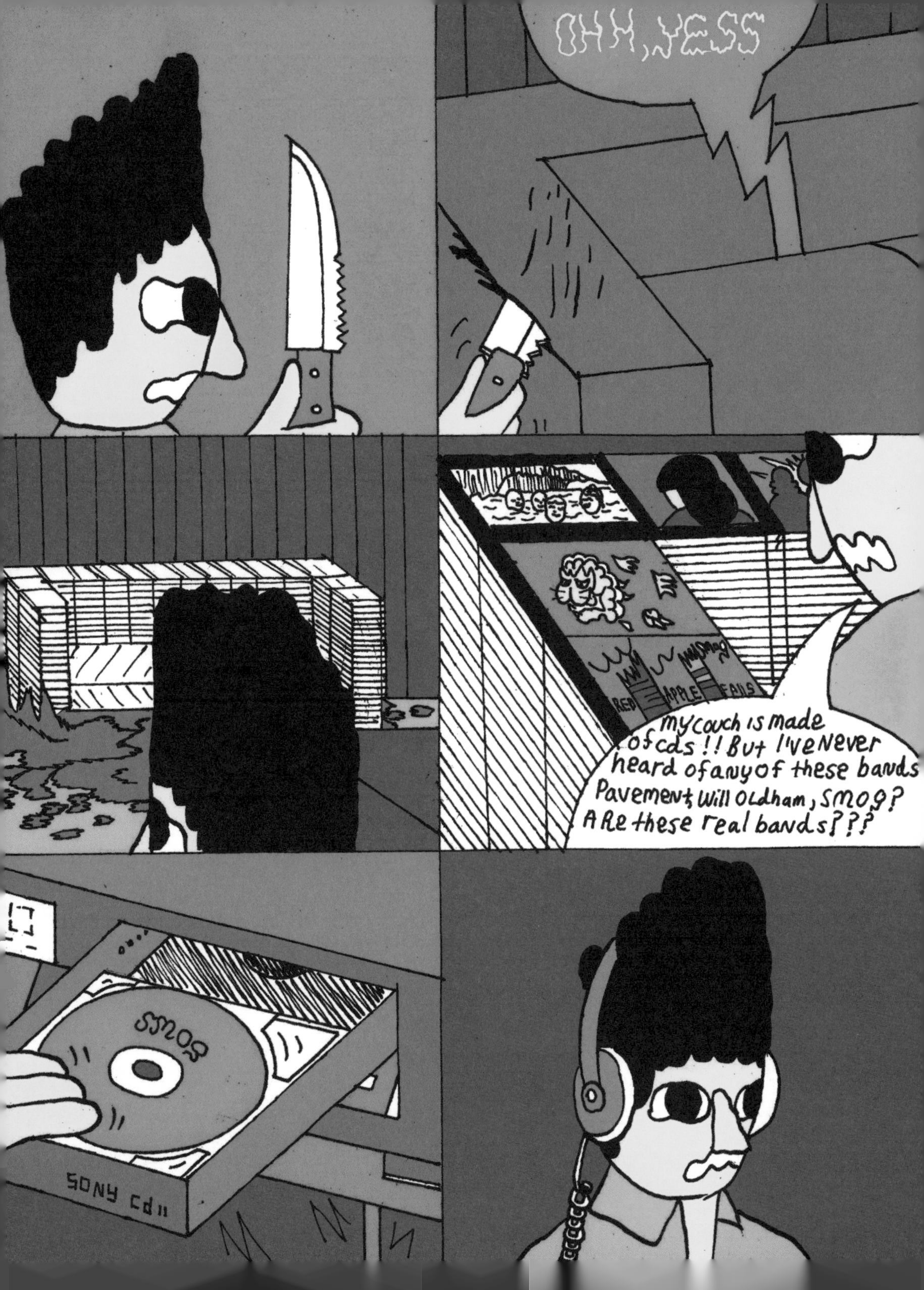
OHH, YESS
RED APPLE FALLS
my couch is made of cds!! But I've Never heard of any of these bands Pavement, Will Oldham, Smog? ARe these real bands???
SMOG
SONY cd11

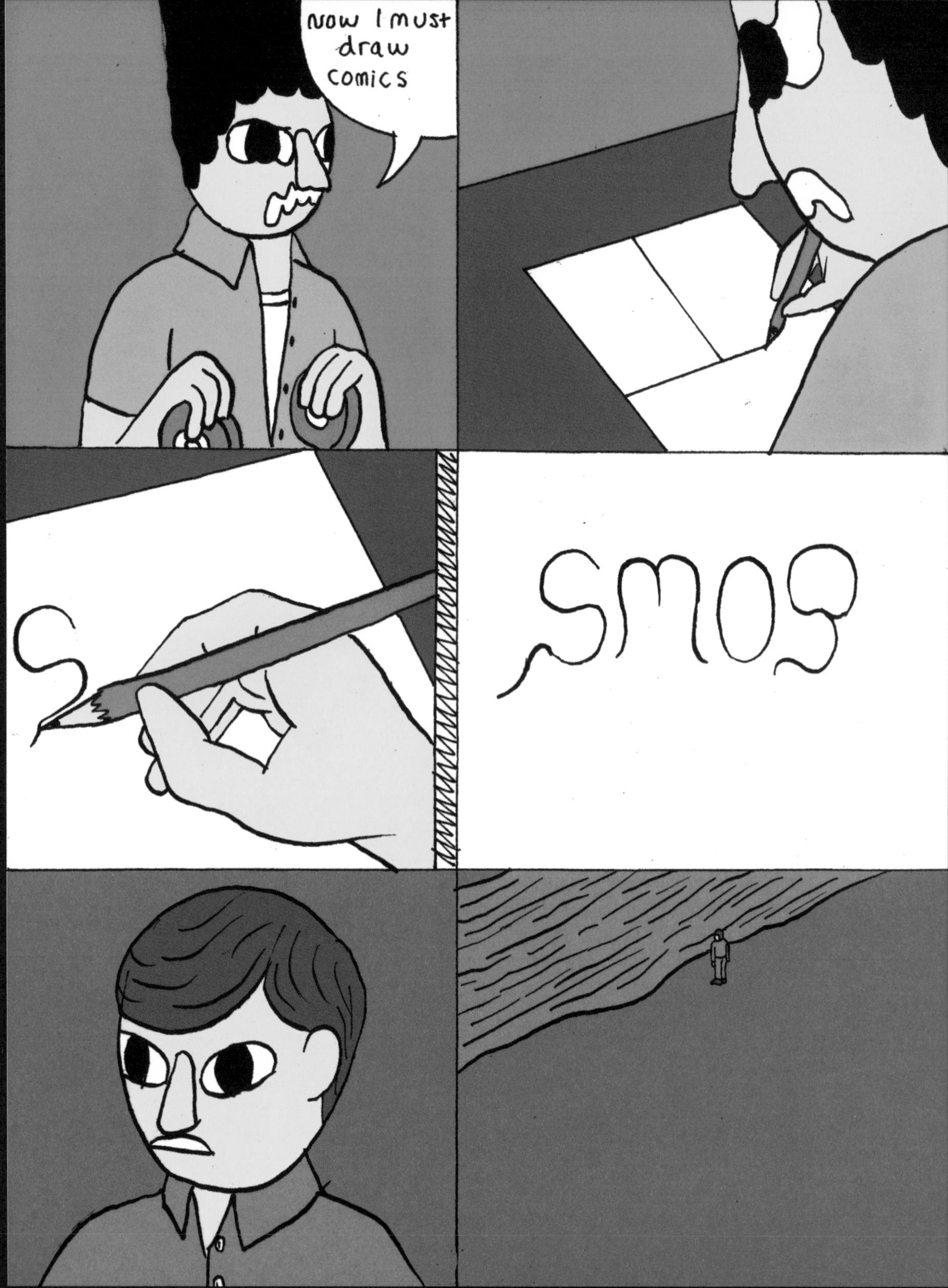
now I must draw comics
SMOG

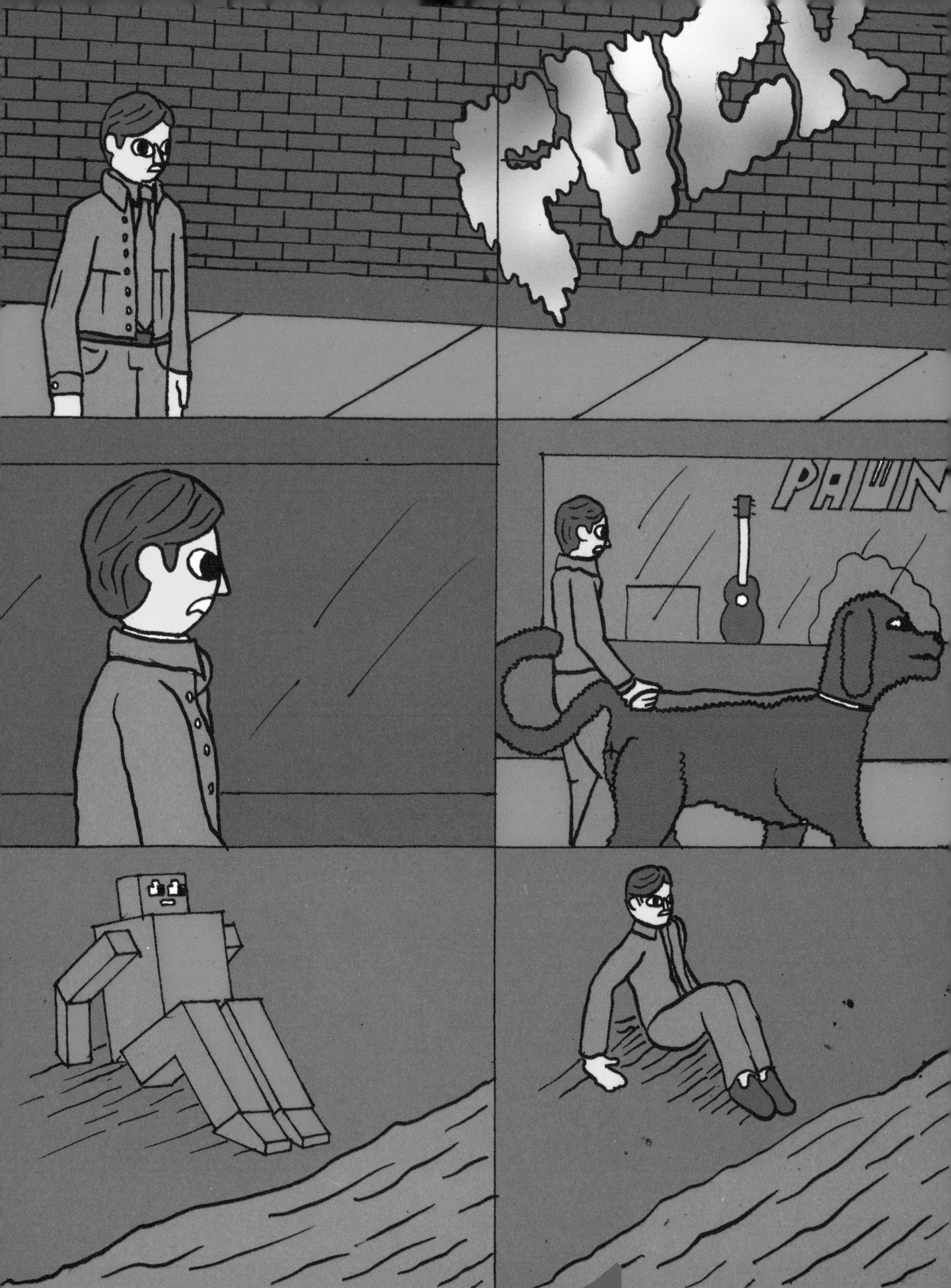
FUCK
PAWN

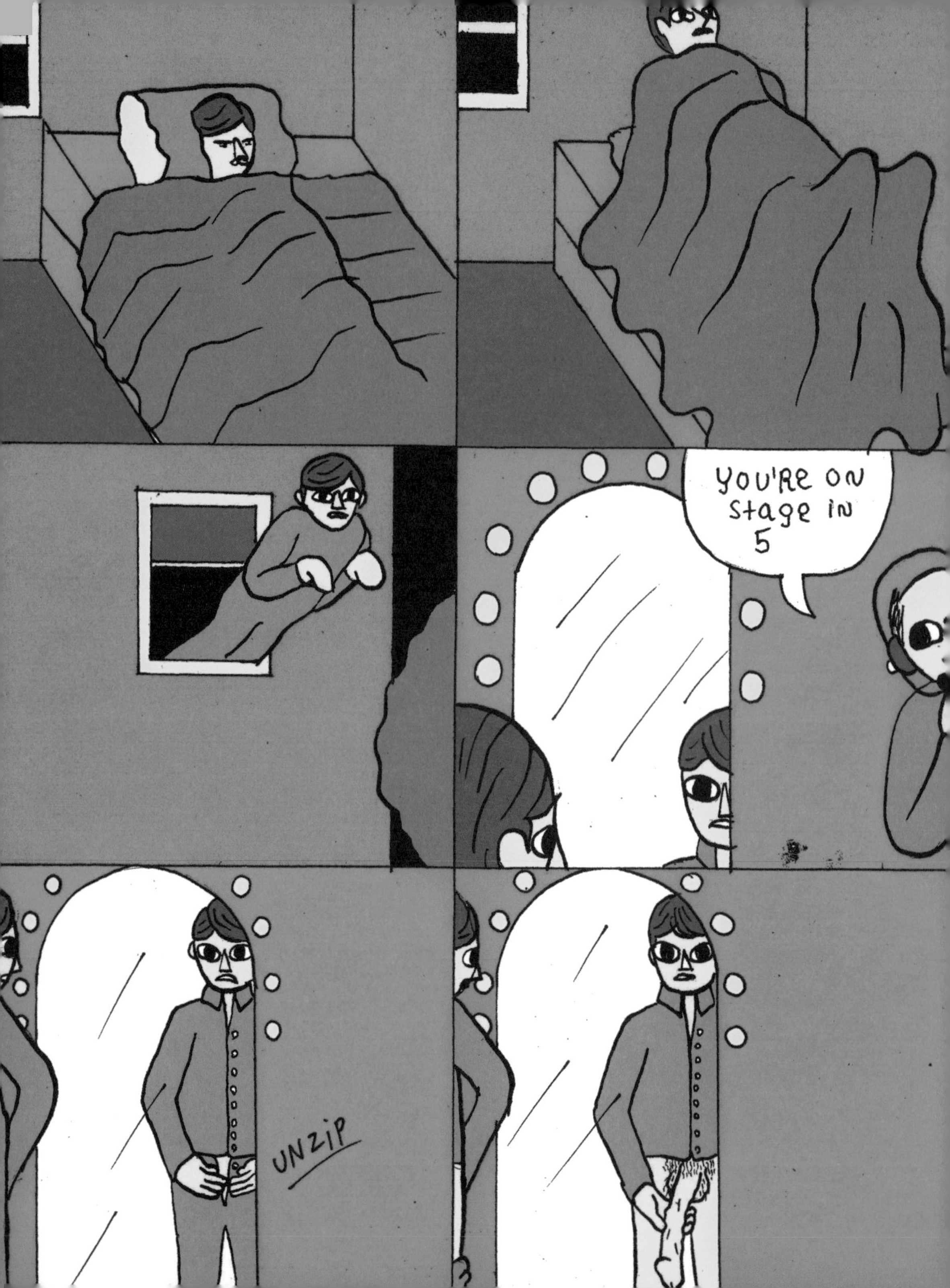
YOU'RE ON stage in 5
UNZIP

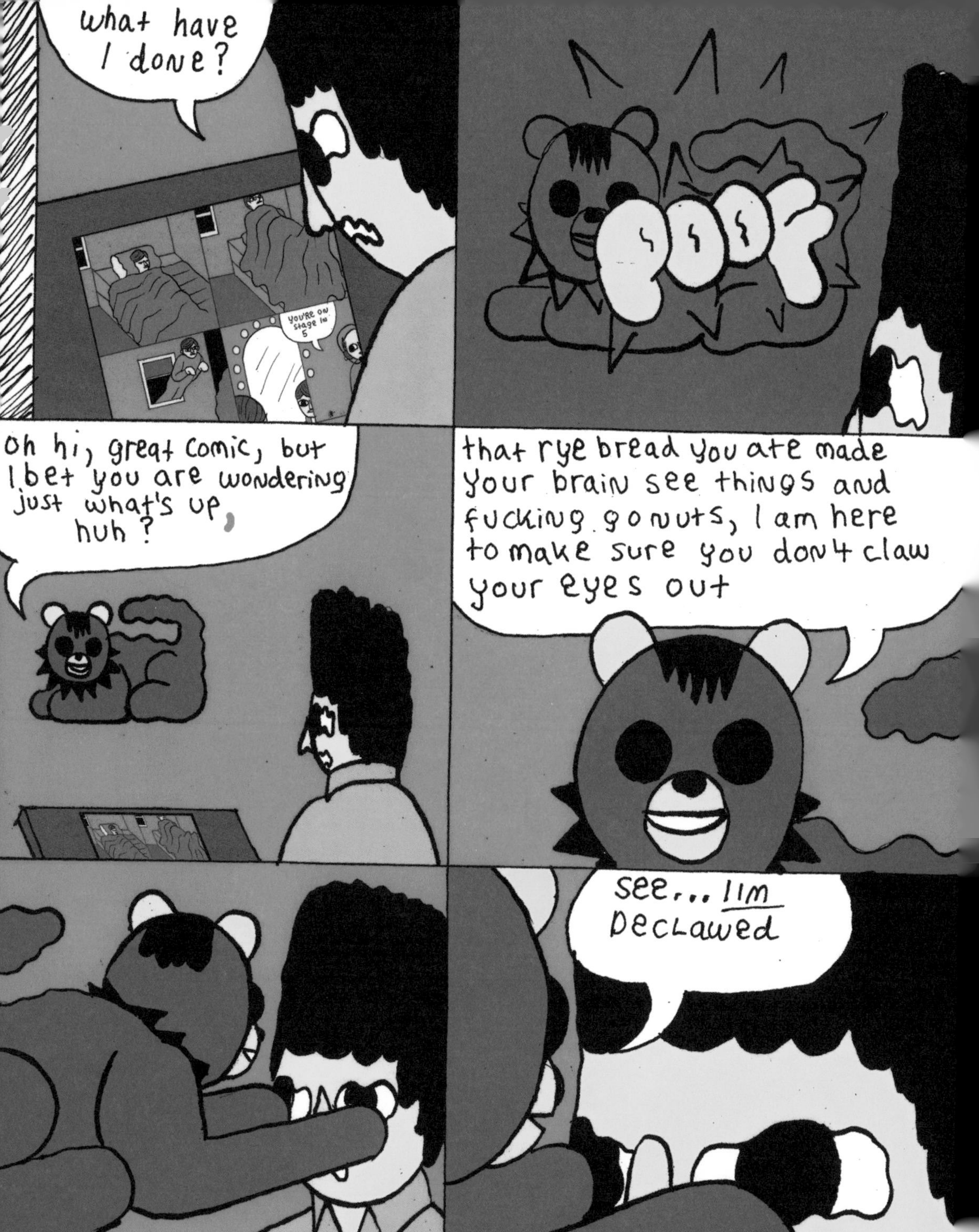
what have I done?
YOU'RE ON stage in 5
POOF
Oh hi, great comic, but I bet you are wondering just what's up, huh?
that rye bread you ate made your brain see things and fucking go nuts, I am here to make sure you don't claw your eyes out
see... I'm declawed

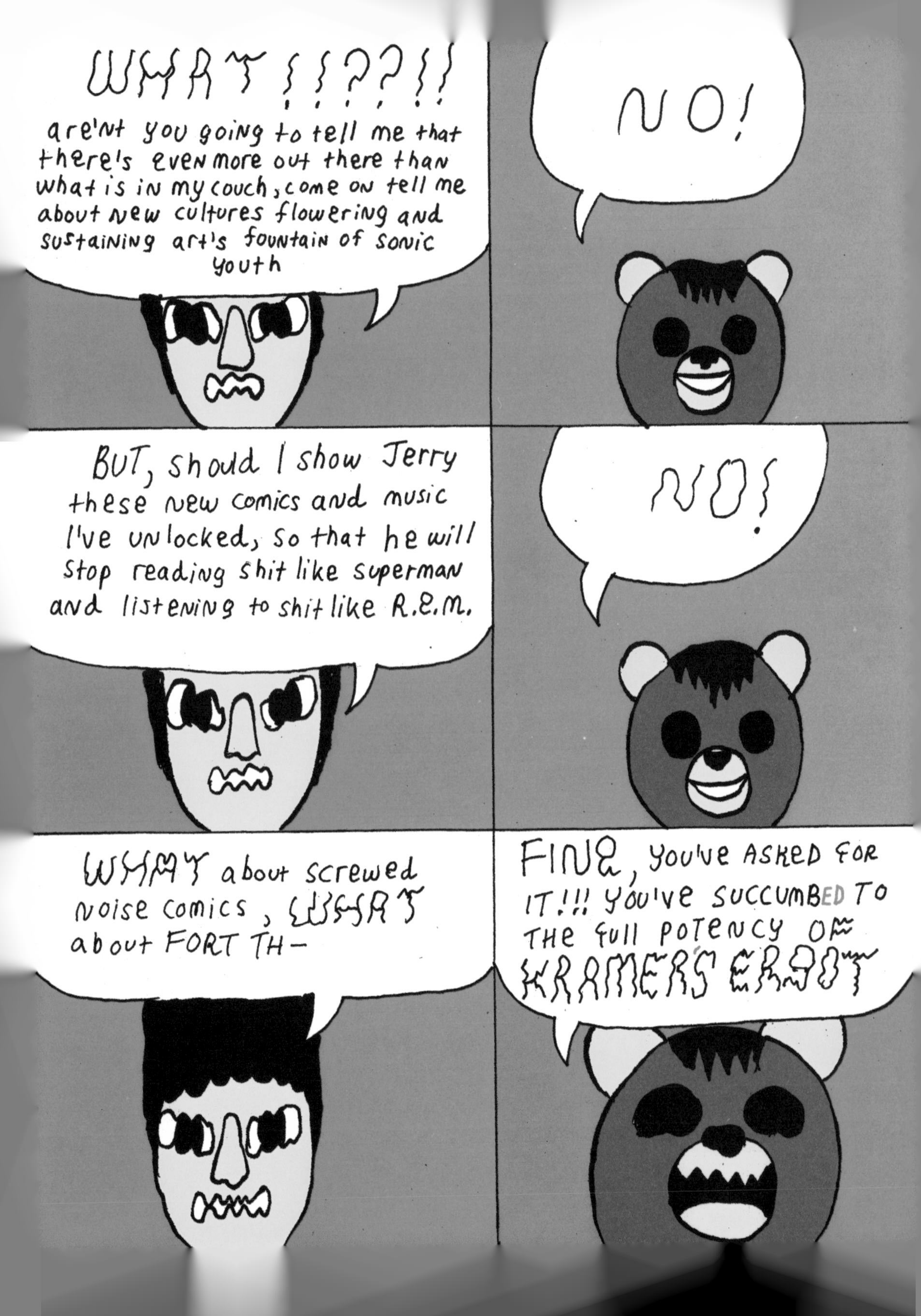
WHAT!!??!!
are'nt you going to tell me that there's even more out there than what is in my couch, come on tell me about new cultures flowering and sustaining art's fountain of sonic youth
NO!
BUT, should I show Jerry these new comics and music I've unlocked, so that he will stop reading shit like superman and listening to shit like R.E.M.
NO!
WHAT about screwed noise comics, WHAT about FORT TH-
FINE, you've ASKED FOR IT!!! You've SUCCUMBED TO THE full POTENCY OF KRAMERS ERGOT

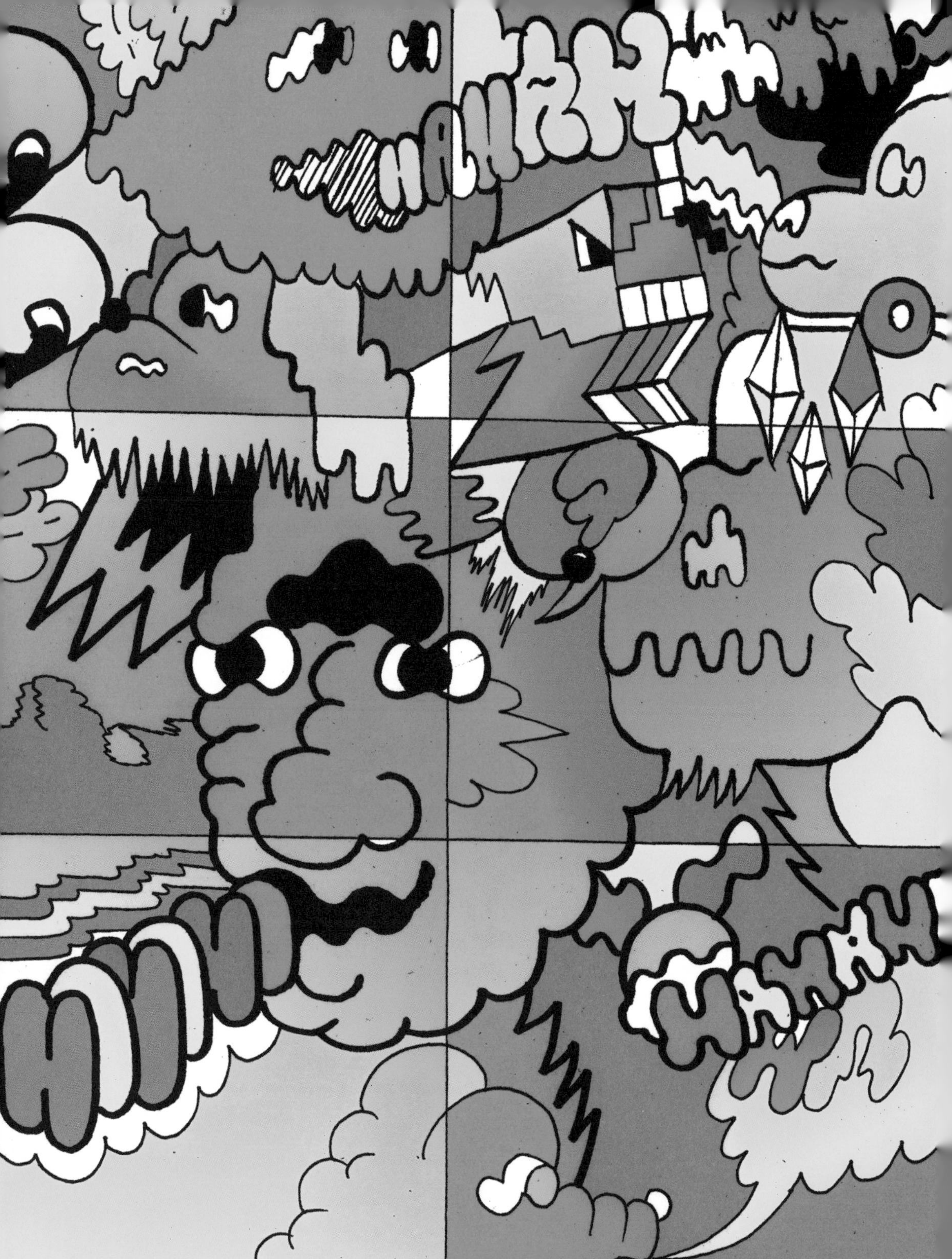

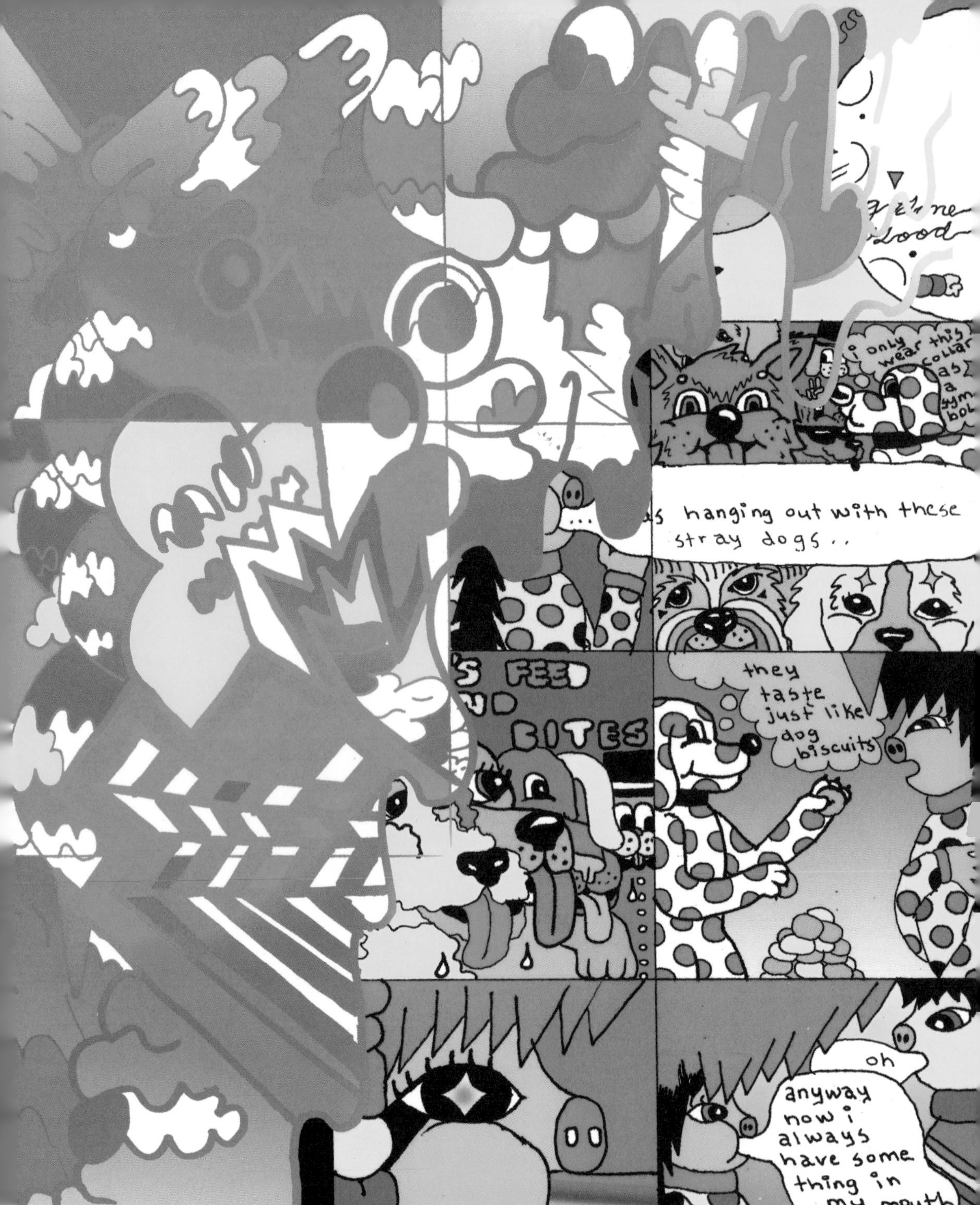
i only wear this collar as a sym bol
hanging out with these stray dogs..
S FEED
BITES
they taste just like dog biscuits
oh
anyway now i always have some thing in my mouth

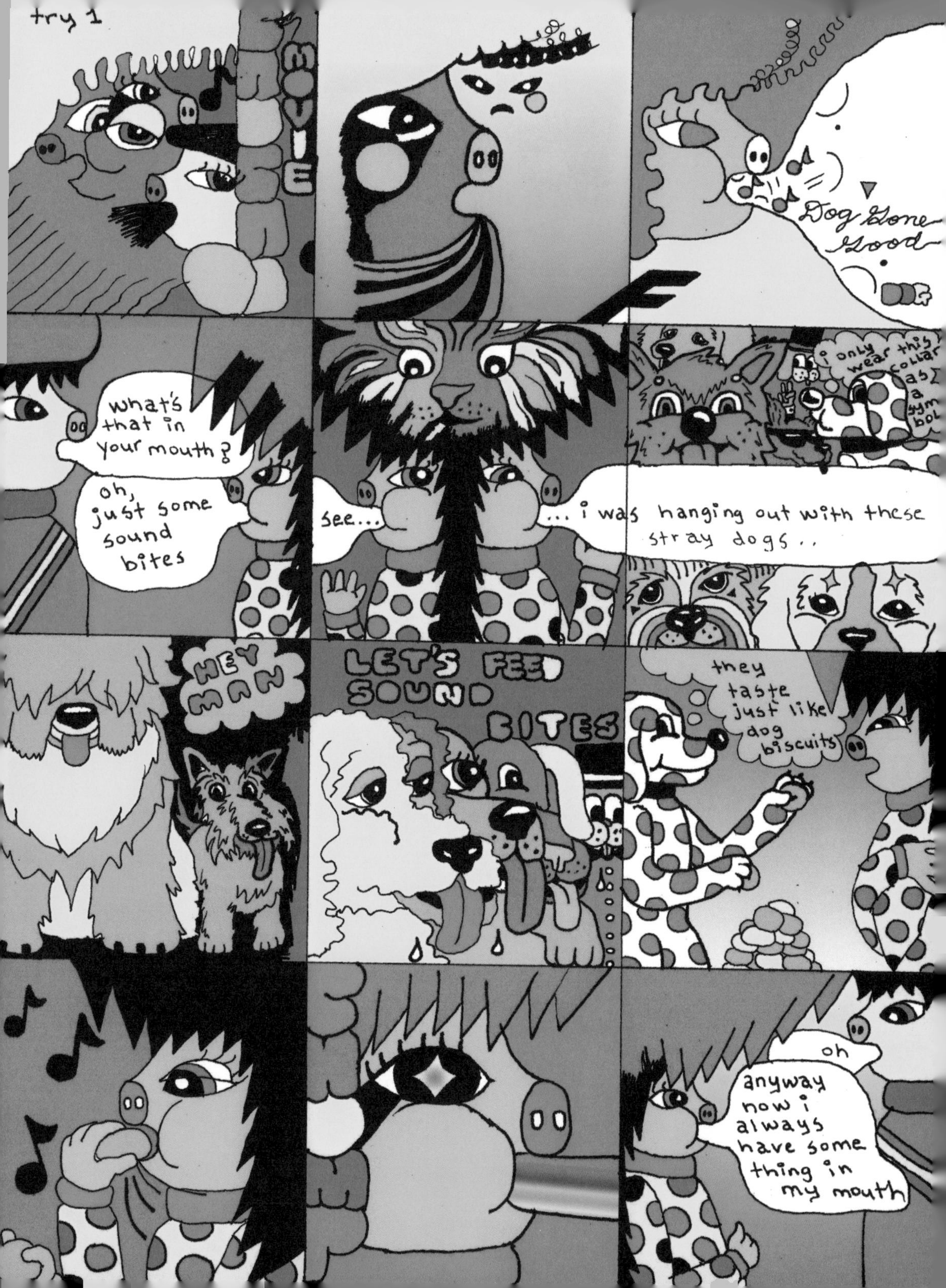
try 1
MOVIE
Dog Gone Good
what's that in your mouth?
oh, just some sound bites
see...
...i was hanging out with these stray dogs..
i only wear this collar as a symbol
HEY MAN
LET'S FEED SOUND BITES
they taste just like dog biscuits
oh
anyway now i always have some thing in my mouth

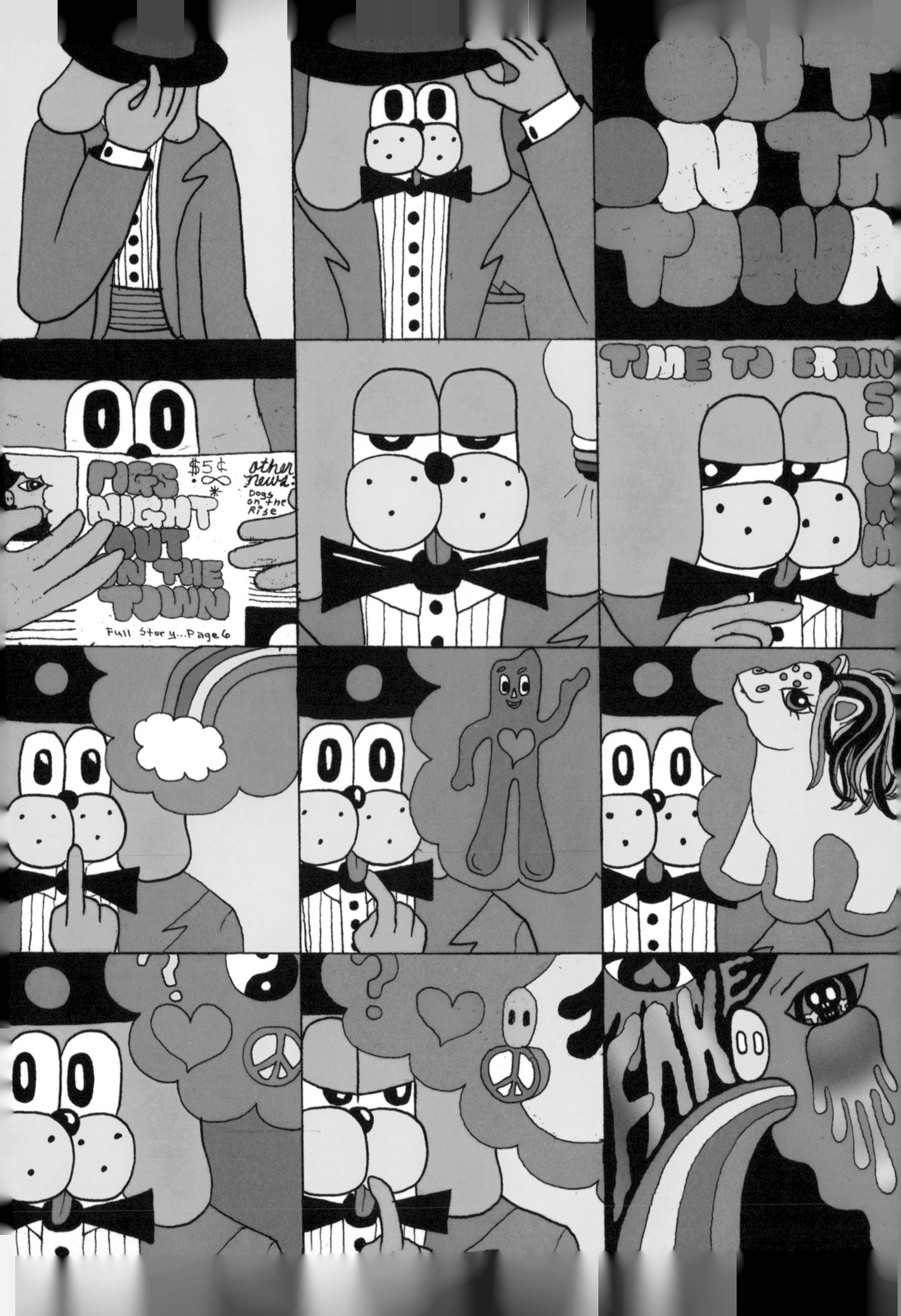
PIGS NIGHT OUT ON THE TOWN
$5¢
other news: Dogs on the Rise
Full Story...Page 6
TIME TO BRAIN STORM
FAKE

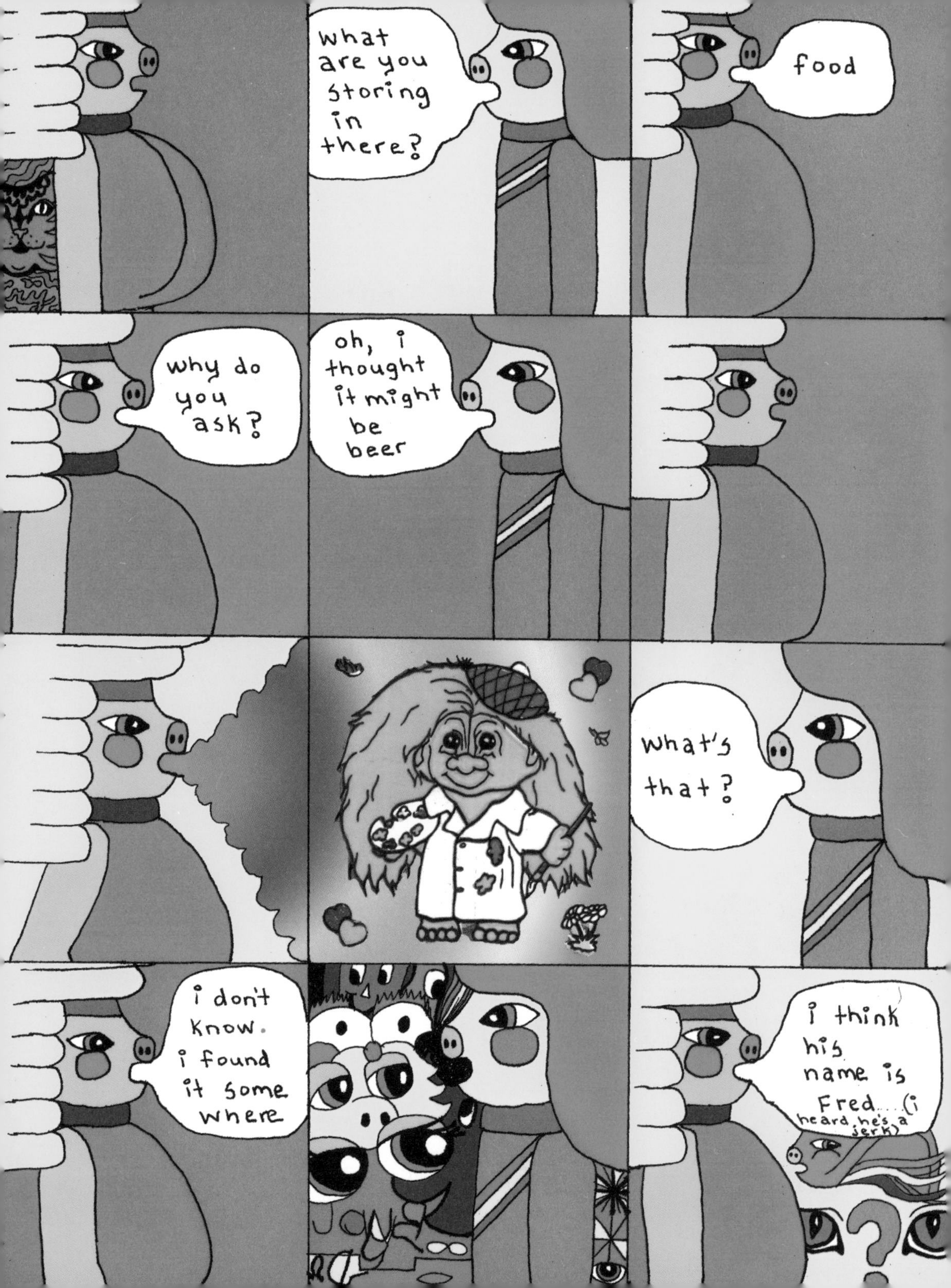
what are you storing in there?
food
why do you ask?
oh, i thought it might be beer
what's that?
i don't know. i found it some where
i think his name is Fred.... (i heard he's a jerk)

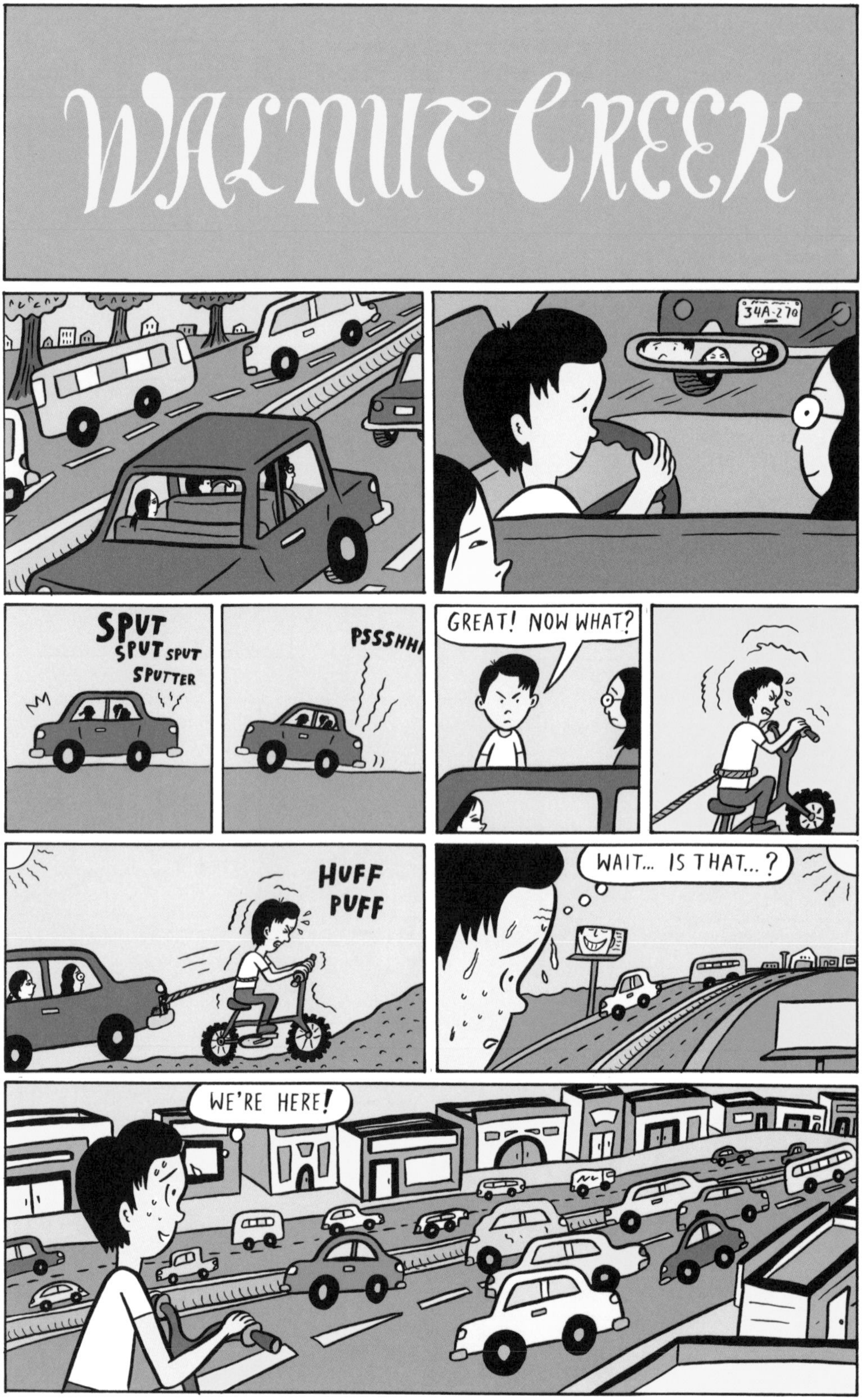
WALNUT CREEK
34A-270
SPUT
SPUT SPUT
SPUTTER
PSSSHH
GREAT! NOW WHAT?
HUFF
PUFF
WAIT... IS THAT...?
WE'RE HERE!

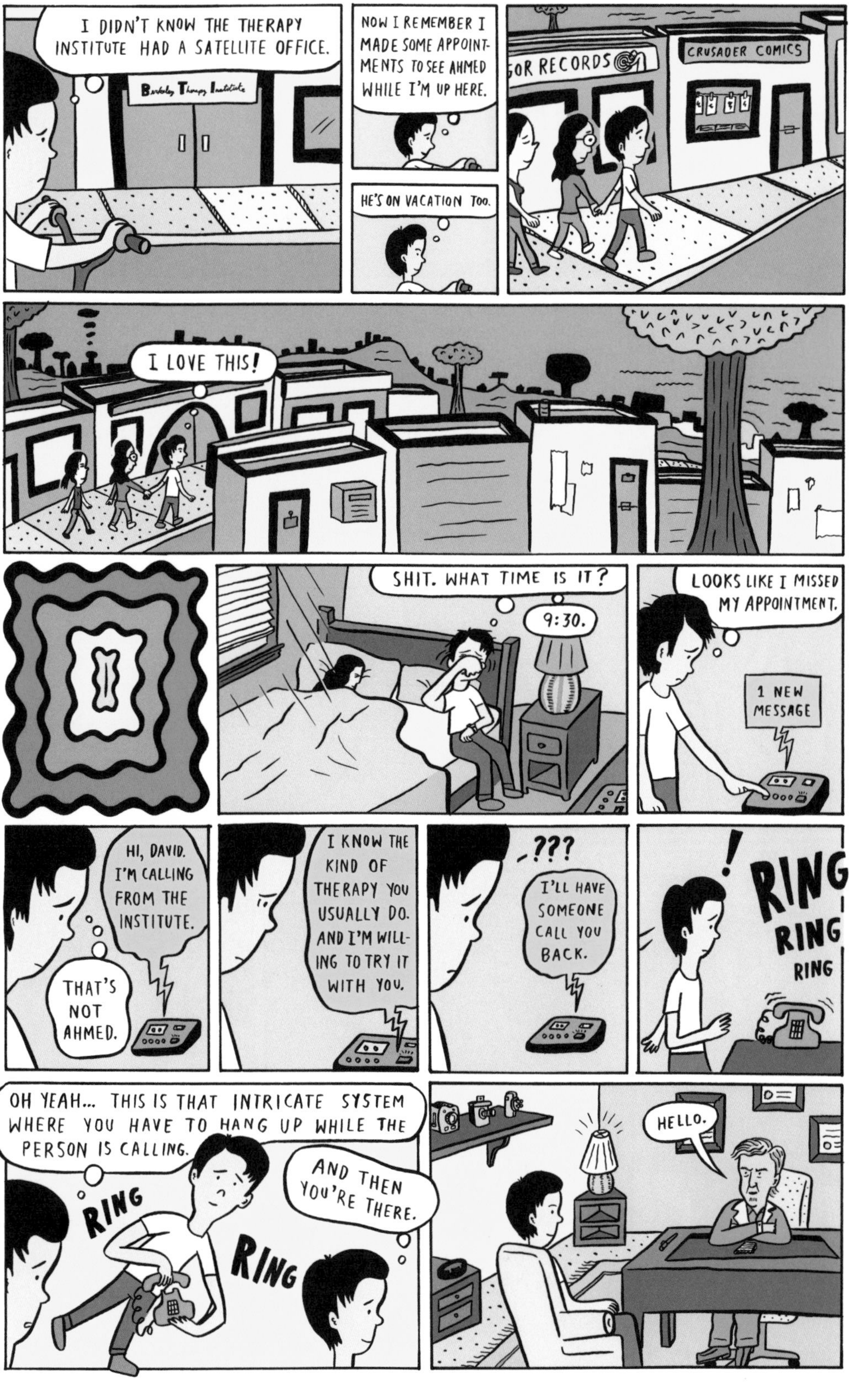
I DIDN'T KNOW THE THERAPY INSTITUTE HAD A SATELLITE OFFICE.
NOW I REMEMBER I MADE SOME APPOINTMENTS TO SEE AHMED WHILE I'M UP HERE.
HE'S ON VACATION TOO.
GOR RECORDS
CRUSADER COMICS
I LOVE THIS!
SHIT. WHAT TIME IS IT?
9:30.
LOOKS LIKE I MISSED MY APPOINTMENT.
1 NEW MESSAGE
HI, DAVID. I'M CALLING FROM THE INSTITUTE.
THAT'S NOT AHMED.
I KNOW THE KIND OF THERAPY YOU USUALLY DO. AND I'M WILLING TO TRY IT WITH YOU.
???
I'LL HAVE SOMEONE CALL YOU BACK.
!
RING
RING
RING
OH YEAH... THIS IS THAT INTRICATE SYSTEM WHERE YOU HAVE TO HANG UP WHILE THE PERSON IS CALLING.
RING
RING
AND THEN YOU'RE THERE.
HELLO.

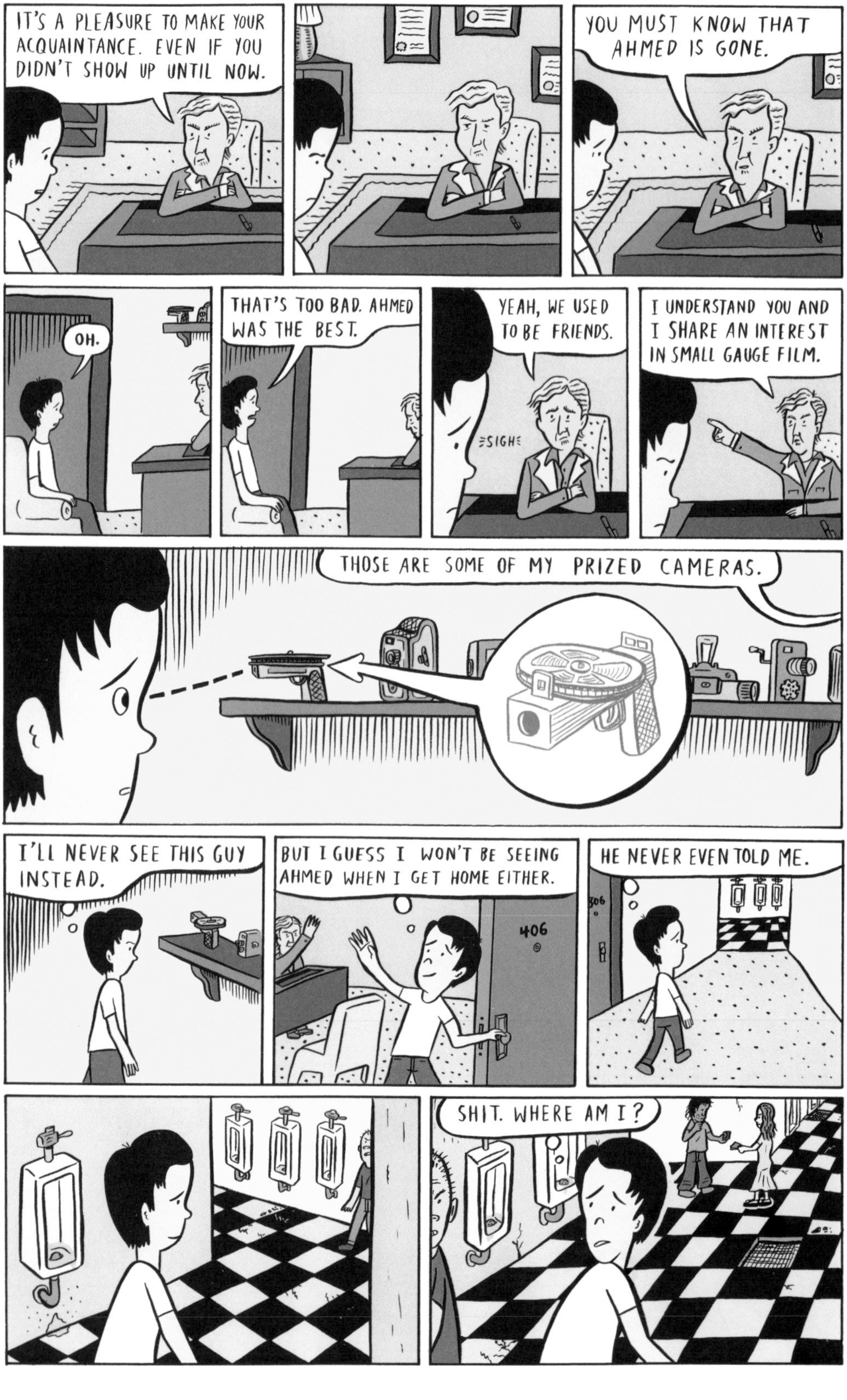
IT'S A PLEASURE TO MAKE YOUR ACQUAINTANCE. EVEN IF YOU DIDN'T SHOW UP UNTIL NOW.
YOU MUST KNOW THAT AHMED IS GONE.
OH.
THAT'S TOO BAD. AHMED WAS THE BEST.
YEAH, WE USED TO BE FRIENDS.
SIGH
I UNDERSTAND YOU AND I SHARE AN INTEREST IN SMALL GAUGE FILM.
THOSE ARE SOME OF MY PRIZED CAMERAS.
I'LL NEVER SEE THIS GUY INSTEAD.
BUT I GUESS I WON'T BE SEEING AHMED WHEN I GET HOME EITHER.
406
HE NEVER EVEN TOLD ME.
SHIT. WHERE AM I?

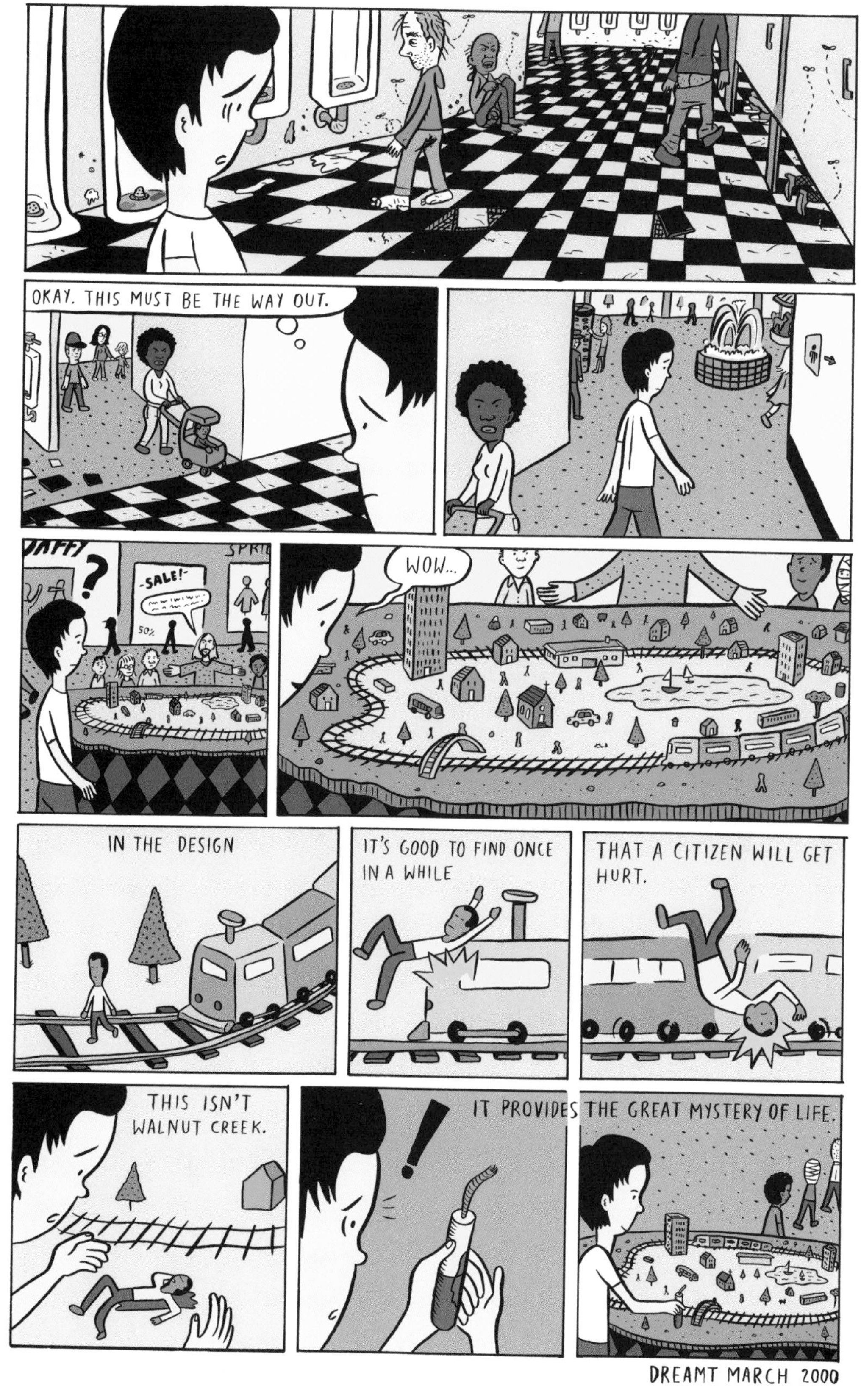
OKAY. THIS MUST BE THE WAY OUT.
?
-SALE!-
50%
WOW...
IN THE DESIGN
IT'S GOOD TO FIND ONCE IN A WHILE
THAT A CITIZEN WILL GET HURT.
THIS ISN'T WALNUT CREEK.
!
IT PROVIDES THE GREAT MYSTERY OF LIFE.

DREAMT MARCH 2000

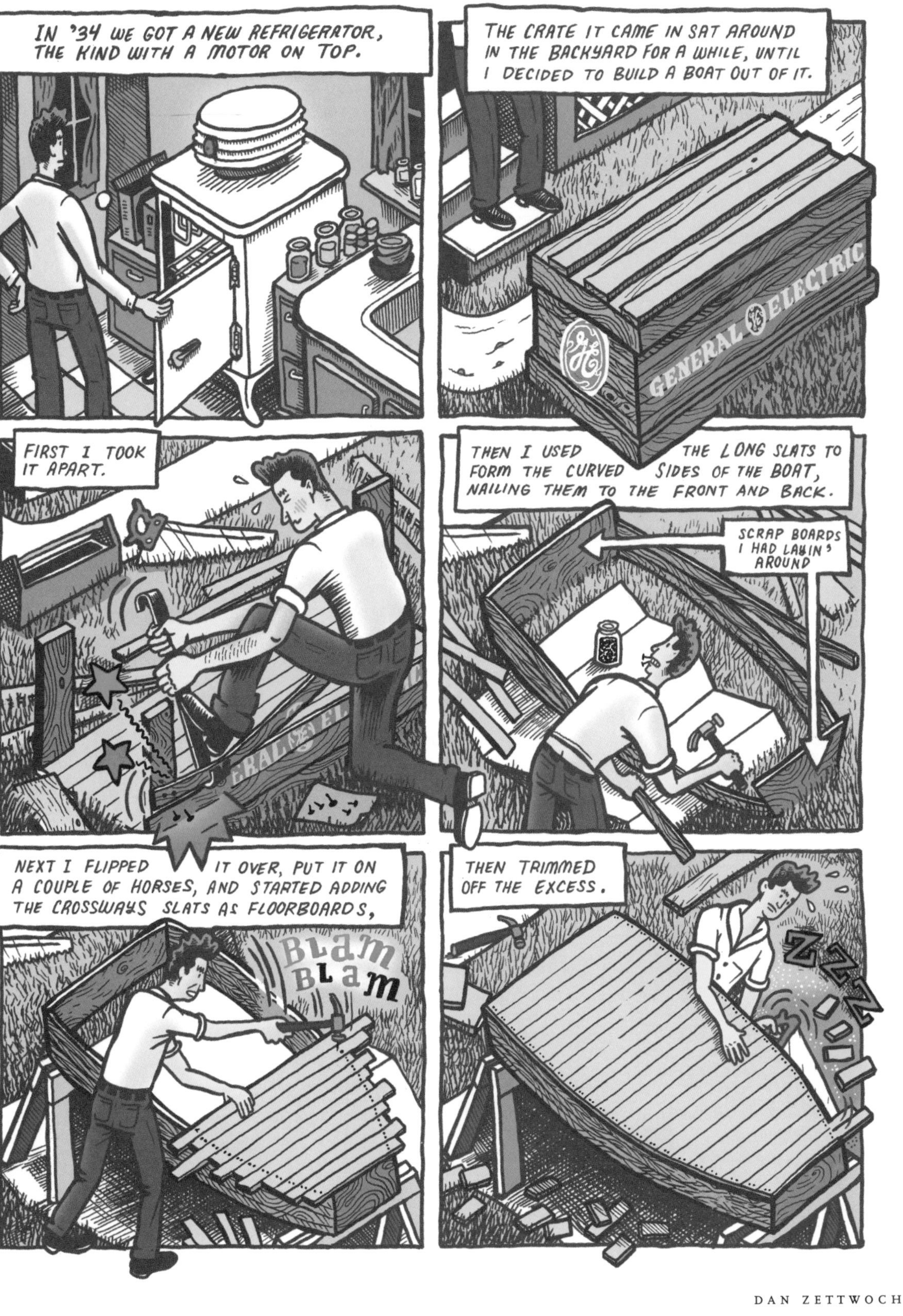
IN '34 WE GOT A NEW REFRIGERATOR, THE KIND WITH A MOTOR ON TOP.
THE CRATE IT CAME IN SAT AROUND IN THE BACKYARD FOR A WHILE, UNTIL I DECIDED TO BUILD A BOAT OUT OF IT.
GENERAL ELECTRIC
FIRST I TOOK IT APART.
THEN I USED THE LONG SLATS TO FORM THE CURVED SIDES OF THE BOAT, NAILING THEM TO THE FRONT AND BACK.
SCRAP BOARDS I HAD LAYIN' AROUND
NEXT I FLIPPED IT OVER, PUT IT ON A COUPLE OF HORSES, AND STARTED ADDING THE CROSSWAYS SLATS AS FLOORBOARDS,
BLAM
BLAM
THEN TRIMMED OFF THE EXCESS.
ZZZZ

DAN ZETTWOCH

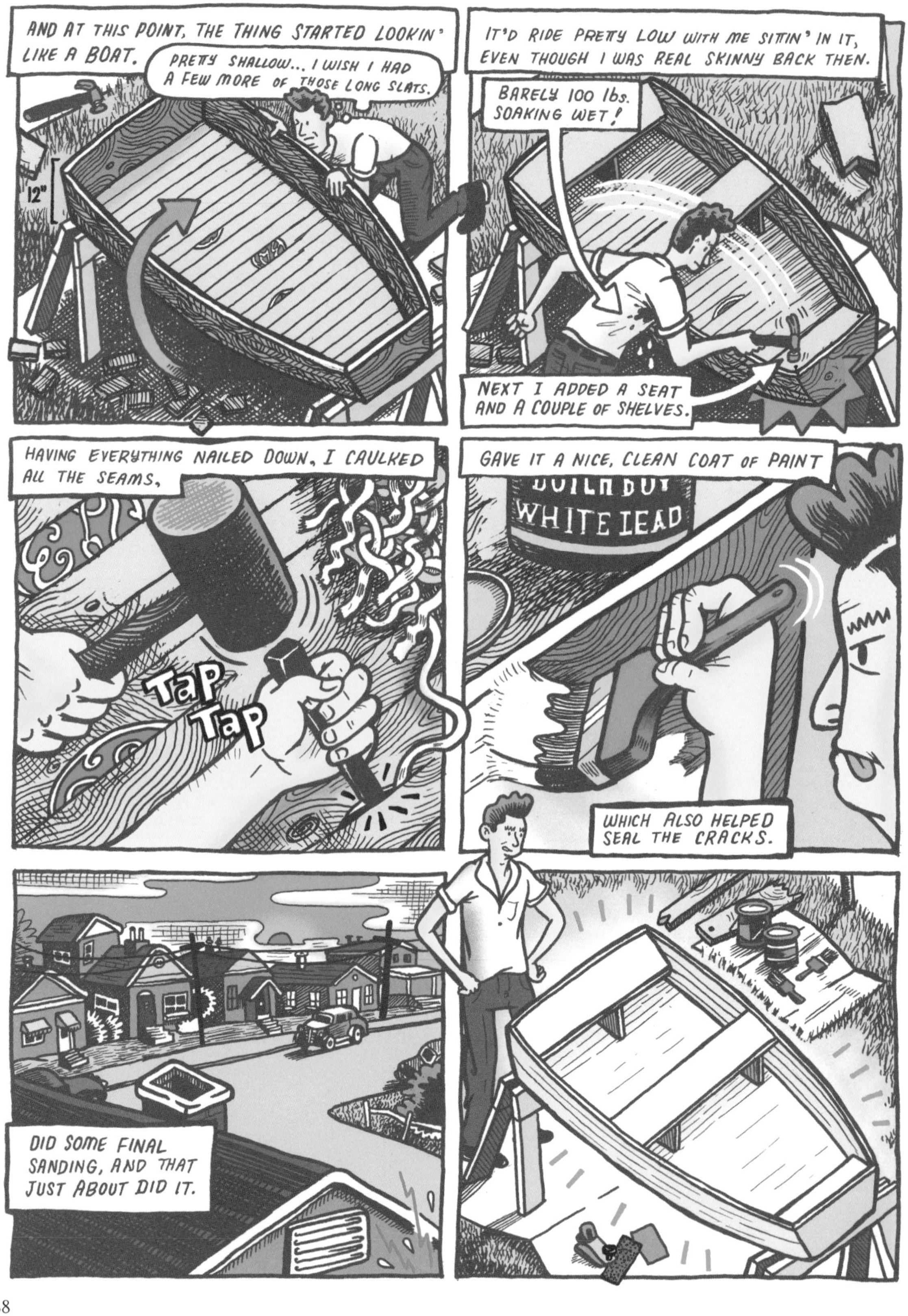

AND AT THIS POINT, THE THING STARTED LOOKIN' LIKE A BOAT.
PRETTY SHALLOW... I WISH I HAD A FEW MORE OF THOSE LONG SLATS.
12"
IT'D RIDE PRETTY LOW WITH ME SITTIN' IN IT, EVEN THOUGH I WAS REAL SKINNY BACK THEN.
BARELY 100 lbs. SOAKING WET!
NEXT I ADDED A SEAT AND A COUPLE OF SHELVES.
HAVING EVERYTHING NAILED DOWN, I CAULKED ALL THE SEAMS,
TAP TAP
GAVE IT A NICE, CLEAN COAT OF PAINT
WHITE LEAD
WHICH ALSO HELPED SEAL THE CRACKS.
DID SOME FINAL SANDING, AND THAT JUST ABOUT DID IT.

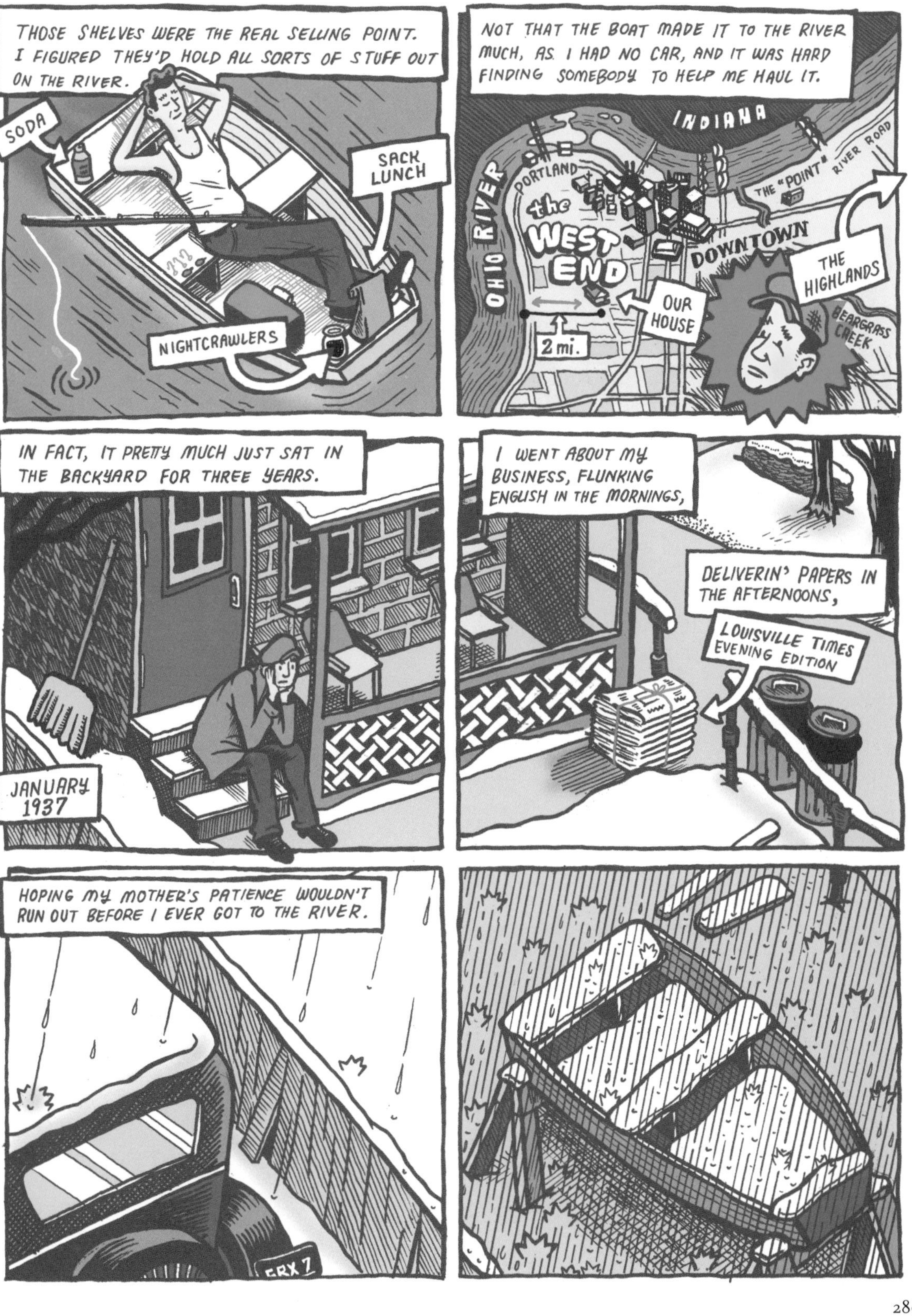
THOSE SHELVES WERE THE REAL SELLING POINT. I FIGURED THEY'D HOLD ALL SORTS OF STUFF OUT ON THE RIVER.
SODA
SACK LUNCH
NIGHTCRAWLERS
NOT THAT THE BOAT MADE IT TO THE RIVER MUCH, AS I HAD NO CAR, AND IT WAS HARD FINDING SOMEBODY TO HELP ME HAUL IT.
INDIANA
PORTLAND
OHIO RIVER
the WEST END
DOWNTOWN
THE "POINT"
RIVER ROAD
THE HIGHLANDS
OUR HOUSE
2 mi.
BEARGRASS CREEK
IN FACT, IT PRETTY MUCH JUST SAT IN THE BACKYARD FOR THREE YEARS.
JANUARY 1937
I WENT ABOUT MY BUSINESS, FLUNKING ENGLISH IN THE MORNINGS,
DELIVERIN' PAPERS IN THE AFTERNOONS,
LOUISVILLE TIMES EVENING EDITION
HOPING MY MOTHER'S PATIENCE WOULDN'T RUN OUT BEFORE I EVER GOT TO THE RIVER.
ERX 7

WON'T BE
THE GREAT '37 FLOOD

THE GATEWAY TO THE SOUTH LOUISVILLE

IT WAS ALREADY the WORST FLOOD ON RECORD, AND THE RAIN WAS STILL COMIN' DOWN.

UNIVERSAL NEWSREEL

LOUISVILLE, KY

COPYRIGHT 1937

THE WHOLE OHIO VALLEY WAS SOAKED, FROM PITTSBURGH TO CAIRO. I'D HEARD ABOUT FREIGHT TRAINS SUNK IN WEST VIRGINIA, THE PRISON BREAK IN FRANKFORT, THE RIVER FULL OF FLAMES IN CINCINNATI, ALL IMPOSSIBLE TO FIGHT.

GIANT, FLOATING POOLS OF SPILT GASOLINE, SPARKED BY DOWNED STREETCAR WIRE

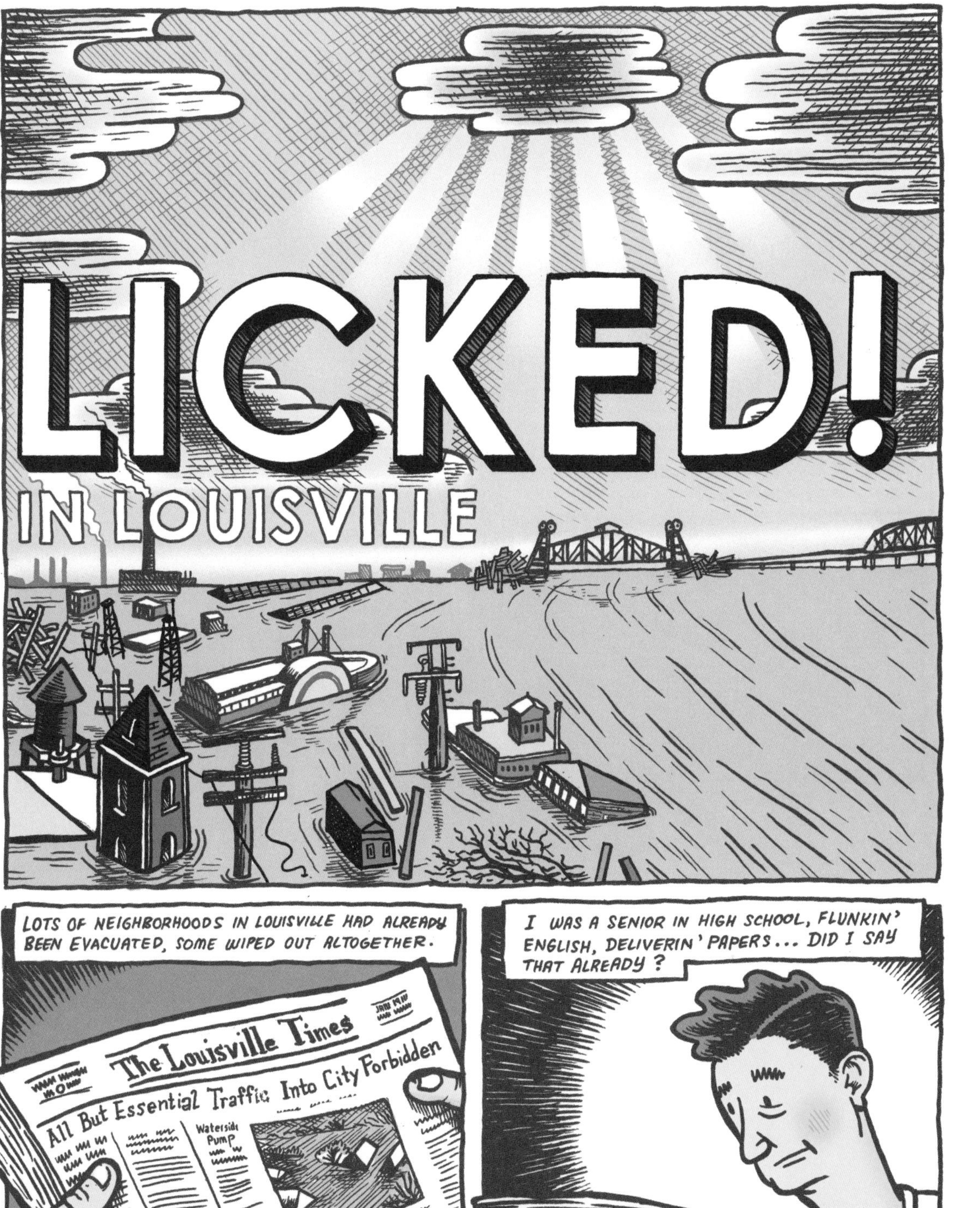
LICKED!
IN LOUISVILLE
LOTS OF NEIGHBORHOODS IN LOUISVILLE HAD ALREADY BEEN EVACUATED, SOME WIPED OUT ALTOGETHER.
The Louisville Times
All But Essential Traffic Into City Forbidden
Waterside Pump
8 New Dead Found
West End Put Under Strict Quarantine
I WAS A SENIOR IN HIGH SCHOOL, FLUNKIN' ENGLISH, DELIVERIN' PAPERS... DID I SAY THAT ALREADY?

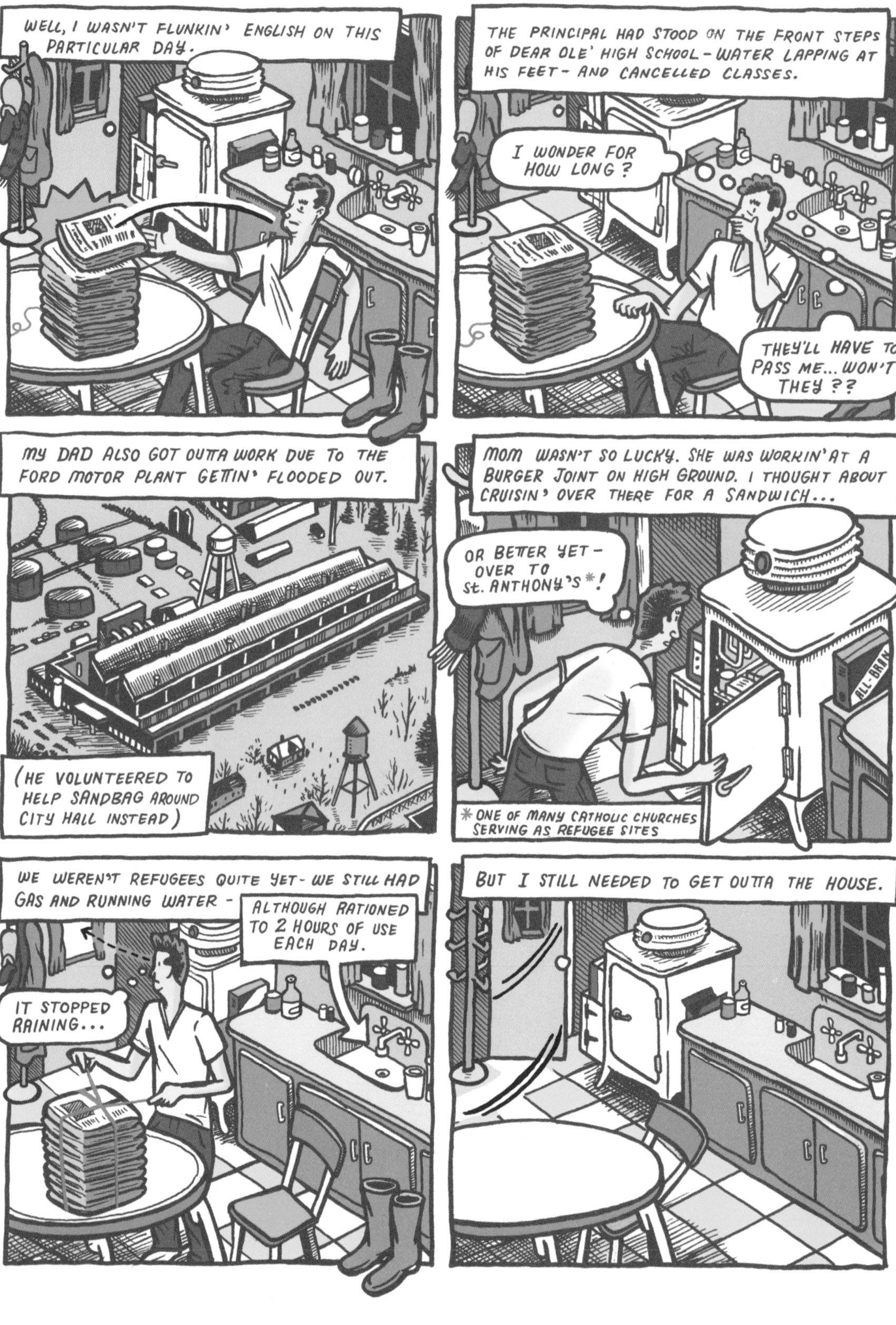

WELL, I WASN'T FLUNKIN' ENGLISH ON THIS PARTICULAR DAY.
THE PRINCIPAL HAD STOOD ON THE FRONT STEPS OF DEAR OLE' HIGH SCHOOL - WATER LAPPING AT HIS FEET - AND CANCELLED CLASSES.
I WONDER FOR HOW LONG?
THEY'LL HAVE TO PASS ME... WON'T THEY??
MY DAD ALSO GOT OUTTA WORK DUE TO THE FORD MOTOR PLANT GETTIN' FLOODED OUT.
(HE VOLUNTEERED TO HELP SANDBAG AROUND CITY HALL INSTEAD)
MOM WASN'T SO LUCKY. SHE WAS WORKIN' AT A BURGER JOINT ON HIGH GROUND. I THOUGHT ABOUT CRUISIN' OVER THERE FOR A SANDWICH...
OR BETTER YET - OVER TO St. ANTHONY'S*!
ALL-BRAN
* ONE OF MANY CATHOLIC CHURCHES SERVING AS REFUGEE SITES
WE WEREN'T REFUGEES QUITE YET - WE STILL HAD GAS AND RUNNING WATER -
ALTHOUGH RATIONED TO 2 HOURS OF USE EACH DAY.
IT STOPPED RAINING...
BUT I STILL NEEDED TO GET OUTTA THE HOUSE.

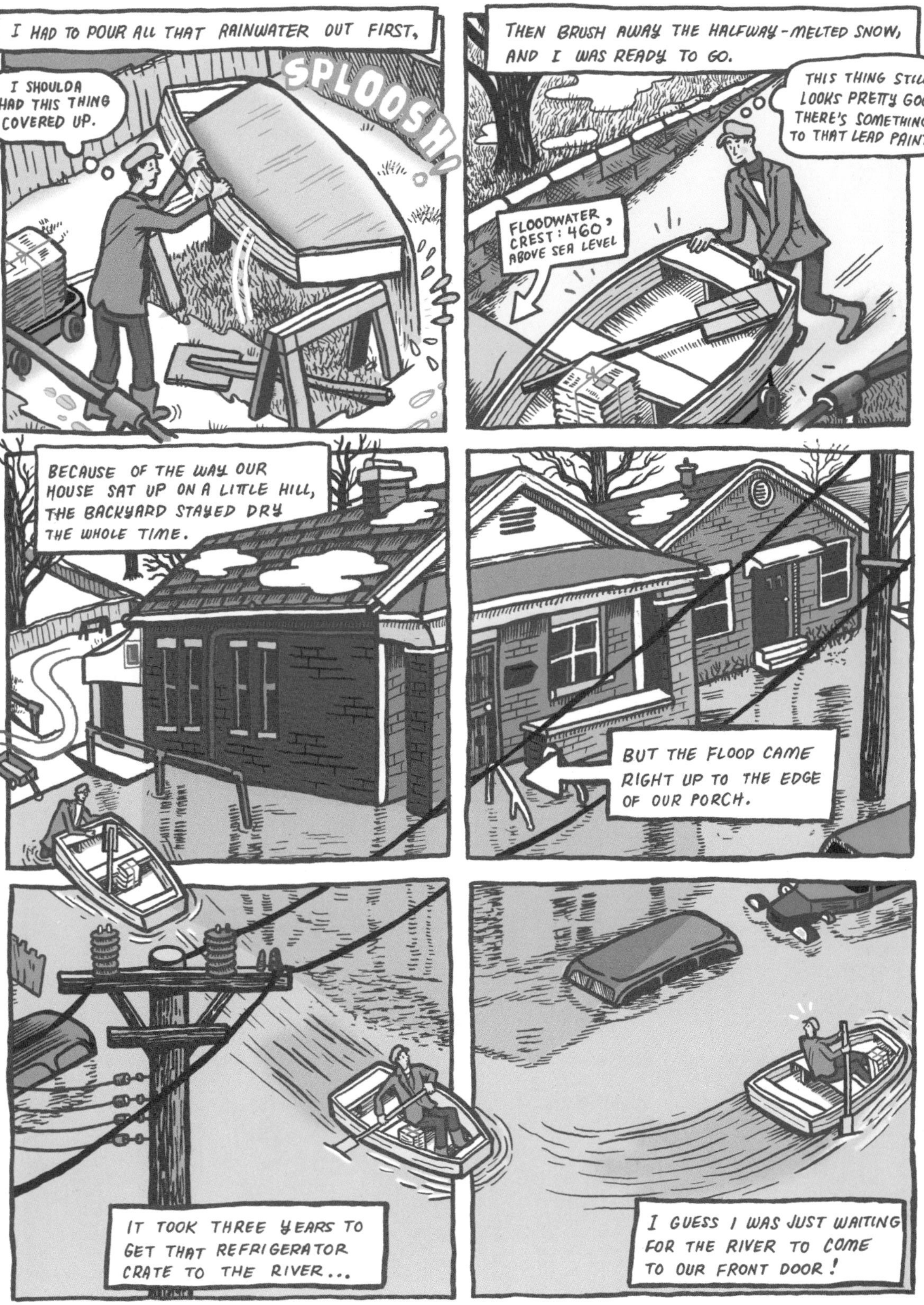
I HAD TO POUR ALL THAT RAINWATER OUT FIRST,
I SHOULDA HAD THIS THING COVERED UP.
SPLOOSH!
THEN BRUSH AWAY THE HALFWAY-MELTED SNOW, AND I WAS READY TO GO.
THIS THING STILL LOOKS PRETTY GOOD. THERE'S SOMETHING TO THAT LEAD PAINT.
FLOODWATER CREST: 460, ABOVE SEA LEVEL
BECAUSE OF THE WAY OUR HOUSE SAT UP ON A LITTLE HILL, THE BACKYARD STAYED DRY THE WHOLE TIME.
BUT THE FLOOD CAME RIGHT UP TO THE EDGE OF OUR PORCH.
IT TOOK THREE YEARS TO GET THAT REFRIGERATOR CRATE TO THE RIVER...
I GUESS I WAS JUST WAITING FOR THE RIVER TO COME TO OUR FRONT DOOR!

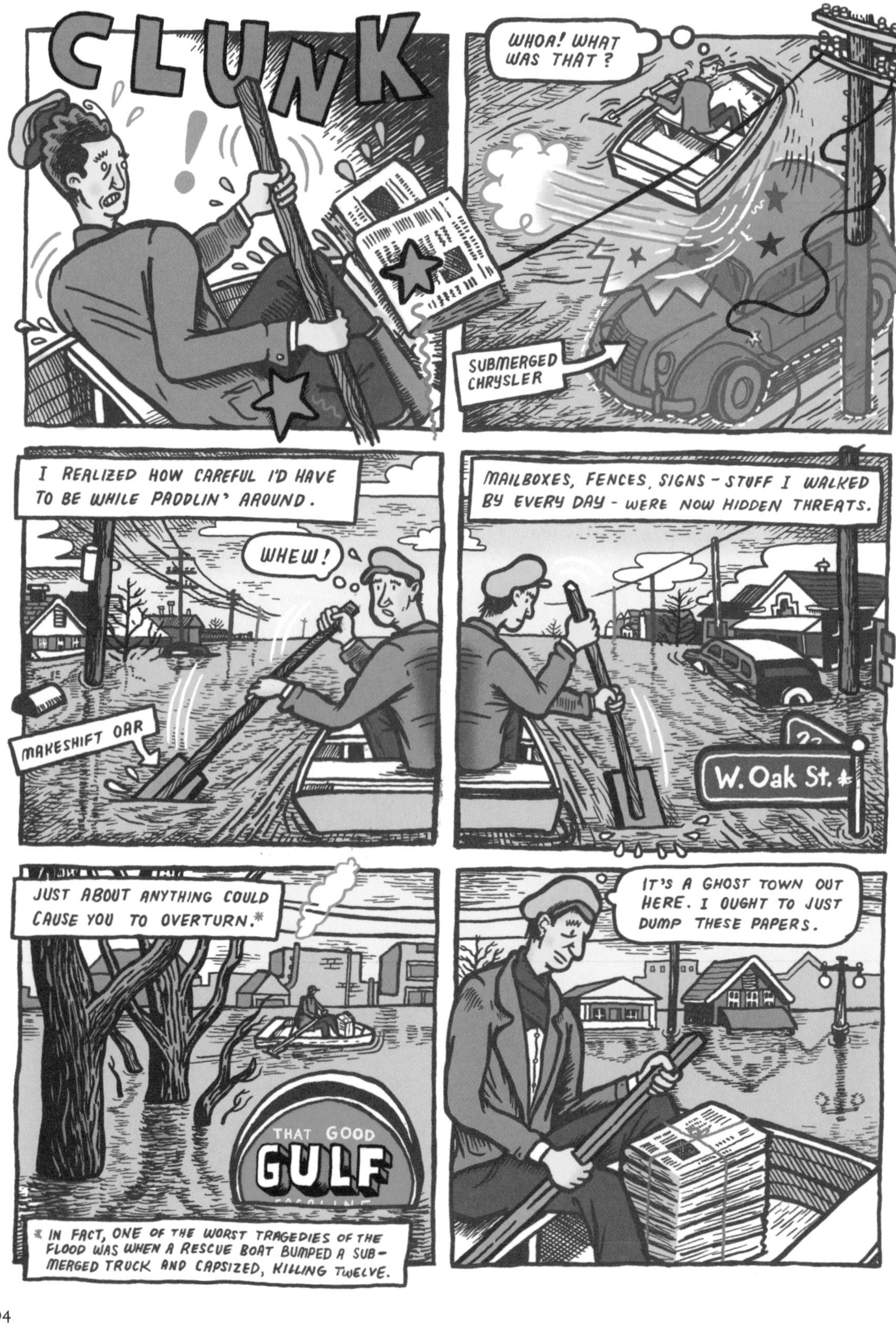
CLUNK
WHOA! WHAT WAS THAT?
SUBMERGED CHRYSLER
I REALIZED HOW CAREFUL I'D HAVE TO BE WHILE PADDLIN' AROUND.
WHEW!
MAKESHIFT OAR
MAILBOXES, FENCES, SIGNS - STUFF I WALKED BY EVERY DAY - WERE NOW HIDDEN THREATS.
W. Oak St.
JUST ABOUT ANYTHING COULD CAUSE YOU TO OVERTURN.*
THAT GOOD
GULF
* IN FACT, ONE OF THE WORST TRAGEDIES OF THE FLOOD WAS WHEN A RESCUE BOAT BUMPED A SUB-MERGED TRUCK AND CAPSIZED, KILLING TWELVE.
IT'S A GHOST TOWN OUT HERE. I OUGHT TO JUST DUMP THESE PAPERS.

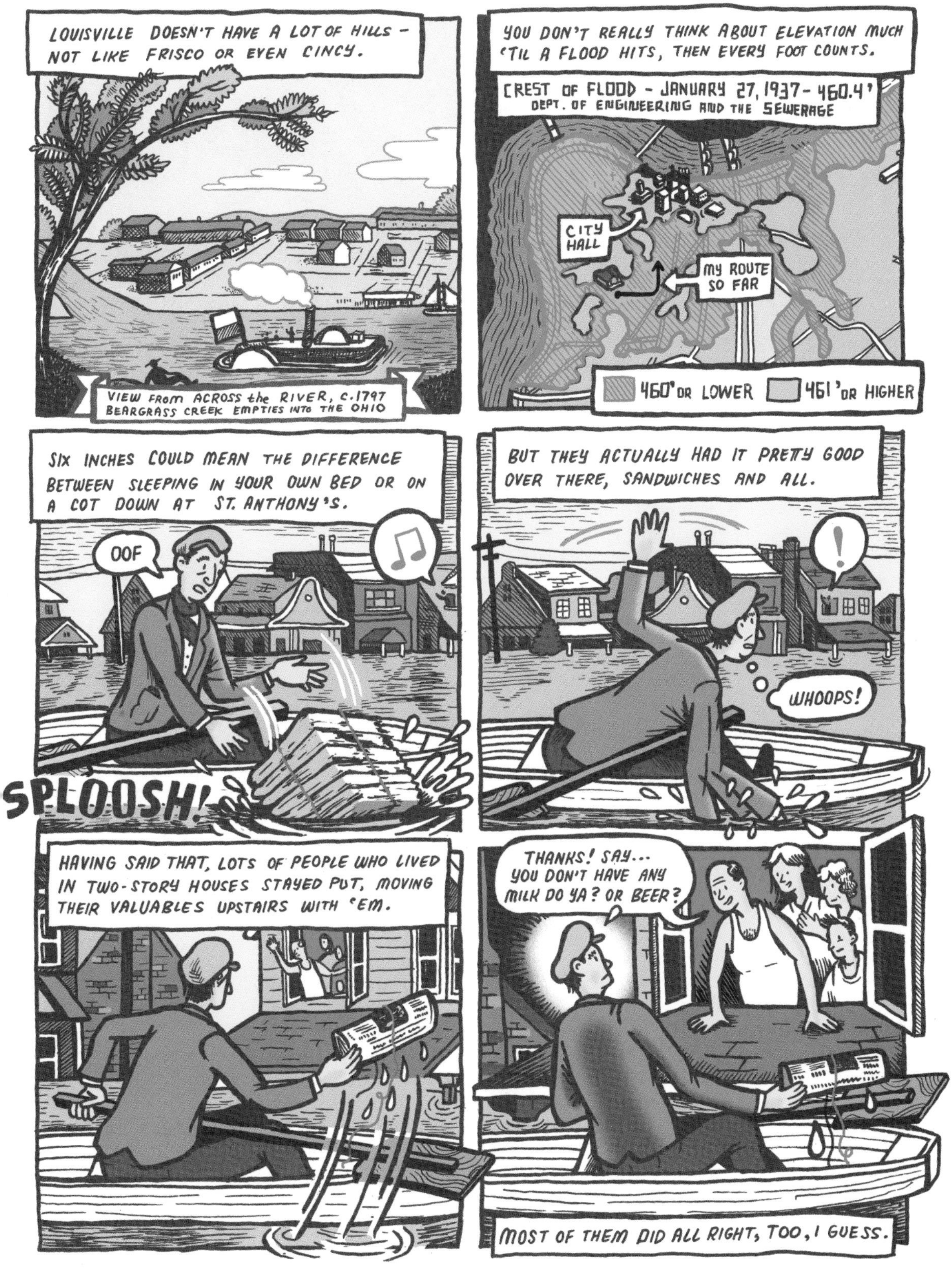
LOUISVILLE DOESN'T HAVE A LOT OF HILLS - NOT LIKE FRISCO OR EVEN CINCY.
VIEW FROM ACROSS the RIVER, c.1797
BEARGRASS CREEK EMPTIES INTO THE OHIO
YOU DON'T REALLY THINK ABOUT ELEVATION MUCH 'TIL A FLOOD HITS, THEN EVERY FOOT COUNTS.
CREST OF FLOOD - JANUARY 27, 1937 - 460.4'
DEPT. OF ENGINEERING AND THE SEWERAGE
CITY HALL
MY ROUTE SO FAR
460' OR LOWER
461' OR HIGHER
SIX INCHES COULD MEAN THE DIFFERENCE BETWEEN SLEEPING IN YOUR OWN BED OR ON A COT DOWN AT ST. ANTHONY'S.
OOF
SPLOOSH!
BUT THEY ACTUALLY HAD IT PRETTY GOOD OVER THERE, SANDWICHES AND ALL.
!
WHOOPS!
HAVING SAID THAT, LOTS OF PEOPLE WHO LIVED IN TWO-STORY HOUSES STAYED PUT, MOVING THEIR VALUABLES UPSTAIRS WITH 'EM.
THANKS! SAY... YOU DON'T HAVE ANY MILK DO YA? OR BEER?
MOST OF THEM DID ALL RIGHT, TOO, I GUESS.

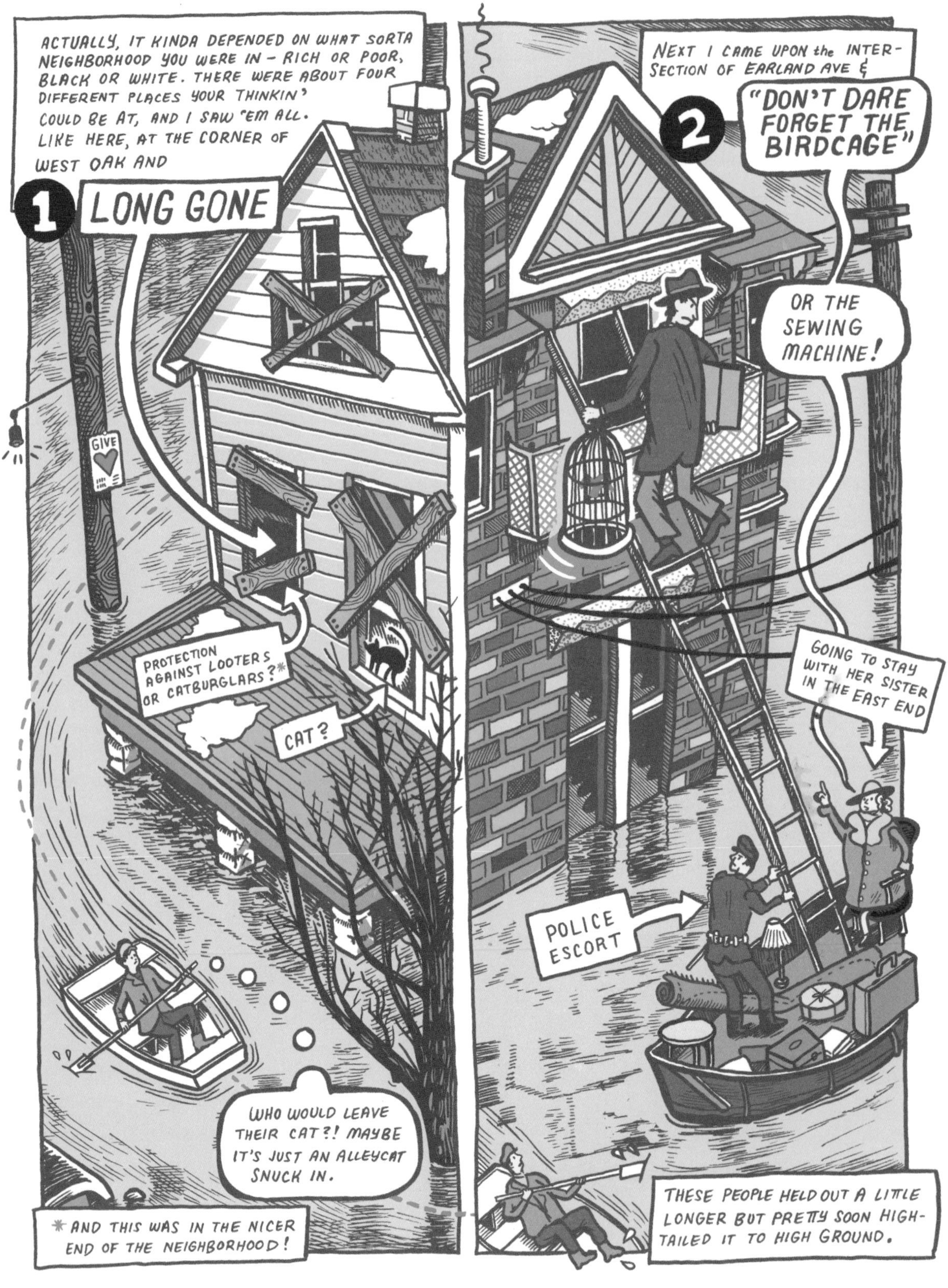
ACTUALLY, IT KINDA DEPENDED ON WHAT SORTA NEIGHBORHOOD YOU WERE IN – RICH OR POOR, BLACK OR WHITE. THERE WERE ABOUT FOUR DIFFERENT PLACES YOUR THINKIN' COULD BE AT, AND I SAW 'EM ALL. LIKE HERE, AT THE CORNER OF WEST OAK AND
1 LONG GONE
GIVE
PROTECTION AGAINST LOOTERS?* OR CATBURGLARS?
CAT?
WHO WOULD LEAVE THEIR CAT?! MAYBE IT'S JUST AN ALLEYCAT SNUCK IN.
* AND THIS WAS IN THE NICER END OF THE NEIGHBORHOOD!
NEXT I CAME UPON the INTERSECTION OF EARLAND AVE &
2 "DON'T DARE FORGET THE BIRDCAGE"
OR THE SEWING MACHINE!
GOING TO STAY WITH HER SISTER IN THE EAST END
POLICE ESCORT
THESE PEOPLE HELD OUT A LITTLE LONGER BUT PRETTY SOON HIGH-TAILED IT TO HIGH GROUND.

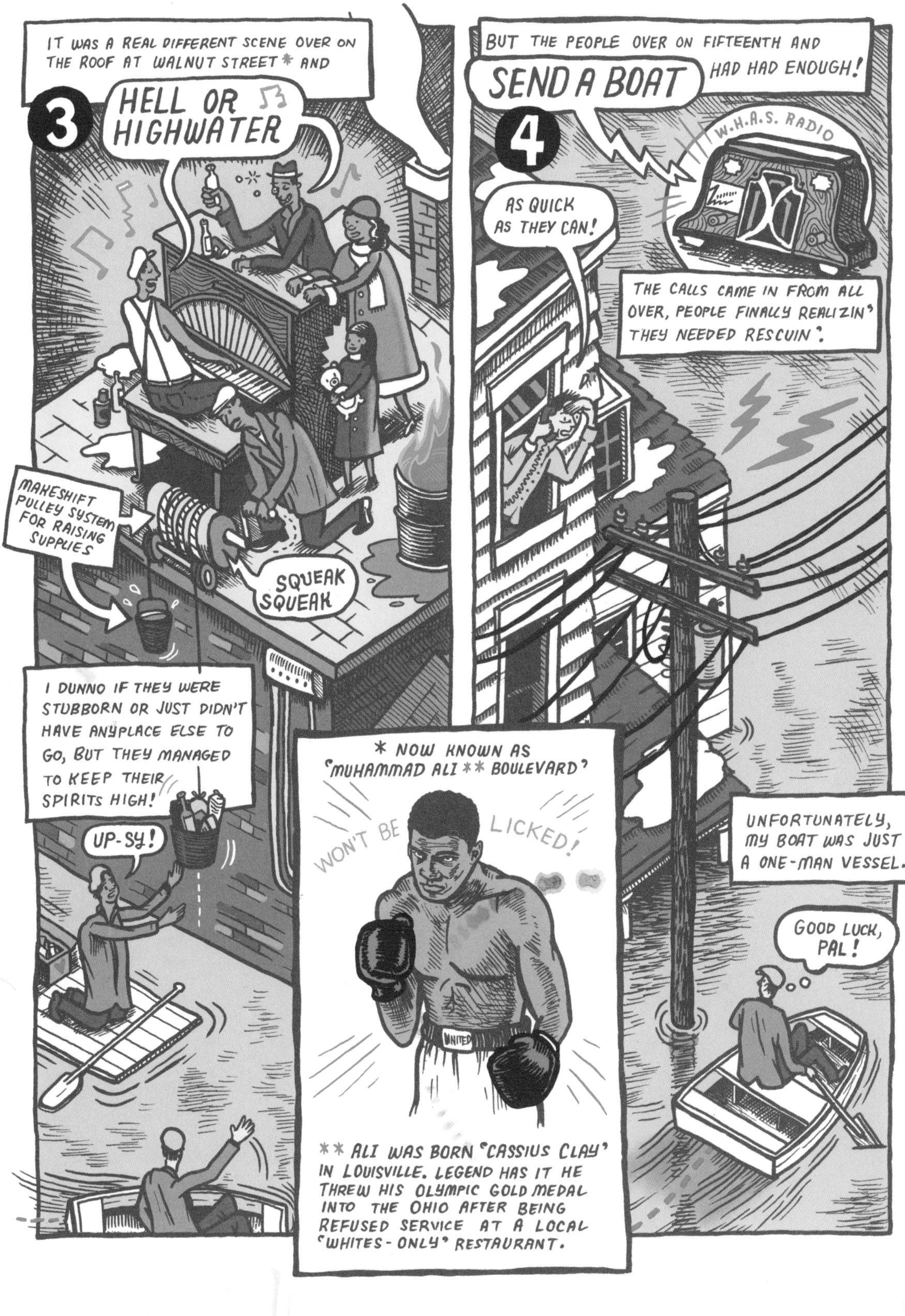
IT WAS A REAL DIFFERENT SCENE OVER ON THE ROOF AT WALNUT STREET * AND
3
HELL OR HIGHWATER
MAKESHIFT PULLEY SYSTEM FOR RAISING SUPPLIES
SQUEAK SQUEAK
I DUNNO IF THEY WERE STUBBORN OR JUST DIDN'T HAVE ANYPLACE ELSE TO GO, BUT THEY MANAGED TO KEEP THEIR SPIRITS HIGH!
UP-SY!
BUT THE PEOPLE OVER ON FIFTEENTH AND
SEND A BOAT
HAD HAD ENOUGH!
4
W.H.A.S. RADIO
AS QUICK AS THEY CAN!
THE CALLS CAME IN FROM ALL OVER, PEOPLE FINALLY REALIZIN' THEY NEEDED RESCUIN'.
UNFORTUNATELY, MY BOAT WAS JUST A ONE-MAN VESSEL.
GOOD LUCK, PAL!
* NOW KNOWN AS "MUHAMMAD ALI ** BOULEVARD"
WON'T BE LICKED!
UNITED
** ALI WAS BORN "CASSIUS CLAY" IN LOUISVILLE. LEGEND HAS IT HE THREW HIS OLYMPIC GOLD MEDAL INTO THE OHIO AFTER BEING REFUSED SERVICE AT A LOCAL "WHITES-ONLY" RESTAURANT.

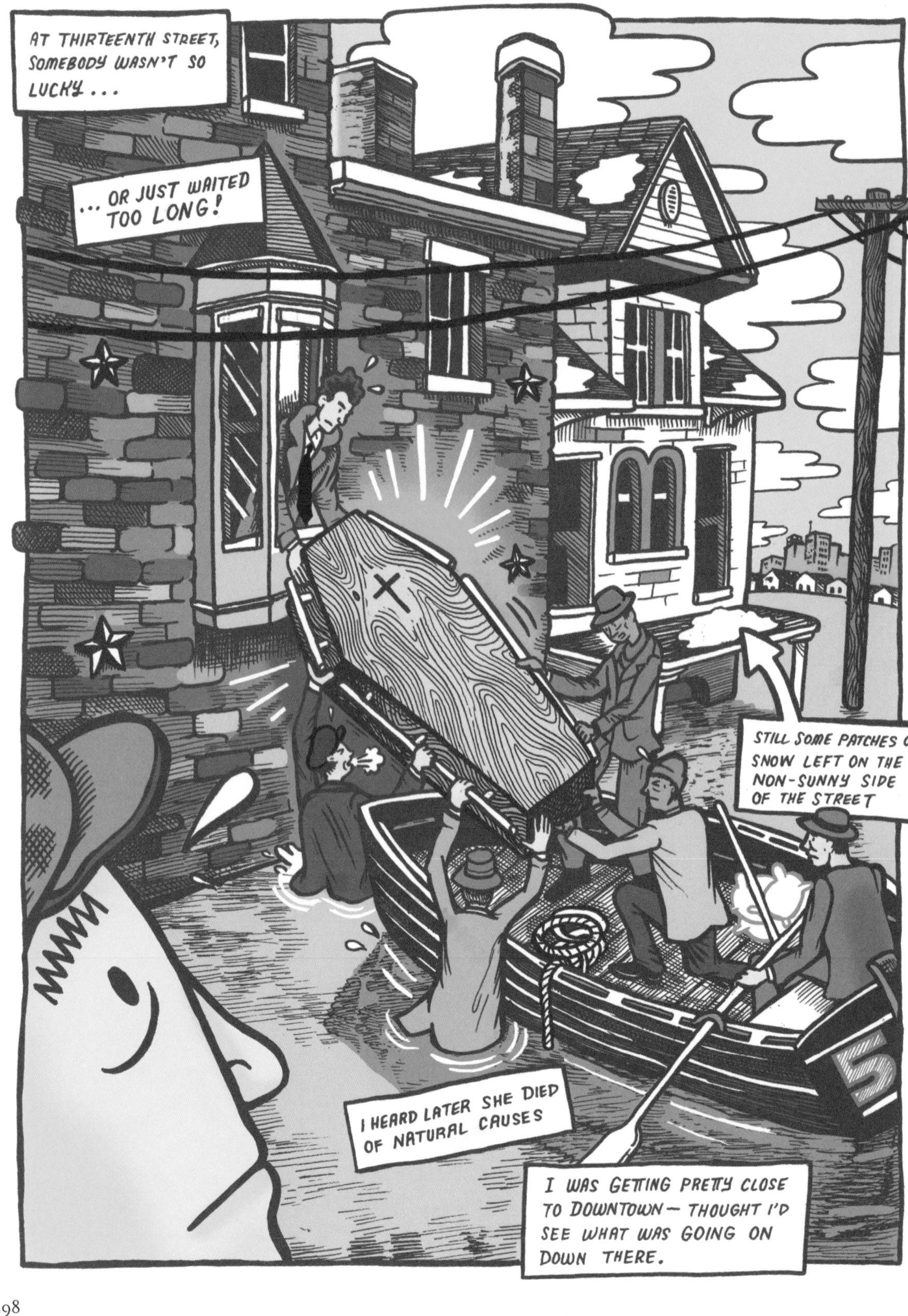
AT THIRTEENTH STREET, SOMEBODY WASN'T SO LUCKY . . .
. . . OR JUST WAITED TOO LONG!
STILL SOME PATCHES OF SNOW LEFT ON THE NON-SUNNY SIDE OF THE STREET
I HEARD LATER SHE DIED OF NATURAL CAUSES
I WAS GETTING PRETTY CLOSE TO DOWNTOWN — THOUGHT I'D SEE WHAT WAS GOING ON DOWN THERE.

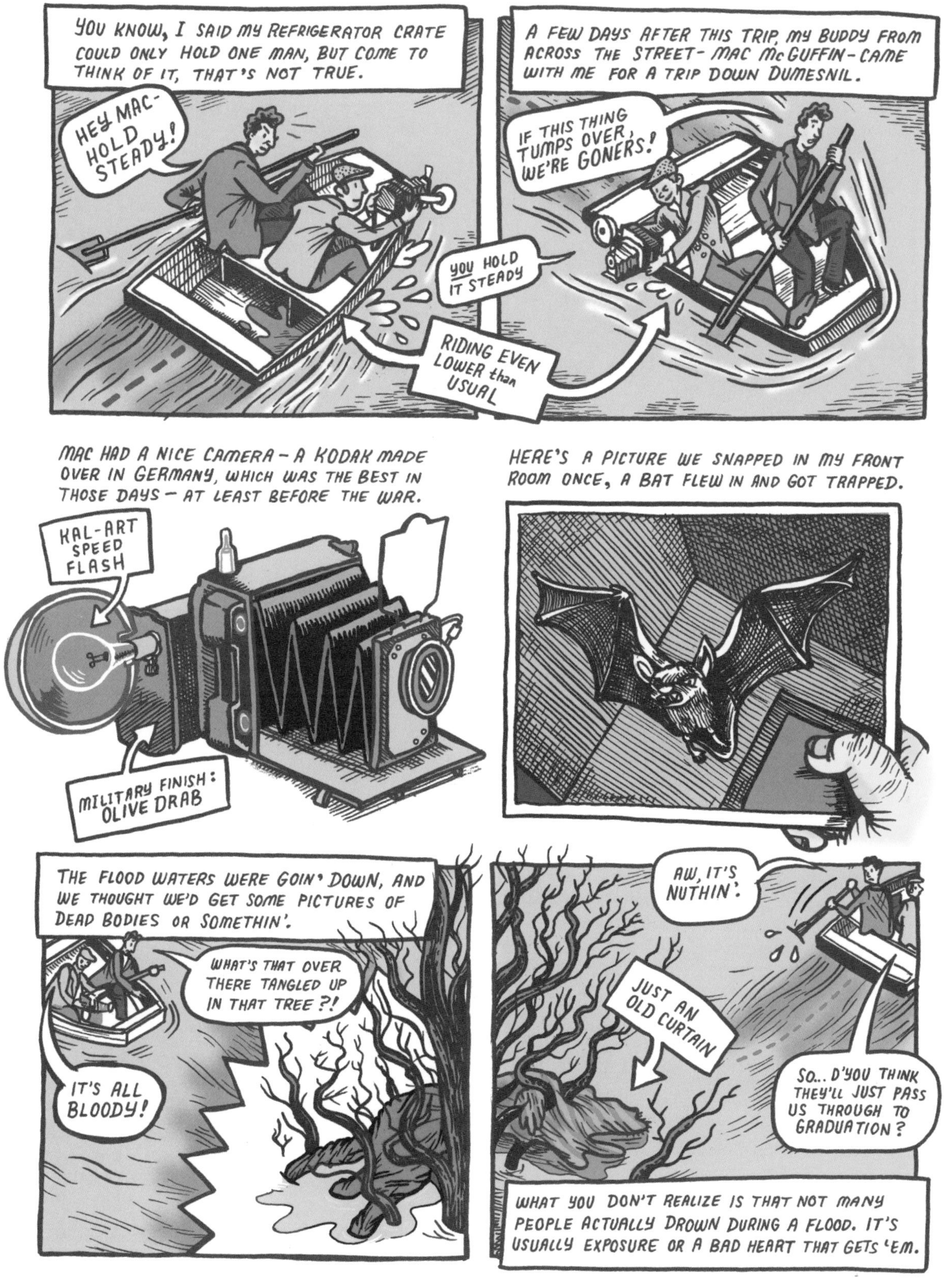
YOU KNOW, I SAID MY REFRIGERATOR CRATE COULD ONLY HOLD ONE MAN, BUT COME TO THINK OF IT, THAT'S NOT TRUE.
HEY MAC-HOLD STEADY!
YOU HOLD IT STEADY
RIDING EVEN LOWER than USUAL
A FEW DAYS AFTER THIS TRIP, MY BUDDY FROM ACROSS THE STREET- MAC McGUFFIN-CAME WITH ME FOR A TRIP DOWN DUMESNIL.
IF THIS THING TUMPS OVER, WE'RE GONERS!
MAC HAD A NICE CAMERA - A KODAK MADE OVER IN GERMANY, WHICH WAS THE BEST IN THOSE DAYS - AT LEAST BEFORE THE WAR.
KAL-ART SPEED FLASH
MILITARY FINISH: OLIVE DRAB
HERE'S A PICTURE WE SNAPPED IN MY FRONT ROOM ONCE, A BAT FLEW IN AND GOT TRAPPED.
THE FLOOD WATERS WERE GOIN' DOWN, AND WE THOUGHT WE'D GET SOME PICTURES OF DEAD BODIES OR SOMETHIN'.
WHAT'S THAT OVER THERE TANGLED UP IN THAT TREE?!
IT'S ALL BLOODY!
AW, IT'S NUTHIN'.
JUST AN OLD CURTAIN
SO... D'YOU THINK THEY'LL JUST PASS US THROUGH TO GRADUATION?
WHAT YOU DON'T REALIZE IS THAT NOT MANY PEOPLE ACTUALLY DROWN DURING A FLOOD. IT'S USUALLY EXPOSURE OR A BAD HEART THAT GETS 'EM.

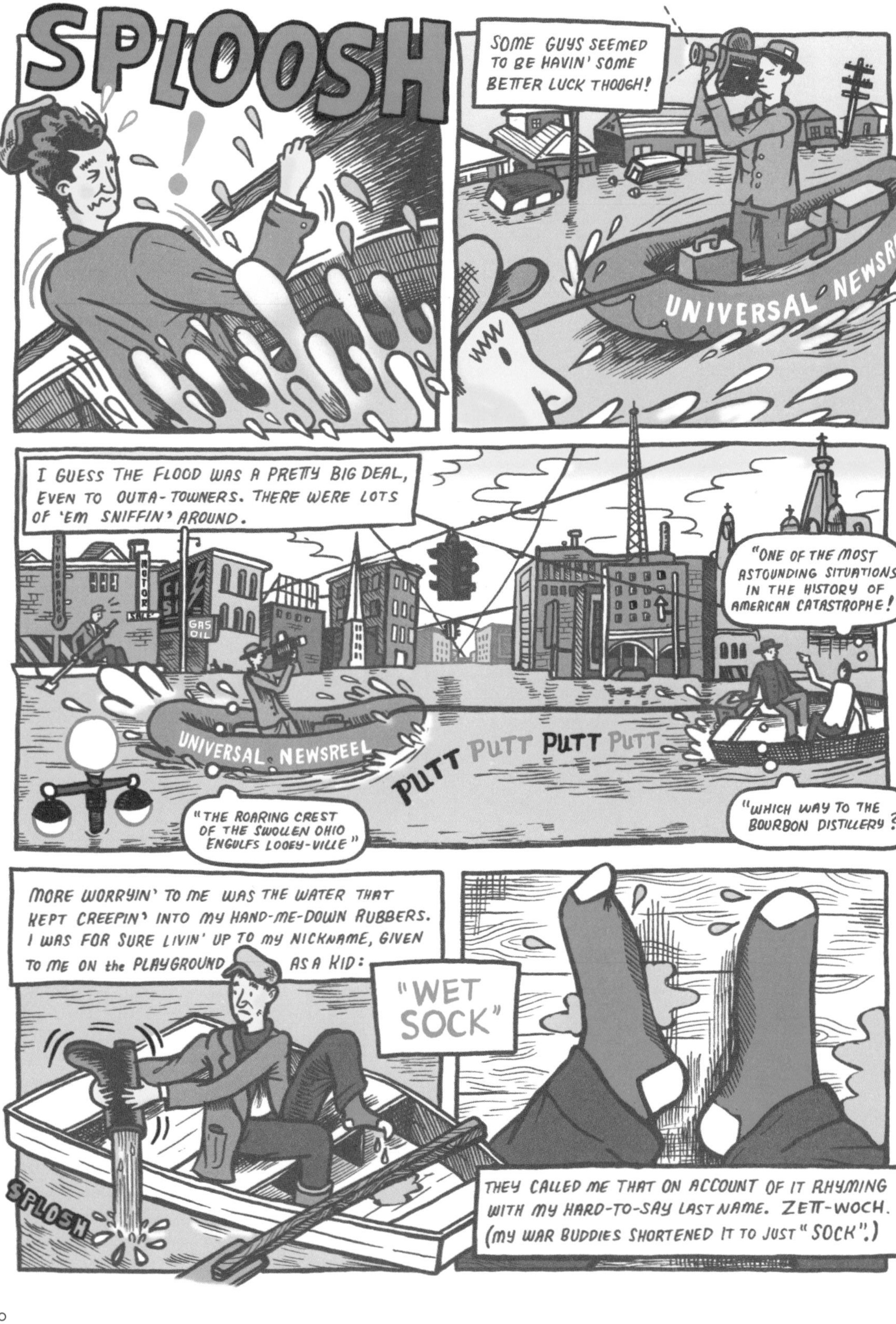
SPLOOSH
SOME GUYS SEEMED TO BE HAVIN' SOME BETTER LUCK THOUGH!
UNIVERSAL NEWSREEL
I GUESS THE FLOOD WAS A PRETTY BIG DEAL, EVEN TO OUTTA-TOWNERS. THERE WERE LOTS OF 'EM SNIFFIN' AROUND.
"ONE OF THE MOST ASTOUNDING SITUATIONS IN THE HISTORY OF AMERICAN CATASTROPHE!"
GAS OIL
UNIVERSAL NEWSREEL
PUTT PUTT PUTT PUTT PUTT
"THE ROARING CREST OF THE SWOLLEN OHIO ENGULFS LOOEY-VILLE"
"WHICH WAY TO THE BOURBON DISTILLERY?"
MORE WORRYIN' TO ME WAS THE WATER THAT KEPT CREEPIN' INTO MY HAND-ME-DOWN RUBBERS. I WAS FOR SURE LIVIN' UP TO MY NICKNAME, GIVEN TO ME ON the PLAYGROUND AS A KID:
"WET SOCK"
SPLOSH
THEY CALLED ME THAT ON ACCOUNT OF IT RHYMING WITH MY HARD-TO-SAY LAST NAME. ZETT-WOCH. (MY WAR BUDDIES SHORTENED IT TO JUST "SOCK".)

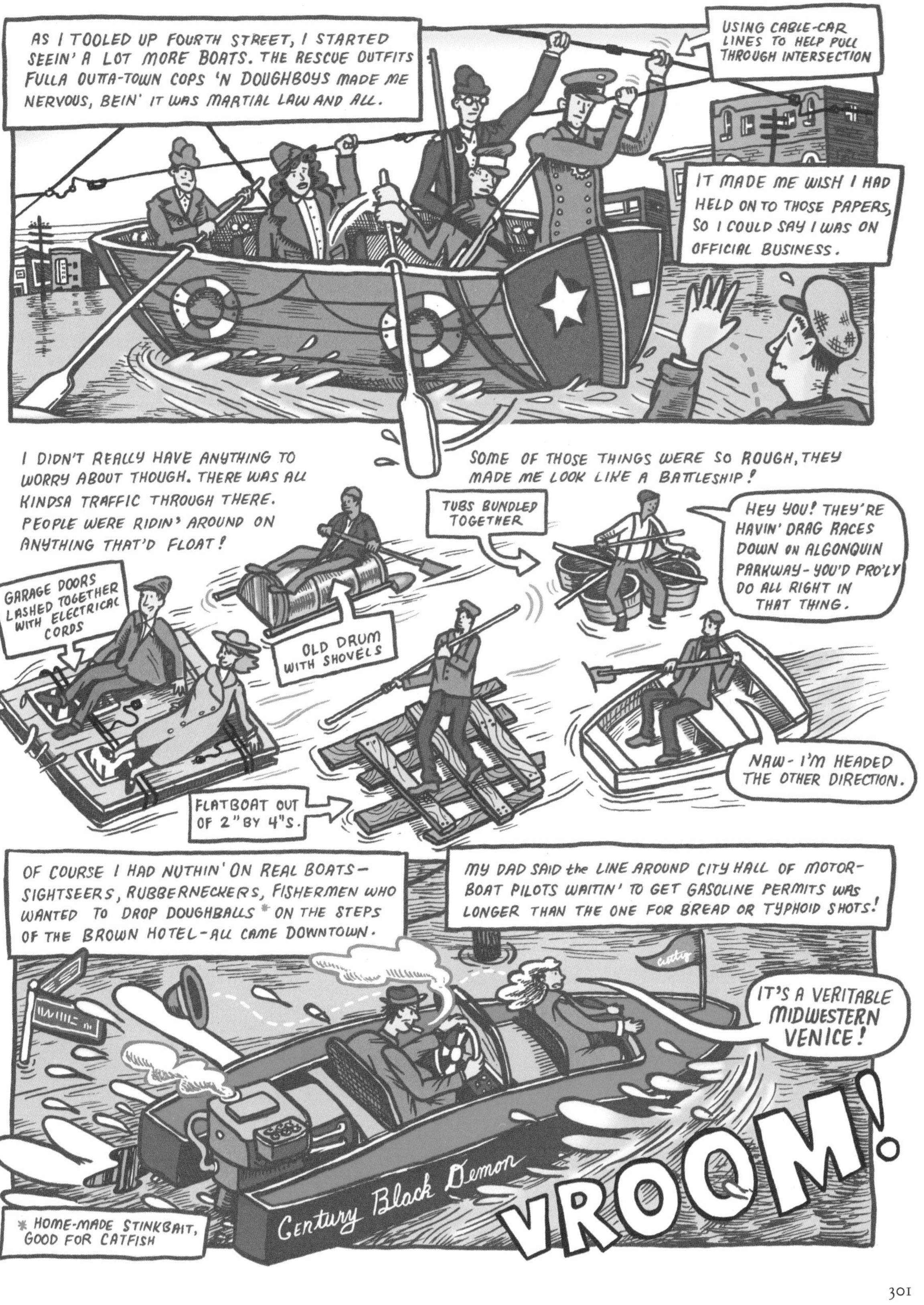

AS I TOOLED UP FOURTH STREET, I STARTED SEEIN' A LOT MORE BOATS. THE RESCUE OUTFITS FULLA OUTTA-TOWN COPS 'N DOUGHBOYS MADE ME NERVOUS, BEIN' IT WAS MARTIAL LAW AND ALL.
USING CABLE-CAR LINES TO HELP PULL THROUGH INTERSECTION
IT MADE ME WISH I HAD HELD ON TO THOSE PAPERS, SO I COULD SAY I WAS ON OFFICIAL BUSINESS.
I DIDN'T REALLY HAVE ANYTHING TO WORRY ABOUT THOUGH. THERE WAS ALL KINDSA TRAFFIC THROUGH THERE. PEOPLE WERE RIDIN' AROUND ON ANYTHING THAT'D FLOAT!
SOME OF THOSE THINGS WERE SO ROUGH, THEY MADE ME LOOK LIKE A BATTLESHIP!
GARAGE DOORS LASHED TOGETHER WITH ELECTRICAL CORDS
OLD DRUM WITH SHOVELS
TUBS BUNDLED TOGETHER
HEY YOU! THEY'RE HAVIN' DRAG RACES DOWN ON ALGONQUIN PARKWAY - YOU'D PRO'LY DO ALL RIGHT IN THAT THING.
FLATBOAT OUT OF 2" BY 4"S.
NAW - I'M HEADED THE OTHER DIRECTION.
OF COURSE I HAD NUTHIN' ON REAL BOATS - SIGHTSEERS, RUBBERNECKERS, FISHERMEN WHO WANTED TO DROP DOUGHBALLS * ON THE STEPS OF THE BROWN HOTEL - ALL CAME DOWNTOWN.
MY DAD SAID the LINE AROUND CITY HALL OF MOTOR-BOAT PILOTS WAITIN' TO GET GASOLINE PERMITS WAS LONGER THAN THE ONE FOR BREAD OR TYPHOID SHOTS!
IT'S A VERITABLE MIDWESTERN VENICE!
Century Black Demon
VROOM!
* HOME-MADE STINKBAIT, GOOD FOR CATFISH

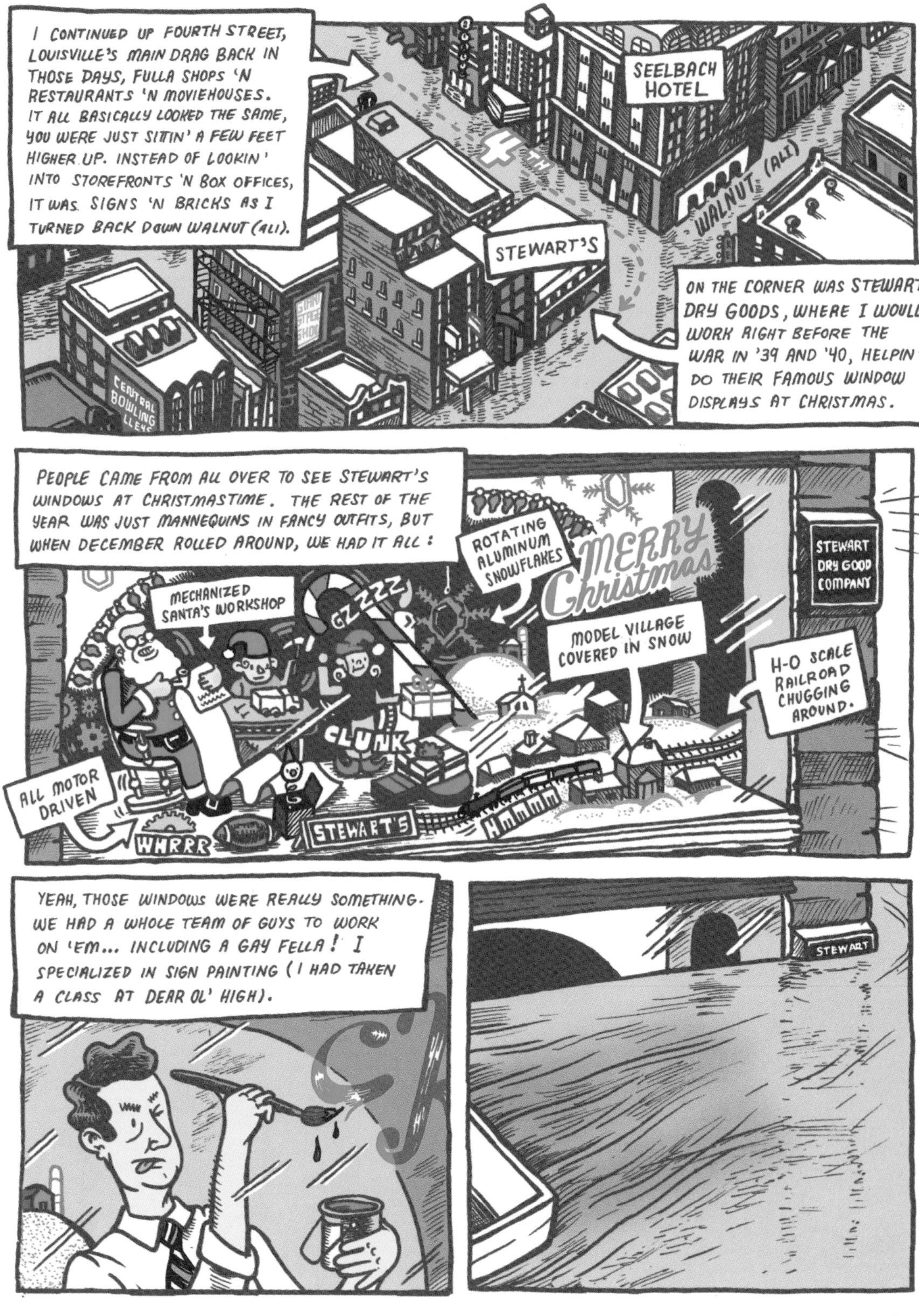

I CONTINUED UP FOURTH STREET, LOUISVILLE'S MAIN DRAG BACK IN THOSE DAYS, FULLA SHOPS 'N RESTAURANTS 'N MOVIEHOUSES. IT ALL BASICALLY LOOKED THE SAME, YOU WERE JUST SITTIN' A FEW FEET HIGHER UP. INSTEAD OF LOOKIN' INTO STOREFRONTS 'N BOX OFFICES, IT WAS SIGNS 'N BRICKS AS I TURNED BACK DOWN WALNUT (ALI).
SEELBACH HOTEL
WALNUT (ALI)
STEWART'S
CENTRAL BOWLING LLEYS
ON THE CORNER WAS STEWART DRY GOODS, WHERE I WOULD WORK RIGHT BEFORE THE WAR IN '39 AND '40, HELPIN' DO THEIR FAMOUS WINDOW DISPLAYS AT CHRISTMAS.
PEOPLE CAME FROM ALL OVER TO SEE STEWART'S WINDOWS AT CHRISTMASTIME. THE REST OF THE YEAR WAS JUST MANNEQUINS IN FANCY OUTFITS, BUT WHEN DECEMBER ROLLED AROUND, WE HAD IT ALL:
ROTATING ALUMINUM SNOWFLAKES
MERRY Christmas
STEWART DRY GOOD COMPANY
MECHANIZED SANTA'S WORKSHOP
ZZZZ
MODEL VILLAGE COVERED IN SNOW
H-O SCALE RAILROAD CHUGGING AROUND.
CLUNK
ALL MOTOR DRIVEN
WHRRR
STEWART'S
YEAH, THOSE WINDOWS WERE REALLY SOMETHING. WE HAD A WHOLE TEAM OF GUYS TO WORK ON 'EM... INCLUDING A GAY FELLA! I SPECIALIZED IN SIGN PAINTING (I HAD TAKEN A CLASS AT DEAR OL' HIGH).
STEWART

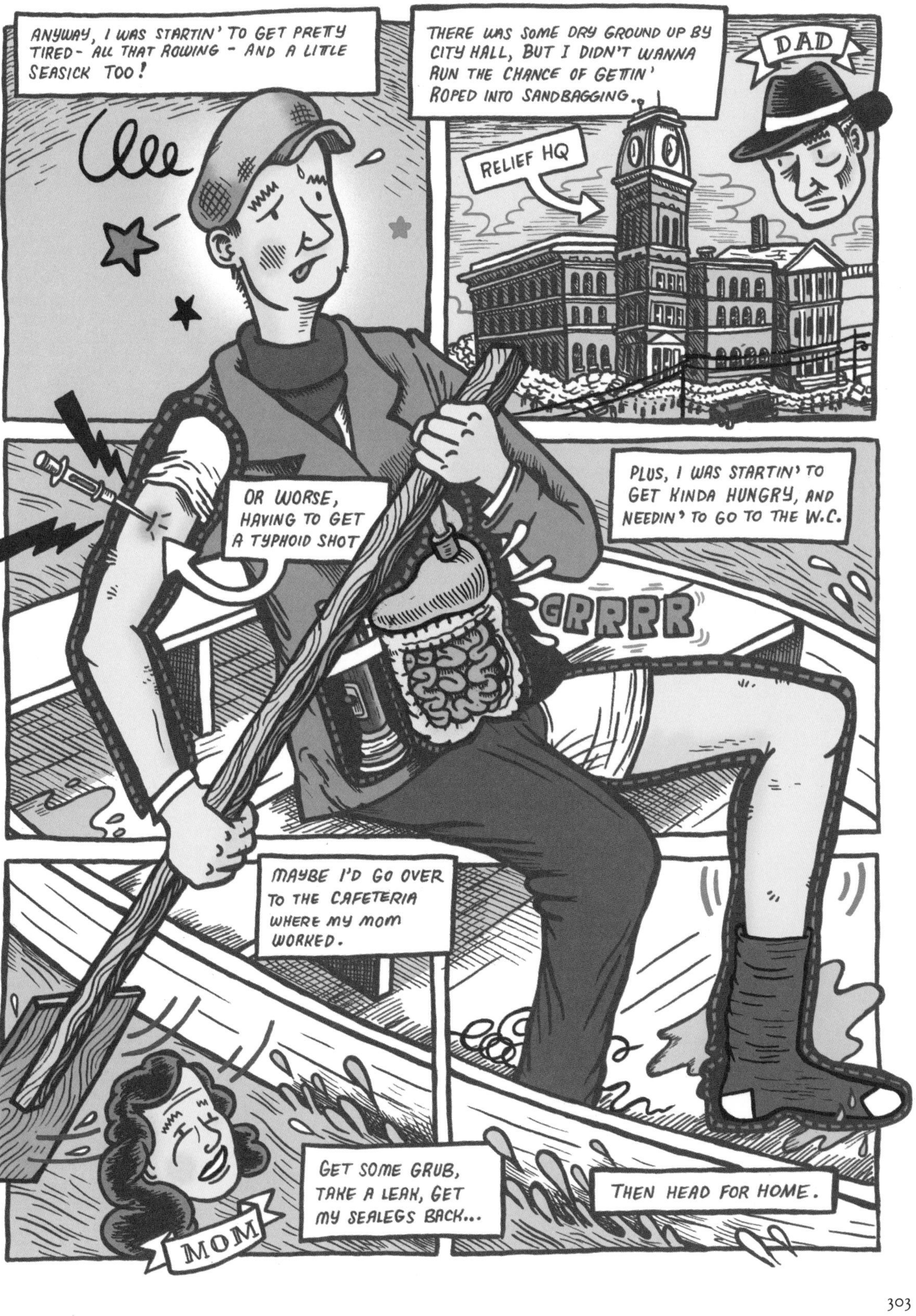
ANYWAY, I WAS STARTIN' TO GET PRETTY TIRED- ALL THAT ROWING - AND A LITTLE SEASICK TOO!
THERE WAS SOME DRY GROUND UP BY CITY HALL, BUT I DIDN'T WANNA RUN THE CHANCE OF GETTIN' ROPED INTO SANDBAGGING..
DAD
RELIEF HQ
OR WORSE, HAVING TO GET A TYPHOID SHOT
PLUS, I WAS STARTIN' TO GET KINDA HUNGRY, AND NEEDIN' TO GO TO THE W.C.
GRRRR
MAYBE I'D GO OVER TO THE CAFETERIA WHERE MY MOM WORKED.
GET SOME GRUB, TAKE A LEAK, GET MY SEALEGS BACK...
THEN HEAD FOR HOME.
MOM

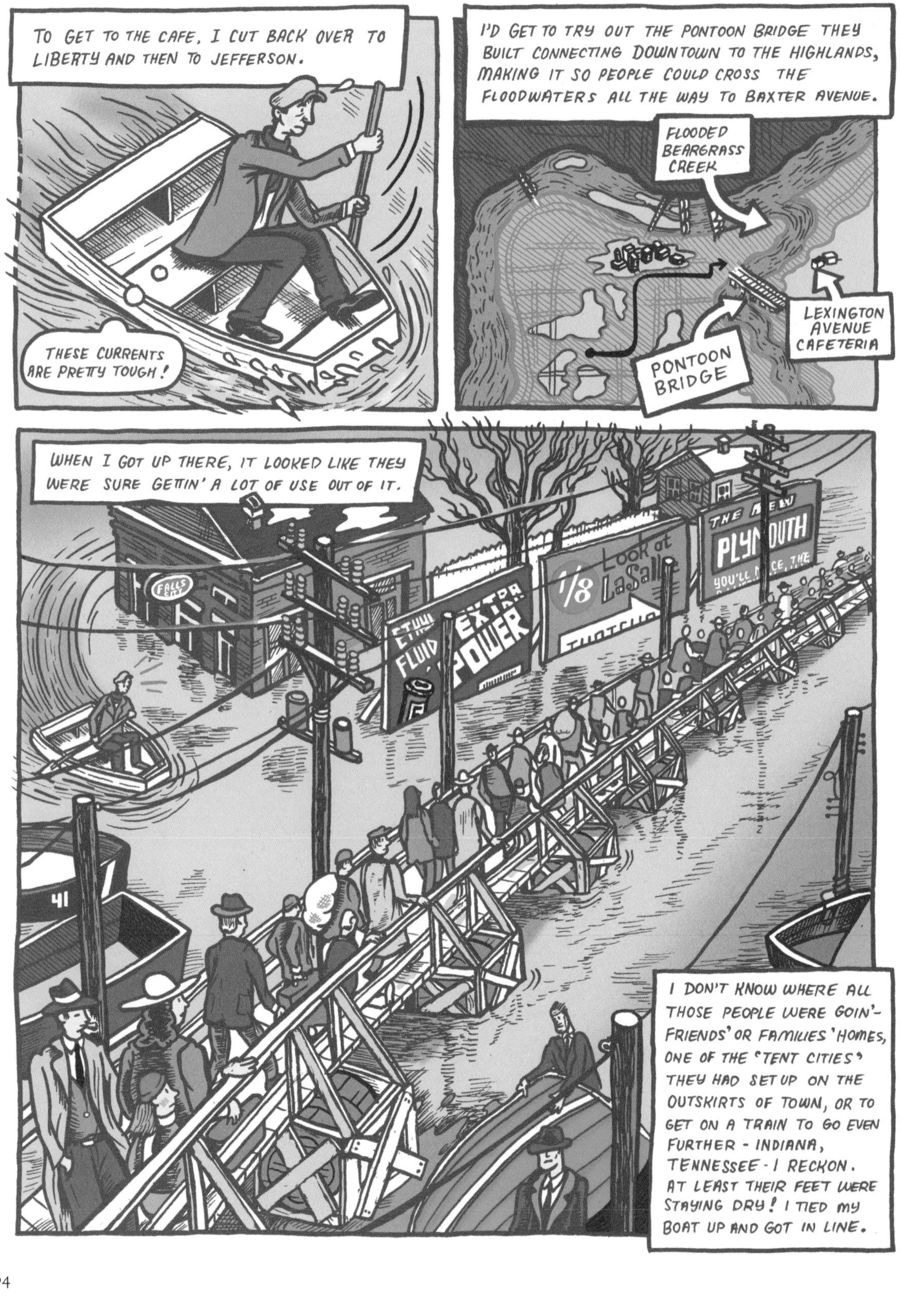
TO GET TO THE CAFE, I CUT BACK OVER TO LIBERTY AND THEN TO JEFFERSON.
THESE CURRENTS ARE PRETTY TOUGH!
I'D GET TO TRY OUT THE PONTOON BRIDGE THEY BUILT CONNECTING DOWNTOWN TO THE HIGHLANDS, MAKING IT SO PEOPLE COULD CROSS THE FLOODWATERS ALL THE WAY TO BAXTER AVENUE.
FLOODED BEARGRASS CREEK
LEXINGTON AVENUE CAFETERIA
PONTOON BRIDGE
WHEN I GOT UP THERE, IT LOOKED LIKE THEY WERE SURE GETTIN' A LOT OF USE OUT OF IT.
FALLS CITY
EXTRA POWER
1/8
Look at LaSalle
I DON'T KNOW WHERE ALL THOSE PEOPLE WERE GOIN'- FRIENDS' OR FAMILIES' HOMES, ONE OF THE "TENT CITIES" THEY HAD SET UP ON THE OUTSKIRTS OF TOWN, OR TO GET ON A TRAIN TO GO EVEN FURTHER - INDIANA, TENNESSEE - I RECKON. AT LEAST THEIR FEET WERE STAYING DRY! I TIED MY BOAT UP AND GOT IN LINE.

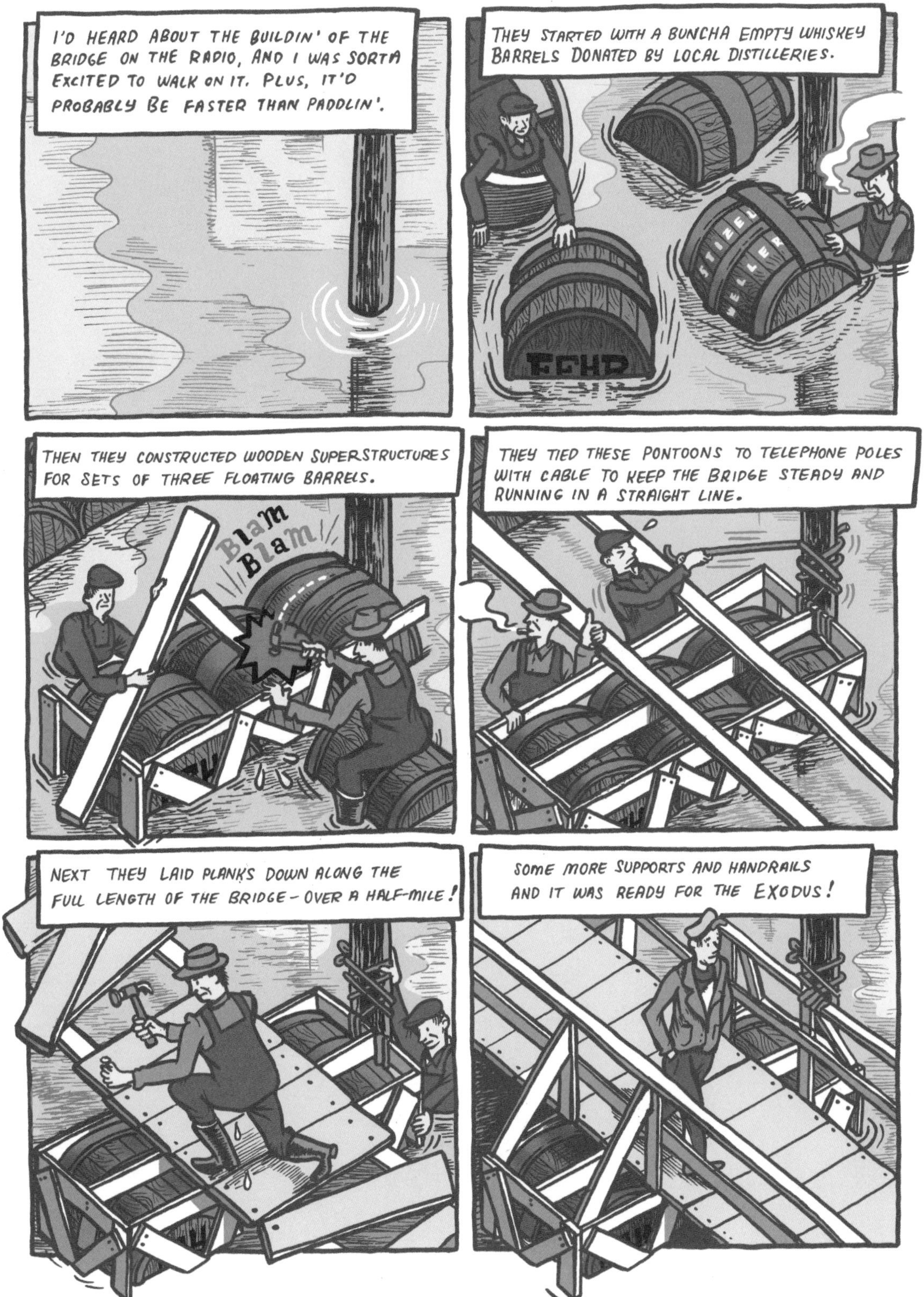
I'D HEARD ABOUT THE BUILDIN' OF THE BRIDGE ON THE RADIO, AND I WAS SORTA EXCITED TO WALK ON IT. PLUS, IT'D PROBABLY BE FASTER THAN PADDLIN'.
THEY STARTED WITH A BUNCHA EMPTY WHISKEY BARRELS DONATED BY LOCAL DISTILLERIES.
STIZEL WELLER
THEN THEY CONSTRUCTED WOODEN SUPERSTRUCTURES FOR SETS OF THREE FLOATING BARRELS.
Blam Blam
THEY TIED THESE PONTOONS TO TELEPHONE POLES WITH CABLE TO KEEP THE BRIDGE STEADY AND RUNNING IN A STRAIGHT LINE.
NEXT THEY LAID PLANKS DOWN ALONG THE FULL LENGTH OF THE BRIDGE - OVER A HALF-MILE!
SOME MORE SUPPORTS AND HANDRAILS AND IT WAS READY FOR THE EXODUS!

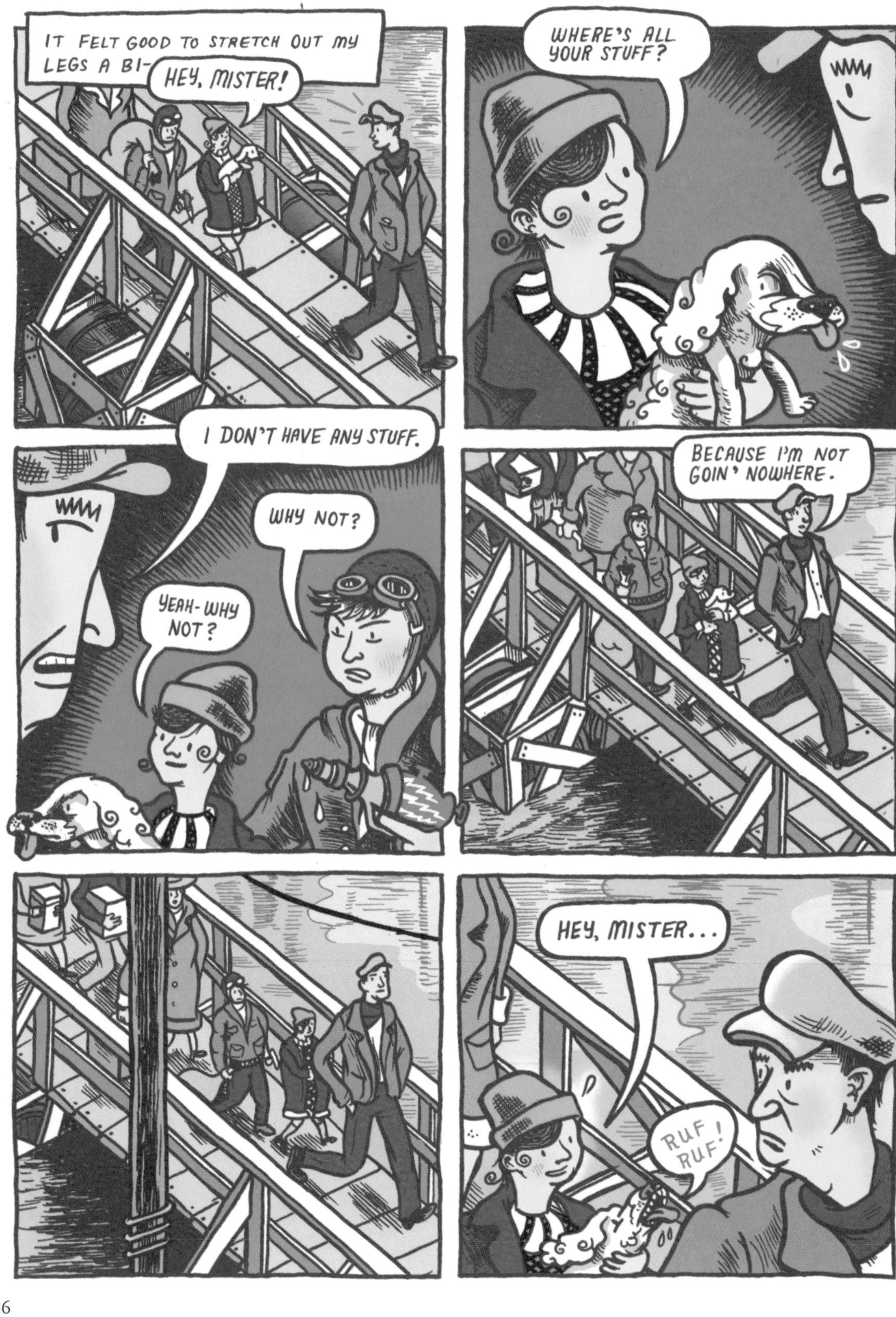
IT FELT GOOD TO STRETCH OUT MY LEGS A BI-
HEY, MISTER!
WHERE'S ALL YOUR STUFF?
I DON'T HAVE ANY STUFF.
WHY NOT?
YEAH- WHY NOT?
BECAUSE I'M NOT GOIN' NOWHERE.
HEY, MISTER...
RUF RUF!

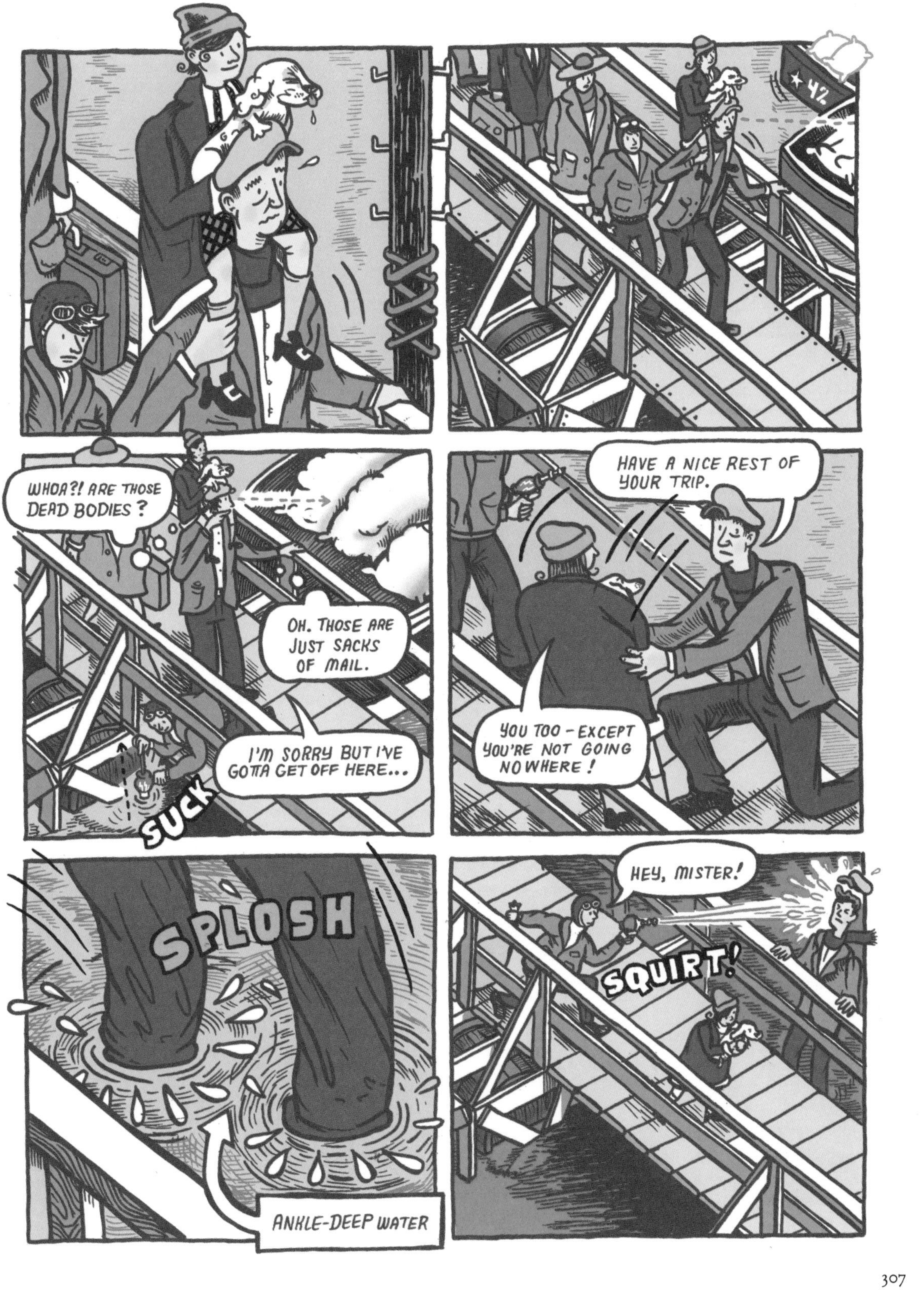

★ 42
WHOA?! ARE THOSE DEAD BODIES?
OH. THOSE ARE JUST SACKS OF MAIL.
I'M SORRY BUT I'VE GOTTA GET OFF HERE...
SUCK
HAVE A NICE REST OF YOUR TRIP.
YOU TOO - EXCEPT YOU'RE NOT GOING NOWHERE!
SPLOSH
ANKLE-DEEP WATER
HEY, MISTER!
SQUIRT!

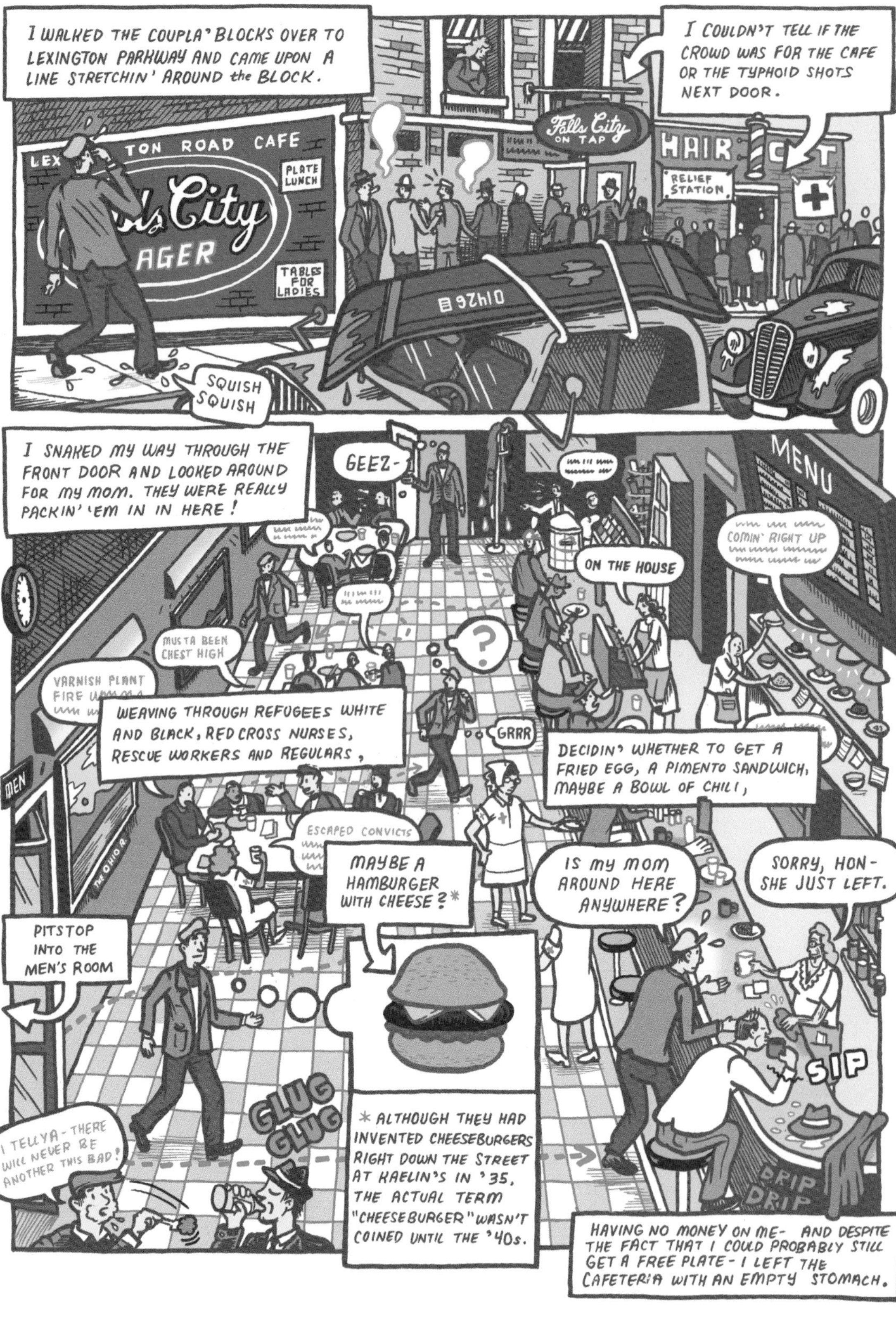
I WALKED THE COUPLA' BLOCKS OVER TO LEXINGTON PARKWAY AND CAME UPON A LINE STRETCHIN' AROUND the BLOCK.
I COULDN'T TELL IF THE CROWD WAS FOR THE CAFE OR THE TYPHOID SHOTS NEXT DOOR.
TON ROAD CAFE
PLATE LUNCH
AGER
TABLES FOR LADIES
Falls City ON TAP
HAIR
RELIEF STATION
SQUISH SQUISH
I SNAKED MY WAY THROUGH THE FRONT DOOR AND LOOKED AROUND FOR MY MOM. THEY WERE REALLY PACKIN' 'EM IN IN HERE!
GEEZ-
MENU
COMIN' RIGHT UP
ON THE HOUSE
MUSTA BEEN CHEST HIGH
VARNISH PLANT FIRE
?
WEAVING THROUGH REFUGEES WHITE AND BLACK, RED CROSS NURSES, RESCUE WORKERS AND REGULARS,
GRRR
DECIDIN' WHETHER TO GET A FRIED EGG, A PIMENTO SANDWICH, MAYBE A BOWL OF CHILI,
MEN
ESCAPED CONVICTS
MAYBE A HAMBURGER WITH CHEESE?*
IS MY MOM AROUND HERE ANYWHERE?
SORRY, HON- SHE JUST LEFT.
PITSTOP INTO THE MEN'S ROOM
SIP
GLUG GLUG
I TELLYA - THERE WILL NEVER BE ANOTHER THIS BAD!
* ALTHOUGH THEY HAD INVENTED CHEESEBURGERS RIGHT DOWN THE STREET AT KAELIN'S IN '35, THE ACTUAL TERM "CHEESEBURGER" WASN'T COINED UNTIL THE '40s.
DRIP DRIP
HAVING NO MONEY ON ME- AND DESPITE THE FACT THAT I COULD PROBABLY STILL GET A FREE PLATE - I LEFT THE CAFETERIA WITH AN EMPTY STOMACH.

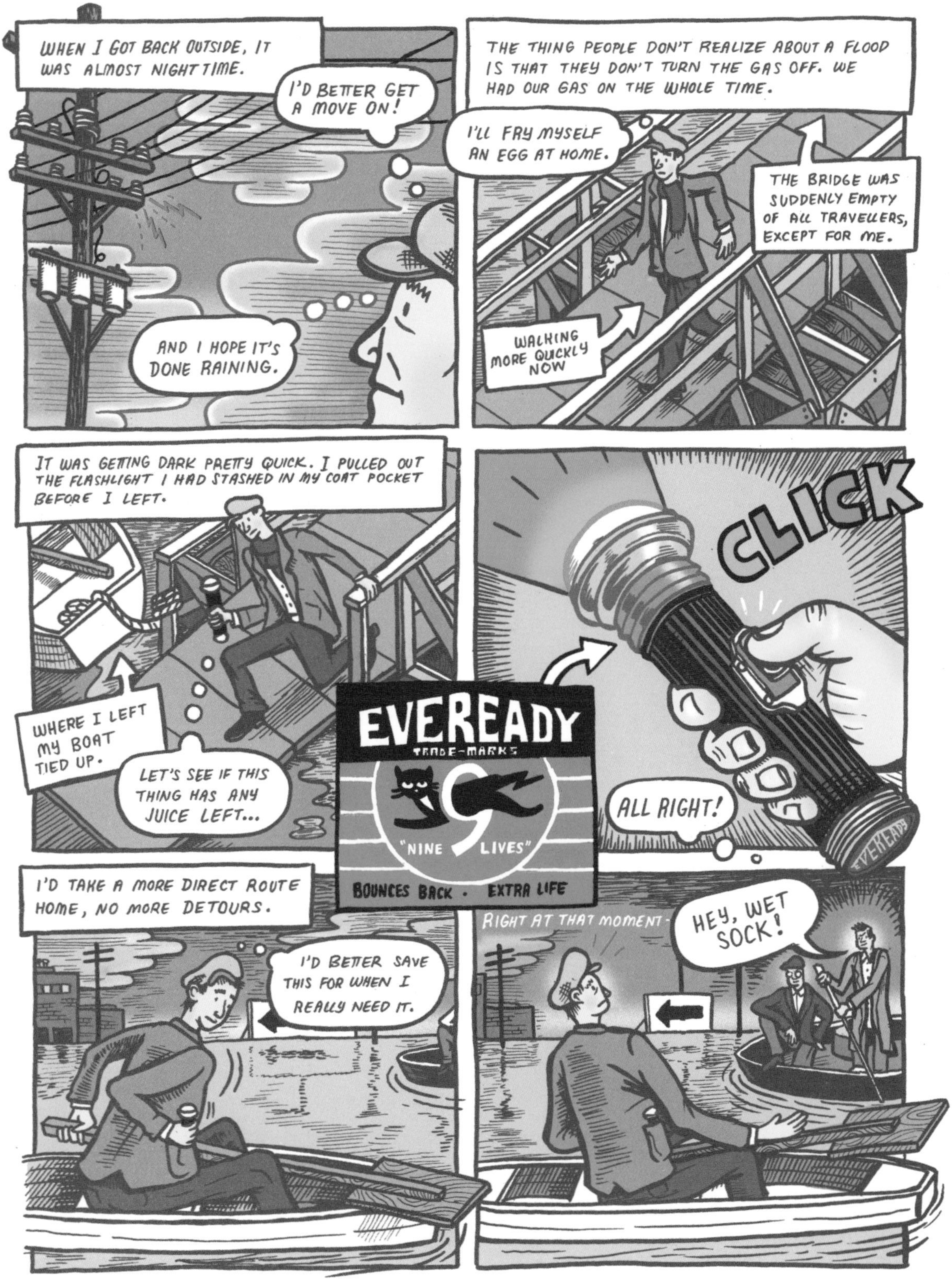

WHEN I GOT BACK OUTSIDE, IT WAS ALMOST NIGHT TIME.
I'D BETTER GET A MOVE ON!
AND I HOPE IT'S DONE RAINING.
THE THING PEOPLE DON'T REALIZE ABOUT A FLOOD IS THAT THEY DON'T TURN THE GAS OFF. WE HAD OUR GAS ON THE WHOLE TIME.
I'LL FRY MYSELF AN EGG AT HOME.
THE BRIDGE WAS SUDDENLY EMPTY OF ALL TRAVELLERS, EXCEPT FOR ME.
WALKING MORE QUICKLY NOW
IT WAS GETTING DARK PRETTY QUICK. I PULLED OUT THE FLASHLIGHT I HAD STASHED IN MY COAT POCKET BEFORE I LEFT.
WHERE I LEFT MY BOAT TIED UP.
LET'S SEE IF THIS THING HAS ANY JUICE LEFT...
CLICK
ALL RIGHT!
EVEREADY
TRADE-MARKS
"NINE LIVES"
BOUNCES BACK · EXTRA LIFE
EVEREADY
I'D TAKE A MORE DIRECT ROUTE HOME, NO MORE DETOURS.
I'D BETTER SAVE THIS FOR WHEN I REALLY NEED IT.
RIGHT AT THAT MOMENT-
HEY, WET SOCK!

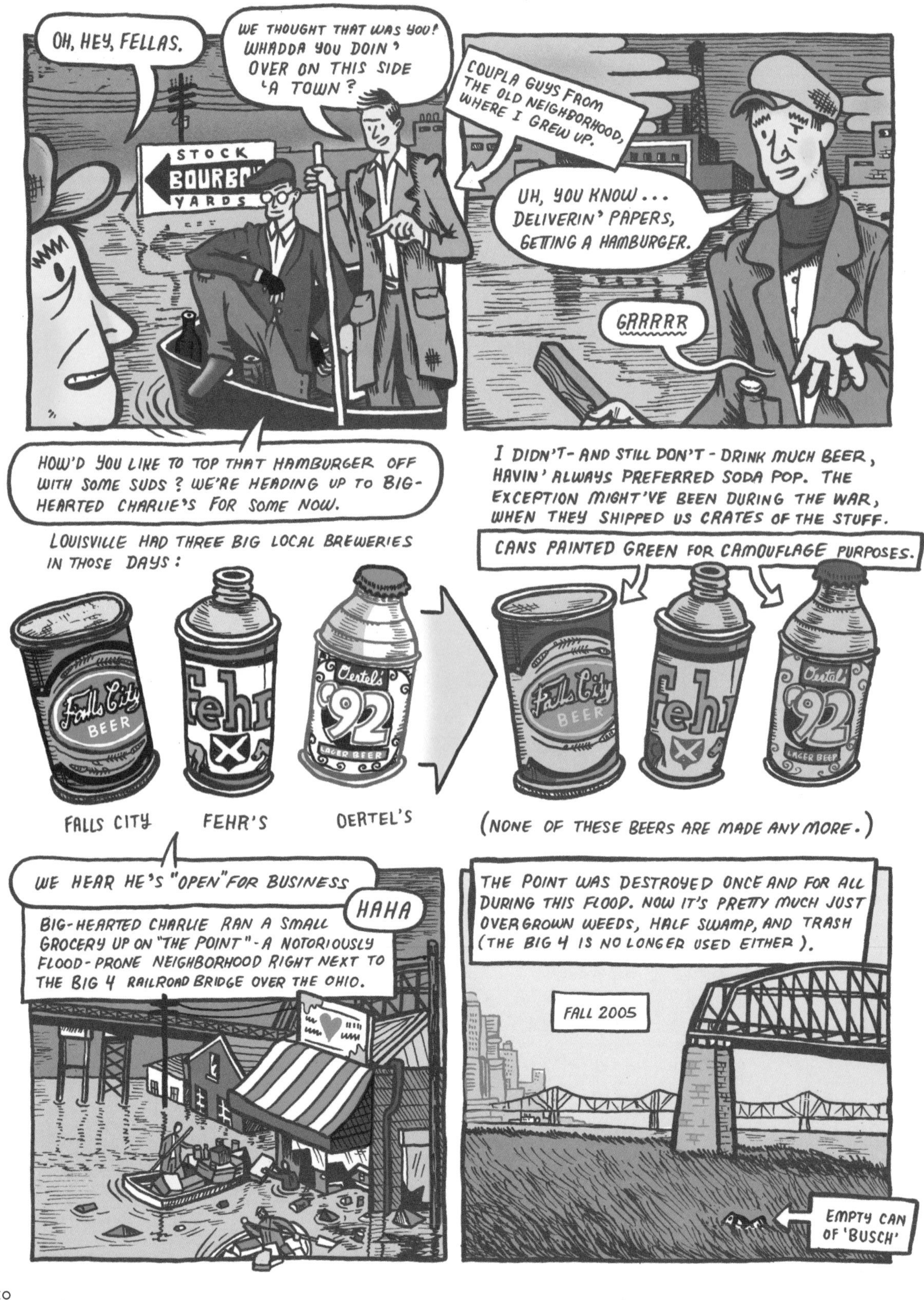
OH, HEY, FELLAS.
WE THOUGHT THAT WAS YOU! WHADDA YOU DOIN' OVER ON THIS SIDE 'A TOWN?
STOCK
YARDS
COUPLA GUYS FROM THE OLD NEIGHBORHOOD, WHERE I GREW UP.
UH, YOU KNOW... DELIVERIN' PAPERS, GETTING A HAMBURGER.
GRRRRR
HOW'D YOU LIKE TO TOP THAT HAMBURGER OFF WITH SOME SUDS? WE'RE HEADING UP TO BIG-HEARTED CHARLIE'S FOR SOME NOW.
I DIDN'T - AND STILL DON'T - DRINK MUCH BEER, HAVIN' ALWAYS PREFERRED SODA POP. THE EXCEPTION MIGHT'VE BEEN DURING THE WAR, WHEN THEY SHIPPED US CRATES OF THE STUFF.
LOUISVILLE HAD THREE BIG LOCAL BREWERIES IN THOSE DAYS:
CANS PAINTED GREEN FOR CAMOUFLAGE PURPOSES.
Falls City BEER
Fehr
Oertel's '92 LAGER BEER
FALLS CITY
FEHR'S
OERTEL'S
(NONE OF THESE BEERS ARE MADE ANY MORE.)
WE HEAR HE'S "OPEN" FOR BUSINESS
HAHA
BIG-HEARTED CHARLIE RAN A SMALL GROCERY UP ON "THE POINT" - A NOTORIOUSLY FLOOD-PRONE NEIGHBORHOOD RIGHT NEXT TO THE BIG 4 RAILROAD BRIDGE OVER THE OHIO.
THE POINT WAS DESTROYED ONCE AND FOR ALL DURING THIS FLOOD. NOW IT'S PRETTY MUCH JUST OVERGROWN WEEDS, HALF SWAMP, AND TRASH (THE BIG 4 IS NO LONGER USED EITHER).
FALL 2005
EMPTY CAN OF 'BUSCH'

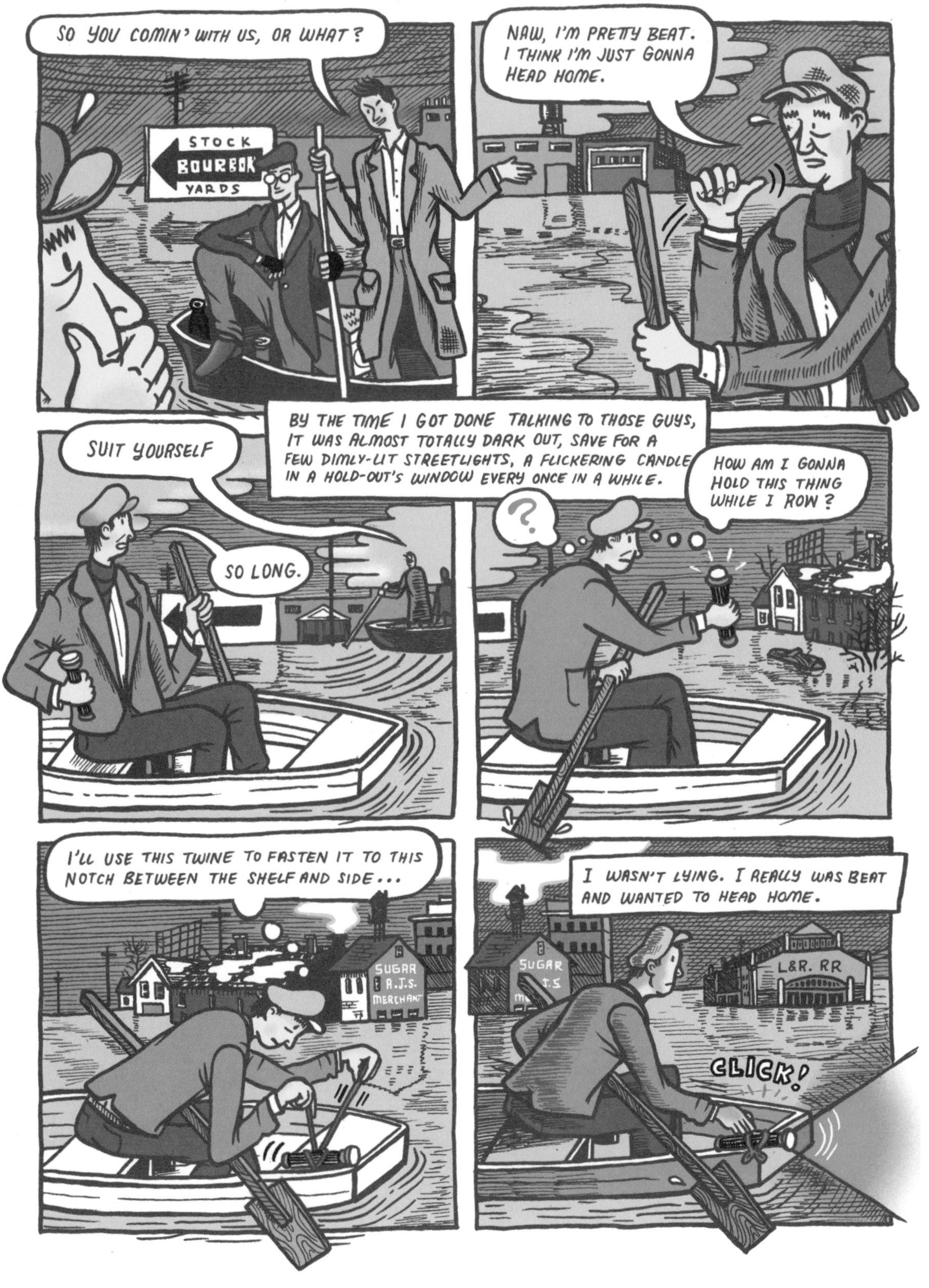
SO YOU COMIN' WITH US, OR WHAT?
STOCK BOURBON YARDS
NAW, I'M PRETTY BEAT. I THINK I'M JUST GONNA HEAD HOME.
SUIT YOURSELF
BY THE TIME I GOT DONE TALKING TO THOSE GUYS, IT WAS ALMOST TOTALLY DARK OUT, SAVE FOR A FEW DIMLY-LIT STREETLIGHTS, A FLICKERING CANDLE IN A HOLD-OUT'S WINDOW EVERY ONCE IN A WHILE.
SO LONG.
?
HOW AM I GONNA HOLD THIS THING WHILE I ROW?
I'LL USE THIS TWINE TO FASTEN IT TO THIS NOTCH BETWEEN THE SHELF AND SIDE...
SUGAR A.J.S. MERCHANT
I WASN'T LYING. I REALLY WAS BEAT AND WANTED TO HEAD HOME.
L&R. RR
CLICK!

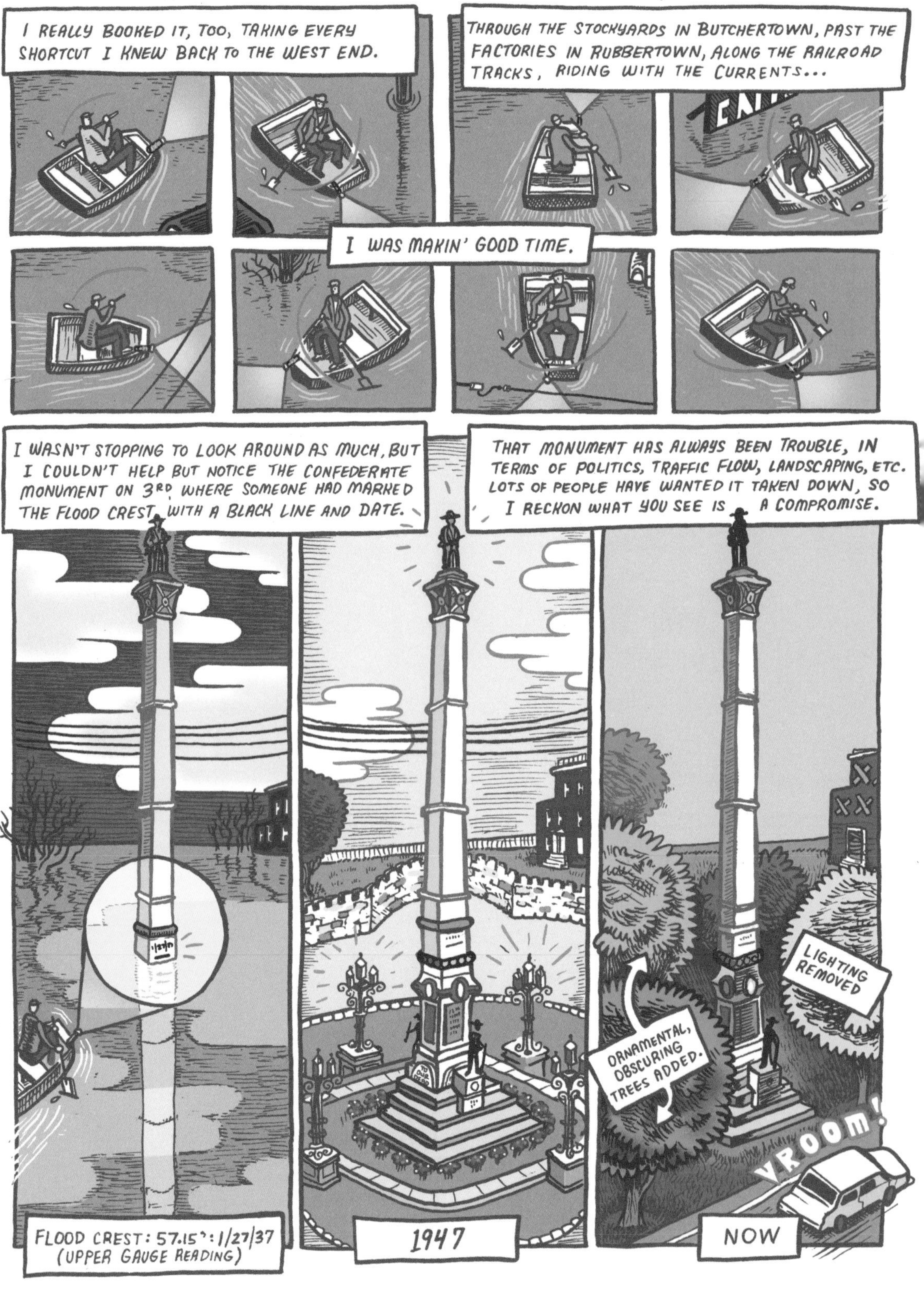

I REALLY BOOKED IT, TOO, TAKING EVERY SHORTCUT I KNEW BACK TO THE WEST END.
THROUGH THE STOCKYARDS IN BUTCHERTOWN, PAST THE FACTORIES IN RUBBERTOWN, ALONG THE RAILROAD TRACKS, RIDING WITH THE CURRENTS...
I WAS MAKIN' GOOD TIME.
I WASN'T STOPPING TO LOOK AROUND AS MUCH, BUT I COULDN'T HELP BUT NOTICE THE CONFEDERATE MONUMENT ON 3RD, WHERE SOMEONE HAD MARKED THE FLOOD CREST WITH A BLACK LINE AND DATE.
THAT MONUMENT HAS ALWAYS BEEN TROUBLE, IN TERMS OF POLITICS, TRAFFIC FLOW, LANDSCAPING, ETC. LOTS OF PEOPLE HAVE WANTED IT TAKEN DOWN, SO I RECKON WHAT YOU SEE IS A COMPROMISE.
FLOOD CREST: 57.15': 1/27/37 (UPPER GAUGE READING)
1947
ORNAMENTAL, OBSCURING TREES ADDED.
LIGHTING REMOVED
VROOM!
NOW

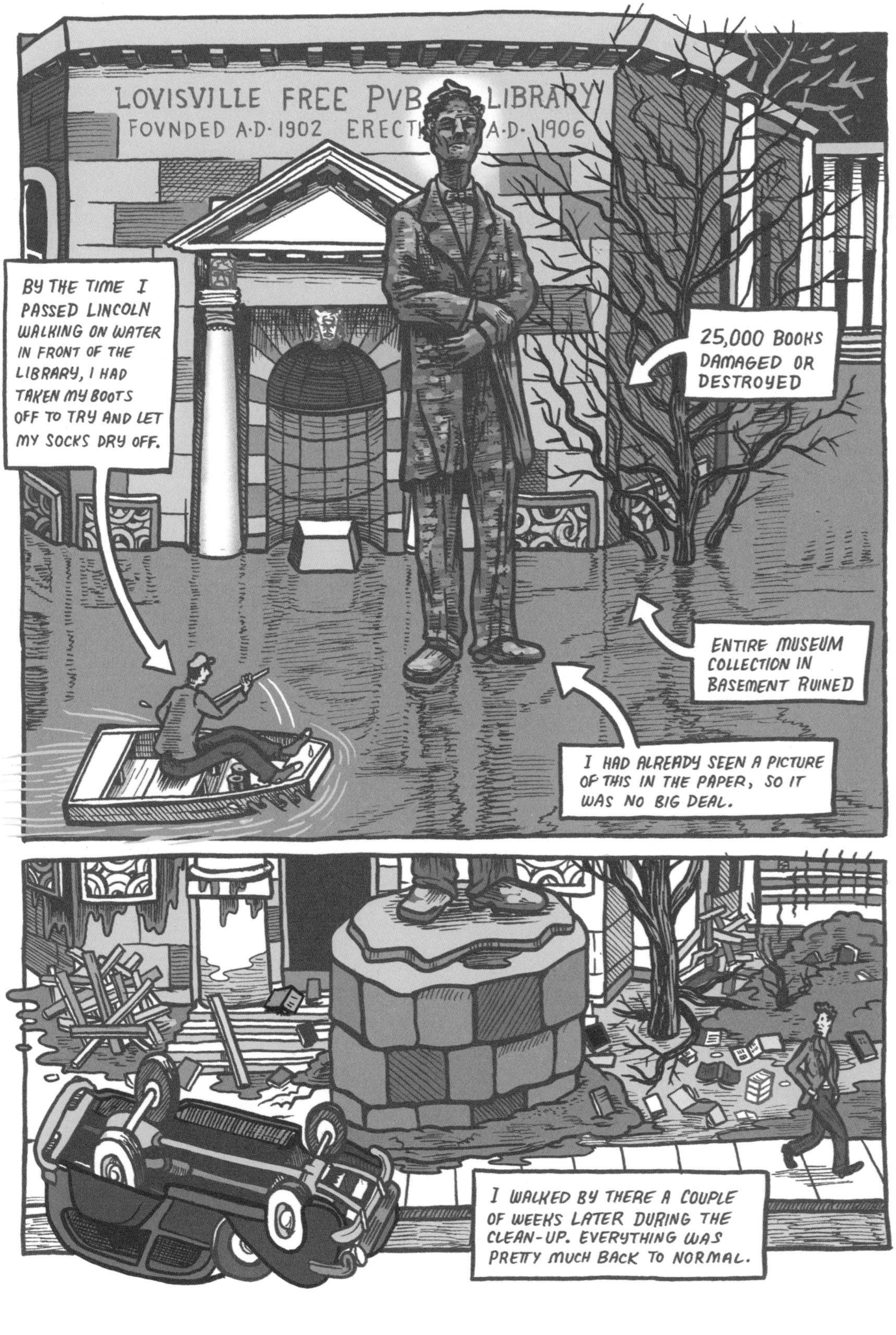
LOVISVILLE FREE PVB LIBRARY
FOVNDED A·D· 1902 ERECT A·D· 1906
BY THE TIME I PASSED LINCOLN WALKING ON WATER IN FRONT OF THE LIBRARY, I HAD TAKEN MY BOOTS OFF TO TRY AND LET MY SOCKS DRY OFF.
25,000 BOOKS DAMAGED OR DESTROYED
ENTIRE MUSEUM COLLECTION IN BASEMENT RUINED
I HAD ALREADY SEEN A PICTURE OF THIS IN THE PAPER, SO IT WAS NO BIG DEAL.
I WALKED BY THERE A COUPLE OF WEEKS LATER DURING THE CLEAN-UP. EVERYTHING WAS PRETTY MUCH BACK TO NORMAL.

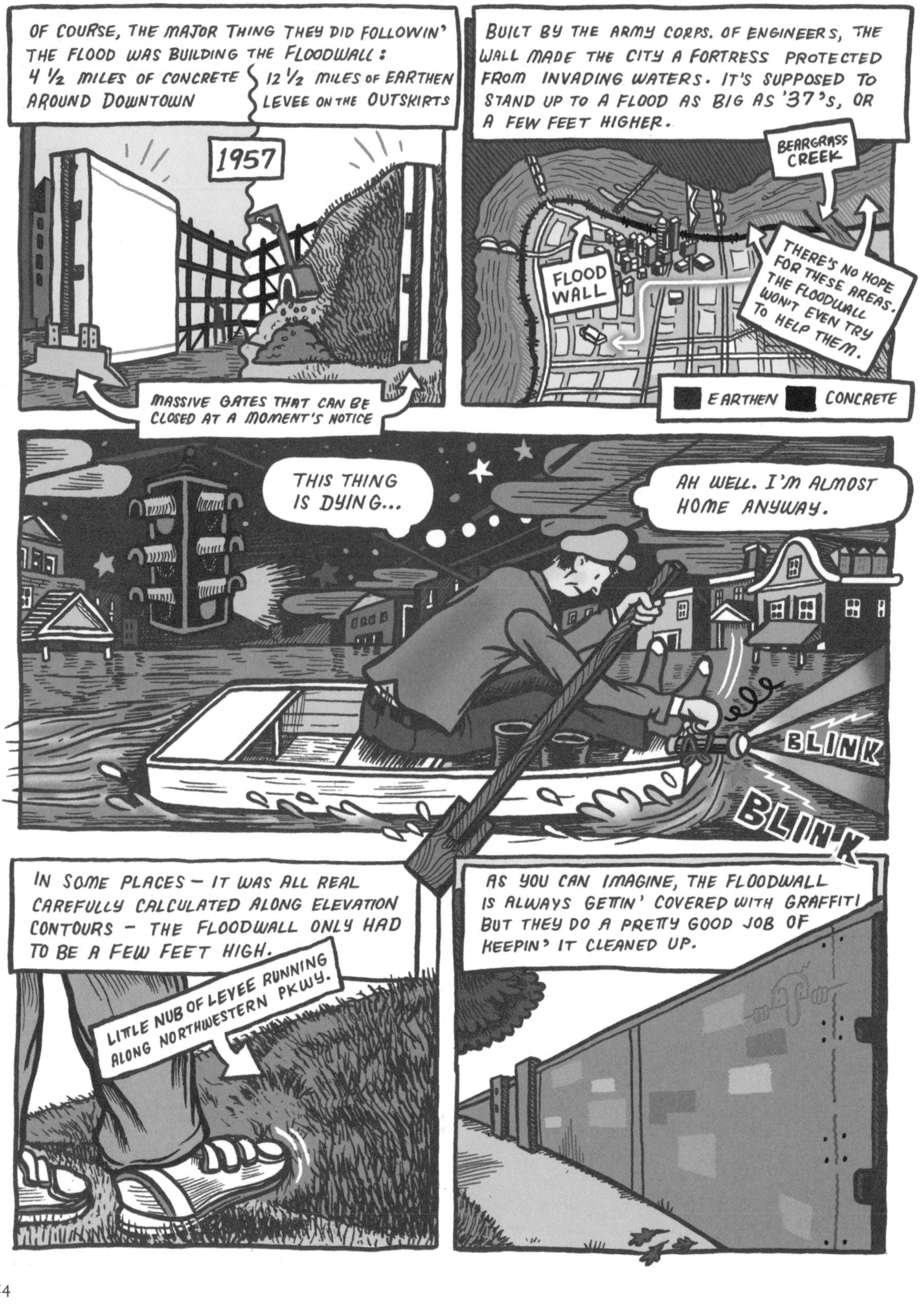
OF COURSE, THE MAJOR THING THEY DID FOLLOWIN' THE FLOOD WAS BUILDING THE FLOODWALL:
4 1/2 MILES OF CONCRETE AROUND DOWNTOWN
12 1/2 MILES OF EARTHEN LEVEE ON THE OUTSKIRTS
1957
MASSIVE GATES THAT CAN BE CLOSED AT A MOMENT'S NOTICE
BUILT BY THE ARMY CORPS. OF ENGINEERS, THE WALL MADE THE CITY A FORTRESS PROTECTED FROM INVADING WATERS. IT'S SUPPOSED TO STAND UP TO A FLOOD AS BIG AS '37'S, OR A FEW FEET HIGHER.
BEARGRASS CREEK
FLOOD WALL
THERE'S NO HOPE FOR THESE AREAS. THE FLOODWALL WON'T EVEN TRY TO HELP THEM.
EARTHEN
CONCRETE
THIS THING IS DYING...
AH WELL. I'M ALMOST HOME ANYWAY.
BLINK
BLINK
IN SOME PLACES – IT WAS ALL REAL CAREFULLY CALCULATED ALONG ELEVATION CONTOURS – THE FLOODWALL ONLY HAD TO BE A FEW FEET HIGH.
LITTLE NUB OF LEVEE RUNNING ALONG NORTHWESTERN PKWY.
AS YOU CAN IMAGINE, THE FLOODWALL IS ALWAYS GETTIN' COVERED WITH GRAFFITI BUT THEY DO A PRETTY GOOD JOB OF KEEPIN' IT CLEANED UP.

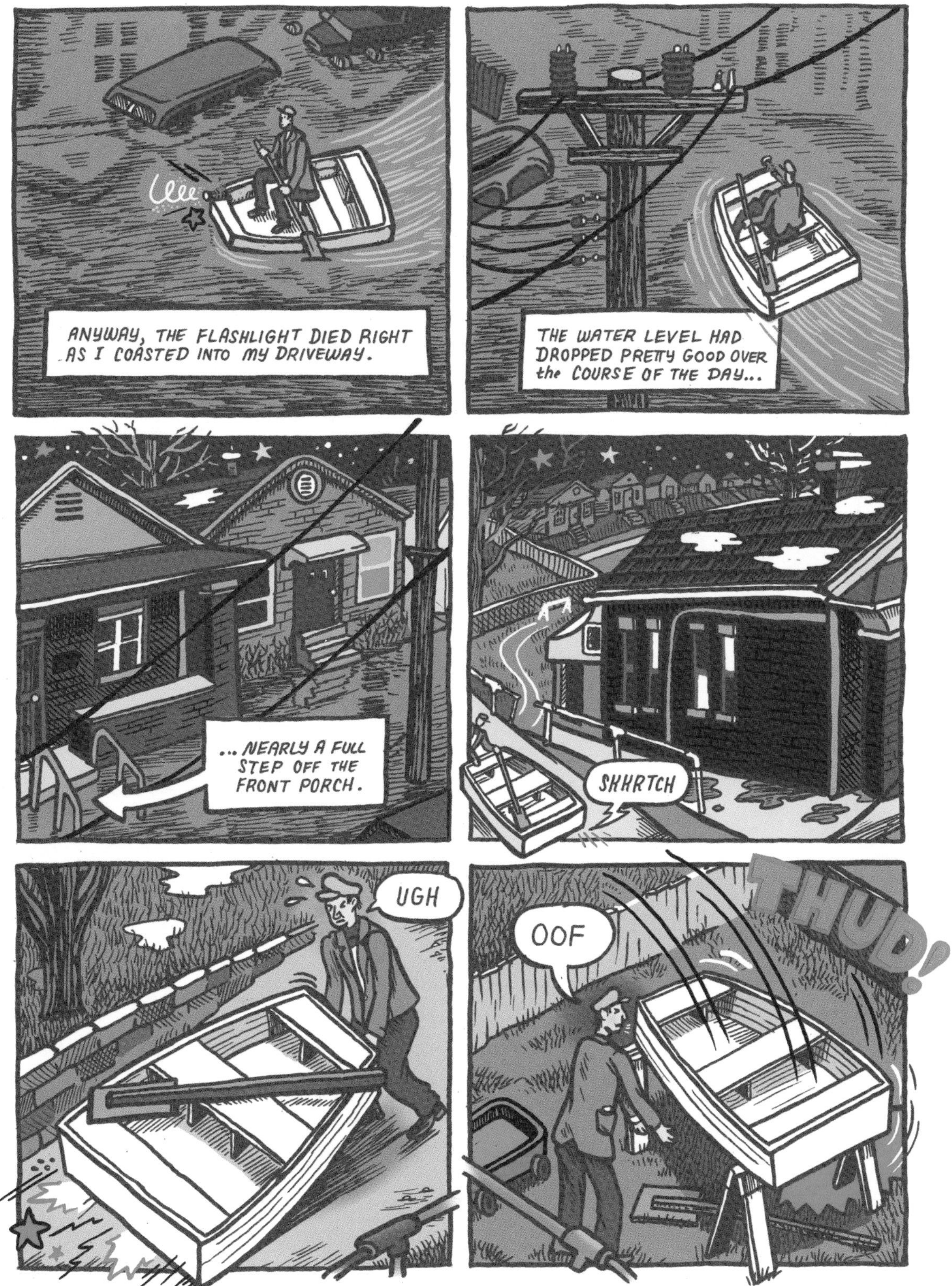

ANYWAY, THE FLASHLIGHT DIED RIGHT AS I COASTED INTO MY DRIVEWAY.
THE WATER LEVEL HAD DROPPED PRETTY GOOD OVER the COURSE OF THE DAY...
...NEARLY A FULL STEP OFF THE FRONT PORCH.
SKKRTCH
UGH
OOF
THUD!

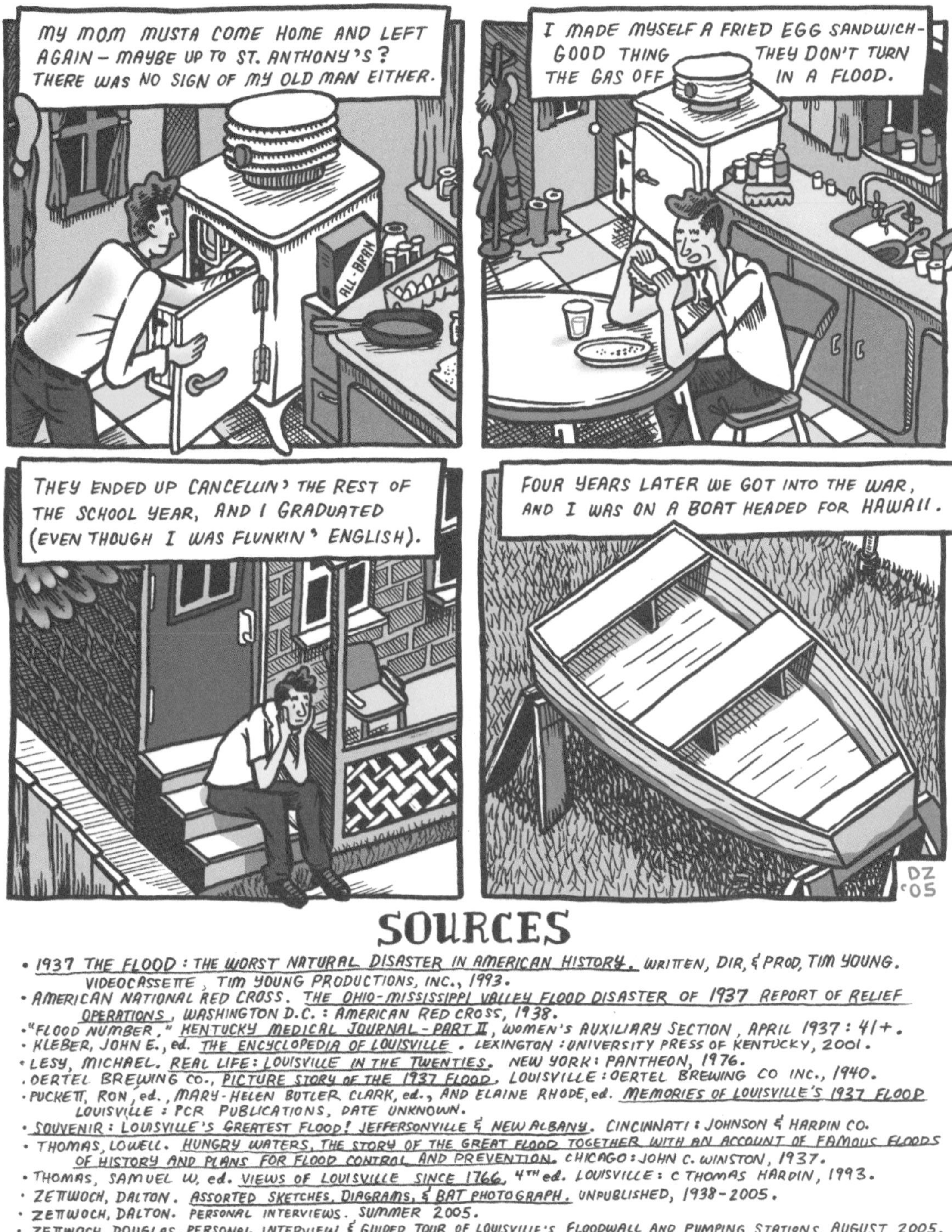
MY MOM MUSTA COME HOME AND LEFT AGAIN – MAYBE UP TO ST. ANTHONY'S? THERE WAS NO SIGN OF MY OLD MAN EITHER.
ALL-BRAN
I MADE MYSELF A FRIED EGG SANDWICH – GOOD THING THEY DON'T TURN THE GAS OFF IN A FLOOD.
THEY ENDED UP CANCELLIN' THE REST OF THE SCHOOL YEAR, AND I GRADUATED (EVEN THOUGH I WAS FLUNKIN' ENGLISH).
FOUR YEARS LATER WE GOT INTO THE WAR, AND I WAS ON A BOAT HEADED FOR HAWAII.
DZ '05

SOURCES

- 1937 THE FLOOD: THE WORST NATURAL DISASTER IN AMERICAN HISTORY. WRITTEN, DIR, & PROD, TIM YOUNG. VIDEOCASSETTE, TIM YOUNG PRODUCTIONS, INC., 1993.
- AMERICAN NATIONAL RED CROSS. THE OHIO-MISSISSIPPI VALLEY FLOOD DISASTER OF 1937 REPORT OF RELIEF OPERATIONS, WASHINGTON D.C.: AMERICAN RED CROSS, 1938.
- "FLOOD NUMBER," KENTUCKY MEDICAL JOURNAL - PART II, WOMEN'S AUXILIARY SECTION, APRIL 1937: 41+.
- KLEBER, JOHN E., ed. THE ENCYCLOPEDIA OF LOUISVILLE. LEXINGTON: UNIVERSITY PRESS OF KENTUCKY, 2001.
- LESY, MICHAEL. REAL LIFE: LOUISVILLE IN THE TWENTIES. NEW YORK: PANTHEON, 1976.
- OERTEL BREWING CO., PICTURE STORY OF THE 1937 FLOOD. LOUISVILLE: OERTEL BREWING CO INC., 1940.
- PUCKETT, RON, ed., MARY-HELEN BUTLER CLARK, ed., AND ELAINE RHODE, ed. MEMORIES OF LOUISVILLE'S 1937 FLOOD LOUISVILLE: PCR PUBLICATIONS, DATE UNKNOWN.
- SOUVENIR: LOUISVILLE'S GREATEST FLOOD! JEFFERSONVILLE & NEW ALBANY. CINCINNATI: JOHNSON & HARDIN CO.
- THOMAS, LOWELL. HUNGRY WATERS, THE STORY OF THE GREAT FLOOD TOGETHER WITH AN ACCOUNT OF FAMOUS FLOODS OF HISTORY AND PLANS FOR FLOOD CONTROL AND PREVENTION. CHICAGO: JOHN C. WINSTON, 1937.
- THOMAS, SAMUEL W, ed. VIEWS OF LOUISVILLE SINCE 1766, 4TH ed. LOUISVILLE: C THOMAS HARDIN, 1993.
- ZETTWOCH, DALTON. ASSORTED SKETCHES, DIAGRAMS, & BAT PHOTOGRAPH. UNPUBLISHED, 1938-2005.
- ZETTWOCH, DALTON. PERSONAL INTERVIEWS. SUMMER 2005.
- ZETTWOCH, DOUGLAS. PERSONAL INTERVIEW & GUIDED TOUR OF LOUISVILLE'S FLOODWALL AND PUMPING STATIONS, AUGUST 2005.
- ZETTWOCH, DONALD. ASSORTED PHOTOGRAPHS OF LOUISVILLE'S WEST END AND THE OLD HOUSE. UNPUBLISHED, 2005.

WON'T BE LICKED!

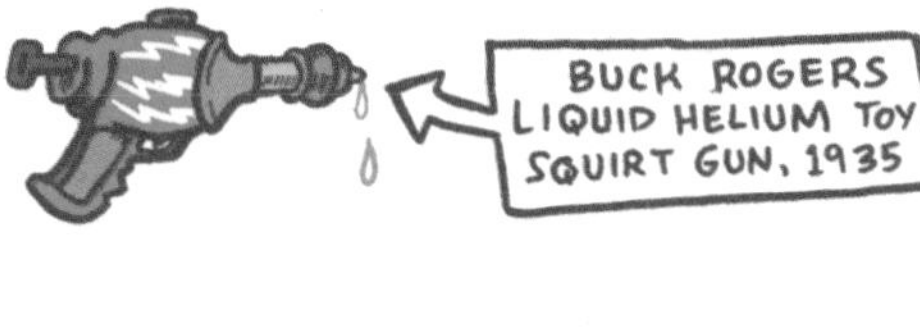
BUCK ROGERS LIQUID HELIUM TOY SQUIRT GUN, 1935

Contributors' Notes

Lynda Barry was born in Wisconsin in 1956, grew up in Seattle, became middle-aged in Chicago, and returned to rural Wisconsin to live out her final days. Her weekly comic strip, *Ernie Pook's Comeek*, will celebrate its thirtieth year in 2008.

■ These strips are from my weekly series. The narrator of the strip has always changed and for the last few years it's been Arna, who is a quieter person than anyone else in the strip. She hardly speaks in the active part of the panels, but in the "thinking" part of it, she says things that no one in her actual world knows she feels, or, for that matter, would care to know. Except maybe for her cousin Freddie, who also pees the bed, has a large inner life, and is often called a fag. Having the strip narrated by a depressed, shy, nearly nonspeaking character who is hardly ever funny has been not so good for business, but I've never had luck trying to make the strip do anything other than what it seems to do on its own if I show up with my brush, ink, paper, and balls. The characters that live in my comic strip have become the kind of steadfast, imaginary friends I always wanted when I was a kid but could never conjure. I'm especially fond of Arna, who shares my love of fungus. Although I'm in fewer papers each year and I'm thankful my strip is published at all, I'd draw it anyway, as there is actually no other way for me to see into that living world and experience what my friends are up to there.

Alison Bechdel was born in 1960 in central Pennsylvania to a family of eccentric schoolteachers whose deep, dark secrets she grew up to expose in her first full-length graphic work, *Fun Home*. She is also the creator of the long-running comic strip *Dykes to Watch Out For*, which in its nearly quarter-century of existence has won some awards and been collected into numerous moderately selling books.

■ This piece is one chapter of my graphic memoir, *Fun Home*, which is the story of growing up with my closeted gay English teacher/mortician/interior decorator father who died when I was nineteen, very possibly by suicide. It's a complicated story, and I found that telling it in a simple chronological way wasn't really possible. I eventually organized the book in chapters around clusters of ideas I had about my father. This chapter is about creativity, in particular the way both my parents' far-flung artistic interests came to shape my own form of creative expression. I realized as I was working on this chapter that it's really about how and why I became a cartoonist. In fact, I think of it in a way as my Cartooning Manifesto. My manifesto has three main tenets: 1) Comics function like maps for me — they're a way of ironing out the chaotic three-dimensional world so I can locate myself and figure out where I'm going. 2) I feel like writing with pictures as well as words enables me to explain things that language on its own can't quite get to. 3) I suspect that drawing comics is a sort of obsessive-compulsive disorder. Maybe *disorder* is the wrong word, because like most cartoonists, I'm pretty high-functioning. But I wouldn't spend my life doing this all-consuming work if I didn't have to.

Gabrielle Bell grew up in Northern California. She first discovered comics as a form of expression in her late teens and has since devoted herself to the medium. In her early twenties, she began producing a series of 32-page mini-comics that were eventually anthologized in her book *When I'm Old and Other Stories*. Her most recent book, *Lucky*, is a collection of diary and autobiographical comics also previously published as mini-comics. She contributes to several anthologies, including *Mome* and *Kramer's Ergot*. She currently lives in Brooklyn and is working on a second volume of *Lucky*.

- When I took a three-week trip to California to visit my family last spring, I decided to do a travelogue in comics form. It was the same formula I had taken with my book *Lucky*; I would turn each day into a comic, choosing one or several incidents and shaping it into a story, and stringing all the stories together to make a larger story. In the end, it took about two days per page instead of one, but I managed to produce eleven pages, and published it in the quarterly Fantagraphics anthology *Mome*.

Jonathan Bennett is a regular contributor to the quarterly Fantagraphics anthology *Mome*, the designer of Todd Hignite's newly expanded periodical *Comic Art*, published by Buenaventura Press, and a designer of book interiors at St. Martin's Press in New York City. He lives in Brooklyn with his wife, Amy.

- Like all my stories that have appeared in *Mome* so far, "Needles and Pins" is an improvised, free-associated story that took me a long time to complete. The spark of "Needles and Pins" was the unfortunately common sight of New York pigeons picking at discarded fried chicken bones on the Brooklyn Heights promenade. Once I sat down at my drawing table, I put down that initial idea and set the scene, trying to let my mind wander "in character." Slowly, as my character responded to his environment, things started to happen. One train of thought led to several visual and physical tangents in the comic strip. Before long, I was able to let the story lead the way in fits.

It's another tale of my mind wandering and trying to convince myself that I'm right there on the page. It's not really important to the story, but I'll say that once I got up to the part where the character's leg falls asleep, I had that Ramones' cover of the song "Needles and Pins" (made famous by The Searchers) stuck in my head. So now whenever I see the title of this story, I hear it with Joey Ramone's extravagantly lethargic phrasing of "Pins-uh."

Jeffrey Brown is an Ignatz Award–winning cartoonist known alternately for his autobiographical graphic novels such as *Clumsy* and his light-hearted parodies such as his most recent *Incredible Change-Bots*. Aside from nearly a dozen books from Top Shelf, Brown also released a collection of strips about his cat, *Cat Getting Out Of A Bag*, with Chronicle Books in the spring of 2007, and a collection of autobiographical short stories entitled *Little Things* (including the story printed in this volume) will be released by Touchstone/Fireside in 2008.

- Most of my autobiographical comics before writing this story had been focused on relationships, but I've also been interested in how things interconnect in life. This was the first story trying to capture that sentiment. It was even tentatively titled "A Small World" at first. I think our minds jump back and forth, one thought leads to something else, and somehow things take on different meanings when we start to realize the associations we have for them. Music is one area that often holds deep meaning for people. I found that over a fairly short period of time, the music of Andrew Bird seemed to have crept in and infiltrated my life in a number of ways, and then I realized this had been happening long before I was aware of it. Somehow his music had become a kind of map to part of my life. I wanted to write about the feelings this map described and at the same time capture a bit of what the music held for me — joy, wonder, nostalgia, introspection, and retrospection.

Ivan Brunetti was born in Mondavio, Italy, in 1967 and moved to Chicago, Illinois, during the blizzard of '76. He has been trapped there ever since. He currently works as a Web designer and has taught classes on editorial illustration and comics at Columbia College, Chicago, and the

University of Chicago. In 2005, he curated *The Cartoonist's Eye,* an exhibit of the work of seventy-five artists, for the A+D Gallery of Columbia College, Chicago; the exhibit was a preview for *An Anthology of Graphic Fiction, Cartoons, and True Stories* (Yale University Press, 2006), which he edited. To date, Fantagraphics Books has published four issues of his comic book series, *Schizo,* two collections of his morally inexcusable gag cartoons (*HAW!* and its miniature companion *HEE!*), and a bound volume of his work, *Misery Loves Comedy.*

▪ These particular strips form a trilogy of sorts, although I was only able to see that after they were completed. The drawings in each are similar, progressing (or perhaps regressing) toward an ever-more-simplified, almost abstract, internal geometry. The first strip condenses seven years of marriage into one page. The second strip encapsulates a much shorter time span, during a much, much healthier relationship, and is a simple and heartfelt tribute to my then-girlfriend and now-wife. The third strip documents the horrible day of an inadvertent act of evil, so thoughtless as to be banal (well, not to the feathered victim). Perhaps it was a cosmic hint, edging me toward abstaining from eating meat; not that I have heeded this karmic call. All three strips reveal me to be quite a horrible person, worthy only of your disdain, dear reader. As always with my comics, they aim for catharsis but end up as mere self-caricature. One day I hope to learn how to draw accurately the world around me, how to notice something other than the swirling matrix of shame and ineptitude that forms my inner core, and hopefully become a better human being as a result. As I type this, I of course realize there is little to no chance of this ever happening. Please move on to the next entry. Sorry.

Charles Burns was born in Washington, D.C., in 1955 and currently lives in Philadelphia with his wife, the painter Susan Moore, and their two daughters. His comics and illustrations have been widely published in Europe and the United States in magazines such as *The New Yorker, The Believer,* and *RAW.* His books include *Black Hole* (2005), *Skin Deep* (2001), *Close Your Eyes* (2001), and *El Borbah* (1999). His recent projects include a book of photographs called *One Eye,* published by Drawn and Quarterly, and work on an animated movie for the French production company Prima Linea, called *Peur(s) du Noir.*

▪ Back in the 1990s, I became obsessed with the concept of a "teen plague" — a disfiguring disease that affects only teenagers. My book *Black Hole* is the result of that obsession. The good news is that my anxiety dreams no longer involve me walking lost and naked in the halls of Roosevelt High School.

R. and Aline Crumb write: "We've been doing this for so long our works are too numerous to list . . . Where would we begin??? We feel like the great-grandparents of the current generation of dazzlingly talented young cartoonists!!! We started working together on the same stories, actually on the same page and even in the same panel, in 1972, when Aline fell and broke her leg and we were stuck inside all winter . . . This work evolved into *Dirty Laundry Comics,* which then led to our more recent collaborations for *The New Yorker.* These later strips are more topical and to the point then the early rambling, often seemingly pointless *Dirty Laundry Comics . . .*"

▪ The "Winta Wundaland" story was done last year when we were in New York visiting our dahling dawder, Sophie, who was living in a squat on the Lower East Side . . . It was inspired by the absurd contradictions in our life and the craziness and anarchy of NYC streets. We're such hicks that we really get overwhelmed and hyperstimulated when we're in a mega city like New York. Also, Aline is like a wild animal released in its natural habitat when she hits the sidewalks of New Yawk . . .

Sophie Crumb was born and raised in rural California until she was nine years old, when her family suddenly moved to a small village in the south of France. "Our family was like a weird cartoon cocoon," she writes. "It was like us against the world. It made me a curious and confused person. I've traveled some, done all kinds of jobs, and lived in various deviant situations. Meanwhile, drawing in my sketchbook, zines, and other underground stuff was the main consistency in my life. Finally, after all this wandering I'm trying to settle down, living in the mountains, attempting to combine tattooing, cartooning, and illustration."

▪ So, see, I have to contribute at least seven pages to Fantagraphics's *Mome* four times a year and that's a lot to me. So, what was it like a year ago, I didn't have enough pages to send so I looked desperately in my sketchbook for a presentable comic or something but I couldn't find anything except that comic. I would have spent more time on it knowing it would be seen by someone else than me!!! Thanks!

Vanessa Davis was born in West Palm Beach, Florida, in 1978, to journalist parents. She began drawing comics, specifically diary comics, in 2003. These were collected into a book, *Spaniel Rage,* published by Buenaventura Press in 2005. Her work has also appeared in such anthologies and publications as *Kramer's Ergot* and the *New York Times,* as well as *The Drama, Vice, Jane,* and *Arthur* magazines. She currently lives in Santa Rosa, California, and is working on her next book, which does not have a title yet.

▪ These diary strips are from a period of time when I was planning to move away from New York to go to California. Before they appeared in *Kramer's Ergot* no. 6, most of my published comics had only been in pencil. The printing of this anthology permitted me to use color, so I took the opportunity to paint and ink my pages. This has become the new way that I've been working lately, but I do think it's funny to apply this technique to such normally spontaneous subject matter.

Kim Deitch was born in Los Angeles, California. He grew up with artistically inclined parents and it rubbed off on him. After bailing from art school about halfway through and knocking around in the world for a while, he drifted into comics, which he decided was an art form that had a lot of room yet for earnest artistic exploration. How true it proved to be, and Deitch has been hard at it ever since the late 1960s, if you can believe it. He's a very hardheaded and diligent fellow. Coming soon from this human comic-book factory is *Alias the Cat,* a graphic novel from Pantheon books. In the works right now is *Deitch's Pictorama,* a book of illustrated fiction (not comics), which he is working on with his two brothers. Last but not least, he is doing a jumbo-sized three-page story for *Kramer's Ergot* that he hopes to make his most elegant-looking comic-book story ever.

▪ The idea for Midgetville came out of an article I read in the *New York Times* that had a title very similar to "No Midgets in Midgetville," about a community of small houses in the town Totowa, New Jersey. I visited the place with low expectations, a jumping-off point, if you will, for me to create the Midgetville of my imagination, influenced to some degree by reports of a midget community that used to be an amusement attraction in the Dreamland amusement park in Coney Island, which burned to the ground in 1911.

C. F. (b. 1979) welcomes mail to P.O. Box 913, Providence, Rhode Island 02901.

▪ This comic I did mostly when I had a fever. While America claps or weeps in unison, thousands of years in the future these other stories are taking place, divorced from the crippling mindsets of today! I hope you enjoy my comic! C.F. 12.24.06.

Sammy Harkham was born in Los Angeles in 1980. Since 1998, he has edited the comics anthology *Kramer's Ergot.* Besides his work in *Kramer's,* Harkham has had work appear in *Drawn & Quarterly Showcase* no. 3, *Best American Nonrequired Reading* 2004, and *Vice.* Now he draws the ongoing comic book, *Crickets,* published by Drawn & Quarterly.

▪ Judaism, especially in the Hassidic branch of the Chabad-Lubavitch world, is concerned with finding the hidden grace innately within mundane reality. I first started learning Hassidic philosophy as a teenager, and it simultaneously confirmed and challenged how I looked at life.

Chabad presents a "system" for living that, ideally, is constantly pushing you forward, always searching, never complacent. It was the exact opposite of what I thought religion was — an intellectual safety zone. And it has affected my entire life till this day. That said, I have avoided including Judaism explicitly in my comics for a long time, as my main concern as a cartoonist is to present the external aspects of life, and to present "answers" of any kind seemed to get in the way of that. At the same time, like any artist, the goal is to always get closer to the truth in the work, to be more honest. In the summer of 2005, I discovered Robert Crumb's strip, "Cave Wimp," the conceit of the strip being Crumb placing his "persona" and concerns in the context of the Stone Age. It inspired a way for me to bring the Jewish concerns in my work to the fore while still making the strip more than just about Judaism and therefore relatable (i.e., readable) to others: autobiography, but set in a different milieu. The effect of which hopefully presents a way of life in a funny way, but also one that's not about how people *once* lived, but still do, although the minor details have changed (at least in California).

The challenge I found once I started on the strip was balancing a lot of different tones. I wanted the strip to be funny but not to make fun of the characters and their lives, as I know there would be readers who have an aversion to religion and would be inclined to laugh at it. At the same time, I didn't want it to be dogmatic. It was important to not give the reader a clear "yes" answer, to not tie everything up in a neat little bow, as Judaism itself is averse to that.

David Heatley is a cartoonist who lives in Queens, New York, with his wife, the writer Rebecca Gopoian, and their children, Maya and Sam. His comics and illustrations have appeared in the *New York Times, McSweeney's, Kramer's Ergot, Mome,* and *Nickelodeon.* A collection of his autobiographical work, *My Brain Is Hanging Upside Down,* will be published some time in 2008. *Overpeck,* a graphic novella, will be published by Fantagraphics some time in 2008. Visit www .davidheatley.com and www.davidheatley.blogspot.com.

- I've been keeping a journal since I was fifteen years old, and I've written down my dreams for almost as long. When I started getting serious about making comics about twelve years ago, I recognized that the best comics have an architecture of good writing and storytelling. I didn't know anything about writing fiction, but I had already been writing for ten years in my journal. Looking back over my entries for material to draw, I could see that my dreams were funny, vivid, bizarre, symbol-ridden, deeply personal, and unlike anything else I was reading in comics (except maybe Julie Doucet's dream comics and Daniel Clowes's "Nature Boy"). They were also material I "knew" (as in the admonition to young writers, "Write what you know"). In short, they were the best fiction I knew how to write, and they were already written. In the last ten years, I've drawn comic strips based on dozens of my dreams. I've also written autobiographical comics about my sex life, race issues, portraits of my parents, and family history and lineage (i.e., my waking life). I think of the dreams as the dark underbelly of my story, where my mind feels free to express the unimaginable. Though they're consciously constructed comics, I try my best to approximate the feelings I had while dreaming them. The dreams chosen for this volume are some of the most recent ones I've drawn and go the furthest in terms of articulating my darkest sides, except for "Walnut Creek," which is obliquely about having a spiritual awakening.

Tim Hensley was born in Bloomington, Indiana, in 1966. He is the author of many songs (some of which comprise a soundtrack recording released in 1993, now out of print, to Daniel Clowes's *Like a Velvet Glove Cast in Iron*). He also drew, Xeroxed, and stapled nine issues of a film criticism zine, *Ticket Stub,* now out of print, at the turn of the century. He is currently working on a comic story called "Gropius" being serialized in the Fantagraphics publication *Mome;* "Meet the Dropouts" is an excerpt.

- Usually I carry a briefcase handcuffed to my wrist with a ten-digit authentication code to encrypt for transmission to subterranean bunkers and submarine flanks, and either red phones ring or keys unlock guidance detonators or flares spatter or galleons raise their black masts. Or I would go to the public library after work and sit in a study carrel and write chicken scratch in a spiral-bound notebook for an hour or so with a copy of a comic book like, say, *The Madhouse Glads,* and anyone glancing as they walked past would've assumed I was mentally ill — only sort of, but not at that time — and later I tried to draw what I wrote, and it was published.

Gilbert Hernandez grew up in Oxnard, California, a small agricultural town just sixty miles above Los Angeles. Comic books, rock-and-roll, and films are his greatest indulgences as well as artistic influences on his work. Real life — and that being attractive women — is the true reason he does anything at all. That and crushing his enemies.

▪ I wanted to create a truthful (and painful) story about how so many men are driven by lust and conquest. The power that an attractive, large-breasted woman can have over so many people, whether she wants it or not, has always amused me. That and how obsession and immaturity drives us in so many ways, to failure many times, but also to success. Most people only want to hear about when it fails people, but I'm more interested in when indulgence brings us happiness. Pain makes great news; happiness does not.

Kevin Huizenga was born in the suburbs of Chicago and now lives near Saint Louis with his wife. His new book *Curses* is published by Drawn & Quarterly. He continues drawing comics for his series *Ganges* for Fantagraphics and *Or Else* for Drawn & Quarterly. *Ganges* no. 1 has been published in six languages and won an Ignatz Award for "Outstanding Story."

▪ "Glenn in Bed" is part of a handful of interconnected stories that makes up my comic book *Ganges* no. 1. Earlier stories tell how Glenn went to the library, got some books, read for a while, and hung out with his wife, Wendy, and drank a lot of coffee. I should explain that when Glenn imagines the other people in bed he's imagining characters from some of the other stories, and when he sees that circular diagram of people in bed, it mirrors another circular diagram in an earlier story. Another thing I could point out is that I didn't fill in all that black with ink — I used Photoshop. It would have taken a long time to fill in all of that black and I'm too impatient. *Ganges* no. 1 is part of the Ignatz line of comic books, not to be confused with the Ignatz Award given out every year at the Small Press Expo. The idea behind Ignatz is to make comics that get published in many different languages at once. It's a great opportunity and I'm honored to be a part of it.

Ben Katchor's weekly strip, "Shoehorn Technique," appears in the *Forward* and the *Chicago Reader.* His monthly strip on the subjects of architecture and design appears in *Metropolis* magazine. He has collaborated with musician Mark Mulcahy on two music-theater productions: *The Slug Bearers of Kayrol Island* and *The Rosenbach Company.* He is a 2006–2007 Fellow at The Dorothy and Lewis B. Cullman Center for Scholars and Writers at the New York Public Library. For more information visit www.katchor.com

▪ My new weekly strip, "Shoehorn Technique," combines my interests in chiropody and atheism. I hope, in the course of this strip, to persuade readers to discard their religious beliefs, whatever they may be, and turn their attention to foot-care and other humanitarian efforts. Doctor Eisbein is based upon a real chiropodist who practiced in Brooklyn, New York, c. 1975. The strip is dedicated to him and other basement practitioners of medicine.

In the year 1996, **Miriam Katin** was working at MTV and a young employee called her up from Human Resources. It seemed that Miriam made a mistake listing the date of her birth. Surely she meant 1972? . . . No . . . 62? . . . No . . . Could it not be 1952? The young woman was unable to go back any further. For her no world, no time, existed so far back. Katin assured her that yes, 1942 was the correct date of her birth, and she was still alive and well sitting on the thirty-sixth floor working on *Beavis and Butthead Do America.* The young employee must have been quite spooked. Miriam Katin had no formal art education. After an apprenticeship in a Tel Aviv advertisement agency, she served in a Graphic Arts Division with the Israel Defense Forces. Later she worked in an animation studio in a kibbutz by the Dead Sea.

▪ My book is the story of our escape and life in hiding during the year of 1944–45. The Germans came into Budapest. The Jewish Law went into effect and it meant deportation and certain death. The stories my mother told me about our survival were like a constant running narrative in my mind through the years. They begged to be told. I could not write but I am an illustrator. With my drawings and some text through the form of comics I found a way to tell our story. I remember very little of that time. I could somehow imagine the places and the people my mother told me about, but a real sense of myself as a small child and the fear and confusion of those times I could understand only by reading the last few letters and postcards my mother had written to my father. Her words and some dark old photographs were the inspiration for this story.

My name is **Jerry Moriarty.**
I was born in 1938 in Binghamton, New York.
I went to Pratt Institute from 1956–60 (BFA).
I did magazine illustration 1960–65 (girlie mostly).
I taught at School of Visual Arts 1963–2006.
I got N.E.A. grant 1977.
I was in *RAW* magazine from 1980–84.
RAW published my book *Jack Survives* in 1984.
I had a one-man show at SVA Museum in 1999.
I had a two-man show at Cue Foundation in NYC 2004.
I had twenty-seven pages of my recent art published in *Kramer's Ergot* no. 6 in 2006.

▪ When I was a kid and learned the art "trick," my father was the main support. He'd come down into the cellar after supper, still in his clothes from work, and watch me paint. Standing quietly behind me, he might say, "How about a little red over there, Jer?" I would gladly do it. Jack Moriarty was a white collar, working-class guy with a ninth-grade education, typical of his generation born in 1900. He loved music and baseball. When someone visited, he'd say to me, "Do you know where that picture is that you did last week?" I would bring it up from the cellar and the visitor would say something nice as my father beamed. My father, who knew nothing about art, is why I am an artist today. He died when I was fifteen, so I have no idea how he'd feel about that. The bald guy is me, as I am now shrunk down to the size of a ten-year-old. Time travel without a machine.

Anders Nilsen is the artist and author of *Big Questions, Don't Go Where I Can't Follow, The End,* and *Dogs and Water.* His work has been translated into several languages and has been featured in *Kramer's Ergot, Chicago Reader,* the *Utne Reader, Mome,* and elsewhere. Nilsen was born in northern New Hampshire in 1973 and grew up there and in Minneapolis. He went to school in New Mexico to study painting and installation before moving to Chicago to go to graduate school at the School of the Art Institute. He dropped out after a year to devote his time and energy to drawing comics and other artwork. He currently works as a cartoonist and illustrator and lives in Chicago.

▪ The piece running here is from a recent chapter of a long story called *Big Questions* that I've been working on since 1999. The story concerns a group of birds living on a plain in the middle of nowhere and three humans with whom they interact and whom they struggle to understand, with mixed results. The plot revolves around an initially unexploded bomb, which the birds mistake for a giant egg, and a crashed airplane they likewise mistake for a giant bird. The bird in this piece, Bayle, seeks a reprise of a previous experience with the person he's following, in which he had, during a moment of absorption in the flavor of a sandwich, been caught off guard and seized by the boy, then let go. The material in the story evolved out of a series of gag strips and a stream-of-consciousness drawing exercise I did as long ago as 1996. I started the present story a few years later and found it compelling enough to give up (for the most part) the other media and subject matter I'd studied and had been working with to that point. As of this writing, the story is about 75 percent complete and just shy of three hundred pages. It is currently being serialized by Drawn & Quarterly.

Oklahoma-born, Texas-reared illustrator, painter, designer, and part-time musician, **Gary Panter** is a child of the '50s who blossomed in the full glare of the psychedelic '60s and, after surviving underground during the '70s, finally made his mark in the '80s as head set designer for the successful kid/adult TV show *Pee Wee's Playhouse,* a job that brought him three Emmy Awards. Possibly the most influential graphic artist of his generation, a fact acknowledged by the Chrysler Design Award he received in 2000, Gary Panter has been everything from an underground cartoonist to an interior designer (for a playroom inside the Philippe Starck–designed Paramount Hotel in New York) to an Internet animator (his *Pink Donkey and the Fly* series can be seen online at Cartoon Network's Web site). He is also the creator of *Jimbo,* a post-nuclear punk-rock cartoon character whose adventures were first chronicled as a comic strip in the '70s LA hardcore-punk paper *Slash* and later in *RAW* magazine. As an illustrator, Panter was one of the first to stop worrying about graphic perfection, preferring instead to push the underground punk attitude he had nurtured since the '70s into his commercial art for established magazines such as *Time, Rolling Stone, Entertainment Weekly,* and *The New Yorker.*

■ In 1988, Pantheon put out a collection of Jimbo comics called *Jimbo in Paradise.* After it was published, I felt sheepish that I had never read Dante's *Paradise* and eventually began to read *The Divine Comedy.* Newcomers to Dante are often blown away by the architecture of his poem and so was I. Fools will dash in.

"**Paper Rad** is a Army, better yet a Navy. Like the Wu Tang Clan, Paper Rad has been forging a street-smart style, full of funky fresh comics and zines, for over two years. Known for their trendy '80s-style art, Paper Rad loves anything kitschy or like 'from the '80s.' On top of that, they got DVDs and are most famous for doing the Lightning Bolt video. So pretty much they are getting pretty pretty pretty famous. What else can I say, '*They rock*'!!!!! Oh, and by the way, they also did a video for Beck, I think, so, yah . . ." — Tom Devlin

While most of the above is wildly false, Paper Rad would like to point out that 90 percent of press about Paper Rad and our immediate community of artists is plagued with falsehoods. Bios, write-ups, and even interviews routinely get the facts messed up. That said, when we are asked to write a bio, it kind of bums us out. *Why?* While we feel really lucky to have a forum to explain ourselves, when we do try to explain ourselves, it gets overshadowed or lost as a result of the ambient hype constantly present in today's society. Now we know how Tom Cruise must feel. Anyway, instead of fighting the uphill battle against the *New York Times, Tokion, Art Review,* and *XLR8R,* all of which have used a combination of the words "collective," "psychedelic," and/or "cartoons" in their kind reviews of our work, we will resist explaining how we don't think we are a collective or any of that other stuff. If you want to know what we are, from our perspective, get some of our books at www.pictureboxinc.com, our DVDs at www.loadrecords.com, our art at www.foxyproduction.com, or some of our soul at www.paperrad.org.

■ The story "Kramer's Ergot 'Fuck You' 9" was written and published before Michael Richards went on his infamous racist comedy tirade. The use of the band Smog is done so in the vein of *Mad* magazine's hilarious satirical comics. I am a big, *big* fan of Smog (excuse the pun), but I want it to be clear that this story is at best an unsanctioned celebration and interpretation of the band. I had seen them play a couple nights before, and the lead singer's lyrics and raw sexuality were stuck in my mind. The other elements of the story need no disclaimer nor explanation. Ironically, this story was also written and printed before the lead singer of Smog's penis reduction surgery . . . *satire!!!*

John Porcellino was born in Chicago in 1968. He began writing and drawing at an early age, compiling his work into small, handmade booklets. His first photocopied zine was produced in 1982, and he began his current series, the autobiographical *King-Cat Comics and Stories,* in 1989. Since then, *King-Cat* has been his predominant means of expression. Porcellino's comics have been translated into French, German, and Spanish, and book collections of his work are available from publishers such as Drawn & Quarterly, La Mano, Reprodukt, and Ego Comme X. His most recent collection is *King-Cat Classix* (Drawn & Quarterly, 2007). Porcellino currently lives in Denver with his wife, Misun, and a small black cat named Maisie Kukoc. For more information, please visit www.king-cat.net.

▪ I wrote "Country Roads — Brighton" for an issue of *King-Cat* that was all about *places.* Specifically, I suppose, this story was inspired by living in San Francisco, where I was struggling with the double whammy of cramped quarters and high rent. I was daydreaming about a way out, a way to really live. I was remembering a dream of what it would feel like to really be alive.

In 1997, when this story was made, **Ron Regé Jr.** was creating zines and mini-comics while living in Cambridge, Massachusetts. He worked every day at a copy shop (to get the things made) and was performing in several bands such as Trollin Withdrawal, swirlies, TacTic, and solo as The Discombobulated Ventriloquist. 2007 finds Regé living in Edendale, California, continuing to make drawings and comics while performing in the band Lavender Diamond, whose album *Imagine Our Love* will be released in May. Ten years of his comics efforts can be found in the books *Skibber Bee-Bye* and *The Awake Field* from Drawn & Quarterly, as well as two installments of his Yeast Hoist series, both available from Buenaventura Press.

▪ I created "FUC 1997: We Share a Happy Secret, but Beware, Because the Modern World Emerges" to appear in the anthology *Coober Skeber* no. 3. This ambitious book was to include signature length, two-color stories by a cast of then unknown cartoonists. Like many large, expensive projects, this one never did see the light of day. When I was invited to include it in *Kramer's Ergot* no. 6, I realized that almost ten years had passed. I still liked the story and decided to finally let it see print. This story was my first attempt at any kind of lengthy narrative. It acted as a bridge between my earlier mini-comics work and my book *Skibber Bee-Bye,* which ended up being 256 pages long.

Seth is a young fogey rapidly turning into an old fogey. He is the author of *It's a Good Life If You Don't Weaken, Clyde Fans Book One,* and *Wimbledon Green* (all published by Drawn & Quarterly). He is the designer of *The Complete Peanuts* and an upcoming series of books on the Canadian cartoonist Doug Wright. This year his strip *George Sprott* (1894–1975) was serialized in the *New York Times.* He was born in 1962 and lives in Guelph, Ontario, Canada, with his wife, Tania, and three old cats.

▪ *Wimbledon Green* was never really meant to be a book at all. It was simply an exercise in my sketchbooks that took on a life of its own. At the time I began it, I was merely trying to experiment with telling a longer story through a series of vignettes. Consequently, the work was much more improvisational than the majority of my published work. I made it up as I went along. The artwork itself was more slapdash too. I wasn't too concerned with the drawing — just interested in getting the story down on paper. "Interested" is a perhaps an understatement. For some indefinable reason, I was rather driven in the creation of this work, turning out the entirety of the book in a short, six-month period. I began the work with a desire to make fun of comic book collectors, but by the middle of the story I had grown to really like ol' Wimbledon Green. By the end of it, I had decided to publish it—warts and all. I shouldn't neglect to mention that the spark of the story was a book I had been reading at the time, *A Gentle Madness* by Nicholas A. Basbanes. This fascinating nonfiction book about bibliophiles served as a good launching point for what I assumed would be a series of strips meant only for my own eyes. When I sat down at my desk to draw the first page, I fished around in my mind for a subject and Basbanes's obsessive book-hoarders filled the bill. I quickly substituted comic book collectors in their place and off I went. I think I had intended the whole thing to be a lot more of a vicious parody of these fellows—but ultimately it turned out to be quite affectionate. Nostalgic even.

Art Spiegelman (born in 1948) was awarded a Special Pulitzer prize in 1992 for his two volumes of *Maus*, a memoir in comics form about his parents' lives as Jews in Hitler's Europe that is considered seminal in the contemporary adult comics landscape. It was first serialized in *RAW*, the influential comics magazine he cofounded in 1980 with his wife, Françoise Mouly, that introduced and championed the work of cartoonists like Charles Burns, Kim Deitch, Gary Panter, and Chris Ware, among many others who now loom large in that landscape. In 2006, Puffin Books released *Big Fat Little Lit,* a gathering of "RAW for kids" coedited by Spiegelman and his wife. His last book, *In the Shadow of No Towers* (Pantheon), was listed as one of the *New York Times* 100 Most Notable Books of 2004. *Time* magazine named Spiegelman one of their Top 100 Most Influential People of 2005, a fact he now cites to prove he is no longer influential. He and Mouly live in lower Manhattan with their two children, Nadja and Dashiell.

▪ When Dan Frank, my editor at Pantheon, expressed interest in republishing *Breakdowns,* a long out-of-print anthology of autobiographical and formally "experimental" underground comix I drew in the '70s, I figured I'd write some sort of brief introduction . . . but then to make my life more complicated I decided to do it in comix form. These "Portrait of the Artist as a Young %@#*!!" sequences will be part of that introduction—memories and notions that shaped me as a cartoonist. I'm almost two years into the project, and the %@#*!! introduction now threatens to become almost as long as the book it's introducing.

Adrian Tomine was born in 1974 in Sacramento, California, and he currently resides in Brooklyn, New York. He is the writer/artist of the comic book series *Optic Nerve,* and his illustrations appear with some regularity in *The New Yorker.* His contribution to this anthology is an excerpt from his graphic novel *Shortcomings,* which will be published by Drawn & Quarterly in the fall of 2007.

▪ I was trying to tell a longer, more developed story than I had in the past, and I wanted it to have the ring of autobiography despite being wholly fictional.

C. Tyler (b. 1951 in Chicago, Illinois, USA) is a critically acclaimed comic book artist/writer who has been nominated for both Harvey and Eisner awards. Tyler's work has been published in numerous magazines and books for the last twenty years. Studs Terkel called her first book, *The Job Thing,* "A Beaut!" And in his introduction to her second and most recent book, *Late Bloomer,* Robert Crumb says, "Her work has the extremely rare quality of genuine, authentic heart. Hers are the only comics that ever brought me to the verge of tears." Tyler's autobiographical stories reflect her struggles as an artist, worker, wife, and mother. *Late Bloomer* was published by Fantagraphics in 2005. Visit her Web site at www.bloomerland.com.

▪ The works featured here were created about ten years apart. "Just a Bad Seed" is a true story of daycare gone wrong. Technically, I was trying to challenge myself with having more than one thing going on layout-wise, and I wanted to experiment with margins usage and bleeds. I drew this story on a card table the summer I spent with my dad when he was battling cancer, or as we called it, "Camp Chemo." More on that in my upcoming book *You'll Never Know*, due out from Fantagraphics in 2008.

The second story, "Once, We Ran" was drawn in an afternoon. I had the time, you see. My daughter had just gotten into a car with her friends as I was watering the rosebush . . .

Lauren Weinstein is a cartoonist. Her most recent book, *Girl Stories*, was published by Henry Holt and has received two ALA nominations. Currently, Lauren teaches drawing and cartooning to children and adults at the 92nd Street Y, the Parsons School of Design, and the School of Visual Arts. In 2003, she was the recipient of a Xeric Grant, allowing her to self-publish her first book, *Inside Vineyland*. In 2004, she received the Ignatz Award for "Promising New Talent." Her comics and illustrations have appeared in the *New York Times*, *Glamour*, *McSweeney's*, *LA Weekly*, *Chicago Reader*, *Kramer's Ergot*, and Seattle's *The Stranger*. Currently she is working on the sequel to *Girl Stories*, tentatively entitled *Calamity*, and a sci-fi fantasy comic entitled *The Goddess of War*.

▪ This excerpt is from *Girl Stories*, a collection of comics that I did over a period of seven years that I loosely based on the beginning of my adolescence. When I was putting the book together, I needed to flesh out the part where John and Lauren first meet each other and go out. I wanted to try and capture all of the immediacy, pain, and nauseous joy that come with a first (reciprocated) romance. I really did have the "classically beautiful" thing happen to me. My dad really did say, "Is he your hero?" in a similar situation. I wish I could make up stuff like that.

Dan Zettwoch was born and raised in Louisville, Kentucky—also birthplace to Muhammad Ali, the cheeseburger, and bubblegum—in 1977. He is a third-generation artist, whose grandfather drew cartoons during WWII and whose father did the same while working for the American Telephone and Telegraph Company. While their talents have gradually transferred to woodworking, painting, and mechanized sculpture, Zettwoch started drawing comics inspired by those found in Jefferson County Flea Market's nickel bins: *Cracked* magazine and *Rom: Space-knight*. He self-published his earliest efforts in hardcore punk fanzines but eventually started stapling together little booklets containing entire comics about things such as professional wrestling, slot-car racing, and Civil War–era battleships. Since then, he has had stories published in *Kramer's Ergot*, *Bogus Dead*, the *Hi-Horse Omnibus*, *SPX* 2001, *Arthur*, and the *Drawn & Quarterly Showcase*. He currently lives and works in Saint Louis, Missouri, where he runs the USS Catastrophe mini-comics shop and works on his new series, *Redbird*.

▪ Louisville's 1937 flood is a major source of Zettwoch family folklore, up there with running moonshine from Uncle Duke's farm and building elaborate golf-ball contraptions down at Shawnee Park. I had heard the story of my Grandpa toolin' around town in a homemade boat fashioned out of a refrigerator crate a hundred times over. I never thought of drawing a comic about it until he did a drawing of the boat for me on a yellow stenographer's pad one afternoon. Later my uncle—a hydrologist for the U.S. Geological Survey—gave me a tour of the old neighborhood, along with historical highwater contour maps of Louisville, and that sealed the deal. *Won't Be Licked* is fictionalized account of one day during the flood and how a young man battled boredom while trying to keep his socks dry. When I finished the comic and gave it to my Grandpa to read, and he said, "The fellow who wrote this . . . it's almost like he was there!"

100 Distinguished Comics

from August 31, 2005, to September 1, 2006

Selected by Anne Elizabeth Moore

GRAHAM ANNABLE
Fishin' Trip. *Nickelodeon*, September 2005.
SERGIO ARAGONÉS
Heroes. *Solo*, August 2006.
I Killed Marty Feldman. *Solo*, August 2006.
ANDRICE ARP
To Captain Ayres. *Mome*, Winter 2006.
PATRICK ATANGAN
Tree of Love. *Song of Our Ancestors* vol. 3.
BRIAN AZZARELLO and DANIJEL ZEZELJ
A Peace of Iron. *Loveless* no. 6.
PETER BAGGE
Tom Paine in the Ass. *Apocalypse Nerd* no. 2.
LIZ BAILLIE
Untitled (Cosmo's Diner). *My Brain Hurts* no. 3.
KYLE BAKER
The Death of Billy Batson. *Plastic Man* no. 19.
LYNDA BARRY
Mood Ring Cycle. *Chicago Reader*, December 2, 2005.
Titles of Poems We Can Never Turn In. *Chicago Reader*, March 10, 2006.
JOSH BAYER
The Fighter. *Comics Are Rad*, 2006.
GABRIELLE BELL
Mike's Café. *Mome*, Winter 2006.
My Affliction, 2006.
NICK BERTOZZI
Sir Ernest Shackleton in: Patience Camp. *SPX*, 2005.
RUBEN BOLLING
The Educa-Fun Page. *Mad*, November 2005.

MATT BROERSMA
The Mesmerist. *Drawn & Quarterly Showcase* no. 3.
Eldorado. *Insomnia* no. 1.
IVAN BRUNETTI
A Little World Made Cunningly. *Chicago Reader*. October 14, 2005.
JOHN CAMPBELL
Stevie Might Be a Bear Maybe, 2006.
SCOTT CAMPBELL
Pyramid Car!, 2006.
The New Favorite Song. *Hickee* no. 2.
LILLI CARRÉ
Untitled (Almost a Full Moon). *Tales of Woodsman Pete* no. 3.
MARTIN CENDREDA
The Magic Marker. *Mome*, Fall 2005.
BRIAN CHIPPENDALE
Maul the Roots. *SPX*, 2005.
GREG COOK
Frankenstein's Monster Is a Competitive High Diver. *Nickelodeon*, December/January 2006.
It Came from the Deep. *Nickelodeon*, February 2006.
JORDAN CRANE
Below the Shade of Night. *Uptight* no. 1.
ANYA DAVIDSON
Nothing Serious. *Whistle Whistle*, 2006.
Whistle Whistle. *Whistle Whistle*, 2006.
MATT DEMBICKI
The Enduring Rain. *Mr. Big* no. 6.
JO DERY
Introducing—The Lounging Animal. *Plant Life for Human Lesson* vol. 2.

The Organ's Song. *Plant Life for Human Lesson* vol. 2.
The Premonition of the Mirrored Children. *Plant Life for Human Lesson* vol. 3.

GENEVIEVE ELVERUM
We're Wolf. *Drawn & Quarterly Showcase* no. 3.

EAMON ESPEY
A Small Victory for a Peeping Tom. *Wormdye* no. 3.
The Blood Is the Cow. *Wormdye* no. 4.

C. F.
Space Ballz, Part 2. *BJ & da Dogs*, 2005.

MATTHEW FORSYTHE
Voodoo. *Flight* vol. 3.

JOSH FRANKEL
Untitled (Trilobite), 2006.

ROBERT GOODIN
Moon Lake. *Après-Shampooing*, 2006.

GEOFFREY GRAHN
The Man Who Saved the World. *Blab* no. 16.

JUSTIN HALL
Pink Dolphins. *The Book of Boy Trouble*, 2006.

JOHN HANKIEWICZ
Lot C (Sometime Later). *Asthma*, 2006.

ANDY HARTZELL
Date with an Angel. *The Book of Boy Trouble*, 2006.

GILBERT HERNANDEZ
Julio's Day. *Love and Rockets* no. 14.

JAIME HERNANDEZ
La Maggie La Loca. *New York Times Magazine*, April 23–August 3, 2006.
Fine to Very Fine. *Love and Rockets* no. 16.

HELLEN JO
Chapter One. *Blister* no. 1.

R. KIKUO JOHNSON
John James Audubon in Pursuit of the Golden Eagle. *Mome*, Spring/Summer 2006.

MEGAN KELSO
Green River. *Roadstrips*, 2005.
Aide de Camp. *The Squirrel Mother*, 2006.
Meow Face. *The Squirrel Mother*, 2006.

MICHAEL KUPPERMAN
Remembering the Thirties. *Tales Designed to Thrizzle* no. 2.
Hercules vs. Zeus in 3D. *Nickelodeon*, March 2006.

HOPE LARSON
Untitled (Blare). *Gray Horses*, 2006.

DAVID LASKY
Diary of a Bread Delivery Guy, January 19, 2005. *Arthur*, January 2006.

MELANIE LEWIS
Salt & Sugar. *P.S. Comics* no. 2.

ALEC LONGSTRETH
Untitled (Basewood Chapter Two). *Phase 7* no. 6.

JASON LUTES
Untitled (Streseman Is Dead). *Berlin* no. 12.

LINDA MEDLEY
Solicitine Part 7. *Castle Waiting*, 2006.
Chapter 1. *Castle Waiting* vol. 2, no. 1.

JASON MILES
Trauma Valley. *Arthur*, January 2006.

ANDERS NILSEN
If You Meet the Buddha on the Road. *Monologues for the Coming Plague*, 2006.
Untitled (I Think I Know What Happened). *Big Questions* no. 8.

DANICA NOVGORODOFF
The Crossing, 2006.

CHRIS OLIVEROS
The Envelope Manufacturer, 2006.

ERIC ORNER
Morning Martyrs. *Stumbling and Raging: More Politically Inspired Fiction*, 2005.

JOHN PORCELLINO
Scott County Memories. *King-Cat Comics and Stories* no. 65.

RON REGÉ JR.
Finding Privacy in the Hypnotist's Ballroom. *Awake Field*, 2006.

JESSE REKLAW
Untitled (My Father). *SPX* 2005.
Our Fred Robinson Story. *Couch Tag* no. 3.

MARC ROSENTHAL
Flotsam and Jetsam. *Blab* no. 16.

FAY RYU
Heart & Brain. *Love Charades* no. 1.

JOE SACCO
Portrait of the Artist as an Aging Lightnin'
Hopkins Enthusiast. *But I Like It*, 2006.

STAN SAKAI
Chanoyu. *Usagi Yojimbo* no. 93.

SOUTHER SALAZAR
Fervler and Razzle. *Kramer's Ergot*, 2006.

ZAK SALLY
Feed the Wife. *Recidivist*, 2005.
Untitled. *Recidivist*, 2005.

SETH
Fine and Dandy: A Short Talk by Wimbledon
Green. *Wimbledon Green*, 2005.
Untitled (July 7, 1966). *Palookaville* no. 18.

ERIC SHANOWER
Betrayal 2. *The Age of Bronze* no. 21.

DASH SHAW
The Haunted Hotel. *Blurred Vision* no 2.

KATIE SKELLY and MATTHEW HAWKINS
Vanilla Gorilla. *Unlucky: True Tales from
Matthew E. Hawkins*, 2005.

ZACK SOTO
The Smog Emperor. *The Secret Voice*
no. 1.

JOSHUA RAY STEPHENS
The Great White Whale. *Compl(I)ementary
Monsters Presents: Tales of Thursday City*,
2006.

CAROL SWAIN
Family Circus. *Hotwire Comix and Capers*,
2006.

JAMIE TANNER
Mine, 2006.

BECCA TAYLOR
Cherchez la Femme. *Papercutter* no. 2.

GIA-BAO TRAN
Contents. *Kaleidoscope* no 2.

C. TYLER
The Outrage (Part I). *Late Bloomer*, 2006.

SARA VARON
Untitled (Boxing). *SPX*, 2005.

BRIAN K. VAUGHAN, GORAN SUDZUKA,
and JOSE MARZAN, JR.
Buttons. *Y the Last Man* no. 41.

ESTHER PEARL WATSON
Part-aye! *Unlovable* no. 4.

LAUREN WEINSTEIN
The Call. *Hotwire Comix and Capers*, 2006.
Women's Lib. *Girl Stories*, 2006.

MACK WHITE
1963. *Roadstrips*, 2005.

BRIAN WOOD and RYAN KELLY
The Last Lonely Day at the Oxford Theatre.
Local no. 5.

DAN ZETTWOCH
CrossFader. *Kramer's Ergot*, 2006.

WIMBLEDON GREEN

GALLERY

I LIKE TO WALK THE CITY STREETS AT NIGHT.
IT BRINGS ME A CLARITY OF THOUGHT I RARELY ACHIEVE DURING THE DAY.
A KIND OF REVERIE OVERTAKES ME...
FREEING MY MIND TO PONDER WHERE MY LIFE IS GOING... AND WHERE IT HAS BEEN.

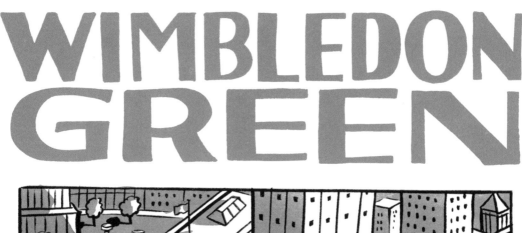

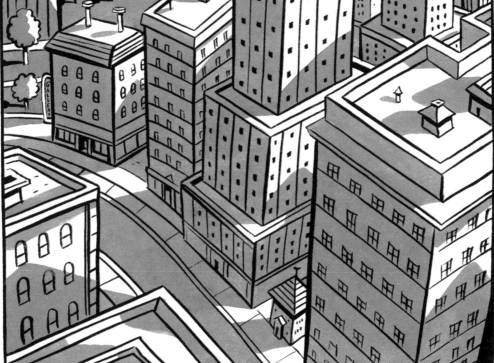

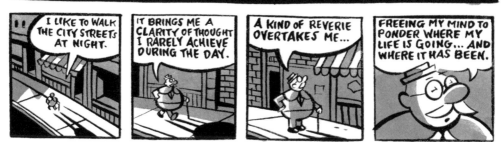

SETH

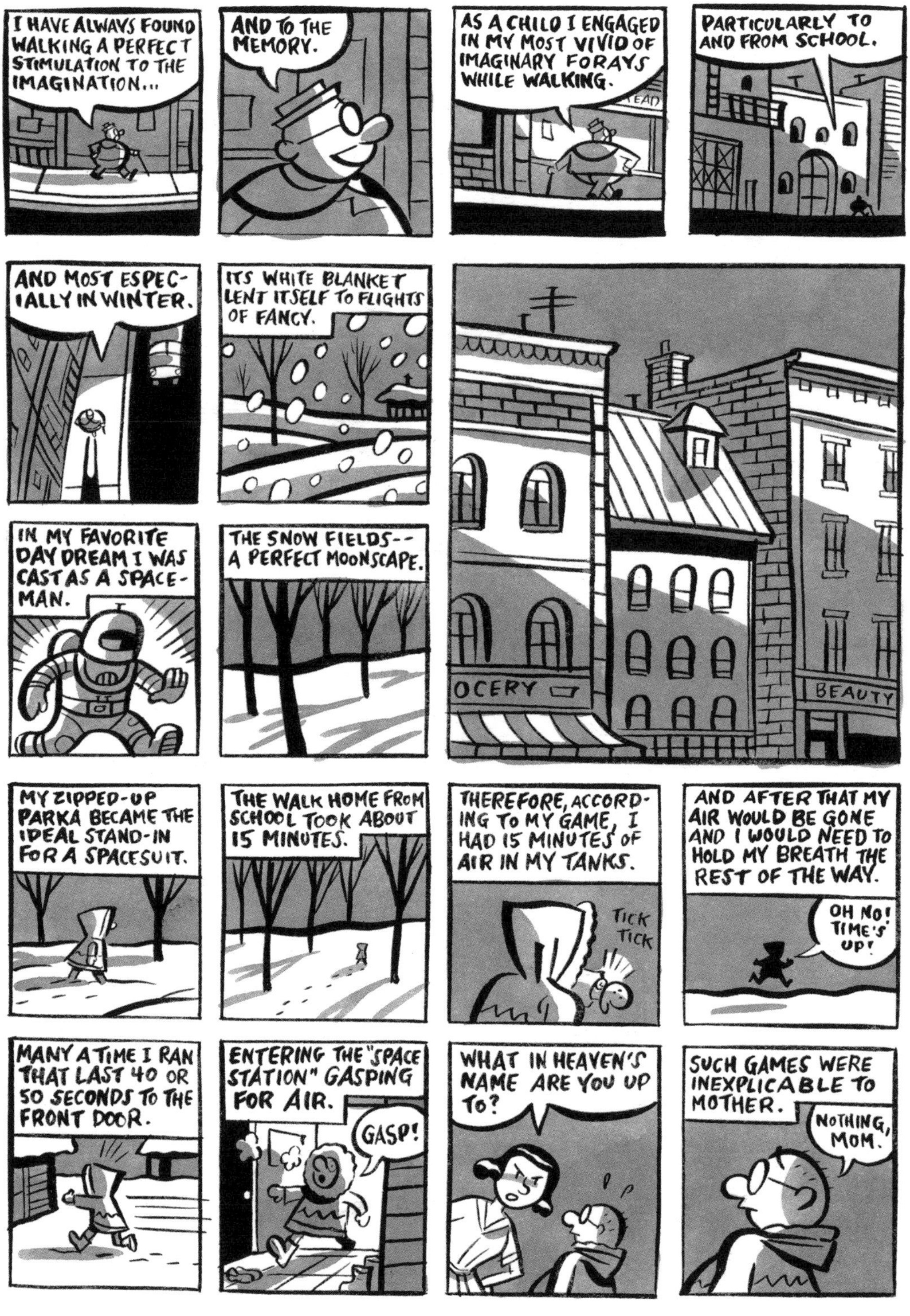
I HAVE ALWAYS FOUND WALKING A PERFECT STIMULATION TO THE IMAGINATION...
AND TO THE MEMORY.
AS A CHILD I ENGAGED IN MY MOST VIVID OF IMAGINARY FORAYS WHILE WALKING.
PARTICULARLY TO AND FROM SCHOOL.
AND MOST ESPECIALLY IN WINTER.
ITS WHITE BLANKET LENT ITSELF TO FLIGHTS OF FANCY.
OCERY
BEAUTY
IN MY FAVORITE DAY DREAM I WAS CAST AS A SPACEMAN.
THE SNOW FIELDS-- A PERFECT MOONSCAPE.
MY ZIPPED-UP PARKA BECAME THE IDEAL STAND-IN FOR A SPACESUIT.
THE WALK HOME FROM SCHOOL TOOK ABOUT 15 MINUTES.
THEREFORE, ACCORDING TO MY GAME, I HAD 15 MINUTES OF AIR IN MY TANKS.
TICK TICK
AND AFTER THAT MY AIR WOULD BE GONE AND I WOULD NEED TO HOLD MY BREATH THE REST OF THE WAY.
OH NO! TIME'S UP!
MANY A TIME I RAN THAT LAST 40 OR 50 SECONDS TO THE FRONT DOOR.
ENTERING THE "SPACE STATION" GASPING FOR AIR.
GASP!
WHAT IN HEAVEN'S NAME ARE YOU UP TO?
SUCH GAMES WERE INEXPLICABLE TO MOTHER.
NOTHING, MOM.

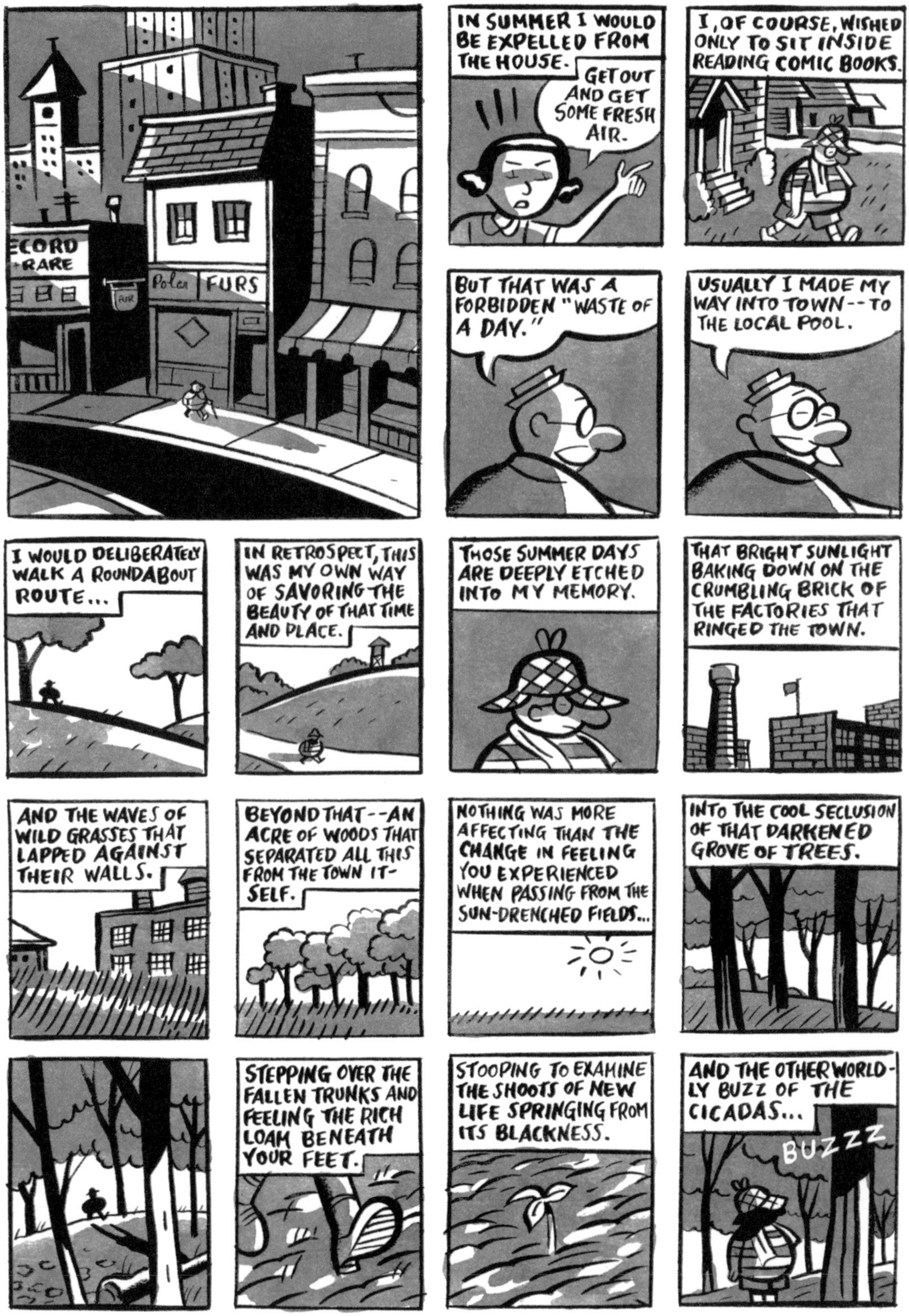
ECORD
+RARE
FURS
IN SUMMER I WOULD BE EXPELLED FROM THE HOUSE.
GET OUT AND GET SOME FRESH AIR.
I, OF COURSE, WISHED ONLY TO SIT INSIDE READING COMIC BOOKS.
BUT THAT WAS A FORBIDDEN "WASTE OF A DAY."
USUALLY I MADE MY WAY INTO TOWN--TO THE LOCAL POOL.
I WOULD DELIBERATELY WALK A ROUNDABOUT ROUTE...
IN RETROSPECT, THIS WAS MY OWN WAY OF SAVORING THE BEAUTY OF THAT TIME AND PLACE.
THOSE SUMMER DAYS ARE DEEPLY ETCHED INTO MY MEMORY.
THAT BRIGHT SUNLIGHT BAKING DOWN ON THE CRUMBLING BRICK OF THE FACTORIES THAT RINGED THE TOWN.
AND THE WAVES OF WILD GRASSES THAT LAPPED AGAINST THEIR WALLS.
BEYOND THAT--AN ACRE OF WOODS THAT SEPARATED ALL THIS FROM THE TOWN IT-SELF.
NOTHING WAS MORE AFFECTING THAN THE CHANGE IN FEELING YOU EXPERIENCED WHEN PASSING FROM THE SUN-DRENCHED FIELDS...
INTO THE COOL SECLUSION OF THAT DARKENED GROVE OF TREES.
STEPPING OVER THE FALLEN TRUNKS AND FEELING THE RICH LOAM BENEATH YOUR FEET.
STOOPING TO EXAMINE THE SHOOTS OF NEW LIFE SPRINGING FROM ITS BLACKNESS.
AND THE OTHERWORLD-LY BUZZ OF THE CICADAS...
BUZZZ

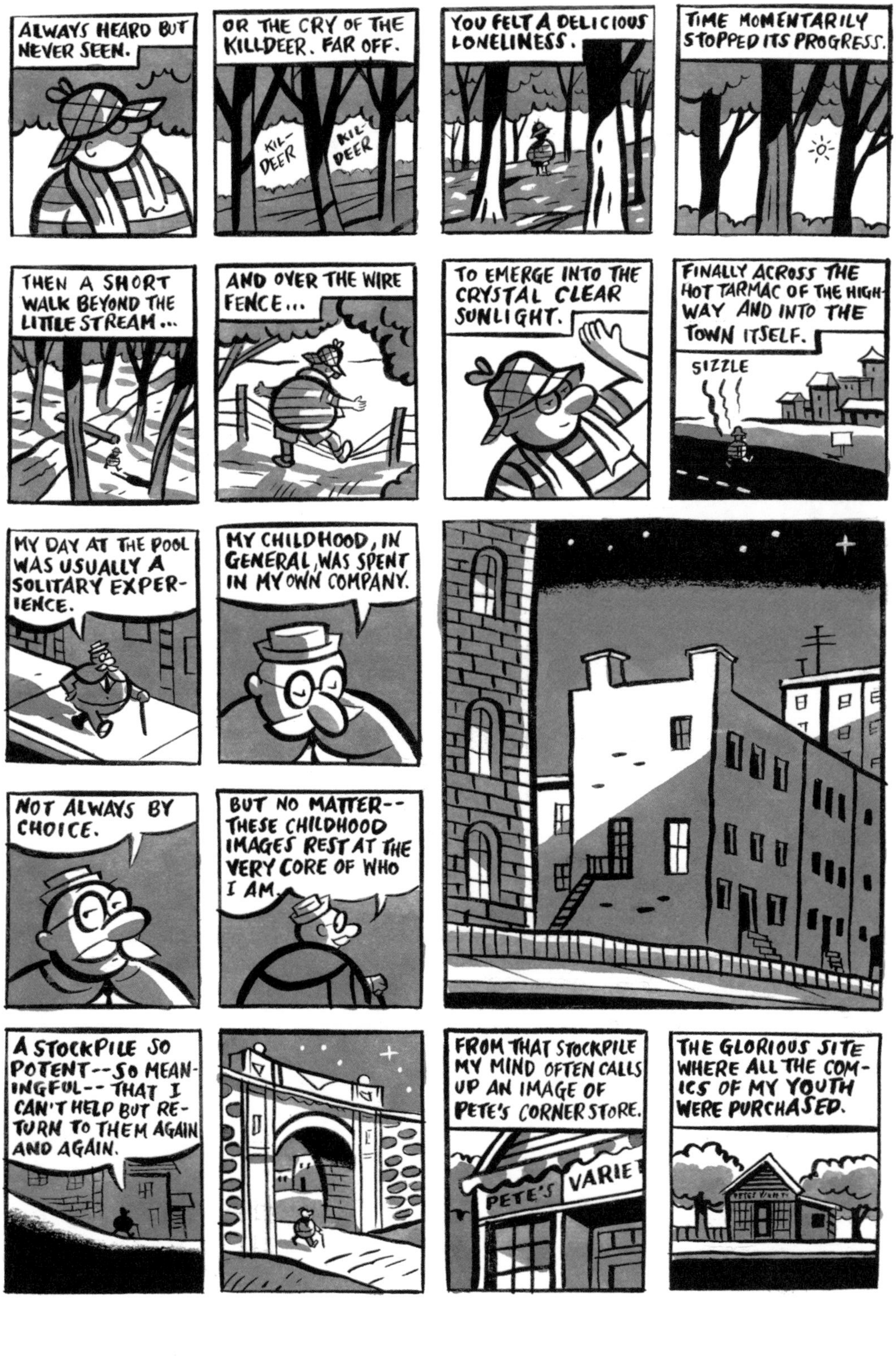
ALWAYS HEARD BUT NEVER SEEN.
OR THE CRY OF THE KILLDEER. FAR OFF.
KIL-DEER
KIL-DEER
YOU FELT A DELICIOUS LONELINESS.
TIME MOMENTARILY STOPPED ITS PROGRESS.
THEN A SHORT WALK BEYOND THE LITTLE STREAM...
AND OVER THE WIRE FENCE...
TO EMERGE INTO THE CRYSTAL CLEAR SUNLIGHT.
FINALLY ACROSS THE HOT TARMAC OF THE HIGH-WAY AND INTO THE TOWN ITSELF.
SIZZLE
MY DAY AT THE POOL WAS USUALLY A SOLITARY EXPER-IENCE.
MY CHILDHOOD, IN GENERAL, WAS SPENT IN MY OWN COMPANY.
NOT ALWAYS BY CHOICE.
BUT NO MATTER-- THESE CHILDHOOD IMAGES REST AT THE VERY CORE OF WHO I AM.
A STOCKPILE SO POTENT--SO MEAN-INGFUL-- THAT I CAN'T HELP BUT RE-TURN TO THEM AGAIN AND AGAIN.
FROM THAT STOCKPILE MY MIND OFTEN CALLS UP AN IMAGE OF PETE'S CORNER STORE.
PETE'S
VARIE
THE GLORIOUS SITE WHERE ALL THE COM-ICS OF MY YOUTH WERE PURCHASED.

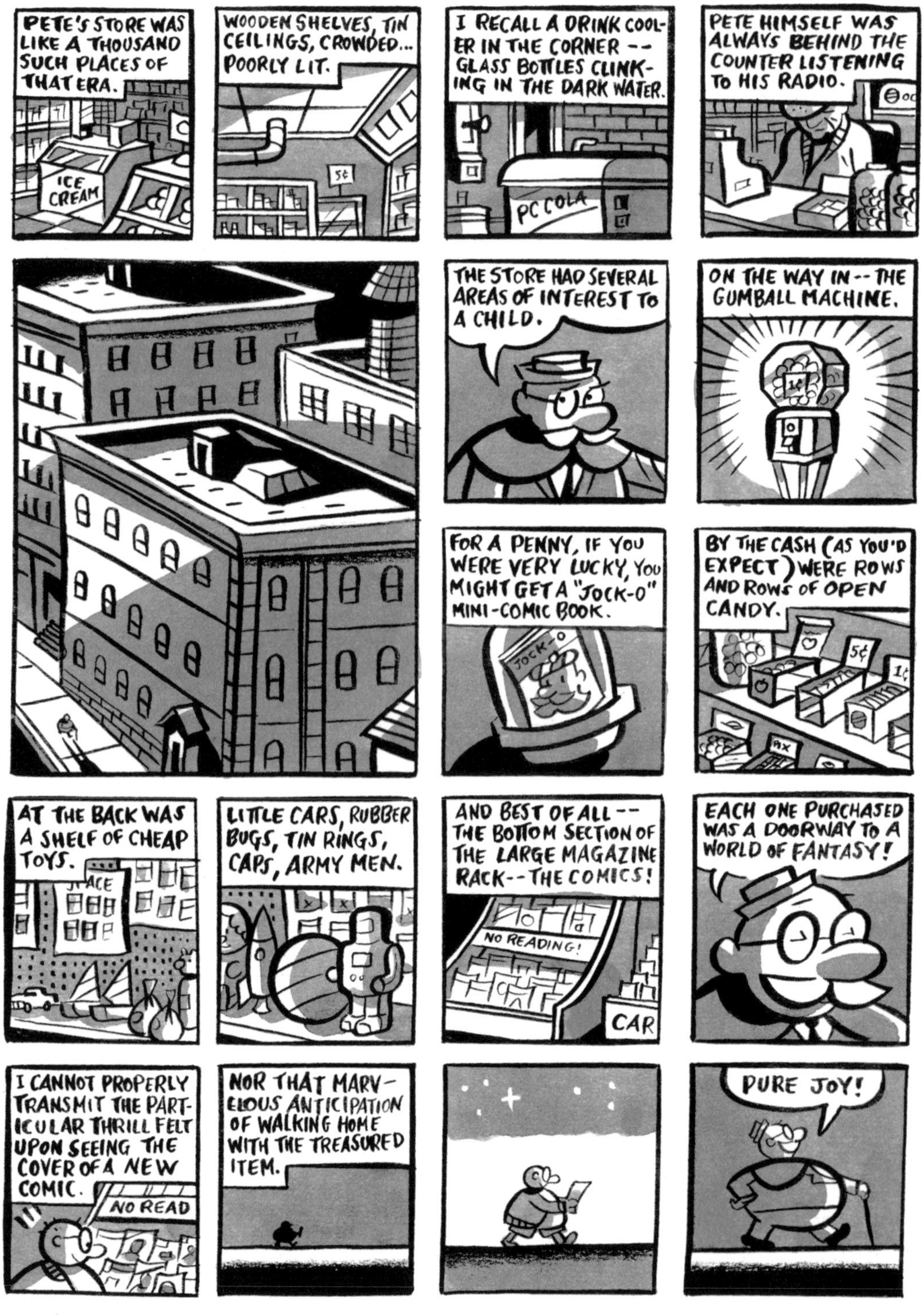
PETE'S STORE WAS LIKE A THOUSAND SUCH PLACES OF THAT ERA.
ICE CREAM
WOODEN SHELVES, TIN CEILINGS, CROWDED... POORLY LIT.
5¢
I RECALL A DRINK COOLER IN THE CORNER -- GLASS BOTTLES CLINKING IN THE DARK WATER.
PC COLA
PETE HIMSELF WAS ALWAYS BEHIND THE COUNTER LISTENING TO HIS RADIO.
THE STORE HAD SEVERAL AREAS OF INTEREST TO A CHILD.
ON THE WAY IN -- THE GUMBALL MACHINE.
1¢
FOR A PENNY, IF YOU WERE VERY LUCKY, YOU MIGHT GET A "JOCK-O" MINI-COMIC BOOK.
JOCK-O
BY THE CASH (AS YOU'D EXPECT) WERE ROWS AND ROWS OF OPEN CANDY.
5¢
1¢
AT THE BACK WAS A SHELF OF CHEAP TOYS.
ACE
LITTLE CARS, RUBBER BUGS, TIN RINGS, CAPS, ARMY MEN.
AND BEST OF ALL -- THE BOTTOM SECTION OF THE LARGE MAGAZINE RACK -- THE COMICS!
NO READING!
CAR
EACH ONE PURCHASED WAS A DOORWAY TO A WORLD OF FANTASY!
I CANNOT PROPERLY TRANSMIT THE PARTICULAR THRILL FELT UPON SEEING THE COVER OF A NEW COMIC.
NO READ
NOR THAT MARVELOUS ANTICIPATION OF WALKING HOME WITH THE TREASURED ITEM.
PURE JOY!

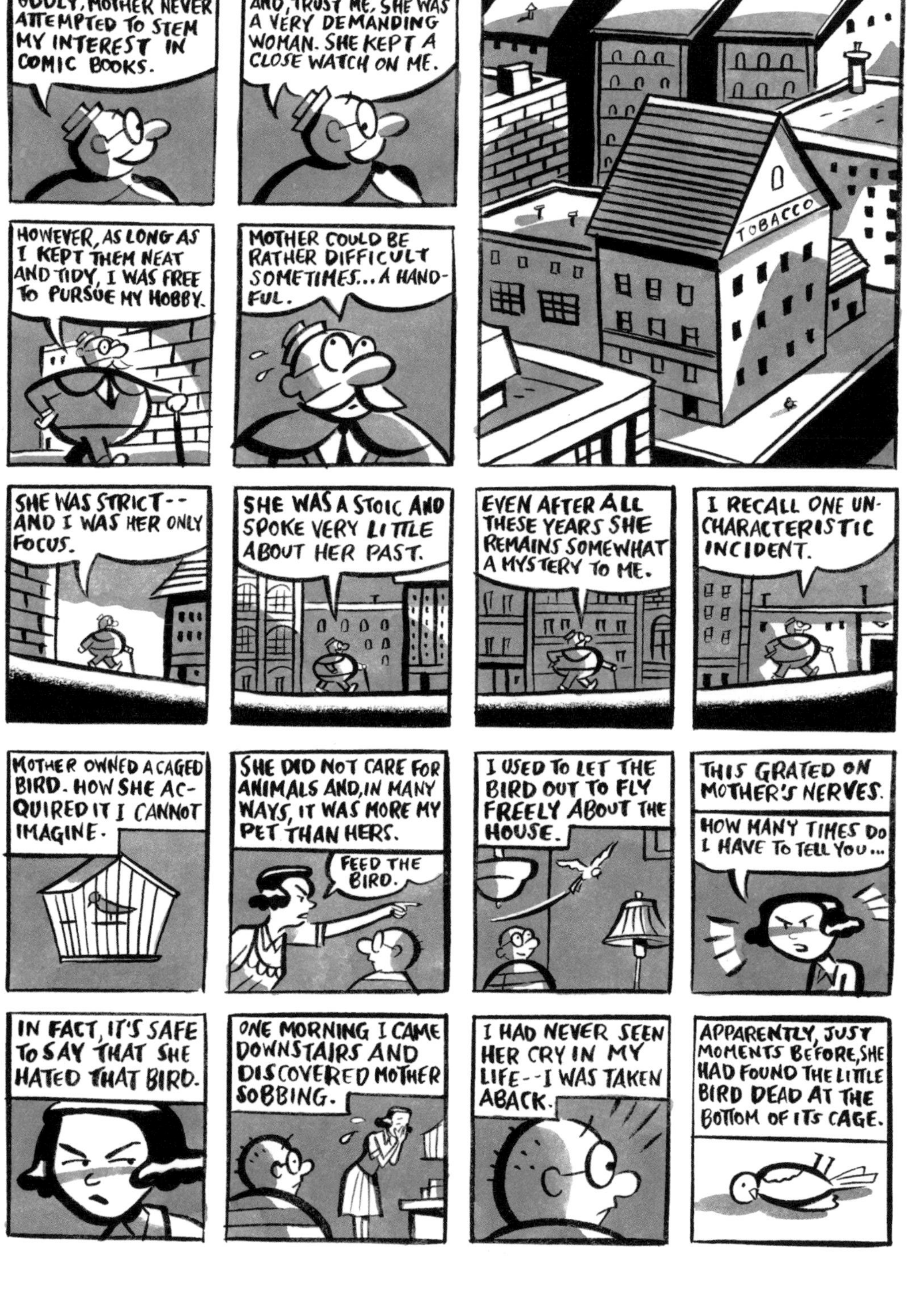
ODDLY, MOTHER NEVER ATTEMPTED TO STEM MY INTEREST IN COMIC BOOKS.
AND, TRUST ME, SHE WAS A VERY DEMANDING WOMAN. SHE KEPT A CLOSE WATCH ON ME.
TOBACCO
HOWEVER, AS LONG AS I KEPT THEM NEAT AND TIDY, I WAS FREE TO PURSUE MY HOBBY.
MOTHER COULD BE RATHER DIFFICULT SOMETIMES... A HANDFUL.
SHE WAS STRICT--AND I WAS HER ONLY FOCUS.
SHE WAS A STOIC AND SPOKE VERY LITTLE ABOUT HER PAST.
EVEN AFTER ALL THESE YEARS SHE REMAINS SOMEWHAT A MYSTERY TO ME.
I RECALL ONE UNCHARACTERISTIC INCIDENT.
MOTHER OWNED A CAGED BIRD. HOW SHE ACQUIRED IT I CANNOT IMAGINE.
SHE DID NOT CARE FOR ANIMALS AND, IN MANY WAYS, IT WAS MORE MY PET THAN HERS.
FEED THE BIRD.
I USED TO LET THE BIRD OUT TO FLY FREELY ABOUT THE HOUSE.
THIS GRATED ON MOTHER'S NERVES.
HOW MANY TIMES DO I HAVE TO TELL YOU...
IN FACT, IT'S SAFE TO SAY THAT SHE HATED THAT BIRD.
ONE MORNING I CAME DOWNSTAIRS AND DISCOVERED MOTHER SOBBING.
I HAD NEVER SEEN HER CRY IN MY LIFE--I WAS TAKEN ABACK.
APPARENTLY, JUST MOMENTS BEFORE, SHE HAD FOUND THE LITTLE BIRD DEAD AT THE BOTTOM OF ITS CAGE.

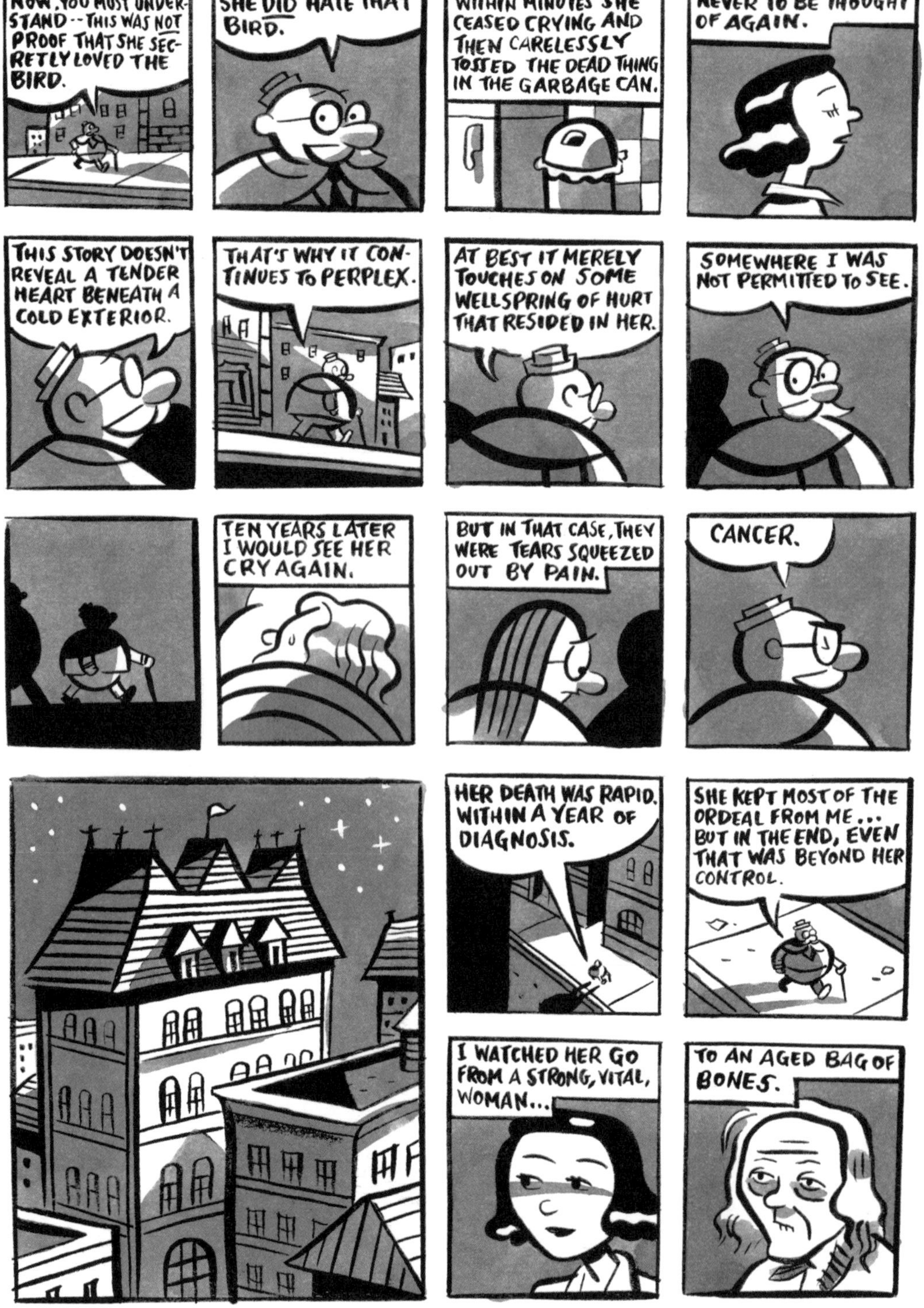
NOW, YOU MUST UNDERSTAND -- THIS WAS NOT PROOF THAT SHE SECRETLY LOVED THE BIRD.
SHE DID HATE THAT BIRD.
WITHIN MINUTES SHE CEASED CRYING AND THEN CARELESSLY TOSSED THE DEAD THING IN THE GARBAGE CAN.
NEVER TO BE THOUGHT OF AGAIN.
THIS STORY DOESN'T REVEAL A TENDER HEART BENEATH A COLD EXTERIOR.
THAT'S WHY IT CONTINUES TO PERPLEX.
AT BEST IT MERELY TOUCHES ON SOME WELLSPRING OF HURT THAT RESIDED IN HER.
SOMEWHERE I WAS NOT PERMITTED TO SEE.
TEN YEARS LATER I WOULD SEE HER CRY AGAIN.
BUT IN THAT CASE, THEY WERE TEARS SQUEEZED OUT BY PAIN.
CANCER.
HER DEATH WAS RAPID. WITHIN A YEAR OF DIAGNOSIS.
SHE KEPT MOST OF THE ORDEAL FROM ME... BUT IN THE END, EVEN THAT WAS BEYOND HER CONTROL.
I WATCHED HER GO FROM A STRONG, VITAL, WOMAN...
TO AN AGED BAG OF BONES.

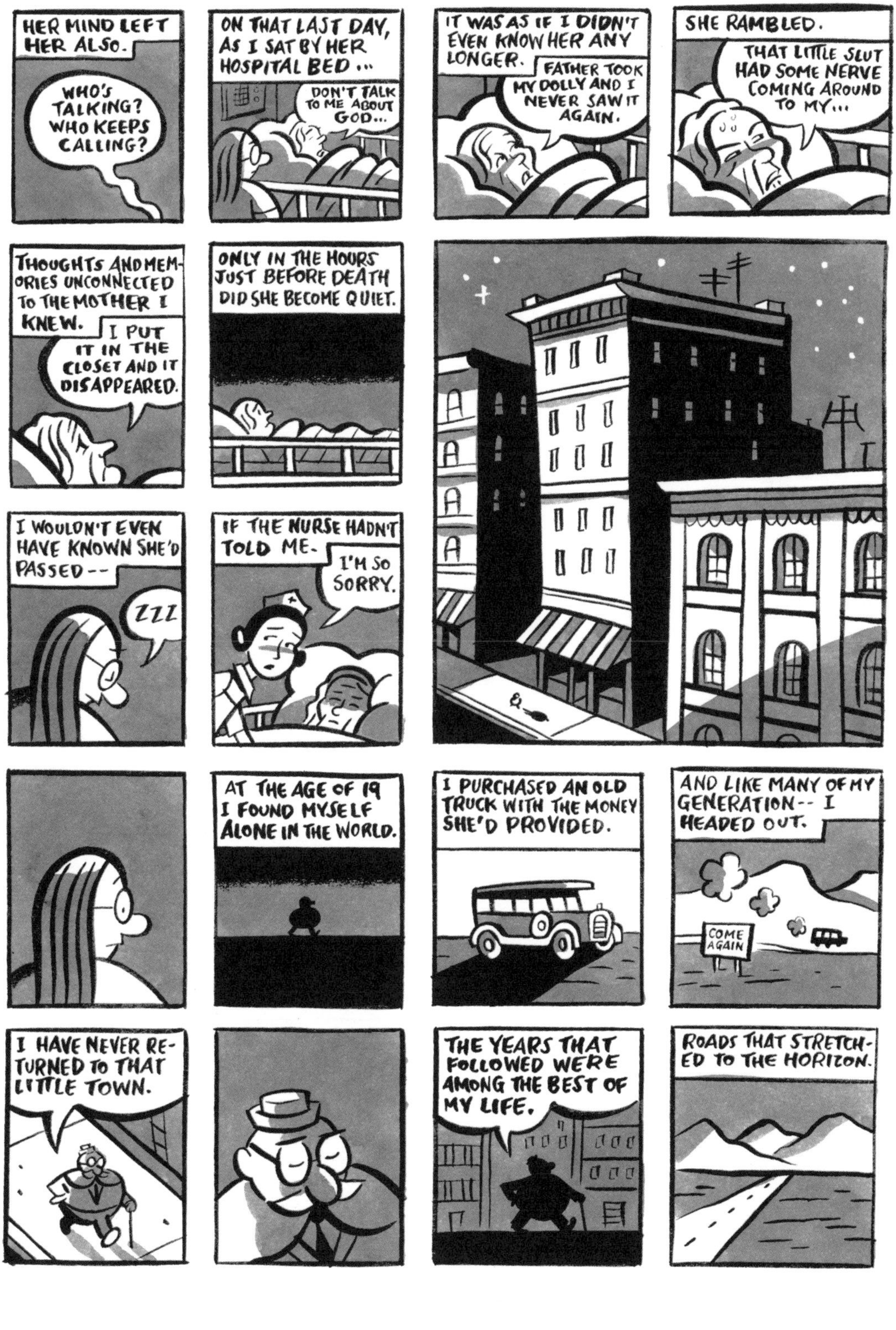
HER MIND LEFT HER ALSO.
WHO'S TALKING? WHO KEEPS CALLING?
ON THAT LAST DAY, AS I SAT BY HER HOSPITAL BED...
DON'T TALK TO ME ABOUT GOD...
IT WAS AS IF I DIDN'T EVEN KNOW HER ANY LONGER.
FATHER TOOK MY DOLLY AND I NEVER SAW IT AGAIN.
SHE RAMBLED.
THAT LITTLE SLUT HAD SOME NERVE COMING AROUND TO MY...
THOUGHTS AND MEMORIES UNCONNECTED TO THE MOTHER I KNEW.
I PUT IT IN THE CLOSET AND IT DISAPPEARED.
ONLY IN THE HOURS JUST BEFORE DEATH DID SHE BECOME QUIET.
I WOULDN'T EVEN HAVE KNOWN SHE'D PASSED--
ZZZ
IF THE NURSE HADN'T TOLD ME.
I'M SO SORRY.
AT THE AGE OF 19 I FOUND MYSELF ALONE IN THE WORLD.
I PURCHASED AN OLD TRUCK WITH THE MONEY SHE'D PROVIDED.
AND LIKE MANY OF MY GENERATION-- I HEADED OUT.
COME AGAIN
I HAVE NEVER RETURNED TO THAT LITTLE TOWN.
THE YEARS THAT FOLLOWED WERE AMONG THE BEST OF MY LIFE.
ROADS THAT STRETCHED TO THE HORIZON.

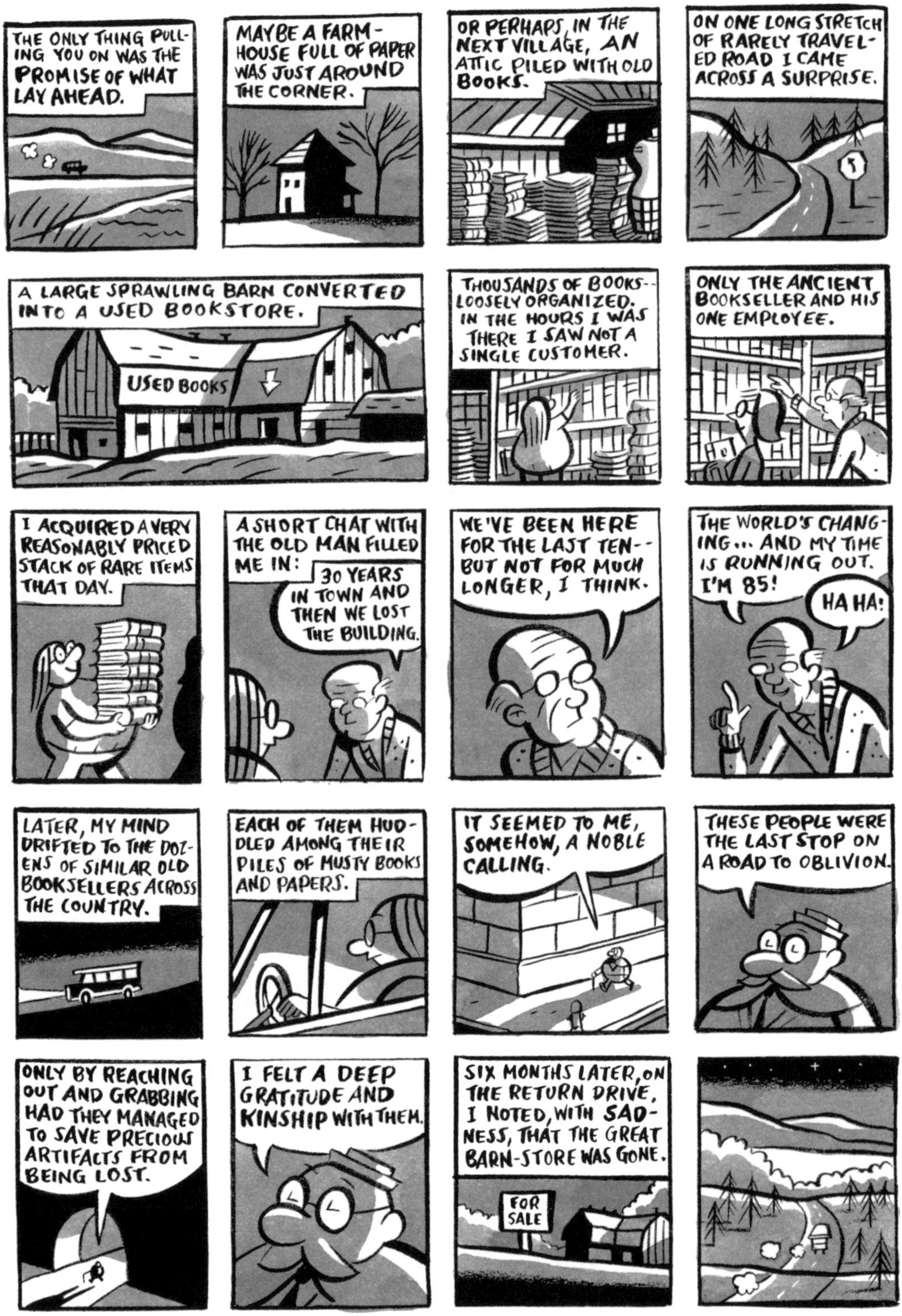
THE ONLY THING PULLING YOU ON WAS THE PROMISE OF WHAT LAY AHEAD.
MAYBE A FARMHOUSE FULL OF PAPER WAS JUST AROUND THE CORNER.
OR PERHAPS, IN THE NEXT VILLAGE, AN ATTIC PILED WITH OLD BOOKS.
ON ONE LONG STRETCH OF RARELY TRAVELED ROAD I CAME ACROSS A SURPRISE.
A LARGE SPRAWLING BARN CONVERTED INTO A USED BOOKSTORE.
USED BOOKS
THOUSANDS OF BOOKS-- LOOSELY ORGANIZED. IN THE HOURS I WAS THERE I SAW NOT A SINGLE CUSTOMER.
ONLY THE ANCIENT BOOKSELLER AND HIS ONE EMPLOYEE.
I ACQUIRED A VERY REASONABLY PRICED STACK OF RARE ITEMS THAT DAY.
A SHORT CHAT WITH THE OLD MAN FILLED ME IN:
30 YEARS IN TOWN AND THEN WE LOST THE BUILDING.
WE'VE BEEN HERE FOR THE LAST TEN-- BUT NOT FOR MUCH LONGER, I THINK.
THE WORLD'S CHANGING... AND MY TIME IS RUNNING OUT. I'M 85!
HA HA!
LATER, MY MIND DRIFTED TO THE DOZENS OF SIMILAR OLD BOOKSELLERS ACROSS THE COUNTRY.
EACH OF THEM HUDDLED AMONG THEIR PILES OF MUSTY BOOKS AND PAPERS.
IT SEEMED TO ME, SOMEHOW, A NOBLE CALLING.
THESE PEOPLE WERE THE LAST STOP ON A ROAD TO OBLIVION.
ONLY BY REACHING OUT AND GRABBING HAD THEY MANAGED TO SAVE PRECIOUS ARTIFACTS FROM BEING LOST.
I FELT A DEEP GRATITUDE AND KINSHIP WITH THEM.
SIX MONTHS LATER, ON THE RETURN DRIVE, I NOTED, WITH SADNESS, THAT THE GREAT BARN-STORE WAS GONE.
FOR SALE

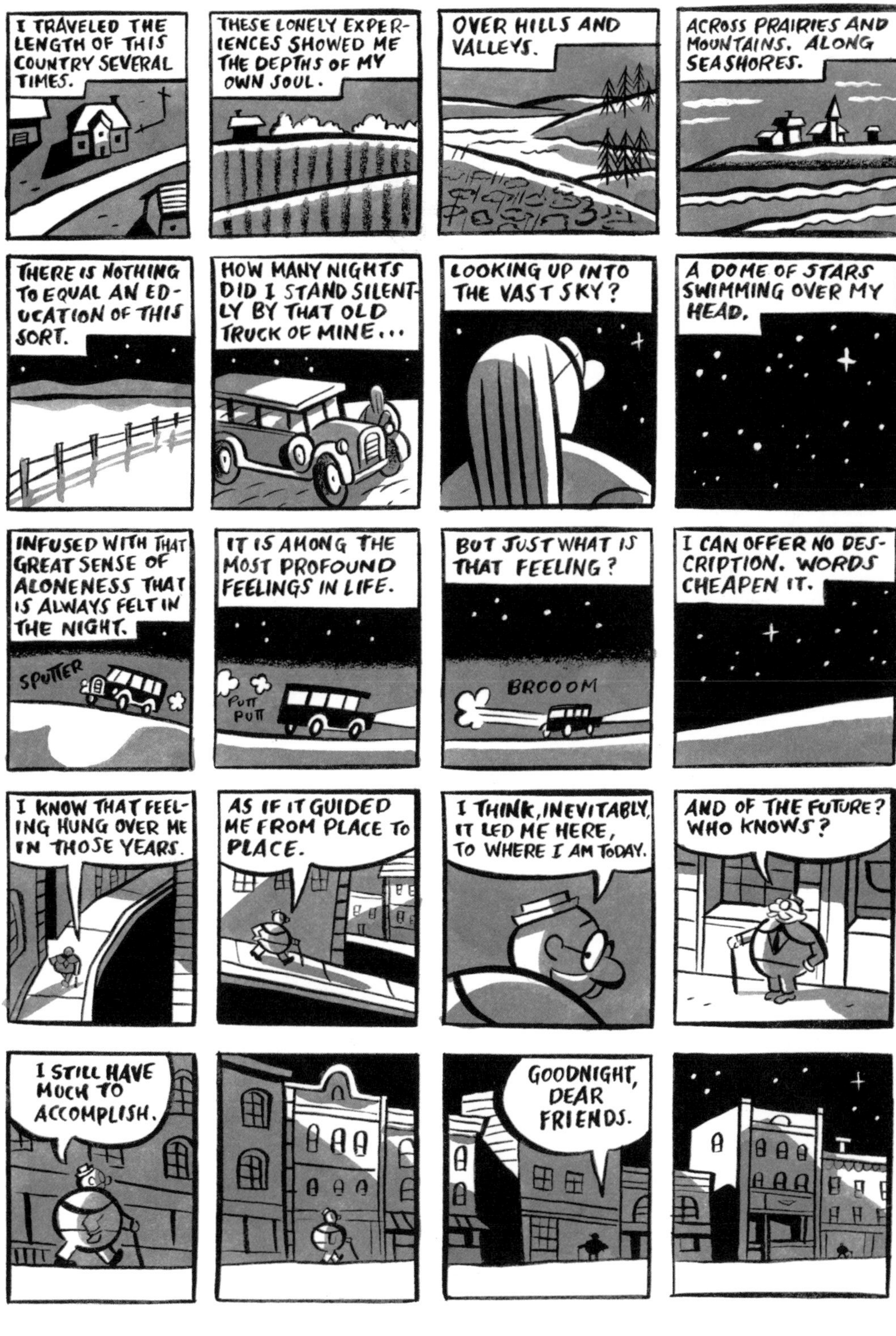
I TRAVELED THE LENGTH OF THIS COUNTRY SEVERAL TIMES.
THESE LONELY EXPERIENCES SHOWED ME THE DEPTHS OF MY OWN SOUL.
OVER HILLS AND VALLEYS.
ACROSS PRAIRIES AND MOUNTAINS. ALONG SEASHORES.
THERE IS NOTHING TO EQUAL AN EDUCATION OF THIS SORT.
HOW MANY NIGHTS DID I STAND SILENTLY BY THAT OLD TRUCK OF MINE...
LOOKING UP INTO THE VAST SKY?
A DOME OF STARS SWIMMING OVER MY HEAD.
INFUSED WITH THAT GREAT SENSE OF ALONENESS THAT IS ALWAYS FELT IN THE NIGHT.
SPUTTER
IT IS AMONG THE MOST PROFOUND FEELINGS IN LIFE.
PUTT PUTT
BUT JUST WHAT IS THAT FEELING?
BROOOM
I CAN OFFER NO DESCRIPTION. WORDS CHEAPEN IT.
I KNOW THAT FEELING HUNG OVER ME IN THOSE YEARS.
AS IF IT GUIDED ME FROM PLACE TO PLACE.
I THINK, INEVITABLY, IT LED ME HERE, TO WHERE I AM TODAY.
AND OF THE FUTURE? WHO KNOWS?
I STILL HAVE MUCH TO ACCOMPLISH.
GOODNIGHT, DEAR FRIENDS.

CREDITS

Excerpt from *Ernie Pook's Comeek* by Lynda Barry. First published in *Ernie Pook*. Copyright © 2006 by Lynda Barry. Reprinted by permission of the author. "The Canary-Colored Caravan of Death" by Alison Bechdel. First published in *Fun Home*, 2006. Copyright © 2006 by Alison Bechdel. Reprinted by permission of Houghton Mifflin Company. "California Journal" by Gabrielle Bell. First published in *Mome*, Fall 2006. Copyright © 2006 by Gabrielle Bell. Reprinted by permission of the author. "Needles and Pins" by Jonathan Bennett. First published in *Mome*, Fall 2005. Copyright © 2006 by Jonathan Bennett. Reprinted by permission of the author. "These Things, These Things" by Jeffrey Brown. First published in *Little Things*, 2006. Copyright © 2006 by Jeffrey Brown. Reprinted by permission of Simon & Schuster. "11:11" lyrics © 2001 Wegawam Music Co. Used by permission. "Lull" lyrics © 2003 Wegawam Music Co. Used by permission. "Sovay" lyrics © 2003 Wegawam Music Co. Used by permission. "The Naming of Things" lyrics © 2005 Wegawam Music Co. Used by permission. "Headsoak" lyrics © 2001 Wegawam Music Co. Used by permission. Special thanks to the New Pornographers for permission to reprint "From Blown Speakers" lyrics. "The Horror of Simply Being Alive," "Six Things I Like About My Girlfriend," and "My Bumbling Corpulent Mass" by Ivan Brunetti. First published in *Schizo* 4, 2006. Copyright © 2006 by Ivan Brunetti. Reprinted by permission of the author. Excerpt from *Black Hole* by Charles Burns. First published in *Black Hole*, 2005. Copyright © 2006 by Charles Burns. Reprinted by permission of the author. "Winta Wundaland" by R. and Aline Crumb. First published in *The New Yorker*, February 13 and 20, 2006. Copyright © 2006 by R. and Aline Crumb. Reprinted by permission of the authors. "Hey, Soph, Whazzup?" by Sophie Crumb. First published in *Mome*, Summer 2006. Copyright © 2006 by Sophie Crumb. Reprinted by permission of the author. "Untitled Diary Strips" by Vanessa Davis. First published in *Kramer's Ergot* #6, 2006. Copyright © 2006 by Vanessa Davis. Reprinted by permission of the author. "No Midgets in Midgetville" by Kim Deitch. First published in *The Stuff of Dreams* #3, August 1, 2005. Copyright © 2006 by Kim Deitch. Reprinted by permission of the author. "Blond Atchen and the Bumble Boys" by C. F. First published in *The Ganzfeld*, 2005. Copyright © 2006 by Christopher Forgues. Reprinted by permission of the author. "Lubavitch, Ukraine, 1876" by Sammy Harkham. First published in *Kramer's Ergot*, 2006. Copyright © 2006 by Samuel Harkham. Reprinted by permission of the author. "Cut Thru," "Sambo," "Laundry Room," and "Walnut Creek" by David Heatley. First published in *Mome*, Spring/Summer 2006. Copyright © 2006 by David Heatley. Reprinted by permission of the author. "Meet the Dropouts" by Tim Hensley. First published in *Mome*, Fall 2006. Copyright © 2006 by Tim Hensley. Reprinted by permission of the author. "Fritz After Dark" by Gilbert Hernandez. First published in *Luba's Comics and Stories* #7, January 1, 2006. Copyright © 2006 by Gilbert Hernandez. Reprinted by permission of the author. "Glenn in Bed" by Kevin Huizenga. First published in *Ganges*, October 1, 2006. Copyright © 2006 by Kevin Huizenga. Reprinted by permission of the author. "Shoehorn Technique" by Ben Katchor. First published in the *Chicago Reader*, March 3–May 19, 2006. Copyright © 2006 by Ben Katchor. Reprinted by permission of the author. "Untitled (The List)" by Miriam Katin. First published in *We Are on Our Own*, May 1, 2006. Copyright © 2006 by Miriam Katin. Reprinted by permission of the author. "Dad Watches" by Jerry Moriarty. First published in *Kramer's Ergot*, 2006. Copyright © 2006 by Jerry Moriarty. Reprinted by permission of the author. "Dinner and a Walk" by Anders Nilsen. First published in *Big Questions #7: Dinner and a Nap*, Fall 2005. Copyright © 2006 by Anders Nilsen. Reprinted by permission of the author. "Untitled (Discrete Operations Vehicle—Burning Gall)" by Gary Panter. First published in *Jimbo's Inferno*, March 1, 2006. Copyright © 2006 by Gary Panter. Reprinted by permission of the author. "Country Roads—Brighton" by John Porcellino. First published in *King-Cat Comics and Stories*, October 1, 2005. Copyright © 2006 by John Porcellino. Reprinted by permission of the author. "Kramer's Ergot" by Paper Rad. First published in *Kramer's Ergot*, 2006. Copyright © 2006 by Benjamin Q. Jones. Reprinted by permission of the author. "FUC 1997: We Share a Happy Secret, But Beware, Because the Modern World Emerges" by Ron Regé Jr. First published in *Kramer's Ergot*, 2006. Copyright © 2006 by Ron Regé Jr. Reprinted by permission of the author. "Wimbledon Green" by Seth. First published in *Wimbledon Green*, October 2005. Copyright © 2006 by Gregory (Seth) Gallant. Reprinted by permission of the author. "Portrait of the Artist as a Young %@#*!" "Discovering America" through "A Father's Guiding Hand." First published in *Virginia Quarterly Review* and *The New Yorker*. Copyright © 2006 by Art Spiegelman. Reprinted by permission of The Wylie Agency, Inc. "Shortcomings" (excerpt) by Adrian Tomine. First published in *Optic Nerve* #10, October 2005. Copyright © 2006 by Adrian Tomine. Reprinted by permission of *Drawn & Quarterly*. "Just a Bad Seed" and "Once, We Ran" by C. Tyler. First published in *Late Bloomer*, 2006. Copyright © 2006 by C. Tyler. Reprinted by permission of the author. "Skate Date," "Waiting," and "John and I Go to the Movies" from *Girl Stories* by Lauren Weinstein. Copyright © 2006 by Lauren R. Weinstein. "Won't Be Licked! The Great '37 Flood in Louisville" by Dan Zettwoch. First published in *Drawn & Quarterly Showcase* #4, 2006. Copyright © 2006 by Dan Zettwoch. Reprinted by permission of the author.

THE BEST AMERICAN SHORT STORIES® 2007.

Stephen King, guest editor, Heidi Pitlor, series editor. This year's most beloved short fiction anthology is edited by Stephen King, author of sixty books, including *Misery, The Green Mile, Cell,* and *Lisey's Story,* as well as about four hundred short stories, including "The Man in the Black Suit," which won the O. Henry Prize in 1996. The collection features stories by Richard Russo, Alice Munro, William Gay, T. C. Boyle, Ann Beattie, and others.

ISBN-13: 978-0-618-71347-9 • ISBN-10: 0-618-71347-6 CL $28.00
ISBN-13: 978-0-618-71348-6 • ISBN-10: 0-618-71348-4 PA $14.00

THE BEST AMERICAN NONREQUIRED READING™

2007. Edited by Dave Eggers, introduction by Sufjan Stevens. This collection boasts the best in fiction, nonfiction, alternative comics, screenplays, blogs, and "anything else that defies categorization" (*USA Today*). With an introduction by singer-songwriter Sufjan Stevens, this volume features writing from Alison Bechdel, Stephen Colbert, Scott Carrier, Lee Klein, Matt Klam, and others.

ISBN-13: 978-0-618-90276-7 • ISBN-10: 0-618-90276-7 CL $28.00
ISBN-13: 978-0-618-90281-1 • ISBN-10: 0-618-90281-3 PA $14.00

THE BEST AMERICAN COMICS™ 2007. Chris Ware,

guest editor, Anne Elizabeth Moore, series editor. The newest addition to the Best American series — "A genuine salute to comics" (*Houston Chronicle*) — returns with a set of both established and up-and-coming contributors. Edited by Chris Ware, author of *Jimmy Corrigan: The Smartest Kid on Earth,* this volume features pieces by Linda Barry, R. and Aline Crumb, David Heatley, Gilbert Hernandez, Adrian Tomine, Lauren Weinstein, and others.

ISBN-13: 978-0-618-71876-4 • ISBN-10: 0-618-71876-1 CL $22.00

THE BEST AMERICAN ESSAYS® 2007. David Foster

Wallace, guest editor, Robert Atwan, series editor. Since 1986, *The Best American Essays* has gathered outstanding nonfiction writing, establishing itself as the premier anthology of its kind. Edited by the acclaimed writer David Foster Wallace, this year's collection brings together "witty, diverse" (*San Antonio Express-News*) essays from such contributors as Jo Ann Beard, Malcolm Gladwell, Louis Menand, and Molly Peacock.

ISBN-13: 978-0-618-70926-7 • ISBN-10: 0-618-70926-6 CL $28.00
ISBN-13: 978-0-618-70927-4 • ISBN-10: 0-618-70927-4 PA $14.00

THE BEST AMERICAN MYSTERY STORIES™ 2007. Carl

Hiaasen, guest editor, Otto Penzler, series editor. This perennially popular anthology is sure to appeal to mystery fans of every variety. The 2007 volume, edited by best-selling novelist Carl Hiaasen, features both mystery veterans and new talents. Contributors include Lawrence Block, James Lee Burke, Louise Erdrich, David Means, and John Sanford.

ISBN-13: 978-0-618-81263-9 • ISBN-10: 0-618-81263-6 CL $28.00
ISBN-13: 978-0-618-81265-3 • ISBN-10: 0-618-81265-2 PA $14.00

THE BEST AMERICAN SPORTS WRITING™ 2007.

David Maraniss, guest editor, Glenn Stout, series editor. "An ongoing centerpiece for all sports collections" (*Booklist*), this series stands in high regard for its extraordinary sports writing and topnotch editors. This year David Maraniss, author of the critically acclaimed biography *Clemente,* brings together pieces by, among others, Michael Lewis, Ian Frazier, Bill Buford, Daniel Coyle, and Mimi Swartz.

ISBN-13: 978-0-618-75115-0 • ISBN-10: 0-618-75115-7 CL $28.00
ISBN-13: 978-0-618-75116-7 • ISBN-10: 0-618-75116-5 PA $14.00

THE BEST AMERICAN TRAVEL WRITING™ 2007.

Susan Orlean, guest editor, Jason Wilson, series editor. Edited by Susan Orlean, staff writer for *The New Yorker* and author of *The Orchid Thief,* this year's collection, like its predecessors, is "a perfect mix of exotic locale and elegant prose" (*Publishers Weekly*) and includes pieces by Elizabeth Gilbert, Ann Patchett, David Halberstam, Peter Hessler, and others.

ISBN-13: 978-0-618-58217-4 • ISBN-10: 0-618-58217-7 CL $28.00
ISBN-13: 978-0-618-58218-1 • ISBN-10: 0-618-58218-5 PA $14.00

THE BEST AMERICAN SCIENCE AND NATURE WRIT-

ING™ 2007. Richard Preston, guest editor, Tim Folger, series editor. This year's collection of the finest science and nature writing is edited by Richard Preston, a leading science writer and author of *The Hot Zone* and *The Wild Trees.* The 2007 edition features a mix of new voices and prize-winning writers, including James Gleick, Neil deGrasse Tyson, John Horgan, William Langewiesche, Heather Pringle, and others.

ISBN-13: 978-0-618-72224-2 • ISBN-10: 0-618-72224-6 CL $28.00
ISBN-13: 978-0-618-72231-0 • ISBN-10: 0-618-72231-9 PA $14.00

THE BEST AMERICAN SPIRITUAL WRITING™ 2007.

Edited by Philip Zaleski, introduction by Harvey Cox. Featuring an introduction by Harvey Cox, author of the groundbreaking *Secular City,* this year's edition of this "excellent annual" (*America*) contains selections that gracefully probe the role of faith in modern life. Contributors include Robert Bly, Adam Gopnik, George Packer, Marilynne Robinson, John Updike, and others.

ISBN-13: 978-0-618-83333-7 • ISBN-10: 0-618-83333-1 CL $28.00
ISBN-13: 978-0-618-83346-7 • ISBN-10: 0-618-83346-3 PA $14.00

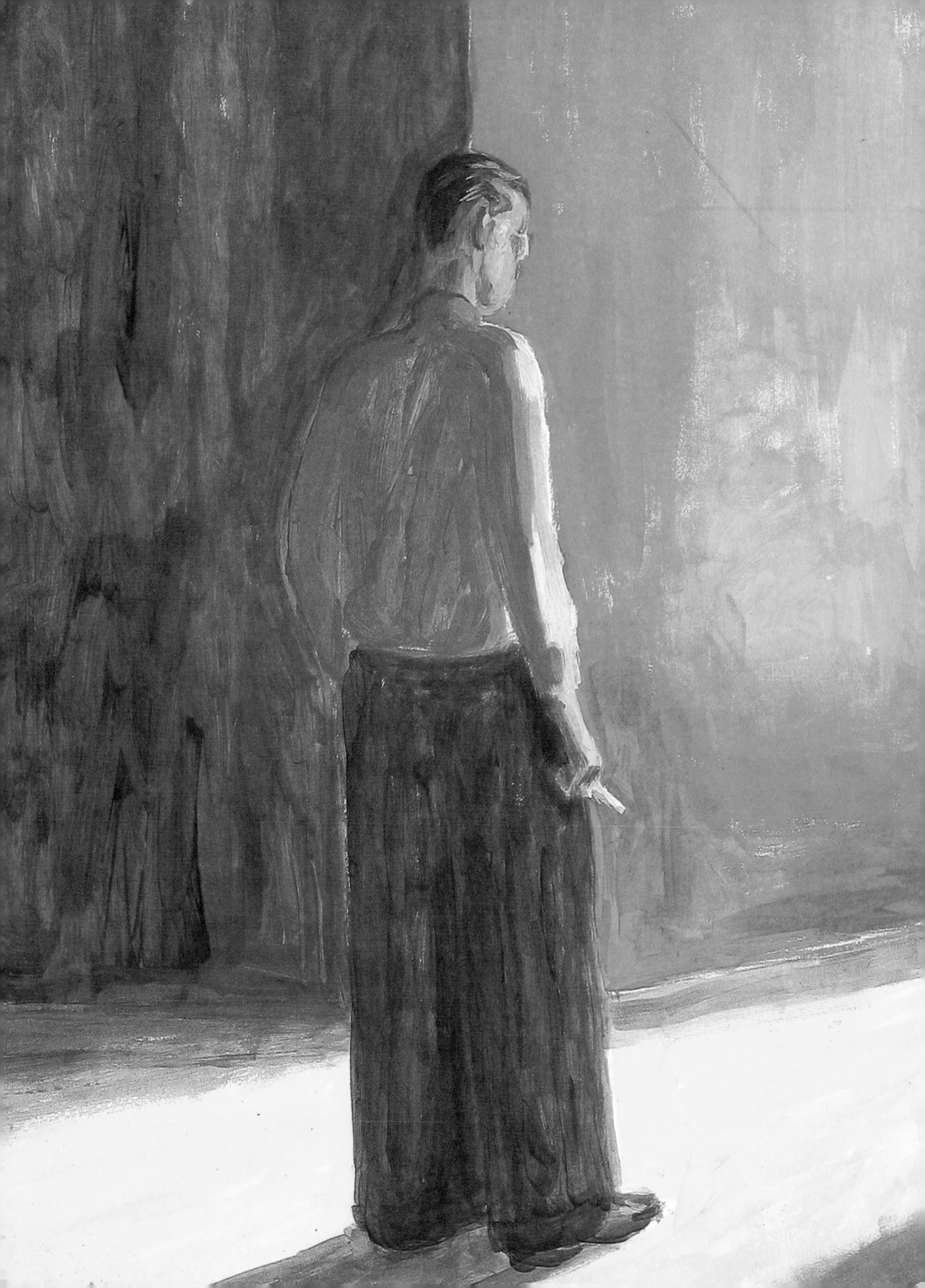